COLORADO
HANDBOOK
SECOND EDITION

COLORADO HANDBOOK

SECOND EDITION

STEPHEN METZGER

MOON
PUBLICATIONS INC.

COLORADO HANDBOOK
SECOND EDITION

Please send all comments, corrections, additions, amendments, and critiques to:

**COLORADO HANDBOOK
c/o MOON PUBLICATIONS, INC.
P.O. BOX 3040
CHICO, CA 95927-3040, USA**

Published by
Moon Publications Inc.
P.O. Box 3040
Chico, California 95927-3040, USA

Printed by
Colorcraft Ltd., Hong Kong

Printing History
1st edition—May 1992
2nd edition—January 1994

Library of Congress Cataloging-in-Publication Data

Metzger, Stephen, 1954-
    Colorado Handbook / Stephen Metzger. — 2nd ed.
        p.   cm.
    Includes bibliographical references and index.
    ISBN 1-56691-013-7
    1. Colorado—Guidebooks.   I. Title.
F774.3.M48   1993
917.8804'33—dc20   93-30739
                                                CIP

Editors: Elizabeth Rhudy, Don Root
Copy Editor: Deana Corbitt
Production and Design: Carey Wilson
Cartographer: Bob Race
Index: Deana Corbitt, Alexandra Foote

Front cover photo of Twin Falls, Yankee Boy Basin,
Uncompahgre National Forest, Colorado by J. C. Leacock

Printed in Hong Kong
Distributed in the USA by Publishers Group West.

For Betsy and Gina

IS THIS BOOK OUT OF DATE?

In the 1930s, Scribners' editor Maxwell Perkins visited Ernest Hemingway in the Florida Keys. One day they went fishing together, and Perkins, taken by the beauty of the landscape, asked Hemingway why he had never written about it. "Because I haven't been away from it for ten years," he answered.

That's the novelist's luxury—to visit a place, reflect on it, and then later describe it, embellishing where necessary. Unfortunately, travel writers can't do that. Readers want to know *exactly* what to expect when they're traveling. So the writer's got to get to work immediately, recording precisely what he saw, and the publisher's got to get the book in the stores as soon as possible. And though ostensibly the result is a general accuracy that makes the reader's trip more enjoyable, there's a trade-off: Because restaurants come and go, motels raise their prices, and new roads get built, some specific details may be irrelevant or just plain wrong by the time you're reading about them.

If that's the case, we want to hear about it. We'll be continually working to revise and update these pages, so if you come across an error or omission in the *Colorado Handbook,* write and let us know. We particularly welcome letters from Coloradoans who want to share an insider's view and from travelers who've run into problems that other visitors should know about. Also, if you find a map or maps difficult to read, or have a suggestion for a map you think would be helpful, please contact us. Be as specific as you can, and document your sources when possible.

Because observations made in the field are usually the most reliable, feel free to jot down notes in the margins of your *Colorado Handbook.* Send it to us, and all contributions will be acknowledged. (Of course we also love to hear from readers who found the book, or sections of it, accurate and useful.)

Address all correspondence to:

Colorado Handbook
c/o Moon Publications, Inc.
P.O. Box 3040
Chico, CA 95927-3040

CONTENTS

MAPS

MAP SYMBOLS

INTERSTATE

U. S. HIGHWAY

STATE HIGHWAY

SKI AREA

POINT OF INTEREST

ACCOMMODATION

WATER

TOWN

CITY

MOUNTAIN

BRIDGE

CAMPGROUND

FREEWAY

MAIN HIGHWAY

OTHER ROADS

UNPAVED ROAD

STATE BORDER

COUNTY BORDER

OTHER BORDER

CHARTS

SPECIAL TOPICS

ABBREVIATIONS

BLM—Bureau of Land Management
CO—Colorado, also Colorado
    State Highway
d—double
elev.—elevation
F—Fahrenheit
Hwy.—U.S. Highway

km—kilometers
pp—per person
pop.—population
RV—recreational vehicle
s—single
tel.—telephone
WPA—Work Projects Administration

ACKNOWLEDGEMENTS

A lot of good people helped me put this book together, and I'm indebted to all of you. Any strengths herein are due to your assistance and kindness; faults, errors, and oversights are my own.

First of all, to Blake and Kristin: thanks for the great hiking, that wonderful day at the American Music Festival, and for letting me bird-sit your apartment in Boulder while you were in Mexico. And while I'm in Boulder, thanks to Karl Kumli and E.J. House. In Summit County, I'm grateful to Steve Metzger (yes, there's *another* one) for your insights and friendship.

Thanks, too, to Jane and Rich at the Twilight Inn in Frisco, George and Connie at the Paradox Lodge in Keystone, Susan Stiff at the Broadmoor Hotel in Colorado Springs, Martin Catmur at the Cristiana Guesthaus in Crested Butte, Dorothy Williams at the Hearthstone Inn in Colorado Springs, and Charles Hillstadt at the Queen Anne Inn in Denver. Your hospitality and graciousness made my work enjoyable and memorable.

I'm also grateful for help from all the chamber of commerce, visitors bureau, and ski area personnel who helped along the way—especially Judy Sheer in Sterling, Barb Bowman and Debbie Kovalik in Grand Junction, Barb Loken and Christina Rosch in Telluride, Carol Pasternak and Killeen Russell in Aspen, Bob Jappe in Summit County, Beth Sharp at Ski the Summit, Patti McCarthy in Durango, Kris Bricker in Colorado Springs, Mary Struzik and Toni Monger in Winter Park, Shelley Helmerick in Boulder, and Jean Anderson in Denver. Above all, thanks to Deborah Cornelius of the Colorado State Department of Tourism for putting me in touch with all these people, as well as for helping Jean arrange Denver lodging.

I'm also thankful to Rebecca Lintz at the Denver Historical Museum, Kathy Swan of the Denver Public Library, and Anne Marie Vellar of the Colorado Department of Corrections for helping to locate and arrange for permission to publish the wonderful historical photos herein.

To Tom Meinen, Mark Stevens, and Lito Tejada-Flores: Thanks for the special topics you contributed to *Colorado Handbook*—and to Mark, especially, for those afternoons at the Wynkoop Brewery and the friendship in an otherwise lonely summer on the road.

Muchisimas gracias also to the professional and dedicated staff at Moon Publications: editors Don Root and Beth Rhudy; illustrators Bob Race, Cathy Carlson, and Karen White; copy editor Deana Corbitt; layout and design artist Carey Wilson; and all the rest of you. Really.

For help on the second edition, thanks to Suzanne "Kate" Robinson, for your phone calls, mailings, and proofreadings. I am also grateful for the criticism and suggestions from Dave Fishell, who straightened me out on the history of Grand Junction; Robert C. Heyder, Superintendent of Mesa Verde National Park, who pointed out several errors in my section on the park; and to Tom Vaughan of the Anasazi Heritage Center in Cortez. And I wish to thank especially Mike Booth of the *Denver Post,* whose essay on Colorado's Amendment 2 (see the special topic) tackles a very difficult and disconcerting problem for residents and tourists alike and which greatly increases this book's attempts to be thorough and virtuous.

Thanks, too, to all the readers of the first edition who took the time to write and point out misteaks, tyops and omis ions, as well as the many chambers of commerce and convention and visitors bureaus that corrected copy and made suggestions for better coverage. It's getting better all the time.

Finally, thanks and love to my family: Betsy, Hannah Rose, and little Gina. "Twenty-thousand roads, I went down, down, down, and they all led me straight back home to you."

BALD EAGLE: Large size, bold markings and majestic manner combine to make bald eagles impressive birds. Being on the top of the wetlands food chain and eating mostly fish, eagles are among those birds whose populations were decimated by the pesticide DDT. Since the banning of DDT in this country, eagles are increasing in some areas, but their real enemy is habitat loss. If places to nest and fish undisturbed are not preserved, these majestic birds will be lost forever. Taking four years to mature to adult plumage of white head and tail, juvenile eagle are mostly brown all over but can vary greatly. Many are "motley," in appearance from patche of white in various parts of their plumage.

© Carl James Freeman 1989

©1983 Carl James Freeman
Bald Eagle

ACKNOWLEDGEMENTS

A lot of good people helped me put this book together, and I'm indebted to all of you. Any strengths herein are due to your assistance and kindness; faults, errors, and oversights are my own.

First of all, to Blake and Kristin: thanks for the great hiking, that wonderful day at the American Music Festival, and for letting me bird-sit your apartment in Boulder while you were in Mexico. And while I'm in Boulder, thanks to Karl Kumli and E.J. House. In Summit County, I'm grateful to Steve Metzger (yes, there's *another* one) for your insights and friendship.

Thanks, too, to Jane and Rich at the Twilight Inn in Frisco, George and Connie at the Paradox Lodge in Keystone, Susan Stiff at the Broadmoor Hotel in Colorado Springs, Martin Catmur at the Cristiana Guesthaus in Crested Butte, Dorothy Williams at the Hearthstone Inn in Colorado Springs, and Charles Hillstadt at the Queen Anne Inn in Denver. Your hospitality and graciousness made my work enjoyable and memorable.

I'm also grateful for help from all the chamber of commerce, visitors bureau, and ski area personnel who helped along the way—especially Judy Sheer in Sterling, Barb Bowman and Debbie Kovalik in Grand Junction, Barb Loken and Christina Rosch in Telluride, Carol Pasternak and Killeen Russell in Aspen, Bob Jappe in Summit County, Beth Sharp at Ski the Summit, Patti McCarthy in Durango, Kris Bricker in Colorado Springs, Mary Struzik and Toni Monger in Winter Park, Shelley Helmerick in Boulder, and Jean Anderson in Denver. Above all, thanks to Deborah Cornelius of the Colorado State Department of Tourism for putting me in touch with all these people, as well as for helping Jean arrange Denver lodging.

I'm also thankful to Rebecca Lintz at the Denver Historical Museum, Kathy Swan of the Denver Public Library, and Anne Marie Vellar of the Colorado Department of Corrections for helping to locate and arrange for permission to publish the wonderful historical photos herein.

To Tom Meinen, Mark Stevens, and Lito Tejada-Flores: Thanks for the special topics you contributed to *Colorado Handbook*—and to Mark, especially, for those afternoons at the Wynkoop Brewery and the friendship in an otherwise lonely summer on the road.

Muchisimas gracias also to the professional and dedicated staff at Moon Publications: editors Don Root and Beth Rhudy; illustrators Bob Race, Cathy Carlson, and Karen White; copy editor Deana Corbitt; layout and design artist Carey Wilson; and all the rest of you. Really.

For help on the second edition, thanks to Suzanne "Kate" Robinson, for your phone calls, mailings, and proofreadings. I am also grateful for the criticism and suggestions from Dave Fishell, who straightened me out on the history of Grand Junction; Robert C. Heyder, Superintendent of Mesa Verde National Park, who pointed out several errors in my section on the park; and to Tom Vaughan of the Anasazi Heritage Center in Cortez. And I wish to thank especially Mike Booth of the *Denver Post*, whose essay on Colorado's Amendment 2 (see the special topic) tackles a very difficult and disconcerting problem for residents and tourists alike and which greatly increases this book's attempts to be thorough and virtuous.

Thanks, too, to all the readers of the first edition who took the time to write and point out misteaks, tyops and omis ions, as well as the many chambers of commerce and convention and visitors bureaus that corrected copy and made suggestions for better coverage. It's getting better all the time.

Finally, thanks and love to my family: Betsy, Hannah Rose, and little Gina. "Twenty-thousand roads, I went down, down, down, and they all led me straight back home to you."

CHARTS

SPECIAL TOPICS

ABBREVIATIONS

BLM—Bureau of Land Management
CO—Colorado, also Colorado
    State Highway
d—double
elev.—elevation
F—Fahrenheit
Hwy.—U.S. Highway

km—kilometers
pp—per person
pop.—population
RV—recreational vehicle
s—single
tel.—telephone
WPA—Work Projects Administration

PREFACE

January, 1973. I am 18 years old and speeding east across Utah on Hwy. 40 in my Mustang convertible. It is sometime between midnight and dawn, and my radio is picking up a megawatt AM rock station out of Oklahoma City or Fort Worth. Between bursts of static, Don McLean is singing about Chevys, levees, American pie, and the day the music died.

I have just graduated from high school, having taken an accelerated course of study in order to finish early. Behind me on the seat is nearly everything I own—a suitcase full of long underwear, flannel shirts, and ragged sweaters; my ski boots; a rolled-up poster of Jean-Claude Killy; a dog-eared copy of *On the Road*; and my notebook. The trunk rack, which I can see through the rear-view mirror and the rip in the plastic back window, holds my skis and poles, which angle into the dark. The heater blasts, does little good.

Before me stretches a Colorado I have never seen, although my mind carries a vague image, drawn from years of magazine articles and "Ski the High Country" ads: big blue sky, cold dry snow, miles and miles of great skiing, Aspen, Vail, Steamboat, and Telluride. My excitement is fueled by a strange love-fear of the unknown that works across my shoulders, down into my chest, and manifests itself in my hand, which trembles slightly when I lift it from the steering wheel.

As the sky grows pink in the east, I stop in Craig for breakfast and coffee, take a seat at the counter of a small diner. A couple of the ranchers and truckers glare at me as though my long hair threatens the existence of free enterprise itself. I eat my hashbrowns and wish I'd had the sense not to put Stevie Wonder on the jukebox.

February. I am sitting inside a lift shack at the top of the Continental Divide. It is my first day of work as a ski-lift operator at Arapahoe Basin. The sky is bluer than I have ever seen it—except where a silvery jet and its trail of vapor slice across it—and the mountains are whiter and more rugged. I am well above the timberline. I watch the skiers ride by on the chairs, unload, tighten their boots, slip their pole straps over their wrists, and take off—some timid, some defiant, all awestruck, as am I, by the peaks and the white and the granite and the sheer majesty of the Rockies at 13,000 feet. At 4 p.m., I stash my notebook in my parka pocket, shut the lift down, lock the door to the shack, and head down with the ski patrol, our skis chattering through the shadows of the closing day.

March. I am standing on the highway just outside Breckenridge, trying to thumb a ride up to Arapahoe. A light snow is falling, but the clouds are growing darker and promise a storm. My Mustang has broken down—two months of neglect in sub-teen temperatures has left it badly in need of a tune-up. But I can't afford that: I have just spent all but a couple of bucks of a two-week paycheck on a brand new pair of skis.

I hoist them onto my shoulder and begin walking, my thumb in the air. A sharp wind blows through the valley. I turn my coat collar up against the cold. Finally, an old Indian in a Rambler station wagon stops and picks me up. We hardly speak, but the sad wisdom of ages clouds his eyes, forming, with the sparkling innocence of my own, a strange and fearless symmetry.

February, 1982. I am sitting at an outdoor café on the Mediterranean coast of Spain in a tiny town north of Barcelona. I have just finished my third cup of espresso, and the novel I am writing—about a young man who comes of age in the Colorado Rockies—is feverishly coming into focus. I don't know if it's any good; that doesn't matter. What matters is that I am beginning to realize what the mountains mean to me, and how being devoted to skiing during such an impressionable period has affected me. From that far away—both in years and miles—I am seeing that skiing can form the perfect metaphor for how we live our lives, or should. When we ski, we are always testing the limits of our abilities; there is a thrill and a passion to skiing only when we push ourselves, because only when we risk falling do we grow. And, too, skiing is largely about friends and family. Though our turns are finally no one's but our own, the experience is far more meaningful when shared—with friends, with family, or even with strangers who become friends for small spots of time during the course of a chairlift ride or a single run. Even falling can be a source of laughter and joy when there are people nearby to help you up.

January, 1991. I am heading southwest on Colorado 133 near Paonia. I have just spent a week in Aspen, and I am bearing down on Telluride. I am excited about being on the road again, about being in the mountains, about skiing. But I am missing my wife and my young daughter; I will learn shortly that another child is on the way.

My Great American Skiing Novel sits in a drawer in California, unpublished; it turned out not to be very good at all. But that doesn't matter. What matters is that I'm back in Colorado— and like so many other times here, the mountains are breathtaking, the morning air crisp and invigorating. In the distance, dark clouds announce the arrival of a mean and nasty storm. I smile. The skiing will be wonderful.

Next fall, I will begin shopping for two very short pairs of skis.

STEPHEN METZGER

INTRODUCTION

THE LAND

Laws change; people die; the land remains.

—Abraham Lincoln

Comprising over 100,000 square miles, Colorado is the country's eighth-largest state—twice the size of New York and 10 times as big as New Hampshire. Its landscapes remarkably diverse, the state stretches from the vast eastern plains to the gently sloping western plateau, the majestic Rocky Mountains running north to south just west of center. The state's topographical relief is nearly 11,000 feet: from the 3,350-foot-high bed of the lower Arkansas River to 14,433-foot Mt. Elbert. And to the observant traveler, the state is a living, breathing geology lesson, with deep canyons carved by ancient waterways exposing hundreds of thousands of years of the land's settling, uplifting, shifting, and erosion.

In The Beginning . . .

During the first part of the Paleozoic Era (240 to 750 million years ago), Colorado was largely flat and entirely submerged beneath the waters of a shallow sea. Toward the end of that era, during the Permian Period, mountains began to rise up, waters receded, and muddy, sediment-filled rivers wandered about the plains. The remains of the first uplifts can be seen in the bizarre redrock formations at Garden of the Gods in Colorado Springs and at Red Rocks Amphitheater near Denver.

During the Mesozoic Era (70 to 230 million years ago), more mountains rose up, and much of the land was lush and marshy. Dinosaurs sloshed through jungles teeming with primitive life-forms. By the end of the era, however, the dinosaurs were gone. In addition, the Gulf of Mexico had crept north to meet the western shores of the Atlantic Ocean, and Colorado was again entirely submerged; the mountains were now underwater reefs.

The Cenozoic Era (beginning 70 million years ago) brought the beginnings of the landscape we see today. Inland seas had receded, though much of the area remained swampy, and mountains were beginning to take forms we might recognize today. During the Pleistocene Epoch, starting less than two million years ago, great glaciers advanced and receded over much of North America. During the most recent ice age, however, between 25,000 and 60,000 years ago, the great continental ice sheet did not creep into Colorado, although smaller glaciers continued to carve away at the Rocky Mountains.

By around 20,000 years ago, the climate had begun to warm, and about that time the first humans probably appeared in Colorado. Nomadic hunters, most likely still en route south after having crossed over the Bering Land Bridge, tracked mastodons, mammoths, ground sloths, and antelope across the eastern plains and the western plateau area.

The Eastern Plains

The Eastern Plains of Colorado actually begin as far east as the Dakotas and eastern Kansas and Nebraska—then come to a screeching halt just west of Denver, where the Rockies' Front Range looms sharp and massive. Comprising roughly 40% of the state, the plains are marked by vast expanses of low rolling hills and yellow-brown fields of prairie grasses.

Thanks to the development of irrigation systems, these otherwise dry lands are the sites of huge ranches and farms. Herds of cattle graze on sprawling spreads that have been in the same families for a century. Sugar beets, wheat, alfalfa, watermelons, honeydew, and other crops are harvested by hardy farmers who do age-old work with high-tech equipment—cellular phones, computers, and thoroughly modern, air-conditioned tractors.

The Rocky Mountains

The backbone not only of Colorado but of the United States, the Rocky Mountains—and the Continental Divide, which snakes through them—mark the division point of the sources of all North American waterways. Even those who have seen the Rockies before—even those who live in the Rockies and see and feel them daily—cannot help but be awed by their immenseness and majesty.

Consider: 54 peaks top 14,000 feet, several roadways wind over 11,000-foot passes, and many towns and communities are nestled in valleys 9,000 feet above sea level. Leadville's elevation is 10,188 feet.

The Western Slope And Plateau Country

The western side of the Rocky Mountains slopes much more gradually than does the steep eastern face, and the area from the Continental Divide west to the Utah border is known generally as the Western Slope. For over a hundred years ranchers have taken advantage of these high-elevation flatlands, and hundreds of thousands of cattle graze in these fields from Craig south to Durango. Make no mistake, though: not all of the Western Slope slopes gently, particularly the towering peaks of the San Juan Mountains around Telluride.

In the northwestern corner of the state, the great plateau is largely shale and underlain with vast fields of coal, oil, and natural gas. Remote river canyons slice deep into the earth. The southwestern corner, meanwhile, particularly the Four Corners area, is a land of redrock canyons and mesas, the dry brown land punctuated by clusters of juniper and piñon.

CLIMATE

In Colorado the joke goes, "If you don't like the weather, just wait 15 minutes." And there's some truth to that, to which anyone who's seen a sunny summer day turn suddenly to rain and thunder can testify. In addition, given the state's dramatic range in geography—from the arid plains to the lush mountain meadows of the Rockies to their windswept peaks—it's difficult to make generalizations.

The Rockies

This is where the weather's the least predictable. Keep in mind that it can get *cold* in the winter. Though it's a dry cold, not nearly as piercing as that damp cold of the coasts, it can still be awfully nasty, especially when the wind blows. Zero-degree temperatures are not at all uncommon in the Colorado Rockies from December to March, and the mercury often drops even lower. Out on the Western Slope, around Gunnison for example, the wind can whip cold and arctic-like across that high plateau. Sub-zero temperatures are not all that rare.

Anyone traveling in the Rocky Mountains in winter should have plenty of warm clothing. Layering is best: Wear a good pair of long underwear, a turtleneck, a wool sweater, and a good, heavy coat, as well as gloves or mittens and a hat. Also, make sure your footwear keeps you not only warm but *dry*. (See "Hypothermia," under "Health and Safety" following.)

Summer days in the Rockies are often pleasant, into the 80s and even 90s, with the high-elevation sun almost mandating shorts. Remember, though, that afternoon storms are *very* common, and you should always have warmer clothes and rain gear handy. Also keep in mind that though summer days are warm, night temperatures drop significantly, down into the mid-50s and lower, and if you plan to be outside at night—especially if you're camping—you should have plenty of warm clothing.

The Plains

The climate's not as dramatic out on Colorado's eastern plains as it is in the Rockies. But there are some things to know. First of all, it gets hot out there, and air-conditioning in your car is more than just awfully nice. Also, summer storms on the plains are common. The temperature might be pushing 90° F or even 100° F in mid-afternoon, when all of a sudden thunderheads start building, leaves and dust start swirling, and shadows fall across wheatfields. In fact, the storms on the plains can be even more threatening than those in the mountains, as they often bring with them high winds and even cyclones. In the summer of 1990, a dark twister twirled through the little town of Limon, east of Denver, upending cars and mobile homes and flattening office buildings.

Ordinarily, of course, summer storms on the plains aren't that bad. Still it would be wise to keep rain gear on hand, as well as a coat and a spare pair of shoes. Also, drive especially carefully when that wind whips up and when water pools on the roadways.

Winter on the plains can be harsh. Temperatures dip into the 30s, and biting winds whip across the vast expanses of open fields. Though snow doesn't fall in the amounts it does in the Rockies, it can still pile up in drifts, and sometimes the wind and snow combine in near whiteouts. On the other hand, when the skies are clear and the winds gentle, day-time temperatures can lift into the 60s. In fact, some winter days on the plains are absolutely gorgeous, with views seeming to stretch forever and a cold but tolerable air invigorating you as you draw deep breaths.

Denver

At the western terminus of the Great Plains, Denver, the "Mile-High City," sits snug up against the Front Range of the Rocky Mountains. Summer days are warm but not hot—though occasional heat waves drive temperatures over 100° F—and they're mostly dry; the city receives less than 15 inches of precipitation a year.

During the winter it can get cold, though it's still quite tolerable. Daytime temperatures are generally in the 40s, though they drop considerably at night, often into the 20s and teens. If you plan to explore Denver between October and April, bring warm clothes. Again, layering is best, starting with wicking long underwear and working out to a good wind- and waterproof coat or jacket.

FLORA AND FAUNA

Colorado's widely varied geography and climate make the state home to a huge range of plant and animal life—from the prairie grasses, yucca, fence lizards, spadefoot toads, and pronghorn antelope of the eastern plains to the aspen, spruce, black bears, bighorn sheep, elk, and mountain goats of the Rocky Mountains. In addition, Colorado is home, either part- or full-time, to many different species of birds—owls, pheasants, grouse, geese, ducks, eagles, turkeys, and hundreds of varieties of small birds.

Colorado's waters—from the low-lying reservoirs of the eastern plains to the tumbling snow-fed streams of the high mountains—hold many different species of warm- and cold-water fish. Bass, walleye, catfish, bluegill, crappie, and other sunfish are found in the lower lakes, notably John Martin Reservoir near Las Animas and Horsetooth Reservoir near Fort Collins. Trout and kokanee salmon are found in the higher lakes and streams; the most common trout are rainbow and brown, while Mackinaw (lake) trout roam some of the larger, deeper lakes (Grand Lake and Blue Mesa Reservoir, for example).

One of the great joys of visiting Colorado, particularly in the spring and early summer, is seeing the abundant wildflowers that blanket meadows and mountain hillsides. Sheets of bright yellow, blue, and purple contrast dramatically with the backdrops of aspen, fir, and spruce, as well as the great granite snowcapped peaks that often loom in the distance. Especially beautiful is Colorado's state flower, the columbine, a delicate, commonly light blue to purplish flower that grows in damp meadows either singly or in clusters.

Aspen Trees

Colorado's aspens have become almost mythical. During the winter, these beautiful white-barked trees lose their leaves and stand stoically in groves, skinny and dormant and contrasting with the evergreens often found in the same forests. In the spring, the trees begin to bud, and the distinctly shaped "quaking" leaves—pale green at first—reappear. In summer, the leaves begin to yellow, and by fall have turned to stunning, electric gold and orange. This is the best time to hike, or drive, into Colorado's aspen forests, though you will not be alone: The vibrant colors attract not only Colorado's color aficionados, but folks from outside the state as well. Tour groups and local boosters have even organized several "color tours" to the various aspen forests.

Bighorn Sheep

One of the other virtual symbols of Colorado is the bighorn sheep. These magnificent beasts, which can weigh up to 350 pounds (and whose horns alone can weigh 35 pounds), are scattered about the state in several specific herds. A recent article in *Colorado Outdoors* (Nov.-Dec., 1991) lists 13 specific "hot spots" where the animals can best be viewed, including: the **Georgetown Wildlife Viewing Area** in Georgetown; **Rocky Mountain National Park; Poudre Canyon,** west of Fort Collins; three spots in the **Salida-Buena Vista** area; and an area on the east side of Hwy. 550 between Ridgway and Ouray.

BOB RACE

bighorn sheep

HISTORY

THE FIRST COLORADANS

Although recent finds in Central and South America have contributed to contemporary theories of the New World's first human inhabitants, the discoveries in the North American southwest turned anthropology on its ear by proving that humans had come across from Asia at least 10,000 years ago, or 8,000 years earlier than previously thought. In the early 1930s, scientists from the University of Denver determined that bones found in northeastern New Mexico were from a post-glacial species of bison, long extinct, and embedded in them were spear points used to kill the animal. Since then, Folsom points, as they have come to be called, have been found throughout the southeastern Colorado plains, as well as on the Western Slope near Montrose—proof that humans wandered in relatively large numbers in the more temperate regions of Colorado some 10,000 years ago, hunting giant ground sloths, woolly mammoths, and mastodons.

The Anasazi

The first people to settle in what is now Colorado were the Anasazi (the word is Navajo and probably best translated as "Enemies of Our Ancestors"). As early as A.D. 550, Anasazi of the Basketmaker Period had begun migrating north from the Rio Grande area of central New Mexico and were building pit houses in the Four Corners area, particularly around Mesa Verde. Between A.D. 750 and 1100, the Developmental Pueblo Period, Anasazi architecture changed from primitive pit houses to above-ground shelters, which were often built in clusters to provide homes and storage for several families. In addition, stone towers 10-15 feet tall were built near these early pueblos, suggesting a need for lookouts. At the same time, they were developing a distinct pottery style, characterized by intricate black designs on a white background, as well as sophisticated water-storage and irrigation systems.

During the Classic Pueblo Period, A.D. 1100-1300, the Anasazi further developed their architecture. Some single pueblos contained over 400 rooms and were four stories tall; some of these pueblo "cities" were home to 5,000 or more people. Around A.D. 1150, many of the Anasazi of southwestern Colorado began to move into cliff-side alcoves. Although no one knows the real reason for the move, anthropologists suspect that it might have been to secure themselves from enemy attack (although no real evidence of enemies or violence has been found) or to protect themselves from the elements. These cliff dwellings are best seen at Mesa Verde National Park, near Durango.

By 1300, the cliff dwellings, as well as the free-standing pueblos scattered about the Four Corners area, had all been abandoned. And again, no one knows why. At one time it was thought that the Navajos and Apaches arrived from the north and drove them out, although modern thinking is that these tribes didn't show up until around 1450. The most commonly accepted theory today is that the Anasazi overfarmed the little valleys in which they grew their corn, beans, and squash; then they simply headed for greener pastures, most likely filtering southwest back toward the Rio Grande area. It's generally assumed that today's Zuni, Acoma, Taos, Sandia, and other Pueblo peoples are descendants of the Anasazi.

The Shoshone And Algonquin Tribes

Between the time the Anasazi disappeared and the white man arrived, Colorado was home to several tribes, most of whom were from the Shoshone and Algonquin linguistic stocks. The most widely spread and the largest in terms of numbers were the Utes, a Shoshonean mountain-dwelling people who roamed from the eastern mountain passes, which they guarded against the Plains tribes, to the lower reaches of the Western Slope.

The Plains tribes, primarily Cheyenne, Comanche, Arapahoe, and Kiowa, hunted the great flatlands east of the Rockies. Often at war with each other, they arrived some time after the Utes, probably having been pushed west by other groups. Other tribes of Colorado included Pawnee, Sioux, and Navajo; Blackfoot and Crow hunting parties probably ventured south into the north central part of the state.

THE ARRIVAL OF THE WHITE MAN

Early Exploration
Most likely the first explorers in Colorado were members of the Francisco Vásquez de Coronado expedition, who might have drifted north from New Mexico in 1541 in their search for the fabled Seven Gold Cities of Cibola. Unlike in New Mexico, where records indicate Coronado was responsible for the widespread rape and murder of native people, the expedition apparently didn't do much damage in Colorado.

During the early 18th century, Spain and France both sought title to the western plains, and the Spanish, pushing up from New Mexico, began to explore the San Luis Valley area of south central Colorado. French trappers and traders, meanwhile, pushed west into the mountains. Spain, however, had a stronger hold on the region, and by 1762, France had ceded to Spain all land west of the Mississippi.

In 1776, friars Francisco Antanasio Dominguez and Silvestre Velez de Escalante traveled through southwestern Colorado in search of an overland route that would connect the missions of New Mexico with those of California. The expedition not only provided the first written record of Colorado exploration but also gave the area many of its place names, including the San Juan and Sangre de Cristo mountains and El Rio de las Animas Perdidos en Purgatorio ("The River of the Lost Souls in Purgatory").

Louisiana Purchase
In 1803, two years after Spain had been forced to turn over its hold on northern Colorado to the French, President Thomas Jefferson bought the Louisiana Territory from Napoléon. Though he was ridiculed at the time for squandering $15 million on real estate that was almost wholly unexplored, the Louisiana Purchase doubled the size of the United States and, as every schoolchild knows, turned out to be a pretty decent deal in the long run.

The First American Explorations
The first American to explore the Colorado area was Zebulon Pike, who pushed into the mountains west of Pueblo and Colorado Springs in 1806. In his journal, Pike described the peak that was named for him as "unscalable."

In 1820, President James Monroe dispatched Major Stephen H. Long to explore the new territory's northern boundary, which had been established a year earlier along the Arkansas River and into the mountains along the Continental Divide. Long's party followed the South Platte River west, then dropped south along the Arkansas, ultimately veering west again near Colorado Springs and venturing as far as Royal Gorge. (One of Long's men, Dr. Edwin James, led the first recorded ascent of Pikes "unscalable" Peak.)

Trappers, Traders, And Colorado Territory
In September 1821, Mexico won its independence from Spain, and almost immediately the United States and Mexico began vigorous trading, with pack trains departing regularly from Missouri for Santa Fe. The Santa Fe Trail, as the route was known, cut across southeastern Colorado and helped further develop this otherwise hostile land. Forts and trading posts were established along the trail, most notably Bent's Fort near Las Animas, providing gathering places for trappers, traders, and mountain men, Americans, French, and Native Americans.

The United States declared war on Mexico on May 13, 1846, and two years later, the Treaty of Guadalupe Hidalgo was signed, which ceded to the U.S. a large chunk of land running from Texas west to California, including some of southern Colorado. Now, all of what is now Colorado belonged to the U.S., although a Colorado Territory was still 15 years down the road.

SILVER THREADS AND GOLDEN NEEDLES

"Pikes Peak Or Bust"
Gold was discovered in September 1858 on several waterways near what is now Denver, and within weeks a number of buildings had sprung up along area riverbanks, forming the first traces of what would soon develop into the state's largest city. Word of the strike quickly spread to the East Coast, and a flood of prospectors began their way west. Their motto, after the prominent landmark just to the south, was "Pikes Peak or Bust."

With the onset of winter, little mining could be done, and while the little settlements grew, so did their inhabitants' anticipation of growing rich. With the thaw, though, came the discovery that the strikes weren't nearly as rich as reported. The summer of 1859 saw thousands of disgruntled fortune seekers heading back the way they'd come, often encountering along the way other Pikes Peak or Busters, many of whom were convinced to turn back long before even reaching the mining camps.

That spring, however, gold was also discovered along Clear Creek in the mountains west of Denver. This time, the strike was for real. Within a matter of days, several mining camps, including Central City, Black Hawk, and Idaho Springs, were teeming with miners. Horace Greeley wrote that at one point 500 men were arriving each day. Over the next few years, dozens of small towns were founded in the nearby mountains, and in 1861, Colorado Territory was officially established.

Early Ranching And Agriculture

During the early days of Colorado Territory, ranchers and farmers began to see the potential of the area's fertile river valleys and vast expanses of grazing lands. The eastern plains and much of the Western Slope were seen as ideal places to raise wheat, corn, and other crops, and to let cattle and sheep roam.

But Wait, Didn't The Land Still Belong To The Indians?

Absolutely, insofar as Native American philosophy allowed for "ownership" at all. And even though the United States now owned this land on paper, the Indians still considered it theirs.

The 1860s and '70s, then, were years of conflict, and often these conflicts were violent and bloody. In 1864, about 30 miles west of the Kansas border, U.S. soldiers under Colonel John Chivington wiped out a Cheyenne village of as many as 500 people, the majority of whom were women and children. Chivington, who claimed he thought the camped Cheyenne were hostile, was court-martialed for the Sand Creek Massacre but never convicted.

Battles also raged in the northwestern part of Colorado, where ranchers and farmers were intruding upon Northern Utes. In 1879, Indian agent Nathan Meeker, known for his lack of

Utes

diplomacy, tried to convince the Utes to give up their hunting lifestyles and turn to farming. Meeker was killed after he sent for troops to support his position. The Utes were subsequently vanquished to a reservation in Utah. Ranchers, farmers, and other settlers now had Colorado all to themselves.

The Iron Horse

One of the biggest influences on the development and settling of Colorado was the railroad. In the 1870s, railroad tracks began to be laid across the land, linking isolated towns and communities, mining camps and supply centers. Almost overnight, the wagon trains and stage coaches were replaced by locomotives, though by foot and burro was still the only way to get over some of the high mountain passes. For the first time, people, cattle, food products, ore, and other items could be transported quickly and reliably across the vast expanses of Colorado Territory. In addition, the new industry brought thousands of jobs to the area, with stations needing to be built about every 100 miles. From Burlington to Grand Junction, from Durango to Julesburg, the railroad significantly

COLORADO HISTORICAL SOCIETY

early railroad passengers on Marshall Pass

COLORADO HISTORICAL SOCIETY

changed the landscape of Colorado and the lifestyles of its people.

In 1876, Colorado achieved statehood.

More Gold And Silver

Between 1880 and the turn of the century, the Colorado mountains were swarming with mining camps. From Aspen to Cripple Creek, from Leadville to Telluride, dozens of tiny communities were bursting at the seams with miners, real estate tycoons, newspapermen (sometimes a town of 5,000 would support 10 newspapers), various bunko artists, and women working to service them. Grand hotels were constructed and lavish parties thrown; elaborate opera houses attracted the biggest names of the day.

After The Gold Rush

And then it all came crashing down. In 1893, silver was devalued, and Colorado's mining camps went into the skids. Mines closed, smelters shut down, and miners hit the road—many of them ending up in Denver where unemployment rates soared. Towns that had once thronged with the newly prosperous were all but deserted. The great hotels and opera houses were boarded up, and banks closed faster than you can say "S and L scandal." Though a handful of towns continued to prosper—Crested Butte, for example, where coal was discovered—Colorado for the most part was in sad shape as the 20th century approached.

THE TWENTIETH CENTURY

The first years of the new century saw great strife between Colorado's mine workers and owners. In Cripple Creek, Victor, and Telluride, particularly, the conflicts were often violent, and on several occasions the National Guard was called in to try to "keep the peace." In 1903 and 1904 miners in Colorado City and Cripple Creek struck to protest a drop in wages, and when "mysterious" explosions in several mine shafts killed a number of workers, labor blamed management and management blamed labor.

In 1914, the United Mine Workers union organized Trinidad-area coal workers, who struck for better wages and working conditions, and in April, after reports of violence in the camps, the Colorado National Guard was sent in. The conflict came to a bloody head on April 20, when several strikers were killed and tent fires killed 13 women and children.

A Short-lived Prosperity

During WW I, silver prices rose, and many Colorado mines reopened. Though the mining towns saw a general caution instead of the wild abandon of the late 19th century, at least some of the little towns could again keep their heads above water. In addition, prices of farm produce, particularly wheat, skyrocketed, and Colorado farmers enjoyed a new prosperity and status.

Which didn't last long.

The Depression hit Colorado hard. Farmers, ranchers, miners, and businessmen found themselves without work and, oftentimes, without homes. Fortunately, the federal government stepped in where it could, and several major projects, including the development of schools and national forests, as well as highway and irrigation systems, provided workers with jobs and the state with a semblance of stability. In 1935 and '36, Colorado revamped its tax systems, with special sales and service taxes set aside for relief.

Another boon to Colorado's economy was the arrival of the military, which largely came about with the advent of WW II. In addition to the United States Air Force Academy just north of Colorado Springs, several other bases were established in the Denver and Colorado Springs areas.

The Ski Industry

As early as the mid-1930s, downhill skiing was already starting to take hold in some of Colorado's tiny mountain communities. Originally just something to keep locals from getting bored during the long winter months, the sport soon caught on, and folks in the lower-lying areas were making weekend treks to the handful of primitive rope tows.

By the late 1960s and early '70s, skiing had grown up, and Colorado was recognized as one of the best places on earth to strap boards afoot, climb aboard a chairlift, and take off through easy wind and downy flake. In fact, not only had the sport grown up, but it had caught on big time, and new resorts were opening each year, while established resorts were cutting new trails and adding new lifts. In the spring of 1973, the first bore of a tunnel through Loveland Pass was completed, which provided Denver-area skiers much easier access to the resorts of Summit County, as well as Vail, just over the next pass. By the late 1980s, Eisenhower Tunnel's four lanes already seemed too few, and on winter weekends traffic bottlenecked horribly as skiers descended in increasing numbers on the ski towns of Dillon, Breckenridge, and Vail.

And the numbers just keep growing. The winter of 1990-91 saw 9.79 million skier-visits in Colorado, with the Forest Service estimating a three percent increase over the next 10 years. So of course, new resorts are being planned, with opposition groups already rightfully positioned—can the forests *handle* more lifts, clearcut trails, condo complexes, parking lots, and *people?* In the early 1990s, at least three new resorts were in the planning stages: Lake Catamount, seven miles south of Steamboat Springs; Adam's Rib, 35 miles west of Vail; and East Fork, 20 miles southwest of Wolf Creek.

What will happen as more and more skiers demand more and more trails in Colorado's decreasing forest areas? Will the state be able to balance the growth of the ski industry with the undeniable need to preserve forests and delicate ecosystems? Will the cost of skiing ($40 a day for a lift ticket, $600 for a pair of skis and boots) naturally curb the sport's growth? Or will the tiny pockets of backwoods Colorado be nothing more than condos and upscale boutiques by the early 21st century? We can only hope that common sense, intelligence, and environmental awareness are the guiding factors.

Recent Developments

In the summer of 1990, Colorado voters approved two measures that will effect significant change, in varying ways, upon the state. The first is legalized gambling. Though limited in scope, gambling was legal in parts of Colorado as of October, 1991. Black Hawk, Central City, and Cripple Creek bettors can now play poker, blackjack, and slots ($5 maximum).

On a more positive note, in the same election voters also approved major-league baseball for Denver. Spring of 1993 saw the addition of a Denver expansion team, and though the Colorado Rockies had an embarrassingly horrible first season, the fans were loyal and the crowds huge. And who knows, with their basement finish in '93, they'll be in a position to pick up some new players and maybe develop into a winning organization.

COLORADO'S AMENDMENT 2:
VOTERS SAY "NO" TO GAY RIGHTS

If you're packing for Colorado, leave your hate behind.

We've got plenty here already, thank you, and production continues unabated.

The anger and emotions generated by Colorado's anti-gay-rights law, Amendment 2, linger long after the 1992 election that put the law on the books. But if you're thinking of avoiding the state altogether, as many have done to honor a boycott launched by gay activists, you'd better think harder if you ever want to travel in the United States again. Buoyed by their unexpected victory in Colorado, religious and secular conservative groups in at least 14 states have announced plans to clone Amendment 2. Conservative legal scholars are so impressed with the Colorado law that many are merely replacing "Colorado" with "Michigan" or "Ohio," while adopting wholesale its wording and mean-spiritedness. The states where similar campaigns are brewing include such tourist meccas as Florida and California, and the number of states voting on anti-gay laws could reach as high as 25 by the end of the 1994 election cycle. The "Boycott Coloado" effort served its purpose early on by focusing the national spotlight on gay issues. But remaining politically correct by avoiding states where conservatism reigns will become increasingly difficult as gay-bashing spreads across the nation.

How could it happen in Colorado, a state defined by its wide open spaces and Birkenstock-Cowboy attitude that says we don't want to be told how to live? Take a look at your own hometown to help answer that touchy question. Doesn't a large segment of the workaday middle class everywhere still flinch at the word "homosexual"? For that matter, don't even most liberal, "politically correct" straights still get flutters in their guts when they picture members of the same sex holding hands, or kissing? That's what Amendment 2 was all about, and that's what campaigns in more than a dozen other states will be about: The gut feeling against gays, narrow minded and silly as it may be, which a significant number of Americans have yet to overcome.

On the surface, Amendment 2 claimed to be about civil rights. According to Colorado for Family Values, the coalition of conservative religious groups that wrote and financed Amendment 2, gays don't deserve protection from discrimination in the same way as "true" minorities, such as African Americans or the disabled. Homosexuality is a behavior, not an immutable and irreversible quality, they argue, and protecting gays from discrimination serves to cheapen the rights of other minority groups while placing an undue burden on employers and landlords. They also won a lot of votes by using the misleading term "special rights," saying gays would eventually seek job quotas and other preferences granted to previously protected minorities, even though gay leaders have never advocated—and would certainly have a difficult time winning—those so-called "special rights."

At the heart of the matter, however, is homosexuality itself. Colorado for Family Values said gays in America have gone too far in seeking not just tolerance but affirmation of their lifestyle. The Bible and thousands of years of cultural disapproval show that homosexuality is wrong, the group claims, and it was time to draw the line. Their cause was aided inestimably by the prominent role of Will Perkins, a Colorado Springs auto dealer and fundamentalist activist who everyone generally agrees would find it easy to sell sand to the Arabs. Perkins, with his mellifluous voice and self-deprecating humor, somehow talks about "militant homosexuals" without sounding hateful, and he struck a chord. Even gay activists find it difficult to hate Perkins; after a two-hour dinner with him, one noted lesbian activist proclaimed that she had a "lovely time."

More than 800,000 votes bought what Perkins was selling in November of 1992. The Colorado gay and liberal activist community was devastated, staring in disbelief at the returns on their TV screens at parties all across the state. Since then, emotions on both sides of the debate have boiled over, with gay leaders claiming the campaign's gay-bashing rhetoric prompted a huge increase in anti-gay violence, and conservatives claiming that the post-election boycott was nothing less than "economic terrorism." A liberal legal team immediately filed suit to have Amendment 2 thrown out as unconstitutional, and a preliminary ruling by the state Supreme Court hints the law is in trouble. But the legal battle promises to rage for years in the state and federal courts, and anti-gay activists say they will simply write another law if their first effort is defeated.

So what is Colorado really like after Amendment 2? Yes, there are pockets of traditional and sometimes extreme conservatism, most notoriously in Colorado Springs, where Colorado for Family Values was born. The city, with its Air Force Academy and multiple military bases, is home to thousands of active and retired military personnel who have always given Colorado Springs and surrounding El Paso County a strong right-wing bent. The Colorado Springs Chamber of Commerce set out a few years ago to attract "clean" development to the area, and the people who showed up were usually fundamentalist Christian activist groups adding further to the conservatism. And Amendment 2 was passed overwhelmingly in a number of eastern plains counties, such as Kiowa County, where civic leaders were quoted by name saying there aren't even any gays in their towns, and if any are found, they'll be run out on a rail.

At the same time, before Amendment 2, three Colorado cities were among the first in the nation to enact local laws protecting gays from discrimination. Denver, Boulder, and Aspen have long been in the forefront of progressive politics, and they remain so. Moreover, tourism-oriented towns like Telluride and Crested Butte defied the restrictions of Amendment 2 to pass their own gay-rights ordinances after the election, hoping to send a signal to visitors that everyone was welcome in the mountains.

And gay activists credit Amendment 2's passage for prompting a new round of grassroots organizing. Nothing brings together and motivates a community like a direct threat, they say. Gays are coming out and forming support groups, theater companies, and political-action committees in small Colorado towns like Grand Junction, where most residents never even knew they had a gay population. Even Colorado Springs, frequently vilified by the Denver and national press as a prehistoric backwater, has seen an explosion in gay awareness and activism, as well as the rapid growth of a moderate watchdog group called Citizens Project, aimed at balancing out the religious right.

In some ways Colorado is a more interesting place to visit than ever. Gay visitors certainly must weigh the psychological impact of a trip to a state that approved a clearly anti-gay constitutional Amendment. But the places where gays and straights alike have always congregated—Denver, Boulder, Aspen, and all the other ski resorts—have reaffirmed their welcome to all visitors, and they mean it. Amendment 2 is a great way to start up a conversation with strangers at any of the dozens of new coffee houses cropping up all over the state. If the stranger is a Colorado resident, he or she will most definitely have an opinion. The grinding political debate over Amendment 2 has done nothing to wear down the majestic Fourteeners, melt the snowpack, or otherwise tarnish all the gorgeous scenery. And remember—the Longs Peak Trail is eight miles, one way, whether you're gay or straight. Whatever your sexual orientation or political persuasion, your legs will still hurt at the top of the mountain, and the view will still be fantastic.

—Michael Booth

Michael Booth is a reporter for the Denver Post, *where he covers Amendment 2.*

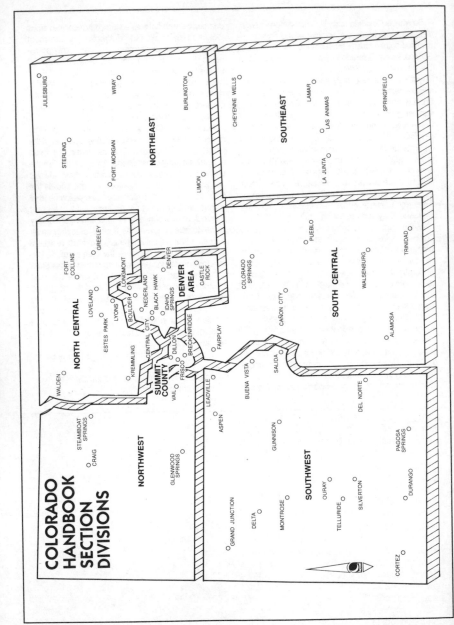

STEPHEN METZGER

PRACTICALITIES

SIGHTSEEING HIGHLIGHTS

The phrase "No visit to Colorado is complete without . . ." probably pops up more than in should in this book. Likewise, when friends ask for help planning itineraries, my list of things I tell them they've *gotta* see and do is probably way too long. But please understand. Not only do I have a passionate love affair with Colorado, but my travels have taken me to so many parts of the state that it's difficult even to come up with a Top-10-type list. So ultimately, I suppose, I defer, dear Reader, to you, as you need to make some decisions about what *kind* of trip yours will be: Will you primarily be sightseeing, or will you be enjoying Colorado's myriad recreational activities? Are you more interested in the state's history than in food, wine, and music festivals? Do you want to explore ancient ruins or modern shopping centers? Do you want to see vast meadows blanketed in white, or mountain hillsides ablaze with brilliant golds and deep, fiery reds?

Once you've answered those questions, you can begin looking at what the state has to offer

a bit more clearly. And though you certainly can't "do" all of Colorado in a two-week trip, you can tailor your trip to make it as rewarding and fulfilling as possible. Herewith, then, are some of what I think are Colorado's highlights. Prioritize them as you will.

THINGS TO SEE

Rocky Mountain National Park probably best encapsulates the beauty and intensity of the rest of the state and the Rocky Mountains. Drive through on the above-timberline Trail Ridge Road, or take off with your backpack or cross-country skis into the backcountry. At **Mesa Verde National Park** you can explore thousand-year-old Anasazi cliff dwellings, and just outside of Colorado Springs you can drive to the top of 14,110-foot Pikes Peak, the "purple mountain" to which Katherine Lee Bates referred in *America the Beautiful*. If you're interested in the state's mining history, don't miss

Cripple Creek, Central City, Black Hawk, and **Leadville,** where you can take mine tours and visit museums that display the tools and equipment of the 1880s, when these towns were bustling with entrepreneurs and entertainers, prospectors and prostitutes.

If you want to see urban Colorado, you need of course to see **Denver.** From its museums and restaurants to its up-scale shopping centers, high-rise hotels, and brand new airport, Denver is at once thoroughly modern and at the same time a town with a palpable link to its past. While in Denver, allow yourself a day to drive up to **Boulder,** an outdoor-oriented university town that seems part Berkeley, part Chamonix, France. Check out the bookstores and street performers on the **Pearl Street Mall** and the coffee shops on **The Hill.**

Another wonderful Colorado town is **Telluride,** though its box-canyon location makes it the kind of town you have to go out of your way to get to (which is part of its charm). Here, Victorian homes cling to hillsides, ski lifts rise just blocks from the main drag through town, and just-passing-through Deadheads share bar space with CEOs.

You might have already formed an opinion about **Aspen,** given its reputation for excellent skiing, expensive lifestyles, and big-bucks resident celebrities. It's a great town, though, and you need neither ski nor be rich to enjoy a visit there—public parks and bike paths allow you to soak in the mountain sunshine, and you can wander the town's little sidestreets, poke your nose into gift shops, and, weather permitting, grab lunch at any of several outdoor cafes.

Just east of Aspen, Colorado 82 lifts up above the treeline to **Independence Pass** (12,095 feet), providing spectacular views before dropping back down again into the gorgeous **Arkansas River Valley.** Several other Colorado mountain passes offer stunning scenery, including **Loveland Pass** and **Berthoud Pass** (both over 11,000 feet) and **Wolf Creek Pass** (10,850 feet). And the entire stretch of **US 550** from **Durango** to **Ouray** seems to take your breath at every turn (and there are lots of them).

THINGS TO DO

Though it's natural to want to relax on vacation, you might not want to do too much of that in Colorado—it'd be a shame not to take advantage of the nearly unlimited recreational opportunities the state affords. Colorado's **skiing** is some of the best in the world, with resorts such as **Aspen, Vail, Crested Butte, Winter Park, Steamboat Springs,** and **Telluride** drawing visitors from as far away as Europe and Asia. Some of the state's lesser-known resorts, though, also offer skiing that locals will tell you rivals that at the big resorts. Not to let the cat out of the bag here, but **A-Basin, Wolf Creek,** and **Purgatory** offer some of the best snow in the Rockies, as well as generally shorter lift lines and an overall more personal and friendly atmosphere than you'll find at some of the larger resorts.

In addition to excellent snow skiing, Colorado also offers first-rate **white-water rafting, mountain biking, fishing, horseback riding, and hiking,** for just about every level of participant— first-timer to expert. Plus, visitors to Colorado can take **four-wheel-drive tours** of remote mountain passes and ghost towns, or rent vehicles and head out on their own. You can also take **narrow-gauge-train rides** along steep cliffsides and over harrowing bridges that cross deep gorges.

Finally, there are the festivals, scores around the state. To name but a few of the best known: Telluride's **bluegrass** and **film** festivals, Boulder's **Shakespeare** and **music** festivals, Aspen's **food-and-wine** and **music** festivals, Winter Park's **American Music** festival, and Vail's **Winterfaire,** as well as golf tournaments, mountain-bike races, and every other imaginable gathering and celebration. (See "Calendar" in specific chapters for dates and other information.)

A lot to see and do? You bet. And I've only skimmed the surface. My advice: Don't try to do it all; you'll only frustrate yourself (believe me!). Instead, take time to enjoy what you do decide on, and then, as they say in the shoe business, Just do it. Besides, perhaps no visit to Colorado, even a lifetime-long one, is ever complete.

RECREATION

Colorado offers a huge array of outdoor activities. Skiing, biking, fishing, golf, camping, rock climbing, whitewater rafting, and kayaking—all are immensely popular. In fact, many folks who've chosen to live here will tell you it's because of the wealth of outdoor recreation. No matter where you are, a lake, stream, golf course, ski slope, hiking trail, or trout stream is nearby.

Skiing

To many people, of course, skiing and Colorado are virtually synonymous. After all, the state is home to some of the world's best, biggest, and most well-known resorts: Vail, Aspen, Winter Park, Steamboat Springs, Crested Butte, Telluride, Copper Mountain, Breckenridge, and Keystone. In addition, more than a dozen other smaller and lesser-known but equally fine resorts lie within Colorado's borders; among them are Arapahoe Basin, Purgatory, and Wolf Creek, favorites of local powderhounds and bumpshredders.

If you're thinking about a ski vacation, you couldn't do much better than Colorado. Fly into Denver, take a shuttle to Vail, Winter Park, or any one of the other resorts within an hour and a half of the airport, and then just spend your time mastering the one mountain; or take a road trip—spread your trip over half a dozen or more resorts. Start at Winter Park, head west to Summit County, then over the pass and on to Vail. Even if you end up as far away as Telluride, you're still less than a day's drive from the airport.

Colorado is also a haven for Nordic skiers. With its thousands of square miles of national forests, as well as many privately run Nordic centers, Colorado welcomes those who'd rather ski quietly off into the woods or crank Telemark turns on a backcountry hillside than stand in lift lines after spending $40 for a ticket. Cross-country skiers will find excellent terrain and Nordic centers near most of the major downhill resorts, including Vail, Aspen, and Telluride, while San Juan, Gunnison, San Isabel, and White River national forests offer exceptional trails, as well as opportunities to explore unmarked backcountry.

For more information on skiing in Colorado, write **Colorado Ski Country USA,** 1560 Broadway, Suite 1440, Denver, CO 80202, or phone (303) 837-0793 or 831-7669 (snow report).

Cycling

While touring is enjoying the same renaissance in Colorado that it is in the rest of the country, mountain biking has taken the state by storm. In fact, Crested Butte and Durango are two of the half dozen or so of the sport's true capitals,

waist-deep powder at Vail

JACK AFFLECK

and both towns not only offer miles and miles of trails and terrain for all levels of ability but also sponsor races, workshops, and various special events throughout the season (generally May through October). In addition, many of Colorado's ski resorts have taken to promoting mountain biking during the summer. At several resorts, including Aspen, Purgatory, Winter Park, and Vail, you can take your bike to the top of the mountain on a ski lift and ride the ski trails back down.

Hiking, Backpacking, And Camping

With the Rocky Mountains as its centerpiece, Colorado claims some of the best hiking, backpacking, and camping in the United States. From the San Juan Mountains to Rocky Mountain National Park north of Boulder, from Colorado National Monument to Great Sand Dunes National Monument, the state offers a wide range of types of trail hiking as well as lengths and degrees of difficulty. You can take short, naturalist-led day-hikes, or you can hike solo

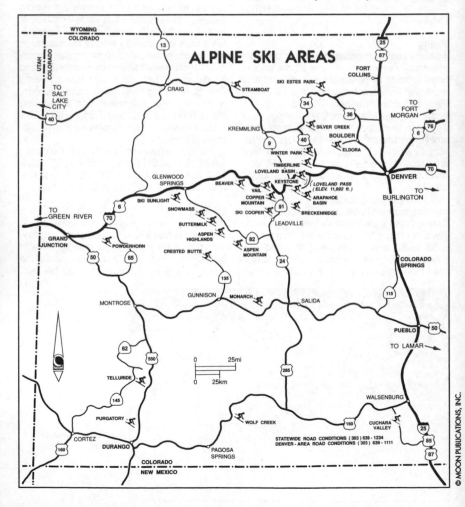

ALPINE SKI AREAS

STATEWIDE ROAD CONDITIONS (303) 639-1234
DENVER-AREA ROAD CONDITIONS (303) 639-1111

© MOON PUBLICATIONS, INC.

WHY SKI COLORADO?

Why do I ski Colorado? You can always duck a "why" question like that by going back to George Leigh-Mallory's answer about climbing Everest: "because it's there." Or be facetious and answer: why not? Or be honest, and say: I ski Colorado because that's where I live, high in the San Juan Mountains in the southwestern corner of the state. But even that was a choice, wasn't it? I moved to Colorado because of a certain tangible magic in these mountains that touches skiing and life in about equal measures. The more interesting question is not why do I ski Colorado, but why do I (and so many others) love skiing here so much?

Start the way skiing itself starts, with snow—great snow. Rocky Mountain snow isn't the whole story, but it's a small miracle. Lighter, drier, more consistent than any snow in the maritime zones of New England or California and other far-west states, Rocky Mountain snow is the stuff skiers' dreams are made of. The small miracle I mentioned is the fact that you, I, all of us, ski better out here than we do at home—if home happens to be anywhere else.

Why is our snow so soft and light? The secret is the continental climate, far from the moist influence of either seacoast, combined with the generally higher elevations of ski areas in Colorado. Not only does Colorado snow fall from the sky as fluff, but often, lowering temperatures after a storm will dry it out even further. Snow here sometimes gets lighter a day after it's fallen. In skiers' terms, this translates into less resistance, less friction, less work to turn and slide. It's as though your skis were always better waxed on Colorado slopes. Powder snow in Colorado is for play not penance, an invitation with no strings attached; and when groomed and packed down into pistes, this stuff becomes a sort of teflon velvet where skis can perform to 110% of their design potential.

Is that all? Hardly. I'd say that on balance Colorado ski resorts are just as special as the snow. Not all perhaps, but most of the resorts here on the backbone of the continent benefit from a special relation to winter, a kind of "skiing culture," a tradition of ski-town hospitality that makes Colorado ski sites more than just overgrown parking lots at the base of lifts. None of the Rocky Mountain states—Colorado, Utah, Wyoming, Montana, Idaho, New Mexico—is exactly experiencing a demographic explosion. These mountains are wild, beautiful, and lonely. And Colorado, although as wild as any of these Rocky Mountain states, is also the most sophisticated of the lot. Take away Denver, and the Rockies look positively empty. No sprawling, tightly packed urban zones to flood the slopes with their clockwork weekend tides. For this reason, most of Colorado's ski spots have become vacation destinations, not weekend rendezvous as is the case with so many eastern and far-western ski areas. In Colorado, necessity and history have transformed the classic base lodge into an even more classic base village.

Here a high percentage of skiers comes from out of state; these folks come from all directions. This means that often the skiers you meet in Colorado lift lines are a more diverse and interesting bunch than you'll find elsewhere. And for that matter, lift lines themselves are on the way out here. The intense competition between Colorado destination resorts for vacationing skiers has fueled a revolution in ski lifts. High-speed detachable quad chairs are fast becoming the norm not the exception at major Colorado resorts. There's no going back, and no nostalgia for the old days of the slow double chair. This is a sweet, almost painless revolution. Higher lift-ticket prices are more than offset by the increased vertical these new lifts deliver. The cost of skiing per thousand feet is actually declining. And for the first time, hard-core skiers are sometimes quitting before the last lift closes, because they have literally skied themselves to exhaustion. A very nice feeling indeed, and a new one in American skiing.

So why do I ski Colorado? And love it so? Because I'm spoiled. Because we're all spoiled.

—Lito Tejada-Flores

Lito Tejada-Flores is an internationally known ski writer and publisher. He has written scores of articles for major magazines, including Ski, Skiing, *and* Powder, *and he is the author of* Breakthrough on Skis.

into remote backcountry wilderness areas; you can even organize a group and hike hut-to-hut through one of Colorado's "hut systems."

In the late 1980s, the Colorado Trail was completed. This 469-mile trail, which stretches from Durango to Denver, offers rich hiking opportunities with specific sections designed for day, overnight, and multi-day hikes. Access points and trailheads are scattered along the trail. One of the best sources for information on hiking in Colorado is the **Colorado Mountain Club,** 2530 W. Alameda Ave., Denver, CO 80219, tel. (303) 922-8315. In addition to publishing a monthly newsletter with articles on climbing and hiking in the state (and beyond), the club sponsors numerous hikes and cross-country ski outings throughout the year.

Colorado's camping opportunities, too, are numerous and varied. Hundreds of public campgrounds are scattered throughout the state in the beautiful San Juan, San Isabel, White River, Pike, Roosevelt, Rio Grande, Grand Mesa, Gunnison, and Arapaho national forests. In addition, Rocky Mountain National Park offers camping in one of most scenic wonderlands in the country, while a handful of national monuments and recreation areas, particularly Curecanti, as well as state parks, also offer good camping.

For more information on camping in Colorado's national forests, write **U.S. Forest Service,** Box 25127, Lakewood, CO 80225, or phone (303) 275-5350.

Rafting And Kayaking

Colorado is a river rat's paradise. Whether your idea of river running is to float lazily down a wide meandering stream in a rubber raft or to shoot Class IV rapids in tiny kayak, whether you prefer organized trips and camaraderie or solo excursions and soul searching, Colorado's waterways will satisfy.

Although rivers throughout the state offer good rafting and kayaking, most of the state's river running is concentrated in the Buena Vista-Salida area (Arkansas River), the Four Corners area (Animas and Dolores rivers), and the northwestern area (Green and Yampa rivers).

For more information on rafting on Colorado rivers, write **Colorado River Outfitters Association,** Box 502, Westminster, CO 80030; tel. (303) 220-8640.

Fishing

While many of Colorado's waterways are tailor-made for rafting, others are trout streams right out of Izaak Walton's *The Compleat Angler* (and some of the rivers are good for both). Unfortunately, mining has destroyed fish habitat in several rivers once rife with trout, though others have been reclaimed, and the Colorado Division of Wildlife, U.S. Fish and Game, and local organizations have successfully reintroduced fish to nearly lost streams.

In addition, sections of several of the state's rivers have special restrictions. Some stretches allow catch-and-release fishing only and/or permit only the use of artificial lures and single barbless hooks. Among the state's favorite streams are the Blue, Roaring Fork, Eagle, Animas, and Gunnison rivers.

Lake fishermen, too, enjoy Colorado angling. Grand Lake and Blue Mesa Reservoir are stocked regularly with decent-size fish, and patient and knowledgeable anglers have taken *huge* Mackinaw from their waters. Reservoirs on the eastern plains offer good warm-water fishing for bass, walleye, catfish, bluegill, and crappie.

Remember that a valid Colorado fishing license is required to fish in all waters except private lakes and a handful of small municipal ponds (usually designated for kids only). For more information on fishing in Colorado, write the **Colorado Division of Wildlife,** 6060 Broadway, Denver, CO 80216, or phone (303) 297-1192.

ACCOMMODATIONS

Colorado's travelers' accommodations run the full gamut from backcountry campgrounds to plush bed and breakfasts, from youth hostels to lavish hotels with valet parking and dining rooms with dress codes. Even the most remote towns usually have a motel or two, and you're rarely far from a national forest campground, where sites run about $7 a night. Colorado's main tourist areas—Denver, Colorado Springs, Summit County, Vail, Aspen, and Durango—have wide ranges of lodging possibilities, including RV campgrounds, luxury hotels, and inexpensive motels. Generally, it's cheaper to stay on the outskirts of town, although you'll sacrifice the convenience of central-location lodging.

Campgrounds

Camping is the least-expensive way to stay in your travels through Colorado, though of course this is recommended for summer travel only (most mountain campgrounds close between October and May). With nightly fees ranging from free to around $18 (for some of the more costly RV sites), the state's campgrounds are generally safe, comfortable, and well maintained. Forest Service campgrounds are not generally equipped with flush toilets or showers, though they do usually have running water.

Bed And Breakfasts

Although generally more expensive than staying in a motel ($50-125 a night), this is one of the best ways to see Colorado. Many of the state's bed and breakfasts are situated in turn-of-the-century (and older) homes and decorated with authentic Victorian furnishings. In addition, most innkeepers go out of their way to provide personal and intimate service. The only disadvantage of bed and breakfasts is that you often must sacrifice a bit of your privacy. Though rooms are usually perfectly private, you may have to share a bath, and often will be eating breakfast in close quarters with—and sometimes at the same table as—the inn's other guests.

For more information on Colorado bed and breakfasts, contact **Bed and Breakfast Colorado, Ltd.,** Box 6061, Boulder, CO 80306, tel. (303) 494-4994; **Bed and Breakfasts of the Rocky Mountains,** Box 804, Colorado Springs, CO 80901, tel. (800) 825-0225; or **Small Bed and Breakfast Inns of Colorado,** 1102 Pikes Peak Ave., Colorado Springs, CO 80904 (for a brochure, send $1 and an SASE).

Dude Ranches

Ranch-style accommodations have been a tradition in Colorado since England's Lord Dun-

19th century digs and diggers

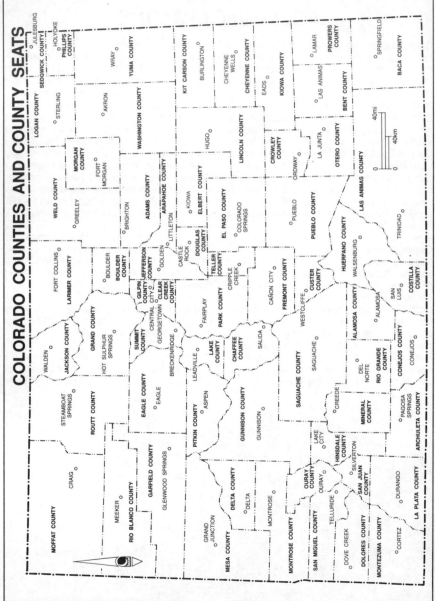

COLORADO COUNTIES AND COUNTY SEATS

© MOON PUBLICATIONS, INC.

raven brought guests from the British Isles to his retreat near Estes Park in the 1870s. Today, there are dude ranches throughout the state, from Durango to Aspen to Steamboat Springs. In addition to offering the proverbial horseback riding, most of the ranches offer a variety of other recreational pursuits as well, including snowmobiling, cross-country skiing, fishing, mountain biking, rafting, and tennis; you can even take part in real ranchhand chores.

For complete information on Colorado dude ranches, write **Colorado Dude/Guest Ranch Association,** Box 300, Tabernash, CO 80478, or phone (303) 887-3128 or (800) 441-6060 (outside Colorado).

Four Distinctive Colorado Hotels
Though there are many excellent hotels in Colorado, particularly in the downtown Denver area, four stand out as places that would make a Colorado vacation especially memorable. **The Broadmoor Hotel** in Colorado Springs was built in the early part of the century and is a sprawling complex that actually consists of three separate hotels, as well as several upscale restaurants, three golf courses, a museum, boutiques, a lake, and an ice-skating arena. One of the classiest and most luxurious hotels in the country, the Broadmoor will take your breath away even if you're prepared to be impressed. Rooms start

at about $120, and suites go for over $1,000.

Downtown Denver's **Brown Palace Hotel** first opened in 1892 and ever since has been accommodating Denver's most discriminating and well-to-do visitors, from Teddy Roosevelt to the Beatles. Rooms start at about $140.

The **Far View Lodge** is located atop Mesa Verde within a couple of miles of some of the Southwest's most fascinating cliff dwellings. Balconies at each room provide the perfect places to listen to the godly silence and to imagine the juniper- and piñon-studded plateau 1,000 years ago, when the Anasazi were developing their mysterious civilization. Rooms start at around $70.

Estes Park's **Stanley Hotel** stands large, white, and sentinel-like on a hillside above town, squaring off with Rocky Mountain National Park. Built in 1909 by F.O. Stanley, who invented the Stanley Steamer, the rustically luxurious Stanley Hotel has hosted many luminaries over the years, including Stephen King, whom the hotel inspired to write *The Shining* (Kubrick and Nicholson hoped to film the movie here but there wasn't enough snow, so the crew moved to the Timberline Lodge on Oregon's Mount Hood). Rooms at the Stanley Hotel start at about $60.

For more information on these hotels, see the "Accommodations" sections in the corresponding chapters.

HEALTH AND SAFETY

Traveling in Colorado is generally very safe, although you should be aware of several specific diseases and climate-caused maladies that could make your visit far less enjoyable and comfortable than it should be. Understanding these problems, and taking the appropriate precautions, will greatly increase the chances of staying healthy while exploring the state. Much of the following information was taken from the American Medical Association's *Encyclopedia of Medicine.*

Altitude Sickness
Also known as mountain sickness, altitude sickness most commonly affects mountain climbers, hikers, and skiers who ascend too rapidly to heights above 8,000 feet. Caused by a reduction in atmospheric pressure, and a corresponding

decrease in oxygen, altitude sickness alters the blood chemistry and affects the nervous system, muscles, heart, and lungs.

Symptoms of altitude sickness include headache, nausea, dizziness, and impaired mental abilities. In severe cases, fluid buildup in the lungs leads to breathlessness, coughing, and a heavy phlegm. Untreated, these symptoms can lead to seizures, hallucinations, and coma. Delays in treatment can even lead to brain damage and death.

The best way to prevent altitude sickness is to ascend *gradually* to elevations above 8,000 feet. Take a day or two for each 2,000-3,000 feet. Victims of altitude sickness should return to lower elevations immediately. If available, pure oxygen can be administered (ski patrol usually keeps oxygen tanks handy).

Dehydration

Dehydration is the result of a drop in the body's water level and oftentimes a subsequent drop in the level of salt. To prevent this you must replace the three (or more) quarts of water your body loses every 24 hours to perspiration and urination. Symptoms of dehydration include severe thirst, dry lips, increased heart and breath rate, dizziness, and confusion. Often the skin is dry and stiff; what little urine is passed is dark. When salt loss is heavy, there will also be headaches, cramps, lethargy, and pallor. Severe cases of dehydration can result in coma.

To prevent dehydration, you must replace the lost water. Even in moderate temperatures and climates, you should be cautious and drink more than you probably think you need; a good rule of thumb is to drink enough water to keep the urine pale. Treatment for dehydration includes fluid and salt replacement—in severe cases intravenously.

Giardia

Giardia, or giardiasis, is an infection of the small intestine caused by the single-celled parasite *Giardia lamblia*. Giardia is spread by direct personal contact or by contaminated food or water; the latter should be of particular concern to hikers and backpackers, as even in remote high-country areas clear-running stream water can be contaminated.

Symptoms of giardia usually begin one to three days after the parasite has entered the system and include violent diarrhea, gas, cramps, loss of appetite, and nausea. To avoid contracting giardia, always wash your hands before handling food, and *do not* drink stream or lake water without first boiling or purifying it. Check sporting goods stores and mountaineering shops for water-purification kits.

Hypothermia

Hypothermia occurs when the body temperature drops below 95° F and is caused by prolonged exposure to cold. Most common among elderly people, whose bodies are unable to generate enough warmth, hypothermia is characterized by a slowed heart rate, puffiness, pale skin, lethargy, and confusion. In severe cases, breathing is also slow.

Hypothermia requires immediate medical attention, and victims are often treated in intensive-care units of hospitals and warmed under controlled conditions. While awaiting medical assistance, move the victim to a warm place, remove wet clothing, and replace it with a warm blanket; if possible, give him something warm (not hot) to drink. *Do not* let the victim walk, do not rub the skin or apply direct heat, and do not give him alcohol.

Sunburn

Sunburn is most common in fair-skinned people and most likely to occur *at high elevations,* where fewer ultraviolet rays are naturally blocked. Skiers and other winter-sports enthusiasts should be especially careful, as the sun's reflection off the snow doubles the effect of harmful rays.

The two best ways to prevent sunburn are by gradual exposure (increasing each day) and by application of a sunscreen with a high sun-protection factor (SPF). Available at pharmacies, sporting-goods stores, and even grocery stores, sunscreens with a high SPF (15 or higher) should be applied liberally and often. Treatment for sunburn includes the application of any of several available lotions and ointments; particularly effective are those with aloe. Severe cases may require medical treatment.

INFORMATION

Your Colorado vacation will be far more enjoyable if you come prepared. In addition to purchasing a thorough and entertaining guide book (which you apparently have already done or are about to do), it's a good idea to send away for any and all information you can get your hands on. One of the best sources for general information is the **Colorado Tourism Board.** Write them at 1625 Broadway, Suite 1700, Denver, CO 80202, or phone (800) 433-2656 (for a vacation kit) or (303) 592-5410 (to speak with someone in the business office). Write the **Denver Metro Convention and Visitor Bureau** at 225 W. Colfax, Denver, CO 80202, or phone (303) 892-1112. Their office, at the same address, is an excellent place to stop in when you first get to town; pick up maps, brochures, and other information, and talk with staff members about everything from where to park to where to find a good sushi bar.

Colorado Welcome Centers
The Colorado Tourism Board has established official Welcome Centers at most ports of entry. These are good places to stop in for information on local, regional, and statewide attractions.

Colorado Welcome Centers are located in **Burlington** (48265 I-70), **Trinidad** (309 N. Nevada Ave.), **Cortez** (928 E. Main St.), **Fruita** (340 Hwy. 40), and **Dinosaur** (in the center of town on Hwy. 40).

Companion Guides
As you'd expect, there are scores of guides to Colorado. Some are thematic; some are regional. Several of these books are excellent and would make ideal companion guides to *Colorado Handbook.* Among these are Lee Gregory's *Colorado Scenic Guide* (Johnson Books, Boulder)—two volumes, northern and southern regions. Of particular value here are the dozens of reprinted U.S. Geologic Survey topo maps, with hiking trails and 4WD routes, as well as the wealth of statistics and facts (including best time of day to take photos). Another good book is Warren Ohlrich's *Aspen-Snowmass Guide to Outdoor Activities* (Warren Ohlrich, Aspen). With over two dozen activities, from Telemark skiing to tennis, from dogsledding to kayaking, this book provides lots of useful first-hand information and tips, as well as listings of shops and agencies specializing in each activity.

For general guides, you'd be hard-pressed to find a book more intriguing than the Works Progress Administration's *Colorado: A Guide to the Highest State.* First published in 1941, this fascinating book is part of the famous series that put some of the country's best writers to work during the lean times of the Depression. The book, available now in used and rare book stores (and re-issued in 1987 as *The WPA Guide to 1930s Colorado* [University Press of Kansas]) includes minutely detailed tours of main routes and back roads, in addition to thorough discussions of the state's history, economy, geography, and population.

For a comprehensive list of other books about Colorado, see the "Booklist."

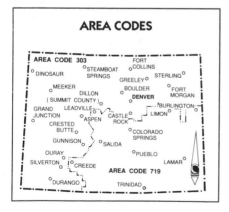

AREA CODES

AREA CODE 303

DINOSAUR   STEAMBOAT SPRINGS   FORT COLLINS   STERLING

MEEKER   DILLON   BOULDER   DENVER   FORT MORGAN

(SUMMIT COUNTY)

GRAND JUNCTION   LEADVILLE   ASPEN   CASTLE ROCK   LIMON   BURLINGTON

CRESTED BUTTE   GUNNISON   SALIDA   COLORADO SPRINGS

OURAY   SILVERTON   CREEDE   PUEBLO   LAMAR

AREA CODE 719

DURANGO   TRINIDAD

USEFUL ADDRESSES AND PHONE NUMBERS

Emergencies: 9-1-1. **Note:** Authorities stress teaching kids to memorize nine-one-one, as opposed to nine-eleven, to keep them from looking for the "11" on the dial.

Aspen Chamber Resort Association, 425 Rio Grande Pl., Aspen, CO 81611, (303) 925-1940

Boulder Chamber of Commerce, 2440 Pearl St., Boulder, CO 80302, (303) 442-2911

Colorado Division of Parks and Recreation, 1313 Sherman St., Denver, CO 80203, (303) 866-3437

Colorado Division of Wildlife, 6060 Broadway, Denver, CO 80216, (303) 297-1192

Colorado Historical Society, 1300 Broadway, Denver, CO 80203, (303) 866-2611

Colorado Springs Convention and Visitors Bureau, 104 S. Cascade, Colorado Springs, CO 80903, (800) 888-4748

Colorado Tourism Board, 1625 Broadway, Suite 1700, Denver, CO 80202, (303) 592-5510

Denver Metro Convention and Visitors Bureau, 225 W. Colfax, Denver, CO 80202, (303) 892-1112

Durango Chamber Resort Association, Box 2587, Durango, CO 81302, (303) 247-0312

National Park Service, 12795 W. Alameda Pkwy., Lakewood, CO 80225, (303) 969-2000

Summit County Chamber of Commerce, Box 214, Frisco, CO 80443, (303) 668-5800

United States Bureau of Land Management, 2850 Youngfield St., Lakewood, CO 80215, (303) 239-3600

United States Fish and Wildlife Service, 134 Union Blvd., Denver, CO 80228, (303) 236-7904

United States Forest Service, Box 25127, Lakewood, CO 80225, (303) 275-5350

Vail Valley Tourism and Covention Bureau , 100 E. Meadows Dr., Vail, CO 81657, (303) 476-1000

TRANSPORTATION

Although several companies offer tours of Colorado—from cliff dwellings to Pikes Peak—and most of the major tourist areas provide excellent public transportation, you're better off with your own rig. Unless you plan to stay in one specific area for your entire visit (which can work very well, especially if all you plan to do is ski), you're probably going to want to get out and do a little exploring. Remember that it's a long way between places you'll want to see, and you'll enjoy the luxury of capricious stops—whether for rest, water, or to explore a mining town or recreation area not on your itinerary.

Colorado By Air

Denver's new International Airport, the first major U.S. airport built in 20 years, is scheduled to open in the fall of 1993. Completely modern in every respect, from appearance to "user friendliness," the new airport will replace Stapleton International Airport and increase the ease of access to Denver and points beyond, particularly the resorts and recreation areas in the nearby mountains. Currently all major U.S. airlines service Stapleton, and from there smaller airlines make regular connecting flights to smaller Colorado towns, including Aspen, Telluride, Montrose, Durango, and Fort Collins. In addition, some of the resort areas, including Telluride, Crested Butte, and Steamboat Springs, offer direct flights from several U.S. cities, such as Phoenix, Chicago, Los Angeles, and Dallas-Fort Worth. There are also large jet airports in Grand Junction and Colorado Springs. Contact your travel agent for specific information about flight schedules and rates.

You'll find rental cars available at Colorado's airports. In addition to the standard chains (Avis,

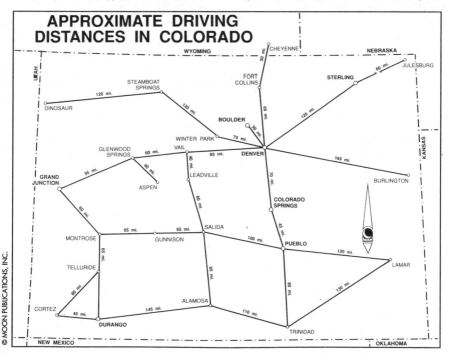

APPROXIMATE DRIVING DISTANCES IN COLORADO

© MOON PUBLICATIONS, INC.

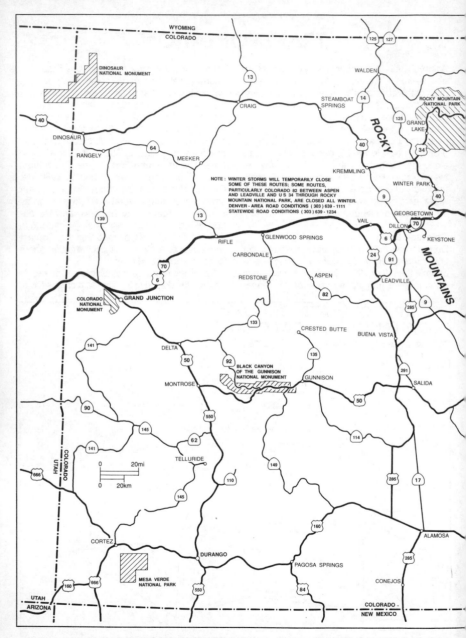

NOTE : WINTER STORMS WILL TEMPORARILY CLOSE
SOME OF THESE ROUTES; SOME ROUTES,
PARTICULARLY COLORADO 82 BETWEEN ASPEN
AND LEADVILLE AND U S 34 THROUGH ROCKY
MOUNTAIN NATIONAL PARK, ARE CLOSED ALL WINTER.
DENVER - AREA ROAD CONDITIONS (303) 639 - 1111
STATEWIDE ROAD CONDITIONS (303) 639 - 1234

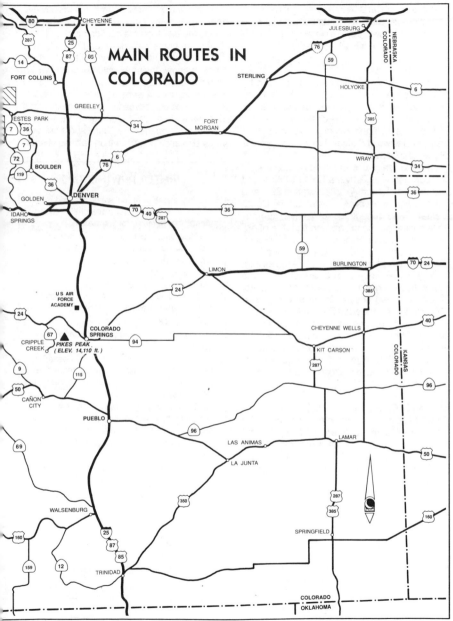

MAIN ROUTES IN COLORADO

© MOON PUBLICATIONS, INC.

Hertz, etc.), several "rent-a-wreck" companies offer discount rates, and a handful of outfits specialize in "snow-ready" vehicles (four-wheel- and front-wheel-drive with ski racks).

By Rail

Colorado's history is defined in large part by the development of the railroad, and by rail is still an excellent way to get here and to see the state. One of **Amtrak**'s major east-west routes cuts across the northern part of Colorado, with stops in Glenwood Springs, Fraser (near Winter Park), and Denver.

The **Ski Train** runs weekends during the ski season between Denver's Union Station and Winter Park. Roundtrip tickets start at $25, and the two-hour trip, which dives under the Continental Divide through Moffat Tunnel, guarantees passengers won't have to fight the oftentimes thick I-70 and Berthoud Pass traffic. For information, phone (303) 296-I-SKI. Also, see "Transportation" under "Winter Park" following.

In addition, several of Colorado's historic towns have begun tourist-oriented train tours. The best-known of these is the **Durango and Silverton Narrow Gauge Railroad,** which hauls over 200,000 passengers a year between the two mountain towns. Rates start at about $40 for the eight-hour trip. For more information, phone (303) 247-2733. Also, see "Durango and Silverton Narrow Gauge Railroad" under "Silverton" following.

Driving In Colorado

Driving in Colorado can be tricky. Even in the summer, when the roads are generally dry and free of snow, you should be very careful. Some of the mountain passes are extremely high and steep, with dramatic switchbacks requiring greatly reduced speed. Make sure your brakes are in good working order.

In the winter, snow drifts across roadways, making visibility difficult, and even when the roads are dry, extreme caution must be taken. When the roads get snowy and wet, it's even more dangerous, and drivers without experience in snow driving should consider waiting until the routes have been cleared. In the spring, melted snow from warm daytime temperatures often trickles across roadways. During the night, this water freezes, resulting in hard-to-see sheets of ice on the road; these spots are even more slick and dangerous than patches of snow.

WINTER DRIVING TIPS

1) Pay attention to highway rules and regulations, including closures and chain requirements; they're meant for your safety.

2) Make sure your brakes are in good working order and that your tires have plenty of tread.

3) Make sure your cooling system has been properly winterized.

4) Check your windshield wipers and wiper fluid—wiper fluid with antifreeze in it is available at auto-parts stores and gas stations.

5) Always carry chains.

6) Do not brake or turn the steering wheel suddenly.

7) If you rent a car, request front-wheel-drive, which offers far greater traction than rear-wheel-drive—4WD vehicles, of course, are best but significantly more expensive.

8) Drive slowly, and always stay in control; remember that your car's stopping distance is greater when the road is wet, snowy, and/or icy.

9) Stop if you begin to lose control or confidence.

10) Keep seatbelts fastened at all times (common sense as well as Colorado state law).

RESPONSIBLE TRAVELING

With each passing day, the world becomes more and more what Marshall McLuhan called a "global village." Television has opened up remote corners of the planet to the eyes of folks sitting in the comfort of their own living rooms in Des Moines and Baton Rouge. Likewise, improved travel technology has opened up the world to tourism. In fact, the recent boom in "adventure travel" has meant package tours to such previously out-of-the-way destinations as Antarctica, the Amazon, and central Africa.

And while all this is generally good (as my colleague Carl Parkes says, "travel spreads prosperity, dissolves political barriers, promotes international peace, and brings about excitement and change"), and host countries do for the most part welcome tourism, there is a dark side to it: Some people who visit native villages forget that people are trying to live their lives there, and the results of such insensitivity can be disastrous. Nor are domestic travelers duty-free of such concerns. Especially in the western states, where native peoples lived for centuries before the first white travelers arrived (in the mid-1500s in some parts of the Southwest, the 18th century in Colorado) and where they are now eking out modest livings on reservations, travelers have immense responsibilities.

The bottom line, of course, is respect and understanding. One organization that has gone to great lengths to encourage this sensitivity is the **North America Center for Responsible Tourism,** whose offices are located in San Anselmo, California. Founded in 1984, the center publishes a newsletter and arranges consultations with groups of travelers. In addition, the center has outlined a "Code of Ethics," which was adapted from a credo written in 1975 by the Asian Council of Churches. The following rules, though originally intended for travelers embarking on trips to remote locations, also apply to American tourists heading out to explore their own backyards.

1) Travel in the spirit of humility and with a genuine desire to meet and talk with local people.

2) Be aware of the feelings of local people; prevent what might be offensive behavior. Photography, particularly, must respect the locals.

3) Cultivate the habit of listening and observing, rather than merely hearing or seeing or knowing all the answers.

4) Realize that other people may have concepts of time and thought patterns that are very different from—not inferior to, just different from—your own.

5) Instead of seeing the "beach paradise" only, seek to discover the richness of another culture and way of life.

6) Get acquainted with local customs; respect them.

7) Remember that you are only one among many visitors; do not expect special privileges.

8) When shopping through bargaining, remember that the poorest merchant will give up a profit rather than give up his personal dignity.

9) Make no promises to local people or to new friends that you cannot implement.

10) Spend time each day reflecting on your experiences in order to deepen your understanding. And remember that what enriches you may be robbing others.

11) If you want a "home away from home," why travel?

RESPONSIBLE TRAVELING (cont.)

In addition to these rules for independent travelers, the center has guidelines for those planning package tours. Asking the following questions will help you decide whether the company allows for responsible travel.

1) Does the tour organizer or travel agent demonstrate a cultural and environmental sensitivity to your destination? How are the local people, and the culture you are to visit, portrayed in advertising brochures and advertising materials?

2) Who benefits from the costs of your trip? Which sectors of the host country benefit? What percentage of your money stays in the country you visit rather than leaking out to transnational industry, the hotel chains, or the airlines?

3) Is a realistic picture of your host country (area) presented, or a version packaged for tourists?

4) Will you use accommodations and modes of travel used by members of the local society?

5) Does your travel plan allow for adequate opportunities for meeting with local people? Does its pacing provide time for you to create and accept opportunities for interacting with local people?

6) Are you committed to engaging in a pre-trip orientation program? Have you thought through ways to share your experiences when you return home, to maintain contact with people and keep informed about the country (area) you visited?

7) Are you allowing sufficient lead time when opting for alternative/local travel services?

8) Do you inform your travel agent/tour organizer about your concerns for justice in travel?

For more information about the Center, send a self-addressed envelope with postage (appropriate for two ounces) to North American Center for Responsible Tourism, 2 Kensington Rd., San Anselmo, CA 94960; you can also phone the Center at (415) 258-6594.

STEPHEN METZGER

NORTHWESTERN COLORADO

The huge northwestern corner of Colorado—comprising Moffat, Routt, Eagle, Rio Blanco, and Garfield counties—is a relatively sparsely populated section of the state, where the highways stretch for miles and miles between tiny little towns. About two-thirds high plateau (the west side) and one-third Rockies' Front Range, northwestern Colorado offers a remarkable variation in scenery. From the barren brown oil shale of the Dinosaur National Monument area to the lush green mountains of White River and Routt national forests, this area is a startling study in contrasts.

Two of the three main east-west routes into the state pass through northwestern Colorado: I-70, which snakes along the Colorado River from the Utah border, then rises up over Vail and Loveland passes; and Hwy. 40, which barrels out of northern Utah making a beeline for Steamboat Springs before being turned south by the Rockies' spine, the Continental Divide. Eventually, just east of Loveland Pass, the two routes join forces and assault Denver in tandem.

Northwestern Colorado is best known today for two things: oil and recreation. The western plateau is thick with fossil fuel, and the world's sixth-largest oil field is just outside Rangely. The eastern side of the plateau area—especially around Craig, Meeker, and (appropriately) Rifle—is very popular with hunters, and the mountains, from Steamboat down to Vail, are world famous for their skiing. In addition, the huge expanses of the forest draw campers, backpackers, rafters, mountain bikers, and anglers to the high mountains when the snow melts.

EAST ALONG INTERSTATE 70

Interstate 70 veers north from Grand Junction, follows the Colorado River, and gradually yet persistently rises up into the heart of Colorado and the Rocky Mountains. En route it passes through or provides access to some of the state's most popular attractions: Aspen, Vail, Summit County, Georgetown and Idaho Springs, and Denver.

Between the Utah border and Glenwood Springs, the largest town between Grand Junction and Vail, the freeway is mostly wide open and flat, passing occasionally through deep canyons carved by the Colorado River. In Glenwood Springs, the valley grows narrow, the canyons often pinching tightly together (see "Glenwood Canyon" under "Glenwood Springs

and Vicinity" following). You can find plenty of inexpensive lodging in Glenwood; this is also where you'll turn south to catch Hwy. 82 to Aspen or Hwy. 113 to Telluride.

Between Glenwood Springs and Vail, the interstate bypasses a number of small towns—Eagle, Edwards, Avon—which also offer lodging and services. At Avon you enter the Vail Valley, a resort region devoted largely to skiing. Three ski areas, Arrowhead, Beaver Creek, and Vail, attract skiers by the thousands (Vail's uphill capacity is 36,000 per hour), not only from Denver, a hundred miles to the east, but from the east coast and around the world. Because of the area's popularity, as well as I-70's importance to cross-country traffic, the road is kept

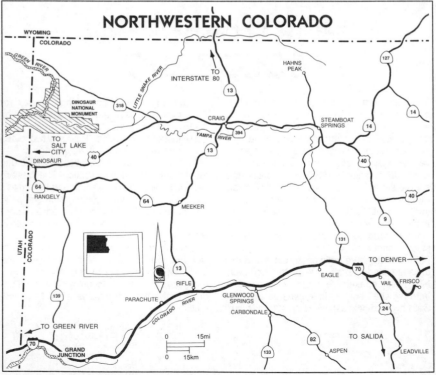

NORTHWESTERN COLORADO

© MOON PUBLICATIONS, INC.

NORTHWESTERN COLORADO HIGHLIGHTS

Dinosaur National Monument: sightseeing, camping, museums

Steamboat Springs: snow skiing, fishing, rafting, hiking, Winter Carnival, Cowboy Roundup Days

Vail: skiing, shopping, cycling, sightseeing, Arrowhead Ski Area, 10th Mountain Hut and Trail System

Glenwood Springs: Frontier Historical Museum, Doc Holliday's Grave, hot springs, Vapor Caves, skiing, fishing

White River and Routt national forests: camping and cross-country skiing

plowed, and even during the severest of storms delays will be few and short-lived (but carry chains anyway!).

PARACHUTE

About an hour east of Grand Junction, Parachute is a little bitty town where you can rest up, gas up, and pick up road pops and other supplies for the cooler. A small picnic area at the turnoff offers a welcome respite for the road weary, who'll also find a booth with tourist information (maps, brochures, etc.) and the Thunder River Trading Post, where you can buy souvenirs, gifts, postcards, T-shirts, and other knick-knacks. In addition to the mini-marts and other small businesses you can see from the road, a City Market (no salad bar or deli) is located up on the hill in the new Battlement Mesa development (follow the signs).

If you're too tired to drive on, Parachute also offers a couple of places to pull off the road to catch some shut-eye, the better to face the road that lies ahead. A **Super 8 Motel,** tel. (303) 285-7936, is located just north of the freeway exit (you can see it from the interstate), and a **Good Sam RV Park** is just over four miles east (stay on the freeway and watch for the sign).

RIFLE

Rifle is located about 75 miles east of Grand Junction at the junction of I-70 and CO 13 north, which shoots straight up to Meeker (40 miles) along the base of the White River Plateau. Long a shopping center and meeting place for area ranchers, Rifle is also a base for folks heading up into the mountains of White River National Forest, just north of town; in the late summer and fall, the area is particularly popular among deer and elk hunters.

According to legend, the town's name came about inadvertently when a mapmaker from an early surveying party left his rifle leaning against a tree, headed back to camp, then suddenly realized his mistake. He grabbed the map he was working on and scribbled the word "rifle" to indicate where the tree was. Later, "rifle" being a prominent word on the only map of the area, folks naturally took to calling the town Rifle. And if you believe that . . .

Rifle Creek Museum
This small museum displays frontier gear (saddles, snowshoes, traps, etc.) as well as early farming and medical equipment and domestic utensils. Located downtown at 337 East Ave., the museum is open Mon. through Fri. 10 a.m.-4 p.m. For further information, phone (303) 625-5862.

Rifle Gap Falls And Lake State Recreation Area
This is where locals go to cool off during the hot summer months, for fishing, swimming, sailing, windsurfing, waterskiing, and even spelunking. Camp beside the Rifle Gap Reservoir, and fish for brown and rainbow trout and smallmouth bass, as well as walleye and other panfish.

Rifle Falls is a broad 50-foot-high waterfall on East Rifle Creek, at the base of which are lush foliage and a series of caves. The caves are large, save for a few narrow crawlways, and perfect for novice explorers.

The lake and falls are located about 15 miles north of Rifle. Take CO 13 north about five miles, and turn right on Hwy. 325. There's a small admission fee to get into the recreation area; additional cost for camping. For further information, phone (303) 625-1607.

Accommodations

Rifle offers several clean, inexpensive, and easy-to-get-to places to bed down for the night, one of the best of which is the **Rusty Cannon Motel,** tel. (303) 625-4004, where singles start at about $30—located just off the interstate. Across the street, the **Red River Inn,** tel. 625-3050, also has inexpensive rooms, starting at about $25 for singles. You'll also find budget rooms across the freeway on the frontage road at the **LaDonna Motel,** tel. 625-1741, an older place that's either nicely shaded or quite overgrown, depending on your perspective.

Food And Drink

If you're heading out of (or through) Rifle in the early morning, stop in at **Country Doughnuts** on E. 3rd St., where you can get doughnuts singly or by the dozen, or, if you're looking for something that'll stick to your ribs a bit longer, big diner-style breakfasts for $2-4. This little café, full of locals talking weather and small-town politics, has a huge map of the United States at the counter, and customers are invited to put pins up marking their home towns. Country Doughnuts is also open for lunch, serving sandwiches, burgers, and salads for $2-5, and dinner, with burgers, chicken, and chimichangas for $3-6.

Village Pizza Factory, 160 Railroad Ave., tel. (303) 625-0835, serves pizzas, sandwiches, salads, and spaghetti dishes Wed. through Sun. for lunch and dinner ($5-12).

The **Red Lion Pub** downtown on Railroad Ave., much less the British-style pub its name implies than the local mountain bar the location suggests, plays loud jukebox music and serves domestic and imported beer in *tall* glasses. The place has a reputation for getting downright rowdy, especially on Friday and Saturday nights, when workers come down out of the mountains to blow off steam.

Services

The offices of the **Rifle Police Department** are at 202 Railroad Ave.; phone (303) 625-2311. Phone the **Garfield County Sheriff** at 625-1899. Rifle's small **Clagett Memorial Hospital** is at 701 E. 5th Avenue, tel. 625-1510. Larger medical facilities are in Glenwood Springs, about 25 mfles west, at **Valley View Hospital,** tel. 945-6535. Rifle's **post office** is at 330 Railroad Ave.; phone 625-1070. Get maps and **Forest Service information** at the White River National Forest—District Office, 94 County Rd. 244; phone 625-2371.

Recycling

Drop off most recyclables at **Blackmore Metals** on the west end of town. Recycle aluminum at the **City Market** at 1320 Railroad Avenue.

*Rifle:
a high-caliber town*

STEPHEN METZGER

Information

The Rifle **Chamber of Commerce** is located in an old railroad car just off the interstate on the south end of town. You'll find information here not only about local attractions, accom-modations, and recreation opportunities, but also about much of the White River National Forest and Glenwood Springs-Aspen areas. You can also write Box 809, Rifle, CO 81650, or phone (303) 625-2085.

GLENWOOD SPRINGS AND VICINITY

One of Colorado's most historically and geo-logically fascinating towns, Glenwood Springs is the site of what it claims is the world's largest natural hot springs pool. Actually comprised of two pools—the larger 405 by 100 feet and con-taining over a million gallons of water—Glen-wood Hot Springs has been attracting travel-ers for centuries, from nomadic Ute, Comanche, Cheyenne, and Arapahoe peoples who believed in the waters' spiritual healing powers to mod-ern-day après-skiers who believe simply in its powers to ease aching muscles.

A gateway to the best ski areas in the state, Glenwood Springs (pop. 6,000; elev. 5,750 feet) has a small ski resort (Ski Sunlight) right in its backyard and is the last decent-sized town you pass through heading east on I-70 before you get into the heart of the Rockies and Colorado's real winter sports arenas: Vail and the ski mecca of Summit County. In addition, Glenwood Springs is at the junction with Hwy. 82, the only road into Aspen in the winter (when the highway southeast of Aspen is closed over Indepen-dence Pass). In fact, not only do a large number of Aspen-area workers live in Glenwood Springs (where housing's much less expensive) and commute the 40 miles every day to the ski town, but many people who live in Aspen drive regu-larly into Glenwood Springs to do their shop-ping; from razor blades to dog food to fresh produce, everyday necessities are far cheaper in Glenwood Springs than in Aspen.

All of which should tell the savvy winter tourist something: If you want to ski Aspen, and you want to save some money, think about staying in Glenwood Springs. Though you'd be hard pressed to find a room in Aspen for much under $80 or $90 a night, Glenwood has several mo-tels where clean rooms start at around $25, as well as a hostel where you can get a bed for about $12. That's a savings of close to $400 a week—which could almost buy you and a date a nice dinner out in Aspen.

HISTORY

Known for centuries to Utes, who, protective of their sacred waters, fought to keep the Cheyenne and Comanche away, Glenwood Springs was first discovered by whites in 1860, when Captain Richard Sopris took sick while exploring the Eagle River Valley and was brought to the waters by the Utes. In the 1870s, the discovery of silver in Leadville brought about a population boom and a flurry of mining-camp construction in the mountains east of Glen-wood. Leadville's John Landis arrived at Yam-pah springs in 1880 and, in true colonial fashion, claimed it for his own.

By the mid-1880s, the Native Americans had been mostly displaced, and white settlers had taken control of much of the fertile Roaring Fork River Valley. In 1885, Walter Devereux, an Aspen miner and engineer, bought the hot springs, incorporated Glenwood Springs, and began to solicit tourism and investment. By the latter part of the 1880s, Glenwood Springs was a rip-roaring town whose nearly two dozen sa-loons were well known to many of the hard-living miners, ranchers, cowboys, merchants, and law-men who opened up the West.

The Denver and Rio Grande Railroad pushed through Glenwood Springs in 1887. A year later, thanks largely to the labor of local prison in-mates who worked to break up the rock-hard ground and divert water from the Colorado River, old Yampah springs had been converted into a concrete pool, with an adjacent bath-house, hotel, and casino.

In 1893, the Hotel Colorado was completed, and the area soon became a popular resort destination for some of the more monied eastern families, including Vanderbilts and Astors. Due in part to the influence of this upscale clientele, as well as to the importance of the horse to Glenwood's development, polo became a cel-ebrated local pastime, and Glenwood teams

TO VAIL AND DENVER →

GLENWOOD SPRINGS
GOLF CLUB

COLORADO RIVER

TO GRAND JUNCTION

GLENWOOD SPRINGS

HOTEL COLORADO

HOT SPRINGS POOL

AMTRAK STATION

POST OFFICE

GLENWOOD SPRINGS HOSTEL

FRONTIER HISTORICAL MUSEUM

COOPER AVE.

9th ST.
10th ST.
11th ST.

CHAMBER OF COMMERCE INFORMATION

CEMETERY RD.

COLORADO AVE.

13th ST.

BENNET AVE.

GRAND AVE.

ROARING FORK

19th ST.

VALLEY VIEW HOSPITAL

BLAKE AVE.

RIVER

27th ST.

NOT TO SCALE

TO ASPEN

TO SKI SUNLIGHT

AIRPORT

82

© MOON PUBLICATIONS, INC.

won national championships in the early part of the century (trophies are on display in the Frontier Historical Museum).

The mid-20th-century was essentially a slow time for Glenwood Springs, as other mountain towns began to draw crowds; however, with the boom in the ski industry (as well as in the health and fitness industries), in addition to an increased interest in local history and heritage, things in Glenwood Springs began to pick up. By the 1970s and '80s, the public was rediscovering the hot springs, realizing the important part this little town played in the development of the state, and taking advantage of its proximity to Aspen and the other nearby ski resorts.

ATTRACTIONS AND PARKS

Frontier Historical Museum

Founded in 1963 by the Glenwood Springs Historical Society, this small museum—originally a home built in 1905 by a local doctor—features a replica of a coal mine, a collection of pioneer-era toys, dolls, and clothing, as well as Native American artifacts and historical maps and photos of Glenwood Springs and the surrounding areas.

Hours are Mon. through Sat. 1-4 p.m. (Thurs.-Sat. only, 1-4 p.m. in winter). Admission is $1 (no charge for kids under 11). Guided group tours are available by appointment. For more infor-

STEPHEN METZGER

Hot Springs Lodge at Glenwood Hot Springs

mation, write Glenwood Springs Historical Museum, 1001 Colorado Ave., Glenwood Springs, CO 81601, or phone (303) 945-4448.

Doc Holliday's Grave, Linwood Cemetery

An easy half-mile trail leads from Cemetery Rd. (off Bennett Ave.) to Linwood Cemetery, where Doc Holliday is reportedly buried: Although a gravestone with his name and the inscription "died in bed" stands in the cemetery, some claim he was buried in an unmarked grave in town. Kid Curry, a member of Butch Cassidy's Hole-in-the-Wall gang, is also buried at Linwood.

In the winter, the trail is perfect for a short Nordic ski excursion.

Glenwood Hot Springs Pool

Advertising itself in the early part of the century as a "Health and Pleasure Resort," serving both "invalids and tourists," this gigantic hot springs has actually been serving travelers for hundreds of years. Utes, who called them Yampah (or "Big Medicine") springs, used the pools, as did early white settlers and several U.S. presidents, including Teddy Roosevelt.

The pools are completely refilled about every eight hours by the three and a half million gallons of 124-degree water that flows from the springs daily—perfect for basking in after a day on the slopes or an afternoon chasing trout in the Colorado or Roaring Fork River. A daily pass is $6 for adults ($3.75 for kids 3-12). There's also a

weight and exercise room, and a water slide. Suits and towels can be rented for a nominal fee. For information, write Hot Springs Lodge and Pool, Box 308, Glenwood Springs, CO 81602, or phone (303) 945-6571, (800) 623-3400 (toll free from Denver), (800) 537-SWIM (toll free from the rest of Colorado).

Vapor Caves

Three caves, heated by mineral hot springs to 115 degrees and approximately 100% humidity, are open to the public seven days a week. At one time part of the Utes' Yampah springs (along with the hot springs pools), the caves are now privately owned. In addition to a cleansing sweat in the caves, you can get a variety of health ministrations: massages, facials, cranial-sacral therapy, Reiki therapy, reflexology, and earwax removal. Afterward, you can relax in the solarium or on the sundeck with a glass of natural juice. Prices start at $5.75 (for a cave visit) and run to $60 (for the full treatment).

The Vapor Caves are open seven days a week 9 a.m.-9 p.m. For more information, phone (303) 945-0667, or write 709 E. 6th St., Glenwood Springs, CO 81601.

City Park

Glenwood Spring's Sayre's Park is right on the main drag through town (Hwy. 82/Grand Ave.) and has picnic facilities, tennis and basketball courts, and spacious lawns.

RECREATION

Skiing

One of Colorado's smaller ski resorts, but a favorite among locals who want to avoid the crowds and pretentiousness of the larger areas, **Ski Sunlight** offers both downhill and cross-country skiing about 10 miles from Glenwood Springs (free shuttles run regularly between town and the resort). With a 2,000-foot vertical drop, Sunlight's 350 acres of trails and runs are 20% novice, 58% intermediate, and 22% advanced—serviced by one triple chair, two doubles, and one surface lift.

Lodging, equipment rental, lessons (downhill, cross-country, and Telemark), and day care are all available at Sunlight, as are package deals with local hotels and motels. For more information, write Ski Sunlight, 10901 County Rd. 117, Glenwood Springs, CO 81601, or phone (303) 945-7491 or (800) 445-7931.

Southwest of Glenwood Springs off Hwy. 82, **Spring Gulch** is a Nordic area with 10 miles of trails. For maps and information, check ski shops in the Glenwood Springs-Carbondale-Aspen area.

Golfing

Glenwood Springs Golf Course is a nine-hole public course located north of the frontage road in west Glenwood Springs. For tee times or further information, phone (303) 945-7086.

Hiking

Virtually surrounded by mountains and national forest lands, Glenwood Springs offers the hiker and backpacker hundreds of miles of trails to explore. Just a few miles east of town, **No Name** and **Hanging Lake** trails are good day hikes. In town, the **Boy Scout Trail** takes hikers from the end of 8th St. to the base of Lookout Mountain—3 1/2 miles, approximately two hours. Bring water. **Red Mountain Trail** will take you from the end of W. 9th St. to the site of Glenwood's first ski area, where the lift towers are still standing. The hikes from Cemetery Rd. to Linwood Cemetery and from the Vapor Caves to the Colorado River are both easy, scenic, and enjoyable.

For maps and more information, contact the Glenwood Springs Chamber of Commerce or the White River National Forest headquarters on Grand Avenue (see "Information" following).

You can also get USGS maps and tips on hiking and backpacking in the area at **Summit Canyon Mountaineering,** 1001 Grand Ave., tel. (303) 945-6994.

Hunting And Fishing

Come winter, you'll likely hear long-time Glenwoodians talking about how full their freezers are. "Didn't think I was gonna get my elk this year, but I finally did, just before the season closed." Deer, too, are popular prey of local (as well as visiting) hunters, though they know the 150 pounds of meat a decent-sized mulie provides is nothing next to what a big bull elk can—upwards of 400 pounds. Good fishing abounds in the Glenwood Springs area, too—rainbows and brown trout in the Colorado River west of town, and brookies and rainbows in the small lakes in the surrounding mountains. For tips on local fishing, stop by **Roaring Fork Anglers,** 2022 Grand Ave., or phone (303) 945-0180.

Rafting

On the confluence of the Roaring Fork and Colorado rivers, Glenwood Springs is a rafter's paradise, and companies based throughout the area offer a variety of trips, from short, two-hour jaunts to three-day excursions. **Rock Gardens Rafting,** tel. (303) 945-6737, offers short tours ($13), half-day ($20), and full-day trips ($35, including lunch); they also have a campground with RV and tent sites. Located off I-70 two miles east of Glenwood Springs, Exit 119. **Blue Sky Adventurers,** 319 6th St., tel. 945-6605, and **Whitewater Rafting,** 51100 Hwys. 6 and 24, tel. 945-8477, can also arrange trips.

TOURS

The Glenwood Springs Chamber of Commerce (see "Information" following) has outlined a historic walking tour of downtown Glenwood Springs. Included are the stone bath house at the hot springs pool, the vapor caves, the Hotel Colorado, the Glenwood Barber Shop (the only remaining portion of the Hotel Glenwood, built before the turn of the century and mostly destroyed by fire in 1945), and over three dozen other buildings of historical significance—homes, banks, and retail stores. The chamber can provide you with a map.

For snowmobile tours of the area (from two-hour trips to overnight excursions that include meals and lodging), contact **Rocky Mountain Sports, Inc.,** 0412 Sun King Dr., Glenwood Springs, CO 81601, tel. (303) 945-8498. In warmer weather, **Crystal River Jeep Tours,** 116 E. Main St., Marble, CO 81623, tel. (303) 963-1991, offers trips to the Yule Marble Quarry, Crystal City, and Lead King Basin.

ACCOMMODATIONS

Hotels And Motels
Glenwood Springs offers a wide range of comfortable rooms, from dorm-style digs at the hostel to relative elegance at the Hotel Colorado, with quite a bit in between. At the **Glenwood Springs Hostel,** 1021 Grand Ave., tel. (303) 945-8545, you can get a bed for about $12, or $70 a week (students and AYH members slightly less). Walking distance from the hot springs, the hostel offers discounts on ski tickets and rental, free pick-up from the bus and train depots (with advance notice), as well as laundry and kitchen facilities and a record library for use by guests.

The **Ponderosa Motel and Cottages** in West Glenwood at 51793 Hwys. 6 and 24, tel. 945-5058, has rooms and cabins starting at under $30, and both the **Super 8 Motel,** tel. 945-8888, and the **Holiday Inn,** tel. 945-8551, also in West Glenwood, have rooms starting at about $40. The **Hot Springs Lodge,** tel. 945-6571 or (800) 537-SWIM (in Colorado only) has doubles starting at about $50, with discounts offered to the pool, while rooms at the historic **Hotel Colorado,** tel. 945-6511 or, toll-free from Denver, (800) 623-3400, start at about $50.

If you're going to be skiing at Ski Sunlight, you'd be hard-pressed to do better than the **Brettelberg Condominiums,** tel. 945-7421 or (800) 634-0481. More a 1940s-style ski lodge than a modern-day condo complex, the Brettelberg is right on the slopes, actually uphill from the base lodge—the ultimate in "ski in and ski out." Rates start at about $70 a night for four people (studio); weekly rates max at about $600 for four. For more information, write Brettleberg Condominiums, 11101 Rd. 117, Glenwood Springs, CO 81601.

Bed And Breakfasts
Glenwood Springs' bed and breakfast accommodations include **Adduccie's Inn,** 1023 Grand Ave., tel. (303) 945-9341, in an old Victorian (most rooms share a shower; one has a private bath); the **Kaiser House,** 932 Copper, tel. 945-8827; the **Sojourners Inn,** 1032 Copper, tel. 945-7162; and the **Talbott House** and the **House Next Door,** a couple adjoining turn-of-the-century homes at 928 Colorado Ave., tel. 945-1039, with both shared- and private-bath rooms and a solar-heated hot tub.

Camping And RVing
Campgrounds are scattered throughout the White River National Forest, large units of which surround the Glenwood Springs area. **Deep Lake** and **Coffee Pot Spring** have free camping at moderately improved sites (pit toilets, no showers—drinking water at Coffee Pot Spring only). For more information, phone the Eagle District Office of the Forest Service at (303) 328-6388; for maps of White River National Forest, stop by forest headquarters on Grand Avenue (see "Information" following).

RV and tent camping are available at **Hideout RV Park,** tel. 945-5621, about a mile up the road toward Ski Sunlight, and at **Ami's Acres Campground,** tel. 945-5340, off I-70 at Exit 114. A **KOA** campground, tel. 984-2240, in New Castle, 11 miles west of Glenwood Springs on I-70, has tent sites, full-hookup RV sites, and cabins, as well as hot showers, laundry facilities, and a small store. Take Exit 105 from I-70, and follow the signs to East Elk Creek Road. Two miles east of Glenwood Springs, **Rock Gardens Camping and Rafting,** tel. 945-6737, offers tent and RV sites as well as half- and full-day raft trips.

FOOD

The Devereux Room at the **Hotel Colorado,** tel. (303) 945-6511, serves breakfast (pancakes, omelettes, etc.), lunch (fish and chips, sandwiches, salads), and dinner (veal, chicken, beef, and Southwestern food) at moderate prices. For an inexpensive and delicious lunch, try **The Loft,** 720 Grand Ave., tel. 945-6808. Sandwiches, salads (dynamite Caesars!), and burritos run $5-8. For dinner try **Peppo Nino's,** 702

Grand Ave., tel. 945-9059. The raviolis and lasagna are wonderful, as is the Dinner for Two (spaghetti, rigatoni, or manicotti, served with salad, French bread, soup, and a half liter of wine for $23). You can also get food to go. Families will enjoy **Andre's Restaurant**, tel. 945-5367, where dolls, puppets, and stuffed animals decorate the walls and an electric train circles overhead in the dining room. Italian entrees and pizzas run $6-10. Located just off I-70 in West Glenwood.

For "Food so good you'll slap yo mama," served by a "well trained . . . and slightly warped staff," try **The Bayou,** on the frontage road in West Glenwood, tel. 945-1047. During ski season, get a free cup of gumbo by showing your lift ticket or ski rental receipt, and a free cocktail if you've got a cast from a ski injury.

About eight miles south of town on Highway 82 (to Aspen) is the **Sopris Restaurant and Lounge,** tel. 945-7771. One of the nicer eateries in the area, the Sopris is popular with everyone from local ranchers and outfitters to Aspen luminaries, who rave about the eclectic menu— from American-standard beef dishes to daily continental specials.

ENTERTAINMENT AND EVENTS

Though there's undoubtedly more going on up the road in Aspen, Glenwood Springs does offer its share of nightlife. **Mother O'Leary's,** 914 Grand Ave., tel. (303) 945-4078, features live rock 'n' roll Thurs.-Sat. nights and country-and-western on Wednesdays and Sundays. In addition, the lounges at the **Sopris Restaurant,** 7215 Hwy. 82, tel. 945-7771, and the **Holiday Inn,** tel. 945-8551, regularly feature live listening and dancing music. For current information on what's going on where, pick up a copy of **Mountain Leisure,** published every Friday by the *Glenwood Post.* You'll find listings of art, recreation, and nightlife happenings, as well as reviews and theater schedules.

Calendar

Glenwood's biggest annual event is the popular **Strawberry Days** in mid-June. Dating from 1863, this is the oldest town festival in Colorado (cancelled only during the food and gasoline rationing of WW II) and features foot and bicycle races, Pony Express rides, a parade, arts-and-crafts fair, beauty pageant (de gustibus non est disputandum . . .), live country-and-western music, and free strawberries and ice cream.

The International Folk Festival and Oktoberfest in the fall in downtown's Sayre Park offers food, drink, and entertainment from around the world.

For exact dates, times, and locations, as well as for more information on other Glenwood Springs events, contact the chamber of commerce (see "Information" following).

SHOPPING

In downtown Glenwood Springs you'll find a handful of souvenir and curio shops, as well as some stores carrying quality arts and crafts. The **Watersweeper and the Dwarf,** 717 Grand Ave., tel. (303) 945-2000, carries handcrafted pieces carved, sculpted, assembled, and molded from silver, gold, clay, glass, and other odds and ends. **Sioux Villa Curio,** tel. 945-6134, one block west of the hot springs pool on 6th St., sells souvenirs and knickknacks, including moccasins, "authentic" Black Hills gold jewelry, and post cards. The Glenwood Springs Mall in west Glenwood has a **JCPenney, K mart,** and over two dozen smaller stores selling everything from hats and shoes to jewelry and pets.

SERVICES

The **Glenwood Springs Police Department** is located at 823 Blake Ave.; phone (303) 945-8566. Phone the **State Patrol** at 945-6198 (24-hour emergency line). Glenwood's **Valley View Hospital** is at 6535 Blake Ave., tel. 945-6535. The main **post office** is at 113 9th St., tel. 945-5611.

Recycling

Glenwood Springs operates two recycling centers, both of which will take aluminum and glass. Locations are 1600 Grand Ave. and the **Wal-Mart** at 3010 Blake. Recycle aluminum only at the **City Market,** 1410 Grand Ave., and **Safeway,** 2001 Grand Ave.

INFORMATION

Stop by or write the **Glenwood Springs Chamber of Commerce** at 1102 Grand Ave., Glenwood Springs, CO 81601, tel. (303) 945-6589. You'll find plenty of information on area history, recreation, dining, and lodging, as well as maps.

For information on the **White River National Forest,** contact either the forest headquarters, 900 Grand Ave., P.O. Box 948, Glenwood Springs, CO 81602, tel. 945-2521; or the Eagle District Office, 125 W. 5th St., P.O. Box 720, Eagle, CO 81631, tel. 328-6388.

The **Book Train** magazine and bookstore, 723 Grand Ave., tel. 945-7045, has an excellent selection of books on Colorado and the Southwest, as well as other travel books, including those Cadillacs of travel guides, Moon Publications' handbooks. The Glenwood Springs branch of the **Garfield County Library** is located at 413 9th St., tel. 945-5958. The Colorado **Mountain College Library** is at the college at 3000 County Rd. 114, tel. 945-7481.

The **Frontier Historical Museum** has a gift shop with books on the area's history, as well as videos for rent. In addition, the museum's archives are available (by appointment only) for more extensive research. Phone 945-4448 or 945-8465.

For **road and weather information,** phone 945-2221.

TRANSPORTATION

Glenwood Springs' **Amtrak** station, tel. (303) 945-9563, is directly across the freeway from the hot springs pool (accessible via footbridge). The **Greyhound** bus depot is at 118 W. 6th St., tel. 945-8501. To rent a car, phone **Defiance Rent-a-Wreck** at 945-7101, located at 1810 Grand Avenue.

Aspen's airport, 40 miles southeast of Glenwood Springs, is serviced by **Continental Express,** tel. 925-3350, and **United Express,** tel. 925-3400. You can rent cars at the Aspen airport (see "Aspen" following).

GLENWOOD SPRINGS TO VAIL

It'd be tough to find a stretch of American interstate prettier than that running east from Glenwood Springs to Vail, up over Vail Pass, through Summit County, over (or under, via tunnel) Loveland Pass, and into Denver. From Glenwood to Vail, it's about 75 miles and when the road is clear takes less than an hour and a half. Allow more time during winter storms (a main east-west artery, this is one of the first roads to be plowed, yet snow can still pile up, making it slick and dangerous).

A half-hour out of Glenwood Springs, you're approaching the soul of Colorado ski country. The Rockies' sharp peaks loom in front of you; the road grows steeper, the air thinner; condominium complexes begin to proliferate and sprawl at freeway exits. Lift towers, chairs and clearcuts punctuate the hillsides. Finally, you roll into the Vail valley, site of one of the world's premier ski resorts and summer vacation areas.

Glenwood Canyon

Just a few miles east of Glenwood Springs, you enter Glenwood Canyon, the most scenic stretch of the Utah-to-Kansas freeway. Here, I-70 snakes through a 15-mile-long crevice carved by the Colorado River, bridging it and flirting with its steep, rocky banks. In some places, the canyon walls are 2,000 feet high.

An important artery for travelers since 1887, when the Denver and Rio Grande Railroad first laid tracks along the river, Glenwood Canyon has seen several generations of roadways. The recently completed Glenwood Canyon Highway, in planning since the mid-1970s and under construction throughout the '80s and early '90s, makes every attempt to wed modern transportation needs with the environmental considerations dire to such a sensitive area. While the road was being built, workers had to conform to strict ecological guidelines and were under the constant scrutiny of environmentalists.

The completed stretch of highway, which includes over 40 bridges (totaling over six miles), used 30 million pounds of structural steel, 30 million pounds of reinforcing steel, and 400,000 cubic yards of concrete.

Four rest areas along this short stretch of road offer access to hiking trails into White River National Forest, as well as to the recreation/bike path (wheelchair accessible) that follows the entire course of the highway through the canyon. One of them, Grizzly Creek Rest Area, also has a launch for kayaks, rafts, and other small boats.

VAIL AND BEAVER CREEK

Located in the Gore Creek Valley between the Gore and Sawatch mountain ranges, Vail has earned a reputation as one of the finest ski areas in the world. Just 100 miles west of Denver via I-70, Vail attracts not only hundreds of thousands of skiers each year, but also more and more summer visitors, who descend on the little community of Vail Village (permanent pop. 5,000) to take part in the virtually limitless recreational opportunities—golfing, tennis, cycling, fishing, horseback riding, and rafting—as well as to wander through the town's cobblestone streets and Tyrolean-style buildings.

Vail, like Aspen, is almost always associated with money. This is one of the playgrounds of the East Coast rich, and hotel rooms can run $300 a night; you can't very well vacation here if you've got to keep a close eye on finances.

Then there's Beaver Creek, Vail's even richer neighbor, where summer homes run into the millions and a suite in a luxury hotel can cost up to $600. People who can afford to stay here don't even blink at the thought of spending $40 for a ski lift ticket (prices are the same at both Vail and Beaver Creek, both of which are owned and operated by Vail Associates).

But don't let it intimidate you. Even though, as F. Scott Fitzgerald once said to Ernest Hemingway, "The rich aren't like you and me," and they do own much of the Vail area, they don't own all of it. And there are ways for a working person to enjoy a visit without going hopelessly into debt. In fact, one of the best parts of visiting Vail is simply wandering around, browsing in the wide range of specialty shops, and strolling along the bike and walking path between the town and the base of the lifts.

History

Compared to Telluride, Breckenridge, Aspen, and many other Colorado ski towns, Vail is a relative newcomer, barely a quarter century old. The area was probably explored to some degree as early as 1850, when Irishman Sir George Gore (whose surname is unfortunately fitting) and a huge hunting party went on a bloodlusty trophy tour of Colorado and southern Wyoming. In 1873, the Hayden Survey Party passed through the valley, with photographer William Henry Jackson lugging 100 pounds of equipment up Notch Mountain to take his now-famous photo of Mount of the Holy Cross. The near-perfect cross in the photo, first displayed at the Philadelphia Centennial Exhibition of 1876, has inspired thousands of pilgrims to the area.

It wasn't until the middle of the next century, though, that the Vail Valley saw any real settlement. In 1942, some 15,000 troops from the Army's 10th Mountain Division were stationed in the mountains south of Vail. Many of these men—trained in backcountry winter survival, including getting around on skis—saw action in Italy's Po River Valley and Apennine Mountains. After the war, a handful of them, led by Peter Seibert, who had been wounded in Italy, returned to the area and began developing their own ski area. Vail saw its first lift-borne skiers on Dec. 15, 1962. By the winter of 1965, a small village had begun to develop, with several restaurants, saloons, hotels, and a medical clinic. The town was incorporated that year.

In the mid-1970s, Vail began to make itself known as one of Colorado's best ski areas, its "Back Bowls" earning the respect of the most discriminating skiers in the country. In 1974, Gerald Ford, who had owned a home in Vail since the mid-1960s, became president of the United States following Richard Nixon's resignation. Photos of Ford at his "Western White House" graced the pages of newspapers throughout the world.

Work on Vail's sister resort, Beaver Creek, was begun by Vail Associates in the late 1970s; it had originally been part of a plan to bid for the 1976 Winter Olympics (defeated by Colorado voters). By the early '80s the two ski areas had developed a reputation not only for some of the best snow in the Rockies, but for some of the best "show." Vail and big money became almost synonymous, and the perception, not wholly inaccurate if obviously stereotypical, of the Vail visitor was one of furs, fancy German cars, expensive state-of-the-art ski equipment, and a foreign accent, either European or Texan.

Also during the early '80s, Vail and Beaver Creek began to expand from primarily winter playgrounds to year-round resorts. More golf courses were built, gondolas and chairlifts were made available to sightseers and mountain bikers, and the village began to sponsor hot-air balloon rallies, tennis tournaments, and concerts, from chamber music to rock 'n' roll. During the summer of 1988, Vail Ski Area's Back Bowls were further developed, more than doubling the amount of skiable terrain on the mountain.

Colorado Ski Museum

Offering an overview of the history of skiing around the world, with an emphasis on Colorado, this small museum features excellent exhibits, including lots of wonderful historical photos and examples of century-old equipment. Check out skis used by early Colorado miners in the 1880s, early "beartrap" bindings, the first buckle boots and metal-edged skis, the infamous K2 Cheeseburger Deluxes, and skis used by recent Olympic-medal winners, as well as equipment once belonging to Gerald Ford. You can also learn more about the Army's 10th Mountain Division and view some of their equipment—tents, skis, white camouflage parkas, etc.

The Colorado Ski Museum is located in Vail Village at the corner of Vail Rd. and E. Meadow Drive. Hours are Tues. through Sun. 10 a.m.-5 p.m. Admission is free. For further information, phone (303) 476-1876.

PARKS AND RECREATION

Recreation is what Vail's all about. Folks come from all over the world to vacation here, to ski the vast expanses of the Back Bowls, to hit golf balls into the 8,000-foot-high, thin mountain air, to toss caddis flies at native rainbow trout. Or just to relax. What better place to hide behind a pair of Foster Grants and a Stephen King novel than beside a pool or at a sidewalk café in Vail Village?

The Vail/Beaver Creek Activities Desk can arrange a wide array of recreational vacations, from kayaking to jeep tours. Phone (303) 949-9090.

WINTER SPORTS

Vail was founded on downhill skiing, and even as the resort has diversified, downhill skiing remains its primary draw. From mid-November through April, weather permitting, Vail's park-

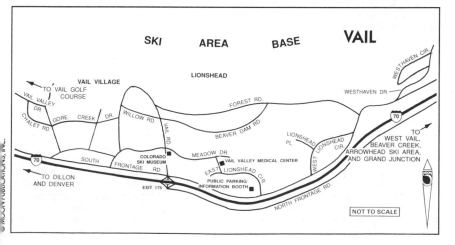

JACK AFFLECK

skiing the Back Bowls at Vail

ing lots are packed with ski-racked 4WD rigs, its streets bustling with ski-booted shoppers, its restaurants and hotels packed to the gills with skiers of all abilities, from complete novices to certified powderhounds and bump bashers. In the winter, just about everything in the Vail valley revolves around snow skiing.

Vail

In a recent *Skiing* magazine article, former Vail ski instructor Lito Tejada-Flores (who has since relocated to Telluride) wrote that Vail's Back Bowls are the "quintessential skiing invitation." In addition, readers' polls sponsored by both *Ski* and *Snow Country* magazines listed Vail as the number one ski area in the country.

Indeed, the resort offers nearly 4,000 acres of wide open skiing terrain divided up fairly evenly for beginner, intermediate, and advanced skiers. The largest single-mountain ski area in the U.S., Vail has a 3,250-foot vertical drop, 20 lifts (including seven high-speed detachable quads), and 120 runs, some of which are over four miles long. Its total uphill capacity is almost 36,000 skiers per hour.

Of course as one of Colorado's premier ski resorts, and certainly its most accessible, the place can get crowded, especially on weekends. Only 100 miles from Denver, Vail is close enough even for day trippers. Still, though, thanks particularly to the new Back Bowls and high-speed

chairs, the mobs are handled relatively gracefully, and you should be able to find a fairly uncrowded slope to crank some turns (though if you'd rather strut your stuff for the masses, there's plenty of opportunity for that too).

Like a luxury hotel, Vail is exclusive in both feel and actual cost, and folks on budgets will have a tough time here: A single day's lift ticket will set you back about $40 (though seniors 70 and older ski free). Still, it's a great splurge, and every serious skier owes it to himself to hit Vail at least once in his lifetime.

Vail has a full-service ski school, including programs for kids (three and older; non-ski programs for kids two months to six years), racers, snowboarders, Telemarkers, and cross-country skiers. Vail also offers NASTAR recreational racing.

For more information on skiing Vail, write Vail Associates, Box 7, Vail, CO 81658, tel. (303) 476-5601. For information about children's ski programs, phone 279-2040; adult ski school, 476-3239; cross-country and Telemark, 476-5601, ext. 4390. For information on **snow conditions,** phone 476-4888 or 476-4889. For information on NASTAR racing, phone 476-5601, ext. 4050.

Complimentary "Meet the Mountain" tours are offered Sun.-Tues. at 1 p.m. beginning at Wildwood Shelter.

Beaver Creek

Vail's little sister, Beaver Creek first opened in the winter of 1980-81. Located 10 miles west of Vail, Beaver Creek's almost 1,000 acres are serviced by 10 lifts providing access to 51 trails. Total vertical drop is a respectable 3,340 feet; uphill capacity is 16,675 skiers per hour.

Beaver Creek was originally designed with the 1976 Olympics in mind. It offers a wide range of skiing for all ability levels, with about 40% of the mountain designated intermediate. The resort offers a children's ski school (for kids three and older), a non-ski program for kids two months to six years, as well as a full range of adult instructional programs, including snowboarding, cross-country skiing, and Telemarking.

For further information about skiing Beaver Creek, write Vail Associates, Box 7, Vail, CO 81658, tel. (303) 476-5601. For information about the nursery and children's ski school, phone 949-2304; adult ski school, 949-5750, ext. 4300; cross-country ski school, 949-5750,

bobsledding at Vail

JACK AFFLECK

ext. 4313. For information on **snow conditions,** phone 476-4888 or 476-4889.

Free "Meet the Mountain" tours are offered Mon. and Wed. at 1 p.m. from Spruce Saddle.

Arrowhead Ski Area
Bordering Beaver Creek Ski Area in the west end of Vail Valley, Arrowhead is a young resort (first opened in 1988) offering a break from Vail's high-end prices and attitude—though it's also correspondingly smaller, its facilities less developed.

Arrowhead is the brainchild of Pete Seibert, Jr., son of one of Vail's principle founders. The resort has one high-speed detachable quad chair, a vertical drop of 1,700 feet, rental facilities, and a ski school; lift tickets are about half the cost of Vail's (and sightseers can ride the chair for free).

For further information on Arrowhead Ski Area, phone (303) 476-1591.

Cross-country Skiing
In addition to the designated cross-country trails systems operated by Vail Associates (Golden Peak Center in Vail and McCoy Park at Beaver Creek), the Vail Valley and surrounding area offers some exceptional opportunities for Nordic skiers of all abilities. You can get out and cruise groomed trails for an hour, or you can head out into serious backcountry, staying in designated huts for a week or longer.

For information on cross-country skiing in the Vail Valley, contact one of the offices of **White**

River National Forest. The Holy Cross Ranger District Office is at 401 Main St. in Minturn, tel. (303) 827-5715. The national forest's headquarters is at 900 Grand Ave., P.O. Box 948, Glenwood Springs, CO 81602, tel. 945-2521.

You can also get information from most of the retail cross-country ski shops in the area, including **Vail Mountaineering** in Lionshead, tel. 476-4223; **Cascade Sports,** 1300 Westhaven Dr., tel. 476-0186; and **Christy Sports,** 293 Bridge St., tel. 476-2244.

Vail Nature Center
Located in East Vail, this is a popular Nordic center and an excellent place to set out for some low-key touring—an eight-mile track snakes along next to Gore Creek. The center also features natural-history exhibits and offers equipment rental. Open daily 9 a.m.-4 p.m. Take Vail Valley Dr. (Frontage Rd.) east from Vail Village.

For information on special programs, phone (303) 479-2261.

10th Mountain Hut And Trail System
Named for the 15,000 U.S. Army troops who trained in the 1940s at Camp Hale in the mountains south of Vail, this network of backcountry trails and huts offers the ultimate Nordic skiing experience. The trail system itself is immense, 300 miles long and linking the towns of Aspen, Leadville, Copper Mountain, and Vail. It would take most of a season to bag the whole thing. And the "huts"? Well, they're not huts as *I* would use the word. Chalets, maybe. Chateaus.

10th Mountain System skiers can either head out on their own or go with guides. The huts, most of which sleep 16, run $22 per person per night (bring your own food). Guides offer three- to eight-day trips, with rates starting at about $60 a day (food and other necessities provided). Though not for the first-timer, most parts of the trail system are suitable for low-intermediate skiers. For further information or reservations (the huts are always booked up in advance), contact the 10th Mountain Trail Association, 1280 Ute Ave., Aspen, CO 81611, tel. (303) 925-5775.

Guided trips can be arranged through **Elk Mountain Guides,** Box 10327, Aspen, CO 81612, tel. 927-9377; **Paragon Guides,** Box 130, Vail, CO 81658, tel. 949-4272; and **Vail/ Beaver Creek Cross Country Ski Centers,** Vail Associates, Box 7, Vail, CO 81657, tel. 476-5601, ext. 4390.

Other Winter Activities

Don't think skiing is the only winter activity for Vail Valley visitors. If you're not into strapping boards afoot, there's still plenty to do. The **John Dobson Ice Arena,** 321 Lionshead Circle, tel. (303) 479-2270, is open to the public daily. Skate rentals available.

If you want to get into the backcountry but don't feel like huffing and puffing your way through drifts of snow, you can take a **Snowcat Tour.** You can arrange tours through the **Vail/Beaver Creek Activities Desk** tel. 476-9090, or through **Nova Guides,** tel. 949-4232.

Those hankering for something a bit more thrilling might want to take a ride on the 3,200-foot-long **bobsled course.** The four-person sleds reach speeds of 40 mph; helmets and instructions provided. Riders 18 and younger must have parents or guardians sign liability releases, and riders must be at least four feet tall. For further information, phone Vail Associates at 949-5750.

Another popular winter activity is **snowmobiling,** tours and rentals offered by several companies, including **Nova Guides,** tel. 949-4232, and **Spraddle Creek Ranch,** tel. 476-6941.

WHEN THE SNOW MELTS

Cycling

One of the first things a summer visitor to Vail will notice is the proliferation of bicyclists. And why not? Not only is this a community where health and fitness are paramount, but cycling is an excellent way to stay in shape for skiing. In addition, the area is ideally suited to cycling, with excellent paved bike paths and hundreds of miles of backcountry trails beckoning mountain bikers. Also, many of the ski shops change their tune in the summer, renting out bikes instead of skis.

From Gore Creek Campground five miles east of East Vail to West Vail Village, this is a perfect valley to explore by bike. Try the mostly flat "recreation path" that winds between the shopping area and the base of the lifts. For something a bit more demanding, head east from the village to the Vail Pass bike path, which you can take all the way into Frisco. Not for the weak of heart, the path tops out at 10,600 feet. If you're up to it, though, you'll find the scenery well worth the effort.

Mountain bikers have most of White River National Forest at their disposal. Maps and information are available from the Forest Service. For tips and advice stop by **Pedal Power,** 555 E. Lionshead Circle, tel. (303) 476-6633.

For the truly ambitious, the **10th Mountain Hut and Trail System** has recently expanded its winter operations to include backcountry bicycle tours. All told, the trail network is 300 miles long, linking Aspen, Leadville, Vail, and several other mountain resort communities. Rent a bunk in one of the 10 huts, which sleep up to 16, for about $22 a night. For information and reservations, contact the 10th Mountain Trail Association, 1280 Ute Ave., Aspen, CO 81611, tel. 925-5775.

Many Vail sporting goods stores and ski shops rent bikes. Try **Cascade Sports,** 1300 Westhaven Dr., tel. 476-0186.

Golfing

The popularity of golfing in Vail shouldn't surprise anyone. After all, this is a town built on a foundation of skiing, and the two sports share some significant similarities, not the least of which are the costs to participate and the resulting generally upscale, monied participants. Also, just as Vail is a premier ski area in anyone's view, the golf courses here are some of the finest in the West, offering challenges, great scenery, and stimulating mountain air.

Vail Golf Course is an 18-hole course and the oldest in the valley. Located at 1778 Vail Valley Dr., the course sponsors several tournaments throughout the season, including the

Jerry Ford Invitational (helmets optional). Phone (303) 476-1330 for information and tee times. The fanciest course in the area is the Robert Trent Jones-designed **Beaver Creek Golf Course,** tel. 949-7123. Greens fees for the 6,400-yard par-70 course are $80 (including cart), with discounts offered in May. In contrast, **Eagle-Vail Golf Course,** tel. 949-5267, is a relatively modest course with considerably lower greens fees ($37 after 4 p.m., cart included). The course is about 10 miles west of Vail in Avon. **Singletree Golf Course,** tel. 926-3533, is located about 15 miles west of Vail at Edwards. Rated by *Golf Digest* one of the top 50 courses in the country, the course is one of the first in the area to open each year, with early-season greens fees (until May 1) a mere $20 (as opposed to $80 when the season's in full swing).

You'll also find several fine golf courses just over Vail Pass in Summit County.

Hiking And Backpacking
Surrounded by national forest lands, the Vail Valley offers nearly unlimited hiking and backpacking opportunities, from short day-hikes to serious backcountry excursions. For maps, information, and advice, stop by the **Holy Cross Ranger District Office,** 401 Main St., Minturn, and phone (303) 827-5715. You can also get information from **White River National Forest Headquarters,** 900 Grand Ave., Box 948, Glenwood Springs, CO 81602, tel. 945-2521. Local book

stores and mountaineering shops carry books and hiking guides that discuss specific routes in detail. A couple of descriptions, following, will provide an idea of the range of hikes available.

One of the shortest but still visually rewarding hikes is the two-miler to **Booth Falls,** a 60-foot waterfall that's the highlight of a series of cascades on Booth Creek. The hike is only moderately demanding. From Vail Village, go east, crossing over to the frontage road on the north side of I-70, and continue to Booth Falls Road.

At the other end of the spectrum is the climb to the top of **Mount of the Holy Cross**—about 12 miles roundtrip. At just over 14,000 feet, the peak offers excellent views of the surrounding mountains.

Camping
White River National Forest also offers superb camping, with scores of campgrounds scattered throughout the forest's two million-plus acres. In addition, backcountry camping is available in the Holy Cross and Eagles Nest wilderness areas.

Forest Service campgrounds in or near the Vail Valley include **Gore Creek Campground,** five miles east of East Vail (take Exit 180 from I-70), as well as **Tigiwon, Half Moon,** and **Gold Park** campgrounds, all south of Vail via Hwy. 24 to Leadville. Contact the Forest Service (see "Hiking and Backpacking" above) for information and reservations.

Fishing
Along with biking and golfing, fishing is one of the sports that truly characterizes summer in Vail. In the very center of Vail Village, in fact, you'll probably see anglers practicing their casts by tossing fly lines out over the pools of **Gore Creek.** (Fishing can actually be respectable right in town.) If you'd rather not fish near boutiques, head upstream to Gore Creek Campground and beyond.

Another popular stream is the **Eagle River,** the South Fork of which parallels Hwy. 24 south of town. When fishing in streams, particularly, be sure to be aware of local restrictions; many stretches of trouty water are designated artificial bait and/or single barbless hooks only.

Local lakes that regularly offer good fishing include **Homestake Reservoir** (take Hwy. 24 south three miles south of Redcliff, and turn

Mount of the Holy Cross near Vail

west on Homestake Rd.), and **Black Lakes** at Vail Pass (lots of traffic, but regularly stocked).

For information and gear, stop in at **Vail Fishing Guides,** 183 E. Gore Creek Dr., tel. (303) 476-3296, where you can also arrange guided tours.

Rafting

One of the best ways to stay cool when the summer sun pierces that thin mountain air, rafting is growing more and more popular in the Vail Valley. Several outfitters offer trips on local waters (the Eagle River), as well as rivers in other parts of the state (the Arkansas and Colorado). Among the local companies offering half- and full-day tours are **Adventures in Rafting,** 1000 Lions Ridge Loop, tel. (303) 476-7645; **Nova Guides,** tel. 949-4232; and **Timberline Tours,** 476-1414.

Ballooning

Though not as popular as in Aspen, where the wider valley is more conducive to expansive views and meandering flights, hot-air ballooning is still a way to see Vail from a unique vantage point. For information and reservations, contact **Balloon America,** 2635 Larkspur Lane, tel. (303) 476-0808, or **Camelot Balloons, Inc.,** Box 1896, Vail, CO 81658, tel. 476-4743.

Horseback Riding

For those who want to see the backcountry without having to tax the ol' heart and soles, horseback is a great alternative. Local outfitters offer a range of rides—from easy, one-hour trips on virtually catatonic critters to more demanding, multi-day adventures on properly spirited steeds. Try **Piney River Ranch,** tel. (303) 476-3941.

Tennis

Many of Vail's condominium complexes have their own tennis courts. Public courts are available at **Booth Creek, Gold Peak, Ford Park,** and **Lionshead.** For more information, phone the **Vail Metropolitan Recreation District** at (303) 479-2296. You can also play at the **Avon Municipal Courts** in Avon, 10 miles west of Vail, tel. 949-4280.

Chairlift Rides

Vail Associates offers both chairlift and gondola rides from shortly after ski season ends into the early fall. For non-skiers, especially, who aren't used to this kind of transportation and the scenery it affords, this can be a wonderful way to see a different side of Vail. The 15-minute gondola ride from Vail's Lionshead to Eagles Nest guarantees stunning panoramas. At the top you can grab a barbecue lunch, take some photos, and climb back in the gondola for the ride back down, or you can hike back to the base on marked trails. Rates for adults are about $12 (seniors 70 and older ride free). Beaver Creek also offers chairlift rides, somewhat scaled down but appropriately more reasonably priced. For more information, phone Vail Associates at (303) 476-5601, ext. 3071.

Take Me Out To The Ball Game

In a town where it seems you're constantly forking out dough to buy, rent, reserve, and tip, it's nice to know there are still some things to do that are absolutely free. Watching a local softball game is one of the most relaxing ways to spend a couple of hours on a weekend afternoon or weekday evening. Grab a lawn chair and set up on the bank above the fields, which are located just off the frontage road in East Vail—you can't miss 'em.

Parks

You'll find several parks throughout the Vail Valley, most of them perfect for a picnic or to park the bike and take a snooze in the shade of a poplar. There's a **children's playground** in East Vail directly behind the softball fields and adjacent to Gore Creek.

ACCOMMODATIONS

Vail is a decidedly upscale ski area, defined in large part by its luxury accommodations—most of which are within a ski pole's toss of the slopes. Keep in mind that this is the playground of the rich and famous, and that you won't have much luck finding bargain-rate lodging. But if you're talking Vail, you're already talking major financial commitment, and if you're gonna pamper yourself, why not go whole hog? Especially if it's for a honeymoon, a special week away from the kids, or that once-in-a-lifetime vacation you've always dreamed about.

On the other hand, if you strictly want the ski experience, and want to cut corners everywhere else, there are possibilities. You'll find less expensive lodging in Eagle (see below) about 30 miles west of Vail, and there are still a handful of relatively inexpensive motels in Frisco and Dillon (see Summit County), over Vail Pass about 25 miles east.

Remember, too, that rates are significantly lower in the off-season (late spring, summer, and fall). Though Vail is growing rapidly as a year-round resort area, winter is still high season. Many of the high-end lodges offer relatively attractive low-season rates with special incentives, such as golf, biking, tennis, and sightseeing packages. Keep in mind that the prices given below should be used for comparison only, and that the *huge* range accounts for seasonal adjustments. The low prices will generally be effective mid-April through mid-November, high prices during the ski season's peak times (Christmas and Easter holidays). Remember, too, that most visitors do opt for multiday stays (most often a "ski week," Mon.-Sun.), when the price *per night* isn't quite so unnerving.

For further information on lodging in Vail, contact the Vail Associates-affiliated **Vail Reservations,** Box 7, Vail, CO 81658, tel. (303) 476-1000 or (800) 237-0643. They can also provide information on air and ground transportation, packages (skiing, golf, etc.), and convention and group facilities.

Hotels

The most "Vaily" Vail lodge is probably the **Westin Resort,** at 1300 Westhaven Dr. in Vail Village, tel. (303) 476-7111 or (800) 228-3000. Offering every imaginable amenity—ski and golf packages, exercise facilities, luxury dining rooms, and kitchens, not to mention its convenient location—the Westin is without doubt among the creamiest of a very creamy crop. Doubles range from $135 to $335. The largest hotel at Vail is the **Marriott Mark,** tel. 476-4444 or (800) 333-3333, which recently underwent a $5-million renovation; rooms go for $125-250. Other classic Vail hotels, all centrally located and offering full amenities, include **The Lodge at Vail,** 174 E. Gore Creek Dr., tel. 476-5011, where doubles run $75-375; **Lodge Tower,** 200 Vail Rd., tel. 476-9530, $80-340; and the **Westwind,** 548 S. Frontage Rd., tel. 476-5031, $60-380.

For Vail tradition, try the **Gasthof Gramshammer,** 231 E. Gore Creek Dr., tel. 476-5626, one of the oldest and most respected lodges in the village. A classic Tyrolean-style inn, the Gramshammer has been Old-World-charming returning visitors for years.

In Beaver Creek, the newly completed **St. James Hotel,** on Village Rd., tel. 949-5750, is unquestionably one of the most luxurious hotels in the state. Doubles here *start* at about $150 and go to nearly $700 (!). The **Hyatt-Regency,** also on Village Rd., tel. 949-1234, has rooms for two running $90-350, and you can stay at the **Inn at Beaver Creek,** tel. 845-7800, for about $90-400 a night.

Motels

You'll find somewhat lower rates at the scattering of motels in Vail, including the **Best Western Vailglo Lodge,** 701 W. Lionshead Circle, tel. (303) 476-5506 or (800) 541-9423, where doubles run $60-200. The **Sitzmark Lodge,** 183 Gore Creek Dr., tel. 476-5001, has rooms for two starting at about $50 and maxing out at $200. The **Comfort Inn** in Avon, Exit 167 from I-70, tel. 949-5511, also has doubles running $70-225. You'll find a handful of other motels in Avon as well. Contact the **Avon Chamber of Commerce,** 400 Benchmark Rd., Avon, CO 81620, tel. 949-5189.

Bed And Breakfasts

Due to the fact that Vail Valley is narrow and development within it therefore concentrated, and that all of the buildings are relatively new, you won't find small back-street bed and breakfasts in old Victorians like you do in Breckenridge and Aspen. Still, some of the inns are moving in that direction, offering either continental or full breakfasts with a night's stay. Two miles west of Lionshead, the **Black Bear Inn,** tel. (303) 476-1304, offers 12 rooms with private baths, ranging from $95-150, including full breakfast. The **Eagle River Inn,** 145 Main St., Minturn, tel. 827-5761, is an adobe Southwestern-style lodge offering a healthful breakfast of yogurt, granola, and fruit. Built in 1894, the Eagle River is decorated with Indian rugs and pottery; each room has a private bath.

For A Real Splurge

If you're looking for totally distinctive deluxe digs, **Trapper's Cabin** may be the answer.

Operated by Vail Associates, this 3,000-square-foot inn, at 9,500 feet between Beaver Creek and Arrowhead, can indulge most every whim—its solitude enhanced by the lack of telephones, televisions, and radios. Use the cabin as a base to explore the mountains by foot, horseback, or cross-country skis. In the evenings dine on elk steak, pheasant breast, duck, or salmon.

Rates: $2,200 a night for up to four people, one night's stay; $2,000 per night, two or four people, two or more nights. For information and reservations, phone Vail Associates' Hospitality Corporation at (303) 949-5750, ext. 6206.

Camping And RVing

The Vail Valley is in the thick of the White River National Forest, and most of the campgrounds in the area are small, Forest Service-administered areas. Some private RV campgrounds can be found nearby though, including **Eagle River Village** in Edwards (about 16 miles west of Vail), tel. (303) 926-3754, and **Best Western Eagle Lodge and RV Park** in Eagle, tel. 328-6316. For information on national forest campgrounds contact the Forest Service (see "Hiking and Backpacking" above).

FOOD

Dining is a big part of the Vail experience. The valley has a number of first-class continental-style restaurants, and Vail Village seems to consist of about one-third eateries, serving everything from pastries to chimichangas to stir-fry. The socializing at many of them is as crucial as the actual eating.

Thankfully, many of the restaurants in Vail post their menus outside, so you can scope out the offerings and prices. Indeed, one of the best parts about a morning's shopping stroll through the village is scanning the various menus and deciding where to have lunch. If the basil-chicken special doesn't grab you, see what's cooking next door.

Start Me Up

Offering a wide range of imported and gourmet coffees, the **Daily Grind,** 288 Bridge St., tel. (303) 476-5856, also serves freshly baked croissants, muffins, bagels, and other pastries daily from 6:30 a.m. For something a little heartier, try an omelette or breakfast burrito at **D.J. Mc-Cadam's,** 616 Lionshead Circle, tel. 476-2336.

Restaurants

The dining room in the **Gasthof Gramshammer,** 231 Gore Creek Dr., tel. (303) 476-5626, is a high-end Vail favorite. Specializing in wild game, the restaurant also serves beef, seafood, and salads in a comfortably rustic Austrian setting. The Westin's **Alfredo's,** 1300 Westhaven Dr., tel. 476-7111, is another of the valley's first-class restaurants, specializing in northern Italian cuisine; also serves Sunday brunch.

For more moderately priced meals, try **Blu's,** 193 E. Gore Creek Dr., tel. 476-3113—fruit and

summertime in Vail Village

yogurt for breakfast, pastas for dinner; the **Bully Ranch,** 20 Vail Rd., tel. 476-5656, for omelettes, salads, and steaks (you can also get rattlesnake stew and buffalo burgers); or the **Ore House,** 228 Bridge St., tel. 476-5100, for steaks, chicken, seafood, salad bar.

For Mexican food, try **Los Amigos,** 476 Bridge St., tel. 476-5847.

ENTERTAINMENT

You shouldn't have too much trouble finding something to do in Vail once the lifts shut down (or it's too dark to find your errant golf ball). Lounges at many of the hotels, including the Westin, offer live music. If you've got something a little rowdier in mind, many of the restaurants in the village feature live music, ranging from acoustic folk to electric rock 'n' roll. For starters, check out **Pepi's,** tel. 476-5626, and the **Red Lion,** tel. 476-7676, two definitive Vail après-ski hang-outs. Also, watch the *Vail Daily* to see who's playing what kind of music where and when.

CALENDAR

Since the early 1980s, when Vail began seriously to court year-round visitors, its schedule of events has been booked. Indeed, there's a festival, concert, gallery opening, bike or ski race, or tennis or golf tournament almost every weekend. Highlights include **Winterfaire,** an annual winter carnival with dog-sled races, ice sculpture, and music; **VailAmerica Days,** a huge Fourth of July celebration, with fireworks, music, arts and crafts, barbecues; the **Colorado Music Festival,** a classical concert series that runs through July and August; and the **Jerry Ford Invitational Golf Tournament,** in late July. For complete information, phone (303) 476-1000 or 476-5601. You should also watch the *Vail Daily,* available in newspaper racks throughout Eagle County; the paper contains a calendar of weekly events, as well as movie and concert listings.

SHOPPING

Any structure in Vail that's not a restaurant or ski shop is most likely a boutique, gift shop, or gallery. And a fun part of visiting Vail is wandering around the shops. You'll find everything from souvenir and knicknack shops to places selling furs that cost more than your Ford. Also *lots* of jewelry (especially Indian) and T-shirt shops.

In addition to the standard gift shops you'd expect in a resort town, Vail has plenty of specialty stores, with something for every interest—shops selling gifts imported from Alaska, fly-fishing gear, and one devoted entirely to Scotch terriers (and their owners). Even if you're not looking to buy, these stores can be fun to poke your head into, and you should allow at least one afternoon to "do" shopping in Vail Village.

SERVICES

The offices of the **Vail Police Department** are at 75 S. Frontage Rd.; phone (303) 479-2200. Phone the **Eagle County Sheriff** at 949-5620, and the **State Patrol** at 328-6343. The full-sevice **Vail Valley Medical Center,** tel. 476-2451 or 476-8085 (in emergencies), is located in Vail Village at 181 W. Meadow Drive. Vail's main **post office** is located at 111 S. Frontage Rd., tel. 476-5217.

Recycling
Recycle aluminum, glass, newspaper, and plastic at **We Recycle,** 111 S. Frontage Rd., Vail, and in Eagle at **Beasely's Food Town,** 212 E. Chambers Road. The **Safeway** in Vail takes aluminum only.

INFORMATION

First-time visitors to Vail should stop at the tourist information center on S. Frontage Rd. in East Vail. Signs to it are posted at freeway exits. The center is staffed with friendly people who can answer just about any question you might have, and you'll also find lots of brochures with information on dining, lodging, shopping, and all manner of recreational activities.

You can also get information from **Vail Associates,** Box 7, Vail, CO 81658, or contact the **Vail Valley Tourism and Convention Bureau,** 100 E. Meadow Dr., Vail, CO 81657; tel. (303) 476-1000. For **road and weather information,** phone 328-6345. For **ski conditions,** phone 476-4888 or 476-4889.

TRANSPORTATION

Getting There

Vail is one of Colorado's most accessible resorts, as well as one of the easiest to get around in once you're here. The valley is 100 miles west of Denver, which is serviced by most major airlines. If you fly into Denver's Stapleton Airport, you can either rent a car there and drive out (less than two hours when the roads are clear) or take a shuttle. See the Denver chapter for names and phone numbers of Stapleton auto-rental agencies, most of which specialize in "winterized" cars (front-wheel- and four-wheel-drive, ski racks).

Vans to Vail, tel. (303) 476-4467 or (800) 222-2212, makes eight trips a day between Vail/Beaver Creek and Stapleton Airport. First Vail departure is 7 a.m., the last at 4:30 p.m.; first Denver departure is 9:30 a.m., the last at 7:30 p.m. One-way fare is about $30. Private charters are available. Other Vail-area shuttle services include **Airport Transportation Service,** tel. 476-7576, and **Colorado Mountain Express,** tel. 949-4227.

You can also fly directly to Eagle County Airport (in Eagle, about 30 miles west of Vail). Phone **American Airlines** at (800) 433-7300 or **America West** at (800) 247-5692, which offer daily nonstop flights from Chicago, Dallas/Fort Worth, Phoenix, and Los Angeles. **Skier's Connection,** tel. (800) 824-1104, offers shuttle between Eagle County Airport and Vail.

Getting Around The Valley

Getting around once you're in Vail is so easy that a car could actually get in the way. Besides, parking, especially in the winter, can be a pain in the neck. **Free shuttles** run daily through the valley, the first bus firing up at 7 a.m. and the last one shutting down at 1:30 a.m. (a bit earlier in the summer and fall); buses run every 10 minutes. For taxi service, phone **Vail Valley Taxi,** at (303) 476-TAXI.

In the Vail area, you can rent cars from **Rent-a-Wreck,** tel. 949-1003; **Budget,** tel. 949-6012; **Hertz,** tel. 476-7707; **National,** tel. 476-6634; and **Thrifty,** tel. 476-8718.

Free parking is provided except during the ski season, with lots conveniently located and well marked.

HIGHWAY 40, UTAH BORDER TO STEAMBOAT SPRINGS

From the Colorado-Utah border to Steamboat Springs is about a 125-mile drive, flat and open with not much traffic. Not a whole lot to look at the first two-thirds of the way, the barren landscape is characterized by miles and miles of flatland, mottled dirty green by the endless sagebrushes. Beyond these horizons, though, the Yampa and Green rivers, as well as the Little Snake, carve deep canyons into the plateau.

This is where the land's true colors are seen. Here the canyon walls form tiered mosaics of countless shades of red, ever changing with the angles of the flirting sun. And on the canyon floors, rivers—churning white, brown, then sleeping in still green pools—continue to carve into the stone. Beneath it all are the still darker pools of fossil fuels—oil and coal, as well as natural gas. In Craig, toward the eastern edge of the plateau, smoke and steam rise from the 15-story-high chimneys of the state's largest coal-fired electrical plant, which processes coal from several nearby mines.

In Craig, the plateau tilts, and the highway slowly begins its apparent assault on the Rockies' Western Slope. This 45-mile stretch follows the course of the Yampa River, winding through the valley, the country growing prettier by the meter. By the time you're face to face with Steamboat Ski Area's Mt. Werner and beginning to climb up Rabbit Ears Pass, you're into the Colorado you'll recognize from postcards and calendars—clear mountain streams and green meadows, with a backdrop of snowy, sawtoothed mountain peaks.

DINOSAUR

Three miles east of the Utah border, the town of Dinosaur is little more than a couple of gas stations, cafés, and dinky old motels. In an otherwise barren, bleak, and mostly humorless country, you'll get a kick out of Dinosaur's street names: The main drag through town (Hwy. 40) is Brontosaurus Blvd., and most other streets are named after dinosaurs as well—Plateosaurus Place, Brachtosaurus Bypass, Stegosaurus Freeway, even Triceratops Terrace. (Don't be surprised if your kids ask where Sharp Tooth lives . . .) The little community was known as Artesia until 1965, when it changed its name to reflect its proximity to Dinosaur National Monument.

Hannah visits the Land Before Time.

STEPHEN METZGER

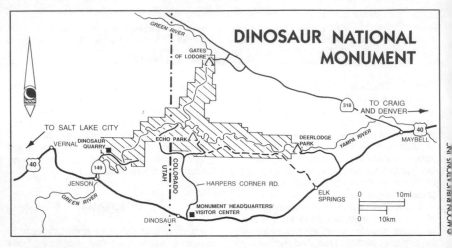

A **Colorado Welcome Center,** open 8 am.-6 p.m. May 1 through Nov. 30, has lots of information on things to do and see in the area and throughout Colorado. Located in the center of town on Hwy. 40. Friendly and helpful staff. Free coffee, restrooms.

Practicalities

If you're heading east, there's not a whole lot along the 90 miles of Hwy. 40 between here and Craig, and if it's getting late you might want to take advantage of Dinosaur's limited lodging options. You can get cheap, no-frills digs at the **Hi-Vu Motel,** tel. (303) 374-2267, the **Park Motel,** tel. 374-2270, or the **Terrace Motel,** tel. 374-2241.

Information

For more information on Dinosaur and the area, write Town of Dinosaur, Box 238, Dinosaur, CO 81610.

DINOSAUR NATIONAL MONUMENT

One of the most remote national monuments in the country, Dinosaur National Monument sprawls over 325 square miles of barren and rugged badlands. It straddles the Colorado-Utah border, its distinctly triangular, three-toed shape itself vaguely resembling a giant dinosaur footprint. A fascinating testimony to the huge reptiles

that sloshed through this part of Colorado some 140 million years ago, Dinosaur National Monument is also evidence of the great powers of nature: The Yampa and Green rivers have sliced far into the plateau, leaving narrow 3,000-foot-deep canyons, whose sheer cliffs ensure darkness even at midday.

Though paleontologists had known for years that northwestern Colorado once teemed with dinosaurs of every size and shape, it wasn't until 1909 that Earl Douglass discovered eight brontosaurus tail bones, apparently undisturbed even after millions of years. The find led to several others nearby, including complete skeletons. In 1915, the site was designated a national monument, and in 1938 the monument was expanded to include the Green and Yampa river canyons.

Dinosaur National Monument is not only unique for the sheer numbers of bones and fossils discovered here (some 350 tons of bones have been sent to museums), but also for the number that remain. At the Dinosaur Quarry building, you can view huge femurs, toes, and vertebrae in states of partial excavation, and watch scientists chipping away at the surrounding rock to better display them.

Dinosaur Quarry

This is the only place in the monument to view dinosaur fossils and bones. Located on the Utah side of the monument, the quarry has a visitors center (open daily 8 a.m.-4:30 p.m.; till 7 p.m. in summer) where you'll get a feel for the variety of life that once thrived here, from prehistoric turtles to brontosauruses. In the summer, a shuttle runs daily from the main parking area to the quarry; take your own rig the rest of the year. The quarry is located seven miles north of Jenson, Utah, on Hwy. 149. Phone the quarry visitors center at (801) 789-2115.

Monument Headquarters And Visitors Center
The visitors center on the Colorado side is located a mile east of the town of Dinosaur. From here, a 31-mile road leads into the monument, past several scenic overlooks, dead-ending at Harpers Corner, where you can view the canyons formed by the Yampa and Green rivers.

The center has lots of books, guides, brochures, and other information, as well as rangers to answer your questions. You can also watch a short video about the monument.

Camping
There are two developed campgrounds within the monument, **Split Mountain** and **Green River** (both accessible from the Utah entrance only). Both can accommodate RVs, although neither hookups nor dump stations are available. You can also camp at any of the five free primitive grounds, three of which are in Colorado. **Echo Park Campground,** in the heart of the park 40 miles from Monument Headquarters, offers excellent views of the river and canyons, as well as river access. A ranger station is open summers only. Take Harpers Corner Rd. north from the visitors center, and turn east on Echo Park Road. **Deerlodge Park Campground** is at the monument's east end and can be reached by turning north on Road 14 at Elk Springs, about 35 miles east of Monument Headquarters. There are no designated sites or drinking water; a ranger station is open summers only. Deerlodge is open summers only; no drinking water is available.

Gates of Lodore Campground is at the far north end of the park and has a ranger station open year round and drinking water available summers only. From the headquarters, take Hwy. 40 east for 60 miles to Maybell; then take Hwy. 318 another 50 miles west to the campground.

Hiking
You'll find several nature trails in the park, most of which are accessible only from the Utah side. On the Colorado side, you'll find trailheads at Harpers Corner and Gates of Lodor Campground, both leading to stunning gorge views. A half-mile marked trail loops out from Plug Hat Butte picnic area, four miles north of the visitors center (not yet technically in the park).

Information
For more information on Dinosaur National Monument, write Park Headquarters, Box 210, Dinosaur, CO 81610, or phone (303) 374-2216. Be sure to ask for a copy of *Echoes, A Guide to Dinosaur National Monument,* which provides detailed information on hiking, backpacking, camping, rafting, and fishing in the park, as well as maps and lists of books for further reading. Phone the Dinosaur Quarry Visitors Center (Utah) at (801) 789-2115. You can also get information by writing **Dinosaurland Travel Board,** 235 E. Main St., Vernal, UT 84078, tel. (801) 789-6932 or (800) 477-5558.

Bill Weir's *Utah Handbook* provides detailed descriptions of the monument's geology, history, and recreational opportunities, and also discusses practicalities (accommodations, etc.) in nearby Utah towns. The book is available from Moon Publications, P.O. Box 3040, Chico, CA 95927, tel. (916) 345-5473.

BROWNS PARK NATIONAL WILDLIFE REFUGE

Situated on the Green River north of Dinosaur National Monument, this 6,000-acre marshland is an excellent (if remote) place to see a variety of wildlife in its natural habitat. A nesting area for thousands of migratory waterfowl, including mallards, teal, canvasbacks, and Canada geese, the region is also home to huge numbers of partridge, grouse, wading birds, and hawks, as well as deer and antelope.

The refuge is located off Hwy. 318 about 10 miles east of the Utah border and is open year round, with two primitive (no water) campgrounds. For further information, write Browns Park National Wildlife Refuge, Greystone Route, Maybell, CO 81640, or phone (303) 365-3695.

RANGELY

A small plateau town that owes its existence solely to the oil and ranching industries, Rangely (pop. 3,000; elev. 5,280 feet), is home to the sixth largest oil field in the country. Its surrounding landscape, flat and sagey and bleak, dominated by pumpjacks chain-link fenced and nodding round the clock, Rangely is 20 miles southeast of Dinosaur via CO 64.

The town dates from 1880, when it was established as a Ute trading post. In the mid-1880s, ranchers began driving huge herds of cattle to the area, and in 1912 the first shipments of sheep arrived. The first signs of oil were probably seen in 1900, when a local rancher noticed a vague slick on the White River, and the first crude, shallow wells were dug in 1903.

In 1933, the California Company, a subsidiary of Standard Oil, drilled 6,000 feet into the ground and discovered a huge oil deposit, although the well was plugged right away. World War II increased the demand for oil, though, and in 1943, the well was unplugged. By late 1945, 56 wells were in operation.

Today Rangely—or "Strangely," as other Coloradans call it—reflects its oil-town legacy. The landscape is scarred, and many of the little town's businesses are boarded up, victims of the industry's capriciousness. On the other hand, Rangely has recently benefitted in other ways from the oilers' presence: In (partial) compensation for wreaking environmental havoc on the surrounding countryside, the oil companies have made financial retributions (which seem huge to such a tiny economy but are of course drops in the bucket of oil conglomerates). Oil money has gone to build Elk Park, which given the size of the town is one of the nicest in the state, as well as a beautiful hillside rec center.

Rangely Museum

Located in Rangely's first schoolhouse, this small museum has good displays of local rocks, minerals, and Indian artifacts, as well as pioneer clothing and other domestic items. Chevron has an exhibit explaining drilling techniques and technology. Summer hours are Mon. through Sat. 10 a.m.-5 p.m., Sun. 1-5 p.m. Admission is free (donations encouraged). The museum is at 434 W. Main. For more information, phone (303) 675-2612.

Elk Park

This huge town park with rolling lawns (big enough to warrant "no golfing" signs) has picnic tables and barbecue grills, basketball and volleyball courts, and a softball field. Take Stanoland three blocks south of Main.

Rangely's **Recreation Center,** on the hill above the park, features a large indoor swimming pool, weight room, racquetball courts, pool and ping-pong table, in addition to jogging and biking trails and an ice-skating rink. Take Stanoland south past Elks Park to the top of

A pumpjack nods just outside downtown Rangely.

the hill. For hours, phone the center at (303) 675-8211.

Petroglyph Tours

The **Rangely Museum Society,** in conjunction with the town of Rangely and Colorado Northwestern Community College, has designated three short self-guided driving tours from which you can view a variety of prehistoric rock art. Petroglyphs include drawings of buffalo, sheep, and deer, as well as many abstract forms and some vaguely resembling humans. The work is from both the Fremont Culture (A.D. 650-1150) and the Ute tribe (1200-1880). Recently a series of prehistoric astronomical sites has been discovered; special directions are needed to get to these sites. Tour maps are available from the Rangely Museum, 434 W. Main St., Rangely, CO 81648, tel. (303) 675-2612.

Practicalities

The **Escalante Trail Motel,** tel. (303) 675-8461, has the best rooms in town (none designated nonsmoking) and is a favorite of oil-rig crews, who sometimes book half a dozen or more rooms for weeks (or more) at a time. Doubles run about $38. The motel is one block off the main drag on S. Grand on the west end of town. The **Rangely Motor Hotel,** tel. 675-2255, is located on the west end of town and has seven rooms. You can camp down in the shade of the cottonwoods at **Rangely Camper Park** for $10 a night; there's also a nice lawn and small kids' play area. Turn north on Nichols at the east end of Rangely.

Pretty slim pickin's in terms of food. A couple of small markets and five small restaurants. The **Last Chance Restaurant,** 302 W. Main, tel. 675-2001, serves good Mexican food and barbecue. You can also try the **Cowboy Corral,** a block east, tel. 675-8986.

Recycling

Recycle at **Town of Rangely Recycling Program,** 214 E. Main, or 825 E. Main. Phone (303) 675-2413.

Information

For more information, write **Town of Rangely,** 209 E. Main St., Rangely, CO 81648, or phone (303) 675-8476.

CRAIG

Seat of Moffat County, the northwesternmost county in the state, Craig (pop. 8,000; elev. 6,190 feet) lies on the Yampa River 42 miles west of Steamboat Springs and 200 miles west of Denver. Rich in natural resources, particularly coal, oil, natural gas, and uranium, Craig is also rich in prehistory and history, with dinosaur fossils, Native American petroglyphs, and remnants of the Old West all within short drives of town. Craig is also a hub of ranching and agricultural activity, particularly sheep, cattle, and wheat.

We approached Craig from the west on a late January afternoon after spending the previous night in Salt Lake City. The high plains were dotted with snow, ice formed along the edges of streams, and the sagebrush looked brittle in the cold. The sun dropping behind us hung shadows across the land. Suddenly out of nowhere a deer darted into the road in front of us. A big mulie buck. Wild-eyed and frightened. *I've really messed up this time,* he must have been thinking. Fortunately I slammed on the brakes, the car swerved dramatically, and he had time to bound to the shoulder, then into the brush, where he quickly, magically, dissolved into sage and shadows.

No fool, I took this as advice to slow down (not to mention to plan to get my brakes adjusted). And once I did that, and our goal was no longer simply to make Craig before dark, we began to see what was really out there: deer. Dozens of them. Alone, in pairs, threes, in herds of six, eight, and more. At every turn, over every rise. I'd never seen so many deer in one stretch. Between Elk Springs and Lay, a distance of some 40 miles, we must have seen more than 200 deer, all within 50 yards of the highway. Who knows how many thousands grazed in the brush beyond our small theater?

As you approach Craig, though, the prevalence of Moffat County wildlife might take a backseat to the airborne residue (a towering, thunderheadlike stack of steam) of Colorado's largest coal-fired electrical generating plant, which processes coal from nearby Trapper Mine, as well as from the Colowyo Mine, 27 miles southwest. Providing the power for the lights, stoves, refrigerators, televisions, VCRs, and microwaves of much of northwestern Colorado, the plant also provides work and a solid economic base for Craig and the surrounding area. In fact, the plant provides weekly paychecks for some 1,200 people.

History
Craig was founded in 1888, seven years after the first homesteader, William Rose, arrived and built a small cabin along Fortification Creek. Though originally called Rose, the community took its current name from the Reverend Bayard

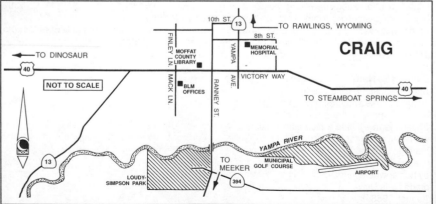

Craig, who, along with W.H. Tucker, arrived in 1887 from Glenwood Springs and helped finance and lay out the town. Within a few years, a hotel and saloon had been built, and in 1891 Clarence Bronaugh founded the town's first newspaper, the *Pentagraph.*

On Valentine's eve, 1897, downtown Craig was mostly destroyed by fire. Originating in the town hall, where there was to be a dance and party the next night, the blaze burned out of control up Yampa Avenue. Though devastated by their loss, the citizens of Craig quickly went about rebuilding their town, and within a year most of the buildings had been reconstructed (many with brick this time).

ATTRACTIONS

Moffat County Museum

Located in the former Armory, at 590 Yampa, this museum documents the history of Craig and Moffat County. For more information, phone (303) 824-6360.

Marcia Railway Car

Built for $25,568 in 1906 for David Moffat (the Denver railroad tycoon), this elegant coach once accommodated 12 passengers and two servants. Hauled by winch along specially built tracks to its present site, the Marcia (named for Moffat's daughter) is 68 feet long, 12 feet wide, and features an ornate interior, with African mahogany with oak inlay, two heating systems, and three ice boxes, as well as a kitchen, observation room, and combination dining/sitting/sleeping room. The car is located on Victory Way near Craig City Park. For tours, phone the Craig Chamber of Commerce at (303) 824-5689.

Sandrocks Nature Trail And Petroglyphs

Sheer sandstone cliffs overlooking the town of Craig, a marked nature trail, and carvings ranging from ancient Anasazian to more recent Shoshonean—this is a nice little side trip that will help you better appreciate Moffat County's heritage and natural history. A joint project of Craig-area 4-H'ers, city council members, nearby homeowners, and faculty and staff from Colorado State University, the trail was dedicated in August, 1988. In addition to carvings of hands,

paws, lightning bolts, horses and other animals—perhaps symbolic, perhaps simply the recording of daily events—you can also view areas where Native Americans sharpened axes and made arrows and arrowheads. Various plants and bushes—prickly pear, Indian rice grass, and rabbit brush—are identified to help you better appreciate other high-desert exploring you may do. Take 9th St. to Alta Vista Dr., and go west.

Colorado-Ute Power Station

Attraction, or *distraction*—it's hard to say. Craig-area boosters boast about it, and in fact, this coal-fired plant is the biggest in Colorado. It also pays enormous amounts of taxes to Moffat County and generates 1,264 megawatts of power. Three and a half miles southwest of Craig, in the softly rolling hills of the high plains, the power plant, whose main building is 25 stories high, spews columns of smoke and steam far into the Colorado sky. Meeting or surpassing all environmental guidelines and restrictions, the plant is primarily emitting steam (after electrostatic precipitators have removed 99.6% of particulate matter from the burning coal).

Tours of the plant are offered by appointment. For information, contact the Craig Chamber of Commerce, tel. (303) 824-5689, or phone the plant at 824-4411. You can also get information by contacting the Communications Group, Colorado-Ute Electric Association, Inc., Box 1149, Montrose, CO 81402, tel. 249-4501.

PARKS AND RECREATION

Town Parks

Located at the corner of 6th and Rose streets, Craig's city park has two swimming pools, tennis and volleyball courts, a playground and picnic facilities. **Loudy Simpson Park,** where S. Ranney crosses the Yampa River, offers fishing, picnicking, a nature trail, jogging paths, a launch area for canoes and rafts, and ice skating.

Elkhead Reservoir

This narrow lake on Elkhead Creek nine miles northeast of Craig is a favorite among sports enthusiasts and folks looking to escape the oftentimes harsh high plains summers. Fishing, boating, waterskiing, and picnicking are all available.

Take Hwy. 40 east to County Rd. 29 and go north to the reservoir.

For New Wavers Only

To paraphrase Brian Wilson, "Catch a wave and you're sitting on top of the plains." The public swimming facilities at Craig's city park have recently expanded, adding an adjacent "wave pool," with 180,000 gallons of churning whitewater. Now in addition to swimming laps in the six-lane, 25-meter Olympic pool, you can frolic in Craig's answer to a surfin' safari. Located at 605 Washington. For hours and prices, phone the **Craig Parks and Recreation Department** at (303) 824-3015. The number for the poolside phone is 824-9993.

Golfing

The **Yampa Valley Golf Course,** tel. (303) 824-3673, is an 18-hole public course along the Yampa River two miles south of town. Phone for tee times and information. Take Ranney St. south to County Rd. 394.

Hiking

The BLM administers some 1.5 million acres of public land in Moffat County. Six miles north of Craig, Cedar Mountain rises 1,000 feet above "plain-level" and offers good hiking and sightseeing opportunities. Take County Rd. 7 from Craig.

You'll also find hiking trails along the Yampa River at Loudy Simpson Park, off S. Ranney St., and at Sandstone Cliffs (see above). For more information, contact the Craig office of the BLM at 455 Emerson, tel. (303) 824-8261, or the Forest Service district office at 356 Ranney, tel. 824-9438.

Hunting And Fishing

Moffat County is prime hunting and fishing country, home of deer, elk, trout, and other game. The Yampa and Green rivers are well known for good trout fishing, and good-sized northern pike are pulled from Elkhead Reservoir. For tips on hot local hunting and fishing spots, as well as for licenses and supplies, stop in at **Craig Sports,** 124 W. Victory Way, tel. (303) 824-4044. **Nielson's Sports,** 538 Pershing, tel. 824-7021, also carries equipment and licenses. The BLM and Forest Service offices in Craig (see "Hiking" above) can provide maps and further information.

Rafting

The Yampa is a popular rafting and canoeing river. You can put in at Loudy Simpson Park or at the Yampa Valley Golf Course. Both private and public lands flank the 50-mile stretch of raftable water; don't trespass on private property (camping is allowed on public lands).

Tours

The Craig Chamber of Commerce has designed several short self-guiding tours of downtown and the surrounding area. The attractions (and excitement levels) vary widely, from the scintillating pass by Craig High School (on Tour #1) to a stop at **Lay Valley Bison Ranch,** where you can pick up a buffalo steak to take home and throw on the barbie. For more information, contact the chamber (see "Information" following).

Helicopter tours over the western Rockies are offered through Yampa Valley Regional Airport; phone (303) 276-3723.

PRACTICALITIES

Accommodations

Of the dozen or so motels in Craig, most are on the main drag (Hwy. 40) through town and very easy to locate. At the west end of town at the junction of Hwy. 40 and Hwy. 13 is a **Holiday Inn,** tel. (303) 824-9455, where doubles for two start at about $45. There's a good-sized indoor pool, Jacuzzi, and a children's play area, with toys to ride and climb on. At the same junction, the **A Bar Z Motel,** tel. 824-7066, has rooms for two starting at about $32, and the **Super 8,** tel. 824-3471, has doubles for about $40. Rooms for two at the **Best Western Inn of Craig,** 755 E. Victory (Hwy. 40), tel. 824-8101, start at $30.

Freeman Campground, about 20 miles north of Craig, has 17 sites, pit toilets, nature trails, and fishing on Freeman Reservoir. Go 13 miles north on CO 13, then nine miles northeast on Forest Service Rd. 113 (dirt). **Wagon Wheels Campground,** tel. 824-5105, about two miles east of Craig on US 40, has 108 RV sites, 13 tent sites, laundry facilities, a small store, and a dump station.

Food

Two restaurants at the Holiday Inn, **Annie Bassett's** and **Cassidy's Bar and Grill,** tel. (303) 824-9455, serve breakfast, lunch, and dinner daily. Dinner entrees (salads, chicken, steaks, seafood) run $5-17. The **Truck Stop Café,** tel. 824-7303, is located downtown at 425 W. Victory and also serves breakfast, lunch, and dinner (American food, reasonable prices). A Safeway and City Market are located on Victory Way.

Shopping
"The shopping hub of Northwestern Colorado," according to the chamber of commerce, Craig has two malls (Centennial and Country) and a downtown shopping center. Included among the de rigueur mall stores are a K mart (2355 W. Victory Way) and a JCPenney and Anthony's (1111 W. Victory).

Calendar
Craig's **Fall-Color Festival** (mid-September) features a parade, fiddle competition, square dancing, and a pancake breakfast. Firework displays on the Fourth of July. Contact the chamber of commerce for exact dates, times, places, and further information.

Services
The offices of the Craig **Police Department** are at 300 W. 4th St.; phone (303) 824-8111. Phone the **Moffat County Sheriff** at 824-4495. **State Patrol** offices are 280 S. Ranney, tel. 824-6501. Craig's **Memorial Hospital,** tel. 824-9411, has 24-hour emergency service, as does **Routt Memorial Hospital,** tel. 879-1322, 40 miles east in Steamboat Springs. Craig's main **post office** is at 556 Pershing; phone 824-5795.

Recycling
Recycle aluminum and glass at **Axis Inc.,** 802 E. 2nd St., and at the **City Market,** 505 W. Victory.

Information
For more information on Craig and Moffat County, write the **Greater Craig Area Chamber of Commerce,** 360 E. Victory Way, Craig, CO 81625, or phone (303) 824-5689. The **Moffat County Visitors Center** is on the south side of E. Victory Way near the corner of Rose Street. The **Moffat County Library** is located at 570 Green St.; for hours, phone 824-5116. Craig's newspaper, the *Colorado Daily Press,* is published five days a week and runs stories of local and statewide interest. For subscription information, write Box 5, Craig, CO 81626, or phone 824-2600.

For more information on outdoor recreation in the area, contact the **Bureau of Land Management,** 455 Emerson, Craig, CO 81625, tel. 824-8261, or the Rabbit Ears District Office of **Routt National Forest,** 356 Ranney, Craig, CO 81625, tel. 824-9438.

For **road and weather information,** phone 824-4765.

Transportation
Continental Express, tel. (303) 879-2468, offers passenger service to Yampa Valley Regional Airport (in Hayden, about 20 miles east of Craig) and to Steamboat Springs (40 miles east). The **Greyhound** terminal is located at 470 Russell; phone 824-5161.

MEEKER AND VICINITY

Colorado 13 drops south out of Craig, follows the course of the Yampa River for 10 miles or so before the river doglegs to the west, then flirts for a few miles with the western border of White River National Forest. Pagoda Peak (elev. 11,120 feet) and Mount Marvin (elev. 12,045 feet) tower to the east. Be sure to gas up in Craig, as no services are available along the 50-mile stretch to Meeker.

MEEKER

Meeker (pop. 2,300; elev. 6,180 feet) is located about midway between Hwy. 40 and I-70 at the western base of the White River Plateau. A quiet and picturesque little town with a strong sense of community and civic pride, Meeker is a favorite among fishers and hunters, especially the latter, who during the fall fill up the town's scattering of lodges and motels, which remain fully booked throughout hunting season.

History

Meeker takes its name from Nathan C. Meeker, an Indian Agent prominent in Colorado affairs. In September, 1879, three years after Colorado achieved statehood, Meeker and 10 of his employees were killed by Utes in what has come to be known as the Meeker Massacre.

Meeker had been appointed to his post at the White River Agency in the spring of the previous year. Apparently not much of a diplomat, Meeker presently set about trying to domesticate the Utes, to convert them from a nomadic, hunting people, which they had been for centuries, into a sedentary aggregation of agriculturists.

The Utes resisted. Accustomed to ritual and grace, they couldn't understand Meeker's lack of civility and decorum. In addition, they were already angry at the government, not only for its attempts to yoke them onto the reservation but for not living up to earlier promises of money and supplies. When Meeker plowed an irrigation channel through an Indian horse-race track and then plowed under some of their best pastureland, they'd had enough.

Hearing war drums echoing down the canyons, Meeker sent for troops. Seeing the troops approach, the Utes got even angrier. They attacked the soldiers, and then the agency. Meeker and most of his men were killed, his wife, daughter, and other women taken hostage. A month later, the hostages were released when the Utes and the government negotiated a peace pact, a condition of which was the northern Utes' banishment to a Utah reservation.

After the massacre, the U.S. government established a fort where downtown Meeker now stands. In 1883, it sold the buildings to settlers

The White River Museum is located in a 19th-century Army cabin.

STEPHEN METZGER

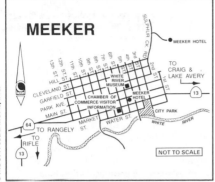

arriving in the area. Three log cabins, once used as barracks, today house the White River Museum. The massacre site can be viewed from Hwy. 64 about four miles west of town. Look for the marker.

White River Museum
Located in an old log cabin built by soldiers who had come following Meeker's massacre, this museum features five rooms of exhibits, including lots of pioneer artifacts (eyeglasses, sewing machine, tack, guns), Native American artifacts, and a wagon that Teddy Roosevelt took from town to the hunting grounds. There are also lots of historical photos, including several of an 1896 bank robbery. Evidently, a group that had been holed up with Butch Cassidy and his gang swept into Meeker, not expecting such violent resistance from the townspeople. Photos show the dead would-be robbers. Nice.

The White River Museum is open Mon. through Sat. 9 a.m.-5 p.m., May 1 to Nov. 15. The rest of the year it's open noon to 4 p.m. You can also arrange special tours. Phone (303) 878-9982. No admission fee; donations accepted. Located at 565 Park, behind the courthouse.

White River National Forest
The northern unit (Blanco District) of the White River National Forest, once a prime hunting ground of Utes, sprawls to the mountains east of Meeker. Gorgeous country, with several peaks topping 12,000 feet, the forest offers virtually unlimited recreational opportunities. Especially popular are hunting, fishing, and camping; the area's also famous for excellent backpacking, cross-country skiing, snowmobiling, and other activities. Take County Rd. 8 east from Meeker.

Fishing
Excellent stream and lake fishing, and trophy-sized brown, rainbow, brook, and cutthroat trout, lure fishermen to the White River area east of Meeker. (In fact, large trout have been caught on the White River within Meeker's city limits.)

Twenty miles east of town is **Lake Avery,** where fishing is good in summer and winter (ice fishermen do *very* well). Another 30 miles into the park is **Trappers Lake,** which, although remote, still gets lots of traffic. The best way to catch fish here is by boat (no motors allowed), which you can rent at **Trappers Lake Lodge,** tel. (303) 878-3336.

Be sure to check local regulations, as some restrictions apply.

Camping
You'll find several excellent Forest Service campgrounds in White River National Forest east of Meeker, including **North Fork Campground,** right on County Rd. 8 (one mile into the forest, 45 units). Also easily accessible and nearby are **South Fork Campground, Marvine Campground,** and **Himes Peak Campground.** There are four separate campgrounds at Trappers Lake, with a total of nearly 60 sites.

Walking Tour
The Meeker Chamber of Commerce has designed a short self-guided walking tour of the historic downtown area. Included are the Meeker Hotel, the White River Museum, St. James Episcopal Church (built in 1889), and several pre-1900 residences. The tour is described in detail in the chamber's *Visitor Information Guide* (see "Information" following).

Accommodations
Because Meeker draws such crowds during the hunting season, plan to make reservations for an autumn stay well in advance. The **Meeker Hotel,** tel. (303) 878-5062 or 878-5596, is on the National Register of Historic Places and has nicely appointed rooms at very reasonable rates. Even if you don't plan to stay here, poke your head in. The place hasn't changed all that much

since Teddy Roosevelt stayed here on a bear-hunting trip. Located right downtown across from the county courthouse. You can also get rooms (and cabins) at the **Rustic Motel**, tel. 878-3136, and the **Valley Motel**, tel. 878-3656.

Trappers Lake Lodge, tel. 878-3336, offers definitively rustic cabins—stoves for heating, no plumbing. Common shower and bathroom area. The lodge also offers pack trips, guided fishing, and canoe, rowboat, and horse rentals. Write 7700 Trappers Lake Rd., Meeker, CO 81641.

There are two campgrounds two miles west of Meeker at the junction of highways 64 and 13. **Rimrock Campground**, tel. 878-4486, is strictly a "passing-through" facility, with basic sites right next to the road. **Stagecoach Park**, tel. 878-4434, offers a bit more privacy, with sites nestled down off the road among the cottonwoods.

Food

The **Sleepy Cat Restaurant**, tel. (303) 878-4413, 20 miles east of town on County Rd. 8, is a 50-year-old Meeker tradition. A classic hunting lodge, its walls lined with trophies, the restaurant is a Meeker favorite, also popular among visiting hunters and anglers and local ranchers. The Sleepy Cat specializes in various beef entrees, but also offers chicken, seafood, and a salad bar.

The **Last Chance Restaurant**, 975 Market, tel. 878-4535, serves Mexican food and Texas barbecue, as well as American standards.

Calendar

Meeker's **Range Call Parade, Rodeo, and Pageant,** on the Fourth of July weekend, was begun in 1885 and is the oldest rodeo in the nation. In addition to providing lots of food, music, and rodeo competition, the pageant offers a re-enactment of the Meeker Massacre, with locals acting out the attack, kidnapping, and murders.

The **Meeker Classic Sheep Dog Trials** are held the second weekend in September. The trials attract upwards of 75 competitors and 2,000 spectators, who not only enjoy watching some of the finest dogs and best trainers in the West, but also get to listen to traditional Irish music and take part in other festivities.

Services

The offices of the **Meeker Police Department** are located at 236 7th St.; phone (303) 878-5555. Phone the **State Patrol** at 675-8311. **Pioneers Hospital** is at 785 Cleveland (turn north on 3rd); phone 878-5047 (in emergencies, 878-5700). The Meeker **post office** is at 656 6th St.; phone 878-5830.

Recycling

Recycle at **Gofer Foods,** 812 Market St., tel. (303) 878-4492.

Information

An excellent source for local information is the chamber of commerce-published *Meeker and White River Country Visitor Information Guide.* Copies are available at the chamber offices on the corner of Hwy. 13 (W. Market) and 7th. Write Box 869, Meeker, CO 81641, or phone (303) 878-5510. The Meeker **public library** is located at 200 Main St., tel. 878-5911.

For information on **White River National Forest,** stop in at the ranger station at 361 7th St., tel. 878-4039.

trainer and sheepdog

STEAMBOAT SPRINGS AND VICINITY

Best known for the ski resort that was built here in 1963, Steamboat Springs, seat of Routt County, is a small town (pop. 6,500; elev. 6,695 feet) surrounded by towering mountains and verdant river valleys. With an economy based largely on ranching (sheep and cattle), farming (hay, wheat, oats, barley), and tourism, Steamboat Springs offers a true taste of the old West, where real cowboys still ride the real range, and at the same time lures upscale travelers looking to escape the trappings of some of the state's glitzier resorts.

HISTORY

Though Steamboat Springs' high-rise hotels and sprawling condominiums attest to the town's membership in the club of modern resorts, the area has actually been a playground of sorts for some 600 years. As early as the 1300s, Utes spent their summers here, hunting buffalo and other large game, and, most likely, taking advantage of the 100-plus-degree hot springs in the Yampa River Valley. The name "Steamboat Springs," in fact, comes from one of the hot springs: A party of 19th-century trappers heard the waters rumbling and bubbling and thought a steamboat was approaching from downriver.

The Utes' summer home was taken from them in 1868 and made the property of the United States—the land was too valuable (particularly because of the pelts the mountain men brought back) for it to remain in the hands of savages, however noble, although the Native Americans continued to believe they had a right to visit (the nerve!). Between 1868 and 1880, when the Utes were finally forced onto a reservation in Utah, several skirmishes took place between various tribes and white settlers, including the Meeker Massacre of 1879.

The Yampa River Valley's first white settler of record was James Crawford, a Missourian, who homesteaded here in 1875, although Crawford's first home was an abandoned log building, suggesting someone had passed through earlier and had stayed long enough to need solid shelter. Evidently respectful of the Utes and their hunting grounds, Crawford became friends with them, and they left him alone while they attacked other settlements in the area, as well as other settlers passing through. Meanwhile, the Yampa Valley was becoming increasingly well known for its high-quality native hay, and in the early 1880s, once the Utes had been vanquished from the valley for good, the region began to see a large influx of farmers and ranchers.

In 1885, Crawford, having obtained financial backing from Boulder businessmen J.P. Maxwell and Andrew Mackay, formed the Steamboat Springs Townsite Company, laid out the streets of the small town, and sold lots. By 1888, the number of buildings in Steamboat Springs had grown from half a dozen to nearly 50. Also germane to the the town's early development was the introduction of Steamboat's first newspaper, the *Routt County Pilot,* which was first printed (on a second-hand foot-powered press hauled over from Boulder) on July 31, 1885.

Also at this time, as farmers and ranchers were establishing themselves in the fertile Yampa Valley, a mine at the base of Hahn's Peak, 30 miles to the north, was drawing miners from throughout the area. This further added to Routt County's population, and though some of these miners were transient and would eventually move on (particularly when the Hahn's Peak mine played out in the early 1890s), some would stay in the area permanently.

Still another crucial stage in Steamboat's development was the arrival of the railroad. The talk of the town since the turn of the century, the railroad to Steamboat was completed on Dec. 13, 1908, and the first passenger train chugged into town a month later on the evening of Jan. 19. The *Routt County Pilot* reported the event the next day: "Steamboat's long-looked-for day has come. . . . Over 75 Steamboat people, including the band, met the train [about eight miles south of town] and rode down, while hundreds more were at the Steamboat Station to cheer it when it arrived."

In 1913, Norwegian cross-country and ski-jumping champion Carl Howelsen arrived in

Steamboat and organized the town's first Winter Carnival. Howelsen so impressed locals with his jumping hill and 110-foot leap that many were inspired to try ski jumping themselves. Local lore has it that some of the jumpers at the first carnival landed in a herd of startled elk grazing nearby.

By 1940, downhill skiing had become popular among Steamboaters, and in 1943 it was added to the curriculum of the local school. In 1963, Steamboat Springs Ski Area was officially opened for business on Storm Peak three miles south of town. A year later, when one of the town's early Winter Olympians, Buddy Werner, was killed in an avalanche in Switzerland, the peak's name was changed to Mt. Werner. Over the last 30 years, the Steamboat Ski Area has grown dramatically: Lifts and a gondola now spoke out over four different mountains, and the base facilities include everything from a golf course (for summer visitors) to bars, restaurants, condominiums, and a fleet of shuttle buses.

ATTRACTIONS

This is a town that bills itself "Ski Town, USA," and of course the main attraction here is the world-class alpine ski resort three miles from downtown. Which means this is largely a winter-sports town, where most everything revolves around the fact that the area's meadows, mountains, and moraines are blanketed with snow from November to May. Still, there's lots to do, even if you're not one to strap boards to your boots and go sliding down mountainsides in search of deep thrills—even in the summer, when all the skis in Ski Town, USA are leaning languidly in closets or hanging from garage rafters.

SKIING AND OTHER WINTER SPORTS

Steamboat Ski Area

With 3,600 vertical feet of skiing, 102 runs, 2,500 skiable acres, an uphill capacity of nearly 30,000 skiers an hour, World Cup races, over 300 inches of snowfall per year, and internationally acclaimed tree and powder skiing, this is without doubt one of the best ski areas in the West (many say in the world).

In a sport that grows more pretentious and exclusive by the season—a sport of doctors, lawyers, and accountants, turbo Saabs, Volvos, and BMWs—Steamboat is a breath of fresh air. Drawing largely on its Old-West heritage, as well as on the real-life Old-West town down the road, Steamboat has managed to maintain its integrity and charm—even in the path of an advancing epidemic of condos, high-rises, and boutiques. Oh, there are still boutiques, and ferny bars, and more real estate and property-management companies than you can shake a ski pole at. But still, it all feels more real here than in some of the Rockies' other big resorts.

Steamboat Village, at the base of the ski lifts

STEPHEN METZGER

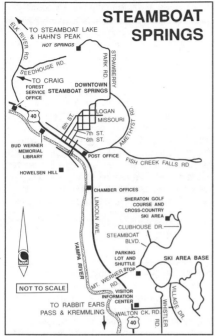

STEAMBOAT SPRINGS

TO STEAMBOAT LAKE & HAHN'S PEAK

HOT SPRINGS

ELK RIVER RD.

SEEDHOUSE RD.

TO CRAIG

FOREST SERVICE OFFICE

DOWNTOWN STEAMBOAT SPRINGS

STRAWBERRY PARK RD.

40

8th ST.

LOGAN

MISSOURI

7th ST.

6th ST.

AMETHYST RD.

BUD WERNER MEMORIAL LIBRARY

POST OFFICE

FISH CREEK FALLS RD.

HOWELSEN HILL

CHAMBER OFFICES

LINCOLN AVE.

SHERATON GOLF COURSE AND CROSS-COUNTRY SKI AREA

CLUBHOUSE DR.

STEAMBOAT BLVD.

YAMPA RIVER

PARKING LOT AND SHUTTLE STOP

SKI AREA BASE

MT. WERNER RD.

NOT TO SCALE

VISITOR INFORMATION CENTER

TO RABBIT EARS PASS & KREMMLING

WALTON CK. RD.

40

WALTON CK. RD.

VILLAGE DR.

WHISTLER

WHISTLER DR.

© MOON PUBLICATIONS, INC.

And it's probably because most everything else here really does take a back seat to skiing. It's a big mountain, and some people come an awfully long way to explore—and, perhaps, master—it. So by day's end, they don't have much energy for shopping. They want to relax, maybe take a hot tub or sauna, and get some food in their bellies for strength for the next day; hardcores with energy left at the end of the day can boogie to live music at several clubs—both on the mountain and in town (see "Entertainment" following).

So, what about that mountain? Well, for starters, it's got a wide variety of terrain for all ability levels, although it's best suited to the intermediate-to-advanced skier, with 54% of its runs designated intermediate (31% are advanced and 15% are beginner). Spread out over four different mountains and rising to 10,385 feet, Steamboat's 2,500 acres of runs and off-piste skiing are serviced by 21 lifts, including an eight-passenger gondola and 17 chairlifts—a quad, seven triples, and nine doubles (which Steamboat returnees claim keep lift lines minimal).

Don't be deceived by what you can see of Steamboat from the base of the mountain. Though it looks big enough, there's lots more. In fact, the majority of the runs and lifts are beyond that first 1,000-foot vertical rise. Experts and advanced skiers will want to check out the runs off of Storm Peak, Sundown, and Priest Creek chair, while Burgess Creek, Sunshine, and Thunderhead offer intermediates a chance to explore and work on their form.

If you can remember back to the 1974 Winter Olympics, or if you read the skiing magazines at all during the late '60s and early '70s, the name Billy Kidd should ring a bell. Perhaps you even have an image of him in your head: the archetypal all-American cowboy-skier, boyish tanned face grinning beneath the brim of his ten-gallon Stetson. Well, Kidd's still around. He's the director of Steamboat's ski school, and he's out on the slopes almost every day. And Kidd's not the only Olympian to have cut his ski teeth in the gates of Steamboat. As of 1990, Steamboat had produced 26 winter Olympic athletes, more than any other town in the United States.

Information
The marketing department of Steamboat Springs Ski Resort will gladly send you more information—from maps of the mountain to complete listings of nearby lodges. Write 2305 Mt. Werner Circle, Steamboat Springs, CO 80487, or phone (303) 879-6111. For **Steamboat Reservations Services,** phone (800) 922-2722.

Howelsen Hill
Named for Carl Howelsen, who at Steamboat's 1914 Winter Carnival jumped 110 feet on skis, this is one of the oldest ski areas in the country. Open seven days a week (night skiing Tues. through Fri. 6-9 p.m.), Howelsen has a 440-foot vertical rise and 30 acres of skiable terrain serviced by two surface lifts.

Best known for its five jumping ramps (20, 30, 50, 70, and 90 meters), Howelsen is the training grounds for the U.S. Ski Jumping Team, and has been the "home field" of many world-class jumpers. Remember "Eddie the Eagle," England's entry in the 1988 Olympic Ski Jumping Competition? Even the Eagle jumped here, having stopped here that year en route to Banff.

The Winter Sports Club, based at Howelsen, offers instruction in downhill, cross-country, and freestyle skiing. There's also an ice-skating rink at the complex, which is located downtown at the south end of the 5th Street Bridge. For more information on Howelsen Hill, phone the Steamboat Springs Parks and Recreation Department at (303) 879-4300, or contact the chamber of commerce.

Backcountry Powder Skiing
For hard-core backcountry skiers and powder-hounds whose idea of graffiti is a series of figure 8s in a remote bowl, **Steamboat Powder Cats** will take you by snowcat up into virgin powder—for both day-trips and overnight excursions. Phone (303) 879-5188 or (800) 288-0543.

Cross-country Skiing
Though better known for its downhill skiing, the Steamboat area also offers excellent opportunities for cross-country skiers—on groomed trails as well as in the backcountry. The **Steamboat Ski Touring Center,** based at the Sheraton Golf Course, has 28 miles of trails winding out over the links and along nearby Fish Creek. The center, which caters to the broadest range of Nordic skiers—from the most cavalier recreational skier to the serious Nordic athlete—is managed by Sven Wiik, who, after immigrating from Sweden in 1949, taught cross-country skiing at Western State College in Gunnison for the next 19 years and coached the United States Olympic team in 1960. Wiik's Scandinavian Lodge offers rentals, lessons, and backcountry tours. For more information, write Steamboat Ski Touring Center, Box 772297, Steamboat Springs, CO 80477, or phone (303) 879-8180.

You'll also find cross-country trails at **Rabbit Ears Pass,** about 10 miles southeast of Steamboat Springs on Hwy. 40, as well as at **Clark Store,** tel. 879-3849, 20 miles north of Steamboat on Elk River Rd. (County Rd. 129). Just off Elk River Rd., **Seedhouse Rd.** offers ungroomed trails along the Elk River; and **Howelsen Hill** (see above) offers rentals, equipment, and trails.

In addition, a number of guest ranches in and around Steamboat offer cross-country skiing. Among them: **Hahn's Peak Guest Ranch,** tel. 879-8638; **Vista Verde Guest and Ski Touring Ranch,** tel. 879-3858; **Elk River Guest Ranch,** tel. 879-3843; and **Dutch Creek Guest Ranch,** tel. 879-8519.

For maps and information on ski touring in Routt National Forest, contact the Hahn's Peak District Office, tel. 879-1870, or the Supervisor's Office at 29587 W. Hwy. 40 in Steamboat, tel. 879-1722.

Other Winter Sports
Those averse to strapping skis afoot have several other options when it comes to winter recreation in Steamboat. Howelsen Hill Ski Complex also offers bobsledding and ice skating, while snowmobiling, snowshoeing, and ice fishing—**Buggywhips Fish and Float Service,** tel. (303) 879-8033—are also available to the winter sports hound. The various activity and reservations centers, as well as the chamber of commerce, have complete listings and schedules.

WHEN THE SNOW MELTS

Don't worry—Ski Town, USA doesn't board up its windows once the chairlifts shut down and wildflowers begin pushing up through the meadows' snowcovers. Quite the contrary. In fact, folks looking for outdoor diversions in the warmer months actually have more to choose from than their winter counterparts do. Golf, for example. Tennis. Cycling (both touring and mountain biking). Rafting. Hiking, backpacking, camping, and fishing. And don't forget hot-air ballooning and horseback riding. You'd have to have the imagination of a hitchin' post not to be able to find something to do in Steamboat once you've put your skis and snowshoes in storage.

Steamboat Lake State Park
Twenty-five miles north of Steamboat Springs on County Rd. 129, this state park on Steamboat and Pearl lakes offers camping, boating, fishing, waterskiing, hiking, and, in winter, snowmobiling. Pit toilets and running water. Phone (303) 879-3922 for more information.

Stagecoach State Recreation Area
South of Steamboat Springs off Hwy. 40, this newly opened recreation area at Stagecoach Reservoir has hiking trails, tent and RV camping facilities, fishing for rainbow and cutthroat trout, and a boat ramp. During the winter, Stagecoach is a popular snowmobiling and cross-country skiing site. For more information, phone (303)

879-3922 or write the Colorado Division of Parks and Outdoor Recreation, 1313 Sherman St., Room 618, Denver CO 80203, tel. 866-3437.

Golf

Steamboat has two golf courses, the 18-hole **Sheraton Steamboat Golf Club,** located at the base of Mt. Werner, and the nine-hole public **Steamboat Golf Club,** at the west end of town off Hwy. 40. The Sheraton Steamboat is a high-class course, affiliated with the Sheraton Hotel (Sheraton guests get discounts on the expensive-anyway greens fees) and designed by Robert Trent Jones. Carts are required, Cadillacs or better recommended. Phone (303) 879-1391 for a tee time, prices, and more information. The Steamboat Golf Club is the town's pleb course, with the attendant retrenched prices and lack of ostentation. Phone 879-4295.

Hiking And Backpacking

Routt National Forest, which sprawls from Steamboat Springs north across the Wyoming border and south nearly to Kremmling (another unit lies east of Kremmling in eastern Rio Blanco and Garfield counties), is an Eden of hiking and backpacking trails and backcountry. Part of this million-plus-acre national forest, the Mt. Zirkel Wilderness Area, about 25 miles north of Steamboat Springs in the gorgeous Park Range, offers lots of backcountry to explore. Take Elk River Rd./County Rd. 129 north to Seedhouse Rd., where you'll find one of several trailheads leading into the wilderness area.

The Forest Service supervisor's office in Steamboat Springs, 29587 Hwy. 40, tel. (303) 879-1722, and the Hahn's Peak District Office, 57 10th St., tel. 879-1870, can provide maps and information.

One of the more popular short hikes for Steamboat visitors is to Fish Creek Falls, a 283-foot waterfall just minutes from town. The quarter-mile trail (restrooms, picnic, and handicap facilities provided) leads to a viewing area, then on to a second waterfall (not nearly as swamped with visitors), and eventually to Dumont Lake, about 11 miles from the trailhead. Take Fish Creek Falls Rd. south from downtown.

Fishing

The lakes and streams in the Steamboat area offer a wide range of fishing possibilities—from easy-to-fool, recently stocked hatchery fish the size of a large pencil to wiley four-pound natives that can tell an artificial fly from the real McCoy at 50 feet. Dumont Lake, on Rabbit Ears Pass 25 miles south of Steamboat via Hwy. 40, is stocked regularly with catchable-sized rainbow trout, as is Steamboat Lake, about 30 miles north of Steamboat off County Rd. 129. The Elk and Yampa rivers also offer good fishing. For guided fishing tours, contact **Buggywhips Fish and Float Service,** tel. (303) 879-8033.

For more information on fishing in Routt County, contact the Steamboat Springs Chamber Resort Association, tel. 879-0880 or (800) 332-3204 (for non-local Colorado calls). Equipment, licenses, and local tips are available at **Steamboat Springs Sporting Goods,** 908 Lincoln Ave., tel. 879-7774; **Straightline,** 744 Lincoln Ave., tel. 879-7568; and **The Grand Tradition,** 906 Lincoln Ave., tel. 879-0916.

Rafting And Kayaking

As you'd expect in a town on two decent-sized rivers, as well as near so many smaller streams, Steamboat is a river rat's paradise, especially those who can settle for water a tad less violent than, say, the Andes' Apurimac. You can put in at a variety of spots along the river, although you need to be careful not to trespass on the private property that flanks much of both rivers.

Buggywhips Fish and Float Service, downtown at 435 Lincoln Ave., tel. (303) 879-8033 or (800) 759-0343, offers a wide range of float trips, from mild to wild. **Mountain Sports Kayak School,** 1835 Central Park Ave., tel. 879-8794, or 879-6910 in winter, provides canoe and kayak rental and instruction. **Mike's Marina** at Steamboat also offers float trips and equipment rentals; phone 879-7019.

Ballooning

Though not cheap, hot-air balloon rides are getting more and more popular each year, with several companies in Steamboat offering quarter-, half-, and full-hour rides daily. **Aero Sports,** tel. (303) 879-7433; **Balloons Over Steamboat,** tel. 879-3298; **Eagle Balloon Tours,** tel. 879-8687; and **Pegasus,** tel. 879-9191, offer various promotional come-ons (free champagne and transportation, senior and group discounts, personalized flights, etc.) to offset the cost of a bird's-eye view of Steamboat in the quietude of the wind-borne schooner.

Horseback Riding

It should come as no suprise in a town such as Steamboat Springs—whose western heritage oozes from every barn wall, saloon door, and Stetson hat—that riding is big here. You may find yourself downtown trying on some après-ski boots while across the store some cowpoke with a wad of chew in his lip is eyeing saddles and tack. And though there are some dude ranches in the area, most of the cowboys in Routt County are for real. This is an area that grew up with horses. And horses still work here.

They're also for hire. A stirrup-ful of outfits in and around Steamboat have horses for rent, as well as guides that will lead tours, instructors that will give lessons, and, if you'd rather ride behind than on a horse, sleighs, coaches, and carts that will make you feel equestrian without risking a bruised posterior. Some of the services provide meals with the trips.

Del's Triangle 3 Ranch, tel. (303) 879-3495 or 879-4109, offers rentals and pack trips, as do **Glen Eden Stables,** tel. 879-3864, and **Steamboat Lake Guides and Outfitters,** tel. 879-3906. **Sunset Ranch,** tel. 879-0954, has horses available for pack trips into the Mt. Zirkel Wilderness Area.

Recreation Information

For more information on what to do in the Steamboat-Routt County area, contact the **Steamboat Activity Center** at (303) 879-2062 or the **Steamboat Springs Chamber Resort Association** at 879-0880 or (800) 332-3204 (for non-local Colorado calls).

TOURS

In addition to the various outfits offering sleigh rides around Steamboat and balloon rides over it (see above), you'll find everything from snowmobile and jeep tours to pack trips and jaunts to hot springs. The **Steamboat Activity Center,** tel. (303) 879-2062, located downtown at 720 Lincoln and in Gondola Square at the base of the lifts, can arrange just about any kind of tour you have in mind, as can **Let Me Entertain You,** tel. 879-8010. For snowmobile tours, try **Elk River Guest Ranch,** tel. 879-3843, **Emerald Mountain Snowmobile Tours,** tel. 879-8065, **Steamboat Snowmobile Tours,** tel. 879-

1551, **Hahn's Peak Guest Ranch,** tel. 879-8638, or **Steamboat Lake Outfitters,** tel. 879-3906 or 879-4404.

Sweet Pea Tours, tel. (303) 879-5820, offers hot-springs tours, which include transportation and admission (bring your own suit and towel).

ACCOMMODATIONS

You won't have an easy time if you go looking for cheap digs in Steamboat Springs—particularly in winter, when some of the best snow in the country has blanketed the runs of Mt. Werner and Sunshine Peak. As in many resort towns, especially those as isolated as Steamboat is, travelers here are more or less at the mercy of the innkeepers and whatever prices they want to charge. If you want to dance, or ski, in Steamboat, you've got to pay the fiddler.

You can save some money, though, by staying in nearby towns. Skiers who don't mind driving 45-60 minutes can get rooms for substantially less in Craig, for example, where rooms at the Holiday Inn start at about $35 (in Steamboat the same room runs $65-145). In addition, advance reservations aren't nearly as crucial if you go outside Steamboat. In town, many rooms are reserved up to a year ahead of time, and in a season of decent snowfall, Steamboat will have fewer rooms available than there were in Bethlehem. Ultimately, you just have to ask (and answer) yourself if the trade-off's worth it. Is what you save by staying 45 miles away worth what you'd gain by staying slope-side, or at least within walking distance to a shuttle stop? Is saving $50 a day on lodging worth missing out on the experience of hanging out after skiing in one of the West's great winter sports towns?

Hotels, Motels, And Condominiums

The newcomer to Steamboat, especially one who's bought into the resort's claim to being a down-to-earth ski town, will most likely be surprised at the number of high-rise hotels and condominiums sprouting from Steamboat Village and the base of the lifts. The ultimate in convenience for the skier who likes to ski right to her doormat, these rooms provide that fine feeling of knowing that when you step out of your skis you're home. No need to worry about finding your car in the parking lot, checking shuttle departure times; no need to fear getting caught in après-ski traffic. In fact, before other skiers have even secured their skis atop their cars, you can be soaking away the day's aches in a hot, swirling Jacuzzi as you pull on a cold one. Not a bad way to close the curtain on the day.

Here are just a few of the slope-side lodges at Steamboat (in addition to the nightly rates given here, most Steamboat inns offer ski-and-lodging package deals, which include lift tickets, and sometimes shuttle transportation, meals, equipment, and other enticements): Doubles at the **Best Western Ptarmigan Inn,** tel. (303) 879-1730 or (800) 538-7519, start at about $60 (summer) and $150 (winter). The **Holiday Inn,** tel. 879-2250 or (800) HOLIDAY, has doubles for $65-145. The **Sheraton Resort and Conference Center,** tel. 879-2220, also located at the lifts, has rooms for two starting at $60 and topping out at $260.

In addition to the ski-in/ski-out lodging facilities at the base of the lifts, you'll find a handful of hotels, motels, and condos three miles away in downtown Steamboat Springs. At the **Rabbit Ears Motel,** tel. 879-1150, you can get a double for around $50 summer, $90 winter. The **Western Lodge,** tel. 879-1050, has rooms for two running $45-100.

Bed And Breakfast

The **Clermont Inn,** tel. (303) 879-3083, in downtown Steamboat Springs, has several small rooms with adjoining baths starting at about $80 a night.

Lodging Information

For more information on the over 50 hotels, motels, and condominiums in Steamboat, as well as complete lists of lodging packages, phone **Steamboat Reservation Services** at (800) 922-2722. Remember, too, that during the height of the ski season you're going to need reservations well in advance—though if you find yourself strapped and desperately needing a Steamboat fix within the month, you might call around to see if there've been any cancellations.

Camping And RVing

A number of campgrounds are available in and around Steamboat Springs, including three that are open year-round with RV facilities. **Ski Town**

Campground, tel. (303) 879-0273, on the Yampa River about two miles west of town on Hwy. 40, has 100 RV sites (tent camping on about a quarter of them) and cabins with nightly, weekly, and monthly rates; shuttle service available. **Fish Creek Campground,** tel. 879-5476, a mile and a half east of Steamboat on Fish Creek, has 15 tent and 30 RV sites, laundry facilities, and a rec room. **Steamboat Lake State Park** (see above), 25 miles north of Steamboat, has 200 tent and RV sites on Pearl Lake. For information and reservations, phone 879-3922.

In addition, several Forest Service campgrounds are scattered throughout the area. **Meadows Campground,** 15 miles southeast of Steamboat; **Dumont Lake,** 10 miles east of Meadows (watch for the sign); and **Summit Lake Campground** (no drinking water), about 15 miles northeast of town (take Strawberry Park Rd. to Forest Service Rd. 60) all have tent and RV sites and pit toilets. Phone the Hahn's Peak District Office of the Forest Service at 879-1870 for more information.

FOOD

Steamboat Traditions

As you'd expect, Steamboat abounds in good places to eat, and just about everyone has a favorite restaurant. **La Montaña,** 2500 Village Way, tel. (303) 879-5800, serves Mexican and Tex-Mex entrees seven nights a week (5:30-10 p.m.) for $7-17; among the favorites are the chili, fajitas, and enchiladas. **Mattie Silk's,** in Ski Time Square, tel. 879-2441, serves seafood, beef, veal, duck, and pasta dishes for $7-20—also open seven days a week 5:30-10 p.m. (6-10 p.m. in summer); check out the huge selection of imported beers. **Mazzola's,** 440 S. Lincoln (between the lifts and downtown), tel. 879-2405, is open for lunch and dinner seven days a week. Specialities include pizzas, calzone, lasagna, pastas, and a salad bar; prices range from about $5 for an Italian meatball sandwich to $15 for the "Seafood Medley," various shellfish served in a white sauce over linguine. Another classic is the **Old Town Pub and Restaurant** downtown at 600 Lincoln, tel. 879-2101. Dinners include burgers, chicken, steak, and seafood ($6-12); also open for breakfast and lunch. **Cantina,** 818 Lincoln, tel. 879-0826, also serves excellent

Mexican food, including enchiladas, burritos, and tacos ($6-9), with your choice of red, green, or cheese sauces. Lots of domestic and Mexican beers available to wash down those nachos (no bangers to complement the Watneys and Guinness on tap, though). For dessert, try the flan, cheesecake, or sopaipillas.

Still Hungry?

For breakfast (served all day), try the **5th Street Café,** at 5th and Lincoln, tel. (303) 879-4106. Crepes, omelettes, and Belgian waffles run $3.50-7. The 5th St. also serves lunch (sandwiches, soups, salads) and dinner (burgers, salads, pastas, chicken). Open 7 a.m.-10 p.m. daily. **Anderson and Friend's Restaurant,** tel. 879-8080, is a low-key little café right at the base of the lifts in Ski Time Square (also at 903 Lincoln in town)—perfect for a healthful and hearty homemade lunch. Salads, vegetarian stir-fry, and quiches are about $5. For dinner, Anderson's serves pastas, seafood, and steak for $7-12. Open 11 a.m-11 p.m. daily. For sports fans (who in Steamboat isn't?), **Mulligan's Sports Bar and Restaurant,** tel. 879-2916, has five large-screen monitors hooked up to a satellite and all the current games, matches, and contests, and, with the aid of an 8- by 12-foot screen, you can even play simulated golf with regulation clubs and balls. Serving food every day till 2 a.m., Mulligan's also has cappuccinos and espressos. Located at the base of the lifts—with outside seating, when the weather allows.

Other favorites among both Steamboat locals and out-of-towners are the **Pine Grove Restaurant,** 1465 Pine Grove Rd., tel. 879-1190, serving buffalo, elk, rabbit, quail, beef, chicken, salad bar; and the **Butcher Shop,** in Ski Time Square, tel. 879-2484, prime rib, seafood, fresh Rocky Mountain trout, salad bar.

ENTERTAINMENT

Many of Steamboat's clubs, restaurants, and hotels offer a variety of après-ski entertainment. For current listings, pick up a copy of *Steamboat Today,* published daily and available free throughout the area. In addition, the **Steamboat Whistle,** published weekly and also free, lists current happenings, theater showings, gallery openings, etc.

If you've still got energy after a day of skiing, check out **The Inferno,** featuring live music and dancing, as well as stand-up comedy by big-name acts. Located at the base of the gondola; phone (303) 879-5111 for more information. The **Old Town Pub,** 600 Lincoln, tel. 879-2101, has live music Sunday and Monday nights, and a big-screen television showing skiing and other sporting events most of the rest of the time. The **Tugboat,** tel. 879-7070, in Ski Time Square in the village has live entertainment 9 p.m.-2 a.m. Another favorite for live entertainment is **P.J.'s,** in the Torian Plum Building, tel. 879-2009.

If you want to combine your dinner and entertainment, check out **Club Majiks** dinner theater, billing itself a "cabaret in the Rockies." Dinner is served Tues. through Sat. from 7-9 p.m. with a show afterward. Phone 879-5848 for more information. Those who want to get a taste of Steamboat outside after dark should consider a sleigh ride. Several outfits offer rides to various restaurants. Among them is **Steamboat Lake Guest Ranch,** tel. 879-8519.

Throughout the winter, **The Saloon,** tel. 879-6303, features live music and regularly offers free country-western dance lessons. Thursday nights, the downtown merchants' association offers free sleigh rides. Phone the chamber for hours and meeting places.

CALENDAR

There's something going on in Steamboat almost every weekend—from on-skis torchlight parades and ski races to local theater productions and rodeos. One of the highlights is the 80-year-old week-long **Winter Carnival,** which takes place in early February each year. Among the events are ice-sculpture competitions, ski jumping, hockey games, and a parade on skis. A local tradition, the festival is marked by a general sense of revelry and nuttiness. For more information, phone (303) 879-0695 or 879-0880. In early June, you can join the runners (and walkers) in the Steamboat Marathon (actually a 10-K course), and a month later, the Fourth of July weekend is **Cowboy Roundup Days,** a potpourri of fireworks, community barbecues, a Rocky Mountain Oyster Fry, and a Cowboy Poetry and Storytelling Jamboree. **Rainbow Weekend,** at the end of July, is an annual hot-air balloon festival, including arts-and-crafts booths, live music, and food.

For exact dates and more information on these events and many more, phone the **Steamboat Springs Chamber of Commerce,** tel. 879-0880. When staying in Steamboat, check out the community calendars in the daily paper *Steamboat Today* and in the weekly *Steamboat Whistle.*

SHOPPING

Though Steamboat's a mecca for lovers of the outdoors, the town and village do offer a variety of gift shops and boutiques as well. While the rest of your party skis, golfs, fishes, balloons, or otherwise explores the area's copious mountains, parks, forests, and lakes, you can venture into the town's world of boutiques, gift shops, galleries, and, alas, tourist traps.

If you drive to Steamboat, you can't miss the zillions of billboards advertising **F. M. Light and Sons,** and most likely you'll be a bit curious. Go ahead and check it out; it's definitely a one-of-a-kind store. Originally a western wear and supply shop dating to the early part of the century, Light's now carries a huge array of apparel—from lizard-skin cowboy boots to Marlboroman ponchos, from after-ski boots to I-Heart-Steamboat sweatshirts. You'll also find postcards and other knicknacks.

The **Elephant's Trunk Boutique** in the Torian Plum Building, tel. (303) 879-3468, sells handsome boots for men, women, and children—from fancy dress to after-ski. **Barton's,** also in the village at the base of the lifts, tel. 879-6777, carries a variety of impressive collectibles—dolls, ceramics, Christmas ornaments, shawls, and wall hangings.

You'll also find a dozen or so galleries in the Steamboat area, both in town and at the village. The **Amer-Indian Gallery,** in Ski Time Square, tel. 879-7116, sells paintings, rugs, baskets, sculpture, and jewelry from over 50 Native American tribes. During the ski season, the gallery offers a series of special shows and lectures; call for more information. **Aristo's,** next door, tel. 879-4392, specializes in imports from Peru, Uruguay, Mexico, Turkey, China, Iran, and Afghanistan. The shop also carries Native American paintings and sculpture. The

Artisans' Market of Steamboat, 624 Lincoln, tel. 879-7512, is a local artists' cooperative, selling the work of a variety of Steamboat and Routt County artists. Open 9:30 a.m.-8:30 p.m. daily. **Emily Ingram Galleries, Ltd.,** 5th and Lincoln, tel. 879-2145, specializes in contemporary Western and Southwestern art—paintings, sculpture, jewelry—with a wide range of quality and price.

SERVICES

The **Steamboat Springs Police Department** is located at 840 Yampa St.; call (303) 849-1144. Phone the **Routt County Sheriff** at 849-1090. **State Patrol** offices are at 29587 W. Hwy. 40; phone 879-4306. Steamboat's **Routt Memorial Hospital** is at 80 Park Ave., tel. 879-1322. The central **post office** is on the east end of town at 200 Lincoln Ave., tel. (303) 879-0363.

Recycling
Recycle aluminum and glass in Steamboat Springs at the **City Market,** 1825 Central Park Avenue. Phone the City of Steamboat **recycling information line** at (303) 879-2060.

INFORMATION

The **Steamboat Springs Chamber Resort Association** is a professional and aggressive group, and a card or phone call will get you on their mailing list, which in turn will get you generous amounts of information (brochures, maps, advertising leaflets, relocation info, etc.). Write Box 774408, Steamboat Springs, CO 80477, or phone (303) 879-0880 or (800) 922-2722.

The **Bud Werner Memorial Library** (Steamboat's public library) is located at 1289 Lincoln Ave., tel. 879-0240; special events are sponsored year round, including children's storytelling.

For maps and information on hiking, snowmobiling, cross-country skiing, and otherwise exploring Steamboat's backcountry, write the district office of the **Routt National Forest,** 57 10th St., Steamboat Springs, CO 80477, or phone 879-1870.

For **road and weather information,** phone 879-1260. For **Steamboat ski conditions,** phone 879-7300.

TRANSPORTATION

Getting around Steamboat, particularly in the wintertime when the shuttles are running full tilt, is relatively easy, as is getting there. Several major airlines, including **American, America West, Continental Express,** and **Northwest,** fly nonstop to Steamboat from cities on both coasts (Los Angeles, San Diego, New York) and in between (Phoenix, Chicago, Dallas, Denver). Check with your travel agent for fares. You might want to fly into Denver instead, as it's considerably cheaper than flying directly into Steamboat, and then either rent your own rig or take a shuttle to the ski area. If you fly into Denver, you can get to Steamboat via **Panorama's Steamboat Express,** tel. (303) 879-3400 or (800) 825-8383.

Once you arrive in Steamboat, whether you're staying downtown or in the village, you don't really need a car to get around. **Steamboat Springs Transit,** tel. 879-3717, has several regular routes around the village, as well as one that runs into town. The "Red Line" and the "Green Line" circle through the condo complexes and will drop you off at the ski area in the morning and virtually at your doorstep at the end of the day. For you night owls, the last bus leaves the village for downtown at 2:03 a.m. (an hour earlier on Sunday). Phone for more information and for non-ski-season schedules.

Alpine Taxi-Limo, Inc., tel. 879-2800 or (800) 232-RIDE (in Colorado) or (800) 343-RIDE (nationwide), offers standard taxi service as well as charters between Steamboat and Denver's Stapleton International Airport, mountain tours, and shuttles between Steamboat lodges and Yampa Valley Airport.

Rent cars in Steamboat from **Budget,** tel. 879-3103, **Dollar,** tel. 879-5969, **Hertz,** tel. 870-0800, **National,** tel. 879-0800, **Rent-a-Dent,** tel. 879-8737, or from **Sam Taylor Auto Rentals,** tel. 879-0928 or (800) 338-5631, specializing in snow-ready front-wheel- and four-wheel-drive rigs. You can also rent cars at Denver's Stapleton International Airport from all major companies, most of which offer special ski vehicles—4WD, ski racks, etc.

SOUTH TO I-70

Highway 40 south to the junction with I-70 near Georgetown is absolutely stunning for its variety of breathtaking scenery. Just south of Steamboat, you arc to the east and begin the climb up and over the Continental Divide at Rabbit Ears Pass (elev. 9,426 feet). Just a few miles later, though, the highway dips south again and back onto the western side of the divide at Muddy Pass (8,722 feet). Then the road drops down into the Blue River Valley and into Kremmling, where you can either continue due south to Dillon via CO 9 and Green Mountain Reservoir or bank east to Granby. At the southwestern corner of Rocky Mountain National Park, Granby offers access to Hwy. 34 through the park to Estes Park (the road is closed in the winter). Continuing on Hwy. 40 south from Granby takes you through the high windswept Fraser River Valley, surrounded by the towering mountains of the deep heart of the Rockies, and into Winter Park. Just past Winter Park, Hwy. 40 begins a nasty series of switchbacks, winding and snaking its way up and over Berthoud Pass (11,307 feet). Views along this stretch are unsurpassed (though you need to make sure your brakes are in good working order . . .). From the junction of Hwy. 40 and I-70 it's less than an hour's drive to Denver.

NORTH CENTRAL COLORADO

Stretching from the Great Plains west to the Continental Divide and from Winter Park north to the Wyoming border, North Central Colorado displays the state's fascinating geological diversity in all its grandness and at its most breathtaking. Here you'll find scores of peaks topping 12,000 feet and several over 14,000, as well as great expanses of prairie grasslands; narrow one-way mountain passes and long, straight stretches of uninteresting interstate; cold, crisp glacier-carved alpine lakes and the muddy South Platte River, which James Michener's *Centennial* narrator described as "the most miserable river in the west."

In addition, North Central Colorado is home to some of the state's best recreation opportunities, from backpacking in Rocky Mountain National Park to windsurfing on Horsetooth Reservoir, from skiing at Winter Park to fishing in Grand Lake or the Cache La Poudre River. In fact, the area offers an amazing amount of public land ideal for exploring by foot, mountain bike, horseback, or cross-country skis—Roo-

sevelt, Routt, and Arapaho national forests, along with Colorado State Forest, combine to occupy about half of North Central Colorado's total area.

The showpiece of North Central Colorado is Rocky Mountain National Park. Accessible from Hwy. 34 either from the east or west (although the road through the park is closed in winter), this 265,200-acre year-round wonderland attracts nearly three million visitors a year. The park features over 350 miles of hiking trails, excellent opportunities to view Colorado wildlife, including bighorn sheep, elk, and deer, and some of the absolutely most spectacular scenery on the planet—alpine meadows blanketed with wildflowers, massive granite peaks white with year-round snow, and lush valleys vibrantly green from summer rains.

The two largest communities in North Central Colorado are Greeley and Fort Collins, both about an hour's drive north of Denver. Fort Collins is home to the 20,000-student Colorado State University, best known for its agriculture

NORTH CENTRAL COLORADO HIGHLIGHTS

Rocky Mountain National Park: sightseeing, camping, hiking, cross-country skiing

Estes Park: hiking and mountain biking in Roosevelt National Park, cross-country skiing, fishing the Colorado, Arkansas, and Cache La Poudre rivers, museums, shopping, Stanley Hotel (majestic, turn-of-the-century hotel), Long's Peak Scottish Festival

Winter Park: skiing and hiking in Arapaho National Forest, 660 miles of mountain-bike trails, American Music Festival, Rocky Mountain Wine and Food Festival, Famous Flame Thrower High Altitude Chili Cook-off

Grand Lake: entry to Rocky Mountain National Park, fishing, camping, hiking, and skiing in Arapaho National Recreation Area, Indian Parks Wilderness Area

Poudre Canyon: sightseeing, fishing, camping

Fort Collins: Anheuser-Busch, Inc. Brewery, Horsetooth Reservoir, hut-to-hut Nordic skiing along the Never Summer Nordic Yurt System, renovated old-town area, shopping, dining, college-town nightlife, Colorado Brewfest, Balloon Festival

Greeley: Fort Vasquez, University of Northern Colorado, Denver Broncos' summer training camp, summer festivals and fairs, museums, shopping, dining (best Rocky Mountain oysters in the state)

programs. Kept vital by its youthful population, Fort Collins is committed to preserving its past, with several historical museums and the recently renovated Old Town shopping area.

Greeley is a ranching and farming area and the central subject of *Centennial*. In the book, Michener describes it as "nothing less than the soul of America . . . as seen in microcosm."

Which could also be said about the whole of North Central Colorado. From its geology and history to its economy and industry, the area is like a living textbook in American studies.

WINTER PARK

Berthoud Pass

The drive up over Berthoud Pass from I-70 to Winter Park is one of the most spectacular in the state. Cutting through sheer canyons and switching back up from the valley floor, finally rising above the timberline and across the Continental Divide, the road affords stunning panoramas of purple mountains and saw-toothed peaks that appear to stretch forever.

At the summit is a plaque marking the Continental Divide. A handful of tables perched precariously on the cliffside let you picnic with a view to the north of Winter Park and on to Rocky Mountain National Park. And if the elevation makes you queasy and you're not sure you can trust your stomach, you can also wait till you get to the bottom, where Midland Picnic Area (in the Arapaho National Forest) will welcome your safe descent.

Located at the foot of Berthoud Pass at the south end of the gorgeous Fraser Valley, Winter Park (pop. 600; elev. 9,000 feet) is a small community devoted almost entirely to tourism and recreation. From Thanksgiving to mid-April, the town is swollen with winter sports enthusiasts of every stripe, while summer sees a proliferation of warm-weather-sports fans, from mountain bikers to trout anglers.

Virtually inseparable from the 54-year-old Winter Park Ski Area, whose runs drop almost to the little town's main drag, Winter Park offers an ideal blend of old-ski-town charm and the latest in high-tech equipment and deluxe lodging facilities. You can stay in a cozy inn or a luxury hotel, take a backwoods sleigh ride or zoom to the top of the mountain via four high-speed detachable quad chairlifts.

Surrounded by towering mountains and Arapaho National Forest, Winter Park sits at the southern end of the beautiful Middle Park region of the Rockies. Winter Park also provides access to the Fraser River Valley, the resort town of Grand Lake, and the western entrance to Rocky Mountain National Park. In fact, the Denver-to-Denver circle—through Winter Park, Rocky Mountain National Park, Estes Park,

Lyons, and Boulder—is one of most breathtaking scenic drives in the country. (Note: The road through Rocky Mountain National Park is closed in the winter.) Highway 40 through Winter Park is also the best way to get to Steamboat Springs from Denver.

History

The Fraser River Valley was first settled in the mid-1800s, although the area had been explored earlier in the century, and hunters and fur trappers frequented the valley in the 1820s and '30s. The valley's first post office was established in Fraser in 1850, and by the 1870s there were enough settlers in the area that local Native Americans were beginning to feel intruded upon. By 1883, the Utes had been relocated to a reservation in Utah following the Meeker Massacre.

Winter Park began to come into its own in 1927 with the completion of the $18-million, seven-mile Moffat Tunnel, which bore through the Continental Divide and linked Denver and the Fraser Valley. The tunnel was named for David H. Moffat, a Denver banker who had

worked for nearly a quarter century to run the Denver and Pacific Northwestern Railroad through the mountains to provide safer and more reliable passage between Denver and Salt Lake City. The tunnel's western terminus is adjacent to the community of Winter Park, which was originally known as West Portal.

In 1937, the Forest Service built an 800-foot rope tow at Berthoud Pass, and by the end of the decade, some 50,000 skiers a year were descending on the little ski resort. Because the area and skiing were growing so popular with Denverites, the city sought a way to open a municipal "winter park" of its own. West Portal was the perfect locale, and Winter Park Ski Area, under management of the City of Denver, first opened on Jan. 28, 1940. Lift tickets that day were $1.

The city ran into difficulties, however, trying to maintain a park on the other side of the Continental Divide, and during the late 1940s, Winter Park fell into disrepair. Sensing the first wave of Colorado's mid-century ski boom, Denver realized it had the opportunity to take part—if it

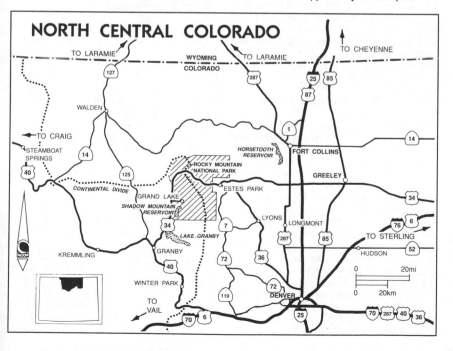

could make Winter Park a viable resort. In 1950, city officials created the Winter Park Recreational Association (WPRA), a 15-member board of trustees that would work independently of the city and run operations at Winter Park. The nonprofit corporation quickly got to work improving the ski area, beginning with a surface lift. The $167,000 City-of-Denver-financed project increased uphill capacity to 1,600 skiers per hour. Since then, the WPRA has remained nonprofit and self-supporting, successfully managing one of Colorado's best ski areas. The 1991 ski season saw $5.3 million in improvements—including construction of a high-speed quad chair, increased snowmaking capabilities, and the remodeling of on-mountain eating facilities.

Sights

Cozens' Ranch House Museum on Hwy. 40 just north of town on the Fraser-Winter Park line was the site of a stage stop and post office dating from 1876. Check out the room commemorating "Doc Suzie," Grand County's first woman doctor, who moved to the area from Cripple Creek in 1907, practiced until 1941, and died in 1960 at age 90. The museum is open 11 a.m.-4:30 p.m.—daily June 15-Sept. 15, and Tues. through Sun. Dec. 15-April 1. For more information, phone (303) 726-5488.

WINTER SPORTS

Winter Park's accessibility to Denver, just 70 miles away via I-70 and Hwy. 40 (broad and well maintained, if a bit steep and harrowing in places), makes it a natural for day-trippers looking for the heart of the snow country. Denver alpine skiers, cross-country skiers, snowboarders, and Telemarkers flock to Winter Park when the snow flies, knowing they can get a good day's skiing in and still be home in time for dinner. In addition, families, honeymooners, and college students from all over the country come to Winter Park for their vacations—by train, plane, and automobile—with the knowledge that they'll find some of the state's best skiing here, as well as one of the West's friendliest mountain towns. And non-skiers know there's a lot to do here besides ski. Though the community's too small to offer a whole lot in the way of nightlife

and other entertainment, the area affords a wide range of other winter recreational opportunities, from ice skating to moonlight sleigh rides.

Downhill Skiing

Recently ranked 13th among *Snow Country* magazine's top 45 North American ski resorts (Sept. 1991), **Winter Park Ski Area** has earned a solid reputation as one of the state's best family ski areas, with terrain suitable for every abil-

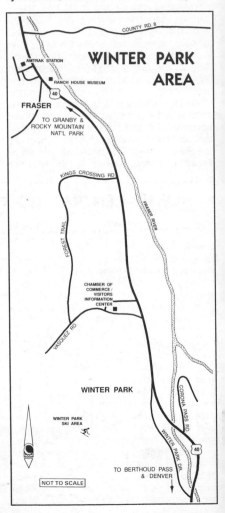

looking east at the Continental Divide from Winter Park

ity level, from snowplower to backcountry bowler. In addition, the resort is held in high esteem worldwide for its commitment to skiers with disabilities—amputees, paraplegics, and the blind.

Winter Park Ski Area sprawls across three separate mountain ridges connected by a sophisticated network of lifts and runs. Combined, **Winter Park, Mary Jane,** and **Vasquez Ridge** offer 20 lifts on 1,301 acres of terrain with an uphill capacity of 29,400 skiers an hour (the second largest in Colorado). The longest run is over five miles.

Winter Park and Vasquez Ridge offer the most skiing for intermediate-range skiers, while Mary Jane has the more demanding runs. In fact, 53% of Mary Jane's runs are designated advanced or expert, and the steep bump runs here are among the nastiest in the state. Only six percent of Mary Jane is designated for beginning skiers.

The true pride of Winter Park, though, is the **National Sports Center for the Disabled.** Founded by Hal O'Leary in the winter of 1969-70, the program started out small. Its goal was to teach children with cancer and leg amputations to ski. Since then, the program has grown to embrace people with over 40 disabilities and provides instruction and adaptive equipment to over 17,000 skiers a year. From single-track skiers (single amputees skiing with outriggers, crutches with short skis on the end) and blind skiers (who follow instructors or partners with bells) to sit skiers (double amputees or paraplegics, who ski in "sleds"), Winter Park's slopes are covered with folks who manage to all but leave their disabilities behind. Don't be surprised to see a single-track skier zip by you demonstrating more élan and control than you can muster on your very best day.

The National Sports Center for the Disabled also offers a number of competitions for disabled skiers, and has recently expanded to offer an array of summer programs, including mountain biking, hiking, and whitewater rafting.

Winter Park Ski Area has a full range of instructional programs for skiers of all abilities and offers complete rental and equipment-repair services. For more information on ticket prices, hours of operation, or instruction, phone (303) 726-5514. For **snow conditions,** phone (900) 950-5550.

Cross-country Skiing

The Winter Park-Fraser Valley areas offer nearly unlimited opportunities for the cross-country skier, thanks to the surrounding Arapaho National Forest. Whether you like to follow old logging roads or break your own trails, you won't be disappointed. For maps and information on exploring Arapaho National Forest on Nordic skis, contact the district office in Granby at 62429 Hwy. 40, tel. (303) 887-3331 (or tel. 887-3165 for a recorded message).

In addition, the area has a number of groomed public trail systems. Winter Park's **Idlewild Center** offers some 25 km of track, a small hill, equipment rental, and instruction. The center is located just east of town at 398 County Rd. 802. For information, phone 726-5564.

Devil's Thumb Guest Ranch and Cross-Country Center, which is connected to the Idlewild Trail System, offers another 50-plus km of trails (fees good at both centers). Explore the quiet backcountry in the woods along the Fraser River. The center is located east of Fraser at 3530 County Rd. 83. For information, phone 726-5632.

You'll also find excellent groomed cross-country trails (about 40 km) at **Snow Mountain Ranch's Nordic Center** about 15 miles north of Winter Park off Hwy. 40. The facility has 65 km of trails on some 4,600 acres of woodsy backcountry, with three km lighted for night skiing. Phone 726-4628 for information.

Snowmobiling

The broad Fraser Valley and sprawling expanses of Arapaho National Forest make the area a natural for exploring by snowmobile; several outfits offer rentals and tours. **Trailblazer Snowmobile Tours,** tel. (303) 726-8452, is based in Fraser and provides a range of tours, as does **Sporting Country Guide Service,** tel. 726-9247 (or tel. 887-3255 in Granby). To rent snowmobiles, contact **Mountain Madness** in Fraser Meadow, tel. 726-4529.

amputee ski racer at Winter Park

ERIK BAKKE

Snowcat Tours

You can tour the Winter Park Ski Area by snowcat, with machines leaving the base of the lifts three times daily. For reservations and information, phone the resort at (303) 726-5514.

Totally Tubular

Snow tubing is a Winter Park tradition. One of the best tubing hills in the Rockies is located just north of town on Hwy. 40 (you'll see it off to your left). Link 'em together to make tube trains, or go solo. Go head, feet, or butt first. Just dress warm—the wind can *really* whip across that meadow. For rates and information, phone the **Fraser Tubing Hill** at (303) 726-5954.

O'er The Fields We Go

In contrast to the gift shops and high-tech lifts, a horse-drawn sleigh will take you out into the quiet moonlit woods for a short scenic tour or a romantic dinner. **Jim's Sleigh Rides,** tel. (303) 726-5527, offers both afternoon and evening rides, with a stop midway for refreshments and warm-up by the fire. **Dinner at the Barn,** tel. 726-4923, provides dinner and evening entertainment rides to a renovated ranch house. You can also take evening dinner rides from **Devil's Thumb Ranch,** tel. 726-5632. It's not the cheapest way to spend an evening, but ideal for a special celebration.

Ice Skating

You'll find ice-skating rinks at **Fraser Valley Elementary School** in Fraser, **Beaver Village Resort** in Winter Park, tel. (303) 726-5741 or (800) 666-0281, and **Snow Mountain Ranch—YMCA of the Rockies** north of town, tel. 726-4628 or, from Denver, tel. 443-4743. For more information on ice skating in the Winter Park-Fraser Valley area, contact the Winter Park Recreational Association at tel. 726-5514.

WHEN THE SNOW MELTS

Don't let the name deceive you. Though best known as one of the state's winter-sports paradises, Winter Park is fast becoming a year-round resort. When skis get hung in racks, out come the mountain bikes, fishing poles, rafts, backpacks, and saddles and tack. Cross-country ski trails become havens for mountain bikers, and ski lifts are open to sightseers. If the little town were to rename itself, it just might choose Year-round Park.

Mountain Biking

This is without doubt the Fraser Valley area's latest rage, and indications are that the sport is here to stay. The old logging trails of Arapaho National Forest offer enough miles of spleen-shaking backcountry riding to keep you rock-hopping all summer, maybe without ever going down the same path twice.

Winter Park's **Fat Tire Society** (FATS) has developed a 660-mile trail system that was recently named "best mountain biking system in Colorado" by *Rocky Mountain Sports Fitness* magazine. FATS publishes a Winter Park mountain biking map, available from the Winter Park Chamber of Commerce and local bike shops, and also sponsors special events throughout the June-Oct. season. You can write the Winter Park Fat Tire Society at Box 1337, Winter Park, CO 80482.

In addition, several companies offer rentals and guided tours. **Mad Adventures,** tel. (303) 726-5290 or (800) 451-4884, accommodates beginning to advanced riders, with instruction, "Jeep Up/Bike Down" trips, and single-track tours. **Colorado Mountain Bike School** has clinics, and its affiliate, **Adventure Works,** (both at tel. 726-8874), rents bikes and offers guided tours. You can also rent bikes at **Alpine Sun,** tel. 726-5107, and many other shops in town.

Golf

The Fraser Valley's public 18-hole **Pole Creek Golf Course** is 10 miles west of Winter Park. Named "Best New Public Course in America" in 1985 by *Golf Digest,* the 6,230-yard Pole Creek remains on the magazine's list of top 50 American courses. The course hosts several tournaments annually, including the infamous **Bert and Ernie Classic** in September. For information and tee times, phone (303) 726-8847.

Grand Lake Golf Club is located 40 minutes north of Winter Park on the east side of Rocky Mountain National Park. Views from this 18-hole course are some of the best anywhere. Phone 627-8008.

Hiking

You'll find lots of excellent hiking opportunities in the Winter Park area. Hiking's best in the morn-

ing, as the sky often clouds up in the afternoon, and hard rains are quite common. **Byer's Peak** (elev. 12,804 feet) towers west of the Fraser Valley and offers a short (just under three miles) but rugged trail to the top. Panoramas are excellent. Go west from Hwy. 40 in Fraser.

For information on hiking in Arapaho National Forest, stop in at the information center at the Sulphur District Office in Granby, or phone (303) 887-3331.

Fishing

The Fraser Valley-Grand County area offers a wide range of mountain fishing for trout and kokanee salmon. Free fishing is provided for kids in the small roadside ponds between Winter Park and Fraser; the lakes are stocked regularly by the local chapter of the Lion's Club. More serious (and older) lake anglers should head up to the Three Lakes Area near Granby and the town of Grand Lake. **Grand Lake, Shadow Mountain Reservoir,** and **Lake Granby** are home to some good-size rainbow, cutthroat, lake (Mackinaw), and brown trout, as well as landlocked kokanee. Fishing is best from a boat, but shore anglers have done well too.

Stream fishermen will want to try the **Colorado** and **Fraser rivers.** The Fraser flows through Winter Park, and offers decent fishing (planters) near the ski area, while a stretch just north of town is designated a Wild Trout Area (be sure to check local fishing restrictions). For information, tackle, and licenses, stop by **Nelson's Fly and Tackle Shop,** north of Winter Park in Tabernash along Hwy. 40, tel. (303) 726-8558.

Rafting

With the North Platte, Colorado, and Arkansas rivers all tumbling through the mountains in Grand County, you can bet there's plenty of rafting action. In Winter Park, several companies offer a variety of trips, from mellow floats to serious whitewater. **Mad Adventures,** tel. (303) 726-5290 or (800) 451-4844, **Rapid Transit Rafting,** tel. 627-3062 or (800) 367-8523, and **Timber Rafting,** tel. 887-2141 or (800) 332-3381, book trips (from half-day to three-day) for all levels of ability and interest. Rates usually begin at around $30 for half-day trips.

Horseback Riding

Beaver Stables, tel. (303) 726-8035 or, after

6 p.m., tel. 726-4311, offers a variety of riding packages—from one- and two-hour jaunts throughout the day to evening rides that include chuckwagon dinners. At **Sombrero Ranch Stables** in Grand Lake, tel. 627-3514, you can also book tours and pack trips or rent horses by the hour.

Chairlift Rides

For spectacular views of the surrounding scenery, it's tough to beat an off-season chairlift ride. **Winter Park Ski Area,** tel. (303) 726-5514, runs lifts during the summer for sightseeing.

Alpine Slide

Winter Park's Alpine slide gives summer visitors a chance to crank turns on the slopes in a completely different fashion, though the ride to the top is the same (via chairlift). Located at the base of the ski hill, the half-mile, 30-turn slide is open June through mid-August and costs $4 a ride (multi-ride discounts are available). Children must be least 45 inches tall. Phone Winter Park Resort at (303) 726-5514 for more information. ·

ACCOMMODATIONS

Much less developed than some of Colorado's major destination ski resorts, Winter Park nonetheless offers the visitor a wide range of lodging options—from an American Youth Hostel to conventional motels to upscale condos with all the bells and whistles. **Note:** It's necessary to make reservations in winter and highly suggested the rest of the year. Also, prices here should be used for comparison; rates often vary significantly from summer to winter.

The **Winter Park Hostel,** tel. (303) 726-5356, offers the least expensive beds in town. Bunks start at about $10 (discounts with American Youth Hostel cards), and guests are asked to help out with a chore or two. Located behind Le Ski Lab in downtown Winter Park; write: Box 3323, Winter Park, CO 80482.

The **Alpenglo Motor Lodge,** tel. 726-5294, or for reservations only, (800) 541-6130, has rooms in the center of town starting at about $50. The **Olympia Motor Lodge,** tel. 726-8843, also downtown, has doubles for about $40. Rooms for two at **Sundowner Motel,** tel. 726-9451 or (800) 521-8279, start at about $45.

Lodges And Condominiums

One of Winter Park's more upscale condo complexes is the **Iron Horse,** tel. (303) 726-8851 or (800) 621-8190, located at the base of the lifts between Winter Park and Mary Jane. Rates start at about $60 for two; ski and golf packages are available.

Gasthaus Eichler, tel. 726-5133 or (800) 543-3899, is located downtown and is better known as a restaurant than as a lodge, though there are rooms upstairs, available with or without meals; doubles run $40-140.

Beaver Village Resort, tel. 726-5741 or (800) 666-0281, offers ski packages in the winter, and in the summer, the lodge bills itself as a "Mountain Bike Dude Ranch." Rates start at $30 and go to $300.

The **Vintage Resort Hotel,** tel. 726-8801 or (800) 472-7017, has a wide range of facilities, from individual rooms to a conference center; golf and ski packages available. Rooms run $50-300.

A favorite among families is the **Snow Mountain Ranch—YMCA of the Rockies,** tel. 726-4628, which offers a variety of lodging options, from individual cabins (sleeping up to 12) to rooms in the central lodge ranging from $25-250 a night. Kids and their parents love it here, as there's always something to do: go hiking or cross-country skiing (with a lodge guide), play in the indoor pool, or even lose yourself in the lodge library. Located just south of Granby at 1344 County Rd. 53 off Hwy. 40, Snow Mountain is a nonprofit operation that's been in business for over 20 years. (YMCA of the Rockies also operates **Estes Park Center**—see Estes Park.) For a brochure with complete information, write Box 169, Winter Park, CO 80482.

Another off-the-beaten-track lodge (yet just a few minutes from Winter Park) is **Devil's Thumb Ranch,** tel. 726-5632 or (800) 826-2280 (in Colorado) or (800) 525-3304 (outside Colorado). Located in a huge meadow three miles north of Fraser, Devil's Thumb is first a cross-country ski lodge, but also a perfect base for a riding, mountain biking, hiking, fishing, or just an I-need-to-get-away-from-the-rush vacation. The rustic restaurant overlooking the meadow is open to non-guests as well. To get to Devil's Thumb, take County Rd. 83 east from Fraser; then go right at the fork in the road.

For total luxury in backwoods lodging, check out the **C Lazy U Guest Ranch,** tel. 887-3344, "the country's only five-star dude ranch." Offering tennis, fishing, horseback rides, cross-country skiing, and many other activities, the C Lazy U is one of the best places around to be pampered. Room prices, which start around $150 (and rise dramatically from there), include three gourmet meals a day. For complete information, write Box 378B, Granby, CO 80446.

Bed And Breakfasts

Winter Park has a number of bed and breakfasts, all of which do well in winter but slack off once the snow's gone and the lifts have shut down. **Nordic Bed and Breakfast,** tel. 726-8459, **Angel West,** tel. 726-5354, **Alpen Rose,** tel. 726-5039, and **Mulligan's Mountain Inn,** tel. 887-2877; **Engelman Pines,** tel. 726-5416, **The Hearthstone,** tel. 726-9710, Beauwest, tel. 726-5145, and **Chalet Zirbisegger,** tel. 726-5416, all are within short drives of Winter Park and offer easy access to summer activities. The Winter Park/Fraser Valley Chamber of Commerce will send you a complete list, with descriptions and rates; phone 726-4118.

Camping And RVing

There are several campgrounds—those operated by the Forest Service, as well as privately run camps—in and around Winter Park. **Robbers Roost** is a small Forest Service campground at the north base of Berthoud Pass, just before the turnoff to Mary Jane Ski Area. A few miles farther north, almost right downtown, **Idlewild Campground** also offers Forest Service-run sites. For information, contact the Winter Park Chamber of Commerce, tel. (303) 726-4118, or the Forest Service district office in Granby, tel. 887-3331.

Elk Valley RV Campground, tel. 887-2380, just south of Granby has RV sites with full hookups, as well as cabins (and horses) for rent.

Information And Reservations

Condominium Management Company handles reservations for half a dozen or so properties, including **Hi Country Haus, Braidwood, Hideaway Village, Timber Run, Crestview Place, The Summit at Silver Creek,** and **Trademark;** phone (303) 726-9421 or (800) 228-1025, or tel. 825-0705 from Denver.

Winter Park Central Reservations, phone 726-5587 or (800) 453-2525, can assist you with booking lodging, as well as air, rail, and shuttle transportation.

FOOD

Start Me Up

Two of Winter Park's favorite breakfast spots are **The Kitchen,** tel. (303) 726-9940, at 78542 Hwy. 40 on the north end of town, and **Bev's Bunnery,** tel. 726-5774. Bev serves up standard American fare with mountain names (the "ptarmigan" is two eggs, home fries, and toast), as well as biscuits and gravy and breakfast burritos—$2-5. Bev also serves fresh-baked pastries, doughnuts, and bran muffins, and is open for lunch, serving soups, salads, and sandwiches (all sandwiches can be prepared to go). **Carlson's Café** on Hwy. 40 on the south end of town is a classic small-town diner, with as much counter space as table space—American breakfasts (delicious pancakes!) run $2-5. Check out the original decor: scores of old ice skates and ice tongs hanging from the ceiling.

Lunch And Dinner

Deno's Swiss House, tel. (303) 726-5332, downtown on Hwy. 40 is part sports bar and part restaurant and has a wide range of food, from chicken-wing appetizers to burgers, fish and chips, and steaks. Prices run $5-20 for dinner. Deno's has several television monitors, as well as an excellent beer selection, making it one of the best places in town to catch a game. **The Last Waltz,** tel. 726-4877, on Hwy. 40 on the north end of town, serves breakfast, lunch, dinner, and Sunday brunch, specializing in Mexican and home-style American dishes. Prices are very reasonable.

A veritable Winter Park institution, **Gasthaus Eichler,** 78786 Hwy. 40, tel. 726-5133, serves lunch and dinner. For lunch try the bratwurst, the quiche of the day, or a salad ($4-7). Dinners include German specialties as well as beef, veal, and seafood and run to $30 (lobster tail). Another local favorite is **Continental Divide,** tel. 726-4900, specializing in Italian food, fish, and chicken. Prices range from $7.50 (salad bar) to around $17 (New York steak). At **Hernando's Pizza and Pasta Pub,** tel. 726-5409, pizzas range from $7-14, and pasta dinners (spaghetti, ravioli, lasagna, etc.) are around $6. **Lani's Place,** tel. 726-9674, is a long-standing favorite of folks looking for good south-of-the-border food, especially those who've spent a day on the slopes (either on skis or bikes) and are as interested in the margaritas and mingling with the lively crowd as they are in the food. For family-style dining, try **Dougal's,** tel. 726-8732, where chicken and beef dinners run $10-15.

Finally, if you're looking for a place to take the kids, try **A'Maze,** tel. 726-9555, next to the Safeway in Fraser. In addition to the human maze, in which kids (and adults) can race against the clock, there's also a video arcade and indoor miniature golf. Oh, and food, too: pizzas, burgers, salads, and ice cream.

ENTERTAINMENT

You're much more likely to find night-owl action in Winter Park in the winter, when skiers are looking for places to boogie after a day on the slopes, than in summer, when the clubs are generally only open weekends. If you like things a bit slower and quieter, though, Winter Park's bars can be downright nice in the summer—you won't have to elbow your way through a crowd to order a beer or a plate of nachos. **The Slope,** tel. (303) 726-5727, just north of the base of the lifts, **Stampede** in Cooper Creek Square, tel. 726-9433, and the **Crooked Creek Saloon** in Fraser, tel. 726-9250, all book live music; Crooked Creek also has pool tables and darts.

A Winter Park tradition is the Grand County Theatre Association's **Balcony Dinner Theater,** which produces a wide range of Broadway-style musicals and comedies. For rates, schedules, and other information, phone 726-0437.

For current information on what to do at night in the Winter Park area, check out *The Guide,* a weekly supplement to the town's newspaper, *Manifest,* available in racks around Winter Park for 50 cents.

CALENDAR

From first snow till the lifts shut down, and again from early June through August, Winter Park sponsors a wide range of events, from ski races and mountain-bike hill climbs to art shows and concerts. Watch *The Guide,* distributed weekly with Winter Park's *Manifest* for the best listing of what's happening where.

Among Winter Park's annual highlights: the **First Interstate Bank Cup** features professional ski races in late January, with excellent opportunities to see top competitors. The **High Country Stampede,** Saturdays in July and August, is Fraser Valley's popular rodeo, attracting top professional and amateur riders from around the country.

A Winter Park classic is the **American Music Festival,** mid-July. The stage is set up at the base of the Winter Park Ski Area, and the audience lines the gentle lower slopes; there ain't a bad seat in the house. Lineups feature mostly American music, with a contemporary country bent. Past acts have included Bonnie Raitt, John Prine, Poco, the Cowboy Junkies, and Leon Russell (shoulda heard him do "Somewhere Over the Rainbow" just as the rain let up).

Winter Park's late-July **Alpine Art Affair,** first held in 1975, features over 100 juried artists from throughout the western United States, as well as food booths and music. In mid-August, the **Rocky Mountain Wine and Food Festival** offers winetasting and seminars, with over 200 wines and champagnes, as well as gourmet meals prepared by the **Colorado Chefs de Cuisine**—a benefit for the National Sports Center for the Disabled. Also in the food category, the **Famous Flamethrower High Altitude Chili Cook-off** in early September is a high-spirited competition between local chefs vying to represent the Rocky Mountain region in the world chili cook-off.

On Christmas Eve, watch the beautiful **Torchlight Parade** wind its way down the runs of Winter Park Ski Area.

For more information or exact dates, contact the **Winter Park Recreational Association,** tel. (303) 726-5514, or the **Winter Park/Fraser Valley Chamber of Commerce,** tel. 726-4118.

SHOPPING

Though you won't find the busy shopping village of a Vail or Aspen, a number of stores carry gifts, souvenirs, and other items. The main drag through town is rife with ski and sports shops, which often unload the previous season's gear and clothing during the summer at "sidewalk" sales. This can be a good time to pick up a pair of ski boots or a parka for a very good price.

SERVICES

Most Winter Park services, including the police and sheriff departments, are based in Hot Sulphur Springs, about 10 miles west of Granby on Hwy. 40. **Police department** offices are at 670 Spring Rd.; tel. (303) 726-5666. The offices of the **Grand County Sheriff** are at 308 Byers; tel. 726-5666. **Winter Park Medical Center,** tel. 726-9616, is in downtown Winter Park, and **7-Mile Clinic,** tel. 726-8066, is at the base of the lifts of Winter Park Ski Area. The Winter Park **post office** is at 78876 Hwy. 40; tel. 726-5495.

Child Care

Winter Park is one of the country's best family ski areas, so it should come as no surprise that children's facilities on the mountain are very highly regarded. A recent article in *Skiing* magazine lauded the resort's **Children's Center,** the oldest in Colorado, giving high praise to the facility's expert and kid-sensitive staff, and to its efficient organization.

The center divides kids into four groups (age three to kindergarten, first to third grade, fourth grade to age 12, and ages 13-16). While the little ones are playing games that acquaint them with the snow, the older ones can ski at their own pace with instructors. The center, operating out of a multistory 32,000-square-foot building, also provides day care for children ages two months to five years. For more information or to make reservations, phone (303) 726-5514, ext. 337.

Recycling

Drop off most recyclables at **Grand Recycles** at the firehouse on Hwy. 40 in Fraser. The Safeway in Fraser (on Hwy. 40) takes aluminum.

INFORMATION

The **Winter Park Chamber of Commerce,** open seven days a week, is an excellent source of information on everything from what to do to where to stay in the area. The office is located just off Hwy. 40 on Vasquez Rd.; write Box 36, Winter Park, CO 80482, or phone 726-5587, (800) 453-2525, or 447-0588 (from Denver). From among the many brochures, maps, and activity guides, be sure to pick up the Grand County *Exploration Guide,* a listing of over 100 historical and geographical places of interest in the county, as well as a copy of *Trails (Tracks* in winter), which lists local events.

For **weather information,** tune your radio to AM 930. If you're padding around in the morning waiting for your coffee to brew, tune your television to channel 5 for news about what's going on in the area.

Winter Park's Children's Center is one of the best ski-area facilities in the country.

STEPHEN METZGER

You can also get **road and weather information** by calling 725-3334.

TRANSPORTATION

Winter Park is only 67 miles from Denver and very easy to get to, despite the taxing drive over Berthoud Pass. **Home James,** tel. (303) 726-5060, offers door-to-door roundtrip (and one-way) shuttle service between Denver and Winter Park (and on to lodges farther north and to Grand Lake). (For information on car rentals at Stapleton or Denver International Airport, see "Colorado by Air" in the Introduction.) You can rent a car in Winter Park by calling Winter Park Central Reservations at (800) 453-2525.

Without doubt, though, the best way to get to Winter Park is by train. **Amtrak** deposits 26,000 skiers a year at the Winter Park Ski Area station in nearby Fraser. For information, phone 726-8816 or (800) USA-RAIL. From downtown Denver, you can ride the **Winter Park Ski Train,** which has been taking skiers to the slopes for over 50 years. The two-hour ride takes you through 29 tunnels and drops you off 100 yards from the lifts. In the winter of 1990-91, the train carried 25,000 passengers. Tickets are $25 for coach, $40 for first-class. For information and reservations, phone 296-ISKI (4754).

peregrine falcon

CATHY CARLSON

NORTH OF WINTER PARK

Highway 40 continues north into the heart of Middle Park, following the Fraser River to Granby then doglegging west toward Hot Sulphur Springs and Kremmling. Just past Granby is the junction with Hwy. 34, which continues north past Lake Granby, Shadow Mountain Reservoir, and the town of Grand Lake, before lifting east into Rocky Mountain National Park and over the Continental Divide (closed in winter).

The scenery throughout this area is stupendous, characterized by long broad mountain valleys surrounded by rugged, saw-toothed peaks, many of which are over 12,000 feet high. Towering just east of the town of Grand Lake is Longs Peak, at 14,256 feet one of the highest mountains in the state. To the north is Mt. Richthofen (elev. 12,940 feet), and to the west is Park View Mountain (elev. 12,296 feet).

GRANBY

Granby (pop. 1,200; elev. 7,600 feet) is a small ranching and farming center in the Fraser River Valley about 20 miles north of Winter Park. Once known especially for its mountain lettuce, Granby served as a railroad shipping point for vegetables and cattle, as well as timber. Many of the valley's older ranches have been converted to guest ranches (see "Accommodations" under

"Winter Park"), and the town now relies heavily on the tourism industry—skiing in the winter, hunting, fishing, mountain biking, and sightseeing in the summer and fall. Granby's Fourth of July fireworks show is the biggest in the state, usually drawing around 75,000 visitors.

Silver Creek Ski Resort
One of Colorado's youngest and smallest ski areas, Silver Creek opened in 1982 as a primarily beginner and intermediate area catering to families and other folks wanting to get away from the crowds. Four lifts service just over 200 acres of skiable terrain with a 970-foot vertical drop. The terrain is rated 20% beginner, 50% intermediate, and 20% advanced, though most sources indicate a certain degree of "slope inflation." (Even the advanced skiing isn't all that challenging at Silver Creek.)

Though barely a decade old, Silver Creek has already established a reputation as a good cross-country area. Nordic skiers can both explore the groomed trails and ride the lifts on the mountain. The **Inn at Silver Creek,** tel. (303) 887-2131 or (800) 526-0590, is a deluxe hotel offering full amenities, including a conference center. Summer rates run about $45-150, and winter rates are about $45-300.

During the summer, the resort complex offers many other recreational activities. For more

the Winter Park
Ski Train

WINTER PARK SKI AREA

information on Silver Creek Resort, phone 887-3384 or (800) 448-9458. The direct line from Denver is tel. 629-1020.

Practicalities
You'll find a handful of motels at the south end of town, including the **Littletree Inn Motel**, tel. (303) 887-2551, where doubles run $30-60. At Granby's north end, the **Blue Spruce Motel**, tel. 887-3300, **Trail Riders Motel**, tel. 887-3738, and the **Elk Monte Motor Inn**, tel. 887-3348 or (800) 282-3348, also offer clean and reasonably priced rooms.

Services
The offices of the local **police department** are located west of town in Hot Sulphur Springs; tel. (303) 887-3866. Phone the **State Patrol** at 725-3393. **St. Anthony Hospital Systems Emergency Medical Center** is at 62801 Hwy. 40 in Granby; tel. 887-2503. The **post office** is at 54 Zero St.; tel. 887-3612.

Information
The **Granby Chamber of Commerce** operates a tourist information booth on the north end of town next to the Blue Spruce Motel. Stop in for maps, activity guides, and dining and lodging brochures, and more information on area guest ranches. You can also write Box 35, Granby, CO 80046, or phone (303) 887-2311 or (800) 325-1661.

GRANBY TO KREMMLING

Highway 40 arcs west just outside Granby following the course of the Fraser River to its confluence with the Colorado at Kremmling. The road is flanked by Routt (north) and Arapaho (south) national forests, and passes through the little historical town of Hot Sulphur Springs. In Kremmling, you can either continue north to Steamboat Springs, or turn south onto CO 9, which follows the Blue River into Summit County, past Green Mountain Reservoir, continuing on to Dillon, Frisco, and Breckenridge.

HOT SULPHUR SPRINGS

Seat of Grand County, Hot Sulphur Springs (pop. 400; elev. 7,655 feet) was named for the nearby springs thought by Native Americans to have medicinal powers. According to legend, a Ute chief, whose tribe had left him to die, appealed to his gods for power. The chief built fires below the bubbling waters, bathed and drank in them, was healed, and rejoined the tribe.

Today, Hot Sulphur Springs is the site of the district offices of Arapaho National Forest, as well as of several local agencies, including police, sheriff, and state patrol. For more information on Hot Sulphur Springs, write **Grand Lake Chamber of Commerce,** Box 57, Grand Lake, CO 80447, or phone (303) 627-3402.

Grand County Museum
Housed in the Hot Sulphur Schoolhouse (1924), this museum exhibits a wide array of historical items, including 8,500-year-old Native American artifacts, pioneer firearms, clothing, utensils, and snow gear (snowshoes, etc.), as well as historical photos. There's also a blacksmith shop, jail, the original county courthouse, and a display commemorating pioneer women and their role in the settling of the area, as well as a recently added 1905 BLM ranger station and a one-room school.

The museum is open daily 10 a.m.-5 p.m. Memorial Day through Labor Day, as well as Wed.-Fri. and the first and third weekends of the month the rest of the year. Admission is $2. For more information, phone (303) 725-3939.

Accommodations
You'll find doubles in the $30-40 range at the **Canyon Motel,** tel. (303) 725-3395, and at the **Ute Trail Motel,** tel. 725-3326. Both are located on Hwy. 40 in town.

KREMMLING

Located on the western side of the Middle Park area at the junction of CO 9 and Hwy. 40, Kremmling offers access to a wide range of recreational pursuits. Borders of Arapaho, Routt, and White River national forests are all within 20 miles of Kremmling, and the nearby waters—the Blue, Fraser, and Colorado rivers all pass through Kremmling—are favorites among kayakers and canoers; there's a put-in one mile south of town on Hwy. 9.

You'll find a **visitor information center** on Hwy. 40 on the west end of town (corner of Park and Center), as well as a park with picnic tables and playground equipment. **Kremmling RV Park,** tel. (303) 724-9593, is located east of town on Hwy. 40 (2200 Central).

NORTH OF KREMMLING

Highway 40 continues north from Kremmling over Muddy and Rabbit Ears passes to Steamboat Springs, then beelines west across the high plateau toward Dinosaur and the Utah border. Just a couple of miles beyond Muddy Pass you can catch CO 14 north to Walden, the isolated seat of isolated Jackson County. From Walden it's only another 20 miles to the Wyoming border, then 50 miles to Laramie.

WALDEN AND NORTH PARK

The North Park/Jackson County area is a high, intermontane glacial basin and is the location of the headwaters of the North Platte River. The basin is rimmed by stunning mountain peaks, some rising to nearly 13,000 feet. Long a favorite hunting ground of the Utes, North Park hosts abundant wildlife, although its harsh winters force many of the critters to lower elevations.

Jackson County's economy relies largely on ranching and farming, although the area is being discovered by outdoor enthusiasts who appreciate its backpacking, hiking, fishing, camping, and cross-country skiing opportunities. Walden's **North Park Pioneer Museum** displays the basin's history, from the days of early settlement through Walden's founding in 1890 and into the 20th century.

In Walden you'll find a number of motels and bed-and-breakfast inns, as well as campgrounds and restaurants. The **North Park Motel,** tel. (303) 723-4271, 625 Main (Walden), is open year-round and has 20 units, some with kitchenettes.

For more information on this remote but gorgeous area, contact the **North Park Tourism Information Center,** Box 489TB, Walden, CO 80480, tel. 723-4344, or the **North Park Chamber of Commerce,** Box 227, Walden, CO 80480, tel. 723-4600.

GRAND LAKE AND VICINITY

Grand Lake (pop. 380; elev. 8,153 feet) is a small summer resort town on the north shore of Grand Lake, the largest natural lake in Colorado. Situated on the western border of Rocky Mountain National Park, the town is a popular stop for tourists heading both into and out of the park. The town itself also attracts its own share of summer visitors, most of whom come to fish and explore the waters and shores of the three nearby lakes, camp in the area's many campgrounds, or hole up in the lodges, guest ranches, and summer homes in town, lakeside, and hidden among the valley's woods and rolling hills. In the summer, the town's population swells to over 1,000. In the winter, though things die down considerably, hardcore outdoorsfolks still prowl the Grand Lake area. Snowmobiling and ice fishing are popular wintertime activities.

Downtown Grand Lake is defined pretty much by the main drag, Grand Ave., which parallels the lake's north shore, and a couple of cross streets that provide access to the water. The downtown section of Grand Ave. is a couple of blocks of gift shops, cafés, taverns, Western-art galleries, and Indian pottery and jewelry stores. There's also the proverbial miniature golf, as well as the obligatory proliferation of T-shirt and souvenir shops. As a resort town, though, Grand Lake doesn't feel *quite* as touristy and gimmicky as other western resort towns do. This is perhaps due to its isolation, as well as its link to Rocky Mountain National Park—one of the most rugged backcountry parks in the nation.

History

Although many of Colorado's resort areas were Native American playgrounds or hunting grounds long before white settlers showed up, the Utes avoided this lake, which they called "Spirit Lake," and the surrounding area. According to legend, a Ute village once stood on the shores of Grand Lake, but it was wiped out by invading Cheyenne and Arapahoes who had come to the area to hunt. Ute men were killed, women and children set adrift on a raft as a storm approached. When the raft reached the lake's deep waters, it capsized. Utes believed that the mists rising from Grand Lake's surface were the spirits of the drowned villagers.

Grand Lake began to develop as a resort area in the late 19th century. Gold had been discovered nearby, and the community started out as a supply stop for prospectors heading into the high country. In the early 1900s, well-to-do Western families began building summer homes around the lake (which explains the large expanses of private property in the area), and in 1905, the Grand Lake Yacht Club was founded. Rocky Mountain National Park was dedicated in 1915, and Grand Lake, on the park's western border, once again became a supply point—this time for motorists heading up to camp in the park or to cross over into Estes Park via Trail Ridge Road.

In the early 1950s, Colorado completed its Big Thompson Water Project, an irrigation system providing water to the farms and ranches on the state's eastern plains. In addition to a 13-mile tunnel through the mountains, the project involved a series of reservoirs, including Lake Granby and Shadow Mountain Reservoir. By mid-century, the area was attracting anglers, boaters, and other summer recreation enthusiasts to its three lakes and to the many resort lodges scattered about its woodsy shores.

Kauffman House Museum

Built in 1892, the Kauffman House was one of Grand Lake's first resort hotels, hosting visitors from around the country for nearly 30 years. In 1921, Ezra Kauffman, the log hotel's builder and owner, died, though his wife and family continued to operate it every summer until the end of WW II. The Kauffman house has been restored and is open to the public for tours (summer only), exhibiting artifacts from Grand County's pioneer days.

The Kauffman House is located at 407 Pitkin. For hours, contact the Grand Lake Area Chamber of Chamber of Commerce at tel. (303) 627-3402 or (800) 531-1091.

PARKS AND RECREATION

Rocky Mountain National Park

This is one of the most spectacular national parks in the country, with breathtaking vistas from virtually every point on the main road, as well as hundreds of miles of backcountry climbing, hiking, and camping. Encompassing over 265,000 acres, Rocky Mountain National Park is one of the country's true wonders and a must for any traveler who wants to see Colorado at its grandest, and nature at its most spellbinding and wondrous.

Trail Ridge Rd., which winds up into the park out of Grand Lake, across the Continental Divide, and down the park's eastern slope to Estes Park, is one of the most scenic drives in the state, offering above-timberline vistas of the Rockies' grandest peaks, over 70 of which are higher than 12,000 feet. The drive also affords chances to view and photograph a wide array of high-mountain wildlife, including mountain goats, bighorn sheep, elk, moose, black bears, and smaller animals.

Visitors who get away from the roads, though, are the ones who see the park at its best. The park offers nearly unlimited hiking, ranging from short, marked nature trails to extended excursions into the park's most remote areas. Visitor centers at both the park's east and west entrances provide complete information on the park, including history, wildlife, and ecology, as well as hiking, camping, sightseeing, and photography opportunities. The **Kawuneeche Visitors Center** is located on the west side of the park just outside the town of Grand Lake. There you'll find books, tape tours, maps, wildlife displays, and rangers to answer any questions you might have.

For general information on Rocky Mountain National Park, phone (303) 586-2371. For **road and weather information** in the park, phone 586-2385.

Arapaho National Recreation Area

Adjacent to Rocky Mountain National Park's southwestern boundary, Arapaho National Recreation Area covers 36,000 acres surrounding Lake Granby and a number of smaller lakes. Popular particularly among anglers, the area offers several campgrounds and picnic areas with boat ramps and shoreline access.

One of the nicer campgrounds is **Willow Creek Campground,** at Willow Creek Reservoir. Located three miles down a well-maintained dirt road, the campground has both RV and walk-in tent sites, as well as a picnic area and launching ramp. To get there, turn west off Hwy. 34 between Granby and Lake Granby (it's well marked). You'll also find picnic areas on the north and south shores of Lake Granby (watch for the signs).

For more information on Arapaho National Recreation Area, phone the Sulphur District Office of Arapaho National Forest in Granby at (303) 887-3331.

view of west side of Rocky Mountain National Park

STEPHEN METZGER

Indian Peaks Wilderness Area

Bordered on the west by Arapaho National Recreation Area, on the north by Rocky Mountain National Park, and on the east by the Continental Divide, this triangle-shaped wilderness is very popular with backcountry hikers, backpackers, fishermen, and hunters. Overnight permits are required, and usually need to be reserved well in advance. For information, contact the **Sulphur District Office** of Arapaho National Forest in Granby at tel. (303) 887-3331.

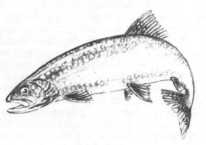

lake trout

BOB RACE

Fishing

Fishing is one of Grand Lake's main draws. The three lakes, Grand, Lake Granby, and Shadow Mountain Reservoir, hold monster trout and kokanee salmon. Mackinaw (lake) trout running 20-25 pounds are not uncommon (though experienced trout fishermen will tell you that lake trout don't put up nearly the fight that smaller rainbow and cutthroat will, and the latter fish are much more fun to catch).

Because of the amount of private property surrounding the lakes, you're better off in a boat. In addition to the several public launching ramps, you can rent boats from a number of marinas, including **Boater's Choice,** 1246 Lake Ave., tel. (303) 627-9273, or **Trail Ridge Marina,** tel. 627-3586.

For tips, tackle, and licenses, stop by **Nelson's Fly and Tackle Shop** in Tabernash, tel. 726-8558, or **Lakeview General Store,** tel. 627-3479, on Hwy. 34 in Grand Lake.

Boating

Sailing, windsurfing, and waterskiing are popular on all three lakes, particularly Grand, and public ramps are scattered about the shore-

lines. At **Boater's Choice,** 11246 Lake Ave., tel. (303) 627-9273, you can rent a range of different boats, including paddleboats, by the hour, or for half-day or full-day outings.

Golf

Grand Lake Golf Course is an 18-hole course whose greens are carved among tall pines at 8,420 feet. Turn west from Hwy. 40 onto County Rd. 48 just north of the turnoff to Grand Lake. For information and tee times, phone (303) 627-8008.

Camping

Surrounded by national forest, park, recreation, and wilderness areas, Grand Lake offers an abundance of camping opportunities, from RV camping (see "Camping and RVing" following) to remote and rugged hike-in-only sites. Keep in mind that even though the area is indeed remote, it gets a lot of traffic, and reservations are a good idea. For information or to make reservations to camp in Arapaho National Forest, contact the Sulphur District Office in Granby at tel. (303) 887-3331. Contact Rocky Mountain National Park at 16018 Hwy. 34, Grand Lake, CO 80447, tel. 627-3471.

In Arapaho National Recreation Area (see above), there are campgrounds at Willow Creek Reservoir, Meadow Creek Reservoir, and the north and east shores of Lake Granby.

Hiking

Grand Lake itself is literally a trailhead for some of the best hiking in the state. Indian Peaks Wilderness Area, east of Lake Granby and south of Rocky Mountain National Forest, offers dozens of miles of marked trails. You can walk along lake shoreline, or hike up into the steep backcountry. Topo maps are available from the Forest Service, tel. (303) 887-3331, and Grand County has published an excellent recreation guide with maps and contact telephone numbers. Pick up a map at any of the Grand County chambers of commerce or visitor centers, or phone the Forest Service.

Cycling

The Grand Lake Metropolitan Recreation District, in conjunction with Arapaho National Forest and local businesses, has recently published a mountain-biking map of the Grand Lake area.

The excellent guide, which implores riders to "tread lightly," lists over two dozen different trails (from two to 15 miles long) around the lakes and into the heart of the national forest. Included are degrees of difficulty, lengths, vertical rises, and other useful information. To get a copy of the guide, or for more information, phone the Grand Lake Metropolitan Recreation District at (303) 627-8328 or Arapaho National Forest at 887-3331.

Horseback Rides
This is a very popular way to explore Arapaho National Forest, Indian Peaks Wilderness Area, and Rocky Mountain National Park. Many of the guest ranches have their own stables and provide both rentals and tours. **Sombrero Ranch,** tel. (303) 627-3514, near the turnoff to Grand Lake, offers a range of services, from hourly rentals and evening steak-fry rides to week-long pack trips. **Winding River Resort,** tel. 627-3215, also offers horseback riding.

Cross-country Skiing
The Three Lakes area is a natural for cross-country skiing, with miles and miles of trails for all ability levels wandering through mountain meadows and deep into steep woods. The **Grand Lake Touring Center** operates at Grand Lake Golf Course with 25 km of track and skating trails. The center's ski shop offers equipment rentals and lessons; phone (303) 627-8008. You can also get information on cross-country skiing by writing the **Grand Lake Metropolitan Recreation District,** Box 590, Grand Lake, CO 80447.

You'll also find excellent Nordic skiing northwest of Grand Lake in Rocky Mountain National Park. Pick up the free booklet, *Ski Touring in Rocky Mountain National Park,* at the Kawuneeche Visitors Center just north of Grand Lake.

Other Winter Activities
In addition to offering cross-country skiing, the Grand Lake area is a favorite of ice fishing enthusiasts, snowshoers, and snowmobilers. Lake Granby, Grand Lake, and Shadow Mountain Reservoir are all open to ice fishing. For information and equipment stop in at **Lakeview General Store,** or **Nelson Fly and Tackle** in Tabernash. Many of the area's summer hiking trails

are ideal for snowshoeing. Pick up maps from the Forest Service or the Grand Lake Chamber of Commerce.

The Grand Lake Metropolitan Recreation District publishes the *Grand Lake Snowmobile Trail Map,* which describes nearly 20 different routes. This excellent guide provides directions to trailheads, lengths, specific precautions, and other indispensable information. Write Box 690, Grand Lake, CO 80447, or phone (303) 627-8008.

Rent snowmobiles from **Grand Lake Motor Sports,** 10438 Hwy. 34, tel. (303) 627-3806; **Spirit Lake Rentals,** tel. 627-9288; **Snowride,** 724 Grand Ave., tel. 627-8866; or **Grand Lake Snowmobile Rental, Inc.,** 801 Grand Ave., tel. 627-8304.

ACCOMMODATIONS

Lodges And Cabins
One of the fanciest lodges in the area is **The Colorado,** located north of Granby off CO 125. Operated by Clarion Resorts, The Colorado offers deluxe accommodations (with meals), and a full range of activities, from skeet shooting, tennis, and horseback rides to cross-country skiing, snowmobiling, and sleigh rides. For rates and information, write Box 497, Granby, CO 80446, or phone (303) 887-3306 or (800) 332-COLO.

A tad more rustic but still quite nice is the **Grand Lake Lodge,** located on the hillside above Grand Lake, tel. 627-3967 or 759-5848. Established in 1921, the lodge retains an early-20th-century feel about it without compromising modern comforts. The **Spirit Lake Lodge,** tel. 544-6593 or (800) 627-3344, is also located very near Grand Lake, with one- and two-bedroom units (some with kitchens).

Just a couple of miles south of Grand Lake, **Pine Ridge Cabins,** tel. 627-3108 or 693-4217, offers small but nice cabins in the trees near Lake Granby. **Gala Marina Motel,** tel. 627-3220, is located right on Lake Granby and has kitchenettes, great views, and decks/patios. Rooms start at about $50. To get to both of these, take County Rd. 64 from Hwy. 34.

Motels
Recommended motels in Grand Lake include the **Lone Eagle Lodge,** 712 Grand Ave., tel.

627-3310 or (800) 282-3311; the **Bighorn Lodge,** 613 Grand Ave., tel. 627-8101 or (800) 621-5923; and the **Gala Motel and Marina,** 828 County Rd. 64, tel. 627-3220.

Camping And RVing

Shadow Mountain Marina RV Park, 12394 Hwy. 40, tel. (303) 627-9971, is located right on the lake. You can also camp at **Winding River Resort Village,** tel. 627-3215, where you'll find 150 sites with horseback rides, volleyball, and other activities.

FOOD

For breakfast, try the **Chuckhole Cafe,** 1119 Grand Ave., tel. (303) 627-5309, serving omelettes, deep-dish pies, and other fare. **Uncle Elmo's Bakery and Cafe,** also on Grand, serves deli sandwiches and a variety of lunch items. The **Red Fox Restaurant,** 411 W. Portal Rd., tel. 627-3418, features up-scale dining overlooking the lake. For family dining and Mexican food, try the **Mountain Inn,** 612 Grand Ave., tel. 627-3385.

There are **picnic tables** throughout the Grand Lake area, many near the water. The city park on the boardwalk also has picnic tables and a kids' playground.

CALENDAR

Every January, Grand Lake hosts its **Winter Carnival,** and in mid-February there's a popular Nordic ski race (10k and 20k). Warm-weather events include Fourth of July fireworks, a parade and buffalo barbecue (late July), the **Lipton Cup Sailing Regatta** (early August), and a couple of golf tournaments (mid-August and early September). For more information, contact the Grand Lake Chamber of Commerce (see "Information" following).

SHOPPING

Gift shops, souvenir stores, and art galleries line the two or three blocks that make up downtown Grand Lake Village. Though it's not exactly a shopper's mecca, you can pick up T-shirts and other knicknacks, as well as some quality jewelry and pottery.

SERVICES

Offices of the Grand Lake **Police Department** are located at 308 Byers in Hot Sulphur Springs; the local phone number is tel. (303) 627-3322. The nearest medical facility is **St. Anthony Medical Center** in Granby; tel. 887-2503. The **post office** is at 520 Center; tel. 627-3340.

Recycling

You can drop off most recyclables at **Grand Recycles** next to the railroad depot in Granby. For information, phone (303) 726-8435.

INFORMATION

An excellent source of information is the **chamber of commerce/tourist information center** on Hwy. 34 at the turnoff to downtown Grand Lake. Staff will answer questions about Grand Lake, Grand County, and Rocky Mountain National Park, and you can also pick up helpful brochures and activity guides. Be sure to pick up Grand County's *Sports and Recreation Map,* which has maps of all the nearby communities, as well as various recreation trails (hiking, cross-country skiing, four-wheeling, etc.). You can write the chamber at Box 57, Grand Lake, CO 80447-0057, or call (303) 627-3402.

Get information on Rocky Mountain National Park from the administrative offices at 16018 Hwy. 34, or phone 627-3471 or 586-2371.

ESTES PARK AND VICINITY

Estes Park (pop. 3,200; elev. 7,522 feet) is a resort town at the eastern gate to Rocky Mountain National Park. Surrounded by some of the most gorgeous country in the Rockies, Estes Park is a popular base camp for folks heading up into the high country, by tour bus, auto, or hiking boot.

Because Rocky Mountain National Park sees fewer than five percent of its visitors in the winter, Estes Park is naturally a summer-oriented town, and many of its lodges, galleries, shops, and other attractions are only open in the warmer months, usually May through September. During those months, though, the town swells with tourists. Sidewalks swarm with souvenir hunters; restaurants and cafés are packed; the town's motels and the valley's many lodges and guest ranches are fully booked; even the backcountry trails and campgrounds can get crowded.

Come winter, though, and the closing of Trail Ridge Rd. (Hwy. 34) through the park, most tourists head for more temperate climes, and Estes Park becomes a quiet, laid-back little mountain town. Some lodge owners and gallery operators themselves leave. Other locals, however, know this is the best time to be in the area. Rocky Mountain National Park offers excellent cross-country skiing and snowshoeing, and there's no denying that the Rockies shrouded in snow are at their most visually arresting and spiritually wondrous.

HISTORY

The lush, sprawling mountain valley that is Estes Park was named for cattle rancher Joel Estes, who arrived here with his family in 1859. Though the area, fertile and bountiful, had probably been a hunting ground for nomadic bands of Ute and Arapahoe tribes, the Estes family found few signs of villages or other settlements.

The winter of 1866 was an unusually harsh one, and Estes herded up his clan and cattle and hit the road, heading for warmer climates. The following year, Griffith J. Evans acquired the property and built a handful of cabins that he rented out to travelers, many of whom used the valley as a base camp for ascents of nearby Longs Peak and explorations into what would become Rocky Mountain National Park. One of the area's first visitors was Albert Bierstadt, and travelers familiar with the painter's work will no doubt recognize the inspirations for some of his huge oils.

Another one of Evans's early guests was English nobleman Lord Dunraven. So impressed with the area was Dunraven that he sought to acquire the valley for himself and turn it into a hunting refuge for his fellow aristocrats. However, settlement and land ownership in the valley was controlled by the Homestead Law, which allowed only 160 acres of land per person. Quite used to having his own way, Dunraven found a way around the law, engineering a classic land-grab scheme. He had the deeds to all the 160-acre parcels in the valley transferred to "loafers and drifters," and, apparently, to some folks residing in local cemeteries. Dunraven then "bought" the land from its new owners, offering the live ones piddling amounts of cash or, in the cases of the dead ones, simply taking possession of the property. It was then just a matter of paying the government a small transfer fee and registering what he called the "English Company," a corporation established in England as the Estes Park Company, Ltd.

In 1907, Dunraven sold out to F.O. Stanley and B.D. Sanborn, who split the valley between them. Stanley immediately went to work building the Stanley Hotel and Stanley Manor House. The hotel opened in 1909 and the Manor House the following year.

Stanley, who had invented the Stanley Steamer, ran a line from the closest railroad terminal, 25 miles away in Lyons, to the hotel, and soon began attracting visitors from around the country. With the success of the hotel, a number of other lodges and cabins were built, and Estes Park began to establish a reputation as a premier resort area. In 1915, Rocky Mountain National Park was born, securing Estes Park as a major tourist destination.

ESTES PARK

H-BAR-G HOSTEL

H-BAR-G RD.

DEVILS GULCH RD.

DRY GULCH RD.

MacGREGOR AVE.

STANLEY HOTEL

TO TRAIL RIDGE RD.
& PARK ENTRANCE

TO LOVELAND
& FT. COLLINS

BIG THOMPSON AVE.

ELKHORN AVE.

FALL RIVER RD.

CHAMBER OF COMMERCE/
VISITOR INFORMATION

LAKE ESTES

34

ROCKY

WONDERVIEW AVE.

RIVER

ST. VRAIN AVE.

34

BIG THOMPSON RIVER

MOUNTAIN

PROSPECT AVE.

ESTES PARK
AREA
HISTORICAL
MUSEUM

N. ST. VRAIN AVE.

NATIONAL

MORAINE AVE.

36

PARK

THOMPSON

MOCASSIN
CIRCLE DR.

STANLEY
AVE.

TO LYONS & BOULDER

TO
TRAIL RIDGE RD.

BIG

RIVERSIDE DR.

HIGH DR.

PARK ENTRANCE
RD.

66

MARY'S LAKE RD.

S. ST. VRAIN AVE.

TO YMCA OF
THE ROCKIES/
ESTES PARK
CENTER

PEAKVIEW DR.

TO ALLENSPARK
& NEDERLAND

MARY'S LAKE

NOT TO SCALE

MOON

7

SIGHTS

Estes Park Area Historical Museum
This museum displays Estes Valley's history from its first settlers, Joel Estes and family, through the founding of Rocky Mountain National Park and the incorporation of the village of Estes Park. Exhibits and buildings include the original headquarters of Rocky Mountain National Park, a Stanley Steamer, and lots of pioneer artifacts and historical photos. May through Sept., the museum is open Mon.-Sat. 10 a.m.-5 p.m. and Sun. 1-5 p.m.; in March and Dec., hours are Tues.-Sat. 10 a.m.-5 p.m. and Sun. 1-

5 p.m. The rest of the year it's open by appointment only.

The Estes Park Area Historical Museum is located at 200 4th Street. For more information or to arrange tours, phone (303) 586-6256.

MacGregor Ranch Museum And Education Center
The MacGregor is a working ranch commemorating the Alexander Q. MacGregor family, one of the valley's largest and most influential ranching families, and displaying life in Estes Park from the 1870s through the mid-20th century. Exhibits include historical photos and documentation of MacGregor's staunch opposition to

Lord Dunraven's land company, as well as family domestic items, including furniture and silver. Cowhands use century-old equipment to display early ranching techniques.

The museum is located at the foot of Twin Owls on Devil's Gulch Rd. about a mile north of Estes Park. Admission is free, donations encouraged. Hours are daily 11 a.m.-5 p.m., Memorial Day through Labor Day. For more information, phone (303) 586-3749.

Enos Mills Cabin

The "Father of Rocky Mountain National Park," Enos Mills was a naturalist, writer, and photographer who homesteaded in Estes Park in the late 19th century. Mills's small cabin, which he built in 1885 at the base of Twin Sisters Mountain, today operates as a nature center and museum. His daughter, Edna Mills Kiley, and other docents offer tours of the house, where his books, photos, and other memorabilia are displayed, and nature trails lead out into the 200-acre property. Copies of his books and photographs are sold in the museum's gift shop.

The Enos Mills Cabin is located just south of Estes Park on CO 7. Admission is free. Open daily 9 a.m.-6 p.m. For more information, phone (303) 586-4706.

Lulu Dorsey Museum

Located at the YMCA of the Rockies—Estes Park Center, this is a hands-on museum displaying antique children's toys and musical instruments, as well as domestic items of historical interest and historical photos, particularly in relation to the founding of the YMCA of the Rockies (see "Lodges and Cabins," under "Accommodations" following).

The Dorsey Museum is located on the grounds of the YMCA at 2515 Tunnel Rd.; open weekdays 9 a.m.-5 p.m., Sat. 9 a.m.-4 p.m., and Sun. noon-4 p.m. Admission is free. For more information, phone (303) 586-3341.

Let's Go Surfin' Now

Huh? A surfing museum in the heart of the Rocky Mountains? Now, I can't vouch for it, as I haven't been there myself, but according to my sources (a brochure and an ad) the **Surfing Museum** at Estes Sport and Surf has the "Rocky Mountain's largest display of collectible surfboards and surfing memorabilia, plus con-

tinuous surfing movies." Check it out, dude. And let me know how it is. It's located at 443 W. Elkhorn in West Park Center, tel. (303) 586-9094.

PARKS AND RECREATION

Rocky Mountain National Park

This is Estes Park's main draw. Every year thousands of tourists use the little village—and its numerous ranches and motels—as a headquarters for exploring the park. See "Hiking" below for complete description.

Bicycling

Though mountain biking's not a full-bore craze here yet, like it is in Summit County, Crested Butte, Durango, and some other Colorado resort areas, the region's ideal for the sport. Roosevelt National Forest's 800,000 acres of public land sprawl east of town, providing lots of excellent trails and logging roads (no off-road riding is permitted in Rocky Mountain National Park).

A recent article in the vacation edition of the Estes Park *Trail-Gazette* discussed some of the area's better rides, including Crossier Mountain, near Glen Haven, seven miles north of town; Pole Hill, three miles east of town on Hwy. 36; and Pearson and Johnny parks, south of town on CO 7.

For maps and more information on cycling in the Estes Park area, stop by the Estes Park Ranger Station at 161 2nd St., tel. (303) 586-3440, or write Roosevelt National Forest, 240 W. Prospect, Fort Collins, CO 80526, tel. 498-1100. You can also get information and rentals from **Colorado Bicycling**, 184 E. Elkhorn Ave., tel. 586-4241.

Golf

The Estes Valley Recreation and Park District maintains two golf courses. The 18-hole **Estes Park Golf Course,** which dates from 1912, is one of the oldest courses in the state. Located at 1080 S. Saint Vrain, the course sprawls through woods at nearly 8,000 feet above sea level. For tee times and information, phone (303) 586-8146. **Lake Estes Executive Golf Course** is a nine-hole course along the banks of the Thompson River, 690 Big Thompson Ave., tel. 586-8176.

Hiking

The Estes Park area is a heaven on earth for hikers, abounding in nature trails to walk, woods to explore, and peaks to climb. The best hiking is in Rocky Mountain National Park, which offers scores of trails with a full range of lengths and difficulty levels. In addition, **Roosevelt National Forest** offers excellent backcountry hiking. Topo maps and information on hiking in the national forest are available from the main office at 240 W. Prospect, Fort Collins, CO 80526, tel. (303) 498-1100, or locally at 161 2nd St., tel. 586-3440. You can also get information, as well as quality equipment, from **Outdoor World**, located in downtown Estes Park Village, tel. 586-2114, and at **The Hiking Hut** in the Park Center Mall downtown, tel. 586-2995.

The **Colorado Mountain Club** has been sponsoring hikes in the Estes Park area since before WW I, and currently runs some 2,000 outings a year. Free literature about the club, including information on hikes, meeting places, degrees of difficulty, etc., is available by phoning 586-6623. You can also get information from their Denver office, 2530 W. Alameda Ave., Denver, CO 80219, tel. 922-8315. The Colorado Mountain Club publishes a monthly newsletter, *Trail And Timberline,* which lists upcoming outings, reviews books on mountains and mountaineering, and tackles sensitive environmental issues.

Reflections of the Rockies Nature Hikes offers naturalist-led hiking tours into Rocky Mountain National Park. For information, write Box 73, Estes Park, CO 80517, or phone 586-8924.

Fishing

Fishing in the Estes Park area ranges from pay-by-the-inch trout farms where no license is required to remote backcountry lakes and streams where wily native trout elude all but the most skilled and patient angler. And of course the scenic rewards of hiking into an isolated lake in Rocky Mountain National Park, even if you get skunked, are far greater for most people than hauling hatchery lunkers from highway-side lagoons.

If you're looking for guarantees, though, you have at least a couple of options. **Trout Haven,** about a mile west of Estes Park on Hwy. 36, tel. (303) 586-2955, and **Rock 'n' River Trout Farm,** about 15 miles southeast of town on Hwy. 36, stock their ponds with rainbows up to 26 inches. Open daily till dusk April 1 through mid-October.

For anglers looking for more of a challenge, the Big Thompson River east of Estes Park offers good trout fishing and decent-size fish. Some stretches are designated artificial lures and flies only. (Always double-check local restrictions.) There's also fishing (and picnicking) just below the dam at the east end of Lake Estes.

For information on fishing in Roosevelt National Forest, stop by the district office at 161 2nd Street, tel. 586-3440.

Rafting

As in most mountain resort towns, whitewater rafting is big here, and several companies offer a range of trips down local rivers. **Estes Park Adventures, Ltd.** books half-, full-, and two-day trips on the Arkansas, Cache La Poudre, and Colorado rivers. Write Box 2924, Estes Park, CO 80517, or phone (303) 586-2303 or (800) 762-5968, ext. 2303. You can also arrange trips with **Rapid Transit Rafting,** Box 4095, Estes Park, CO 80517, tel. 586-8852 or (800) 367-8523; **Mad Adventures,** tel. (800) 451-4844; and **Colorado Wilderness Sports,** 358 E. Elkhorn, tel. 586-6548.

Horseback Riding

This is a popular way to explore both Rocky Mountain National Park and Roosevelt National Forest, and several outfitters in the area offer tours and rentals. **Hi Country Stables,** with two centers within the boundaries of Rocky Mountain National Park, runs a range of tours into some of the park's most scenic spots, including Bierstadt and Bear lakes. Phone (303) 586-5890 or 586-6269. **Sombrero Ranch** offers several types of rides, from one-hour to several-day pack trips, as well as pancake breakfast and evening chuck-wagon rides. For information and reservations, phone 586-4577. **Elkhorn Stables** also offers rides, ranging from one to eight hours, some with meals. Phone 586-3291.

Tram Rides

For a bird's-eye view of the Estes Park Valley, as well as of towering Longs Peak and other Rocky Mountain National Park peaks, take the 12-passenger aerial tram to the summit of Prospect

Mountain (elev. 8,800 feet). Check out the gift shop and snack bar at the top; open daily mid-May through mid-Sept., 9 a.m.-6:30 p.m. The base of the tram and ticket office are located at 420 E. Riverside Drive. For rates and more information, phone (303) 586-3675.

Downhill Skiing

Estes Park is far less a winter than a summer resort, yet this is after all Colorado, and folks gotta have a place to crank turns. **Ski Estes Park** is a small family-oriented ski area inside Rocky Mountain National Park (Trail Ridge Rd. carves across the slopes.) The resort has rentals, a ski school, cafeteria, and children's center. For information, phone (303) 586-8173.

Cross-country Skiing

Most visitors to Estes Park come to hike the nearby trails and explore Rocky Mountain National Park backcountry under a warm summer sun. Yet some of those very same trails and woods also offer excellent opportunities for Nordic skiers. The best cross-country skiing is in the park (see "Rocky Mountain National Park" following), although Roosevelt National Forest also has hundreds of square miles of picture-book Nordic terrain. Get maps and information from the Forest Service district office at 161 2nd St., tel. (303) 586-3440; rent equipment and get expert advice from **Colorado Wilderness Sports,** 358 E. Elkhorn, tel. 586-6548. Another excellent source of information on cross-country skiing in the area is the **Colorado Mountain Club,** tel. 586-6623, which sponsors some 2,000 hiking and cross-country skiing trips a year and publishes literature on trails and specific areas.

ACCOMMODATIONS

If you're new to Estes Park, you'll be amazed at the number of inns, lodges, motels, cabins, hotels, and combinations thereof. With its ideal location adjacent to Rocky Mountain National Park, Estes Park has zillions of rooms and campsites available for passers-through, as well as for travelers who want to use the town as a base to do some exploring in the area. For complete listings of available lodging, contact the Estes Park Chamber of Commerce, which publishes several accommodations guides to the area. Their toll-free telephone number is (800) 44-ESTES.

Hotels

Of the first-class lodges in the Rockies, the **Stanley Hotel,** tel. (303) 586-3371 or (800) ROCKIES, is without doubt one of the most elegant and glorious. Standing high on the hillside, castlelike, and looking out over the town, the valley, and west toward the towering Rockies, the Stanley, like the wizened resident it is, seems to be casting a cynical eye over the rest of Estes Park and some of its more touristy trappings and Johnny-come-lately attendants. First opened in 1909, after three years' construction, the Stanley was the brainchild of F.O. Stanley, whose guests arrived at the lodge via Stanley Steamer, which he invented. At the time, the Stanley was known as one of the most luxurious hotels in the West, and in addition to its fancy furnishings offered guests a golf course, stables, bowling, billiards, and theater.

Though some people claim the hotel was used in the Stanley Kubrick film *The Shining,* anyone who's seen both the movie and the hotel can tell you this isn't true. It is true, however, that the hotel inspired one of its guests, Stephen King, to write the novel upon which the film was based. The filming crew, faced with a lack of snow at the Stanley, shot the movie at the Timberline Lodge on Oregon's Mt. Hood.

Double rooms at the Stanley Hotel range from about $60 to $150 a night, and it's a good idea to make reservations ahead of time.

Though paling in comparison to the Stanley, several other Estes Park hotels offer upscale lodging. The **Estes Park Inn,** tel. 586-5363, (800) 438-7269 (in Colorado), or (800) 458-1182 (outside Colorado), on the east side of town on Hwy. 34, is a full-fledged resort offering meeting facilities and access to golf and skiing. The **Holiday Inn,** tel. 586-2332 or 534-4775 (from Denver) is located in town at the junction of Hwy. 36 and CO 7 and also offers meeting and convention facilities.

Lodges And Cabins

One of the most unusual lodges in the area is **Estes Park Center—YMCA of the Rockies,** tel. (303) 586-3341 or (800) 228-3947 (in Colorado). Like its sister, Snow Mountain Resort (see "Winter Park" above), this is a sprawling, self-contained resort complex offering a huge range of lodging options, facilities, and amenities. Situated on 1,400 acres adjacent to Rocky Mountain National Park, the Estes Park Center has furnished two- and four-bedroom cabins as well as a variety of lodge-style rooms. Activities include hiking, horseback riding, tennis, cross-country skiing, and snow tubing. Perfect for families, the lodge has lots of kid-oriented programs, as well as its own library, museum, grocery store, and gift shop. For rates and reservations, write YMCA of the Rockies, Estes Park, CO 80511-2550.

Located on the North St. Vrain River 14 miles east of Estes Park, **Shelly's Cottages,** tel. 823-6326, offers convenience and quiet privacy. Cabins for two run about $40-70. You can also get reasonably priced cabins at the family-owned **Edgewater Heights Cottages,** tel. 586-8493, two miles east of Estes Park at 2550 Big Thompson along the Big Thompson River. Another popular Estes Park lodge is the **Longs Peak Inn and Guest Ranch,** tel. 586-2110, about 10 miles south of town at the base of Longs Peak. Longs Peak Inn offers a full range of dude ranch-style amenities, including meals and campfire programs, as well as guided hiking and riding tours, fishing ponds, and day care.

Motels
You'll find bizillions of motels in Estes Park, though that shouldn't keep you from making reservations in advance, especially in the height of the summer. The **Mountain 8 Inn,** 1220 Big Thompson, tel. (303) 586-4421, has among the least expensive rooms in town, with doubles starting at about $30. The **Landmark Motel,** just east of town on Hwy. 36, tel. 586-4523, has doubles for about $40. Rooms for two at the **Alpine Trail Ridge Inn,** 927 Moraine Ave., tel. 586-4585 or (800) 233-5023 (doubles, some with kitchens) run $35-90.

Hostel
The **H-Bar-G Hostel,** tel. (303) 586-3688, is a member of the American Youth Hostel system and provides the least expensive lodging in the area ($7.25 for members, slightly more for non-members). Open summers only, the H-Bar-G is just north of Estes Park with a variety of hiking trails leading from the property into Roosevelt National Forest. In addition, the hostel has ten-

nis and volleyball courts and a game room. Write: Box 1260, Estes Park, CO 80517 (May-Sept.) or 700 Flagstaff Star Rt., Boulder, CO 80302 (Oct.-late April).

Camping And RVing
Estes Park is surrounded by public campgrounds, administered either by the National Park Service or the Forest Service. **Olive Ridge Campground** is in Roosevelt National Forest about eight miles south of Estes Park on Hwy. 7 (see "Rocky Mountain National Park," following, for camping information).

Privately administered RV campgrounds, generally open May-Sept., include a **KOA,** two miles east of town on Hwy. 34, tel. (303) 586-2888; **Park Place Camping Resort,** six miles southeast of Estes Park on Hwy. 36 (also cabins), tel. 586-4230; **National Park Campground and Resort,** right at the park's Fall River entrance, tel. 586-4563; and **Estes Park Campground,** about five miles southwest of Estes Park on Hwy. 66, tel. 586-4188.

FOOD

A resort town catering to free-spending passers-through, Estes Park is packed with cafés and restaurants. For breakfast, try **The Other Side,** 900 Moraine Ave., tel. (303) 586-2171, open daily at 7 a.m. with a health-conscious menu. Another breakfast spot worth checking out is the **Mountaineer Restaurant,** 540 S. Saint Vrain, tel. 586-9001. The Mountaineer opens at 6 a.m. and specializes in biscuits and gravy and homemade cinnamon rolls.

For Mexican food, try **La Casa,** 222 E. Elkhorn, tel. 586-2807, a favorite among locals and tourists alike. In addition to Mexican standards, La Casa also serves Cajun and American dishes—outdoor patio seating, too. A favorite for Italian food is the **Dunraven Inn,** 2470 Hwy. 66, tel. 586-6409, which calls itself the "Rome of the Rockies." About seven miles south of town on Hwy. 7, the **Baldpate Inn,** tel. 586-6151, has a reputation for excellent food, particularly the soup-and-salad buffet and homemade breads and pies. The Baldpate also offers bed-and-breakfast accommodations.

If you're looking for picnic fixin's before heading up into Rocky Mountain National Park, stop at the **Safeway** on the hill above downtown, where you'll find a deli and salad bar.

ENTERTAINMENT

The **Gaslight,** 246 Moraine Ave., tel. (303) 586-5978, features live Irish music daily, 4-8 p.m., and dancing to live country music Mon.-Sat. nights 8:30 p.m. till closing. British beers on tap. The **Park Village Playhouse,** 900 Moraine Ave., tel. 586-2171, offers a variety of different kinds of live music, from cowboy to big band, as well as special comedy nights and community theater productions. Call for schedule and reservations.

For dinner theater, try **Centennial Playhouse,** tel. 586-2885, where you can join in the fun of a classic melodrama.

CALENDAR

Estes Park has a rather idiosyncratic lineup of annual events, ranging from the proverbial fireworks-over-the-lake on the Fourth of July to a wild Celtic celebration. Though there are a handful of wintertime affairs, including the **Ski Estes Park Snow Festival** in late March, things don't really kick off until early June, when Trail Ridge Rd. through Rocky Mountain National Park traditionally opens. The Stanley Hotel hosts a variety of music throughout the summer, most notably the classical **Summer Concert Series;** phone (303) 586-3371 for information. The YMCA of the Rockies sponsors its **Summerfest Concert Series,** with music ranging from classical to jazz to bluegrass; phone 586-3341.

Fall's highlight is the two-day Celtic fair in September (sorry, basketball fans—the "C" here is hard, not soft, these players blow bagpipes, not games to the Pistons, and they wear skirts, not gym shorts). Officially known as the Longs Peak Scottish Fair, it usually draws some 20,000 people and features a parade (with over two dozen bagpipe bands), athletic competitions (including the hammer and tree-trunk tosses), and a general craziness that usually lasts into the wee hours. For complete information, phone 586-6308. For more information on Estes Park's wide range of annual events, phone the chamber of commerce at (800) 44-ESTES.

SHOPPING

Estes Park has one of the state's largest concentrations of gift shops and galleries, selling gifts and souvenirs ranging from hopelessly tacky to museum quality. You'll find lots of Native American art, photos and renderings in various other media of Rocky Mountain National Park, as well as Christmas stores, boutiques, and jewelers. Part of the fun is simply wandering around the village, poking your head into the various shops.

A handful of the galleries are particularly worth checking out. The **Art Center,** in the lower level of Stanley Village, features a wide range of quality art, with exhibits changing monthly. The center also offers classes and demonstrations. **Artisans of Colorado,** 157 W. Elkhorn, has work by over 75 of the state's best artists and artisans. The **Ricker-Bartlett Casting Studios and Gallery,** two miles east of town on Hwy. 34, is the world's largest pewter-casting studio. Pieces from the studio have been presented to several U.S. presidents, and some are in the Smithsonian Institution. Among the displays is a 300-square-foot re-creation of an American small town at the turn of the century. Phone (303) 586-2030 for complete information.

The **Charles Eagle Plume Gallery and Museum of Native American Arts,** 10 miles south of Estes Park on CO 7, has been around since 1917 and has a huge collection of baskets, jewelry, rugs, and other art and artifacts on display and for sale. Charles Eagle Plume, the shop's owner and curator, graduated from the University of Colorado in 1932 and has been active in Native American rights for the better part of this century. Eagle Plume has been awarded an honorary Doctorate of Humanities from the University of Colorado. The museum and gallery is open summers only. Phone 586-4710 for more information.

The **Fine Arts Guild of the Rockies** publishes the *Estes Park Gallery Guide,* which lists some 20 galleries and shops in town. Write the guild at Box 1165, Estes Park, CO 80517, or phone the chamber of commerce at 586-4431 or (800)44-ESTES.

SERVICES

The offices of the Estes Park **Police Department** are located at 170 MacGregor; phone (303) 586-5331. Phone the Larimer County **Sheriff** at 586-9511 and the **State Patrol** at 484-4020 (Fort Collins). **Estes Park Medical Center** is located at 555 Prospect, tel. 586-2317. The **post office** is at 215 W. Riverside, tel. 586-8177.

Recycling
The transfer station for **Estes Park Recycling Center** is located on Elm Rd. and will take aluminum, glass, and newspaper. For information, phone (303) 586-3772.

INFORMATION

An excellent place to begin your visit to Estes Park is at the chamber of commerce's **visitor information center,** located at 500 Big Thompson Avenue. You'll find tons of info on Estes, the surrounding area, and Rocky Mountain National Park. You can also write the chamber at Box 3050, Estes Park, CO 80517, or call (303) 586-4431 or (800) 443-7837. The **public library** is located at 225 E. Elkhorn, tel. 586-8116. **MacDonald Book Shop,** 152 E. Elkhorn, tel. 586-3450, has a good selection of books on Rocky Mountain National Park, the Estes Park area, and Colorado.

For information on Rocky Mountain National Park, phone the headquarters at 586-2371 or the backcountry office at tel. 586-3440. You can get a 24-hour recorded message by dialing 586-2385.

For **road and weather information** phone 586-4000.

TRANSPORTATION

Estes Park is situated at the junctions of Highways 34 and 36 and CO 7, making it approachable from the south, east, and west (except during the winter, when Hwy. 34 to the west, through Rocky Mountain National Park, is closed). **Charles Limousine Service** runs at least four shuttle buses daily between Estes Park and Stapleton Airport in Denver; roundtrip fares start at $35. Phone (303) 586-5151 or (800) 950-3274. Charles also provides taxi service in town (tel. 586-8440), as well as tours of Rocky Mountain National Park, backcountry 4WD trips, and hiking and fishing tours.

SOUTH OF ESTES PARK

Colorado 7 drops south out of Estes Park, paralleling the eastern border of Rocky Mountain National Park for about 18 miles. Affording excellent views, both of the park (particularly Longs Peak) and of the valley to the east, the route has several places worth stopping at along the way. The stretch from Estes Park south to Central City, which includes Colorado Highways 7, 72 through Nederland, and 119, has been designated the **Peak to Peak Highway,** and offers breathtaking vistas and panoramas around virtually every turn.

About five miles out of Estes Park is **Lilly Lake Picnic Area,** a day-use-only area administered by Roosevelt National Forest. In addition to picnicking, you can explore the shores of this lovely little alpine lake via a number of hiking trails that begin near the parking lot.

A couple of miles south of Lilly Lake is **Twin Sisters Trailhead,** which leads to Twin Sisters Peak (elev. 11,248 feet) in a small isolated unit of Rocky Mountain National Park east of the highway.

Longs Peak Campground (in Rocky Mountain National Park) is about nine miles south of Estes Park. The campground is designated for tents only. Between Longs Peak Campground and Allenspark (about seven miles), you'll find several Rocky Mountain National Park trailheads, including access to Wild Basin. A mile north of Allenspark is Roosevelt National Forest's **Olive Ridge Campground** (56 sites, pit toilets, no showers).

Allenspark and Ferncliff are two quaint little towns just off the highway at the southeastern edge of Rocky Mountain National Park. You can get rooms at the **Ferncliff Motel and Cabins,** tel. (303) 747-2531, for about $35 and cabins for two for $45. The **Allenspark Lodge,** tel. 747-2552, is a rustic old inn that would be perfect for one of those occasionally mandatory getaways when you just want to shut out the world and not let *anyone* know where you are. Doubles start at about $40.

Four miles south of Allenspark the road arcs east, and you can either continue on to Lyons or catch CO 72 south for Nederland, where you can shoot into Boulder the back way.

ROCKY MOUNTAIN NATIONAL PARK

Without doubt one of the most gorgeous and breathtaking of Colorado's natural wonders, Rocky Mountain National Park includes over 265,000 acres of towering peaks, rolling alpine meadows, pristine lakes, and dense forests of aspen, fir, spruce, and pine. A paradise for hikers, backpackers, mountain climbers, and sightseers, the park attracts nearly three million visitors a year, the greatest percentage of whom come between May and October (the main road through the park—see "Driving Through the Park" following—is closed in winter).

A microcosm of the greater Rocky Mountains' geology, Rocky Mountain National Park is like a giant wedge of cheese, gently sloping up from the west, then dropping dramatically at the Front Range to the flatlands below. Within the boundaries of the park are more than 75 peaks towering 12,000 feet or more above sea level, including several over 13,000. The highest point in the park is Longs Peak, at 14,255 feet. Trail Ridge Rd., the main road through the park, passes through 12,000-foot-high meadows, with wildflowers and grasses waving softly in mountain breezes. Five small alpine glaciers, vestiges of the great ice floes that carved valleys and lakes from the heaving mountains, remain within the park's boundaries.

Not surprisingly, the park is full of wildlife: bighorn sheep, mountain goats, elk, deer, bear, and many smaller animals, from marmots and beavers to coyotes and mountain lions. Thankfully, no hunting is allowed.

History
Rocky Mountain National Park's history dates from just after the turn of the century, when naturalist, writer, and photographer Enos Mills, who had been living in a small cabin just outside Estes, began a campaign to protect the land. Although Mills soon had enough support to convince the Federal government to set aside some land, the first designation was as a national forest. But conservationists were not yet satisfied.

A small but vocal group, spearheaded by the newly founded Colorado Mountain Club, sought national park status, against the wishes of the Forest Service and landowners.

The group, led by Mills, and the club, got its way. In January 1915 the land was officially designated Rocky Mountain National Park.

One of the park's most influential administrators was its third superintendent, Roger Toll, who took office in 1920. Toll, an avid mountain climber and preservationist, made first ascents of many of the park's peaks and wrote the park's first climbing guide, *Mountaineering in Rocky Mountain National Park* (Department of the Interior), as well as the classic *The Mountain Peaks of Colorado* (Colorado Mountain Club). Toll also oversaw construction of Bear Lake Rd. (1920), Trail Ridge Rd. (1932), and many of the park's first trails, which opened up much of the backcountry to visitors. Toll served until 1936, when he was killed in a car crash en route to Mexico to consult with U.S. and Mexican authorities about establishing game preserves along the border. In 1940, the name of Ute Horn was changed to Mt. Toll, and in 1941, the Toll Memorial was erected on Sundance Mountain near Trail Ridge Road.

VISITOR CENTERS

There are excellent visitor centers at both the east and west entrances to Rocky Mountain National Park, as well as at the summit of Trail Ridge Road. You'll find a wide range of books, maps, and brochures, as well as staff members to answer all questions. The **Park Headquarters Visitors Center** is located on Hwy. 36 just west of Estes Park, tel. (303) 586-2371. Also on the Estes Park side is the **Moraine Park Museum,** tel. 586-3777, where you can study the park's geology, history, and wildlife, and take a hike on a half-mile, self-guided nature trail. The museum is open mid-May through September.

The **Kawuneeche Visitors Center,** tel. 627-3471, is located on the park's west side just north of Grand Lake. The **Alpine Visitors Center,** tel. 586-4927, is near the top of Trail Ridge Rd. at Fall River Pass (elev. 11,796 feet) in the heart of the park. You'll find exhibits about the surrounding alpine tundra, plus other park information. Closed in winter.

DRIVING THROUGH THE PARK

The main road through Rocky Mountain National Park is **Trail Ridge Rd.,** a 50-mile stretch of Hwy. 34 that offers some of the most spectacular scenery on the planet. Its summit at 12,183 feet, Trail Ridge Rd. lifts up past the treeline and meanders along the ridgetop through meadows of alpine tundra. Allow three to four hours, as along the way you'll want to get out of your car to take pictures or simply appreciate the scenery. There are also several short hikes to scenic overlooks.

Old Fall River Rd. is the original road through the park. Completed in 1920, the one-way (east-to-west) 11-mile gravel road parallels Trail Ridge Rd. from Endovalley to the Alpine Visitors Center. Don't expect the sweeping panoramas you get on Trail Ridge. Motor homes and trailers are not allowed.

Bear Lake Rd. leads from the Moraine Park Museum to Bear Lake, where a number of trails lead to waterfalls and other lakes. The road is paved and gets a lot of traffic, and the two parking lots at the lake are usually full in the summer in midday. To avoid parking, you can take a Park Service shuttle from Glacier Basin Campground, about three miles past the museum (watch for the signs).

At the visitor centers you can pick up cassette tapes with recorded information on the drive through the park. The narrator points out areas of geological and historical interest, and also discusses Native American legends and wildlife. Tapes cost about $12 and include maps. They're available at the park visitor centers, as well as at gift shops in Estes Park. You can order tapes from **CCInc. Auto Tape Tours,** Box 631, Goldens Bridge, NY 10526, tel. (914) 232-0322.

Tours
If you'd rather leave the driving to someone else, you can tour the park with **Rocky Mountain National Park Tours,** which offers three different trips. The Grand Lake trip takes a full day with lunch in Grand Lake. Weather permitting, you'll take both Trail Ridge Rd. and Fall River Road. The tour departs at 9 a.m. and costs about $18 per person. The half-day Trail Ridge tour takes you to the Alpine Visitors Center via Fall River Rd. and back on Trail Ridge Road. Tours start at 9 a.m. and 2 p.m. and cost about $13. The Bear Lake at Dusk tour takes you into Bear Lake "when the crowds leave," at 6:30 p.m., about $12. For information and reservations, phone (303) 586-8687.

Rocky Mountain National Park's Trail Ridge Road rises well above the treeline on its 12,183-foot summit.

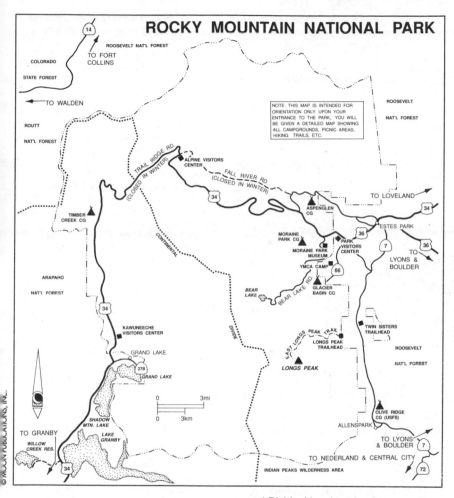

HIKING AND BACKPACKING

You could spend a lifetime exploring the trails and backcountry of Rocky Mountain National Park (and some folks have). Over 350 miles of marked trails weave in and out of forests and meadows, up mountainsides, and along meandering streams. They range from short paths between parking lots and scenic overlooks, to trails that cross the park from one side to the other, *over* the Conti-

nental Divide. Your best bet is to stop in at one of the visitor centers to check out the several available hiking guides. They range from the brief Park Service-published brochure to full-blown books with maps, charts, descriptions, difficulty levels, and any information you could possibly need. A popular (very!) short hike is the half-miler around **Bear Lake.** Take Bear Lake Rd. to the trailhead. In addition to the short Bear Lake Trail, several other hikes of varying lengths and degrees of difficulty begin here.

The **Sprague Lake Five Senses Trail** is specifically designed with disabled visitors in mind; the half-mile trail is level, wide enough to accommodate wheelchairs, and encourages appreciation of the park, and nature, through all five senses. Take Bear Lake Rd. about three miles past the Moraine Park Museum.

Just west of the Fall River Entrance Station (on Hwy. 34), you'll find a turnoff to Aspenglen Campground. Several trails wander through this lush valley and along the Fall River (this is before the road begins to climb up to Trail Ridge). There are also hiking and nature trails at all the visitor centers.

At the other end of the spectrum are the **Longs Peak trails.** The highest peak in the park (elev. 14,255 feet), Longs can be reached by at least two routes. The most popular is the main trail from the Longs Peak trailhead, located south of Estes Park just off CO 7. The 16-mile roundtrip is for experienced hikers only, although no climbing equipment is required; allow about 12 hours. **Note:** The Park Service recommends getting an early start and being on your way down by early afternoon to avoid the proverbial summer storms.

Remember, too, that hiking in Rocky Mountain National Park is serious business, and that even though you don't need a permit for a day hike, you should always let someone else know where you're going and when you expect to return. Backcountry hiking is limited to seven nights June-Sept. (15 nights the rest of the year). Camp in designated areas only, unless authorized by permit, available at the visitor centers, tel. (303) 586-2371.

Camping

Rocky Mountain National Park has five campgrounds. **Longs Peak, Moraine Park, Glacier Basin,** and **Aspenglen** are out of Estes Park on the east side of Fall River Pass; **Timber Creek Campground** is on the west side, out of Grand Lake. None of the campgrounds has

electrical outlets or water or sewer connections, and all are full by noon (earlier in June, July, and August). Longs Peak Campground is designated tents only, and stays are limited to three days. You can camp up to seven days at the others.

Permits to camp in the backcountry are available at the visitor centers. Be sure to read regulations carefully and to follow them closely. They're designed for your safety and the health of the park. For more information, phone park headquarters at (303) 586-2371.

CROSS-COUNTRY SKIING

The lower valleys of Rocky Mountain National Park are perfect for exploring on cross-country skis, and roads to several of the lower trailheads are plowed throughout the winter. Aspenglen, Longs Peak, and Timber Creek campgrounds are open year-round (though Aspenglen is the only one plowed), providing access to a wide range of excellent trails and woodsy backcountry. There are also trails at Glacier Basin Campground and at Bear Lake.

For more information on cross-country skiing in Rocky Mountain National Park, stop by **Colorado Wilderness Sports,** 358 E. Elkhorn in Estes Park, tel. (303) 586-6548. You can also get information from the **Colorado Mountain Club,** tel. 586-6623. The club, founded in 1912 as an offshoot of the Colorado Mountain Climbing Club (itself founded in 1896), sponsors a wide range of trips into the park each season.

Information

For more information, write Rocky Mountain National Park, Estes Park, CO 80517. You can also phone (303) 586-2371 (headquarters), 586-2385 (recorded information), or 586-3440 (backcountry office).

In your car, tune your radio to AM 1470 for recorded visitor information.

GREELEY AND VICINITY

Located near the confluence of the Cache La Poudre and South Platte rivers about 60 miles north of Denver, Greeley (pop. 68,000; elev. 4,663 feet) is a proud and civic-minded community whose roots are in cattle ranching and agriculture. Weld County, of which Greeley is the seat, comprises two million acres and ranks fourth in the nation and first in the state in the value of its agricultural products, primarily corn, wheat, and alfalfa.

Greeley is home to the University of Northern Colorado as well as the summer training camp of the Denver Broncos. Several Fortune 500 companies, including Hewlett Packard and Eastman Kodak, have facilities nearby. Greeley's size and western plains location ensures a laid-back, small-town lifestyle and a relatively mild climate. At the same time, it's just an hour from the Denver nightlife or the rugged backcountry of Rocky Mountain National Park.

In 1989, Greeley scored a major coup. In May of that year it was selected as one of the 10 All-American Cities by the National Civic League of Chicago. Focusing primarily on the candidates' senses of community, the 40-year-old program seeks "to encourage and recognize civic excellence." Among the 10 judging criteria are citizen participation, community leadership, government performance, volunteerism, and civic education.

Walking the streets of Greeley, you can see it. There's a genuine wholesomeness and classic Western friendliness here. And there's an almost palpable sense that folks who live here are proud of themselves and their community, and wouldn't live anywhere else.

History

Greeley was named for *New York Tribune* editor Horace Greeley, who visited Colorado Territory in 1859 and returned with his exhortation, "Go West, young man, and grow with the country." Impressed by the land's immense potential for farming, Greeley, along with his agriculture

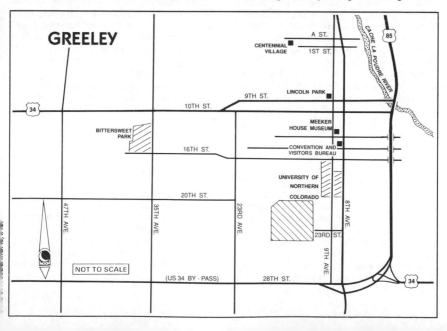

editor, Nathan Meeker, campaigned to establish a utopian community in Colorado based on religion, temperance, and cooperative farming. According to the WPA's 1930 Colorado guidebook, Meeker circulated flyers and advertised in eastern papers, emphasizing that "the idle, immoral, intemperate, or inefficient need not apply." In 1869, Meeker bought 12,000 acres of land on the banks of the Cache La Poudre River in the South Platte Valley, with provisional title to another 60,000. The following year he led a group of 50 New England families to the site, traveling from Cheyenne on the newly completed Denver Pacific Railroad. There the group established the Union Colony, each member paying $5 to belong and $150 for no more than 160 acres of land. A 100-by-150-foot townsite was also laid out.

Work began immediately on housing and irrigation ditches, though one of the first construction projects on the agenda was a church, in which services were held within two weeks of the colonists' arrival. One of the new community's commandments was, "Thou shalt not sell liquid damnation within the lines of Union Colony."

By the mid-1870s, homes, stores, and office buildings had been built, and water was being run into the fields to irrigate tomatoes, potatoes, melons, cucumbers, and fruit trees. In October of that year, Horace Greeley visited for the first time the town that had taken his name.

In 1877, Greeley was designated seat of old Weld County, which included almost all of what is now northeastern Colorado, including Logan, Washington, Morgan, Sedgwick, Phillips, and Yuma counties. Weld County, named for Lewis Leyard Weld, whom Abraham Lincoln appointed Colorado Territory's first Secretary in 1861, was reduced to its present size in 1899.

During the last quarter of the 19th century and into the 20th, Greeley began to grow proportionately more potatoes, and "Greeley Spuds" earned a national reputation. In addition, the surrounding area began to develop as a ranching center, with huge herds of beef cattle blanketing the plains. In 1890, Greeley citizens matched $10,000 in state funding to establish the University of Northern Colorado, which opened its doors in 1899.

Shortly after the turn of the century, farmers in Weld and other Platte River Valley counties began to contract with sugar companies to grow sugar beets. Sugar factories were built in Greeley and other nearby towns. From the early 1900s through the 1930s, the area attracted large numbers of immigrants, who came to work in the newly built factories and in the productive fields, as well as to take advantage of homesteading opportunities. According to a recent edition of *Greeley Style Magazine*, many current residents' German, Russian, Japanese, and Hispanic roots date to early 20th-century recruiting.

Greeley remained true to the vision of its founding fathers for its first 100 years, and it wasn't until 1969 that the sale of liquor was allowed within the city limits. In the 1980s, James Michener lived in Greeley while he researched and wrote *Centennial,* his fictionalized account of the history of the town and area. Anyone looking to learn more about Greeley and Weld County would do well by Michener's novel.

SIGHTS

Meeker House Museum

Listed on the National Register of Historic Places, this was the home of Greeley founder Nathan Meeker, who built the two-story brick house in 1870. The museum offers docent-led tours of the adobe building and offers an opportunity to view some of Meeker's personal belongings and furniture, as well as other artifacts collected from the area.

The Meeker Museum is located at 1324 9th Avenue. Memorial Day through Labor Day, the museum is open Tues.-Sat. 10 a.m.-5 p.m., and the rest of the year it's open Tues.-Sat. 10 a.m.-3 p.m. Admission is $2.50 ($1 for kids 6-12 and seniors 60 and older). Costs also include admission to Centennial Village (see below). For more information, phone (303) 350-9221.

Centennial Village Museum

This multi-structure museum complex occupies five acres and offers an interpretive history of Greeley and Weld County from 1860-1920. Exhibits and buildings include an 1863 log courthouse, an 1872 cottage, and a turn-of-the-century church and one-room schoolhouse, as well as displays emphasizing the importance of agriculture, such as a granary and an early-20th-century sugar beet shanty. Guided tours take about an hour. There's also a small gift shop, where you can buy souvenirs, books on local history, and homemade candy.

The Centennial Village Museum, at 1475 A St., is open Memorial Day through Labor Day, Tues.-Sat. 10 a.m.-5 p.m. and Sun. 1-5 p.m. The rest of the year it's open Tues.-Sat. 10 a.m.-3 p.m. Admission is $2.50 ($1 for kids 6-12 and seniors 60 and older), which includes entrance to the Meeker House Museum (see above). For more information, phone (303) 350-9224.

Greeley Municipal Museum

A gallery and research center, this museum exhibits traveling displays and stores archives on the history of Greeley and Weld County. In addition, the museum houses the Colorado Collection: rare, out-of-print, and contemporary books and journals on all aspects of the state. The museum is located at 919 7th St. and is open Tues.-Sat. 9 a.m.-5 p.m. Admission is free, tours available. For more information, phone (303) 350-9220.

Fort Vasquez

Located on Hwy. 85 in Platteville, about 18 miles south of Greeley, this National Historical Society site is a WPA-constructed model of the original Fort Vasquez, which was built in 1835. Originally established as a trading post where mountain men and Plains tribes swapped furs, weapons, and tools, the Fort Vasquez enterprise was a relatively short-lived one. Today the visitor center next to the fort offers an overview of early-19th-century South Platte Valley fur trade. In addition to viewing the displays in the visitor center, you can also tour the fort itself.

Fort Vasquez is open to visitors Memorial Day through Labor Day, Mon.-Sat. 10 a.m.-5 p.m. and Sun. 1-5 p.m. For more information, phone (303) 785-2832.

PARKS AND RECREATION

City Parks

Greeley's got over two dozen city parks scattered within its boundaries. **Lincoln Park,** across the street from the downtown mall, has lush lawns and shade trees and is perfect for picnicking. Another nice city park is **Bittersweet Park,** at 16th St. and 35th Ave., which has lawns, shade, and playground equipment. For more information on Greeley's city parks, contact the **Parks and Recreation Department,** 651 10th Ave., tel. (303) 350-9400.

Golf

Greeley's **Highland Hills Municipal Golf Course** is located on the west side of town off 20th St. (2200 Clubhouse Dr.). For information and tee times, phone (303) 330-7327. The **Eaton Country Club,** in Eaton about 10 miles north of Greeley on Hwy. 85, is an 18-hole "championship course" with a restaurant and banquet room. Phone 454-2106.

ACCOMMODATIONS

You'll find accommodations in Greeley ranging from mom-and-pop motels to convention-center complexes and a bed and breakfast. A **Motel 6,** tel. (303) 351-6481, is located on the south side of town at 3015 8th Avenue. The **Best Western Ramkota Inn and Conference Center,** tel. 353-8444, is right downtown kitty-corner from the Greeley Mall; doubles run about $60. At the Greeley **Holiday Inn,** 609 8th Ave., tel. 356-3000, you can also get doubles for around $60.

The **Sterling House,** tel. 351-8805, is a very tastefully done bed and breakfast in a gorgeous 1886 Victorian home at 818 12th St. (only two rooms available). Full breakfast included, and evening meals can be arranged with advance notice.

Greeley Campground and RV Park, tel. 353-6476, a mile east of town on Hwy. 34, has 95 sites on 10 acres.

FOOD

Bruce's

Call them what you will, bull fries, prairie oysters, swinging steaks, or the more popular Rocky Mountain oysters, but the best, well, bull testicles around are (reportedly!) served up at Bruce's, located west of Greeley in Severance. Sliced thin, breaded, and deep fried, Bruce's fries are very popular—folks go nuts for 'em. In fact, Bruce's owners Ruth and Betty Schott sell between 20 and 25 tons of the things a year and have been known to let patrons think they were eating "headless and tailless shrimp." A recent *Rocky Mountain News* article quoted Schott as saying, "I always tell people to come to Severance and have a ball." Travelers watching their weight or red-meat intake might want to try the turkey variety.

Like something out of *Thelma and Louise,* Bruce's doubles as a Western bar and has been open since 1958. Regular customers include members of the Denver Broncos, whose summer training camp is in Greeley. Outside the restaurant are murals of bulls holding picket signs reading "Unfair" and "Very Unfair." Inside is a painting of a rather startled and angry-looking bull experiencing "the procedure." Saturday nights, locals come to dance and drink beer. You can also get a freshly shot goose cleaned for $6.

To get there, take Hwy. 85 north about 10 miles to Eaton, and go west another nine miles. Phone (303) 686-2320.

Other Greeley Food

If you don't have the stomach for Rocky Mountain oysters, or don't feel like driving up to Severance, you'll find plenty of more conventional cuisine in Greeley—lots of fast-food places and other restaurants. A favorite is **Potato Brumbaugh's,** 2400 17th St., tel. (303) 356-6340, named for the fictional owner of Brumbaugh Feed Lots in *Centennial.* Specialties include steaks, chicken, and seafood.

ENTERTAINMENT

With the 10,000-student University of Northern Colorado in town, Greeley offers more in the way of entertainment than the many other plains communities that roll up the sidewalk when the sun goes down. In addition to clubs that book live dance music—from bluegrass to rock 'n' roll—Greeley also has a philharmonic orchestra, chamber orchestra, and a number of community theater groups. One of the most popular and successful is UNC's **Little Theatre of the Rockies,** which has been producing plays since 1934. Performances, including comedy, drama, and musicals, run throughout July on the university campus. For information and schedules, write Little

Theater of the Rockies, College of Performing and Visual Arts, University of Northern Colorado, Greeley, CO 80639, or phone (303) 351-2200.

CALENDAR

Semana Latina ("Latin Week") in early May is a week-long celebration of the area's Hispanic heritage. Festivities include music, dance, and poetry readings, and exhibits demonstrate contributions to politics, education, and other aspects of Greeley and Weld County life. The event is designed to highlight Cinco de Mayo. For more information, contact the Greeley Cultural Affairs Office, 919 7th St., Greeley, CO 80631, tel. (303) 353-6123.

No urban cowboys, Greeley's bronc riders are the real McCoy.

One of Greeley's most popular annual events is the **Greeley Independence Stampede,** running from late June through the Fourth of July. The eight-day celebration features rodeos, barbecues, lots of live music, and a Fourth of July parade, culminating with an evening of fireworks displays. For information, phone 356-BULL. The **Weld County Fair** in August provides a forum for local farmers and ranchers to display their prize crops and critters, as well as for local bakers, canners, and sewing hobbyists to compete for best pies, peaches, and quilts. Contact the Weld County Extension Office, tel. 356-4000.

For more information or for a complete calendar of events, contact the convention and visitors bureau.

SHOPPING

Greeley's downtown mall is a very pleasant retail shopping area, with a full range of shops and boutiques, as well as cafés, benches, and shade trees. Ideally located across the street from Lincoln Park, the mall offers an excellent opportunity to stroll about to get a feel for Greeley and its people.

The newly built Greeley Mall is a generic mall located at the Hwy. 34 bypass and 23rd Avenue. You'll find what you expect: Sears, JCPenney, Joslin's, etc.

SERVICES

Phone the **Greeley Police** at (303) 350-9605, the **Weld County Sheriff** at 356-4000. **North Colorado Medical Center** is located at 1801 16th St., tel. 352-4121. The Greeley **post office** is at 925 11th Ave., tel. 353-0398.

Recycling
You can drop off most recyclables in Greeley at the **King Soopers** store at 2712 11th Ave., or at **Greeley-Weld Recycle** with locations at 310 8th St. and 2699 47th Avenue. For more information, phone (303) 352-8312.

INFORMATION

The **Greeley Convention and Visitors Bureau** publishes several guides and directories you'll probably find very useful. Stop by their offices at 1407 8th Ave., or phone (303) 352-3566. Be sure to ask for a copy of *Greeley Style Magazine,* which runs stories on Greeley and Weld County history, reviews restaurants, and profiles local businesspeople. For subscription information, write Box 5195, Greeley, CO 80631.

The **Greeley Municipal Museum** contains the Colorado Collection: new, rare, and out-of-print books on the area and state. The museum is located at 919 7th St. and is open Tues.-Sat. 9 a.m.-5 p.m., tel. 350-9220. You can also get information on Greeley, Weld County, and Colorado at the Greeley **public library,** 917 7th Street.

TRANSPORTATION

The **Greeley/Weld County Airport** is located at 600 Crosier Ave., tel. (303) 356-9141. Rent cars from most national agencies, plus **Econo Rent-A-Car,** 1030 7th Ave., tel. 351-6969, and **Garnesy and Wheeler Rent-A-Car,** 1108 8th Ave., tel. 353-1111. For taxi service, phone **Shamrock Taxi** at 352-3000.

Public transportation is available on Greeley's "The Bus," which has routes throughout town. For schedule information, phone 350-9BUS.

NORTH OF GREELEY

Highway 85 continues north from Greeley, paralleling I-25 all the way to Cheyenne. Between Nunn and Rockport, a distance of about 20 miles, the highway skirts the western edge of **Pawnee National Grassland.** The area is open to the public and offers the amateur geologist a fascinating case study. For a description of the region, see "The Interstate 76-South Platte Corridor" in the following chapter. You can get information and maps from the Grasslands headquarters, located in Greeley at 660 O St., tel. (303) 353-5004.

FORT COLLINS AND VICINITY

Fort Collins (pop. 94,000; elev. 5,004 feet) is located 60 miles north of Denver on the Cache La Poudre River just east of sprawling Roosevelt National Forest. A college town, Fort Collins offers plenty of outdoor as well as indoor activities: What better way to wind up a day on the lake than by quaffing a locally made ale and digging a local blues band's rendition of "Good Mornin', Little School Girl"?

Though the Fort Collins-area economy has traditionally relied on ranching and farming for its stability, the last decade has seen an influx of modern industry, with several large companies, including Hewlett-Packard and NCR, building plants nearby. In addition, Colorado State University has a growing reputation as a center for high-caliber research and has been instrumental in linking academia and agriculture. The result has been an increase in the efficiency and productivity of local farmers and a state-of-the-art agricultural technology that Fort Collins proudly exports. About 20,000 students attend the university, which is the city's largest employer (nearly 8,000).

Fort Collins's plains location guarantees a fairly moderate climate (local boosters claim the sun shines some 300 days a year), yet the city is close enough to the Front Range of the Rockies to allow for daytrips to some of the state's best hiking, backpacking, mountain biking, skiing, and other sports. One of the highlights of the downtown area is the newly renovated Old Town, a couple of square blocks where you can visit boutiques and bookstores, gift shops and galleries, and pubs and restaurants with fountain-side outdoor seating perfect for people-watching. Cart vendors also sell a variety of items, from tie-dyed T-shirts and novelty sunglasses to frozen yogurt.

HISTORY

As one of the last stops for fur trappers heading west into the rugged Rocky Mountains, the prairie lands surrounding what is now Fort Collins, as well as the various local waterways and routes leading into the high country, were well known by early-19th-century mountain men and the Native Americans with whom they traded and sometimes fought. In fact, the Cache La Poudre River, which runs north of town, takes its name from the French trappers who, to lighten their loads before heading up into the snow, often stashed their powder barrels in the lower river basin.

The Colorado gold rushes of the mid-1800s brought the first real settlers to the Fort Collins area—many of them frustrated miners who hadn't hit pay dirt in the mountains. In 1862, Camp Collins (named for U.S. Cavalry Lt. Col. William O. Collins) was established to protect traders traveling the Overland Trail, which passed about five miles north of present-day Fort Collins. On June 9, 1864, the camp was wiped out by flood, and three months later a new post (Fort Collins) was established downstream. During the 1870s and '80s, a series of irrigation canals was built in the area, allowing for much more efficient farming—primarily wheat, oats, and barley—and establishing the economic base that still exists. By 1872, Fort Collins could claim a hotel, general store, and post office.

In 1876, the town was hit by a horde of grasshoppers, which, along with the failure of Fort Collins's first bank, almost destroyed it. In fact it might have, were it not for the Colorado Central Railroad, which arrived the following year. In 1879, the first building of what would become Colorado State University was constructed—on land donated by the townspeople—and the Agricultural College of Colorado opened its doors for the first time in September of that year.

By the end of the 19th century, local farmers had begun to harvest sugar beets and alfalfa, and in the early 1900s the area was also prime cattle- and sheep-raising country. In 1910 the population of the town was over 8,000; by that time, however, Fort Collins's population had divided itself into two disparate camps, the "wets" and the "drys," the infamous Blue Laws having been enacted in 1896 (Fort Collins remained "dry" until 1969).

The addition of a college to Fort Collins proved fortuitous, as students and professors worked together on projects that greatly improved farming conditions and the quality of the crops. Eventually, the school began to earn a reputation as a frontrunner among the nation's agricultural colleges and began to attract students from beyond the nearby fields. Colorado State University, as it came to be known, was largely responsible for the town's increase in population, which doubled in the 1950s and '60s.

During the 1970s, the people of Fort Collins began to realize the importance of their own past (the Fort Collins Historical Society was founded in 1974), and by the 1980s the town was at work restoring itself: Old Town Square was an early '80s project that sought at once

to recognize the town's history and to attract shoppers and tourists by restoring the downtown area.

SIGHTS

Fort Collins Museum
Specializing in historical artifacts pertinent to the settling of the Fort Collins area, the Fort Collins Museum also curates a handful of the area's original buildings, which have been moved to the Library Park site just off College Avenue. A log cabin built by fur trapper Antoine Janis and purportedly one of the oldest buildings

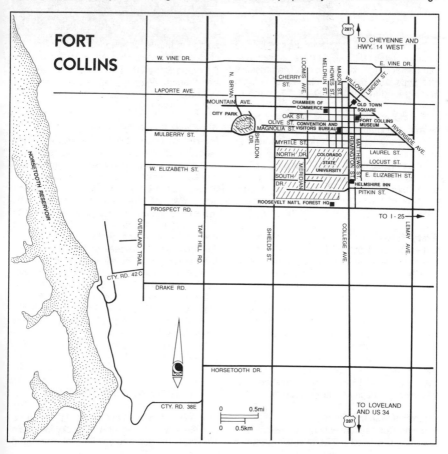

Fort Collins Museum is just two blocks from Old Town.

in the state, a stone cabin from the 1860s, and a schoolhouse built in 1884 have all been dismantled and moved to the park. The museum also houses an excellent selection of Folsom points found in the 1920s and '30s north of town.

The museum sits on a city block surrounded by lawn and shade trees, with picnic tables and a playground—the perfect post-museum-tour picnic site.

The Fort Collins Museum, located at 200 Matthews St. (two blocks east of College), is open Tues.-Sat. 10 a.m.-5 p.m. and Sun. from noon-5 p.m. Closed on Mondays and holidays. For more information, phone (303) 221-6738.

Avery House

Listed on the National Register of Historic Places, the sandstone Avery House was built in 1879 by Franklin C. Avery, a Fort Collins architect and banker. Descendants of Mr. Avery lived in the house until 1962, when it was obtained by the city, restored, and turned into a museum. The house contains original Avery-family furniture and decorations, in addition to other authentic period pieces.

The Avery House is located at 328 W. Mountain and is open the second and fourth Wednesdays of each month. For more information, contact the convention and visitors bureau.

Historical Walking Tours

The Fort Collins Convention and Visitors Bureau has designed a 22-site walking tour of some landmarks of historical Fort Collins. Included are the Avery House, several of the first Colorado State University buildings, and an early church, drugstore, and hotel. For a list of the sites and addresses, contact the convention and visitors bureau.

Anheuser-Busch, Inc. Brewery

Free tours of the state's fastest brewery (not to be confused with its largest, the Coors plant in Golden, or its best, the Wynkoop in Denver) are offered at this facility year-round. (Smaller-quantity and home brewers scorn both speed and size; how much beer and how fast you can make it are generally in opposite proportion to its quality.) In addition to viewing the brewing and packaging processes, visitors also get to see the Budweiser Clydesdales and taste some beer before browsing in the gift shop (natch!).

A relative newcomer to Colorado brewing, having opened for production in 1988, the Bud brewery is open to visitors daily 10 a.m.-5 p.m., May-Oct., and Wed.-Sun. 9 a.m.-4 p.m., Nov.-April. To get there, take I-25 north from town to Mountain Vista Dr. (Exit 271), and turn right onto Busch Drive. For more information, phone (303) 490-4691.

PARKS AND RECREATION

Fort Collins's location at the foot of the Rockies and virtually in the shadow of Rocky Mountain National Park guarantees plenty of year-round outdoor activity for residents and passers-through. Not to be overlooked, though, are the great numbers of recreational possibilities outside the park and mountains—from fishing in nearby lakes and streams to cycling, hiking, and golf in the warmer months to cross-country skiing in the winter.

City Parks

Fort Collins has several large city parks and many smaller neighborhood parks. **City Park,** 1500 W. Mulberry, has lots of lawns for tossing Frisbees or napping, picnic facilities, a fitness course, and fishing (at the small lake). For tennis or horseshoes, try **Edora Park,** 1420 E. Stuart, where you'll also find a public swimming pool and ice-skating rink. **Lee Martinez Park** features picnic facilities, tennis courts, and softball fields. You can also visit Martinez Park's 12-acre farm and experience first-hand the responsibilities of raising animals and harvesting crops (kids can pet the animals). For information, phone (303) 221-6665. **Roland Moore Park,** 2201 S. Shields, has indoor handball and racquetball courts, in addition to hiking and biking trails and a picnic area.

For more information on Fort Collins city parks, phone the **Parks and Recreation Department** at 221-6640.

Horsetooth Reservoir

Horsetooth Reservoir is a popular recreational area just southwest of Fort Collins. The 4,000 acres of water and its rocky shoreline attract lots of outdoor enthusiasts, particularly in the warmer months when folks flock to the water to escape the heat. **Horsetooth Mountain Park** borders the lake and offers fishing (for bass, trout, and landlocked salmon), waterskiing, windsurfing, picnicking, horseback riding, mountain biking, and backcountry camping. For information, contact the **Larimer County Parks Department** at (303) 226-4517.

Lory State Park is located on the northwest shore of Horsetooth Reservoir. In addition to hiking and

mountain biking on the park's two-dozen-plus miles of trails, you can explore the area on horseback. At **Double Diamond Stables** you can rent horses by the hour, join a group on a breakfast, lunch, or dinner ride, or rent a carriage. For information, write 710 Lodgepole, Bellvue, CO, or phone 224-4200. Lory State Park also offers fishing and birdwatching, and is a favorite place to check out the wildflowers in spring and early summer. For more on Lory State Park, contact the **Colorado Division of Parks and Outdoor Recreation,** 3842 S. Mason, Fort Collins, CO 80525, tel. 226-6641.

To get to Horsetooth, head west from downtown to Overland Trail; then take County Rd. 42C (which runs into Overland between Prospect and Drake). You can also get there by heading west on Hwy. 287 through LaPorte and turning west at the Bellvue exit.

Colorado State Forest

Located about 70 miles west of Fort Collins via Hwy. 287 and CO 14 (and 10,276-foot Cameron Pass), Colorado State Forest offers excellent hiking and backpacking, as well as camping, fishing, and sightseeing. Write Colorado State Forest, Star Route Box 91, Walden, CO 80480, or phone (303) 723-8366.

Cycling

Any self-respecting college town's got to have its share of bike paths and mountain-bike trails, where students can go to alleviate post-exam stress (or avoid thinking about an exam on the horizon). No exception, Fort Collins has nearly 60 miles of city bikeways, and the city is dedicated to making cycling safe and convenient. The *Tour de Fort Bike Guide* is a city map that designates a variety of interconnecting routes, including some set aside for pedestrians and cyclists only. The guides are available at local bike shops, as well as from the chamber of commerce and the convention and visitors bureau.

Local mountain bikers like to head into Roosevelt National Forest or Colorado State Forest, west of town via CO 14. For maps and

BOB RACE

information on biking in the national forest, stop by its headquarters at 240 W. Prospect, or phone (303) 498-1100. State forest information is available from the main office in Walden; phone 723-8366.

The **Never Summer Nordic Yurt System** is a hut-to-hut cross-country skiing system open in the summer to mountain bikers. There are three yurts (small cabins that sleep six) and an interconnecting series of trails. The area is located in Colorado State Forest about 70 miles west of Fort Collins (east of Walden). For reservations and more information, write Box 1254, Fort Collins, CO 80522, or phone 484-3903.

Closer to town, **Horsetooth Reservoir** offers a decent amount and range of off-road cycling on 2,100 acres of public land (county maintained). Small entrance fee.

Golf

The city of Fort Collins maintains three municipal golf courses, and there are a handful of private courses in the area. **City Park Nine** is a nine-hole course at City Park (411 S. Bryan). For information and tee times, phone (303) 221-6650. The other two city courses are **Collindale Golf Course,** 1441 E. Horsetooth, tel. 221-6651, and **Southridge Greens,** 5750 S. Lemay, tel. 226-2828, both 18-hole courses.

Link-N-Greens, 777 E. Lincoln, tel. 221-4818, is a public course offering nine holes and a lighted driving range. Private courses include the **Fort Collins Country Club,** north of town on Country Club Dr. (off College), tel. 482-1336.

Hiking

Fort Collins is located close to some of the state's best hiking areas. Rocky Mountain National Park and Roosevelt National Forest offer hundreds of miles of trails to wander, woods to explore, and peaks to bag.

The **Colorado Mountain Club,** based in Estes Park, hosts day and overnight trips into the backcountry. Phone their main office at (303) 586-6623; for the name and number of the current Fort Collins Outing Chairman, phone the Denver office at 922-8315.

The **Mountain Shop,** 632 S. Mason, tel. 493-5720, is an excellent source for expert advice and quality equipment; they also carry maps and rent gear.

Fishing

Several of the lakes in the Fort Collins area offer good fishing for bass, crappie, walleye, and other warm-water fish. At Horsetooth Reservoir, you can cast for warm-water fish as well as trout and kokanee salmon; the reservoir is especially well regarded for its large lake trout. There are public boat launches and marinas at Horsetooth, though fishing can be productive from the shore as well. Kids might enjoy fishing for panfish at the small lake at City Park.

If you'd rather not take chances of getting skunked (or if you don't want to buy a license), **Frank's Trout Pond,** 2912 W. Mulberry, tel. (303) 482-5102, is stocked with hungry fish you pay for by the inch. (See also "West of Fort Collins," following.)

Rafting

Several companies in Fort Collins and the surrounding area offer whitewater rafting trips on the Cache La Poudre, Arkansas, and Green rivers. Phone **Adrift Adventures** at (303) 493-4005 or (800) 824-0150 (from Denver). Trips are also offered by **Wildwater, Inc.,** tel. 224-3379, and **Wanderlust Adventures,** tel. 484-1219.

Cross-country Skiing

Excellent cross-country skiing opportunities await the Fort Collins-area three-pinner—from the woods of Roosevelt National Forest to the valleys of Rocky Mountain National Park, and a lot closer to town as well, including the trails around Horsetooth Reservoir.

The **Never Summer Nordic Yurt System** offers hut-to-hut Nordic skiing in Colorado State Forest. Sleeping six people each, the three yurts are connected by an intricate series of backcountry trails. For reservations and more information, write Box 1254, Fort Collins, CO 80522, or phone (303) 484-3903.

The best source for information on Nordic skiing around Fort Collins is **The Mountain Shop,** 632 S. Mason, tel. 493-5270. In addition to providing advice, rental gear, and maps, the store also stocks quality equipment and clothing.

You can also get information and maps from Roosevelt National Forest Headquarters, 240 W. Prospect, Fort Collins, CO 80526, tel. 498-1100.

Crested Butte is one of the country's great ski towns.
(Crested Butte Mountain Resort Association, Grafton Marshall Smith)

(top) totally tubular, Fraser tubing hill north of Winter Park; (bottom) over the river and through the woods, near Redstone (both photos: Stephen Metzger)

ACCOMMODATIONS

A college town that attracts everyone from students' parents and visiting professors to students' party buds and other low-budget travelers looking for cheap digs must offer a wide range of accommodations options, and Fort Collins does. At one end, the **Motel 6,** tel. (303) 382-6466, offers its proverbially clean albeit systemically homogenized rooms at about $30 for doubles; located at 3900 E. Mulberry. Doubles at the **Inn at Fort Collins,** just south of the college at 2612 S. College Ave., tel. 226-2600, start at about $35. You'll find at least a dozen more motels on the north end of town on College Ave. (Hwy. 287).

For more upscale lodging, the **Helmshire Inn,** tel. 493-4683, on College Ave. right across from the school, offers rooms for two in a converted hotel for about $70, which includes a continental breakfast and access to health club facilities. The Fort Collins **Holiday Inn,** 425 W. Prospect, tel. 482-2626, has doubles for $45-70. At the **Ramada Inn,** 3709 E. Mulberry, tel. 493-7800, you can get a room for two for about $45. The Fort Collins **Marriott,** 350 E. Horsetooth, tel. 226-5200 or (800) 548-2635, has doubles for about $80-100.

The Fort Collins **Mile High KOA** campground, tel. 493-9758, is located about 10 miles northwest of town on Hwy. 287.

FOOD

Start Me Up

For breakfast, it's tough to find a place with a better reputation than the **Silver Grill Café,** 218 Walnut, tel. (303) 484-4656. Serving the residents of Fort Collins since the 1930s, the Silver Grill specializes in gargantuan cinnamon rolls, and it dishes up other standard American fare as well.

The **Patio Café** in Old Town Square is also a very nice place to relax over breakfast. With seating on the mall (and inside as well), this little restaurant specializes in dishes with a Southwestern bent (breakfast burritos), as well as elegant egg dishes (various versions of eggs Benedict); prices range from $3.50-5.50.

Lunch And Dinner

If you're looking for a lunch spot with lots of local flavor, stop in at **Coopersmith's Brew Pub,** tel. (303) 498-0483, in Old Town Square. Quaff a beer (Scottish Ale, India Pale, or Oatmeal Stout) while you munch on bangers and mash, fish and chips, bratwurst, or a burger with artichoke hearts, scallions, and sour cream. Coopersmith's also serves stir fry, steaks, salads, and homemade desserts; lunches and dinners run $4-8. Open Mon.-Sat. 11 a.m.-2 a.m. and Sun. 11 a.m.-midnight.

Across the square, **Old Town Ale House,** tel. 493-2213, also serves pub fare—soups, salads, and sandwiches run $4-8—with one of the best beer selections in town, including several British Isle beers on tap. **Chesterfield, Bottomsley, and Potts,** 1415 W. Elizabeth, tel. 221-1139, is a sports bar (eight big-screen TVs) very popular with the college crowd. Over 50 imported beers, and the local paper's pick as "best burger in town" for three years in a row.

One of Fort Collins's hot spots for south-of-the-border fare is the **Rio Grande Mexican Restaurant,** 150 N. College, tel. 224-5428, which serves traditional Mexican food, as well as Tex-Mex, with dinners running $5-8; lunch specials are $4-6, and you can get a mini-margarita for 99 cents. (The Rio Grande has a sister restaurant in Boulder just below the Pearl Street Mall.)

Another standby is **Old Chicago,** 147 S. College, tel. 482-8599, serving pizza, pastas, salads, over 125 types of beer, and patio dining. Open for lunch and dinner. Prices range from $5-12.

Also popular for Italian food is **Canino's,** 613 S. College, tel. 493-7205. A long-time family-owned favorite, Canino's offers take-out and delivery as well.

If you start feeling guilty after gorging yourself on pub fare, pasta, burritos de pollo, and local brew, and you're looking for something healthful to pack for the road, stop in at **Fort Collins Food Co-op,** tel. 484-7448, 250 E. Mountain (just around the corner from Old Town Square). The little shop carries organically grown fruits and vegetables, in addition to juices, nuts, breads, and other goods.

For the best Rocky Mountain oysters in the area, check out **Bruce's** in Severance, just southeast of Fort Collins (see "Food" under "Greeley and Vicinity" above).

ENTERTAINMENT

Any college town has got to have places where folks can let loose on weekends, and Fort Collins doesn't disappoint. **Mishawaka Inn,** tel. (303) 482-4420, located about 14 miles up Poudre Canyon north of town, regularly features surprisingly big-name acts, which have included Hot Tuna, Jerry Jeff Walker, and Asleep at the Wheel.

In Old Town Square, the **Old Town Ale House,** tel. 493-2213, features live music most nights, while just across the mall, the **Comedy Works,** tel. 221-5481, books local and club-circuit comics. **The Page,** tel. 482-1714, is a small club at 181 N. College where you can dance to live rock, blues, and jazz.

A favorite of the college crowd is **Fort Ram,** 450 N. Linden, tel. 482-5026—live music from time to time, but other nights, DJs play dance music. **Linden's,** 214 Linden, tel. 482-9291, specializes in blues—Chicago and Delta—and also books pure rock 'n' roll bands. Open jam sessions Monday nights.

CALENDAR

There's an event or festival of one kind or another almost every weekend in Fort Collins, either at the university or downtown. Highlights include the **Colorado Brewfest** in late June, where you can sample the pilsners and porters of Colorado's many microbreweries, munch from a wide range of food booths, and listen to a variety of ethnic music. On the **Fourth of July** there's a fair with food, music, and fireworks at City Park, and in mid-September balloons from the Fort Collins **Balloon Festival** fill the sky. The **Octoberfest,** during the first week of October, features street dancing, traditional food and drink, and a general sense of revelry and carrying on.

For a complete calendar of Fort Collins's annual events, contact the chamber of commerce or convention and visitors bureau.

SHOPPING

Old Town Square, located in one of Fort Collins's original financial centers, is one of the town's true delights. Built in the early 1980s, with a fountain to keep it cool and several cafés with patio seating, the little shopping mall offers several different retail shops, galleries, as well as cart vendors selling T-shirts, jewelry, and souvenirs. **Children's Mercantile** has tons of kids' games, toys, and an exceptional selection of books. **Colorado Classics** carries menswear and specializes in Western duds, particularly Pendleton shirts. **Trimble Court Artisans** and **Walnut Street Gallery** are worth poking your head into if you're interested in prints, posters, and art by local craftspeople.

Farmers Market

Every Wednesday 3-6 p.m., local farmers (and remember, this is one of the agricultural capitals of the state) sell their freshly picked wares in the parking lot at the corner of College Ave. and History Cabin.

SERVICES

The offices of the Fort Collins **Police Department** are at 300 Laporte; phone (303) 221-6540. Phone the Larimer County **Sheriff** at 221-7000; offices are located at 200 W. Oak. **State Patrol** offices are at 2412 E. Mulberry; phone 484-4020. **Poudre Valley Hospital,** tel. 482-4111 or (800) 284-5241, is located at 1024 S. Lemay Avenue.

Fort Collins's main **post office** is located in the Federal Building; phone 482-2837.

Recycling

The **King Soopers** stores at 1015 Taft Hill Rd. and 2325 S. College take aluminum, glass, newspaper, and plastics.

INFORMATION

The offices of the **Fort Collins Convention and Visitors Bureau,** tel. (303) 482-5821 or (800) 274-FORT, are at 420 S. Howes St., Suite 101, where you'll also find the Fort Collins Information Center; the folks here are always good for information on things to do and see (and where to spend your money) in the area. The **Fort Collins Chamber of Commerce,** tel. 482-3746, is located at 225 S. Meldrun, across College Ave. from Old Town Square. Be sure to pick up a copy of *The Guide to Fort Collins,* which contains listings of parks, restaurants, nightclubs, shopping centers, and other attractions. The Fort Collins **public library** is at 201 Peterson, tel. 221-6740.

Stone Lion Books, tel. 493-0030, in Old Town Square, has a wide selection of books on local and state history, as well as on recreation.

The local daily is the *Fort Collins Coloradan,* a Gannett paper. For subscription information, phone 224-7730.

TRANSPORTATION

America West, Continental, and **Delta** airlines fly into **Fort Collins-Loveland Municipal Airport,** tel. (303) 221-1300, about five miles south of town off I-25. Private-plane pilots can fly directly into **Fort Collins Airpark,** located near the downtown area; phone 484-4186 or 482-6588.

Airport Express, tel. 482-0505, has shuttle service between Denver's Stapleton Airport and Fort Collins (as well as between Fort Collins and Cheyenne and Fort Collins and Laramie). Fort Collins's public transportation is **Transfort,** with regular routes throughout town; phone 221-6620 for rates and route information. For taxi service, phone **Yellow Cab** at tel. 493-8200 or **Shamrock Taxi** at tel. 224-2222.

Rent cars in Fort Collins from **Altra Auto Rental,** 115 E. Harmony Rd., tel. 226-3171; **Budget,** 516 S. College Ave., tel. 484-5574; **Choice Rent-a-Car,** tel. 226-6772; **Econo-Rate Rent-a-Car,** 3836 S. College Ave., tel. 221-2722; **Hertz,** 1235 N. College Ave., tel. 484-0077; **National,** 3404 E. Harmony, tel. 229-0704; **Rent-a-Wreck,** 134 W. Wilcox, tel. 224-3478; or **Ugly Duckling,** 602 S. College Ave., tel. 484-7443.

WEST OF FORT COLLINS

Highway 287 continues north through Fort Collins for a couple of miles, hooks to the west, then meanders north again, crossing the border into Wyoming and rolling into Laramie. From Fort Collins, it's about 68 miles to Laramie. Fourteen miles northwest of Fort Collins, you can catch CO 14 west through the Poudre River Canyon, Roosevelt National Forest, and Colorado State Forest, eventually arriving in the small town of Walden.

This is a wonderfully scenic route, taking you along the shores of the Cache La Poudre, past some excellent fishing spots and camping and picnic areas, through the Medicine Bow Mountains, and over Cameron Pass (elev. 10,276 feet) near the northwest corner of Rocky Mountain National Park. Along the 80-mile stretch from LaPort to Gould are numerous Forest Service access roads leading to more campgrounds. Be sure to check local fishing regulations, as some stretches of the Cache La Poudre have special restrictions.

Forest Service campgrounds along CO 14 include **Ansel Watrous,** 18 miles west of LaPort (open all year, pit toilets, no showers); **Kelly Flats,** 30 miles west (open mid-May to mid-Nov., pit toilets, no showers); and **Chambers Lake** (60 miles west, open June through Oct., pit toilets, no showers). In addition, camping is available in the **Red Feather Lakes** area northwest of Fort Collins, where a series of lakes offers good trout fishing just north of the Poudre River Canyon. Be sure to check local regulations; some of the waters have special restrictions. To get there, turn north onto Feather Lakes Rd. at Rustic.

For information on lodging and camping in the Feather Lakes Area, write **Poudre River— Red Feather Lakes Tourist Council,** Box 505, Red Feather Lakes, CO 80545, or phone (800) 462-5870. For information on the other Forest Service campgrounds accessible from CO 14, contact the offices of **Roosevelt National Forest,** 240 W. Prospect Rd., Fort Collins, CO 80526, tel. (303) 498-1100.

STEPHEN METZGER

NORTHEASTERN COLORADO

NORTHEASTERN COLORADO HIGHLIGHTS

Fort Morgan: museum, Pawnee National Grassland, Pawnee Buttes

Sterling: Overland Trail Museum, parks, boating, fishing, Sugar Beet Days

Tamarack Ranch State Wildlife Area (Crook): 7,000-acre refuge

Limon: Twilight Train rides

Burlington: museum and Kit Carson County Carousel (national historic register)

This is not the Colorado most imagine when they think of the state. It's not John Denver's "Rocky Mountain High" or Boulder's progressive politics and New Ageism; nor is it Cripple Creek's Victorian shops or Colorado Springs' mountain vistas. Yet this part of Colorado offers the traveler something just as much a part of the state's soul and heartland: the plains, where people have been farming, ranching, and drawing their livelihoods from the soil and the sky for generations. It's a place where bumper stickers advise you to Eat Beef, where acres of sugar beets and alfalfa stretch as far as you can see, where folks haul ass on long, straight unpaved backroads in pickups and Cadillacs, like characters out of Larry McMurtry novels. It's a place where you can get not only a sense of rural Colorado and hard-working Coloradans but a very real taste of something that is truly and uniquely American as well.

Just listen to the names of some of the towns out here: Yuma, Burlington, Holyoke, Sedgwick, Heartstrong, Haxtun, Crook—most of them blink-and-you'll-miss-it towns where things are so slow and the citizenry so insulated that if you do slow down you're likely to be given the once-over by just about everyone you pass on the street, from the kid in the high-school letter jacket and his young adoring girlfriend to the retired

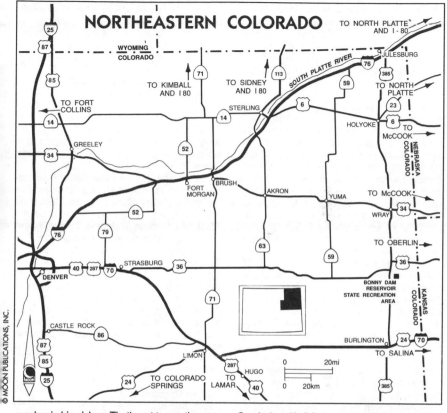

rancher in his pickup. That's not to say the people out here aren't friendly. On the contrary, they welcome passers-through, and they'll usually go out of their way to help you find a restaurant or coffee shop, campground, park or picnic area. In fact, get a local talking about his town—or, more accurately, his county—and you'll have a tough time getting him to stop. These are proud people, and they love their county fairs, livestock shows, and harvest festivals.

Long before the white man arrived here, these grasslands had been home to roaming bands of Cheyenne and Arapahoe, who hunted the prairie's great herds of buffalo. As early as the 1820s, though, traders and trappers began infringing on Native American lands, working the South Platte area (which parallels present-day I-76 from Julesburg to Fort Morgan, then veers northwest to

Greeley) and building a series of forts and trading posts. Like the buffalo, though, which within a few years would be all but extinct on the American plains, the beaver, which had once been abundant in the South Platte, were quickly too few to be very profitable. By the 1850s, interest in trapping along the South Platte was dying out.

Toward the end of the 1850s, however, gold was discovered at Pikes Peak and Cherry Creek (near what is now Englewood, a suburb of Denver), and prospectors began streaming across Colorado, many of them following the South Platte corridor. In 1860, Julesburg became a stop on the short-lived Pony Express Trail, and though that enterprise only lasted a year, when the Union Pacific Railroad arrived in Julesburg in 1867, the sleepy little hamlet was transformed almost overnight: Its dance halls and saloons, prostitutes and gamblers earned it the nickname, "the wickedest little town in the West." (Actually, the present town of Julesburg is not in the same location as the Julesburg of the 1860s; there were, in fact, four separate Julesburgs, the current one having been founded in 1881.)

During the early 20th century, the South Platte Valley became prized for its sugar beets, and although other crops—including alfalfa, wheat, and other grains—are grown out on these plains, it's the beets that have been sweetening the local economy for most of the century. Several northeastern Colorado towns, including Haxtun, Sterling, Merino, and Atwood, have relied heavily over the years on the annual beet harvest (beginning in October) for their economic survival. And even the towns whose economies are primarily livestock related also rely on the beets; ranchers in Fort Morgan, for example, fatten sheep on beet pulp.

Traveling through Northeastern Colorado today, whether by interstate or back road (the latter is advised), is in a way like stepping back in time. The pace in these little towns is a lot slower than it is in Denver, Colorado Springs, or Boulder. The stockyards are much the same as they were a hundred years ago, though ranching has changed considerably. Today, ranchers buy and sell by computer and telephone (don't be surprised to see them sitting in coffee shops or behind the wheels of their pickups, talking into cellular phones), though the weather, with its ability to capriciously determine fates, still dominates conversation.

But don't write Northeastern Colorado off as strictly a bunch of lazy cowtowns. Even if you're just passing through on your way to Vail, take the time to get off the main highways. Check out the Fort Morgan Museum, with its Glenn Miller display (Miller grew up in Fort Morgan), the Overland Trail Museum in Sterling, or the Kit Carson County Carousel (a hand-carved merry-go-round) built in 1905 and designated a National Historic Landmark). Or just take the time to drive through the grasslands, imagining a time when the country wasn't in such a hurry.

Northeastern Colorado Information
You'll find a **Northeast Colorado Gateway Information Center** at the Julesburg exit off of I-76. Pick up brochures and publications promoting areas of historical and recreational interest, as well as information on lodging, dining, and sightseeing throughout the northeastern part of the state.

The **Northeast Colorado Visitor Information Center** is located just east of downtown Sterling between I-76 and the Platte River (take the Sterling exit). In Burlington, check out the **State of Colorado Welcome Center,** where you can get information on northeastern Colorado as well as on the rest of the state. The Colorado Tourism Board publishes the *Centennial Country Travel Guide,* which discusses the area's history, highlights specific areas of interest, and suggests several different tours. The publication is available at visitor centers, as well as at the Logan County and Sterling chambers of commerce. To receive prepared tourist packets of information on Northeastern Colorado, phone (800) 544-8609, or write Box 1683, Sterling, CO 80751.

Further Reading
James Michener's typically sprawling historical novel *Centennial* explores in great depth and detail the history of this part of Colorado, as well as the area just to the west. As in most Michener novels, in which the setting becomes a central character, the plains play a pivotal part. Locals claim the town in which most of the book takes place was based on Greeley, Colorado (see "North Central Colorado").

THE INTERSTATE 76-
SOUTH PLATTE CORRIDOR

Interstate 76 angles from Denver up to a point about as close to the precise northeastern corner of Colorado as you can get. The drive from Denver to Julesburg, just two miles from the Nebraska border, is a little over 200 miles and it's flat, fast, and arrow straight. Without stopping, it will take less than four hours. Along the way, though, are a handful of museums and other diversions that are well worth exploring if you've got the time. The Overland Trail Museum in Sterling, for example, with its displays from the 19th century, will give you a better sense of the area's history and of its land and people. Another good way to better appreciate the region is to stay off the interstate entirely: A series of two-lane highways parallels both the South Platte and I-76, from Fort Morgan to Julesburg, passing through several tiny farming and ranching towns and communities along the way. The little general stores and watering holes provide great opportunities to experience local color.

FORT MORGAN AND VICINITY

Fort Morgan (pop. 8,628; elev. 4,330 feet) is the seat of Morgan County, one of the smallest (1,296 square miles) but most agriculturally rich counties in the state. Producing a wide variety of crops, including sugar beets, wheat, beans, alfalfa, onions, barley, and potatoes, Morgan County relies on Fort Morgan as a shipping and distribution hub. The area is also known for its beef, sheep, and dairy ranches.

Founded in 1864 as a military post to protect gold rushers and other travelers on the Overland Trail, Fort Morgan was originally called Camp Tyler, then Camp Wardell. The town assumed its present name in 1866 in honor of Colonel C.A. Morgan, the post's first commanding officer. The town today is one of quiet tree-lined streets, many with beautiful, well-maintained homes and large lush yards.

Fort Morgan Museum
Depicting Morgan County from the first nomadic bands of hunters up to bandleader Glenn Miller, who grew up here, this small museum displays artifacts and photos that testify to the area's varied history. Particularly worth checking out is the Koehler Site display, which explains the 1980 discovery at a nearby landfill of a prehistoric campsite. Also on display are Plains tribe moccasins, belts, and pipes, as well as an exhibit devoted to Miller, with many intriguing

The Northeastern Colorado Visitor Information Center in Sterling is a good source for advice and literature on the area.

STEPHEN METZGER

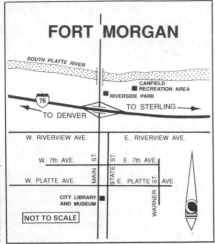

FORT MORGAN

SOUTH PLATTE RIVER

CANFIELD RECREATION AREA
RIVERSIDE PARK

76

TO DENVER

TO STERLING →

W. RIVERVIEW AVE.   E. RIVERVIEW AVE.

W. 7th AVE.   E. 7th AVE.

W. PLATTE AVE.   E. PLATTE AVE.

MAIN ST.   STATE ST.   WARNER ST.

CITY LIBRARY
AND MUSEUM

NOT TO SCALE

© MOON PUBLICATIONS, INC.

photos of him as a teenager and young man (Miller graduated from Fort Morgan High School in 1921), as well as a recreated soda fountain from the old Hillrose Drugstore, and a room reserved for traveling exhibits (usually with Western themes, from Navajo blankets to Charles Russell's paintings).

Museum hours are Mon. through Fri. 10 a.m.-5 p.m., Tues. through Thurs. evenings 6-8 p.m., and Sat. 11 a.m.-5 p.m. The Fort Morgan Museum is located at 414 Main Street. For more information, phone (303) 867-6331.

Riverside Park And Canfield Recreation Area

This large and beautiful city park just off the freeway (Exit 80) tempts the weary road warrior with shaded lawns, picnic tables, restrooms, volleyball, basketball, and tennis courts, horseshoe pits, and (for winter travelers) an ice-skating rink, as well as tons of playground equipment. The park is a perfect stop for a quick leg-stretch or maybe even a long afternoon nap under a shade tree. In addition, the park offers free overnight camping and has a swimming pool that's free and open to the public.

Pawnee National Grassland And Pawnee Buttes

The two separate units of Pawnee National Grassland sprawl on the plains of northern Weld

County, north of Greeley and Fort Morgan. Desolate, dry, and sparsely populated, the grasslands don't offer the traveler much in the way of views, especially when compared to the eastern slope of the Rockies looming just to the west. There are two startling exceptions, though, to all this flatness: Pawnee Buttes.

Rising over 250 feet above the plain, the two buttes, comprised of sedimentary rock protected by a layer of hard sandstone, have resisted the forces that have eroded the surrounding area. Of great interest to paleontologists and anthropologists, the buttes have yielded several prehistoric animals, including *Alticamelus*, a giraffe-like camel, and *Amphycyon*, a large animal that would appear today part dog and part bear, as well as an abundance of Native American artifacts (the area was once the hunting grounds of the Pawnee).

The Pawnee National Grassland and Buttes are open to the public, though getting to the Buttes does require some backroading. For more information and specific directions, see Lee Gregory's excellent book, *Colorado Scenic Guide, Northern Region*. You can also get more information, including maps, from the Pawnee National Grassland Office of the Forest Service, located in Greeley at 660 O St.; phone (303) 353-5004.

Golfing

The **Fort Morgan Municipal Golf Course,** tel. (303) 867-5990, is adjacent to Riverside Park and open to the public.

Accommodations

You can get good clean rooms right downtown at the **Park Terrace Best Western,** 725 Main St., tel. (303) 867-8256, as well as the **Econo Lodge,** 1409 Barlow (Exit 82), tel. 867-9481 or (800) 446-6900.

Services

Fort Morgan Police can be reached at (303) 867-5678. The offices of the **Morgan County Sheriff** are at 400 Warner; phone 867-2461. Phone the **State Patrol** at 867-6844 (emergencies) and 867-6657 (non-emergencies). **Fort Morgan Community Hospital** is located at 1000 Lincoln, tel. 867-3391. The central **post office** in Fort Morgan is at 300 State; phone 867-7111.

Recycling
Drop off most recyclables at **K and K Recycling,** 125 Park St. The **Safeway,** 620 W. Platte, takes aluminum. For more information on recycling in the Fort Morgan area, phone **All Trash Recycling** at (303) 867-3275 or 867-6196.

Information
The Fort Morgan **public library**, tel. (303) 867-9456, is located next door to the Fort Morgan Museum at 414 Main Street. For more information on Fort Morgan and Morgan County, phone the **Fort Morgan Chamber of Commerce**, tel. 867-6702, or write 300 Main St., Box 971, Fort Morgan, CO 80701. For **road and weather information**, phone 867-2021.

STERLING

The largest town in the ranching and farming country of the northeastern corner of Colorado, Sterling (pop. 1,200; elev. 3,945 feet), seat of Logan County, is a quiet little community with towering shade trees and old homes with long front porches. Only the southwestern end of town has been invaded by the proverbial Wal-Mart, K mart, Taco John's and other fast-food franchises. Its economy supported by cattle, sugar beets, corn, and alfalfa, Sterling hosts several agricultural and livestock festivals each year; the whole town'll turn out for a 4-H show or the annual alfalfa festival.

Calling itself the "City of Living Trees," Sterling is particularly proud of the dozen or so sculptures scattered around town, carved "on location" by Brad Rhea out of, well, living trees. These include "Skygrazers," a herd of giraffes stretching skyward; "The Dreamer," a clown; "Minute Man," and "The Golfer," the latter located, of course, at the Sterling Country Club.

In 1871, railroad surveyor David Leavitt passed through the area and was impressed enough with the valley to return the following year to begin ranching. The town of Sterling was founded a decade later in 1881, and originally settled by pioneers from Mississippi and Tennessee. The little town's riverside location led to rapid growth, and throughout the early- and mid-20th century, it served as a hub for area beet farmers. Today, many of Sterling's buildings, including the Logan County Courthouse, are on the National Register of Historic Places. Sterling's Northeastern Junior College, founded in 1941, offers a wide variety of fully accredited two-year programs in several different fields, including agriculture, humanities, business, sciences, and social sciences. For information on admissions or visiting the college, phone (303) 522-6600, ext. 651.

Overland Trail Museum
One of the best small-town museums in the state, the Overland Trail Museum features excellent displays of Native American clothing, tools, and weapons, pioneer clothing and domestic utensils, a grand piano shipped from Mississippi to

You might have trouble finding tofu burgers in parts of Colorado.

STEPHEN METZGER

one of Brad Rhea's "living" sculptures

STEPHEN METZGER

Sterling in 1889, and, out back, a reconstructed blacksmith's shop with tools and items typically made by a smithy (horseshoes, spades, plow hardware, etc.). Also out back is an old schoolhouse used these days as a summer school by Sterling teachers and students, who dress as pioneers. Be sure to spend a few minutes looking over the native grasses display between the parking lot and front door. There's also a nice shaded picnic area next to the museum.

The Overland Trail Museum is open April 1 to Oct. 1, Mon. through Sat. 9 a.m.-5 p.m. and Sundays and holidays 10 a.m.-5 p.m. Phone (303) 522-3895. Admission is free.

Parks And Recreation

Columbine Park, on Hwy. 6 between S. 3rd Ave. and Division Ave., is huge, shady, and lawny, with picnic tables, swings, and other playground equipment, as well as two of the "Living Tree" sculptures. **Pioneer Park,** two miles west of downtown on Main St., has horseshoe pits, tennis courts, a merry-go-round, a series of nature trails among 14 acres, and campsites. For more information, contact the **Sterling Recreation Department,** 421 N. 1st St., tel. (303) 522-9700. You can phone the offices of Pioneer Park at 522-0441.

Other Recreation

North Sterling Reservoir, as well as nearby Jumbo and Prewitt reservoirs, offers fishing for catfish, bass, walleye, and other warm-water fish. Even if you're not into waterskiing, boating or fishing, take a drive out to the lake in the evening. It's quiet out there, except for the sound of an occasional fish rising, and the prairie seems to stretch endlessly, to the horizon and into the past—it's easy to forget the 20th century out there, and imagine yourself a westbound pioneer, one of the first settlers crossing the Great Plains.

Sterling also has four golf courses, including the public **Riverview,** tel. (303) 522-3035, and the private **Sterling Country Club,** tel. 522-5523. For swimming, racquetball, and other indoor sports (the pool is indoor), check out the **Sterling Recreation Center,** 808 Elm, tel. 522-7882.

Accommodations

Anachronistic out here on the high plains, where lodging usually consists of small motels on main drags, the **Crest House** bed and breakfast, 516 Division, tel. (303) 522-3753, offers an opportunity to stay in a gorgeous Victorian home. A private residence until September 1989, when current owners Barbara and Julius Rico purchased it, the building has beveled-glass windows, cherrywood bearing posts, and is furnished with four-poster beds and other antiques. Adjacent to the house is a small motel. Singles in the house go for $30 (with breakfast), and rooms in the motel are $17.

Just off the freeway, the **Ramada Inn,** tel. 522-2625, has good, comfortable rooms at reasonable rates (indoor pool, whirlpool and sauna, exercise room, etc.). You can also get a good clean room at a decent price at the **Sundowner Motel,** tel. 522-6265, also just off the freeway.

Buffalo Hills Camper Park, tel. 522-2233, has tent and RV sites, laundromat, recreation room, and heated pool.

Food

A favorite hangout for local ranchers and merchants, the **J and L Café,** 423 N. 3rd, tel. (303) 522-3625, has been serving meals for nearly 40 years. A classic small-town café—its atmosphere defined by cigarette smoke and formica—the J and L serves breakfast, the meal it's best known for, all day. Steak and eggs are $4.50, German sausages $3.75, and hot cakes, rolls, and other standard fare run $2-4. Another favorite breakfast place is **Thompson's Bakery,** where locals swear you can get the best doughnuts in town. For lunch, try **Fergie's,** a small bar and restaurant specializing in sandwiches (Italian subs and barbecue beef), soups, and nachos. Hours are Mon. through Fri. 11:30 a.m. to 2 a.m. While you're waiting, amuse yourself with the *Far Side* cartoons on the back of the menu.

Cocina Alvarado, tel. 522-8884, is an authentic Mexican restaurant (though I was disappointed with the store-bought chips, as well as the ground beef in the tacos), with daily specials

running $3-5. There's also a full-service restaurant at the **Ramada Inn,** tel. 522-2625, with a seafood buffet on Friday nights and a Sunday brunch.

Calendar

Among Sterling's annual events are the **Northeastern Junior College Rodeo,** in May; **Hay Days,** in June; and the **Logan County Fair** and **Sugar Beet Days,** in August. For specific dates, phone the Northeastern Colorado Visitor Information Center at (800) 544-8609.

Services

Phone the **Sterling Police** at (303) 522-3512, the **Logan County Sheriff** at 522-1373, and the **State Patrol** at 867-6844 (Fort Morgan). **Sterling Regional Medical Center** is located at 615 Fairhurst, tel. 522-0122. A larger facility, **Fort Morgan Community Hospital,** is in Fort Morgan at 1000 Lincoln, tel. 867-3391. The main **post office** is at 306 Poplar, tel. 522-1105.

Recycling

Recycle aluminum at **Pioneer Distributing,** 915 State St., tel. (303) 522-0706.

Information

The independently published *Journal-Advocate,* tel. (303) 522-1990, is Sterling's daily

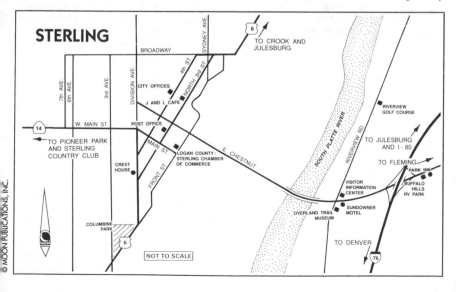

newspaper, a good source to get a feel of the town, as well as to find out about what's going on in the area, from movies to alfalfa fairs. Published weekday afternoons and Saturday mornings, the paper is available in racks around town.

You'll find a Northeastern Colorado **Visitor Information Center** just east of town between I-76 and the South Platte (across the street from the Overland Trail Museum). Pick up brochures and other information on Sterling, Logan County, and much of the northeastern corner of the state. Phone them at (800) 544-8609 or write Box 1683, Sterling, CO 80751.

The **Logan County Chamber of Commerce** is in Sterling at 300 Main St. (corner of Front); phone 522-5070, or write Box 1683, Sterling, CO 80751. The **Sterling Chamber of Commerce** is at 113 S. 2nd St., tel. 522-5070.

You can also get information on Sterling and Logan County by phoning the **Centennial Country** branch of the Colorado Tourism Board, located in Sterling, at (800) 544-8609.

The Sterling **public library,** tel. 522-2023, is located at the corner of 5th and Walnut. For **road and weather information,** phone 522-4848.

JULESBURG

If you're heading east on I-76, Julesburg will be the last you'll see of Colorado before lifting up over the border into Nebraska (two miles from town). At various times over the history of the region, the name Julesburg was given to three

BOB RACE

different communities in the same vicinity. It was finally affixed to the present townsite in 1881, when the town was founded as a division point on the main line of the Union Pacific Cutoff to Denver. Today, Julesburg is one of the area's major agricultural shipping stations.

The **Fort Sedgwick Depot Museum,** 202 W. 1st St., tel. (303) 474-2264, is open Memorial Day through Labor Day and exhibits prehistoric and Native American artifacts, pioneer gear (from bullets and casings found at battle sites to hat pins and carriages), and historical photos. Hours are Mon. through Sat. 9 a.m.-5 p.m. and Sun. 11 a.m.-5 p.m. Tours are also offered by appointment; phone 474-3682. There's a nice picnic area right next door.

If you're looking to spend the night, you can get lodging at the **Platte Valley Inn Motel,** tel. 474-3336. A popular local chow house is **Dan's Seafood and Steak House,** tel. 474-3757, at the junction of I-76 and Hwy. 385.

HIGHWAY 34 TO NEBRASKA

BRUSH

Ten miles from Fort Morgan, where Hwy. 34 forks off of I-76 and shoots due east into the heart of the plains, Brush is a small plains town that has historically been dependent on agriculture and the local beef industry. Huge ranches and muddy stockyards packed with lowing cattle punctuate the surrounding prairie, and billboards claim Nothing Satisfies Like Beef. Ranchers in dusty Ford pickups, often with Queensland blue heelers or border collies in the back, zoom down highways and bump over rutted dirt backroads.

Named for Jared L. Brush, one of northeastern Colorado's pioneer cattlemen, Brush also relies heavily on agriculture, particularly sugar beets. The town itself is one of quiet streets shaded by huge numbers of fir, pine, and cedar trees, obviously not indigenous to the area and looking a bit incongruous against the prairie backdrop. You'll find free camping, with electrical hookups for RVs, at **Brush City Campground** (take Clayton St. four blocks south of Hwy. 34), as well as shaded lawns, picnic tables, playground equipment, a pool, showers, and restrooms. Brush's **Best Western Inn** is located at 1208 N. Colorado, tel. (303) 842-5146.

For more information on Brush, write the **Brush Area Chamber of Commerce,** 301 Edison St., Brush, CO 80723, or phone 842-2666.

AKRON

About midway between Brush and Yuma, Akron has been a division point on the Burlington Railroad since 1882, when it was the only townsite on the line. Akron is the seat of Washington County. You'll find a picnic area with barbecue grills and restrooms at the corner of Hwy. 34 and Custer. Lodging is available at the **Crestwood Manor Motel,** tel. (303) 345-2231, and at the **4 B's Motel,** tel. 345-2028.

YUMA

Incorporated in 1887, Yuma is located on the western edge of Yuma County, where the local economies are chiefly dependent on agriculture and ranching; Yuma County grows more corn than any other county in the state. Other crops include oats, winter rye, wheat, pinto beans, soybeans, sunflowers, and alfalfa. At one time, Yuma was known for the Federal Agricultural Experiment Station here, which developed new methods of soil conservation. Tourist information is available at the **Yuma Chamber of Commerce,** 413 S. Main St., tel. (303) 848-2704. The **Yuma Historical Society Museum,** at the corner of Hwy. 59 and E. 3rd Ave., is open weekends only.

WRAY

Seat of Yuma County, Wray is a sort of oasis on the prairie flatlands: It's got actual hills, shaded with indigenous trees, and the North Fork of the Republican River tumbles through town. The **Wray Museum,** 205 3rd St., tel. (303) 332-5063, displays Native American arrowheads, barbed wire, local brands, a 1907 switchboard, dolls, and military uniforms and weapons. Hours are Tues. through Sat. 10 a.m.-5 p.m., Sunday 1-4 p.m. Admission is $1.

Free tent camping is available at West City Park on Hwy. 34 on the west end of town, where you'll also find a picnic area with barbecue grills, a playground, and restrooms. You can get lodging in Wray at the **Butte Motel,** tel. 332-4828, and the **Traveler's Inn,** tel. 332-4848, both located on Hwy. 34 in town. The **Sandhiller Restaurant,** tel. 332-4134, has an all-you-can-eat lunch buffet daily 11 a.m.-2 p.m. for $4.25. Dinners (chicken, steak, seafood) run $8-22. **Augustino's,** tel. 332-3177, serves sandwiches, lasagna, stews, and chili for $2-4, and pizzas run $4-13; the salad bar is $4. There's a **Safeway** on the east end of town.

For more information on Wray, phone the chamber of commerce at 332-4609. Tourist information is also available at the Butte Motel.

OTHER PLATTE RIVER CORRIDOR TOWNS

If you take Hwy. 6 from Fort Morgan up to Sterling and then continue on Hwy. 138 to Julesburg, you'll pass through a handful of intriguing little towns, including Merino, Atwood, Iliff, Proctor, Sedgwick, and Crook. If you want to get even more off the beaten path, you can explore CO 113 north (where you'll find the little town of Peetz, just a few miles from the Nebraska border), or Hwy. 6 east (where you'll pass through Fleming and Haxtun before arriving in Holyoke, the seat of Phillips County).

For specific information on any of these towns, call or write the **Centennial Country** branch of the Colorado Tourism Board, Box 1683, Sterling, CO 80751, tel. (800) 544-8609.

MERINO

Originally known as "Buffalo," and the site of the area's first school (1874), Merino was given its present name in 1881 by railroad workers who saw sheep grazing on the nearby plains. Though Merino is in the heart of traditional farming and ranching country, one ranch has animals you won't see on others. Ostriches, llamas, and draft and miniature horses are raised by the Vogt family, who will be happy to show you around if you call ahead; phone (303) 522-0936. Merino is also home to Brad Rhea, who does the "Living Trees" sculptures in Sterling.

ATWOOD

Just southeast of Atwood is the **Summit Springs Battlefield**, site of the last major battle between the United States Cavalry and the indigenous Plains people. On July 11, 1869, Cheyenne Chief Tall Bull and his warriors were attacked by eight companies of the Fifth Cavalry and 150 Pawnee scouts—the Cheyennes, in a last desperate attempt to fend off the encroaching whites, had kidnapped two white women on a "rampage" through Kansas. Fifty-two Cheyennes, including Tall Bull, were killed in the battle, and the soldiers took 12 Indian prisoners. According to reports, one of the kidnapped women was rescued, though the other died, having been tomahawked before the battle began.

PEETZ

Just south of the Nebraska border on CO 113, Peetz is a tiny community made up largely of ranchers and farmers who are descendants of the area's original white settlers. Though this part of Colorado is mostly flat prairie, grasslands seeming to roll oceanlike forever toward all horizons, the plain is broken up, and quite dramatically, about 15 miles west of Peetz. There, the plain breaks, and the Chimney Canyons rise, their mesa-tops towering 250 feet above the prairie, in stark contrast to their flat surroundings. To get there from Peetz, take County Rd. 74 west to 37, then 37 south to 70 and go west again.

First settled in 1885, by homesteaders Peter Peetz and Nick Treinan, the town has a reputation for mischief that's belied by today's quiet community. Local legend has it that early 20th-century Peetzians, particularly those living in the area during Prohibition, were a fiercely independent folk and did not take kindly to the restrictions the feds attempted to levy on their lifestyles. Some say there was a "still over every hill." There's even a story of one woman who supposedly took out the backseat of her Model T, which she then filled with her homemade potables, making housecalls along the area's dusty country backroads. In keeping with the town's bibulous tradition, the **Hot Spot,** tel. (303) 334-2265, is a watering hole popular among locals throughout the county.

CROOK

Best known in the area for the **Tamarack Ranch State Wildlife Area,** a hunting and bird- and wildlife-watching refuge (wild turkeys, geese, pheasant, deer, antelope, etc.) on 7,000 acres of river-bottom land, Crook is another small ranching and farming community in the fertile Platte River valley. Two Overland Trail stage stops, Spring Hill and Lillian Springs stations, both designated with historical markers, are just outside Crook on the Tamarack Ranch. For more information on the Tamarack Ranch State Wildlife Area, phone (303) 671-4500 or (800) 365-2267.

In town, named for General George F. Crook, to whom Geronimo surrendered in New Mexico in 1866, you'll find the **Crook Museum,** tel. 886-2782 or 886-2992. The museum displays pioneer artifacts, local brands and tack, and a gor-

geous 19th-century rosewood piano originally purchased for 50 cents. The museum is open Sundays 2-4 p.m., Memorial Day to Labor Day, and by appointment. There's also a small community park and picnic area in Crook, as well as **Bobbi's Tavern,** tel. 886-3241, which serves wild game (goose, wild turkey, antelope, etc.) in season. Another restaurant popular among locals is **Nelson's Cafe,** tel. 886-2402.

HIGHWAY 6 TO NEBRASKA

FLEMING

About 20 miles east of Sterling on Hwy. 6, Fleming was first settled in the 1880s and incorporated in 1917. Another agriculture-dependent small town, Fleming relies heavily on wheat, alfalfa, and corn. The town has two small museums of interest to passers-through. The **Fleming Heritage Museum and Park,** tel. (303) 265-2591, at the old Burlington Northern Train Depot, displays items of local historical interest (the park has restrooms, playground equipment, and picnic shelters). **Al's Country and Western Museum** has antique wagons, surreys, carriages, and automobiles. Ask locals for information on and directions to some of the area's first homesites: a rock house, "soddies" (early sod houses), and two homes ordered pre-cut from an early-20th-century Sears-Roebuck catalog.

HOLYOKE

Holyoke, at the junction of Hwys. 6 and 385, is a small town of beautiful brick homes with nicely maintained yards. Very young mothers push strollers along the sidewalks of sleepy, shady streets. *It's a Wonderful Life* could have been filmed here.

Just 15 miles from the Nebraska border, Holyoke, seat of Phillips County, is a hub for area ranchers and farmers; the main crops are alfafa, wheat, and corn. Passers-through will find two nice parks, one on the north end of town (on Hwy. 385), with a picnic area and kids' playground; the other, on the town's south end (also on Hwy. 385), is a bit bigger and also has tennis and basketball courts, and a swimming pool. You can get lodging at the **Cedar Motel,** tel. (303) 854-2525. For more information on Holyoke, write the Information Center at 100 Emerson, Holyoke, CO 80734, or phone 854-3517.

EAST ON INTERSTATE 70

LIMON

Limon (rhymes with "rhymin'") is located in the heart of Colorado's "outback" about midway between the Rockies' Front Range and the Kansas border. If you're westbound on I-70, you can either continue on the interstate at Limon (pop. 1,800; elev. 5,360 feet) where it veers north toward Denver (about 75 miles), or you can catch Hwy. 24 and drop southwest to Colorado Springs (also about 75 miles).

Ordinarily a typically quiet little plains community, Limon roared and crashed and turned topsy-turvy for about 10 minutes one evening in the summer of 1990. On June 6, the skies over Colorado's plains began to darken and churn—not particularly unusual for that time of the year—and a series of tornadoes was reported touching down in remote plains locations. What was unusual that night, though, was that the winds didn't settle down; they got angrier, and one of the tornadoes happened to choose to twist, moving slowly and forcefully, right through the middle of downtown Limon, demoniacally, like some hell-born evil bent on destruction, spitting hail and turning almost everything that had been Limon to rubble.

When the tornado was gone, so was most of the town: Homes had been slashed apart (70 mobile homes were destroyed). Town Hall totalled. Retail stores and banks leveled, or pummeled beyond recognition (23 businesses were destroyed). Cars upended, lifted clear off the ground, and dumped like toys in heaps. Crops and fields ruined (agricultural damage was estimated to be well over $1 million). Total damage: over $20 million.

As you'd expect in a small farming community such as Limon, the townspeople banded together, offering moral, emotional, and financial help to each other. The Salvation Army and the American Red Cross also helped out, as did Colorado grocery stores (including Albertson's, King Soopers, and Safeway) and other businesses, and Limon has mostly recovered. In fact, within weeks, most businesses (especially those on the edges of town, where the damage

wasn't so severe) were back to normal operations. By late spring, 1991, even most of downtown had been rebuilt, and in June the governor came to dedicate "New" Limon.

Limon Twilight Train Rides

For an authentic taste of the history and wildlife of Colorado's "outback," take this two-hour sunset ride through a private game reserve. The restored 1924 coach, from the Rock Island Line, will take you out onto the plains, "where the deer and the antelope play." En route, listen to live music and a historical narrative, and cap the evening off with dessert. A gift shop and museum at the depot at the end of the line sells and displays Native American artifacts and railroad memorabilia.

The train runs Saturdays June 1 to Sept. 1; departures are at 7 p.m. Museum hours are Mon. through Fri. 1-5 p.m. and Sat. 1-9 p.m. For more information, write Twilight Train Ride and Heritage Society, Box 341, Limon, CO 80828, or phone (719) 775-2373.

Tarado Mansion

Located in the fields just south of Arriba, a tiny farming community 20 miles east of Limon, this Greek-revival building is a reconstruction of the historic Adam's Hotel (moved from downtown Arriba in 1972). The mansion is furnished with a potpourri of antiques, including a harp that once belonged to General George Custer's wife, 18th-century Italian porcelain, Chinese pieces dating to the Ming Dynasty, Victorian furniture, and a re-created 19th-century country kitchen and dining room. In December the mansion is decked out for Christmas. A huge tree is decorated with antique ornaments, and miniature lights and candles are strung throughout the many rooms. Guided tours are offered daily 10 a.m.-5 p.m. The mansion also offers bed and breakfast accommodations. For more information, write Torado Mansion, Route 1, Box 53, Arriba, CO 80804, or phone (719) 768-3468.

Practicalities

Passers-through looking for lodging in Limon have several options. The **Budget Host Silver**

Spur Motel, tel. 775-2807, and the **Preferred Motor Inn,** tel. 775-2385, (both at Exit 361 off I-70) have rooms starting at around $35. Downtown, the **Midwest Motel and Country Inn,** tel. 775-2373, also has rooms for around $35.

For more information on points of interest, events, and services in the Limon area, write the **Limon Chamber of Commerce** at Box 101, Limon, CO 80828. Chamber Representative Harold Lowe can be reached at the Midwest Motel and Country Inn.

BURLINGTON

Twelve miles from the Kansas border, Burlington (pop. 3,000; elev. 4,160 feet) is home to a historic carousel still offering rides to the public, and Old Town, a reconstructed frontier town featuring a museum and some two dozen historic buildings (some are restorations, some are new). Seat of Kit Carson County, Burlington was once the largest grain-shipping point between Omaha and Denver. If you're arriving from the east, be sure to stop at the **State Welcome Center** just off the interstate, where you can get brochures and information on the Burlington/Kit Carson County area, as well as on the rest of Colorado.

Kit Carson County Carousel
Built in 1905 by the Philadelphia Toboggan Company for Denver's Elitch Gardens (where it operated until sold to Kit Carson County in 1928),

the carousel is a National Historic Landmark. Among the 46 hand-carved animals on whose backs you can ride are horses, giraffes, zebras, camels, goats, and a "hippocampus" (seahorse), all of which parade in lines of three to the robust and throaty music of a Wurlitzer Monster Military Band Organ, built in 1909. The details on the animals, including tigers' snarling mouths, lions' saddles adorned with cherubs, and a snake crawling up a giraffe's neck, are exquisite.

The Kit Carson County Carousel is open from late May through mid-Sept. in afternoons and early evenings. A ride will set you back all of a quarter. For more information, phone (719) 348-5562.

Old Town Museum
With melodrama, cancan girls, gunfights, and hayrides, as well as a saloon, drugstore, blacksmith shop, and bank, Burlington's Old Town Museum offers an attractive break from the tedium of long-haul cross-plains travel. You can either wander through the grounds on your own (detailed maps are available) or take a guided tour. You can also take a wagon ride from Old Town to the Kit Carson County Carousel.

Old Town Museum is open June through Sept. 9 a.m.-9 p.m. For hours of operation and information, phone (719) 346-8404. Signs throughout town will direct you there.

Bonny State Recreation Area
About 22 miles north of Burlington off Hwy. 385, this 7,000-acre park offers picnicking, camping,

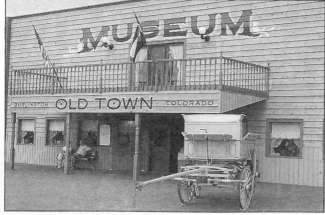

Old Town Museum in Burlington

STEPHEN METZGER

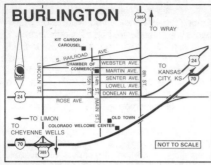

fishing, birdwatching, and boating. Four different campgrounds (with 200 sites) range from rather primitive (pit toilets) to more developed (flush toilets, showers, and laundry facilities). Camping is free on weekdays; a small fee is charged on weekends. At the Bonny Marina, tel. (303) 354-7306, you can rent boats and buy fishing tackle, licenses, and groceries.

For more information on Bonny State Recreation Area, write Box 78-A, Idalia, CO 80735, or phone the Bonny Marina. You can also get information from the Colorado Division of Parks and Recreation, 1313 Sherman St. #618, Denver, CO 80203.

Accommodations
You'll find a handful of motels just off the interstate in Burlington. Try the **Burlington Super 8,** 2100 Fay, tel. (719) 346-5627 or (800) 843-1991; the **Econo Lodge,** 450 S. Lincoln, tel. 346-5555; the **Burlington Inn,** 118 8th St., tel. 346-8613; or the **Western Motor Inn,** 222 Rose Ave., tel. 346-5371. You'll also find several campgrounds, suitable for either tents or RVs: **Campland,** 4th and Rose, tel. 346-8763; and **Sloan's Trailer Park,** 1901 Rose, tel. 346-5333.

Food
Like most out-in-the-middle-of-nowhere American towns, especially those that lie along interstates, Burlington has its share of fast-food restaurants—a Pizza Hut, Dairy Queen, Sonic Drive In, Arby's. You can also get decent grub at the **Hoof and Horn Restaurant,** tel. (719) 346-7107 (about a mile west of town on Hwy. 24); the **Interstate House,** tel. 346-8010 (at the junction of I-70 and Hwy. 385—open 24 hours); and at the restaurant at the **Western Motor Inn,** tel. 346-9974 (junction of Hwy. 24 and Hwy. 385). The **Main Street Donut and Deli** is located at 415 14th Street.

Services
The **Burlington Police Department** is at 1394 Webster; phone (719) 346-8353. The offices of the **State Police** are located at 179 Webster; phone 346-5430. **Kit Carson County Memorial Hospital** is at 286 16th Street, tel. 346-5311. The main **post office** is at 259 14th St., phone 346-8964.

Information
For more information on Burlington and Kit Carson County, contact the **Burlington Chamber of Commerce** at 415 15th St., Burlington, CO 80807, tel. (719) 346-8070. The **public library** is at 321 14th St., tel. 346-8109.

STEPHEN METZGER

SOUTHEASTERN COLORADO

At first glance, Southeastern Colorado may appear much like the northeastern corner of the state. Both are comprised of mostly barren prairie land stretching from the Rockies' Front Range to the state's eastern border, and both are primarily agricultural regions, divided by important waterways, which, with headwaters in the Rockies, eventually reach the Missouri-Mississippi River system and the Gulf of Mexico. A closer inspection, however, will reveal significant differences in the two eastern corners of Colorado—in their histories, people, and even in the geology and the composition of the prairie itself.

If you come into southeastern Colorado from the north, you'll note gradual changes in the flora of the plains. Its makeup shifts from waving wheat fields and rolling grasslands to deserty stretches of yucca and sage, and the hills are dotted with juniper and piñon. This is the southwestern United States, and it looks a whole lot more like New Mexico than it does Kansas.

In addition, as you get farther south into Colorado, you'll find the proportion of people of Span-

ish descent increases dramatically. This is reflected in the region's place names (the towns of La Junta, Las Animas, Granada, and Campo, as well as Baca and Otero counties) and its cooking (you tend to see more authentic Mexican restaurants out this way than you do burger shacks). Why the change in demographics? Is it simply because you're that much closer to Mexico? In part, yes. But the reason's also historical: From the early 1820s until the late 1870s, the Santa Fe Trail cut across this part of Colorado, linking Santa Fe, New Mexico—then *old* Mexico's major northern trade center—with Independence, Missouri. Goods, and people, were transported along the rutted dirt highway, creating a natural amalgamation of cultures.

Settlement of Southeastern Colorado began in the late 1820s, when traders Ceran St. Vrain and Charles and William Bent built a trading post along the Santa Fe Trail between what are now the cities of La Junta and Las Animas. A major hub of trading activity—for mountain men, Cheyennes, and Mexican and American troops—the outpost at

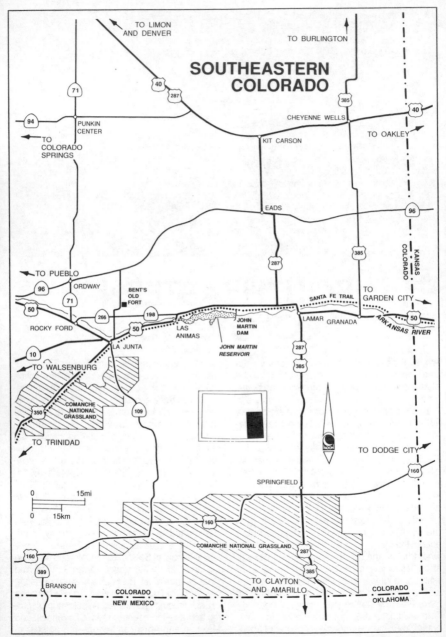

one time employed over 100 men. The fort was abandoned in 1852, although it has recently been reconstructed and is an excellent stop for modern travelers interested in the history of the West (see "Bent's Old Fort National Historic Site" under "Las Animas" following).

The railroad arrived in Southeastern Colorado in the 1870s, and during the 1880s the area was prime cattle-grazing country, with huge herds of longhorns roaming freely. It was largely this cattle-ization and railroad-ization of eastern Colorado that marked the end of the area as a wilderness populated by the great indigenous animals: Bison and bears fell victim to sharpshooters, government, and bounty hunters. "It was the livestock industry that finished off the grizzly [bear] in the more arid states," writes Doug Peacock in his excellent book *Grizzly Years.* "The principal reason given for killing grizzlies was protection of livestock. But few bears actually preyed on domestic animals, though the reprisals were always unrelenting and unforgiving. Bears were shot on sight out of ignorance, irrational hatred, and because of illusions about what constituted duty or sport."

By the early 20th century, the great cattle roundups had gone the way of the bison, wolf, grizzly, and Indian. Ranchers and farmers had turned to poultry, lamb, dairy cattle, and irrigated crops, particularly melons and sugar beets. Holly, after the sugar company of the same name, and Sugar City are both located in this part of the state.

In many ways, Southeastern Colorado has not changed much since its conversion from cattle-grazing country to agriculture. Melons and sugar beets are still primary crops, and the little towns and farming communities, miles and miles from the state's sprawling metropolitan centers and chic resort areas, remain slow paced, close knit, and timelessly and essentially yoked to the earth and their own landscape.

Modern travelers in Southeastern Colorado, though not afforded the mountain vistas and cultural centers of other parts of the state, can take advantage of several museums, including the restored Bent's Fort and a fascinating Native American museum in La Junta. In addition, motorists can follow the route of the Old Santa Fe Trail, from Holly, near the Kansas border, to Trinidad, where the route drops down into New Mexico. Campers and fisherpersons can explore the Arkansas River, as well as John Martin Reservoir, where the river is dammed, about midway between Las Animas and Lamar.

Before You Go

If you're coming into the area from the south, stop in Trinidad at the state welcome and tourist center, where you'll find information not only on Southeastern Colorado but on the rest of the state as well. Pick up brochures on everything from historical sites to recreation. There's also a welcome center in Burlington that provides lots of information on eastern Colorado. For information on specific towns and areas in Southeastern Colorado, contact the local chambers of commerce, whose phone numbers and addresses are provided below.

ARKANSAS RIVER CORRIDOR AND HIGHWAY 50

Dropping down out of the Rocky Mountains west of Pueblo and slicing across the Southeastern Colorado plains to the Kansas border, the 2,000-mile Arkansas River, which drains nearly 190,000 square miles, is the greatest tributary of the Missouri-Mississippi river system. Highway 50 follows this main artery of Southeastern Colorado, passing through a number of small towns and communities, including Holly, about four and a half miles from the border, Lamar, Las Animas, and La Junta (Hwy. 50 and the Arkansas continue to run parallel west through Pueblo, Cañon City, and Salida, where the river drops down from its headwaters near Leadville).

LAMAR

Named for L.Q.C. Lamar, President Cleveland's Secretary of the Interior, Lamar (pop. 8,000; elev. 3,500 feet) still feels like the rowdy cowboy town it was during the late 19th and early 20th centuries. As late as 1928, four bank robbers rode into Lamar, held up the First National Bank (shooting the president and his son and kidnapping an employee, who was also eventually shot), and escaped with nearly a quarter of a million dollars.

Today Lamar is the seat of Prowers County, as well as home to Lamar Community College. In the fall, the town, which calls itself the "Goose Hunting Capital of the World," fills up with bird hunters, who pour into town by the barrel, fill up most of the motels, and spend their days working the sprawling fields and wetlands.

Big Timbers Museum

Admission is free to this pioneer museum, named for a stretch of the Animas River where William Bent and company had camps during the height of their trading empire (see "Bent's Old Fort National Historic Site" following). In addition to historical photos, you'll find an array of

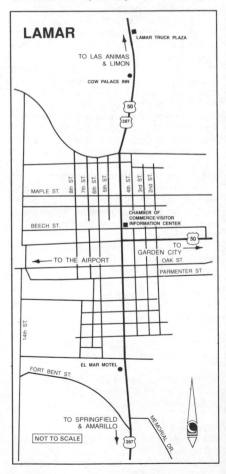

CATHY CARLSON

Canada goose

domestic tools and equipment, as well as clothing from the mid-19th century. The museum is open daily 1:30-4:30 p.m. It's located at 7515 Hwy. 50 just north of Lamar. Phone (719) 336-2472 for more information.

Practicalities

The nicest lodging in town is the **Cow Palace Inn Best Western,** 1301 N. Main, tel. (719) 336-7753. Doubles start at about $60. You'll find less expensive rooms (doubles about $35) at the **El Mar Motel,** 1210 S. Main, tel. 336-4331. The dining room at the **Cow Palace Inn** has good food at reasonable prices, with buffets Sun. 11 a.m.-2 p.m. and Fri. evenings (Mexican specialties). The Lamar **KOA** campground, tel. 336-7625, is located about five miles west of town on Hwy. 50. **Hud's Good Sam Campground,** tel. 829-4344, about 15 miles west of Lamar, has nice RV sites in the shade of cottonwoods, as well as a small grocery store. **Ranchers 24-Hour Family Restaurant,** tel. 336-3445, at the Lamar Truck Plaza, three miles west of town at the junction of Highways 50 and 287, serves BIG truckers' breakfasts for $2-5, sandwiches and burgers for $3-6, and there's a soup and salad bar.

Services

The offices of the **Lamar Police Department** are located at 505 Main St.; phone (719) 336-4341. Phone the **Prowers County Sheriff** at 336-5234 and the **State Patrol** at 336-7403. **Prowers Medical Center** is located at 2101 S. Memorial Drive, tel. 336-4343. The central **post office** is at 300 S. 5th St.; phone 336-4421.

Recycling

Recycle aluminum at the **Safeway,** 405 E. Olive St., and aluminum and glass at the **Lamar Area Hospice,** 1001 S. Main.

Information

The **Lamar Chamber of Commerce** is downtown at 17 S. Main, tel. (719) 336-4379. The **public library** is at 104 E. Parmenter; phone 336-4632. You can also get tourist information at the KOA campground west of town.

LAS ANIMAS

Highway 50 beelines due west for 30 miles from Lamar to Las Animas, following the courses of the Arkansas River, the Santa Fe Trail, and the Atchison, Topeka, and Santa Fe Railroad. Not a whole lot to look at along here—mostly dry, brown, and flat—though you can pull off at John Martin Reservoir to camp or do some warm-water fishing. Also watch along the highway for communities of prairie dogs

Las Animas (pop. 2,800; elev. 3,900 feet) was founded in 1869 at the confluence of the Arkansas and Purgatoire rivers and near the site of Fort Lyon, a U.S. Army post built in 1860 to house cavalry troops and to protect Santa Fe Trail travelers. Between the mid-1870s and about 1915, the Las Animas area was the scene of huge cattle roundups, though the region has long been rich in agriculture as well. As early as 1866, Thomas O. Boggs and John Prowers were experimenting with irrigated crops on a farm two miles south of present-day Las Animas. Boggsville, as the community came to be known, eventually became a regional center for cattle, sheep, and a variety of crops, and it was the first seat of Bent County. Kit Carson died in 1868 in a cabin in Las Animas and was buried near Bent's Fort with his third wife, Maria Josefa Jaramarillo, though their remains were later moved to Taos, New Mexico. The abandoned Boggsville was acquired in 1985 by the Pioneer Historical Society of Bent County, which is in the process of restoring the community.

Kit Carson Museum

If you think this place is odd to look at, with the word "MUSEUM" spelled out on letters atop tall poles, like an advertisement for some tacky motel, get a load of the building's history: Built of adobe in 1940, it originally housed German prisoners of war captured in North Africa. After the war, it was home to Jamaican field workers, and was later a home for widows and the poor. Don't expect upscale displays here with high-tech dioramas and fancy collections. This is a pioneer museum pure and simple. Wander through the historical displays of the main building—Native American artifacts, early farming equipment, domestic gear. Then wander out back to the several historical buildings that have been moved onto the site: the first Las Animas jail, built in 1882; the original Bent County Jail; an 1860s log stage station, originally located between Bent's Fort and Pueblo; a one-room school, a blacksmith shop, and a carriage house. (Be sure to check out the replica of the gallows in the field across the street from the museum.)

Kit Carson Museum is open Memorial Day through Labor Day and is located on 9th St. near the junction of Hwy. 50 and Colorado 101. Watch for the sign (you can't miss it). For more information, phone the Las Animas/Bent County Chamber of Commerce at (719) 456-0453.

John Martin Reservoir And Lake Hasty

Located about 15 miles east of Las Animas, this large reservoir and smaller, nearby lake offer a variety of water sports, as well as sightseeing, picnicking, and camping, with lots of very nice campsites right on the water. Originally part of a federal flood-control and irrigation project, the dam was completed in 1946. It's over two miles long and rises over 100 feet above the river; the spillway is over 1,000 feet long. Seventy-five-acre Lake Hasty is immediately downstream and was formed when earth was moved to build the dam.

Stop in at the visitor center in the Project Office, where you can pick up maps and other information about the facilities. Tours can also be arranged by calling in advance. For information, or to book tours, phone (719) 336-3476; or write John Martin Reservoir Resident Office, U.S. Army Engineers, Star Route, Hasty, CO 81044.

Bent's Old Fort National Historical Site

Anyone with even a moderate interest in history will find this fort absolutely fascinating, definitely one of the highlights of a visit to this part of the state. Completed in 1833, the adobe fort for nearly 20 years was a critical trading hub—the most important stop between Independence, Missouri, and Santa Fe, New Mexico—where Native Americans, mountain men, U.S. Army troops, and Mexican soldiers gathered to swap furs, manufactured goods, and tales of life in the rugged West, as they swigged the notorious Taos Lightning.

The trading company was the brainchild of two brothers, Charles and William Bent, along with Ceran St. Vrain, the three of whom had left St. Louis to make their fortunes in fur trading. William Bent, historians tell us, was unusually sensitive to the Native Americans, whose lands their trading empire encompassed (Southern Cheyenne, Arapahoe, Ute, Northern Apache, Kiowa, and Comanche). The business-savvy William went to great lengths to ensure that the post saw large numbers of traders; he encouraged rival tribes to make peace with each other, and in 1837 he even married a Cheyenne woman, apparently primarily to look better in the eyes of potential native traders.

By the late 1840s, Santa Fe Trail trade was already on the wane—due to the Mexican-American War, increasing native uprisings, Charles's death in Taos, St. Vrain's departure, and finally, in 1849, cholera, which decimated the tribes upon which William relied for trade.

Bent's Old Fort has been restored to approximate its 1830s prime, and it's one of the best examples in the West of a "living museum." A costumed guide takes visitors through the fort's many rooms—blacksmith's shop, military and trappers' quarters, billiard room, and warehouse—while employees, also in costume, quietly go about their work, as though it were a century and a half earlier. Be sure to check out the orientation film before going through the fort (if only to hear the attempt at a French accent by whoever's doing the voice of Ceran St. Vrain).

The fort is open daily 8 a.m.-6 p.m., Memorial Day through Labor Day, and 8 a.m.-4:30 p.m. the rest of the year. Closed New Year's Day, Thanksgiving, and Christmas. To get there take CO 194 or Hwy. 50 west from Las Animas, or Hwy. 50 east from La Junta, and watch for the

*Don't miss
Bent's Old Fort
between Las Animas
and La Junta.*

signs. A 200-yard paved walkway leads from the parking lot to the fort; rides are provided for disabled visitors. For more information, phone (719) 384-2596, or write 35110 Hwy. 194 East, La Junta, CO 81050-9523.

Practicalities

In addition to a handful of independently run motels in Las Animas, you can get rooms at the **Best Western Bent's Fort Inn,** 10950 Hwy. 50, tel. (719) 456-0011; doubles will run about $40. The **Troll Haus Restaurant,** 616 Locust, tel. 456-0062, is a local favorite.

Services

The **Las Animas Police Department** is located at 326 Prowers Court; phone (719) 456-1313. Phone the **Bent County Sheriff** at 456-1363 and the **State Patrol** at 384-2562 (La Junta). The nearest hospital is the **Arkansas Valley Regional Medical Clinic** in La Junta at 1100 Carson Dr.; phone 456-2088 from Las Animas, 384-5412 from La Junta. The Las Animas **post office** is at 513 W. 6th St.; phone 456-0310.

Recycling

Recycle aluminum and glass in La Junta at **Greenstreet Distributing Company,** 706 E. 1st St. (call ahead: 719-384-8761), or at **Safeway,** 315 W. 2nd Street.

Information

For more information on the Las Animas area, write **Las Animas/Bent County Chamber of Commerce,** 511 Ambassador Thompson Blvd., Las Animas, CO 81054, or phone (719) 456-0453. In town, stop by the Las Animas **public library** at 308 W. 5th St., tel. 456-0111.

LA JUNTA

Seat of Otero County, La Junta (Spanish for "The Junction," though mispronounced La-HUNT-a) is located about 20 miles west of Las Animas, at the junction of the old Navajo and Santa Fe trails. At La Junta, Hwy. 350, following the Santa Fe Trail, splits off Hwy. 50 and drops down through the Comanche National Grassland to Trinidad. La Junta is also at the junction of the Santa Fe Railroad's main line and its Denver branch, and so has long been an important shipping town. It was founded in 1875 and originally called Otero, after Spanish settler Miguel Otero.

One of the prettier towns on the southeastern plains, La Junta is characterized by huge hillside homes and nicely kept lawns and gardens. Its city park is perfect for a picnic and/or an afternoon snooze.

Koshare Indian Museum

It might be tempting to zip through La Junta without stopping, but it'd be a shame to miss this wonderful museum. Among the highlights are Crow, Cree, Shoshone, and Flathead buckskin clothing, moccasins, and hide paintings, in addition to Zuni pottery, Hopi, Zuni, and Navajo silver, Hopi Katchinas, and Hupa baskets. There's also a full-size model of a kiva, where a local Boy Scout troop performs authentic Native American dances Saturday evenings in the

STEPHEN METZGER

LA JUNTA

TO ROCKY FORD & PUEBLO

ARKANSAS RIVER

TO WALSENBURG

TO TRINIDAD

ANDERSON

SANTA FE AVE.

SAN JUAN AVE.

COLORADO AVE.

RATÓN AVE.

2nd ST.

10th St.

CITY PARK

14th ST.

OTERO JUNIOR COLLEGE
KOSHARE INDIAN MUSEUM

TO BENT'S OLD FORT & LAS ANIMAS

NOT TO SCALE

© MOON PUBLICATIONS, INC.

summer and during holidays (the group started in the 1930s and has earned a national reputation for itself, performing around the country). A gift shop sells quality Native American artwork, as well as souvenirs and knicknacks.

The museum is open daily 9 a.m.-5 p.m. June through Aug., and noon-5 p.m. the rest of the year. It's located on the Otero Junior College campus. Take Santa Fe Ave. south to 18th St. (Santa Fe is interrupted by the city park; circle around it). Small entrance fee. For more information, phone (719) 384-4801, or write 115 W. 18th St., Box 580, La Junta, CO 81050.

Otero Museum

This pioneer museum, located in a turn-of-the-century building listed on the National Register of Historic Places, displays artifacts from the area's history, emphasizing the arrival of the railroad and the development of agriculture. Exhibits include grocery items (the building was originally a grocery store), farming and ranching tools and equipment, and even a mid-19th-century stagecoach.

The museum, located at 2nd and Anderson, is open daily 1-5 p.m. June through September. Phone (719) 384-7406 for more information.

City Park

Just north of the Koshare Museum and Otero Community College is a large city park with hilly lawns, shade, picnic tables, and a large pond.

Practicalities

You'll find a handful of motels and inns in La Junta. The **La Junta Budget Inn**, 110 E. 1st St., tel. (719) 384-2504, has doubles for about $30, while rooms for two run about $40 at the **Luxury Inn**, Hwy. 50 W, tel. 384-4408, and about $50 at the **Quality Inn**, 1325 E. 3rd St., tel. 384-2571.

Predictably, there are *muchos restaurantes Mexicanos* in La Junta. Try **El Axteca**, 710 W. 3rd., tel. 384-4215, **El Cid**, 1617 Ratón Ave., tel. 384-9818, or **Felicia's**, 27948 Frontage Rd., tel. 384-4814. There's also an A & W, McDonald's, Kentucky Fried Chicken, and K-Bob's Steak House.

Services

You can reach the **La Junta Police** at (719) 384-2525, the **Otero County Sheriff** at 384-5941, and the **Colorado State Patrol** at 384-8981. La Junta's **Arkansas Valley Regional Medical Center** is located at 1100 Carson Ave.; phone 384-5412. The main **post office** is at 4th and Colorado; phone 384-5944.

Recycling

Recycle aluminum and glass at **Greenstreet Distributing Company,** 706 E. 1st St., tel. (719) 384-8761 (call ahead), and aluminum at **Safeway,** 315 W. 2nd Street.

Information

La Junta's **Woodruff Memorial Library** is located at 522 Colorado Ave.; phone (719) 384-4612. The **La Junta Chamber of Commerce** is at 110 Santa Fe Ave., tel. 384-7411. Check the **Book Stop,** 318 Santa Fe, tel. 384-8839, for books of local interest.

WEST OF LA JUNTA

If you've been out poking around on the eastern plains you're probably growing a bit weary of all the flatness and barrenness and nothingness. Driving west out of La Junta, then, offers cheap thrills. To wit: an actual, bona fide view of mountains. Yes, whether you take Hwy. 50 to Pueblo, CO 10 to Walsenburg, or Hwy. 350 to Trinidad, somewhere about a half hour out of La Junta (sooner on clear days) you see them: the Rockies, looming snowcapped in the distance. Truly a sight for sore eyes.

The 65-mile stretch of Hwy. 50 from La Junta to Pueblo takes you through a handful of small farming towns and communities, including Swink, Rocky Ford, Manzanola, Fowler, and Avondale. Pueblo sits at the foot of the Front Range, and from there it's just a half-hour or so before you're winding up into some serious mountains.

Rocky Ford

This little agricultural community, about 15 miles west of La Junta, is known nationwide for its melons. The Rocky Ford cantaloupe, particularly, but locally grown watermelons as well, attract buyers from throughout the country. Each summer, in mid-August, Rocky Ford hosts the Arkansas Valley Fair, which celebrates the region's multicultural heritage and agricultural harvests.

Information

For more information on Rocky Ford or the Arkansas Valley Fair, write the **Rocky Ford Chamber of Commerce,** 105 N. Main St., Rocky Ford, CO 81067, or phone (719) 254-7483.

La Junta To Walsenburg and Trinidad

From La Junta to Walsenburg it's about 75 miles, the drive straight and unbroken, with little to amuse, save for two exciting crosses over county lines. Best, then, simply to get on with it.

La Junta to Trinidad is about an 80-mile drive, Hwy. 350 following the Santa Fe Trail southwest then dropping nearly due south at Trinidad and the junction with I-25. From there it's just 90 miles to Ratón Pass and the New Mexico border. In fact, along this stretch of Hwy. 350 the landscape begins to look even more Southwestern, the brown bluffs and mesas dotted with yucca and cane cholla. Then, just about 15 miles out of Trinidad, the flora turns dramatically green, the valleys lush and fertile. Readers heading on to New Mexico and heartbroken about having to glovebox the witty traveling companion that has guided them thus far, or those simply intrigued with the mystery and seductiveness of that wonderful state, would do well to invest 17 bucks in the thoroughly researched, intelligently written, and critically acclaimed *New Mexico Handbook,* by yours truly (and humbly); it's available at your local bookstore, or from Moon Publications, P.O. Box 3040, Chico, CA 95927, tel. (916) 345-5413.

Anasazi pottery

BOB RACE

STEPHEN METZGER

SOUTH CENTRAL COLORADO

The diversity of South Central Colorado makes it in a very real sense a microcosm of the rest of the state. This one region, stretching north from the New Mexico border to Colorado Springs and Fairplay and west from the Great Plains to the towering Rocky Mountains, offers fascinating lessons in the state's geology, history, and demographics, as well as myriad sightseeing and recreation opportunities.

South Central Colorado is split lengthwise by I-25, which crosses over from New Mexico at Ratón Pass, then follows the plains' western edge north through Trinidad, Pueblo, and Colorado Springs, and continues on through Denver and up into northern Wyoming. Highway 50 bisects I-25 at Pueblo, cutting east to west across South Central Colorado from the plains up into the foothills of the Cañon City area and then on to Salida, Gunnison, Grand Junction, and west to California. Just north of the New Mexico border, between Del Norte and the Sangre de Cristo Mountains, is the San Luis Valley, a 50- by 125-mile pocket of austere beauty surrounded by

mountains—the San Juans, Sangre de Cristos, La Garitas, and Conejos-Brazos.

This was the first part of Colorado to be explored by nonnative peoples. Perhaps as early as the mid-16th century, Spanish expeditions were pushing up from the south. San Luis, a small community a half-hour from the New Mexico border at the junction of CO 159 and CO 142, is the oldest town in the state. Because the Spanish were the first to explore and settle this area, it still maintains its Hispanic heritage—evident in its architecture, cooking, folk art, and the surnames of a large proportion of the people.

In the mid-19th century, South Central Colorado was the scene of important mining activity. The mines of Cripple Creek, in the high mountains west of Colorado Springs, produced millions of dollars in gold and silver and made fortunes for their owners, who built palatial homes, opera houses, and resorts in Denver and Colorado Springs.

Today South Central Colorado offers the traveler lots to see and do. Drive up to the top

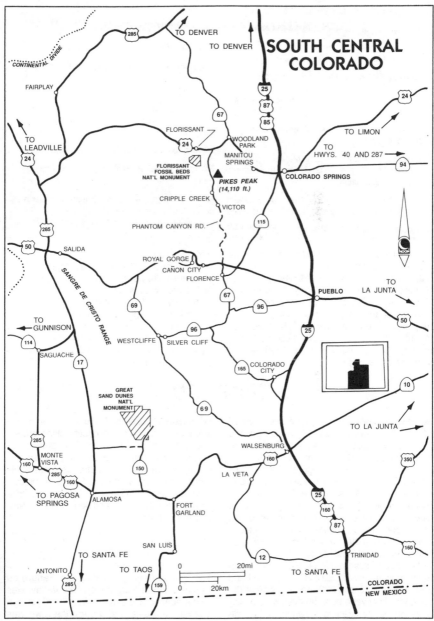

SOUTH CENTRAL COLORADO

TO DENVER
TO DENVER
TO LIMON
TO HWYS. 40 AND 287
TO LA JUNTA
TO LA JUNTA
TO GUNNISON
TO LEADVILLE
TO PAGOSA SPRINGS
TO SANTA FE
TO TAOS
TO SANTA FE

CONTINENTAL DIVIDE
FAIRPLAY
FLORISSANT
WOODLAND PARK
MANITOU SPRINGS
COLORADO SPRINGS
FLORISSANT FOSSIL BEDS NAT'L MONUMENT
PIKES PEAK (14,110 ft.)
CRIPPLE CREEK
VICTOR
PHANTOM CANYON RD.
SALIDA
ROYAL GORGE
CAÑON CITY
FLORENCE
PUEBLO
SANGRE DE CRISTO RANGE
SAGUACHE
WESTCLIFFE
SILVER CLIFF
COLORADO CITY
GREAT SAND DUNES NAT'L MONUMENT
MONTE VISTA
WALSENBURG
LA VETA
ALAMOSA
FORT GARLAND
SAN LUIS
ANTONITO
TRINIDAD
COLORADO
NEW MEXICO

0   20mi
0   20km

© MOON PUBLICATIONS, INC.

SOUTH CENTRAL COLORADO HIGHLIGHTS

Trinidad: museums, the Bloom Mansion, Sangre de Cristo Mountains, fishing, camping

Highway 12, Trinidad to Walsenburg: San Isabel National Forest, Monument Lake, wildflowers in the Cuchara Valley, Spanish Peaks, fishing, camping, skiing

Great Sand Dunes National Monument: sightseeing, camping

Pueblo: Rosemount House Museum, Mineral Palace Park, city zoo, Colorado State Fair, fishing, camping, sightseeing

Cañon City: Colorado Territorial Prison Museum and Park, museums, sightseeing, whitewater rafting

Royal Gorge: sightseeing, tram rides, camping

Cripple Creek: Narrow-Gauge Railroad, Mollie Kathleen Mine Tour, sightseeing, museums, gambling, shopping

Colorado Springs: museums, U.S. Olympic Sports Complex, Will Rogers Shrine of the Sun, ProRodeo Hall of Fame, Broadmoor Hotel

Bishop Castle (Westcliffe): modern stone castle

Pikes Peak: Pikes Peak Highway, cog railway, hiking

Manitou Springs: historical tours, museums, Garden of the Gods (national natural landmark)

---

of Pikes Peak. Visit the United States Air Force Academy or ProRodeo Hall of Fame in Colorado Springs. Explore the old mining towns of Victor and Cripple Creek, or a stretch of the Old Santa Fe Trail. Camp in the gorgeous San Isabel and Pike national forests. Take a narrow-gauge train over into New Mexico. Wander into the tallest sand dunes in the country. Or just enjoy some of the prettiest scenery in the state.

Before You Go

If you're coming in from the south, stop at the **Colorado Welcome Center** in Trinidad, 309 N. Nevada Ave., tel. (719) 846-9512. You'll find a friendly staff and lots of information and brochures on things to do and see in the area, as well as the rest of the state; the center also provides information about lodging and camping. Be sure to pick up a copy of *Spirit: The Magazine of Southern Colorado.*

TRINIDAD

Situated just east of the Sangre de Cristo ("Blood of Christ") Mountains and 20 miles from the New Mexico border, Trinidad (pop. 9,500; elev. 6,025 feet), seat of Las Animas County, maintains a strong sense of its Spanish heritage. Its narrow, hilly brick streets, stone churches, and mellow, Old-World pace, as well as the nearby place names (Segundo, Aguilar, Isabel, Cuchara, La Veta) are evidence of the town's ties to the Spanish Colonial era and, later, to the period when the surrounding area was part of the Territory of New Mexico.

The hub of several highways, Trinidad is a funny town to drive in, as I-25, Hwys. 160 and 350, and CO 12 and 239, not to mention the railroad, all convene near the river, winding linguini-like before heading out again in their different directions. The downtown area, Corazon

de Trinidad ("Heart of Trinidad"), is an excellent spot to spend a few hours poking around and getting a feel for a part of the state that's very different from the resort towns and sprawling urban centers to the north. Also, take a few minutes to drive up into the hills on Trinidad's east side above the Pioneer Museum; the brick streets are truly unique and add a distinct flavor to the little town.

HISTORY

The Trinidad area, including the Sangre de Cristos and the Purgatoire River Valley, was long a hunting and ceremonial ground for various Indian tribes, and though the town was never actually attacked, early European settlers were accustomed to threats by Ute war parties. Long before the Comanches, Utes, and other groups arrived, prehistoric people were living in caves and crude shelters in the nearby hills.

Shortly after 1598, when Juan de Oñate arrived in the Santa Fe area from Spain, he led a group north into the Purgatoire River Valley. Over the next two centuries, Spanish priests, explorers, and soldiers continued to probe the area north of Santa Fe, and between 1822 and the late 1870s, Trinidad was the last stop on the Santa Fe Trail before Ratón Pass and the drop down into Santa Fe.

On May 13, 1847, the United States declared war on Mexico, and a month later, Stephen Watts Kearny, after passing through what is now Trinidad, arrived in Santa Fe and took control of that town without resistance. In 1859, New Mexican Gabriel Gutierrez came north to Trinidad to herd sheep, and his cabin was the first building of record.

Gradually, Trinidad saw more and more settlers, at first mostly from the south. Soon, though, people began to arrive from the north as well, and for a time the rambunctious town seemed to symbolize the larger frictions between the United States and Mexico; fights between the two groups were commonplace. On Christmas Day, 1867, nearly a thousand people took part in a rumble of sorts, which resulted in several deaths and could only be brought under control by the U.S. cavalry, who declared martial law. That year also saw the opening of Trinidad's first coal mine.

The arrival of the railroad in the late 1870s helped encourage cattle ranchers to come to the area, boosting the local economy; the town was incorporated in 1877. On April 20, 1914, striking coal workers, with support from the United Mine Workers, battled U.S. militiamen, who had been called in to keep the peace. During the ensuing gunfight, which took place about 12 miles north of Trinidad, six coal miners were shot, and 11 children and two women killed when the tent in which they were hiding burned. (If you find this period of history interesting or are intrigued by the early American labor movement, see Peter Weir's excellent

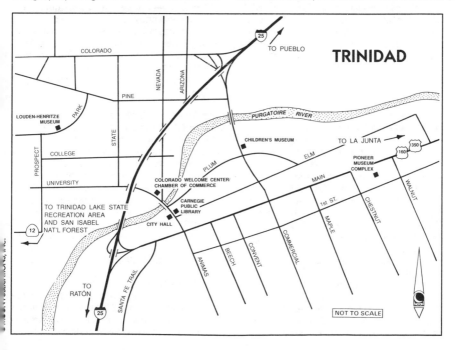

horses grazing in the Purgatoire River Valley near Weston on CO 12

STEPHEN METZGER

film *Matewan,* which, based on a true story, examines the deplorable working conditions in the mines and the resistance labor organizers met when they tried to improve them.)

The United Mine Workers of America has erected a monument near the Ludlow Exit north of Trinidad in recognition of those killed. In June 1990, the 100th anniversary of the founding of the UMWA, labor leaders from around the country gathered at the site of the monument to commemorate the massacre.

MUSEUMS

Baca House, Bloom House, And Pioneer Museum

This three-museum complex occupies the 300 block of E. Main Street. A small entrance fee gets you a guided tour of all three buildings.

The **Baca House,** made of adobe and dating from 1869, is the oldest still-standing building in Trinidad. Built by Pennsylvanian John S. Hough and sold a year later to Felipe Baca, a Spanish sheep rancher, shipping tycoon, and politician, the house has been redecorated with period furnishings.

The 13-room **Bloom House** is reportedly the state's best example of Second Empire French architecture; it was built in 1882 for cattle rancher and banker Frank L. Bloom. All of the furnishings in the mansion are either original or exact duplicates. Bloom House highlights include elaborate draperies and wallpapers and a Victorian garden, complete with waterfall.

Occupying what were once the stables and servants' quarters for the Baca House, Trinidad's **Pioneer Museum** displays an array of artifacts from the Santa Fe Trail and from Trinidad's past, including Indian arrowheads, carriages, guns, and historical photos.

The museum complex is open Memorial Day through Labor Day, Mon. through Sat. 10 a.m.-4 p.m., Sun. 1-4 p.m., and later in September by appointment only. For information on all three museums, write 300 E. Main St., Trinidad, CO 81082, or phone (719) 846-7217.

Louden-Henritze Museum Of Archaeology

Located in the library of Trinidad State Junior College, this small museum features dioramas of nearby Trinchera Cave, which was occupied thousands of years ago by nomadic hunters. The museum also displays arrowheads, fossils, and samples of local gems and minerals. Some of the artifacts come from a 1962 excavation of hundreds of sites now deep beneath the waters of Trinidad Reservoir.

The museum is open June-Aug., daily noon-4 p.m. Admission is free. For more information, phone (719) 846-5508.

Children's Museum

Located in an old firehouse, which was also the town's first city hall and jail, this is a museum full of hands-on displays, including a firecart, fire engine, and primitive alarm system.

(top) rock climber in Garden of the Gods, near Colorado Springs;
(bottom) Glenwood Hot Springs Pool (both photos: Stephen Metzger)

(top) Visitors explore cliff dwellings at Mesa Verde National Park. (Durango Chamber Resort Association and Mesa Verde National Park); (bottom) stark cliffs and spires in Colorado National Monument (Stephen Metzger

The museum is at 314 N. Commercial Street. For more information, or to book tours, phone (719) 846-7721.

A.R. Mitchell Museum Of Western Art

Famous for his Western paintings, as well as the scores of covers he did for Western dime novels, Arthur Roy Mitchell died in 1977. The Trinidad gallery displays some 200 of his original oils, in addition to work by other Western-style painters, including Harvey Dunn and Grant Reynard. The museum also exhibits a collection of Spanish folk art, and a gift shop sells jewelry, paintings, cards, and souvenirs. Admission to the museum, located at 150 E. Main, is free. Hours are Mon. through Sat. 10 a.m.-4 p.m., mid-April through September. For more information, phone (719) 846-4224.

PARKS AND RECREATION

City Parks

Kit Carson Park, located northwest of the downtown area at San Pedro St. and Kansas Ave., has picnic facilities, lawns, shade trees, and a kids' playground, as well as a turn-of-the-century bandstand and a statue of Carson. **Central Park,** west of I-25 at Stonewall and San Juan, has softball fields, a small lake, picnic tables, a playground, and a jogging trail. **Southside Park,** on Benshoar Dr., has a jogging trail, horseshoe pits, softball fields, picnic tables, and a playground. For more information, phone the Trinidad Community Center at (719) 846-4454.

Trinidad Lake State Recreation Area

This 2,300-acre park, with a 900-acre lake, located about four miles west of Trinidad on CO 12, offers a wide range of recreational activities, including hiking, fishing, boating, picnicking, swimming, and camping (tenting and RVing). You'll find 62 campsites, running water, flush toilets, and hot showers, as well as laundry and RV-dump facilities. Fish for rainbow and brown trout, largemouth bass, channel catfish, bluegill, walleye, and crappie. Two short nature trails (Carpios Ridge Trail, one mile, and Levsa Canyon Trail, 1 1/2 miles) have been laid out for hikers.

For more information on Trinidad Lake State Recreation Area, write 32610 Hwy. 12, Trinidad, CO 81082, or phone (719) 846-6951.

Call to reserve campsites or group picnic areas. You can also get information from the **Colorado Division of Parks and Outdoor Recreation,** Department of Natural Resources, 1313 Sherman #618, Denver, CO 80203, tel. (303) 866-3437.

Highway 12 And San Isabel National Forest

Highway 12, which winds west out of Trinidad, up into the gorgeous Sangre de Cristo Mountains of San Isabel National Forest, over 9,941-foot Cucharas Pass, then back down through La Veta and into Walsenburg, offers excellent camping (three Forest Service campgrounds just east of Cucharas Pass) and fishing opportunities, as well as spectacular sightseeing. The 82-mile drive is discussed in detail under "North to Walsenburg Via Hwy. 12" following. Monument Lake Resort, about 35 miles west of Trinidad, is owned by the city. For further information on San Isabel National Forest, write 1920 Valley Dr., Pueblo, CO 81008, or phone (719) 545-8737.

Golfing

The **Trinidad Municipal Golf Course,** tel. (719) 846-4015, located just south of town, is a nine-hole course open year-round and sponsors various local tournaments.

PRACTICALITIES

Accommodations

The **Trinidad Motor Inn,** tel. (719) 846-2271, is located just off I-25 (Exit 13B) and has doubles starting around $40. Doubles at the **Best Western Country Club Inn,** tel. 846-2215, Exit 13A, will run $45-65 depending on the season. The **Derrick Motel Budget Host,** tel. 846-3307, has doubles starting at $30. There's also a **Holiday Inn,** tel. 846-4491 or (800) HOLIDAY; take Exit 11. Rooms for two at **Blue House Bed and Breakfast,** 824 W. Colorado, tel. 846-4507, are about $45.

Food

This close to New Mexico, and with such a large Hispanic population, Trinidad offers cooking that leans south—toward green chiles, sopaipillas, tamales. I stumbled on an unpretentious little hole-in-the-wall called **La Fiesta**, 510 W. Main St., tel. (719) 846-9006. Specializing in green chile stew and burgers, La Fiesta is open daily except Sunday 8 a.m. to 8 p.m., with complete dinners running $3-5, and à la carte burritos $1-3 (they also serve American breakfasts and offer take-out). Other Mexican restaurants include **El Capitan**, 321 State St., tel. 846-9903, and **Maria's,** 219 W. Main St., tel. 846-4962.

The **Stagecoach Dining Room** in the Trinidad Motor Inn, tel. 846-2271, serves chicken, fish, and beef dinners, as well as Mexican and Italian food. You can also get Italian food at **Nana and Nano's Pasta House,** 415 University St., tel. 846-2697. **Monteleone's Deli**, on the west side of town en route to Trinidad Lake, sells homemade Italian sandwiches (meatball, Italian sausage, etc.).

Calendar

Each June (usually around the second weekend), Trinidad sponsors the **Santa Fe Trail Festival,** which features arts-and-crafts shows, costume competitions, and lots of food and live entertainment. There's also a staged melodrama. For information and exact dates, contact the chamber of commerce (see "Information" following).

Services

The offices of the **Trinidad Police Department,** tel. (719) 846-4441, and the **Las Animas County Sheriff,** tel. 846-2211, are downtown next to city hall. Phone the **Colorado State Patrol** in Trinidad at 846-2227. **Mt. San Rafael Hospital** is at 410 Benedicta, tel. 846-9213. The main **post office** is at 301 E. Main; phone 846-6871.

Recycling

Recycle aluminum at the **Las Animas County Rehabilitation Center,** 1205 Congress Dr., and at **Safeway,** 457 W. Main.

Information

In addition to the Colorado Welcome Center in Trinidad, you'll find a Trinidad **visitor center,** in the train caboose in the parking lot near Safeway and city hall. Pick up information on recreation, dining, lodging, as well as maps of the area and of a self-guided historical walking tour. Write the **Trinidad Chamber of Commerce** at 309 Nevada St., Trinidad, CO 81082, or phone (719) 846-9285.

Trinidad's historical **Carnegie Public Library** is at 202 N. Animas, tel. 846-6841. Watch Trinidad's daily newspaper, the *Chronicle-News,* tel. 846-3311, for listings of current events and other happenings.

For **road conditions,** phone 846-9262.

Transportation

Although Trinidad's a weird town to drive in, with all the different highways converging, the downtown area is pretty square and easy to walk. To make it even easier to get around, the city offers the **Trinidad Trolley,** with stops at parks and historical sites. Departures are hourly from the parking lot next to the city hall (summer only).

NORTH TO WALSENBURG VIA HIGHWAY 12

Though this route will take you at least an hour and a half out of your way (I-25 to Walsenburg takes 40 minutes, max), this scenic byway, one of the prettiest in the state, is definitely worth the extra time. The highway first drops southwest out of Trinidad, passes by Trinidad Lake State Recreation Area and the historical mining town of Cokedale, winds through the lush Purgatoire River Valley, then begins to climb up into the high mountains, offering breathtaking vistas along the way. You'll pass through a number of tiny resort communities, San Isabel National Forest, up over 9,941-foot Cucharas Pass, and past several pristine alpine lakes near, or above, timberline. Linguists take note: Occasionally in the Purgatoire River Valley, you'll see the word "Picketwire" in place names. This is an Anglo bastardization of "Purgatoire," French for Purgatory.

Cokedale
Now a National Historic District, Cokedale was founded in 1906 by the American Refining and Smelting Company. Though the community bustled with work and workers during the early part of the century, when coke from the town's ovens was shipped to Leadville, today the town's all but abandoned. Dirt streets wind past dilapidated houses—some still occupied—which cling to the hillside in last-gasp efforts to remain standing.

Segundo
About 10 miles past Cokedale, the tiny town of Segundo is little more than a gas station and small market and deli (Ringo's). Earlier in the century, citizens of Spanish descent painted the doors and window frames of Segundo homes and businesses bright blue to keep the devil away.

Stonewall
Named for the gigantic granite stone wall you can see through the trees on the west side of the highway, this town was established by Juan Gutierrez (nephew of Gabriel Gutierrez, one of Trinidad's founding fathers) in the late 1860s.

Long a resort community for fishermen, as well as for people simply wanting to escape the heat of the lowlands, Stonewall still offers a couple of inns tucked away in a beautiful valley setting, highlighted by the rushing river, green meadows, and tall pines and cottonwoods. The **Picketwire Lodge,** tel. (719) 868-2265, has rooms with kitchens and is open year-round for hunting, fishing, and cross-country skiing. The **Stonewall Guest Ranch,** tel. 868-2270, has cabins, RV sites, a playground, and a trout pond. The **Mountain Inn Motel,** tel. 868-2294, has cabins, RV sites, and a small store with groceries and basic camping and fishing supplies.

You can also get fishing licenses and equipment, as well as tips on how to catch the big ones, from **The Shopping Bag** in Stonewall.

Monument Lake
With a large granite stone sticking straight up out of its deep blue waters, Monument Lake is a perfect place to stop and picnic and set up camp for a couple of days. **Monument Lake Resort and Campground,** tel. (719) 868-2226, which is owned and operated by the city of Trinidad, offers a full range of accommodations, from tent and RV sites to cabins and luxury rooms in the adobe lodge; there's also a full-service restaurant, lounge, and gift shop. Tent sites run $8, cabins and rooms start at about $40 for two. Write Star Route #1, Box 81A, CO 81091 for more information.

Cucharas Pass
The views from this pass are stunning. In the early summer, columbines sheet the steep meadows, and the variegated mountainsides are mottled green with aspen, fir, spruce, and pine. Several of the lakes along the road offer excellent fishing, although you should check the restrictions—some are flies or artifical lures only. Just north of the pass is a turnoff to a rocky dirt road leading to three Forest Service campgrounds (pit toilets only, no showers). The first, **Cucharas Pass** (22 sites), is a half mile from the highway, **Blue Lake** (15 sites) is four miles, and **Bear Lake** (14 sites) is five.

Spanish Peaks is a private campground also on the north side of the pass, with nicely sheltered tent and RV sites ($8 and $13, including showers).

Cuchara

Cuchara is a 90-year-old resort between the gorgeous Cucharas Pass and the lush Cuchara Valley. Though primarily a summer resort, the area began to attract visitors in 1981, when the small Panadero Ski Resort opened up the road. The name was shortly changed to Cuchara Valley Resort, and in 1985 the area was expanded to cover 135 acres with 24 runs and a vertical drop of 1,562 feet. In 1986, the resort's loan was foreclosed upon. Its new owners? Summit Savings in Dallas, which operated the area until November 1989, when it announced quite unexpectedly that it was shutting down the lifts.

Then in 1991, the resort was purchased by Dick Davis, a Texas businessman whose goal was to turn Cuchara Valley Resort into a family-oriented area that emphasized affordability and fun (adult lift tickets were $25 in the winter of 1992-93). And with the community largely behind him, Davis seems to be revitalizing Cuchara. It probably won't be long before word gets out that this out-of-the-way resort is worth going out of your way for.

You'll find a variety of lodging options in Cuchara, including **Yellow Pines Guest Ranch,** 15846 State Hwy. 12, Cuchara, CO 81055, tel. (719) 742-3528; **Misty Haven Cabins,** 178 Hill Rd., Cuchara, CO 81055, tel. 742-3433; the **Cuchara Inn,** tel. 742-3685; and the rustic **Cuchara Lodge,** tel. 742-3254. For information on lodging at the Cuchara Valley Resort (ski area), phone 742-3163 or (800) 227-4436.

The Cuchara Valley

Just past Cuchara, CO 12 drops down out of the high mountains and begins its gentle roll through the Cuchara Valley back toward I-25 and the western edge of the plains. During the summer, the valley meadows are ablaze with wildflowers—especially impressive are June's wild irises and July's columbines. This verdant valley offers spectacular views of the Spanish Peaks, or Las Cumbres Españolas, which have been landmarks for travelers for hundreds of years. To the Native Americans, the mountains were known as Huajotolla (which I've seen trans-

lated both as "the Twins" and as "the Breasts of the World"), and as early as 1654 New Mexico governor Diego de Vargas reported having spotted them on a trip north from Santa Fe. The mountains, rising 13,610 and 12,669 feet, have also been called Dos Hermanos ("Two Brothers"), the Mexican Mountains, and Twin Peaks.

LA VETA

La Veta is a kick-back little resort town and artists' community in the shadow of the Spanish Peaks and on the banks of the slowly tumbling Cucharas River. Founded in the mid-19th century, La Veta ("The Vein") served as a trading center for about a hundred years. Today, La Veta caters to folks looking to escape lowland heat and urban craziness, whether they come to rejuvenate for a weekend or relocate for a lifetime. Passers-through can stop in at the town's impressive historical museum, play a round of golf at the club, or camp at one of the many nearby campgrounds.

Fort Francisco Museum

Built in 1862 by Colonel John M. Francisco and Judge Henry Daigre, both to serve as a trade center and to protect local settlers from Indian attacks, this was the first structure in the Cuchara Valley. In 1871, the area's first post office opened at the fort. When the railroad arrived in the valley in the late 1870s, and the depot was built a few blocks north, the community's merchants and traders all but abandoned this once-thriving hub.

In 1957, the Huerfano County Historical Society obtained the fort and shortly thereafter opened it as a museum. Many of the buildings and furnishings are original, and descendants of local settlers have donated artifacts of historical interest. Exhibits include the old saloon (which over the years also served as a pool hall, restaurant, post office, roller rink, and general store), barbershop, one-room school, blacksmith shop, and mining museum. The museum has an excellent collection of historical letters and documents, including Kit Carson's will. A gift shop sells souvenirs, cards, and locally made crafts.

The Gallery

Established in 1975, La Veta's Friends of the Arts Guild displays and sells work by local artists.

The Gallery was built in 1983. In addition to exhibiting artwork, the building also serves as a classroom and meeting place for guild members, who are spread throughout the area. Ordinarily, the Gallery displays the work of over two dozen artists, with media ranging from charcoal and pencil drawings to weaving, woodwork, and stained glass. The Gallery is located on W. Ryus. For information and business hours, contact the La Veta/Cuchara Valley Chamber of Commerce (see "Information" following).

Golfing

La Veta's **Grandote** (gran-DOH-tay) **Golf and Country Club** is an 18-hole course designed by famous golfer Tom Wieskopf. One of the state's newest golf courses (it opened in 1986), Grandote hosts a number of tournaments throughout the summer and fall. For information on greens fees and tee times, phone (719) 742-3123.

Practicalities

For such a small community, La Veta offers a relatively large number of accommodations options, from RV campgrounds to bed and breakfasts. The **1899 Inn,** tel. (719) 742-3576, is an extremely nice and unassuming little getaway on Main St.; rooms with private baths start at about $40 (about $32 for shared bath). *Huge* breakfast included. **Circle the Wagons** RV Park, tel. 742-3233, offers RV sites for $9, plus, for square dancers, a variety of "dance packages." You can also get rooms at the **Log Haven RV Park**

and Motel, tel. 742-3252, and the **La Veta Motel,** tel. 742-5598.

The **Cajun Eatery,** located downtown at 222 Main, tel. 742-3004, specializes in New Orleans fried chicken, poorboy sandwiches, and other southern favorites; prices are very reasonable. The **Covered Wagon Steakhouse,** 205 S. Main, tel. 742-3679, is a local favorite, serving a variety of beefy entrees, fowl, salads, etc. If you're looking for a place to grab a hot dog, some fries, and a cold one, try the new **Sports Pub and Grub** at 923 Oak, tel. 742-3093, open Sun. through Thurs. 11 a.m.-midnight and Fri. and Sat. 11 a.m. till 2 a.m.

Recycling

Recycle aluminum, glass, and newspapers at 121 E. Ryus.

Information

The **La Veta/Cuchara Valley Chamber of Commerce,** Box 32, La Veta, CO 81055, tel. (719) 742-3676, has assembled a thorough package of tourist information, including a *La Veta/Cuchara Tour Map and Guide,* which features hot springs, hiking trails, geological highlights, and other points of interest in the area. The chamber can also provide a complete list of restaurants, retailers, accommodations, and other information services.

You can also get information on the area from the **Cuchara Tourist Association.** Write Box 2111, Cuchara, CO 81055, or phone 742-3685 or 742-3450.

pika

MARK MORRIS

WEST TO ALAMOSA

Hwy. 160 runs west out of Walsenburg, up over North La Veta Pass (elev. 9,413 feet), then cuts across northern Costilla County, through Fort Garland, Blanca, and into Alamosa. The 75-mile stretch follows pretty closely the Denver and Rio Grande Western Railroad route.

This southern prairie pocket of Colorado, roughly 125 miles north to south and 50 miles across, is the San Luis Valley, long a hunting area for Utes and Comanches. One of the first parts of Colorado to be explored by the Spanish, as early as 1761, the San Luis Valley still claims a great many Hispanic citizens, many of whom are descendants of original mid-18th-century Mexican land-grant settlers.

As you approach Fort Garland, watch the mountains to the north. Four "14ers" are clustered within a few miles of each other: Mt. Lindsey (14,042 feet), Little Bear Peak (14,037 feet), Blanca Peak (14,345 feet), and Ellingwood Point (14,042 feet).

FORT GARLAND

The first U.S. outpost in the San Luis Valley was Fort Massachusetts, built in 1852 about five miles northeast of Fort Garland. The fort only saw active duty for six years, however, as it was built on swampland, and the army had trouble providing fresh drinking water for the troops. Fort Garland, named for Brigadier General John Garland, was built in 1858, when Fort Massachusetts was abandoned. For some 25 years, Fort Garland served both to protect settlers from Utes, who were attempting to save their land and herds, and also to provide a social and trading center in an otherwise lonely and barren region. Kit Carson was assigned to the fort from 1866-67; it was his last military post.

Sixteen miles south of Fort Garland on CO 159 is the little town of San Luis, the oldest community in the state.

Fort Garland Museum
Reconstructed to provide visitors with a genuine sense of life on the lonesome frontier in the mid-19th century, the old fort displays a wide range of Native American, Mexican, and Anglo historical artifacts, including original military uniforms and weaponry. There's also a sampling of Hispanic folk art from the area.

The museum is located at the junction of Hwy. 160 and CO 159. For hours and more information, write Box 368, Fort Garland, CO 81133, or phone (719) 379-3512.

ALAMOSA

Alamosa (pop. 7,000; elev. 7,500 feet) is the largest town in the San Luis Valley, as well as the last decent-sized town in Colorado as you head south on Hwy. 285 toward Santa Fe, New Mexico. It's also the closest town to Great Sand Dunes National Monument. Long a hub town and shipping center, particularly for potatoes, the San Luis Valley's principal crop, Alamosa ("Cottonwood Grove") today is the seat of Alamosa County, as well as home to Adams State College, a popular teacher-training institution.

History
In 1878, Alamosa's founding father, A.C. Hunt, president of the Denver and Rio Grande Construction Company, loaded up flatcars with stores, churches, and houses and moved them from Garland City, which until then had been

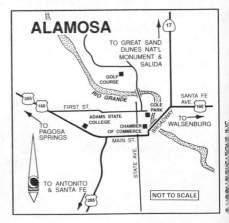

*cooling off in the creek
at the base of the
sand dunes*

the railroad's terminus, and plunked them down at the site of the new one. *Voilà.* Alamosa.

A rambunctious town from the get-go, early Alamosa saw more than its share of ramblers, gamblers, and frontier crazies, particularly the notoriously rowdy railroad construction workers. Lynchings are said to have been commonplace, with one particular riverside cottonwood designated the "hangin' tree."

Later, things mellowed out some, and Alamosa became a central shipping point for San Luis potatoes, as well as wheat, oats, alfalfa, lettuce, cauliflower, and peas, which were commonly fed to hogs, another Alamosa-area export.

Great Sand Dunes National Monument
Created by winds blowing Rio Grande-eroded particles of valley floor east across the San Luis Valley and up against the Sangre de Cristo range, these sand dunes, which reach heights of 700 feet, are the tallest in the country. A true geological oddity, the 39 square miles of dunes stand in stark contrast to both the snowcapped mountains behind them and the desert valley at their base.

Great Sand Dunes National Monument offers year-round camping (both in developed and in primitive backcountry areas), picnicking, and hiking, as well as a chance simply to goof around in this huge and most unlikely of sandboxes. Though much of the dune area is off limits, a short hike from the parking lot, one mile past the visitors center, will take you into sand completely undisturbed by anything save the

wind and the handful of small critters that make their homes there.

The visitors center, open daily 8 a.m. to 5 p.m. (with extended summer hours) has brochures, maps, books, wildlife and geology displays, explanatory videos, and a self-guided nature trail, as well as rangers to answer your questions.

To get to Great Sand Dunes National Monument, take Hwy. 160 16 miles east from Alamosa and then CO 150 20 miles north. You can also go north 14 miles from Alamosa on CO 17 and turn east on County Lane 6 one mile north of Mosca.

City Park
Alamosa's **Cole Park** is located on the east end of town on the banks of the upper Rio Grande. Huge lawns, cottonwoods for shade, and picnic tables—all just yards from the Alamosa tourist information center (chamber of commerce).

Golfing
There are four public golf courses within driving distance of Alamosa. **Alamosa Golf Course** is an 18-hole course at 6678 River Rd.; phone (719) 589-5330. The **Monte Vista Golf Club** (nine holes) is located in Monte Vista west of Alamosa via Hwy. 160; phone 852-9995. North of town, off CO 17 in Crestone, **Los Cumbres Golf Course** is another nine-hole course; phone 256-4856. **Great Sand Dunes Country Club and Resort** is about seven miles south of Great Sand Dunes National Monument; phone 378-2357.

Accommodations

Not a whole lot to choose from here, although since it's most likely not your honeymoon you shouldn't be too disappointed. The least expensive rooms are probably at the **Sky-Vue Motel,** tel. (719) 589-4945, on the east end of town at 250 Broadway. For about $45 a night you can get a room at any of a handful of places, including the **Alamosa Inn Best Western,** 1919 Main, tel. 589-2567; the **Lamplighter,** 425 Main, tel. 589-6636; and the **Luxury 8 Inn,** 224 O'Keefe Parkway (US 160 on the east side of town), tel. 589-9037. The Alamosa **Holiday Inn,** right next door to the Luxury 8, tel. 589-5833, has doubles for about $55.

Camping And RVing

There are RV campgrounds both on Alamosa's east and west side. A **KOA,** tel. (719) 589-9757, is on Hwy. 160 as you pull into town from the east, and **Navajo Trails Campground,** tel. 589-9460, on Hwy. 160 on the west side offers mini golf. There's also camping at Great Sand Dunes National Monument, about 35 miles northeast of Alamosa (see above). **Great Sand Dunes Oasis and RV Park,** tel. 378-2222, is located three miles south of the visitors center on Hwy. 150. There's also a small grocery and souvenir store, and you can book scenic 4WD tours. **Blanca RV Park,** tel. 379-3201, is about 30 miles south of the park in Blanca.

Food

Passers-through can fill up ice chests at the City Market and Safeway in Alamosa (west side of town, Hwy. 160). If you'd rather sit down and eat than buy picnic fixin's, **Oscar's,** right downtown at 710 Main, tel. (719) 589-9320, serves Mexican lunches and dinners daily 11 a.m.-9 p.m. For Asian food, try **Hunan Chinese Restaurant** at 419 Main, tel. 589-9002—serving Hunan, Szechuan, and Cantonese dishes. A handful of other restaurants and cafés are located in downtown Alamosa.

Shopping

The **Rio Grande Art Market,** downtown at the corner of State and Main streets, carries a wide range of traditional and contemporary work from artists throughout the San Luis Valley—from traditional weavings to jewelry, pot-tery, furniture, basketry, and bronze. Hours are Mon. through Sat. 10 a.m.-8 p.m.; phone (719) 589-5557.

Services

The offices of the **Alamosa Police Department** are at 425 4th St.; phone (719) 589-2548 (589-5807 in emergencies). Phone the **Alamosa County Sheriff** at 589-6608 (589-5807 in emergencies). The **State Patrol** offices are at 1205 West; phone 589-2503. The **San Luis Valley Regional Medical Center** is in Alamosa at 106 Blanca Ave.; phone 589-2511. There are also branch clinics in La Jara, tel. 274-4007, and in Monte Vista, tel. 852-2448.

Alamosa's **post office** is behind the chamber of commerce at 505 3rd St.; phone 589-4908.

Recycling

Recycle aluminum and glass at the **City Market,** 131 Market St., and aluminum, glass, newpapers, and plastic containers at **Villa Mall, Adams State College,** and the **Loaf & Jug** (6988 S. Hwy. 17). For more information, phone **San Luis Valley Recyclers** at (719) 589-5193.

Information

Located at Cole Park, along the Rio Grande just off Hwy. 160 on the east side of town, the **Alamosa Chamber of Commerce** has lots of brochures, maps, and other information on Alamosa and the San Luis Valley. Write Alamosa Chamber of Commerce, Cole Park, Alamosa, CO 81101, or phone (719) 589-3681. For maps and information on the San Luis Valley, write the **Bureau of Land Management,** 1921 State Ave., Alamosa, CO 81101; phone 589-4975.

A book's throw across the parking lot is the Alamosa **Southern Peaks Public Library,** 424 4th St.; phone 589-6592. **Narrow Gauge Newsstand,** 604 Main St., tel. 589-6712, has books on the area, its history, and recreational guidebooks.

Alamosa's daily newspaper is the *Valley Courier,* which serves the San Luis Valley. For information or subscriptions, write Box 1099, Alamosa, CO 81101, or phone 589-2553 or 359-0742.

For **road and weather information,** phone 589-9024.

Transportation

Alamosa is located at the junctions of Hwy. 160 running east to west, Hwy. 285 running north to south, and CO 17, which runs north from Conejos (northbound termination point of the Cumbres-Toltec Railroad), through Alamosa, and north toward Salida.

Air transportation is provided by **Continental Express,** tel. (719) 589-3804, to San Luis Valley Airport (tel. 589-2593)—connecting flights from Denver's Stapleton International. You can rent cars in Alamosa from **Freedom Rent-a-Car,** tel. 589-5466, **Hertz,** tel. 589-6559 or (800) 645-3131, or **Silver State Auto Rental,** tel. 589-4651. Phone Alamosa's **Valley Wide Taxi Service** at 589-4445.

Tours

If you prefer guided tours of the San Luis Valley area to exploring it on your own, **Sierra Vista Tours,** tel. (719) 379-3277 or (800) 637-3469, offers jaunts to several of the local attractions, including Great Sand Dunes National Monument, the Cumbres and Toltec Scenic Railroad, museums, fishing holes, and ski areas. Write Box 207, Blanca, CO 81123. You can arrange 4WD tours of the Great Sand Dunes area through **Great Sand Dunes Oasis and RV Park,** tel. 378-2222.

SOUTH TO ANTONITO AND NEW MEXICO

From Alamosa, it's only a half-hour drive south on Hwy. 285 to Antonito and the northern terminus of the Cumbres and Toltec Scenic Railroad, and from there it's just five miles to the New Mexico border. A fairly straight shot this, beelining down along the western side of the San Luis Valley.

A mile north of La Jara, or about 14 miles out of Alamosa, you'll find the **Conejos Peak Ranger Station** for the Rio Grande National Forest, where you can get maps and information on camping in the forest (which stretches to the west from Del Norte nearly to Silverton). At the junction of CO 142, about seven miles past La Jara, you can turn east to Manassa, birthplace of Jack Dempsey, the "Manassa Mauler," and visit the **Jack Dempsey Museum.** Though Dempsey left the tiny town as a young teenager to fight in the mining camps to the north, and by 1950 was famous worldwide as one of the greatest heavyweight boxers of all time, he kept in close contact with his friends and family in Manassa, until he died in 1983. The museum, located downtown, displays boxing artifacts and photos of young Jack and his family. For hours and more information, write Box 130, Manassa, CO 81141.

From Manassa, continue east to San Luis, one of the oldest towns in Colorado. Founded in 1851 by Spanish settlers, the town has remained largely isolated, and its citizenry is still almost entirely Hispanic. The **San Luis Museum, Cultural, and Commercial Center** there displays Hispanic folk art, as well as graphic explanations of the culture of the San Luis Valley. The museum, located at 402 Church Place, is open weekdays year-round 8:30 a.m.-4:30 p.m. and in the summer on weekends 11 a.m.-5 p.m. For information, phone (719) 672-3611.

For more information on San Luis, write the **San Luis Visitor Center,** Box 307, San Luis, CO 81152, or phone 672-4441.

Antonito

The northern terminus of the **Cumbres and Toltec Scenic Railroad,** Antonito is little more than a train depot and a couple of motels and small cafés. Beginning in Chama, New Mexico, the 1880-vintage railroad winds 64 miles through some of the most beautiful country in the Rockies—through tunnels and pristine vales, and across high trestles over deep mountain gorges—crisscrossing the border several times. The summit is 10,022-foot Cumbres Pass, where the Spanish first entered Colorado.

From Antonito to Chama is a full-day ride, and you can return by van. Another option is to stop at Osier, the halfway point, for lunch, and to return to Antonito. Either way it's one full day. Fare from Antonito to Chama, including return by van, is about $45. Reservations are highly recommended. For more information, contact Cumbres and Toltec Scenic Railroad, Box 668, Antonito, CO 81120, tel. (719) 376-5483, or Box 789, Chama, NM 87520, tel. (505) 756-2151.

The **Antonito Tourist Information Center and Chamber of Commerce** is located at the south end of town across from the railroad tracks. Write Box 427, Antonito, CO 81120, or phone (719) 376-5441. You can get lodging in Antonito at the **Narrow Gauge Railroad Inn,** tel. 376-5441.

WALSENBURG AND VICINITY

From La Veta to Walsenburg (pop. 5,100; elev. 6,186 feet) is about 17 miles, CO 12 joining Hwy. 160 about 12 miles west of town. Predictably, it gets flatter and drier as you drop back down onto the prairie. About five miles west of Walsenburg, you'll pass Martin and Horseshoe lakes and Lathrop State Park, where you'll find facilities for camping, boating, fishing, swimming, and other activities (see below).

Founded by Spanish farmers in the mid-19th century as Plaza de los Leones, Walsenburg was renamed in the 1870s for Fred Walsen, one of the town's early merchants. Today it's a true hub town, at the junction of I-25, Hwys. 160 and 87, and CO 10.

Lathrop State Park
With a commanding view of Spanish Peaks in the distance, this recreation area offers a watery and scenic respite from the heat of the plains. Whether it's waterskiing, sailing, windsurfing, fishing (for trout, bass, catfish, walleye, bluegill,

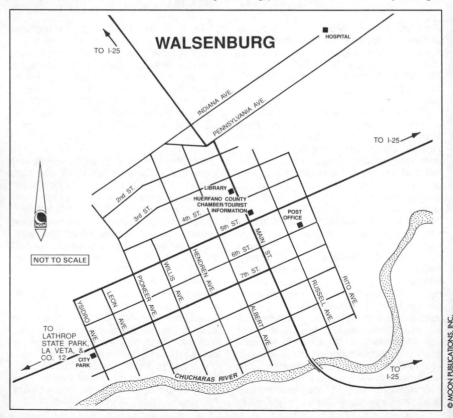

and crappie), swimming, camping, picnicking, golfing, or just plain sightseeing, the two lakes and surrounding area offer a bit of relaxation for just about everyone. The two campgrounds, **Piñon** and **Yucca,** have a total of nearly 100 campsites, and much of the park is handicapped accessible.

Even if you're just passing through, you might want to stop at the visitor center, where nature trails help you identify local flora and you can pick up maps, books, area guides, and postcards. For more information, write Lathrop State Park, 70 County Rd., Walsenburg, CO 81089, or call (719) 738-2376. For information on the golf course, phone 738-2730.

City Park
You'll find a nice, lawny, shady park as you come into town from the west. The park has a public pool, picnic facilities, and playground equipment.

Accommodations
The **Rio Cucharas Inn,** tel. (719) 738-1427, is the first lodge you'll see if you're coming in from the west. From I-25, take Exit 52 to the **Best Western Rambler,** tel. 738-1121; doubles run $40-60 (low in winter, high in summer). You can get nice rooms in town at the **Anchor Motel,** 1001 S. Main, tel. 738-2800, for about $30 for two. Campers can either pull in at **Lathrop State Park** (see above), **Dakota Campground,** tel. 738-9912, or **Budget Host,** tel. 738-3800, both of which are located north of town on Pueblo Rd./Hwy. 85-87. There's a **Day's Inn,** five miles north of Walsenburg on just off I-25; phone 738-2167. A handful of other motels are situated on the north end of Walsen Ave. on the way to Interstate 25.

Malachite Farmstay
The Malachite Farm and School is a nonprofit education organization focusing on nature and humanity's "responsibility to build anew and to cultivate healthy relationships between people and the planet through an awareness that all we create comes from within." Located west of Gardner and surrounded by gorgeous peaks,

the school offers bed-and-breakfast, dorm-style accommodations ($20 per person) and camping ($12 per person). Dinner and lunch menus feature locally grown organic produce and farm-raised rabbit, chicken, pork, and beef.

To get there, take CO 69 west 25 miles to Gardner, and then turn south on the west side of town at the sign for Redwing. Continue south for five miles; then turn left when you see the row of mailboxes. Follow the dirt road for a mile, and watch for the sign for Malachite.

For more information, write Malachite School and Farm, 8055 County Rd. 570, Gardner, CO 81040, or phone (719) 746-2412.

Food
The **Alpine Rose Café,** downtown on Main St., tel. (719) 738-1157, is a classic small-town eatery, offering breakfast, lunch, and dinner at reasonable prices.

Services
The **Walsenburg Police Department** is located at 202 W. 6th St.; phone (719) 738-1044. The **Huerfano County Sheriff** is at 112 W. 5th St.; phone 738-1600. The **State Patrol** offices are at 500 S. Albert, tel. 738-1600. The **Huerfano Medical Center,** tel. 738-5100, is five miles west of Walsenburg on Hwy. 160. The main **post office** is 204 E. 6th, tel. 738-2100.

Recycling
Recycle aluminum at the **Safeway** at 457 W. Main.

Information
The **Huerfano County Chamber of Commerce** can provide extensive information on Walsenburg, Huerfano County, and the surrounding area, including local histories and dining, lodging, and recreation guides, as well as information helpful if you're thinking of relocating. Write Box 493, Walsenburg, CO 81089, or phone (719) 738-1065. If you're in town, stop by their offices in the train depot on Main St. between 4th and 5th. The Walsenburg **public library** is at 323 Main St.; phone 738-2774. The local paper is the *Huerfano World,* tel. 738-1720, with offices at 111 W. 7th.

NORTH FROM WALSENBURG

The 50-mile, less-than-an-hour stretch of I-25 from Walsenburg to Pueblo is largely nondescript, save for the impressive views of the Wet Mountains, a Rockies' sub-range, standing massive and snowcapped to the west. Two miles north of Walsenburg, CO 69 shoots northwest off the interstate, follows the Huerfano River to Gardner, snakes between the two largest units of San Isabel National Forest, passes through the beautiful Wet Mountain Valley and Westcliffe, then intersects with Hwy. 50 west of Cañon City and Royal Gorge. To the west, just south of Westcliffe, you'll be able to see five mountain peaks topping 14,000 feet. Known collectively as the Crestone Needle Peaks, they include Kit Carson Mountain (14,165 feet), Crestone Peak (14,294 feet), Crestone Needle (14,191 feet), Challenger Peak (14,080 feet), and Humboldt Peak (14,064 feet). At both Westcliffe and Hillside you can turn west off Hwy. 69 to campgrounds in San Isabel National Forest.

WESTCLIFFE

At the junction of Hwys. 69 and 96 and nestled between the Wet and Sangre de Cristo mountains, Westcliffe is the seat of Custer County, long one of Colorado's important ranching regions. Westcliffe was founded in 1885 by transplanted Englishman Dr. J.W. Bell, who named it after Westcliffe-on-the-Sea, where he was born. Today Westcliffe, along with its sister city, Silver Cliff, once a booming silver town a mile east, is a base for hikers, backpackers, anglers, cross-country skiers, climbers, and hunters heading either west or east up into the mountains.

Bishop Castle

A legitimate candidate for Ripley's "Believe It Or Not," this is one of the state's most unlikely attractions—a three-story (and growing!) medieval stone castle, complete with buttresses and ornamental iron. The obsession of one man, Jim Bishop, who has been building it at a rate of 1,000 stones a year since 1969, the as-yet-uncompleted castle stands nearly 60 feet tall, less than half as high as it's projected to be upon completion. (It will also have a moat and drawbridge.)

Bishop Castle, which stands partially hidden among the mountain pines and firs, is open to the public free of charge. It's located about 28 miles southeast of Westcliffe. Take CO 96 east, turn south on 165, and watch for the signs. For more information, write Bishop Castle, HCR 75, Box 179, Rye, CO 81069.

Practicalities

Lodging is available in Westcliffe at the **Alpine Lodge,** tel. (719) 783-2660, the **Antler Motel,** tel. 783-2426, the **Castile Lodge,** tel. 783-9701, and a couple of other inns. The Alpine Lodge also has a dining room popular among locals. For more information on lodging, dining, camping, etc., in the Custer County area, write the **Custer County Chamber of Commerce,** Box 81, Westcliffe, CO 81252, or phone 783-9163.

black-footed ferret

CATHY CARLSON

PUEBLO AND VICINITY

Though Pueblo doesn't have the greatest reputation among other Coloradans, who invariably describe it as dull and drab, and who point to its sagging economy and desperate efforts to entice businesses to relocate here, it's actually a pleasant little city, with many quiet, tree-lined streets, stunning Victorian homes, and a population that's largely quite happy here, thank you, and wouldn't live anywhere else.

Pueblo (pop. 102,000; elev, 4,690 feet) is situated on the very edge of America's Great Plains. Just a couple of miles west of town, the Rockies begin their gradual yet unrelenting ascent from foothills to deep forested mountains. Short drives west from Pueblo take you into some of Colorado's most scenic, as well as most historically significant, areas. In fact, one of the best ways to get to Cripple Creek is to head west from Pueblo and then just east of Cañon City to take Phantom Canyon Road (well-maintained gravel) up into Victor and the historic high mining country.

HISTORY

Long a popular hunting ground for bands of plains and mountain native tribes, particularly Comanche, Kiowa, Arapahoe, Cheyenne, and Ute, the Pueblo area was first explored by Europeans in the mid-17th century, when Spaniards from Santa Fe came looking for gold and convertible pagans, as well as to investigate rumors that the French were beginning to colonize the area. The first recorded accounts of actual encampments at the site of present-day Pueblo are from 1706, when a group of Santa Feans rested here briefly on their quest for escaped Native American slaves. Over the next century, the area was explored by trappers, soldiers, prospectors, and Spanish priests.

In 1806, Lieutenant Zebulon Pike erected Pueblo's first structure—a five-foot-high log shelter in which his party camped for a week—and in 1822, Major Jacob Fowler and a small party of trappers and traders built a three-room log house on the banks of the Arkansas River. Twenty years later, James Beckwourth and his party built a small trading post, attracting to the site a couple of dozen settlers, whom Beckwourth put to work building a small adobe fortress, which he dubbed Fort Pueblo.

Between 1842 and 1854, Pueblo attracted a wide range of settlers, from a splinter group of a westbound Mormon party to Indian agents, trappers, traders, and rambunctious pioneers. One of the most famous traders to pass through Pueblo was Richens Lacy "Uncle Dick" Wooten, who would later make a fortune building a 27-mile road over Ratón Pass into New Mexico, erecting a toll gate, and charging every trader, trapper, soldier, and outlaw that passed through. In 1854, a year after he had driven 9,000 head of sheep from New Mexico to California, Wooten settled briefly in Pueblo. At Christmas that year, the inhabitants of the fort, against Wooten's advice, invited local Utes to join in their celebrations. The Utes, taking advantage of the Puebloans' drunkenness, massacred all of them save for three children and one man. By 1855, Pueblo was all but abandoned, former traders avoiding it, believing it haunted by the ghosts of the Christmas massacre.

Pueblo City was actually established in 1860. By 1863, the town had its own post office and by 1868 its first newspaper. The town was incorporated in 1870. Two years later the narrow-gauge Denver and Rio Grande Railroad arrived, and four years after that the rails of the Atchison, Topeka, and Santa Fe railroad were laid to Pueblo. The late 19th century saw the development of Pueblo as an industrial area, with the construction of several smelters, and in the early 20th century a number of steel mills were built.

One of the city's most painful memories can still be recalled by Pueblo old-timers: On July 3, 1921, the Arkansas River overflowed its banks, submerging the downtown area in over 10 feet of water. Hundreds of homes and businesses were washed away, destroyed, or damaged, and scores of people were killed. Two years later the capricious river was rerouted, domesticated with concrete channels and levees.

the Rosemount
House Museum

STEPHEN METZGER

MUSEUMS

Rosemount House Museum

This gorgeous 37-room Victorian was built in 1893 for banker and merchant John A. Thatcher, who amassed his fortunes in mining, ranching, and farming. The 24,000-square-foot house is constructed of pink rhyolite stone and features extensive marble and silverplate tile, elaborate gold, silver, and brass lighting fixtures, and an oak dining table that seats 36. The house cost $60,000 to build.

Tours of the home, located at 419 W. 14th St., are offered during the summer every half hour, Tues. through Sat. 10 a.m.-3:30 p.m. and Sun. 2-3:30; the rest of the year tours are Tues. through Sat. 1-3:30 p.m. and Sun. 2-3:30. Closed in January. Small fee. For information, phone (719) 545-5290.

El Pueblo Museum

Operated by the Colorado Historical Society, this museum displays the history and culture of Pueblo and Pueblo County. Included are both permanent exhibits (the contributions of iron and steel to the area) and traveling displays, arranged by the Colorado Historical Society. During the school year, the museum works with local educational groups, offering a variety of historical programs.

El Pueblo Museum is located at 324 W. 1st St. and is open Mon.-Sat. 10 a.m.-4:30 p.m. and Sun. noon-3 p.m. Admission is $2.50 for adults and $2 for kids and seniors. You can also arrange group tours. For more information, or to book tours, phone (719) 564-5274.

Fred E. Weisbrod Aircraft Museum

Located east of town at the airport, this outdoor museum lets you wander among a wide array of once-important aircraft, including a Lockheed F-80 fighter plane, a B-29 (with original crew members listed on display stand), an F-101 Voodoo, a Douglas C-47 Skytrain, and the B-47E "Might in Flight." Statistics, including passenger or load capacity, crew, special uses, etc., about each craft are given on display plaques. Open daily 9 a.m. to sunset. Free.

International B-24 Memorial Museum

Located across the street from the Aircraft Museum, the B-24 Museum is dedicated to the crews of WW II B-24 Liberators. Exhibited here are historical photos, uniforms, documents, and other artifacts. Open Mon. through Fri. 10 a.m.-4 p.m. and Sat. 10 a.m.-3 p.m. For information, phone (719) 948-9219.

Pueblo Fire Museum

Located at 102 Broadway, this museum displays historical fire-fighting gear, including an 1881 hand-drawn fire-hose cart, a fire truck from 1917, a collection of helmets from around the world, as well as ladders, nozzles, rescue equipment, and historical photos. Open by reservations only. For more information, phone (719) 544-4548, or write Box 4127, Pueblo, CO 81004.

Historical Walking Tours

Local historical groups have developed self-guided walking tours of two Pueblo districts. The **Union Avenue District** tour includes homes and businesses in the Union and Grand Avenue areas, many dating from the 1880s. Some 40 buildings are on the National Register of Historic Places. The **Mesa Junction** tour, on the other side of the Arkansas River, explores the 1880s shopping area where two trolley lines met.

Maps and more information on the tours, as well as detailed discussions of the buildings, are available from the Pueblo Chamber of Commerce (see "Information" following).

Sangre De Cristo Arts And Conference Center

This two-building complex, with four art galleries, a 500-seat theater, and a hands-on children's museum, attracts upwards of 200,000 visitors a year. The galleries feature both permanent and traveling displays, and the center offers dance and music workshops, as well as a summer concert series. There's also a gift shop.

The center's art galleries are open Mon. through Sat. 11 a.m.-4 p.m. The children's museum is open Mon. through Sat. 11 a.m.-5 p.m. For information, or to arrange free tours, phone (719) 543-0130. The center is located at 210 N. Santa Fe.

PARKS AND RECREATION

Lake Pueblo State Recreation Area

An excellent place to beat the heat of a Pueblo summer afternoon, Pueblo Reservoir offers a variety of water sports, including sailing, windsurfing, fishing, and swimming (permitted only in the Rock Canyon Swim Area), in addition to camping, horseback riding, hiking, wildlife viewing, and sightseeing. Though its 60-mile shoreline is mostly barren, surrounded by treeless bluffs and rocky cliffs, the lake still affords a stark, high-plains sort of beauty, especially against the massive Rockies in whose shadow it lies.

First open in the early 1970s, the recreation area has several different campgrounds, with hot water, flush toilets, and RV hookups—nearly 300 campsites all told. Fish for trout, black bass, crappie, and bluegill, from the shore or boat, or hoist a sail and run on the wind. To get there,

take Hwy. 50 west and watch for the signs. For information, write 640 Pueblo Reservoir Rd., Pueblo, CO 81004, or phone (719) 561-9320.

Greenway And Nature Center

Located on the Arkansas River below the Pueblo Reservoir Dam, the center offers picnicking, fishing (from a large deck out over the river), volleyball courts, and raft, kayak, and canoe put-ins. Cyclists will enjoy the 20 miles of bike trails, while hikers can follow the short nature trail (wheelchair accessible). Canoes and bikes are available to rent.

Above the greenway is a small nature center displaying much of the flora and fauna found in the area, and the nearby Raptor Rehabilitation Center cares for injured hawks, owls, falcons, and eagles, with the hope of returning them to the wild. The Nature Center, tel. (719) 545-9114, is open daily 9 a.m.-5 p.m., and the Raptor Rehabilitation Center, tel. 545-7117, is open daily 11 a.m.-4 p.m. To get there, take Hwy. 50 west to Pueblo Blvd./CO 45, turn south, and follow the signs.

City Park And Zoo

This is a very popular weekend destination for locals as well as passers-through. Highlights include a carousel built at the turn of the century (moved to its present site in 1940), a small lake (open for fishing to kids 15 and under and disabled people only), and a train that loops you out around the lake. The park also has other amusement-park rides, playground equipment, tennis courts, a softball field, golf course, and picnic facilities.

The **Pueblo Zoo,** adjacent to the park, has over 70 different kinds of animals, including Bengal tigers, camels, American bison, and an Andean condor, as well as the state's largest herpatology display. The zoo is open in the summer 10 a.m.-5 p.m. and the rest of the year 9 a.m.-4 p.m. A nominal admission fee is charged. To get there, take Pueblo Blvd. to Thatcher. From downtown, take 4th St. west till it turns to Lincoln, then Lincoln west to Thatcher.

Mineral Palace Park

This huge city park, with gorgeous gardens, lawns, and tall shade trees is frequently the site of weddings. A perfect place to picnic after wandering around Pueblo, the park also has a public swimming pool and vita-course. From down-

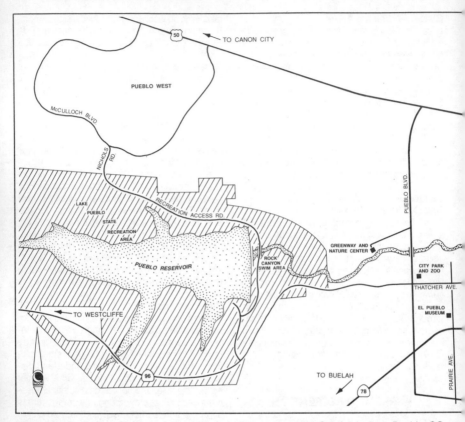

town, take Santa Fe or Main north; from Elizabeth or Greenwood, turn east on 17th.

Golfing

Pueblo's 18-hole municipal golf course is located at City Park at Pueblo Blvd. and Thatcher. For information and tee times, phone (719) 561-4946. Other area courses include the **Pueblo West Golf Club,** tel. 547-2280, eight miles west of town off Hwy. 50 in the Pueblo West development, and the **Hollydot Course,** tel. 676-3341, 25 miles south of Pueblo on I-25 (Exit 74).

Cycling

The Pueblo area has miles and miles of biking trails. For maps, contact the chamber of commerce or the **Pueblo Parks and Recreation Department,** 800 Goodnight Ave., Pueblo, CO 81005, tel. (719) 566-1745. For maps of cycling trails in Pueblo, Colorado Springs, Cañon City, and Trinidad, write **Colorado Division of Parks and Outdoor Recreation,** 1313 Sherman St., Denver, CO 80203, or phone (303) 866-3437.

ACCOMMODATIONS

Motels And Hotels

Pueblo has several franchise-type lodges easily accessible from I-25. They include a **Motel 6,** 4103 N. Elizabeth, tel. 543-6221; **Pueblo Plaza,** 800 Hwy. 50 W, tel. 543-6820; **Super 8,** 1100 Hwy 50 W, tel. 545-4104; **Holiday Inn,** 4001 N. Elizabeth, tel. 543-8050; and **Hotel Pueblo,** Hwy. 50 E and Hudson Ave. (I-25 Exit 100A), tel.

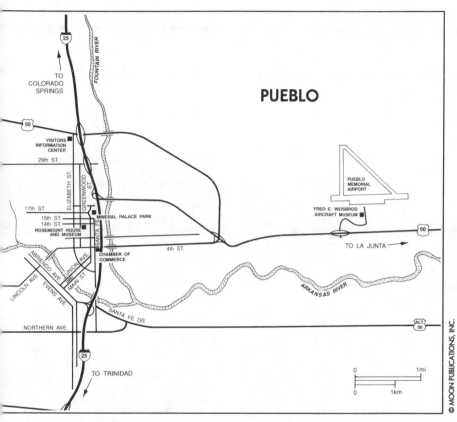

© MOON PUBLICATIONS, INC.

542-3750. The **Inn At Pueblo West Best Western** is eight miles west of town on Hwy. 50, tel. 547-2111.

Bed And Breakfasts

The **Abriendo Inn,** located at 300 W. Abriendo, tel. (719) 544-2703, in the elegant and beautifully restored 1906 home of brewing magnate Martin Walter, is one of the classiest and most comfortable bed and breakfasts around. Hostess Kerrelyn McCafferty serves up huge and delicious homemade breakfasts, the menu changing daily. If your timing's right, there just might be some bearclaws or poppyseed cake waiting for you in the sunny dining room. Doubles at the Abriendo start at around $50. Bed and breakfast accommodations are also available at the **Storyteller Inn,** 414 Broadway, tel. 544-1025.

Camping And RVing

In addition to the campgrounds at **Lake Pueblo State Recreation Area** (see above), there are a number of private RV campgrounds in and around the Pueblo area. The Pueblo **KOA** campground, tel. (719) 542-2273, is located five miles north of town off I-25 (take Exit 108). **West Pueblo Kampground,** tel. 547-2101, is just west of town on Hwy. 50.

FOOD

Start Me Up

A popular morning hangout among the Abriendo-area business crowd, the **Pantry Restaurant,** 107½ E. Abriendo, tel. (719) 543-8072, is a down-home and home-style restaurant. For a taste of local blue-collar color, try **Don's Café,** tel. 543-5814, on Elizabeth just a couple of blocks soúth of the Hwy. 50 W exit from I-25 (and near both the Holiday Inn and Motel 6). A classic diner, Don's serves American breakfasts (including pork chops and eggs) for $2-4, and lunch and dinner (sandwiches, liver and onions, chicken, soup and salad) for $5-12.

Mexican Food

As you'd expect, Pueblo has lots of excellent Mexican restaurants, ranging from neighborhood holes in the wall to upscale dining rooms. A sure bet is **El Valle Mexican Restaurant,** 208 W. Northern, tel. (719) 564-9983, a family-run joint that's been in business since 1937. Open every day but Thursday, El Valle offers huge lunch specials for about $4, while combination dinners run $7-8. You can also get shrimp, pork, chicken, avocado, and beef burritos for about $6; a bowl of menudo is $3.25. For dessert, try the conchas—sopaipillas stuffed with apple, pineapple, or cherry for $1.75. El Valle is located on Central Ave. near the junction with I-25. From the freeway, take the Central Ave. exit and go north one block. Another Mexican favorite is **Jorge's,** tel. 564-6486. Famous for burritos, Jorge's also serves enchiladas Tejanas (with eggs and chicken) for $4.25 and tamales and stuffed sopaipillas for $3-5. Jorge's is also open for breakfast, serving Mexican and American food for $3-5. **Nacho's,** 215 N. Main, tel. 544-0733, is yet another favorite, serving lunch and dinner burritos, tostadas, and taco plates for $2.50-4.50. A bowl of menudo is $2.95. A bit more upscale, in fact, described by a local as a "California-style Mexican restaurant—you know, great atmosphere, lots of lettuce, fruit, stuff like that . . .," the **Cactus Flower,** tel. 545-8218, serves blue-corn enchiladas, pollo dishes, as well as carne asada, crab chimichangas, and *pescado Veracruz* for $7-11.

Other Mexican standbys include **Los Hombres,** 3015 W. Northern, tel. 561-8800; and **Stifino's,** 625 W. Abriendo, tel. 544-4019.

"But I'm Tired Of Mexican Food"

Understandable. But fear not. Though this town is no San Francisco, there *are* alternatives. (In fact, Pueblo bills itself as, ahem, "a cultural cornucopia.") And though you might not find much in the way of, say, Senegalese food in town, you will find restaurants that serve food besides tacos. To wit: The **Irish Pub and Grille,** 108 W. 3rd, tel. (719) 542-9974, serves, according to Pueblo gourmands, excellent (I'm not making this up) Chinese food. Locals swear by the fried rice, chicken chow mein, huge beer selection, and friendly after-work atmosphere. The fried chicken is also said to be good.

Hardcore meat lovers might forego the Mexican food, no matter how highly recommended, for the equally highly touted steaks at **Park East,** 720 Goodnight Ave., tel. 561-8707—also serving seafood, chicken, and prime rib. Prices run $7-16. **Mico's,** 1310 Hwy. 50 W, tel. 545-8770, also has an excellent reputation, for prime rib, chicken, trout, and scampi dinners running $10-18.

For Italian food, try **Ianne's Pizzeria,** 515 W. Northern, tel. 542-5942. In addition to pizza, you can get a variety of pasta, including homemade lasagna, as well as chicken and barbecued ribs (about $8). Also good salads. There's also an **Ianne's** at 2912 N. Elizabeth, tel. 543-3230.

Another downhome friendly place, highly respected for its "home-style cooking" is **LaTronica's,** at the corner of E. Mesa and Abriendo, tel. 542-1113.

If you happen to be near (or in) the Rosemount House Museum around lunchtime, try **Lindy's Restaurant,** right next door, tel. 544-9593. Specials include gourmet salads (asparagus mousse, for example) and sandwiches. Open Mon. through Fri., 11 a.m.-2 p.m.

ENTERTAINMENT

The Bars

Downtown Pueblo is a strange blend of modern-looking office buildings and neighborhood taverns, ranging from biker bars to sports pubs. Some of the downtown joints feature live music on weekends. **The Gold Dust Saloon,** 130 S. Union, tel. (719) 545-0741, is a friendly little place where you can munch popcorn or peanuts while tossing darts or catching a game on one of the several television screens.

Pueblo Pooch Races

A popular Pueblo pastime is dog racing. At **Pueblo Greyhound Park** you can participate in parimutuel greyhound racing. Located at Lake Ave. and Pueblo Blvd. South. Phone (719) 564-5274 for starting times and information.

CALENDAR

Pueblo's big annual event is the **Colorado State Fair.** In addition to offering the standard rides, livestock shows, and booths where you can win a mirror etched with a likeness of Elvis or of a large-breasted woman on a Harley, this huge and highly anticipated fair also features big-name entertainment. Headliners at the 1990 fair were Bob Dylan and Wayne Newton (no truth to the rumor they got together for a duet on "Tangled Up In Blue"), and other acts included Waylon Jennings, Kenny Rogers, and Los Lobos. Held in late August, the Colorado State Fair attracts thousands of people from all over the Southwest. For information, phone (719) 561-8484 or (800) 444-FAIR.

Pueblo also hosts a number of other events over the course of the year, from arts-and-crafts and home-and-garden shows to rodeos and concerts. For information on what's going on in Pueblo, check the *Pueblo Chieftain,* or phone the city Events Line (weekly listing), 542-1776, or the Community Calendar (coming events), 542-1704.

SHOPPING

Downtown Areas
Combine your shopping with historical tours at three downtown shopping areas, **Mesa Junction, Downtown,** and **Union Avenue Historic District.** You'll find gift shops, bookstores, boutiques, and other specialty shops located in restored 19th-century buildings. There are also restaurants and neighborhood pubs for refreshment.

Pueblo Mall
The Pueblo Mall has (surprise!) a JCPenney, Mervyn's, Ward's, Joslin's, 10 shoe stores, seven jewelers and a whole lot of other stores. Located at I-25 and Hwy. 47 East. A slew of strip malls is located near the corner of Pueblo and Northern—K mart, Wal-Mart, SuperCuts, fast-food franchises, etc.

SERVICES

The offices of the **Pueblo Police Department** are located at 130 Central; phone (719) 549-1200. The **Pueblo County Sheriff** is at 909 Court; phone 546-1123. Phone the **Colorado State Patrol** in emergencies at 544-2424 (546-5465 in non-emergencies). **Parkview Episcopal Medical Center** is located at 400 W. 16th (Exit 99B off I-25); phone 584-4000. **St. Mary-Corwin Regional Medical Center** is at 1008 Minnequa (Exit 96 off I-25); phone 560-4000. The main **post office** is at 421 Main St., and there's also one at 6th and Central.

Recycling
Recycle aluminum, glass, newspapers, and plastic at the **King Soopers** stores: 3050 W. Northern and 102 W. 29th. Recycle aluminum at the **Safeways:** 1322 E. 8th St., 617 W. 29th St., and 1231 S. Prairie.

INFORMATION

Chamber Of Commerce And Tourist Information
Contact the Pueblo **Chamber of Commerce** at 302 N. Santa Fe, Pueblo, CO 81003; phone (719) 542-1704. There's also a **Visitor Information Center** in the K mart parking lot at Hwy. 50 W. and Elizabeth St. (from I-25, take Exit 101); phone 543-1742. The offices of the **Parks and Recreation Department** are at 3400 Nuckolls Ave.; phone 566-1745. Offices for **Pike** and **San Isabel national forests** are at 1920 Valley Dr.; phone 545-8737.

For **road and weather information,** phone 545-8520.

Bookstores and Libraries
The **Bookery,** 129 E. Abriendo, tel. (719) 544-1135, has a good selection of books on Colorado—history, travel, etc. For used books and rare books, check out **Tumbleweed Books,** 687 S. Union, tel. 544-3420, which specializes in, among other subjects, Western Americana. There's a **Waldenbooks** in the Pueblo Mall.

The main branch of the **Pueblo Library District** is at 100 E. Abriendo; phone 543-9600. There are also branches at 1515 Bonforte, tel. 544-5040, and 2525 S. Pueblo, tel. 564-8382.

The independently published ***Pueblo Chieftain,*** first printed in 1868, comes out Mon. through Sat. and is available in racks around town. Offices are located at 825 W. 6th Street. Write Box 4040, Pueblo, CO 81003, or phone 544-3520.

TRANSPORTATION

Pueblo is an easy town to get around in, though it does get a bit messy downtown, where streets change names and loop around each other. It helps to remember when driving that the main north-south arteries are Elizabeth, Greenwood, Abriendo, Santa Fe, and, on the west side, Prairie and Pueblo. East-west thoroughfares are Northern, 4th St. (which, heading west, turns into Lincoln, which turns into Thatcher), Midtown, 29th St., and Hwy. 50. Remember, too, that the numbered *streets* run east to west and the numbered *avenues* run north to south.

Pueblo Airport is served by **America West, Continental Express,** and **TWA.** The phone number for airport administration is (719) 948-3355. **Greyhound/Trailways** has passenger service to Pueblo; phone 544-6295. Rent cars in Pueblo from **Avis,** tel. (800) 331-1212; **Budget,** tel. 948-3363; **Hertz,** tel. 948-3345; **National,** tel. 948-3343; and **U-Save,** tel. 544-6222.

WEST TO CAÑON CITY

On the north side of Pueblo, Hwy. 50 rises up out of the plains and into the scrubby Rocky foothills, loosely following the courses of the Arkansas River and the Atchison, Topeka, and Santa Fe Railroad. Eight miles out of Pueblo, you'll pass the planned community of Pueblo West, a scattering of rather sterile-looking newer homes, many owned by retirees. You can turn south here, wind your way through Pueblo West and down to Lake Pueblo State Recreation Area (see above), where you'll find boating, camping, fishing, etc. Forty miles out of Pueblo, CO 115 tees into the highway, dropping back to the northeast to Colorado Springs, and following the western boundary of Fort Carson en route. Turn south at this junction onto Colorado 115 to **Florence,** site of the oldest continually producing oil well in the world. Long an important oil and coal town (Petroleum Ave. is one of the main north-south streets), Florence (pop. 3,000) today is the seat of Fremont County. The **Price Pioneer Museum** on the corner of Pikes Peak and Front St. displays mining and domestic artifacts. Open June through mid-September. A city park and public swimming pool are located on Pikes Peak between 3rd and 4th. For information about Florence, write **Florence Chamber of Commerce,** Rialto Theatre Building, Box 145, Florence, CO 81226, or phone (719) 784-3544.

Hayden Expedition, 1870—pausing for espressos and croissants

Four miles past the junction with 115, you can turn north onto **Phantom Canyon Road**, which follows the old Denver and Rio Grande Railroad line up into the historic mining towns of Victor and Cripple Creek. A seldom-used route, this well-maintained dirt road takes you gradually up into the high mountains, offering some excellent scenery along the way. From this turnoff it's about eight miles to Cañon City.

CAÑON CITY

As a gateway town, Cañon City (pop. 14,700; elev. 5,343 feet) offers access to some excellent recreational and sightseeing opportunities: thousands of square miles of national forest land (for camping, hiking, cross-country skiing), as well as some of Colorado's favorite stretches of white water and the 1,000-foot-deep, eight-mile-long Royal Gorge. Not really sure how to define itself, Cañon City is at once both proud of its fascinating history and scenic wonders and at the same time somehow determined to exploit them in silly and embarrassing ways.

HISTORY

With its mild climate and proximity to so much natural bounty, the Cañon City area was a favorite hunting ground and base camp of Utes long before the first white settlers showed up. The first nonnatives to explore the area were most likely Zebulon Pike and his party, who camped here in December, 1806 (although he mistook the Arkansas River for Texas's Red River). The next half century or so, though, the area remained solely Ute land, and it wasn't until 1859 that the first miners started to arrive.

The early town's economy was a hybrid, derived from both mining (gold and silver) and agriculture (fruits and vegetables). Writer Joaquin Miller was one of Cañon City's first administrators, serving as mayor, judge, and minister.

In 1868, Colorado Territory gave Cañon City a choice. It could be the site of either the state university or the state penitentiary. Cañon City chose the latter, figuring attendance would be better at prison than at school. The university, of course, went to Boulder. And, as the University of Colorado has largely given definition to the city of Boulder since then, so has Colorado State Penitentiary defined Cañon City. Today, the Department of Corrections is Fremont County's largest employer, and the towns-people thank the prison system for the stability it provides.

In the late 1870s, as the West's railroads competed for rights to key routes, Cañon City, because of its choice location—near the mouth of Royal Gorge, a crucial passage west—became an unwitting participant in the fray. The Denver and Rio Grande and the Santa Fe railroads went to court over the rights to the canyon, with the rights ultimately being awarded to the Denver and Rio Grande. The Santa Fe had to run its line south from Pueblo and then west from Ratón.

In 1908, Cañon City acquired Royal Gorge Park, and in 1929, a suspension bridge, still the highest in the world (1,053 feet), was built across it. Since then, Cañon City has appealed to tourism, attracting upwards of a half million visitors a year, who, in addition to being awed by the bridge, also

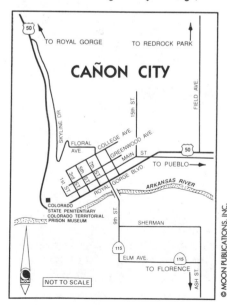

CAÑON CITY

NOT TO SCALE

© MOON PUBLICATIONS, INC.

appreciate the canyon's sheer beauty, the aerial tramway across, and the railroad rising 1,500 feet from the river to the canyon's rim.

SIGHTS

Colorado Territorial Prison Museum And Park

A genuinely unique and perversely intriguing experience, a tour of this museum offers a realistic view of the 120-year history of Colorado State Penitentiary. Originally a single, two-story stone structure, the prison saw 77 executions (45 by hanging, 32 by gas) and a number of escapes and riots; the bloody aftermath of one of which has been re-created with broken cell doors and blood on floors. There's also a fascinating collection of historical photos, including shots of Alferd Packard (who served 15 years for cannibalism), John Dockerty (Colorado's first convicted abortionist), and Anton Wood (at 11, the state's youngest prisoner of record—sentenced to 25 years for murdering a neighbor in a dispute over a watch). The grisliest photos are of the hanging of one George Witherall.

COLORADO HISTORICAL SOCIETY

Cañon City still has a number of fine bars.

The Colorado Territorial House and Museum, located at 1st and Macon, is open daily 10 a.m.-6 p.m., May 1 to Oct. 1 and Wed. through Sun. 10 a.m.-5 p.m. the rest of the year. Admission for adults is $3. For more information, phone (719) 269-3015.

Cañon City Municipal Museum

Housed in a complex that includes the second and third floors of the Cañon City municipal building, as well as three historic buildings behind the city hall, this museum displays a wide range of items from the Fremont County area's history. Included are rocks and minerals from the region, the mounted heads of the last of the area's buffalos (shot by poachers in 1897), Ute artifacts, replicas of a saloon and blacksmith shop, as well as antique furniture and clothing and other personal belongings and domestic items.

The museum, located at Royal Gorge Blvd. and 6th St., is open May 15 to Sept. 15, Mon. through Sat. 9 a.m.-5 p.m., Sun. 1-5 p.m.; Sept. 16 to May 14, the museum is open daily 1-5 p.m. Admission is free; donations are appreciated. For information, phone (719) 269-9018.

Scenic Drives

Eight miles east of Cañon City is the junction with **Phantom Canyon Road**, where you can turn north and drive into Victor and Cripple Creek the back way. The twisting, turning, well-maintained 35-mile dirt-and-gravel road, which follows the old Denver and Rio Grande Railroad line, is not recommended for large (over 35 feet) RVs. Three-mile **Skyline Drive**, which was built in 1906 with convict labor and stones from every state in the union, takes you 800 feet above the town. The one-way road begins just west of Cañon City on Hwy. 50; follow the signs.

PARKS AND RECREATION

Surrounded by lush national forests, steep mountains, and countless lakes, streams, and rivers, Cañon City is an outdoor-lover's paradise. Particularly popular is river rafting, with several guide services offering half- and full-day trips on the Arkansas and other area rivers. Of course, the scenery, too, is wonderful, and the area offers excellent sightseeing opportunities.

City Parks

Twelve miles north of Cañon City is 500-acre city-owned **Redrock Park,** characterized by its bizarre redrock formations. It offers sightseeing, hiking trails, and picnic facilities. Take Field Ave. north from town.

Temple Canyon Park is also owned by Cañon City and also offers picnicking, hiking, and sightseeing. A natural amphitheater along one of the hiking trails is reportedly an ancient Ute ceremonial site. Take 1st St. south from town.

Whitewater Rafting

The section of the Arkansas River between Cañon City and Salida is a favorite among river rats, and even those new to the sport can get in on the fun. Half- and full-day trips can be arranged. No problem finding an outfitter/guide, as the countryside, particularly right at Royal Gorge, is studded with billboards advertising the services. Rafting companies include **Brown's Royal Gorge Rafting and Helicopter Tours,** tel. 275-5161 or 275-7238; and **Lazy J Resort and Rafting Company,** tel. 942-4274. Prices usually start at about $35 per person (half day).

Camping

With San Isabel National Forest to the south and southwest, and Pike National Forest to the west and north, Cañon City offers almost unlimited camping possibilities (in addition to the RV camping at Royal Gorge—see that section, following). For maps and information, stop by the Forest Service office in town at 300 Dozier, tel. (719) 275-4119, or the BLM office at 3170 E. Main, tel. 275-0631.

Golfing

The private **Shadow Hills Golf Club** is open to nonmembers with some restrictions. Built shortly after WW II, the course has long been a local favorite. Take 4th St. south from town; phone (719) 275-0603 for tee times and information.

Horseback Riding

This is another activity popular in the Cañon City-Royal Gorge area, with several companies offering rentals and rides. Among them: **Buckskin Joe's,** tel. (719) 275-5149, and **Lazy-J Resort and Rafting Company,** tel. 942-4274,

headquartered in Coaldale, about 35 miles west of Cañon City on Hwy. 50.

PRACTICALITIES

Accommodations

Among the many motels in Cañon City is the **Best Western Royal Gorge Motel,** 1925 Fremont, tel. (719) 275-3377, where doubles range from $35 to $65, depending on the season. Doubles at the **Cañon Inn,** at Hwy. 50 and Dozier, tel. 275-8676, run $45-75, while rooms for two at the **Super 8,** 209 North 19th, tel. 275-8687, will cost between $40 and $60.

In addition to the RV campgrounds at Royal Gorge (see that section, following), you can also camp at **RV Station and Campground,** in town at 3120 E. Main, tel. 275-4576. Much more isolated, in fact pretty much out in the proverbial middle of nowhere, **Indian Springs Ranch Campground,** tel. 372-3907, is located at the end of a four-mile dirt road which forks off Phantom Canyon Rd. east of Cañon City (no vehicles over 25 feet).

Food

For sandwiches, nachos, green-chile burritos, and a taste of the local scene (albeit a bit of a smoky one), stop in at **My Brother's Place,** tel. (719) 275-9954, located right downtown on Main—also great for a cold beer and a game of pool. For what locals claim are the best burgers around, try the **Burger Baron,** 1006 Royal Gorge, tel. 275-8513; they also serve milkshakes and ice cream. Another favorite is **Merlino's Belvedere,** 1330 Elm/CO 115, tel. 275-5558, which serves a wide range of Italian food, as well as steaks, seafood, and chicken. For Mexican food, try **Ortega's,** 2301 Main, tel. 275-9437. The **Dragon Gate,** 507 Main, tel. 275-4759, has a daily all-you-can-eat Chinese buffet lunch.

For picnic packin', there's a **City Market** on Hwy. 50 on the east end of town.

Shopping

One of the joys of researching travel books is discovering bizarre little businesses with bizarre little names. This one in Cañon City tops 'em all, though: **Fluff 'em, Buff 'em, and Stuff 'em.** Representing a true milestone in the history of marketing, advertising, promotion, and taste, this little place offers one-stop hairstyling, car restoration, and taxidermy.

If you'd rather stick to more conventional shopping, you might want to wander the Main Street area, where you'll find a handful of boutiques and galleries, including **RSVP,** at 515 Main, which carries some nice Native American art and jewelry.

SERVICES

The offices of the **Cañon City Police Department** are at 816 Royal Gorge Blvd.; phone (719) 275-8638. Phone the **Fremont County Sheriff** at 275-2000 or 275-1553. The **Colorado State Patrol** can be reached at 275-0015 or 275-1558. Cañon City's **St. Thomas More Hospital** is located at 1019 Sheridan; phone 275-3381. The main **post office** is at 505 Macon; phone 275-6877.

Recycling

Recycle aluminum and glass at the **City Market** on the east end of town off Hwy. 50. Recycle aluminum, cardboard, glass, newspapers, tin, etc., at **Recycling Opportunities,** in the Alco Parking lot, Sat. 10 a.m.-4 p.m., and at **Florence Super Foods,** (in Florence) Tues. noon-4 p.m.

INFORMATION

You'll find a tourist information booth just off Hwy. 50 on the east end of town. Pick up information on lodging, recreation, and other attractions. You can also get information from the **Cañon City Chamber of Commerce,** 1032 Royal Gorge. Write Box 749, Cañon City, CO 81212, or phone (719) 275-2331.

To learn more about the history of the town and surrounding area, visit the **Local History Center,** tel. 269-9020, which collects newspapers (from 1860); historical periodicals, journals, and photographs; oral histories and transcripts; and maps and extensive prison records and publications. Located downstairs in the **Cañon City Public Library,** 516 Macon, the center is open Mon. through Fri. noon-5 p.m. and Sat. 10:30 a.m.-2 p.m.

The **Book Corral,** 621 Main, tel. 275-8923, has an excellent selection of books about Colorado, from histories to recreational and backcountry guides. The local newspaper is the *Daily Record,* which comes out weekday afternoons and Saturday mornings. Watch for the weekly insert "This Week in the Royal Gorge Region," which lists current events and highlights particular points of interest. For information, phone 275-7565.

For information on the Pike or San Isabel national forests, contact the district offices at 300 Dozier, Cañon City, CO 81212; phone 274-4119. Or write the central offices at 1920 Valley Dr., Pueblo, CO 81008, tel. 545-8737. The local office of the BLM is at 3170 E. Main; phone 275-0631.

For **road and weather conditions,** phone 275-1637.

ROYAL GORGE

A bizarre blend of absolutely stunning scenery and god-awful promotion and exploitation, Royal Gorge can be enjoyed on a number of levels, and for a range of prices. If you've got the time and money, you can take in the entire experience: Take the aerial tram, the "Scenic Railway," the train to the bottom, and/or a helicopter tour; view a "25-minute sight and sound extravaganza" in the Royal Gorge "Plaza Theatre"; buy some deer food "for a buck" from the human-type beings dressed as a chipmunk and a miner; stay at "Yogi Bear's Jellystone Park RV Camp and Resort" (I'm not kidding).

Or . . .

Drive up to the toll gate, turn around, park, and walk over through the piñons to the cliffside (protected with chain-link fence), and take a look. For free. There's also a free picnic area just east of the toll gate. The problem is, you may have been turned off already by the tackiness of it all, the way the natural beauty has been subjugated, hidden away behind the waterslide and the billboards advertising "buffalo burgers" and "Pepsi, the Official Soft Drink of Royal Gorge." What's truly stunning, though, is that nature still manages somehow to awe and inspire despite it all. But just think what it must have been like in the days B.C. (Before Commercialism).

Buckskin Joe's

A theme park next to Royal Gorge offering gold panning, gunfights (11 a day!), horseback riding, and country music. For information, phone (719) 275-5149.

Steam Train And Antique Car Museum

This recently opened museum features a collection of hand-built steam trains, as well as a gondola, a caboose, tank cars, box cars, and cattle cars. The collection also includes many beautifully restored vintage American automobiles. Open daily through the summer. For information, contact the Cañon City Chamber of Commerce, tel. (719) 275-2331.

Accommodations

Although a number of private RV campgrounds at Royal Gorge vie for your patronage, you can camp free at what's probably the nicest area anyway. **Cañon City Campground** is a sprawling area with isolated sites (no water), located between the turnoff from Hwy. 50 and the toll gate about a mile down a well-maintained dirt road. Among the private campgrounds: **Camp Eight Eighty,** tel. (719) 269-3211; **KOA,** tel. 275-6116; **Royal View RV Campground,** tel. 275-1900; and **Yogi Bear Jellystone Park RV Camp and Resort,** tel. 275-2128.

suspension bridge over 1,053-foot-deep Royal Gorge

STEPHEN METZGER

Food

You'll find a Bavarian restaurant at the Highway 50 turnoff to Royal Gorge, serving authentic Bavarian food and buffalo burgers (about $4). There's also a restaurant at Buckskin Joe's and a cafeteria and a beer and pizza garden inside the toll gate at Royal Gorge Bridge.

Information

For more information on Royal Gorge, write Box 549, Cañon City, CO 81212-0549, or phone (719) 275-7507. To make reservations for whitewater rafting or helicopter tours, phone 275-5161 or 275-7238. You can also get information from the **Cañon City Chamber of Commerce,** Box Bin 749, Cañon City, CO 81215-0749, tel. 275-2331.

elk

BOB RACE

COLORADO SPRINGS

Snug up against the Rocky Mountains' forested eastern slope, with Pikes Peak rising towerfully just a few miles to the west, Colorado Springs (pop. 375,000; elev. 5,900 feet) is one of the state's more popular tourist destinations. With a huge variety of historical, recreational, and geological attractions, Colorado Springs could keep a traveler charmed for weeks.

A planned community dating from the late 1880s, Colorado Springs still reflects its original design—the downtown streets are wide, the sidewalks broad, and there are lush parks throughout the city. You'll find a scattering of outdoor cafés, buildings that have been remodeled but not overly gentrified, and small shops. The centerpiece of the downtown area is Acacia Park, a lovely central park and plaza that looks like something out of *The Music Man* or Norman Rockwell. Until recently the park had gone to seed (locals had taken to calling it "Needle Park"), but it has been "reclaimed," and on summer evenings these days is full of families, young couples, and old-timers. Some sit on benches enjoying ice cream cones from Michelle's across the street; others pack the shuffleboard courts or just idly watch the wonderfully summer-paced competition.

HISTORY

Between modern downtown Colorado Springs and Manitou Springs is Colorado City, or "Old Town." Founded in 1858 as "El Paso" (the site was chosen for its location at the base of popular Ute Pass Trail) by a group of Kansas miners, the town changed its name to El Dorado City just a year later, when a second group of Kansans laid out streets and housing sites. By the late 1850s the community was known as Colorado City, and by the early '60s it had some 300 homes and cabins; for a few short years Colorado City was the territorial capital.

In 1871, William J. Palmer, a Denver and Rio Grande Western Railroad baron and former Civil War general, bought 10,000 acres of land east of Colorado City and went about designing what he foresaw as a thoroughly modern and "upright" community, complete with schools, parks,

and churches. Calling his new town Fountain Colony, Palmer discouraged industry of all kinds, as well as saloons and gambling houses, which he believed were better left to the still-wild-and-woolly Colorado City. In fact, the new town was so bent on maintaining a "temperate" community that all city deeds had specific contracts disallowing the manufacture and sale of alcoholic beverages. Colorado Springs remained "dry" until the repeal of the 18th Amendment in 1933.

Little London

Although one of Colorado Springs' original aims was to set itself apart from the rowdy Manitou Springs, a road between the two communities was built within a year of the construction of Palmer's first buildings. Soon visitors, drawn to Colorado Springs by the railroad companies' boasts of pure, medicinal mineral waters and a dry and healthful year-round climate, were regularly making the short trek to Manitou. Meanwhile, Colorado Springs grew from its original buildings—a post office, hotel, and railroad office—to a bustling resort community with elegant mansions, polo and cricket fields, and golf courses. So popular was Palmer's Colorado Springs with easterners and Europeans, who gave it a decidedly cosmopolitan flair, that Palmer's resort city earned itself the nickname, "Little London." During these same years, several sanitoriums were built to accommodate the increasing numbers of tuberculosis patients moving to the area. Evidence of Colorado Springs' TB days can be seen today in the huge porches on hillside houses, as well as in the immense number of towering trees, originally planted to increase the city's air quality.

Like many Colorado cities and towns, early Colorado Springs was shaped to a large degree by the railroad (or, more precisely, the railroads). In the mid-1880s, the Colorado Midland Railroad ran a line west from Colorado Springs to facilitate ore transportation from the thriving mountain camps, and four years later, the city was designated as the far-western stop on the Chicago, Rock Island, and Pacific Railway. In 1890, a cog railway was built to the top of Pikes Peak (see "Pikes Peak Area" following).

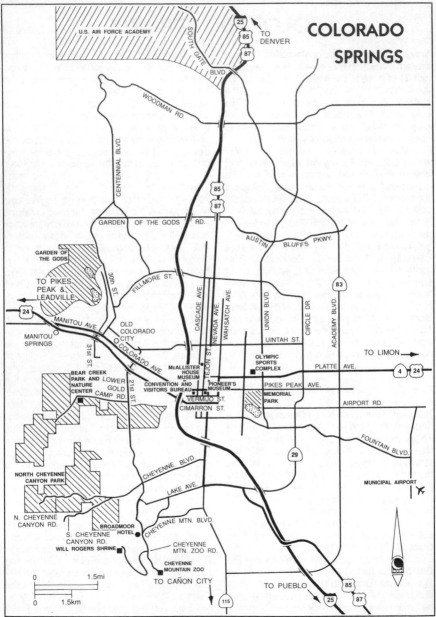

COLORADO SPRINGS

The Town Hits Pay Dirt

The development of Colorado Springs ground to a near standstill in the early 1890s when the silver market went bust; at the same time, the once-thriving Colorado City all but shut down. A few years later, however, things picked up again when the mines of Cripple Creek began producing vast quantities of gold. By the end of the century, Colorado Springs, as well as Colorado City, was back on its feet.

Colorado Springs continued to grow as a resort town, attracting large numbers of wealthy investors and vacationers. In addition, many of the miners who had struck it rich in the Rocky Mountain mines moved to the young town, building huge homes and establishing an up-scale social order, the remains of which can still be seen today in their palaces around the Broadmoor Hotel (see "Accommodations" below) and in the almost Old-World-like separation of the people who live in them from the working class. From 1900 to 1910, Colorado Springs' per-capita wealth was the highest in the country.

Meanwhile, Colorado City, whose economy relied largely on wages and on those who did the grunt work for the mine owners, ran into hard times when the mines played out. By the 1920s, most of the community's mills had been shut down and its saloon doors boarded up.

During the early 1940s, Colorado Springs began to take on the shape it has today, as military presence grew more and more part of the city's personality. In 1942, Fort Carson (originally called Camp Carson) was built, and a few years later Peterson Air Force Base and the North American Aerospace Defense Command were part of the city's landscape. Work on the United States Air Force Academy, today the state's third most popular tourist attraction (see "Vicinity of Colorado Springs" following), was begun in 1954.

Modern Colorado Springs

The 1970s and '80s saw a huge boost in Colorado Springs' appeal to tourism. Many of Colorado City's and Manitou Springs' old buildings were converted to specialty shops, and the area's many geological wonders—from Royal Gorge and Pikes Peak to Garden of the Gods and Cave of the Winds—began to solicit visitors with more aggressive pitches, from elaborately slick brochures to monstrously hideous billboards that often screened off and scarred the mountains' otherwise scenic landscapes.

By the late '80s and the beginning of the century's last decade, Colorado Springs had taken on the feel of so many of the country's larger urban centers. Though the mountains keep the town from sprawling very much to the west, and the downtown area is nicely preserved, the east side, and to some degree the north end, have fallen victim to suburban blight, with miles and miles of housing developments, all looking very much alike, seeming to roll forever toward the plains.

SIGHTS

Pioneers Museum

Don't let the name mislead you: The Pioneers Museum, though basically historical in concept, displays a wide range of artifacts from the Pikes Peak area. The museum's highlights are temporary exhibits (often on loan from places such as the Smithsonian), as well as several permanent displays: Pikes Peak Natives, for example, which includes Paleo-Indian and more modern Native American cultures; a look at the area's medical history, with an emphasis on tuberculosis—patients and cures; and the gift shop, which has an excellent selection of books. Also unique to this museum is its location: in the old El Paso County Courthouse, which opened in 1903, was restored in 1972, and dedicated as Pioneers Museum in 1979. Today the exhibits are in the original court rooms; mock trials, open to the public, are held from time to time.

The Pioneers Museum, at 215 S. Tejon St., is open Mon. through Sat. 10 a.m.-5 p.m. and Sun. 1-5 p.m. Admission is free.

McAllister House Museum

Built in 1873 by Henry McAllister, one of General Palmer's protégés and an early civic leader, this was one of early Colorado Springs' first landmarks and showplaces. Listed on the National Register of Historic Places, the house had three white marble mantlepieces, shipped from Philadelphia, as well as running water. The home has been restored to its original elegance and appointed with authentic Victorian furnishings and decorations.

Today the McAllister House, located at 423 N. Cascade (on the east side of the street; park in the alley), is open for tours and viewing. Hours are Wed. through Sat. 10 a.m.-4 p.m. and Sun. noon-4 p.m. (May through Aug.); Thurs. through Sat. 10 a.m.-4 p.m. (Sept. through April).

Colorado Springs Fine Arts Center

With both rotating and permanent exhibits, this museum displays a wide array of 19th-century, modern, and postmodern art. The Charles Russell Room contains sketches and letters by the artist, as well as original manuscript pages from his autobiography. The museum also houses pieces by Georgia O'Keeffe, Peter Hurd, and Edward Hopper.

The museum is located at 30 W. Dale (one block off N. Cascade). Hours are Tues. through Fri. 9 a.m.-5 p.m., Sat. 10 a.m.-5 p.m., and Sun. 1-5 p.m. Admission is free. For more information, phone (719) 634-5581.

U.S. Olympic Sports Complex

Colorado Springs is one of the most outdoors- and sports-oriented areas in the country, so it's no surprise that the city is home to this 36-acre training complex, which is also headquarters for the U.S. Olympic Committee. Stop by to watch athletes working out (the thin air at 6,000 feet is ideal for training)—at everything from fencing to gymnastics to volleyball. Guided 90-minute tours take you through the facilities, beginning with a 90-minute film on the Olympics. There's also a gift and souvenir shop.

The complex is located at 1750 E. Boulder. Tours are offered during the summer Mon. through Sat. 9 a.m.-5 p.m. and Sun. 10 a.m.-4 p.m.; the rest of the year Mon. through Sat. 9 a.m.-4 p.m. and Sun. noon-4 p.m. Admission is free. Phone the visitors center at (719) 578-4618 or the **Events Hotline** at 578-4644.

World Figure Skating Hall Of Fame And Museum

A true special-interest museum, this complex commemorates the history of ice-skating and honors famous skaters such as Sonja Henie and Peggy Fleming (who hails from Colorado Springs and the rink at the Broadmoor Hotel). Besides costumes, medals, and trophies, the museum also houses a library of ice-skating books and what it claims is the world's largest collection of ice-skating art.

Hours are Mon. through Sat. 10 a.m.-4 p.m., June through Aug., and Mon. through Fri. 10 a.m.-4 p.m. the rest of the year. No charge for admission. Located near the Broadmoor at 20 1st Street. For information, phone (719) 635-5200.

Carriage House Museum

This is a real sleeper—not many people even know about it. But right across Lake Circle from the main building of the Broadmoor Hotel, this little museum displays the carriage (and other vehicle) collection of Spencer Penrose, who built the Broadmoor Hotel in 1918. In perfect

Not known for their wit or sense of humor, giraffes just can't keep tongue in cheek.

STEPHEN METZGER

The Will Rogers
Shrine of the Sun
offers excellent views
of Colorado Springs.

condition, all 33 of them, they include a one-horse carromat and caliza (from the Philippines), an 1890 opera bus (for two or four horses), an Abbott Downing and Company Concord Coach, built in 1850 and shipped around the Horn to be used for mail service in Mendocino County, California. There's also a beautiful 1928 Cadillac and an antique gun collection, including several examples of dueling pistols. A bonus is the two friendly and knowledgeable gentlemen who tend the museum. As classy as the carriages themselves.

The museum is open daily 9 a.m.-noon and 1-5 p.m. Admission is free, though donations are accepted.

Cheyenne Mountain Zoo

Located on the hillside above the Broadmoor complex and southern Colorado Springs, this small zoo features some 800 animals in a natural setting lush with flora. Wind your way from cage to cage along narrow pathways overgrown with tall bushes. Highlights: gorgeous snow leopards, giraffes that eat out of your hand, and a monkey house.

Of course, a zoo is a zoo, and particularly on hot days one tends to wonder at the absurdity of locking wild animals in cages hundreds of times smaller than what they'd ordinarily need to sustain themselves—so that we can stare and ooh and aww and say, "How cute!" But given that, this zoo tends to be environmentally responsible, with attention drawn to the plights of endangered species (many of which are represented here), as well as scheduled workshops for local school groups.

Zoo hours are 9 a.m.-5 p.m. in the summer and 9 a.m.-4 p.m. the rest of the year. The $5.75 admission also gets you into the Will Rogers Shrine (see below). To get to the zoo, take Lake Ave. from S. Nevada (CO 115), and follow the signs. The route is well marked. For information, phone (719) 475-9555.

Will Rogers Shrine Of The Sun

Even if you're not necessarily interested in Will Rogers, a drive up to this shrine is well worth your time. Clinging to the steep mountainside above southern Colorado Springs, the stone tower, made of indigenous gray-pink granite, offers excellent views of the city, particularly of the Broadmoor area (from here, you can really see the property's sprawling majesty).

Begun in 1934 and dedicated in September, 1937, the shrine was commissioned by Spencer Penrose, who owned the Broadmoor Hotel. When Penrose's friend Will Rogers died in 1935, Penrose decided to name the tower in his honor. (One story, perhaps apocryphal, is that Penrose—not known for his modesty—originally intended to honor himself with the shrine.)

Today, a tape of a Will Rogers monologue plays continually, and the interior of the tower is decorated with lots of photos of Rogers, including the plane crash that took his life, as well as with painted murals depicting Colorado's history. The shrine is open to the public Memorial Day through Labor Day, 9 a.m.-5:30 p.m.; 9 a.m.-4:30 p.m.

the rest of the year. Follow Mirada Rd. through Cheyenne Mountain Zoo (see above), admission to which includes entrance to the shrine.

Seven Falls

This is a beautiful series of seven waterfalls cascading into a tiny pool. If you've been faithful to your stairmaster, or are in moderately good shape, you can climb the *steep* steps to the tops of the two viewing platforms. The first clings to the canyon's side across from the falls (there's a snack bar and gift shop at the top); the second climbs the granite alongside the falls themselves and takes you to a trail that follows the meandering upper creek back into the woods. Native American dances are performed at the falls' base several times daily.

Admission is $5.75 for adults, $3 for kids 6-12. Take Cheyenne Blvd. and watch for the signs. For information, phone (719) 632-0741.

PARKS AND RECREATION

Located near some of the finest outdoor recreation areas in the country, Colorado Springs is a natural for just about any sport or activity you can name (well, maybe not *surfing* . . .). And the folks who live here take advantage of it. They're an outdoorsy bunch—runners, skiers, hikers, climbers, cyclers, golfers, all enjoying that crisp mountain air and fabulous scenery.

Several city-maintained parks are scattered around town, offering grass, shade, and picnicking. **Memorial Park** is located near downtown Colorado Springs (at Pikes Peak and Union) and has a public swimming pool, tennis courts, picnic facilities, huge lawns, shade trees, and a small lake. **Quail Lake Park,** just east of Nevada Ave./Hwy. 115 on Cheyenne Mountain Rd., is a very nice little community park with lush lawns, picnic tables, grills, hiking and biking trails, boating and fishing, and a wonderful kids' playground. **North Cheyenne Canyon Park,** located on the west side of town at the end of Cheyenne Canyon Rd., offers hiking trails, guided nature walks, and interpretive programs, as well as rock-climbing and picnicking. For information, phone (719) 634-9320 or 578-6640. At **Bear Creek Regional Park,** 245 Bear Creek Rd., you can hike the five miles of nature trails, join in a guided walk, or explore the **Bear Creek Nature Center.** For more information, phone 520-6387.

Golfing

Colorado Springs has several excellent golf courses, public and private. The courses at the **Broadmoor Hotel** complex, tel. (719) 634-7711, attract some of the best (and wealthiest) golfers in the country. Open to members and hotel guests only. The 18-hole Robert Trent Jones course at the **U.S. Air Force Academy** is open to military personnel only (including retirees). Phone 472-3456 for information and tee times. **Colorado Springs Country Club** is located at 3333 Templeton Gap Rd., tel. 473-1782.

If you've got neither the bucks nor the connections to play a private course, don't be putt off: the city has places for plebes too. **Pine Creek Golf Club,** 9850 Divot Dr., tel. 594-9999, is an 18-hole public course open year-round, as are the **Patty Jewett Golf Course,** 900 E. Espanola, tel. 578-6825, and **Valley-Hi Golf Course,** 610 S. Chelton Rd., tel. 578-6926.

Hiking

Hiking and backpacking opportunities in the Colorado Springs area range from nature walks at the city parks (see above) to full-bore excursions into serious backcountry and treks to the top of Pikes Peak. The most popular route up Pikes Peak is **Barr Trail,** which begins above the hydroelectric plant in Manitou Springs off Ruxton Avenue. Overnight shelters along the 13-mile (one way) trail are provided at the 6.8-mile (Barr Camp Cabins) and 8.5-mile (Timberline A-frame) points. For information on camping, phone the Pike National Forest office at (719) 636-1602. **North Cheyenne Canyon Trail** will take you on an easy 10-mile (roundtrip) day hike with good views of Colorado Springs and the mountains. The trailhead is located just past the entrance to North Cheyenne Canyon at the end of Cheyenne Canyon Rd.

For more information on hiking and backpacking in the Colorado Springs area, write the **El Paso County Parks and Recreation Department** at 1045 W. Rio Grande, Colorado Springs, CO, or phone 520-6375.

Swimming

Public swimming pools in Colorado Springs include the **Manitou Springs Pools,** 202 W. Manitou in Manitou Springs, tel. (719) 685-9735, and more than a half dozen Colorado Springs municipal pools, including **Memorial Park Pool,** tel. 578-6634, and **Valley-Hi Pool,** tel. 471-9085. For a complete list of municipal pools, phone the County Parks and Rec. Dept. at 520-6375.

Cycling

As in the rest of the country, bicycling is enjoying a renaissance in Colorado Springs. This is due in large part to the overnight explosion in the popularity of mountain biking, though the interest in touring has also been rekindled. For maps and information on mountain biking and touring in the area, stop by **Mountain Chalet Sports,** 226 N. Tejon; **Criterium Bicycles,** 829 N. Tejon or 5660 N. Academy; **Mountain Tour Cycles,** 1813 N. Circle (where you can also rent mountain bikes; phone 719-389-0780).

Climbing

The steep sandstone spires and cliffs of the **Garden of the Gods** attract highly skilled rock climbers, as well as photographers and others awed by these athletes' arachnid ability to cling to vertical surfaces. Climbers need to register at the visitors center before heading up.

Mountain Chalet Sports, 226 N. Tejon in Colorado Springs, tel. (719) 633-0732, carries climbing equipment, maps, and local guidebooks, and also rents gear.

Skiing

Colorado Springs is close enough to the state's major resorts that (weather permitting) serious shredders can head up for the day and be stepping into skis at, say, Monarch or A-Basin when the lifts open.

Cross-country skiers need not go all the way to Summit County to find some good fluff, as some excellent trails await in nearby **Pike National Forest.** For cross-country rentals, as well as advice on where to head, stop by **Mountain Chalet Sports,** 226 N. Tejon.

TOURS

Gray Line, tel. (719) 633-1181, offers tours to Pikes Peak, Royal Gorge, and other area attractions, including Seven Falls and Cave of the Winds. Gray Line also offers whitewater-rafting trips.

You can also tour the area on foot. **Gentle Earth Tours, Ltd.,** tel. 633-2301, offers naturalist-led half- and full-day hikes, as well as night hikes into the Pikes Peak-area hills and forests. For more information, write 2301 W. Vermijo Ave., Colorado Springs, CO 80904.

ACCOMMODATIONS

Hotels

Without doubt one of the grandest of all hotels west of the Mississippi, **The Broadmoor,** tel. (719) 634-7711, will take your breath away even if you've prepared yourself to be impressed. Built in 1918, and added onto and renovated several times over the years, the 30-building complex—looking more like an Italian villa than an American hotel—sprawls beautifully at the foot of the Rocky Mountains.

Of course, none of the 560 rooms here is cheap, but for those rare occasions when you really want to toss caution to the wind, the Broadmoor offers you first class all the way. Doubles start at about $120 (low season: Oct. to May); suites range from $220-1540. Lodging plans range from no-frills digs to packages that include meals, champagne, golf, skiing, and tours of the area.

To get there, take Nevada Ave. south from downtown, and turn right on Lake Ave. (you'll see the signs).

Another Colorado Springs institution is **The Antlers Hotel,** 4 S. Cascade Ave., tel. 473-5600, originally built in 1883 by William Palmer. Though today the Antlers and the Broadmoor share owners, for much of this century the two were fierce rivals. One story goes that the "A" in the Broadmoor's logo (which is a different design than the rest of the word) came about as a poke at the Antlers, after Penrose had spent a wild night in that hotel's bar. Rooms for two at the Antlers start at about $90.

You'll also find many of the chain hotels in Colorado Springs. Doubles at these usually run about $50-90, with lower rates on weekends, when business people, whose companies are picking up their tabs, are less likely to be traveling. The following hotels all offer easy access for travelers: **Embassy Suites,** tel. 599-9100 (Exit 149 from I-25); **Hampton Inn,** tel. 593-9700 (Exit 149); **Hilton Inn,** tel. 598-7656; **Marriott,** tel. 260-1800 (Exit 147 from I-25); and two **Ramada Inns,** tel. 596-7660 (at the airport), and tel. 594-0700 (Exit 146 from I-25).

the Broadmoor Hotel,
one of the classiest
lodges in the West

STEPHEN METZGER

Motels

Colorado Springs has a wide range of motels, from historical places with lots of character to sterile freeway-side numbers that are nonetheless fine for a night's shut-eye for passers-through. The adobe **El Colorado Lodge,** tel. (719) 685-5485 or (800) 442-4884, is a rusti-cally handsome motel on the east end of Mani-tou Springs. Doubles range from $35-70. Also in Manitou are **Garden of the Gods Motel,** 2922 W. Colorado Ave., tel. 636-5271, where dou-bles run about $30-50, and the **Apache Motel,** 3401 W. Pikes Ave., tel. 471-9440, where you can get a room for two for starting at about $30.

Most of the city's chain motels are located at or near the major freeway exits from I-25. You'll find two **Holiday Inns,** tel. (800) HOLIDAY, one at Exit 141, and one north, at Exit 145; rooms for two start around $45. At the Colorado Springs **Comfort Inn,** tel. 598-6700 (Exit 150A), and **Quality Inn,** tel. 593-9119 (Exit 146), doubles run $45-65.

In addition, you'll find at least two "motel rows" in Colorado Springs. You can get cheap rooms at any of several motels along S. Nevada near the railroad tracks (where you'll also find the pawn shops and bail bondsmen). A nicer slew is on Colorado Ave. between Colorado City and Manitou Springs.

Bed And Breakfasts

The Colorado Springs area has several won-derful bed-and-breakfast inns. In fact, right down-town you'll find one of the nicest and best-known in the state, **The Hearthstone,** 506 N. Cas-cade, tel. (719) 473-4413. Remodeled from two side-by-side Victorians, now joined with a breezeway, the Hearthstone has 25 different rooms, each beautifully decorated in a specific theme and most with private baths. Rates range from about $60 for "The Dormer," the smallest room (no bath), to $130 for "The Fireside," which has a fireplace and its own private porch.

The **Holden House,** 1102 W. Pikes Peak Ave., tel. 471-3980, is another elegantly re-stored Victorian (built in 1902). Named for his-torically important Colorado towns (Cripple Creek, Silverton), the Holden House's rooms are decorated with authentic furnishings from Colorado's past. Rates run about $60-90.

Bed and breakfasts in Manitou Springs in-clude the **Onaledge,** 336 El Paso, tel. 685-4265, and **Redstone Castle,** tel. 685-5070.

Youth Hostel

Colorado Springs' **American Youth Hostel,** tel. (719) 475-9450, is located at Garden of the Gods Campground in Manitou Springs. Over 100 tent sites, as well as a dozen cabins with bunks. Beds run about $8.

Camping And RVing

You'll find virtually limitless camping opportuni-ties in **Pike National Forest** west of Colorado Springs, from improved areas with running water to backcountry sites where no one else may ever have camped. For maps and information on Pike National Forest, stop by the district ranger office at 601 S. Weber, or phone (719) 636-1602. Another great source is **Mountain Chalet Sports,** 226 N. Tejon, tel. 633-0732, where you can pick up books and maps and talk to experts on camping and exploring the Colorado backcountry.

There's also lots of RV camping in the Colorado Springs area. Situated on 1,000 isolated acres four miles south of town on CO 115, **Golden Eagle Ranch RV Park,** tel. 576-0450, has 500 RV campsites. It's also right next to the May Museum of Natural History (see "Vicinity of Colorado Springs" following). **Garden of the Gods Campground,** tel. 475-9450, is located adjacent to Garden of the Gods in Manitou and has 300 RV sites, as well as tent sites and cabins. Bus and trolley service to Manitou Springs and lots of social events (barbecues, watermelon feeds, Sunday pancake brunches). You'll also find several RV campgrounds west of Colorado Springs on Hwy. 24 (between Green Mountain Falls and Woodland Park).

FOOD

Start Me Up
Looking for an espresso to get the wheels turning? **La Baguette,** tel. (719) 577-4818, at 2417 W. Colorado in old Colorado City between Colorado Springs and Manitou, serves gourmet coffees and a variety of pastries and breads. (La Baguette faithfully donates unsold bread to homeless shelters.) You can also get coffee and pastries at **La Creperie,** 204 N. Tejon, tel. 632-0984, as well as crepe specials (stuffed with chicken, turkey, asparagus, etc.) for dinner ($6-8).

Downtown's **Country Kettle,** 23 S. Tejon, tel. 520-0449, serves breakfast daily from 6 a.m. **The Olive Branch,** 333 N. Tejon, tel. 475-1199, specializes in healthful breakfasts, including vegetarian dishes (there's a second Olive Branch at 2140 Vickers).

Inexpensive To Moderate
A favorite among both locals and passersthrough, particularly families, is **Giuseppe's,** tel. (719) 635-3111, serving good solid Italian food at reasonable prices—in the Old Depot (just a cou-

ple of blocks from downtown), where trains roar by regularly just outside the back door (ask for a window table to get the best view of the tracks). Specializing in pasta dishes (the lasagna is superb), sandwiches, and pizzas, as well as prime rib, steaks, and seafood, Giuseppe's also has a soup and salad bar and desserts (if you're not yet dragging your caboose).

Giuseppe's is located at 10 S. Sierra Madre. From downtown, go about three blocks west—it's between the train tracks and old Engine 168, the power that pulled the first passenger train from Denver to Ogden, Utah, on May 21, 1883.

Another favorite for Italian food is **Old Chicago,** downtown at 118 N. Tejon, tel. 634-8812, serving excellent pasta dishes, deep-dish pizzas, and Italian sandwiches ($5-10). The place does tend to get a bit crowded, especially on Friday evenings (when the downtown business crowd flocks in to wind down), but waiting for a table here is half the fun. The bar features over a hundred different kinds of beer from around the world, as well as a couple of television sets usually tuned to the seasonally appropriate sport. Old Chicago also offers take-out.

Just down the street at 222 N. Tejon is another hoppin' place, **Jose Muldoon's,** tel. 636-2312, serving steaks, seafood, chicken, and Mexican and New Mexican food for $6-$12. The **Ritz Grill,** 15 S. Tejon, tel. 635-8484, serves pastas, fish and stir-fry for $5-14, as well as soups, sandwiches, and salads for $2-6. **Luigi's,** 947 S. Tejon, tel. 632-7339, is a family-owned Colorado Springs tradition, where you can get chicken, veal, pastas, and pizzas for $6-13. Specials include homemade lasagna Wednesday and manicotti Friday.

Another Colorado Springs tradition and favorite for Mexican food is **Henri's,** 2427 W. Colorado in Colorado City, tel. 634-9031, serving stuffed sopaipillas, shrimp chiles rellenos and other dinners ($7-9), as well as à la carte tacos, tostadas, etc., for $2-4.

For classic American food, you have several excellent choices. Rated by in-the-know Colorado Springs gourmets as one of the best downhome restaurants in the area, **Juniper Valley Ranch,** tel. 576-0741, 15 miles south of town on CO 115, has been serving fried chicken, baked ham, and other American standards at reasonable prices for over 40 years. For closer-to-town American food (burgers, chicken-fried steak, fried catfish), try **Gunther Toody's Diner,** 3952 N. Academy, tel. 597-1950. Dinners are $3-8. If you'd rather eat on the lighter (and more healthful) side, check out the **Dale Street Cafe,** 115 E. Dale St., tel. 578-9898. Salads (Caesar, Niçoise, spinach, tabbouleh, etc.), pastas, and Mediterranean pizzas run $5-8.

More Expensive

As a resort town founded primarily by big money, Colorado Springs has its share of upscale restaurants, most notably those located in the Broadmoor Hotel. In fact, the Broadmoor complex includes eight separate restaurants, ranging from casual (relatively speaking) dining rooms off the golf course to those in the main buildings, with dress codes and don't-ask-the-prices menus.

The Broadmoor's classiest, fanciest, and most expensive restaurant is **Charles Court,** tel. (719) 577-5774, in the west lobby. The **Penrose Room,** tel. 577-5773, in Broadmoor South, specializes in continental cuisine. Both require coats and ties for men and dresses or suits for women. The **Tavern,** tel. 634-7711, in the Broadmoor Main, serves excellent food—steaks, prime rib, and seafood, as well as daily specials—at more affordable prices (dinners run about $12-24). Live music nightly.

For more information on dining at the Broadmoor Hotel, phone 577-5252.

The **Steaksmith,** 3802 Maizeland Rd., tel. 596-9300, is said to have the best steaks in town, as well as excellent seafood and desserts. Dinners run $12-22.

ENTERTAINMENT

Colorado Springs is a big enough city that you're likely to find live music and other entertainment just about every night of the week, ranging from lounge music to comedy to hard-core rock 'n' roll. Check the *Gazette-Telegraph,* Colorado Springs' daily newspaper, for listings of who's playing where and when. Friday's edition carries the "Scene" supplement, geared specifically to entertainment.

Clubs

A great place to go with family and friends is the **Golden Bee,** in the International Center at the Broadmoor. Gather round a table, order up a yard-long schooner of beer, pass around the house songbooks, and join the crowd accompanying the tavern's pianist.

To quaff a few with the downtown locals, stop by **Old Chicago,** 118 N. Tejon, tel. (719) 634-8812, especially on a Friday around Happy Hour.

Jeff Valdez' Comedy Corner, 204 N. Union, tel. 591-0707, features live stand-up comedy Wed. through Sunday.

Dinner Theater

A casual dinner out and a show by local talent is one of the best ways to spend an evening anywhere. Colorado Springs groups include **About Town Dinner Theater,** tel. (719) 471-9356 (578-6629 for reservations), performing at the Curtain Call Café, 221 E. Kiowa. Dinner and a show will run you about $15. Reservations required. You can also attend dinner theater at **McKenna's Pub,** 3725 Austin Bluffs Parkway, tel. 599-3020. Tickets about the same price. Call for information and reservations.

Take Me Out To The Ball Game

As anyone who's been to a minor league baseball game knows, these games have a charm and attraction all their own. You don't have to fight crowds, all the seats are good (and cheap!), the young players, while working hard to make it to the Bigs, are having great fun, and the fans are absolutely *rabid.* The **Colorado Springs Sky Sox** is the AAA team of the Cleveland Indians. Take in an afternoon or evening game and watch these young players on their way up (and some on their way down . . .). All seats are under $5. For information and tickets, phone (719) 597-1449.

CALENDAR

From chili cook-offs to rodeos, auto races, and arts-and-crafts festivals, there's something going on nearly every weekend in Colorado Springs. The town's biggies are the **Air Force Academy Graduation,** in late May; the **Fourth of July Celebration and Fireworks;** the **Pikes Peak Auto Hill Climb,** in July (past winners include Bobby and Al Unser and Mario Andretti); **Pikes Peak or Bust Rodeo,** in mid-August; and the **International Balloon Classic,** Labor Day

Weekend. Watch the *Gazette-Telegraph* for listings of events. You can also get up-to-date information by phoning the convention and visitors bureau's **FunFone Events Line,** (719) 635-1723.

SHOPPING

The Colorado Springs area has several nice places to shop for souvenirs and other gifts. Be sure to allow some time to explore Old Colorado City, a National Historic District located between the 2400 and 2700 blocks of Colorado Ave. (west of downtown). Lots of boutiques, art galleries, and cafés are housed in 1860s-era buildings that once served as supply stores and saloons for Cripple Creek miners. Check out **Michael Garman Galleries,** tel. (719) 471-1600, for miniature figurines and dioramas of street scenes. Equally impressive is **Simpich Character Dolls,** tel. 636-3272, where you can get (or just look at) exquisitely detailed, handmade ceramic and fabric miniature dolls, with an emphasis on Christmas figures. The dolls come to life in the **Simpich Marionette Theatre,** where past productions include *A Christmas Carol, Heidi,* and *Beauty and the Beast.* Phone the theater at 636-3539 for more information.

You'll also want to spend some time exploring the boutiques, galleries, and arcades in Manitou Springs. Shops range from some rather tacky rubber-tomahawk "trading posts" to legitimate and classy galleries and boutiques selling quality jewelry, pottery, and other crafts and artwork. When you're done shopping, or just need a break, there are lots of sidewalk cafés, as well as vendors selling soft drinks and saltwater taffy.

SERVICES

In emergencies in Colorado Springs, always dial **9-1-1.** For non-emergencies, phone the **Colorado Springs Police** at (719) 635-6611; the **El Paso County Sheriff** at 390-5555; and the **Colorado State Patrol** at 635-3581.

Colorado Springs' **Memorial Hospital** is located at 1400 E. Boulder; phone 475-5000. The **Penrose-St. Francis Healthcare System** maintains three separate facilities: **Penrose Community Hospital,** 3205 N. Academy, tel. 591-3000; **Penrose Hospital,** 2215 N. Cascade, tel. 630-5000; and **St. Francis Hospital,** 825 E. Pikes Peak, tel. 636-8800. For information, phone their **Healthline** at 630-5555.

The downtown branch of the **post office** is at 210 E. Pikes Peak; phone 570-5343. For information, or for locations of other branches, phone 570-5339.

Recycling

Colorado Springs is a relatively big city, and there are scores of places to recycle just about anything you've managed to collect on your trip. Recycle aluminum, glass, newspapers, and plastic containers at all Colorado Springs **King Soopers,** including those at the following locations: 1750 W. Uintah, 2720 Palmer Park, 6930 N. Academy, and the corner of Hancock and Academy. You can also recycle aluminum, glass, newspaper, at two **Recycle America** locations, 419 E. Vermijo and 1965 Commercial, as well as at **Springs Recycling,** 3436 W. Colorado Avenue. Colorado Springs **Safeways** will recycle aluminum and grocery bags.

For more information on where to recycle in the Colorado Springs area, contact **Waste Management of Colorado Springs,** tel. (719) 632-8877.

INFORMATION

For more information about Colorado Springs and the Pikes Peak-Manitou Springs area, contact the **Colorado Springs Convention and Visitors Bureau,** tel. (719) 635-1632 or (800) 88-VISIT. The bureau's offices are located downtown at 104 S. Cascade (free parking at entrance on Colorado Ave. and camper parking one block west). Stop in to pick up brochures on area attractions, as well as dining, lodging, and events guides; particularly useful is the free Colorado Springs *Official Visitors Guide.* Write the **Colorado Springs Chamber of Commerce** at Drawer B, Colorado Springs, CO 80901, or phone 635-1551.

The information center for the **Pikes Peak Library District** is located at 5550 N. Union Blvd.; phone 531-6333. The district's downtown branch is the **Penrose Public Library,** tel. 473-2080, located at Kiowa and Cascade.

One of the area's best bookstores is **The Chinook Bookshop,** downtown at 210 N. Tejon, tel. 635-1195. It's got an excellent selection of books (travel, recreation, histories, etc.) on the Colorado Springs area, as well as on the rest of Colorado and the West, including a large section of Native American works. For used books, check out **Poor Richard's,** 324 N. Tejon, tel. 578-0012, where you'll also find a café and espresso bar.

Colorado Springs' daily newspaper is the *Gazette-Telegraph.* For subscription information, phone 632-5511 or write Box 1779, Colorado Springs, CO 80901.

For information on **road and weather conditions,** phone 635-7623.

Further Reading

One of the best histories of the area is Marshall Sprague's *Newport of the Rockies.* Available in most Colorado Springs-area bookstores, this book documents the city from its beginnings under General William Palmer, through its popularity with health- and cure-seekers, particularly tuberculosis patients, and into the later 20th century. Sprague's *Money Mountain, the Story of Cripple Creek Gold* will also interest travelers who want to learn about the area's past. Sprague writes as though he were telling you yarns as you sat around a campfire at the base of Pikes Peak.

TRANSPORTATION

Getting There

Colorado Springs Municipal Airport is serviced by several major carriers, including **American Airlines, America West, Continental,** **Delta, TWA, United,** and **United Express. Airport Transportation Service,** tel. (719) 635-3518, offers regular shuttles from the airport to Colorado Springs hotels and private residences. Colorado Springs' bus terminal is located at 327 S. Weber; phone **Greyhound/Trailways** at 636-1505 or (800) 527-1566.

Automobile rentals are available both downtown and at the airport. Rent from **Avis,** tel. 596-2751; **Budget,** tel. 473-6535; **Dollar,** tel. 591-6464; **Hertz,** tel. 596-1863; **Payless,** tel. 597-4444 (airport) or 471-4444 (downtown); and **Thrifty Car Rental,** tel. 574-2472. Phone **Yellow Cab** at 634-5000.

Getting Around

Getting around in Colorado Springs is not difficult. **Colorado Springs Transit** buses serve most of the metropolitan area. For route information, phone (719) 475-9733.

When driving, remember that the major north-south arteries are I-25, CO 115, Academy/CO 83, Wahsatch, Nevada, Tejon, and Cascade; major east-west arteries include Fountain, Hwy. 24/Platte, Colorado (which connects Colorado Springs and Manitou Springs and becomes Pikes Peak Blvd. east of Hwy. 24), Constitution, Fillmore, and Austin Bluffs Parkway. It's helpful, too, to keep a bit of history in mind: Queen Palmer, wife of founding father General William Palmer, named Colorado Springs' original north-south streets, or those parallel with the Rockies, after other mountain ranges (Cascade, Sierra Madre, Wahsatch) and east-west streets after rivers (Cimarron, Cuchara, Rio Grande, Las Animas, Colorado, Platte, Willamette). Finally, remember that Pikes Peak and the Rocky Mountains are always to the *west*— you couldn't ask for a better landmark.

VICINITY OF COLORADO SPRINGS

In addition to the many things to do and see in town, the surrounding area has a wide range of other attractions, from museums, railways, and shopping areas to mountains, forests, and red-rock canyons—enough to keep the budding naturalist exploring happily for weeks on end. Whether your bent is to watch white-capped cadets marching in formation at the U.S. Air Force Academy or to hike to the top of Pikes Peak and take in the incredible vistas, you're sure to find plenty to do.

SIGHTS

United States Air Force Academy

One of Colorado Springs' main tourist attractions, this 18,000-acre officer-training campus is impressive (even if you're not a military buff) for its military importance, its intriguing architecture and layout, and the gorgeous grounds, rife with wild game, in the forests at the foot of the Rocky Mountains.

Though much of the campus is off-limits to visitors, you can take a self-guided driving tour through the grounds, with a number of stops along the way. The huge visitor center, open daily 9 a.m.-5 p.m. (till 6 in summer), has displays on the academy's beginnings (founded in 1954), a map with pins showing home towns of current cadets, textual and photo exhibits of the school's educational programs, the requisite display showing how being a cadet "builds character," and a gift shop, where you can get Air Force sweatshirts and other souvenirs. Regularly scheduled guided tours are offered free of charge. Admission to the visitor center is also free.

To get there, take Exit 156B from I-25 to the academy's north entrance, and follow the signs. At the gate, you'll be given a map to help guide you through the grounds and to the visitor center and other parts of the campus open to tourists, including the chapel, planetarium, parade ground, and nature trail.

For more information, write **Visitor Services Division,** Directorate of Public Affairs, HQ USAFA/PAV, USAF Academy, CO 80840-5151; or phone (719) 472-2555.

ProRodeo Hall Of Fame And Museum

Even if you didn't grow up ropin' and ridin', and even if the closest you've come to a rodeo is the pages of a Larry McMurtry novel, you'll still get a boot out of this museum.

Displays include works by Gary Morton, of New Mexico's Bell Ranch (paintings), who's also a cowboy ("I'll keep on ridin' for my pleasure

B-52 Bomber in field on the campus of the U.S. Air Force Academy

STEPHEN METZGER

statue outside Colorado Springs' ProRodeo Hall of Fame and Museum

and paintin' the cowboy's domain"); a memorial to Casey Tibbs, with memorial by Charlie Daniels (his gold record for "Simple Man" and a poem, "Casey's Last Ride" dedicated to Tibbs); and lots of great photos, including shots of clowns *working* (saving bronc riders in BIG trouble), trophies, silver spurs, gold buckles, and beautifully tooled saddles.

The museum, located north of town at Exit 147 off I-25, is open daily 9 a.m.-5 p.m. Admission is $5 for adults; group rates available. For information, phone (719) 593-8847.

Western Museum Of Mining And Industry

A nonprofit and low-key outfit, this is one of Colorado Springs' true gems, one that avoids the touristy trappings of some of the other attractions. Tours begin with a short slide show (sponsored in part by the National Endowment for the Humanities) on the history of western mining, and then you're taken through displays of various steam engines (which your tour guide will fire up), and even to a sluice box (where you'll learn how to pan for gold). In all, there are over 15,000 square feet of exhibits in several different buildings. An 8,000-volume library is open to museum members and students (by appointment only).

Admission, including the tour, is $5 for adults, $4 for senior and students, and $2 for kids 5-12. Group rates (the museum is a natural for field trips!) are available. Hours are Mon. through Sat. 9 a.m.-4 p.m. and Sun. noon-4 p.m.

Take Exit 125A (Gleneagle Dr.) from I-25 and follow the signs (east side of highway). For more information, phone (719) 488-0880.

May Museum Of Natural History And Space Museum

A couple of the area's quirkiest museums, these two display the lifetime collections of artifacts owned by John May. The Museum of Natural History actually specializes in entomology, as you would have guessed from seeing the giant beetle at the turnoff. But even for non-bug fans, this is some interesting stuff—butterflies, moths, spiders, and beetles of every imaginable size, shape, color, and attitude, all well displayed and safely dead, thank you. Check out the 20-inch-long Karabidionaustrala monster from New Guinea (something like a giant praying mantis), the megasoma beetle from South America (just smaller than a Volkswagen), a Peruvian tarantula scarfing a humming bird, and foot-long Venezuelan centipedes.

There's also a small gift store, where you can pick up an odd assortment of souvenirs—how 'bout a shiny gold black widow lapel pin?

The Space Museum, off in the woods a hundred feet or so from the bug museum, is even more peculiar—but for entirely different reasons. First of all, it's in an old musky-smelling house trailer, with warped paneling, like something out of *Twin Peaks*. And then there are the displays—model airplanes and photos and maps, most of which look like they were picked up in dime stores and in gift shops at other museums. There's also an early-flight exhibit, and a display, with news clippings and photos, of the American space program.

Again, a quirky little place, where a sense of humor will get you a long way. Entrance fee to both museums is $4.50. Open 8 a.m.-5 p.m. in May; 8 a.m.-9 p.m. June through Sept.; closed the rest of the year. To get there, take CO 115 south of town, past Fort Carson, and watch for the giant beetle on the west side of the road. The Golden Eagle Ranch RV Park is adjacent to the museum and administered by the same people—see "Accommodations" under

"Colorado Springs" above. For more information, phone (719) 576-0450.

PIKES PEAK AREA

Of course, the main attraction here is Pikes Peak itself, the flagship of the Front Range. First spotted in 1806 by Zebulon Pike, the mountain had been known to the Utes for years as "The Long One." In the 1850s, the mountain was a welcome sight to westbound gold seekers, whose covered wagons often bore their motto, "Pikes Peak or bust." Pikes Peak was also the "purple mountain . . . above the fruited plains" to which Katherine Lee Bates was referring when she wrote *America the Beautiful.* Each summer in July, top race-car drivers from around the world compete in the Pikes Peak Hill Climb, or the "Race to the Sky." There's also an annual footrace to the top.

Pikes Peak Highway
In 1916, a road was cut to the top of Pikes Peak, and for the next 20 years was maintained with funds collected at the toll gate ($2 per car), providing a popular, if somewhat nerve-rattling, manner in which to test the guts, and brakes, of early motorcars. Between 1936 and 1948, the Forest Service took over the highway's operations and allowed passage free of charge, although without the funds to maintain the road, it quickly fell into a state of decline. The City of

Colorado Springs took over the highway in 1948 and has been managing it since.

Pikes Peak Highway is open daily April through Oct. (weather permitting). The nearly 20-mile (one way) route, which rises about 7,000 feet, is paved about the first third of the way. Allow at least two hours roundtrip. At the 13-mile point is the **Glen Cove Inn,** where you'll find a snack bar, souvenirs, and restrooms. The road quickly gets steep, zigzagging dramatically up the mountainside, past the treeline, then rolling out onto some positively lunar landscape. Watch for bighorn sheep, deer, and marmot, as well as figure-8s made by skiers. The views along the way, of Denver, the San Juans, the plains, are stunning.

At the top is the **Summit House,** a second gift shop, and a doughnut shop and snack bar. If you plan to get out, bring a sweater: It may be warm down in Colorado Springs, but it'll be *cold* up top, most likely with a biting wind.

Unfortunately, the toll is per person, not per car, so it can get a bit steep, although all proceeds go to road maintenance. Toll: age 12 and up, $5; age six to 11, $2; five and younger, free. The toll gate is open 9 a.m.-3 p.m. in April and May and 7 a.m.-6:30 p.m. through the summer. Be sure to get a map and information brochure, and pay attention to its driving tips. To get there, take Hwy. 24 west from Manitou Springs to Cascade Rd. and watch for the signs. For more information and road conditions, phone (719) 684-9383.

looking down on Pikes Peak Highway from near the summit

STEPHEN METZGER

Hiking Trails

The in-shape and adventurous can hike to the summit of Pikes Peak, something Zebulon Pike wrote would never be possible. Many hikers take Barr Trail (named for Fred Barr, the trail's designer) and allow two days to make the 26-mile roundtrip. You can spend the night at either of two camps about halfway up from the trailhead (see "Hiking" under Colorado Springs above). For maps and more information, stop by the office of Pike National Forest, 601 S. Weber St., or phone (719) 636-1602.

Pikes Peak Cog Railway

If you don't trust your rig, or your nerves, you can instead get to the top of Pikes Peak by rail. The seven-mile ride offers equally stunning views and takes just over three hours roundtrip (the old Swiss-made trains chug s-l-o-w-l-y up the 26% grade). The train runs about every hour and a half from 8 a.m.-5:20 p.m., departing from Manitou Springs. Cost is $20.50 for adults and $9 for kids 5-11; no charge for kids five and younger if they're held on laps.

To get to the depot, take Manitou Ave. to Ruxton, go left, and watch for the signs. For information, write Cog Road Depot, Box 1329, Manitou Springs, CO 80901, or phone (719) 685-5401.

North Pole/Santa's Workshop

Located in a beautiful mountain setting at the foot of Pikes Peak, this amusement park offers a variety of rides, shows, and other diversions for kids from one to ninety-two. You can pet Santa's reindeer and other animals, see toys being made for Christmas delivery, ride the antique carousel, take a train ride, and then stop for a milk shake or hot chocolate in the ice-cream parlor.

The North Pole is open mid-May until Christmas Eve. In May, hours are Fri. through Wed. 9:30 a.m.-6 p.m.; June 1 through Aug. 31, daily 9 a.m.-6:00 p.m.; and Sept. 1 through Dec. 24, Fri. through Tues. 10 a.m.-5 p.m. Phone (719) 684-9432.

MANITOU SPRINGS

Located about 10 miles west of Colorado Springs on Hwy. 24, Manitou Springs was named for the two dozen mineral springs that have been attracting health seekers for centuries. Long before white settlers arrived in the mid-19th century, Native American hunting parties visited the springs when passing through the area. In the 1860s and '70s, miners heading into or out of the Cripple Creek area would stop here. Many of them eventually settled, turning Manitou into a sort of frontier resort.

Manitou Springs today is part artists' community, part resort, and part tourist trap—a blend of galleries, gift shops, quiet city parks, tastefully remodeled Queen Anne homes, and Coney Island-type arcades. A National Historic District, Manitou Springs offers a wide range of history-oriented attractions, from turn-of-the-century stone castles and old stagecoach stops to "trading posts," wax museums, and reproductions of Anasazi cliff dwellings.

Garden Of The Gods

One of the most popular attractions in the Colorado Springs area, Garden of the Gods is a geologic oddity of bizarre red Morrison sandstone rock formations, some angry, jagged, and jutting, others softly and sensuously eroded. American novelist and campaigner for so-

CATHY CARLSON

CARLSON

Pikes Peak Cog Railway

cial justice Helen Hunt Jackson described the gardens in the 1880s as "colossal monstrosities looking like elephants, like gargoyles, like giants . . . all motionless and silent, with a strange look of having been stopped and held back in the very climax of some supernatural catastrophe." Dedicated in 1909, this city park is not only a geologist's dream come true, but it's also a hiker's, horseback-rider's, and climber's paradise. And—here's the best part—this 1,350-acre registered National Natural Landmark is absolutely *free*. An oddity in itself in a region where it's routine to shell out 20 bucks so the family can view paraffin approximations of American historical figures waxing nostalgic under museum lights.

The lunarlike landscape of the Garden of the Gods began to take shape some 300 million years ago, long before the Rockies pushed up to their modern (in geological terms) elevation and eminence. Some of the spires you see standing above the garden floor—the tallest of which is 300 feet—have withstood the eroding powers of wind and rain that long.

A series of loop roads will take you out into the gardens (past several picnic areas), and even if you don't get out and do much exploring, you ought to stop in at the **visitor center,** where you'll find a variety of geology, history, and wildlife displays, as well as a small theater for ranger-led nature talks. A short trail is punctuated with identified flora from the area. You can also sign up for guided nature walks. Rock climbers must register with rangers here.

You might also want to stop at **High Point,** near the park's south entrance, for the best views of the gardens as well as of Pikes Peak. For a different kind of view, step inside the **Camera Obscura,** whose 13-foot lens provides a magnified 360-degree look at the area (small fee). At the **Trading Post,** you can buy gifts and souvenirs, ranging from the proverbial your-name-here key rings to quality artwork, including Native American pottery, jewelry, rugs, and sandpaintings. There's also a small restaurant. **Hidden Inn** is a snack bar, gift shop, and information center.

Garden of the Gods is open year-round. Summer hours are 5 a.m.-11 p.m.; reduced hours the rest of the year. To get there, take Hwy. 24 from Colorado to Manitou Springs, turn north on

Ridge Rd., and follow the signs. For more information on Garden of the Gods, write 1401 Recreation Way, Colorado Springs, CO 80905, or phone (719) 578-6640. Phone the Trading Post at 685-9045.

Glen Eyrie

This sprawling estate and castle, listed on the National Register of Historic Places, was built in 1904 by Colorado Springs' founding father William Palmer for his wife, Queen. The property includes stables, lagoons, a schoolhouse, and a dairy, as well as the castle itself, decorated with furnishings from Europe and heated by 24 fireplaces, many of which were also brought from abroad—one was carved by Benedictine monks in the late Middle Ages.

Tours of Glen Eyrie, which begin at 1:30 p.m. and 3:30 p.m., are offered Mon. through Fri., June through Aug.; Sundays only Sept. through May. Tours take approximately 75 minutes and cost $5, less for kids and seniors (no charge for ages 12 and younger). Reservations are highly recommended. Irregularly, Glen Eyrie offers **Sunday Brunch Tours** as part of a bed-and-breakfast package; phone for dates. Groups of 15 or more should schedule at least a month in advance.

For information and reservations, phone (719) 598-1212, ext. 269. To get there, take Garden of the Gods Rd. west from I-25, and turn left on 30th St., or take 30th or 31st north from Colorado Ave. in Manitou. Glen Eyrie is located just north of Garden of the Gods.

Miramont Castle Museum

If Garden of the Gods is Manitou Springs' geologic oddity, then Miramont Castle is its architectural one. Dating from just before the turn of the century, this four-story, 14,000-square-foot structure, with its two-foot-thick stone walls, looks like it's part medieval castle, part Swiss chalet, and part San Francisco Victorian. In fact, the castle's original design drew on nine distinct architectural styles.

Commissioned in 1895 by Father Jean Baptiste Francolon, an ailing but wealthy French priest who came to Manitou with his mother for the mineral springs, the castle has 46 rooms ranging from open and airy sitting rooms to small and dark bedrooms barely bigger than closets. After the priest died, the castle was used as a sanatorium and later as an apartment building. It was put on the National Register of Historic Places in 1977.

Today, the castle is open to the public. Some of the rooms have been restored to approximate their original flavor, while others house various displays—a doll museum, railroad museum, and a miniature reproduction of turn-of-the-century Colorado Springs, complete with an in-progress baseball game. The castle also has a restaurant and hosts weddings and other groups and parties.

Summer hours are daily 10 a.m.-5 p.m., the restaurant serving from 11 a.m.-4 p.m. September through May, the castle is open 1-3 p.m. daily, and the restaurant is open for lunch and dinner by reservation only. Small admission fee to the castle. For more information, or to book tours, phone (719) 685-1011. You can also write Miramont Castle, 9 Capitol Hill Ave., Manitou Springs, CO 80829. To get there, take Manitou Ave. west to Ruxton, turn left, and then go right on Capitol Hill Road.

Cave Of The Winds

A strange blend of nature at its most impressive and commercialism at its most shameless, Cave of the Winds is a mile-deep cavern, tours of which are so orchestrated and slick that you feel more like you're at Universal Studios than deep underground. Look beyond the fancy lights and talking rocks, though, as well as the corny group photo and the push to buy a print at tour's end ($4), and you'll find the cave quite fascinating. Discovered in 1880 by children who were playing nearby, the cave is named for the sound the wind makes as it whistles through the subterranean tunnels.

Of particular interest is the nature display, where area birds and minerals are identified, and kids can use blocks to make wolf, deer, raccoon, coyote, and other animal tracks in the sand. The gift and souvenir shop has the standard key chains, mugs, T-shirts, and Native American jewelry; there's also a snack bar.

The $8-per-adult price is steeper than the walkways inside the cave (tours are 45 minutes), but if you've never been inside a large cave before, you will have been once you've been in Cave of the Winds. Take Hwy. 24 west and watch for the signs. For more information, phone (719) 685-5444.

Manitou Cliff Dwellings

Not to be mistaken for the real McCoys—in New Mexico, Arizona, and southwestern Colorado—these cliff dwellings were built here in 1906, some 600 years after the last Anasazi packed his spare loin cloth into his Samsonite, checked out of his room, and climbed down off Mesa Verde. Actually a decent facsimile, the dwellings were made of rocks hauled from the Four Corners area with the best of intentions—to preserve the remains of a culture that was disappearing as fast as its people once did. Regular dances by Plains (?) Native Americans indicate a possible nomination for an Unclear-on-Concept Award.

In addition to the dwellings, there's a small museum, where you can get a sense of 13th-century pueblo life, as well as of the dwellings' construction, by viewing dioramas and Anasazi and Mogollon pottery and other artifacts.

Summer hours are daily 8 a.m.-9 p.m.; in May, Sept., and Oct., the museum's open 10 a.m.-5 p.m. Admission is $4, less for kids and seniors. For information, phone (719) 685-5242.

Ghost Town

Though a bit on the gimmicky side, Ghost Town offers a wide array of authentic historical artifacts and knicknacks, arranged to simulate an American frontier town. There's a general store, with candy jars, hog tonic, hats, corsets, and washbowls, a barbershop, jail, post office, bank, and a stagecoach that ran between Denver and Cheyenne in 1868. You can also view Roosevelt's 1942 bullet-proof Lincoln limousine (and wonder what the hell it's doing here), as well as the proverbial two-headed calf. Exit, of course, through the "Trading Post" (read, gift shop).

Summer hours are weekdays 9 a.m.-7 p.m. and Sundays 1-6 p.m. Also open weekdays 9 a.m.-5 p.m. and Sun. 1:30-5 p.m. May 1 through Memorial Day and Labor Day through mid-October. Admission for adults is $3.75, less for kids and seniors. To get there, turn south on 21st St. from Hwy. 24 West. For more information, phone (719) 634-0696.

Buffalo Bill Wax Museum

Offering a general overview of the West, this museum features wax likenesses of many of the characters from western American history and mythology, many of them acting out the scenes for which they're most famous. See Black

Bart in mid-holdup, the shoot-out at the OK Corral, Black Jack Ketchum's hanging in Clayton, New Mexico—also Buffalo Bill and Annie Oakley (good taste precludes a re-creation of what *they* were best known for . . .), the James Gang, mountain men Jim Bridger and Jim Bowie, and western writers Mark Twain, Bret Harte, and Ned Buntline. A highlight is the authentic western music, à la Sons of the Pioneers.

Buffalo Bill Wax Museum is located in Manitou Springs at 404 W. Manitou. In summer, it's open daily 8 a.m.-5:30 p.m.; in April, May, and Sept. daily 8 a.m.-5 p.m. Admission is $3.50 for adults and $1.50 for kids 6-16—no charge for children five and younger. For information, phone (719) 685-5900.

Hall Of The Presidents Living Wax Studio
Featuring wax figures from Madame Tussaud's London studio, Hall of the Presidents depicts U.S. presidents (and other political figures) through Reagan at historical moments: Thomas

STEPHEN METZGER

a wax Richard Nixon at the Hall of Presidents Living Wax Museum, but no mention of his checkered past

Jefferson signing the Declaration of Independence, John Adams and Benjamin Franklin at the Court of Versailles in 1782, the assassination of Garfield in 1881, and Reagan nodding off during a summit conference. The museum also has a wax Pinocchio, Alice in Wonderland, and Snow White and the Seven Dwarfs.

Hall of the Presidents, located at 1050 S. 21st Street, is open daily in the summer 9 a.m.-9 p.m. and Oct. through April Thurs.-Mon. 1-5 p.m., Sat. 10 a.m.-5 p.m. Admission is $4 for adults, less for kids and seniors. For more information, phone (719) 635-3553.

Van Briggles Art Pottery
Billed as an art studio offering free instructive tours, Van Briggles has been in business since 1899, and the uniquely gorgeous pottery is one of the prides of Manitou. Paris-taught founder Artus Van Briggle was world famous and won numerous awards for his work, many of which are on display in the studio.

Maybe I'm naive to the ways of the business world, but I was expecting more from my visit than a sales pitch. Most of the five-minute "free tour" is spent watching a potter at work on a wheel while your tour guide explains the process of "throwing"—the whole thing really just a gimmick to get you into the "showroom" and the clutches of too many eager salespeople. Too bad, because the work is beautiful, and it'd be nice to be able to enjoy it without feeling pressured.

The studio, located at the corner of Colorado Ave. and 21st St., is open Mon. through Fri. 8 a.m.-5 p.m. and Sat. 8:30 a.m.-5 p.m. For more information, phone (719) 633-7729.

Flying W Ranch
A tourist and family favorite, the Flying W is a working cattle ranch that features western stage shows complete with singing cowboys and chuckwagon dinners. You can also wander around the western town/museum complex, which includes a blacksmith shop (watch the smithy at work between 6 p.m. and 7 p.m. daily) and other outbuildings. Reservations are required for dinner, seatings for which are at 5 p.m. and 8 p.m. daily mid-May through September. Phone (719) 598-4000 or (800) 748-3999. To get there from I-25, take Garden of the Gods Rd. west to 30th St., turn right, and

then go left on Flying W Ranch Road. From Manitou, take 30th St. north past Garden of the Gods to Flying W Ranch Road.

Manitou Springs-Area Dining

Manitou Springs is home to several excellent restaurants, as well as many small cafés, many with sidewalk seating. **The Stagecoach Inn,** 702 Manitou Ave., tel. (719) 685-9335, is located in an 1880s-era stagecoach stop that was also a summer home for novelist Helen Hunt Jackson. The perfect place for a light, casual lunch, the Stagecoach specializes in salads, soups, quiches, etc. ($5-8), and also serves dinner. The **Briarhurst,** 404 Manitou, tel. 685-1864, specializes in meals cooked with organically home-grown herbs, fruits, and vegetables, and home-smoked meats and fish. **Antonio's,** 301 Garden of the Gods Rd., tel. 531-7177, serves chicken, veal, and pasta dinners, in addition to several vegetarian specialties. Prices run $7-16.

If you're out wandering around in Manitou Springs and feel like snacking but aren't in the mood for the cotton candy, fudge, and caramel corn the arcades are pushing, check out **Market La Rue Too** just off the main drag at 102 Canyon. This unpretentious little grocery store sells organically grown produce, natural sodas, and other healthful treats.

Manitou Springs Information

The **Manitou Springs Chamber of Commerce** is located at 354 Manitou Ave., Manitou Springs, CO 80829. Write or stop by for maps and brochures. Phone the office at (719) 685-5089.

WEST OF COLORADO SPRINGS

Highway 24 West from Colorado Springs rises quickly into beautiful mountain country, skirts the northeast flank of Pikes Peak, and passes through the southern section of Pike National Forest. About midway between Colorado Springs and Woodland Park, you'll pass turnoffs to Cascade, Chipeta Park, and Green Mountain Falls, small resort communities nestled at the base of Pikes Peak.

Cascade was founded in 1886 by transplanted Kansans, who built a number of small cottages along Fountain Creek. Among those who spent summers here was Indiana lawyer John Milton Hay, assistant secretary to President Lincoln. Hay wrote much of his ten-volume *Abraham Lincoln: A Life History* in Cascade, as well as his *Pike County Ballads*. Chipeta Park was named after Ute Chief Ouray's wife, Chipeta.

In Green Mountain Falls, you'll find a nice shady picnic area just off the highway, as well as a public swimming pool and a small lake with a tiny island and gazebo. The **Outlook Lodge**, tel. (719) 684-2303, in Green Mountain Falls is a quiet bed and breakfast located on a forested hillside. Rooms with private baths start at about $45 (call ahead—the eight rooms book up way in advance). The **Falls Motel**, tel. 684-9745, is situated right on the lake and has rooms (many with kitchens) starting at about $35.

In Woodland Park, you can either turn north onto CO 67, which will take you up through the national forest to Deckers, or you can stay on Hwy. 24, which continues west over Ute and Wilkerson passes, to Buena Vista and Leadville. Seven miles past Woodland Park is the turnoff to Cripple Creek, an important western historical site and one of Colorado's most popular tourist attractions.

Colorado 67 South to Cripple Creek is one of the highlights of exploring this part of the state. Winding up through Pike National Forest, along aspen- and spruce-sided mountains, and through a rickety, log-lined one-way tunnel, the 20-mile stretch offers more great views per mile than many of even the most famously scenic of Colorado highways. It's also one of the state's least nerve-wracking high-mountain passes, the road unfolding gently across above-timberline alpine meadows—you half expect to hear distant singing, and then to see the Von Trapp family appearing blonde and knickered over a wind-swept knoll.

WOODLAND PARK

Woodland Park (pop. 4,300; elev. 8,500 feet) is an attractive and vital mountain community just 20 miles west of Colorado Springs. With its crisp mountain air and omnipresent view of Pikes Peak, Woodland Park attracts many Colorado Springs workers, who find the under-half-an-hour commute a fair price to pay for the slower and more healthful mountain lifestyle. The town was founded in the early 1880s, and until the early 20th century was an important lumber supply center, serving both Cripple Creek and Colorado Springs.

Woodland Park Practicalities

You can get good inexpensive rooms at **The Lofthouse**, tel. (719) 687-9187, located at 222 E. Henrietta on the hillside above the downtown area. The rooms, some of which have kitchenettes, are smoky, well-stocked with murder mysteries, and feel like the kind of places where Officers Gannon and Friday might stay while investigating some insidious crime. Rooms at **Pikes Peak Paradise Bed and Breakfast**, tel. 687-6656 or (800) 728-8282, run $60-75.

If you're passing through Woodland Park in the early hours, stop in at the locally popular **Donut Mill** at 310 W. Hwy. 24. In addition to doughnuts and fritters, you can get biscuits and gravy, as well as eggs with burritos—all for under $3. **Grandmother's Kitchen** at 212 Hwy. 24 serves early-bird specials from 6-8 a.m. (all breakfasts except steak and eggs are $2). For dinner, try **Pazano's Italian Restaurant**, 730 E. Hwy. 24, tel. 687-9898, where you can get complete dinners (excellent lasagna) for $5-$10. **Tres Hombres Tex-Mex Cantina**, 116 1/2 Midland (Hwy. 24), tel. 687-0625, serves good burritos, chimichangas, etc., for $4-7; live music most nights.

For more information on Woodland Park and the surrounding area, stop by the the **Chamber of Commerce** at the junction of Hwy. 24 and CO 67 North. You can also write Box W, Woodland Park, CO 80866, or phone 687-9885.

CRIPPLE CREEK

To get a proper perspective on Cripple Creek's importance to the state, as well as to the history of the west, consider: Between 1891 and 1916, Cripple Creek produced $340 million worth of gold. By 1952, 625 tons, or 20 million ounces, of the stuff had been taken from Cripple Creek mines for a total value of over $413 million (figured at the long-running mid-century rate of $20.67 an ounce). Cripple Creek produced twice as much gold as California's famed Mother Lode, and nearly $100 million more than Nevada's Comstock produced in gold and silver combined. Alaska's and the Yukon's gold camps—Klondike, Fairbanks, Nome—pale in comparison to Cripple Creek's. In fact, no single geological deposit on earth has produced as much gold as Cripple Creek.

According to Colorado Springs historian Marshall Sprague, Cripple Creek's population increased from 15 to 50,000 between 1891 and 1900, its monthly payroll from $50 to $1,000,000. During the same period, the town's annual production went from "$2,000 worth of calves to $20 million worth of gold bricks." Among those who cashed in on Cripple Creek's boom was Winfield Scott Stratton, who left his $3-a-day carpentry job in Colorado Springs, staked a claim in Cripple, and later sold his mine for $10 million. According to the WPA guide to Colorado, just after the turn of the century, Cripple Creek had 41 assay offices, 91 lawyers, 88 doctors, 70 saloons, and 14 newspapers.

Today, Cripple Creek is a major tourist destination, many of the old buildings having been converted to boutiques, restaurants, and gift and specialty shops. Walking Cripple Creek's main drag, and touring mines where huge fortunes were made, you can easily imagine how it must have been a century ago, when the camp was roaring with gambling saloons, bars, and brothels, and the very existence of every citizen and visitor—from wealthy mine owner to exploited mine worker, from postal clerk to pick-

pocket—was inextricably linked to the goldfields. In fact, seeing Cripple Creek—a small town so germane to the development of the state—crystalizes one's understanding and appreciation of Colorado.

In part because here you can also see close up the ugly side of it all.

In addition to bringing wealth and prosperity to Colorado, mining—and its myopic policymakers—also caused great environmental harm. One need not look too awfully hard to see the scars and ugly mine dumps that remain on the bare mountainsides surrounding the little town. Look a little more closely, or talk to people who live in the area, and you'll come to know mining's more subtle and perhaps longer-ranging consequences: the contamination of soils and waters from gold mining processes. In short, there's a much bigger lesson in a visit to Cripple Creek. As Sprague wrote in 1952, "Cripple's story . . . is a capsule history of the United States from country bumpkin to world power." He might add today that its subsequent fall—marked by depression, environmental destruction, desperate appeal to tourism through commercial exploitation, and, finally, in a last-ditch effort to prop itself back up, legalized gambling—resembles the recent sad stumble this country's taken.

Today during the summer, Cripple Creek's sidewalks are packed with visitors clinging to shopping bags, and its sidestreets are lined with motorhomes with out-of-state plates and Volvo station wagons piled high with ice chests, tents, lawn chairs, and tricycles.

History
During the 1860s and early '70s, the valley in which Cripple Creek lies was known as Poverty Gulch, through which meandered a small stream. Actually the crater of a long-extinct volcano, the valley was blessed with sides steep enough to contain cattle, and the first settlers in the area were ranchers, one of whom was Levi Welty, who, according to a perhaps apocryphal story, gave the town its name.

One day Welty and his three sons were building a cabin in the valley when they lost their grip on a heavy log, which rolled into one of the boys. In the commotion, Levi Welty's shotgun discharged, injuring his hand and frightening a pet calf that was grazing nearby. The calf tried to jump the stream, but stumbled and broke its leg. His son, his hand, and his calf all injured, Levi later supposedly lamented, "Well boys, this sure is some cripple creek!"

One of the valley's more colorful characters was Bob ("Crazy Bob") Womack, a cowboy who had come to Colorado from Kentucky and taken over the Welty ranch. Apparently rarely sober—which is probably why his claims of gold in the area were not taken seriously—Womack in 1886 did finally manage to haul some gold out of a Poverty Gulch mine, the El Paso. Womack sent specimens to an assayer's office in old Colorado City, where it was found to be of high quality. On a Christmas morning years later, after watching tiny Poverty Gulch transform into the bustling Cripple Creek Mining District, Bobby Womack would stand on a street corner in Cripple Creek, drunk and holding the $500 for which he had sold his share of the mine the night before. There, in the cold of that wintry morning, Womack handed out a one-dollar bill to each child that passed by, until a long line formed and Womack realized he was giving money to adults. At that point, an embittered Womack slugged the next person in line, who slugged back, knocking Womack to the ground. Womack was taken home by the deputy sheriff and the next day left Cripple Creek, never to return. The El Paso would go on to produce gold worth over $5 million.

By 1896, 10,000 people were living in Cripple Creek, and the little town's reputation for wild times and wilder women, particularly those employed at the "pleasure palaces," was well known throughout the country. On a Saturday afternoon in late April of that year, a couple fighting in their apartment above the Central Dance Hall knocked over a lighted gasoline stove, igniting a fire in the building that quickly spread up and across the street. The fire, which only lasted three hours but was abetted by stiff breezes, destroyed some 40 homes, the Cripple Creek Mining Exchange, the First National Bank, the post office, and several "one-girl cribs," including "The Library" and "Old Faithful." By the time it was over, 1,500 people were homeless.

A determined and uneasily daunted lot, Cripple Creekians quickly set about rebuilding their town. The Cripple Creek *Times* moved into a new office and put out a paper the very next day; carpenters began construction on new buildings; and many of the dance halls, some partly burned, were once again raucous and rolling.

For three days.

Then on Wednesday another fire broke out. This one, buffeted by even stronger winds, destroyed 10 saloons and numerous other homes, stores, and businesses. Many people were seriously injured, including six firemen who were hurt when a boiler exploded, and 5,000 people were left without homes. Still, the cloud of fires had its silver lining: The phoenix that rose from the ashes was largely brick and all in all much better constructed; Cripple Creek was less a mining camp now, bastion of rascals

Cripple Creek's first newspaper office, 1892

and con artists, and much more a legitimate town, an alliance of businesspeople and civic leaders.

Which isn't to say that Cripple Creek became an instant model of righteousness. Indeed, though in general the town did take more pride in itself, the lowlife faction was decidedly still extant. Just before the turn of the century, the murder rate rose from one to eight a month.

In the early 1900s, labor-management relations in Cripple Creek began to grow strained. Workers' attempts to unionize were violently resisted. According to some reports, as many as 500 laborers simply "disappeared" from Cripple Creek's streets.

By 1915, the price of gold had fallen, and Cripple Creek's mines were mostly played out. In 1920, fewer than 10% of the district's mines were still in operation. Still, ore continued to be taken from the hillsides, though by mid-century most of the remaining mines were owned by large conglomerates. The days of individual ownership—the days of Womack, Stratton, and the rest—were long gone. In the 1970s and 1980s, Cripple Creek began to appeal to tourism. Mine tours were offered, artisans opened up shop in some of the old buildings, and boutiques and gift shops appeared in others. Town boosters hoped the tourist dollar would facilitate a second boom for the little mountain town.

Then, in the late summer of 1990, holding what it hoped was one last wild card up its sleeve, Cripple Creek looked its tourists in the eye and upped the ante. Cripple Creek, along with Central City and Black Hawk, legalized gambling. Though limited in scope, especially compared to the virtually-anything-goes wagering you'll find in Nevada, gambling is now a major part of Cripple Creek's personality, with many of the old buildings having been converted to casinos. In addition, the community has built a new mini-mall, and larger grocery stores have sprung up to accommodate the increase in visitors.

Meanwhile, Coloradans—from legislators to investors to nickle-slot players—are keeping a close eye on what happens. For if gambling does for Cripple Creek what proponents claim it will, if it increases the town's draw and helps breathe new life into the economy, then it's likely that other Colorado historical districts—Leadville, Georgetown, and others—will follow suit.

Cripple Creek District Museum

With a large collection of mining artifacts, including equipment and tools, ore samples, mine models, and a reconstructed assay office, this small museum offers an opportunity to see what made Cripple Creek tick between 1890 and early 20th century. Also on display are domestic items and Victorian-era clothing. Open daily 10 a.m. to 5 p.m., May 30 to mid-October, weekends noon to 4 p.m. the rest of the year. Located on Bennett Avenue (east end). Small admission fee. For more information, phone (719) 689-2634.

Historical Tours

The Cripple Creek Chamber of Commerce has designed a self-guided historical tour of the Cripple Creek Mining District, including the town of Victor (see that section, following). The 18-mile (roundtrip) auto tour takes about 45 minutes. For a map and guide, stop by the office at 107 E. Eaton. **Ghost Town Tours** offers guided trips through the area. Legitimate historians (not college kids doing summer work), the guides provide in-depth explanations of the mining district and the various mines. The hour-and-a-half tours, beginning at 451 E. Bennett, are offered daily from 8:30 a.m. until 5 p.m.; $6 for adults. When you're finished, stick around for the 30-minute "Story of Cripple Creek" video. For more information, phone (719) 689-3000.

Mollie Kathleen Mine Tour

In continuous operation between 1892 and 1961, "the Mollie" offers miner-led tours 1,000 feet into its recesses. View the equipment that miners used to extract the gold and convey it to the surface; listen to stories and explanations of how the shafts were dynamited. Take a look at what real gold looks like before it finds it way to earrings and necklaces. Learn what to look for should you find yourself getting "the fever."

Tours of the Mollie Kathleen are offered daily 9 a.m. to 5 p.m., May through October. Admission is $7 for adults, with reduced rates for kids. Take Bennett Dr. east, turn north on CO 67, and follow the signs. For more information, phone (719) 689-2465.

Cripple Creek And
Victor Narrow Gauge Railroad

This four-mile run from Cripple Creek to Anaconda provides an authentic way to get a sense

shops and hotels in downtown Cripple Creek

of the mining district's past (at one time 56 ore-laden trains left Cripple Creek daily). The coal-burning steam engine hauls you out past several abandoned mines (and the attendant dumps and junk piles), and offers views of many historical sites, including Bobby Womack's "Poverty Gulch." Trains run daily 10 a.m. to 5 p.m. Memorial Day through Labor Day, departing from the Cripple District Museum; the trip takes 45 minutes. Cost is $6.50 for adults, $6 for seniors, and $3.25 for kids. For more information, phone (719) 689-2640.

Imperial Hotel Melodrama

Established in 1948, this old-time theater group is one of the most famous in the country, having been written up in *Time*, *The New York Times*, and many other publications. Season is mid-June through Labor Day; show times are Tues.-Sat. 2 p.m. and 7:45 p.m., and Sun. 1 p.m. and 4 p.m. Tickets run $8-10, with discounts for kids and at matinees. Located in the Imperial Hotel and Casino, 123 N. 3rd Street. For reservations or more information, phone (719) 689-7777.

Shopping

Downtown Cripple Creek consists of several blocks of turn-of-the-century (and earlier) buildings that have been converted to restaurants, boutiques, gift shops, and souvenir shacks. Which means, of course, there's no shortage of places to pick up T-shirts, mugs, hats, and key chains. Yet a handful of the shops carry quality gifts and art work. **Phenix Rising Gallery** [*sic*] sells contemporary painting, sculpture, and pottery with a Southwestern and Native American feel. The **Scott Stearman Gallery** has contemporary Native American bronze sculptures. **John's Jewelry** carries an excellent selection of Hopi work, including rings, bolos, pendants, bracelets.

Scenic Drives

If you're in Cripple Creek, you've taken at least one scenic drive: there's no way to get here without passing through some of the state's most beautiful country. If you've come in from the north and are looking for an alternative route out, you have several (well-maintained gravel) options. **Phantom Canyon Road** runs south out of Cripple Creek through Victor and down toward Cañon City. **Gold Camp Road** follows the old rail line between Cripple Creek and Colorado Springs. Both of these offer gorgeous views and exceedingly light traffic.

Accommodations

For a real taste of historic Cripple Creek, the **Imperial Hotel**, 123 N. 3rd St., tel. (719) 689-7777, has doubles running $60-80. Built in 1896, it's the only one of Cripple Creek's original hotels still standing. The Imperial also hosts melodrama theater during the summer (see above). You can also get lodging at the **Cripple Creek Motel**, 201 Bison, tel. 689-2491; the **Best Western Gold Rush Hotel and Casino**, 209 E. Bennett, tel. 689-2646; **Bronco Billie's**, 233 E. Bennett, tel. 689-2142; the **Midnight Rose Hotel and Casino,** 256 E. Bennett, tel. 689-2865 (also has a kids' arcade); the **Palace Hotel and Casino,** 2nd and Bennett, tel. 689-2992, and the **Longbranch Saloon and Casino,** tel. 689-3242 (featuring stand-up comedy).

Two miles northeast of town on CO 67, **Cripple Creek Gold Campground,** tel. 689-2342, offers very nice secluded campsites, for both tents and RVs.

Food

You'll find on-site restaurants at most of the hotel/casinos, including the **Gold Rush,** tel. (719) 689-2646; **Bronco Billie's,** tel. 689-2142 (which also has a sports bar); and the **Midnight Rose,** tel. 689-2865. The **Imperial Hotel and Casino,** tel. 689-7777, has a long-standing tradition of excellent dinners, with specialties including beef, seafood, and chicken. Another favorite is the **Red Lantern,** 353 Myers, tel. 689-2519, where you can get steaks, burgers, and barbecued chicken dinners for $8-$12.

Services

The offices of the Cripple Creek **Police Department** are in the city hall building on E. Bennett; phone (719) 689-2655. Phone the **Teller County Sheriff** at 689-2644. The **post office** is at the corner of 2nd St. and Masonic; phone 689-2423.

Information

The **Cripple Creek Chamber of Commerce** can provide you with an extensive visitors package, with complete information on attractions, lodging, dining, etc. Write Box 650, Cripple Creek, CO 80813, or phone (719) 689-2169. Cripple Creek's **Franklin-Ferguson Memorial Library** is on the northwest side of town at the corner of B St. and Galena; phone 689-2800.

VICTOR

The second-largest city in the Cripple Creek Mining District, Victor was once home to 18,000 people. Lowell Thomas spent a good portion of his youth here, jump-starting his journalism career by delivering newspapers in the town's redlight district. Jack Dempsey once trained and fought in the city hall building. Today fewer than 300 people live in Victor.

History

Though over the years Victor and Cripple Creek have been rival cities, Victor was largely to thank not only for helping put out Cripple's 1896 fires but also for sending men and supplies and for helping shelter the 6,000-plus residents the fires left homeless. Victor's streets are said to be literally "paved with gold": In the district's early days only the highest-grade ore was trucked out, the low grade used for road surfacing.

In 1893, after mine owners attempted to reduce the district's $3-a-day wage, some 800 Cripple Creek and Victor members of the Western Federation of Miners went on strike. Arbitration, and the National Guard, kept things from

The Lowell Thomas Museum in Victor offers illuminating glimpses into frontier Colorado.

getting out of hand, and the workers' wages remained unchanged. In 1903, some of the mines began shipping ore to a nonunion mine in Colorado City, and Cripple Creek and Victor members of the WFM struck in sympathy. Tension escalated, with many miners refusing to work while others broke strike and kept working. In September, the militia was called in, and by December the entire Cripple Creek Mining District was under martial law.

In early 1904, there were both a "mysterious" mine explosion and a mine "accident" involving a broken cable hoist. Many men were killed, management claiming the mines had been sabotaged and workers claiming management was attempting to discredit the union. Two more men were killed when rioting broke out in tne streets of Victor. Eventually, troops were again called in, and union members unconvinced it would be in their best interest to leave of their own accord were escorted down off the mountain. The Cripple Creek Mining District's chapter of the WFM was effectively dismantled.

Victor today is a crumbling remnant of its once-booming self. Though a couple of hundred of the old red-brick buildings still stand, they lean tiredly and wistfully into the hillside. Still, Victor has its own special draw, in part its refreshing lack of tacky souvenir shops. Walking the steep streets of Victor one can, perhaps more easily than in Cripple Creek, imagine ghosts of Victorian-era miners lurking in doorways and dissolving before the future's great wash.

Lowell Thomas Museum

This is at once both a monument to Victor's history and to the early life of Lowell Thomas, who moved here with his family just after the turn of the century. Thomas delivered the *Denver Post* and the *Victor Daily Record* in the area, worked in the mines in 1911, and for a short time was editor of the *Victor Daily News*. He left Victor in 1912.

In addition to old miners' gear, a fire truck, slot machine, mail-order catalogs, quilts, dolls, clocks, typewriters, and historical photos, the museum displays Lowell Thomas memorabilia, including various editions of the many books he wrote. Some of the rooms have been reconstructed to approximate the Thomas family's home.

Admission is $1. For hours and more information, phone the Cripple Creek Chamber of Commerce at (719) 689-2169.

UTE PASS WEST TO FAIRPLAY

Ute Pass (elev. 9,165 feet) has long been an important gateway between the central Rockies and the eastern foothills. Until 1859, when whites came looking for gold, the pass was a stronghold of the Utes, who took advantage of its narrowness and steep granite walls to keep the Plains tribes at bay. Even into the early 20th century, Utes maintained small fortresses in the area. Today, Hwy. 24 climbs up out of Divide, over the pass, winds through a broad alpine valley, through the tiny towns of Florissant and Lake George, and then climbs up again, over Wilkerson Pass (elev. 9,507 feet), before dropping down into the South Park basin. There, the highway crosses CO 9, which shoots north through the basin to Fairplay (18 miles) or south to meet Hwy. 50 between Cañon City and Royal Gorge (50 miles).

Florissant Fossil Beds National Monument

Located three miles south of Florissant, this is natural paradise for the budding paleontologist. Between 26 and 38 million years ago, the area was lush waterland, with palm trees, towering redwoods, and tall birches and willows lining the shores of Lake Florissant. There were also thousands of species of insects. Toward the end of that period, volcanoes began spewing ash and lava into the air, which settled onto the thriving ecosystem, preserving it and providing for visitors today one of the world's most extensive fossil records.

Visiting Florissant Fossil Beds is a good way to get an overview of what life in Colorado was like during the Oligocene Period. The visitors center has excellent fossil displays and books, and also offers guided walks out into the fossils. In addition, you can take a self-guided tour on a series of hiking trails, ranging from one-half to four miles long, where you can view petrified redwood trees (some estimated to have been 350 feet tall) and other 35-million-year-old specimens. Open daily; small admission fee. For more information, write Box 185, Florissant, CO 80816, or phone (719) 748-3253.

Lake George

This small town is little more than a roadside market and a couple of RV campgrounds, **Stage Stop Campground**, tel. (719) 748-3393, and **Homestead Motel and Campground**, tel. 748-3822. Just past Lake George is the turnoff to Pike National Forest's **Round Mountain Campground**, where you'll find a couple of dozen sites nicely set back in the aspens and ponderosas (pump water and pit toilets only).

Forest Service Information

A district office for Pike National Forest is located at Wilkerson Pass. Stop in for information on camping and other activities in the area, as well as for maps.

FAIRPLAY

Though not as well known as Cripple Creek or Leadville, Fairplay, too, was once a thriving mining town. Named by prospectors who'd been run out of Tarryall, another gold camp, about 20 miles east, Fairplay (pop. 500; elev. 10,000 feet) is the seat of Park County and the largest community in South Park. From Fairplay, you can continue north on CO 9 to Summit County (about 35 miles to Frisco), turn south on Hwy. 285 to Buena Vista (35 miles), or head back to Denver on Hwy. 285 (85 miles). All routes guarantee breathtaking scenery—high mountain passes and lush forests.

South Park City Museum

Comprised of 30 different buildings, this museum is a model of a Victorian-era town, with arti-facts from throughout the state. Included are a general store, assay office, drugstore, saloon, and brewery, all furnished with authentic period artifacts. Open daily mid-May through mid-Oct.; small admission fee. For more information, phone (719) 836-2387.

Practicalities

Two historic hotels in the Fairplay area offer accommodations and dining in genuine Victorian-era settings. The **Fairplay Hotel**, at 500 Main St., tel. (719) 836-2565, has reasonably priced rooms with and without private baths; the hotel also has a dining room and saloon. The **Hand Hotel**, 531 Front St., tel. 836-3595, has 10 bed-and-breakfast rooms and a dining room. You'll also find in Fairplay two motels, three secluded guest cottages, and a handful of restaurants.

Cross-Country Skiing

The **Fairplay Nordic Center,** tel. (719) 836-2658 or 836-2120, offers 20 km of groomed trails with views of the South Park area. Instruction and rentals available.

Fishing

Ten miles south of Fairplay is the **Middle Fork of the South Platte River,** a designated Gold Medal trout stream known for its 20-inch (and larger) fish.

Information

For more information on activities in the Fairplay area, as well as on lodging and dining, contact the **Park County Tourism Office,** Box 701, Fairplay, CO 80440, or phone (719) 836-2771, ext. 279.

STEPHEN METZGER

SOUTHWESTERN COLORADO

Most folks who know Colorado have soft spots in their hearts for the southwestern corner of the state. They know this area offers as much scenic beauty, history, culture, and recreation as any similar-sized area in the country—perhaps more. From the towering peaks of the San Juan Mountains to the deep gorges of Black Canyon of the Gunnison, from the sharp Continental Divide to the gently falling Western Slope, from the high lakes of Grand Mesa to the western reaches of the San Luis Valley, and from the cliff dwellings at Mesa Verde National Park to the trendy boutiques in Aspen, Southwestern Colorado offers enough to see and do to keep you here for weeks on end, or for a lifetime, to which many transplanted locals will testify.

The first thing that'll most likely strike you is the pure scenic wonder of the area. Drive in from the south, over Wolf Creek Pass, or drop down out of Carbondale, through the Crystal River Valley. Head north from Durango over the "Million Dollar Highway" to Silverton and Ouray, or explore the Maroon Lakes area just outside Aspen. Out here, even cynics shake their heads and mutter things about "God's Country."

The history, too, is fascinating. Mining and railroads. Drive up to Leadville and take a tour of the famous Matchless Mine. Ride an 1880s coal-powered narrow-gauge train from Durango to Silverton. Stay in an historic hotel in Telluride or Aspen, or toss back a shot and a beer at a 19th-century bar in Crested Butte.

And then check out the culture: 1,000-year-old Anasazi ruins, as well as museums and heritage centers in the Four Corners area; film, jazz, rock, and bluegrass festivals in Telluride; film, classical music, and wine and food festivals in Aspen. Plus scores of local historical society museums scattered about the area, many with excellent displays of Native American, mining, and railroad artifacts.

And *then* there's recreation. World-class snow skiing at Telluride, Aspen, and Crested Butte, as well as excellent skiing at out-of-the-way areas such as Wolf Creek Pass and Purgatory.

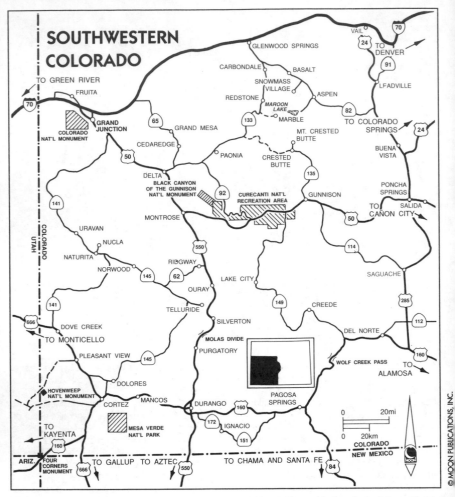

SOUTHWESTERN COLORADO

Jeep touring over high mountain passes and through ghosts of 19th-century mining towns. Fly-fishing for wily native rainbow trout or trolling for landlocked salmon. Whitewater rafting in Class V rapids. Hiking, snowshoeing, hot-air ballooning, camping, golfing, horseback riding.

And the nice thing about it is that much of Southwestern Colorado is remote enough that you won't be fighting the crowds to do it. Oh, sure, Aspen gets packed with tourists, summer and winter alike, and when the train's running in Durango, it's tough sometimes just to find a place to park in the little town. But for the most part, Southwestern Colorado—and its sprawling San Juan, Rio Grande, Gunnison, Uncompahgre, and Grand Mesa national forests—offers the traveler an excellent opportunity to lose herself. To get away from the trappings of this fast-paced and overcrowded world. To simply enjoy being outside in one of the country's prettiest spots.

GRAND JUNCTION

Grand Junction (pop. 30,000; elev. 4,590 feet) is the largest town between Salt Lake City and Denver. Situated in the irrigated Grand Valley at the junction of the Colorado and Gunnison rivers, Grand Junction is mainly a small industrial and agricultural community; its major crops are corn, alfalfa, and fruit, particularly apples and peaches. Other important crops are beans, small grains, pears, cherries, and apricots. The Grand Valley also supports large herds of cattle, and many sheep ranchers summer their animals in the area.

Grand Junction and the Grand Valley are surrounded by remarkable landscapes. To the northeast are the Little Bookcliffs, a miles-long row of mesa-side cliffs that drop dramatically to the valley floor. East of town, the Colorado River carves deep canyons into the rugged Colorado Plateau, and to the southeast, Grand Mesa, the world's largest flat-topped mountain, rises powerfully into the clouds. Just a half hour from Grand Junction, Grand Mesa National Forest is a treasure of alpine lakes, pine, fir, and aspen trees, and that invigorating high-country air. To the west are the soft redrock canyons, stark sandstone spires, and juniper- and piñon-dotted mesa-tops of Colorado National Monument.

Which adds up to lots of wonderful country to explore. Whether by foot, Nordic skis, mountain bike, horse, or car, the Grand Junction area offers plenty of open space to wander in. As well as wonderfully friendly folks to point you in the right directions.

HISTORY

Although white settlement didn't begin in the Grand Valley and surrounding area until 1881, several Spanish and United States exploration parties had passed through in the late 18th and mid-19th centuries. The first Spanish explorers in the area were friars Francisco Antanasio Dominguez and Silvestre Velez de Escalante, who traveled through in search of a route connecting the missions of New Mexico with those in California. In 1821, after Mexico won its independence from Spain, the region was claimed for the United States, and in 1853, the area was partially mapped by two U.S. expeditions—those of John C. Frémont and John Gunnison—attempting to establish a cross-country railroad route. The United States Geological Survey

---

SOUTHWESTERN COLORADO HIGHLIGHTS

Grand Junction: Colorado National Monument, museums, mountain biking along Kokopelli's Trail (125 miles), camping, fishing, and other recreation

Aspen: downhill skiing on Buttermilk Mountain, Snowmass, Aspen Mountain and Aspen Highlands, hut-to-hut Nordic skiing on the Tenth Mountain Trail Association Hut System, dogsledding, fishing along the Roaring Fork River, hiking in the White River National Forest, festivals such as Winteröl, and the Aspen-Snowmass Food and Wine Classic

Leadville: mining tours on the Leadville, Colorado, and Southern Railroad, hiking up Mt. Elbert (state's highest peak), museums, camping, fishing, skiing, Oro City Festival

Salida/Buena Vista: rafting on the Arkansas River, museums, camping, hot springs, Aspen-Salida Music Festival, Yard-of-the-Month Awards

Crested Butte/Gunnison: alpine skiing at Mt. Crested Butte, fishing in the Taylor, East, and Gunnison rivers, 4WD tours, biking, hiking, camping, American Indian Cultural Festival, Fat Tire Week, Festival of the Arts

Ouray/Silverton/Durango: Durango-Silverton Narrow Gauge Railroad, hiking, mountain biking in the San Juan National Forest, fishing and rafting on the Animas River, Purgatory Ski Area, Trimble Hot Springs, Durango Cowboy Gathering, Mesa Verde National Park

Telluride: skiing, mountain biking, 4WD tours, film and music festivals

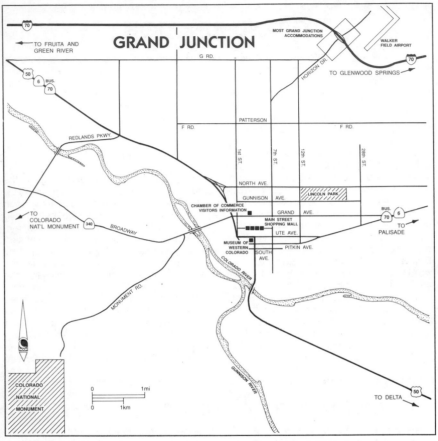

© MOON PUBLICATIONS, INC.

studied the area in detail in the early 1870s, and the resulting book of maps, the Hayden Survey, was published and sold across the country in 1876.

Settlers began to arrive in September 1881, once the Utes had been moved to their reservation, and within four months irrigation projects were underway, a store had been built and the town of Grand Junction was incorporated. Its first winter, the new town claimed just 150 residents. But 1882 saw the the arrival of the Denver and Rio Grande Railroad, as well as the town's first hotel, and soon nearly a thousand citizens were supporting a bustling business district, including a drug store, two blacksmith shops, and five hotels and restaurants. By the end of the year, 11 more saloons had been built, providing rest and recreation for cowboys who worked ranches in the area (from 15 to 75 miles away) and would come to town to hit the saloons and red-light districts.

As Grand Junction's downtown area continued to grow, increased irrigation in the surrounding Grand Valley led to successful peach, pear, and apple orchards. Farming continued to provide stability to Grand Junction's economy into the 20th century, as improved irrigation turned the valley into one of the lushest and most productive in the state—the area was now exporting cherries, apricots, grapes, and other crops as well. The Grand Valley area was drawn to the nation's attention again in 1911, when Colorado National Monument was established.

During the early and mid-1900s, oil and uranium wells were drilled throughout the northern Western Slope area, from Rangely south to the Grand Junction area. Grand Junction, as the largest town between Salt Lake City and Denver, again became an important shipping center, for both product and workers, and the area saw a cycle of booms and busts. The biggest boom, fueled by the post-war demand for uranium, brought worldwide publicity to Grand Junction, though the bust of the early 1960s caused major social and economic problems.

Most recently, Grand Junction has begun to capitalize on its nearby recreation, and to appeal to tourism. Still defined largely by farming, the Grand Junction area nonetheless is becoming better and better known for its excellent hiking, mountain biking, and other sports, as well as for the gorgeous forests and startlingly beautiful mesa lands and canyons nearby. At the same time, downtown Grand Junction has begun to honor its history and celebrate its diversity, with museums, galleries, art shows, and various festivals throughout the year.

MUSEUMS

Museum Of Western Colorado

This museum complex includes the main museum downtown, the Dinosaur Valley paleontology center, and the Cross Orchards Historic Site.

The small but interesting **Main Museum** displays the geology, prehistory, history, and culture of western Colorado. Exhibits include a Colorado timeline (1880-1950), with tools, clothing, and artifacts from each era; Ute baskets, beadwork, and bows and arrows; Fremont culture petroglyphs, awls, fetishes; and Mimbres pottery. The museum also has a gift and book store, specializing in Colorado history. The museum is located at 248 S. 4th Street (corner of Ute). Hours are Mon. through Sat. 10 a.m. to 4:30 p.m., Memorial Day through Labor Day; Tues. through Sat. 10 a.m. to 4:30 p.m. the rest of year. Admission is $2 for adults, $1 for kids 2-17. For more information, phone (303) 242-0971.

Dinosaur Valley, located on the Main Street Mall, is a veritable course in dinosaurs and pa-

leontology. Follow the huge green footprints past several *large* animated dinosaurs, including a *Stegosaurus, Allosaurus,* and *Tyrannosaurus rex,* all of which move in startlingly lifelike fashion and growl ferociously. Other features include reconstructed dinosaur skeletons, fossilized eggs and footprints, timelines explaining when the different dinosaur periods were, a video room, and an explanation of continental drift. Don't miss the life-size reconstructed head of a *Tyrannosaurus rex;* it's downright scary (in fact, though the museum is wonderful for kids, some of the younger ones might be a bit put off by all the growling and moving). Admission is $4.50, $2.50 for kids 2-12.

The adjoining gift shop sells a variety of dinosaur-oriented items, including dinosaur kites, coffee mugs, T-shirts, backpacks, books, posters, and even inflatable dinosaurs.

Dinosaur Valley is located right downtown at 362 Main and is open daily 9 a.m. to 5:30 p.m. Memorial Day through Labor Day; Tues. through Sat. 10 a.m. to 4:30 p.m. the rest of the year. For more information, phone tel. (303) 241-9210.

Cross Orchards Historic Site offers thorough tours of a working apple orchard that has been in operation since the late 1890s. Founded by Isabelle K. Cross of Massachusetts (heiress to the Red Cross Shoe Company fortune), the Cross was at one time one of the largest and most productive orchards in the country; it covered nearly 250 acres when the average orchard was under 10.

An ideal school field trip, a Cross Orchards tour demonstrates planting and harvesting techniques and also takes you into the workers' bunkhouses, a dining room, and kitchen. Tour participants get to taste apples (in season) and are given fresh-baked sugar cookies. A gift shop sells cards, crafts, candy, and other items. A number of annual events are held here, including a quilt show, pumpkin hunt, and "country Christmas."

Cross Orchards is open to the public 10 a.m. to 4 p.m. daily, mid-May to Nov. 1, as well as during special events. Admission is $1.50 for kids 2-12, $3 for ages 13-59, and $2.50 for seniors. For more information, write Cross Orchards Historic Site, 3073 Patterson/F Road, Grand Junction, CO 81504, or phone 434-9158.

The museum also administers **Dinosaur Hill** and **Riggs Hill,** sites of historic dinosaur excavations. One-mile loop trails provide access to both of these historic quarries. **Rabbit Valley Research Area and Trail Through Time** is administered by the museum and the BLM. Dinosaur bones, plant fossils, and geology can be seen along this 1½-mile self-guided trail.

For more information on the Museum of Western Colorado complex, write 248 S. 4th St., Box 20000-5020, Grand Junction, CO 81502, or phone 242-0971.

Western Colorado Center For The Arts

Located at 1803 N. 7th St., this museum features a wide variety of rotating displays. Though the emphasis is on Western and Native American art, the museum also exhibits other art in various forms from around the country. On permanent display is an excellent collection of Navajo rugs. This is also a center for performing arts, with concerts held throughout the year. Hours are Tues. through Sat. 10 a.m. to 5 p.m. For more information, phone (303) 243-7337.

PARKS AND RECREATION

Colorado National Monument

Sheer redrock cliffs, sandstone spires rising dramatically up from valley floors, desolate mesas, and shadowed canyons dotted with juniper and piñon—Colorado National Monument sprawls just west of Grand Junction over 32 square miles of some of the Southwest's most austerely beautiful landscapes. **Rimrock Drive,** the main road through the park, rises from the lowlands of the Colorado River Valley up through the canyons to the top of a broad plateau. The 23-mile road provides access to the park's visitor center, a campground, several picnic areas, over a dozen hiking trails, and many scenic overlooks.

Be sure to stop in at the visitor center, where you'll find displays of the park's geology, flora, and fauna. You can also get information on guided nature walks and campfire programs, and pick up books, maps, and other useful literature. **Saddlehorn Campground** has 81 sites available on a first-come, first-served basis; flush toilets, no showers, $7 per night. Backcountry camping is also allowed throughout the park; some restrictions apply.

Hiking trails in Colorado National Monument range from short nature walks and quarter-mile paths leading to scenic overlooks, to seven- and eight-mile backcountry routes through remote canyons. Some of the trails offer excellent cross-country skiing in the winter.

There are both east and west accesses to Colorado National Monument. To get to the east entrance, take Monument Road west from downtown. To get to the west entrance, take Broadway west from downtown or I-70 west to Fruita and follow the signs. Admission is $4 per vehicle for a seven-day pass.

For further information, write Colorado National Monument, Fruita, CO 81521, or phone (303) 858-3617.

hiking trails in Colorado National Monument

STEPHEN METZGER

City Parks

Lincoln Park, on N. 12th between North and Gunnison, is the community's largest and best town park. There are volleyball courts, swimming pools, picnic areas, a great kids' playground, huge lawns, and shade trees. Smaller, but also nice, is **Hawthorne Park,** at 5th and Gunnison; you'll find a picnic area, playground, lawns, and shade trees. For more information on Grand Junction parks, phone the **Parks and Recreation Department** at (303) 244-3866.

Child's Play

Grand Junction is a wonderfully "kid oriented" town. In addition to the excellent city parks, the community offers two unique diversions for kids. **Moon Farm** is a day and summer camp catering to kids ages 5-12. Originally founded over 30 years ago when the Moon family hosted son Dave's end-of-the-year kindergarten party, the farm, located on a huge spread west of town, has grown to include a huge and bizarre array of things for kids to do, with an emphasis on multicultural understanding They can try on wooden shoes at the Dutch House; play in the "saloon"; explore the Egypt House (where they can learn papyrus painting, the Egyptian alphabet, etc.); learn about Arabic cultures in the Middle East House; dig in a real fossil pit; feed the many animals, from Vietnamese pigs to goats and peacocks. They can also play soccer, volleyball, basketball, go horseback riding, practice archery, make videos, explore the Witch's Castle—with 180-200 other children (and one employee per 15 kids).

Moon Farm offers both daily and weekly programs, with bus service provided from downtown Grand Junction, and you can either stay with your kids or turn them over to trained staff. Day-camp rate is $10 per child per day. For more information on rates, hours, and special programs, write Moon Farm, Inc., 1360 18½ Rd., Fruita, CO 81521, or phone (303) 858-7176. To visit Moon Farms, go south on Hwy. 50 to 18½ Road.

On a smaller scale, but equally attractive, the **Doo Zoo Children's Museum** offers a wide range of diversions for kids from about three to eight. From play cars to a "sea" of blue plastic balls for "swimming," from a post office to a grocery store, the Doo Zoo offers enough to keep kids occupied for hours. Lots of hands-on learning toys, including typewriters and computers, are available. A small admission fee is charged, and parents should stay with their kids.

The Doo Zoo is located right downtown at 635 Main. Hours are Mon. through Sat. 10 a.m. to 5:30 p.m. For more information, phone 241-5225.

Cycling

The Grand Junction area offers excellent touring and mountain biking. Rimrock Drive through Colorado National Monument is a wonderful if admittedly arduous road tour. The route rises 2,000 feet from the valley floor to the top of the plateau and back down in 23 miles; the loop from Grand Junction through the park and back to town is about 36 miles.

Kokopelli's Trail is a recently developed mountain-bike trail that winds 128 miles from Grand Junction to Moab, Utah. Kokopelli's Trail (named for the humpbacked, flute-playing Anasazi god of fertility) begins 15 miles west of Grand Junction at Loma (Exit 15 from I-70), parallels the interstate for about 40 miles then drops south at Cisco, Utah, and winds down just south of Arches National Park. The trail is just one leg of the Colorado Plateau Mountain-Bike Trail System, which also includes the **Tabeguache Trail** to Montrose and when completed will ultimately comprise a half dozen other routes interconnecting Crested Butte, Aspen, Telluride, Grand Junction, Montrose, Moab, and Green River. The designers of the system are dedicated to political awareness and environmental preservation (Kokopelli's Trail is largely old jeep trails, so little actual construction had to be done). For a map of Kokopelli's Trail or more information on the Colorado Plateau Mountain-Bike Trail Association, write Box 4602, Grand Junction, CO 81502, or phone (303) 241-9561. Information is also available from the BLM, 764 Horizon Dr., Grand Junction, CO 81506, tel. 244-3000, as well as from Grand Junction-area bike shops, including **The Cycle Center,** 141 N. 7th, tel. 242-2541, **The Bike Peddler,** 710 N. 1st, tel. 243-5602; and **Tompkins Cycle Sports,** 225 E. Aspen (Fruita), tel. 858-9606.

Golf

Grand Junction's public golf courses include the small, nine-hole **Lincoln Park Golf Course** in town at 12th and Gunnison, tel. (303) 242-6394, and the 18-hole **Tiara Rado Golf Course** between Grand Junction and Colorado National Monument (go west on Broadway), tel. 245-8085.

Hiking

The Grand Junction area's two best hiking areas are **Colorado National Monument** and **Grand Mesa** (see "Grand Mesa," following, for information on hiking in Grand Mesa National Forest). Colorado National Monument offers excellent hiking for all levels of ability and seriousness. A half dozen or so short marked trails (from one-quarter- to one-mile long) will get you out of the car for a breather, while backcountry trails ranging 4-8½ miles will take up to 16 hours roundtrip. The park has published a map and guide with descriptions of the different trails, including lengths in miles and approximate time allowances. You'll be given the guide when you enter the park. You can also get information on hiking in the park from the visitor center or by writing Colorado National Monument, Fruita, CO 81521; tel. (303) 858-3617.

Just west of the national monument is little-known **Rattlesnake Canyon,** a desolate and rugged area accessible only by foot or 4WD vehicle. Hardy backcountry hikers will be rewarded with some of the most austere beauty on the Western Slope—sandstone cliffs, piñon-dotted mesas, and several natural arches. For information on Rattlesnake Canyon, contact the regional BLM office at 764 Horizon Dr., Grand Junction, CO 81506; tel. 243-3000.

Fishing

The Colorado and Gunnison rivers were probably once full of healthy lunker trout, though as victims of irrigation and mining, the rivers don't offer much to modern anglers. The Grand Mesa area (see that section, following) has over 200 lakes and offers decent fishing. For information and licenses in Grand Junction, stop in at **Surplus City,** 1st and Grand, tel. (303) 243-3604.

Rafting

Grand Junction's Western Slope location makes it ideal as a base for river running, from kayaking in boiling whitewater to floating down broad, lazy stretches of calm riverwater. **Adventure Bound, Inc.** is a Grand Junction-based company that offers trips on the Colorado, Yampa, and Green rivers in Colorado and Utah. Trips range in length from one to five days. Explore the canyons of Dinosaur National Monument and Utah's Green Wilderness. For a brochure with more details, including prices and reservation information, write Adventure Bound River Expeditions, 2392 H Rd., Grand Junction, CO 81505, or phone (303) 241-5633 or (800) 423-4668.

You can also book raft trips on the Colorado River through **Rimrock Deer Park and Outdoor Center.** Rates range from $13 (1½-hour trip) to $135 (two days). You can also rent canoes. Write Box 604, Fruita, CO 81521, or phone 858-9555.

Horseback Riding

Grand Junction's roots are in ranching and farming, and it remains a very Western town—lots of Stetsons, string ties, and horse trailers. Several outfitters in the area rent horses and offer tours, one of the best ways to see Colorado National Monument. **Rimrock Deer Park,** whose stables are located near the west entrance to the monument, offers one- and two-hour rides, as well as half-day, full-day, and overnight pack trips. Rates start at about $12 for a one-hour ride. For further information, phone (303) 858-9555.

Downhill Skiing

One of Colorado's lesser-known ski resorts, **Powderhorn,** is located just 35 miles from Grand Junction via I-70 and Hwy. 65. Powderhorn and the surrounding Grand Mesa National Forest also offer good Nordic skiing. For information on skiing Powderhorn, see Grand Mesa, below.

ACCOMMODATIONS

Hotels And Motels

Most of Grand Junction's hotels and motels are concentrated on Horizon Dr just off I-70 (airport exit, Exit 31). You'll find **Ramada Inn,** tel. (303) 241-8411; **Holiday Inn,** tel. 243-6790; **Super 8,** tel. 248-8080; **Sandman Best Western,** tel. 243-4150; **Horizon Inn Best Western,** tel. 245-1410; **Budget Host Inn,** tel. 243-6050; **Hilton,** tel. 241-8888; **Motel 6,** tel. 243-2628; and several others.

The closest motel to Colorado National Monument is the **West Gate Inn,** at I-70 Exit 26, tel. 241-3020. Doubles run about $40-50.

Bed And Breakfasts

The **Junction Country Inn,** 861 Grand Ave., tel. (303) 241-2817, is a centrally located bed and breakfast in a remodeled 1907 home. Within walking distance of many of the city's parks and other attractions, the inn is also on a relatively busy (for Grand Junction) street. If you'd rather be out and away from the hustle and bustle of town, try the **Orchard House,** 3573 E-1/2 Rd. (Palisade), tel. 464-0529. About 10 miles east of Grand Junction on a hillside above the little town of Palisade, the Orchard House looks out over the farms and orchards of the Grand Valley.

Camping And RVing

In addition to Saddlehorn Campground at Colorado National Monument (see above) and the Forest Service campgrounds on Grand Mesa (see that section, following), the Grand Junction area also offers several privately owned camping areas. The Grand Junction/Clifton **KOA** campground, tel. (303) 434-6644, is located just east of town at 3238 E. Business-70 (take Exit 37 from I-70). On the other side of town are the **Junction West RV Park,** 799 Rd. 22 (Exit 26 off I-70), tel. 245-8531, and **Fruita Junction RV Park and Campground,** tel. 858-3155, off I-70 in Fruita adjacent to the Colorado Welcome Center and near the west entrance to Colorado National Monument.

FOOD

Start Me Up

If you're just passing through, you'll find plenty of fast-food restaurants at the major exits off I-70, particularly at the airport exit (Exit 31). **Good Pastures,** tel. (303) 243-3058, at the Friendship Inn at 733 Horizon Dr. (Exit 31 from I-70) is Grand Junction's answer to a health food restaurant. Beginning with fresh juices (celery, carrot, apple, etc.), Good Pastures offers several low-fat, healthful dishes, including some vegetarian specials; at breakfast, you have your choice of sausage, Canadian bacon, or "soysage." For a different kind of breakfast experience, try **Talley's,** downtown right next to the Doo Zoo. A local hangout, Talley's features standard American food, complete with the smoke and Formica of a traditional small-town café.

Other Restaurants

One of the best restaurants in town is **The River City Cafe and Bar,** 748 North, tel. (303) 245-8040. Offering an eccentric menu with an emphasis on healthful foods, River City serves pizzas (with eggplant and feta cheese), soups, salads, and a variety of Mexican and Southwestern dishes. River City specializes in black-bean and other vegetarian dishes, including delicious black-bean burgers. Dinners run $5-12.

For authentic Mexican food, try **La Mexicana,** 1310 Ute, tel. 245-2737. Dinners run about $4-7, and Friday and Saturday nights, the stage comes alive with authentic Mexican folk dancing, focusing on a different state in Mexico each evening.

Sweetwaters, 336 Main (on the Mall), tel. 243-3900, has very good Italian food at decent prices: fish, meat and seafood dinners run about $9-14, but you can get pasta specials for $7-10.

Just Desserts

Pappy's Ice Cream Parlor, on the Main Street Mall at 560 Main, tel. (303) 241-5600, features excellent homemade ice cream (using Ben and Jerry's recipes), fresh-squeezed lime- and lemonade, fresh-ground coffees, and gourmet candies.

ENTERTAINMENT

Those expecting Boulder-like nightlife in Grand Junction will be disappointed. Though there are a handful of places to listen to live music, your choices are limited, and you're probably better off taking advantage of the area's daytime recreational opportunities. If nighttime finds you antsy to get out, though, try **Cahoot's,** 490 28-1/4 Rd., tel. (303) 241-2282, which features live rock 'n' roll, or **The Rose,** 2993 North Ave., tel. 245-0606, where you can dance to live country-and-western music. **Bailey's,** at the Ramada Inn, 2790 Crossroads, tel. 241-8411, is a nightclub/disco with DJ dancing, and **Cinnamon's,** in the Holiday Inn, 755 Horizon, tel. 243-6790, has live music. **Charade's,** in the Hilton, 743 Horizon, tel. 241-8888, features live comedy on Tuesday nights. The **River City Cafe and Bar,** 748 North, tel. 245-8040, also books live music from time to time.

CALENDAR

From music festivals to baseball tournaments to bike races, Grand Junction's got something going on just about every weekend. The best sources for what's happening when and where are the *Daily Sentinel* and the Grand Junction Area Chamber of Commerce.

Among the highlights: The **JUCO** (Junior College) **Baseball World Series** in late May; the **Hot-Air Balloon Rally** early June; the **Colorado Stampede** (rodeo, music, cowboy poetry), mid-June; **Country Jam USA Music Festival** late June; **Dinosaur Days,** late July; the **Mesa County Fair,** early August; **Palisade Peach Festival,** late August; **Renaissance Faire,** mid-September; and the **Colorado Mountain Winefest,** late September.

Throughout the summer, downtown Grand Junction features **Art on the Corner,** with a diverse group of the state's sculptors displaying their work outside on streetcorners. The **Grand Junction Symphony Orchestra** hosts a concert series each year, with special shows attracting big-name guest conductors and musicians. For information, phone the symphony at (303) 243-6787.

SHOPPING

Try to allow yourself some time to explore downtown's Main Street Mall. Though the street has been remodeled, it's refreshingly free of Yup-scale boutiques and trendy (and pricy) shops. Instead, you'll find classic small-town clothing, band-instrument, shoe, stationery, and gift stores. There's even a nurses' uniform store, a formal-wear rental shop, and a Woolworth's. Be sure to check out **A Haggle of Vendors Emporium,** 510 Main, where every imaginable nook and cranny is packed with imports, antiques, and junk—everything from toys and fabrics to picture frames, plates, mugs, and glassware.

SERVICES

The offices of the Grand Junction **Police Department** are located at 625 Ute; phone (303) 244-3538. The Mesa County **Sheriff** is at 215 Rice; phone 244-3500. Both of Grand Junction's hospitals offer emergency and non-emergency medical care. **St. Mary's Hospital and Regional Medical Center** is at the corner of 7th and Patterson; phone 244-2273. **Grand Junction Community Hospital** is at 12th and Walnut; phone 242-0920. Grand Junction's main **post office** is at 241 N. 4th; for information on other branches or Grand Junction-area zip codes, phone 244-3400.

Recycling

Recycle at **United Waste and Recycle,** 2948 I-70 Business, and **Western Colorado Recycling,** 2379 G Road. You can also drop off most recyclables at Grand Junction's **City Markets,** 2770 Hwy. 50, 1909 N. 1st St., 569 32nd Ave., and 200 Rood Avenue.

INFORMATION

Just west of town in Fruita is a Colorado State **Welcome Center,** where you can pick up brochures on what to do and see in the Grand Junction area, as well as in the rest of the state.

The **Grand Junction Area Chamber of Commerce,** tel. (303) 242-3214, and the **Visitors and Convention Bureau,** tel. 244-1480 or (800) 962-2547, are located in the same building two blocks off the Main Street Mall at 360 Grand Avenue. Lots of brochures and information on things to do in Grand Junction, on the Western Slope, and in the rest of Colorado. The Visitors and Convention Bureau operates a visitor center on Horizon Dr. just off I-70.

One of the best places in town for Colorado books, maps, and magazines is **Readmore Book and Magazine Stand,** 344 Main St., next to Sweetwaters on the Main Street Mall. The shop carries an excellent selection of everything from coffee-table-size photo books to small-press histories, with a special section of books by local authors. The main branch of the **Mesa County Public Library** is located in Grand Junction at 530 Grand Ave.; phone 243-4442.

Grand Junction's *Daily Sentinel,* which comes out weekday afternoons and Saturday and Sunday mornings, has information on current events, local movie and television listings, and weather. For subscription information, phone 242-5050.

(top) downtown Crested Butte in summer; (bottom) Mountain bikers explore the Crested Butte area. (both photos: Crested Butte Mountain Resort Association, Grafton Marshall Smith)

Victorian home in Georgetown (Stephen Metzger)

TRANSPORTATION

Located just south of Interstate 70 about 250 miles west of Denver, Grand Junction is easily approachable by either car or bus. The **Greyhound-Trailways** bus depot is downtown at 230 S. 5th; for information on rates and schedules, phone (303) 242-6012. You can also get to Grand Junction via **Amtrak,** whose passenger station is at 2nd and South Ave.; for information, phone 241-2733 or (800) 872-7245.

Grand Junction's **Walker Field Airport** is the largest airport in the state west of Denver and is serviced by several major airlines, with flights from cities around the country as well as connecting flights from Denver. Phone the airport at 244-9100. For airport transportation services, phone **A Touch With Class,** tel. 245-5466.

Most of the major car-rental agencies have booths at Walker Field, including **Avis,** tel. 244-9170; **Budget,** tel. 244-9155; **Hertz,** tel. 243-0747; and **National,** tel. 243-6626. Offices of **Thrifty Rental,** tel. 243-7556, are at 752 Horizon.

For taxi service in Grand Junction, phone **Sunshine Taxi** at 245-TAXI.

SOUTH AND EAST OF GRAND JUNCTION

COLORADO 141 SOUTH

Colorado 141 winds south from Grand Junction to Dove Creek, coursing through western Colorado's remote canyon country and passing through a handful of ramshackle old mining towns. Along the way, the 150-mile stretch of highway flirts with the Utah border, twice approaching within 10 miles of the state line. Known as the **Unaweep/Tabeguache Byway,** the road slices below Grand Mesa, across the Uncompahgre Plateau, and follows the course of the Dolores River for some 30 miles. Ribboning through ancient Native American hunting grounds, the route takes its name from the Utes: "Unaweep" means "Canyon With Two Mouths," and "Tabeguache" ("TAB-a-wash") means "Place Where The Snow Melts First."

Unaweep Canyon is a harshly scenic draw that slices through the plateau nearly from Whitewater to Gateway. Its floor lush and green and sometimes seemingly endless, its walls towering sharp and sheer, the canyon has that unmistakably familiar ability to help travelers find perspective. Out here, where the lines between nature's beauty and her cold indifference become blurred, you, and your problems, can seem awfully small.

In the late 1880s, a seven-mile wooden flume was built along the Dolores River just north of Uravan. Used to carry water from the San Miguel River to the Lone Tree Placer Site, **Hanging Flume** clings precariously to the sheer sandstone cliffs 150 feet above the water's surface. A turnout and interpretive sign provide an excellent view, as well as historical background.

Uravan was a company town founded in 1936 and named for the two elements found in the area's carnotite ore, uranium and vanadium. During the 1940s, the U.S. Army sent uranium from the tailings from the vanadium mill to Los Alamos, New Mexico, where Oppenheimer and crew used it in the Manhattan Project, the world's first atomic bomb. The mill was shut down in 1984.

For a complete guide to the Unaweep-Tabeguache Byway, contact the Grand Junction Visitors and Convention Bureau. The thorough and well-written guide describes 35 points of interest along the route from Whitewater to Placerville and also provides information on the geology, history, and wildlife of the area. Write 360 Grand Ave., Grand Junction, CO 81501, or phone (303) 244-1480 or (800) 962-2547.

Nucla, Naturita, And Norwood

Naturita is a small town west of the junction of CO 141 and CO 145 with several businesses flanking the highway for a couple of blocks. The town was founded in 1882 and serves today as a supply center for nearby ranchers and farmers. In addition, a handful of small motels provide base camps for the hunters who find their way out here in the summer and fall. **Children's Memorial Park** is just off the highway (at 2nd St.), next to the **Rimrock Historical Museum** (for hours and more information phone 303-865-2554).

THE GREAT COLORADO PRAIRIE-DOG SHOOT

Here's a pop quiz to test your sensitivity toward delicate environmental issues: Pick the Colorado tourist brochure image that seems just a tad bit out of whack.

a) A black bear lounging by a gurgling mountain creek.

b) Elks grazing in a meadow rimmed by 14,000-foot peaks.

c) A cross-country skier cruising through an aspen grove, oblivious to the doe and fawn nearby.

d) A fisherman snagging a fiesty rainbow from a rushing river.

e) Hunters and weekend sharpshooters with rifles using innocent, furry, photogenic, cuddly little prairie dogs for target practice in a competition to determine who can obliterate the most varmints with 50 squeezes of the trigger and win a $10,000 jackpot.

Hmmmmm. The elks? Doesn't seem likely. Time's up.

Careful readers will note the quiz writer slipped a couple of emotion-charged words into the right answer, "e." Innocent was sort of a giveaway.

To some, the Top Dog World Prairie Dog Shoot in the western Colorado town of Nucla—as close as you can get to nowhere and still be on the map—is cause for shame. To Nucla-ites, though, the staging of the annual competition (every June) serves a host of useful purposes. First, it removes several thousand of the pesky rodents from the nearby fields. In Colorado, there are an estimated 20 million prairie dogs and only about three million people. Second, the shoot pumps thousands of dollars into the local economy—no different, residents argue, than money from state-licensed hunters who stalk deer and elk each fall. And third, it's an excellent source of humor. "This shoot is a lot like sex and the Catholic Church," one local told the *Denver Post.* "Everyone agrees the job has to be done. The controversy is whether we get to enjoy it."

. There have been cries of anguish in metro Denver as prairie-dog populations are eliminated to make room for the sprawl, but nobody thought the workers gassing prairie-dog holes were there for the enjoyment of the experience. In Nucla, it's a different story. The idea of purposeful killing, with competition no less, prompted animal-rights ac-

tivists to picket the inaugural shoot in 1990. They deemed it a bloodthirsty example of man's inhumanity to other creatures. The slaughter of 3,000 rodents may have helped them prove their point. The next year, the activists decided that the hordes of media drawn by their protest only served to bulk up the coffers of the very people benefitting from the event, the residents of Nucla and nearby Naturita. So the 1991 demonstration was staged about 250 miles away, in Denver.

Nucla and Naturita, 110 miles south of Grand Junction, were founded by white settlers in the late 19th century. These towns, and many others like them throughout the mountains and eastern plains, give the state its independent, conservative edge. There are hundreds of hamlets throughout the state that have struggled and survived rough years—a crash in the markets for silver, a glut in the oil market. The silver crash led, over the decades, to Aspen becoming a mecca for skiers and the glamorous life. The low price of oil made the prospect of extracting crude from shale rock unlikely in Battlement Mesa, currently being touted as a retirement community. The thinking in Nucla was that simple. Why not take advantage of an overpopulation of prairie dogs?

Few visitors who head down this way will be disappointed by the scenery. Besides, the argument went, nobody cared about the plight of the prairie dogs when they were being gassed or shot by lone farmers simply trying to make their fields more productive. The fuss over a few thousand critters dying en masse one weekend each year, however, painted a different picture, one that Governor Roy Romer, in 1990, didn't want promoted. But as soon as he took sides in the debate, the controversy flared anew.

Nobody could have been happier than the folks in Nucla, who didn't really mind the attention and held their own Prairie Dog Plebescite to determine the fate of the event. The vote, rather lopsided, was 317-4.

There was nothing better, to locals, than being able to tell the governor to go meddle in somebody else's affairs. The folks in Nucla were simply trying to make a bigger mark on the map—the tourist brochures be damned.

—Mark Stevens

Five miles northeast of Naturita is the town of Nucla. Shortly before the turn of the century, the Colorado Cooperative Community established the town as an experiment in communal living. Designed as a community where "equality and service rather than greed and competition [would be] the basis of conduct," Nucla was made up of businesses that were all cooperatively owned. In addition, labor was evenly divided, and any product of community labor—the town's irrigation ditch, for example—became community property. Nucla was chosen for the town's name as its founders saw it as the nucleus of a socialist society that would eventually spread throughout the country. But it was not to be—the experiment was short-lived.

About 20 miles southeast of the junction of CO 145 and CO 141 is the little mesa-top ranching town of Norwood. Popular with outdoor enthusiasts, particularly hunters and anglers, the Norwood area is one of Colorado's little pockets of relatively undisturbed natural beauty. You can enjoy fishing and boating at nearby Miramonte Reservoir. For information on the area, phone the **Norwood Chamber of Commerce** at 327-4238.

GRAND MESA

Less than an hour east of Grand Junction via I-70 and CO 65, Grand Mesa is startling in its contrast to the Grand Valley sprawling at the base of its steep sides. Here a mountain highway winds and climbs and switches back from the scrubby canyon country up into the firs, spruces, and aspens of Grand Mesa National Forest. The mesa is 10,000 feet above sea level (and over 5,000 feet above Grand Junction) and covers over 50 square miles.

With over 200 lakes, 15 campgrounds, and miles of riding, hiking, snowmobiling, and cross-country ski trails, as well as Powderhorn downhill ski area, Grand Mesa offers some of the best recreational opportunities in the region. In addition, the mesa affords absolutely spectacular scenery. On the drive down the back side of the mesa, there are places where you can see the San Juan Mountains shouldering massively into the sky over a hundred miles to the south. Oftentimes in the summer, late-afternoon storms roll in, cold rains angle across the sky, washing the needles and leaves of the trees, and the sunlight plays strange tricks with the mist and the distant clouds. Rainbows arc across the sky, and the greens shine electric.

A word of caution: Even when it's warm in the valley, it can get downright cold on the mesa. I drove up one day in mid-June when it was pushing 90° F in Grand Junction, and by the time I got onto the mesa it was *snowing*. Even if it seems crazy, bring a coat or sweater.

Grand Mesa Lodging

The **Grand Mesa Lodge,** tel. (303) 856-3211, offers cabins that sleep up to six, and the **Mesa Lakes Resort,** tel. 268-5467, has small rustic cabins (no running water), larger, more modern cabins, and a central motel. Each lodge has a small restaurant and grocery and tackle shop.

Camping

Grand Mesa's campground's are generally open only from Memorial Day through Labor Day, thanks to the large amount of snowfall. Sometimes, there's even too much snow to open the areas until mid-June or later. **Jumbo** and **Spruce Grove** campgrounds have tent and RV sites, pit toilets, and access to hiking trails.

Hiking

Grand Mesa National Forest offers hundreds of miles of trails and backcountry to explore. One of the more popular trails is **Crag Crest Trail** on the highest point of Grand Mesa. The 10-mile trail provides access to broad clearings where you'll want to stop to take in the view, as well as to dense forests and beautiful mountain lakes. The Forest Service can provide topo maps and more information on specific parts of the mesa that are best for hiking.

Fishing

The lakes on Grand Mesa are open year-round, with ice fishing popular among die-hard trouters. Most of the lakes are quite small and get a lot of traffic. The shores of the more accessible lakes are lined with hopeful anglers, their RVs parked nearby. Even the more remote lakes are rather heavily fished.

For licenses, tackle, and information on current hot spots, stop in at the **Mesa General Store** in Mesa on CO 65 on the north slope.

view to the southwest
from Grand Mesa

STEPHEN METZGER

Skiing

Though primarily an intermediate area, Powderhorn offers good skiing away from the pomp and snobbery of some of the state's better-known resorts. Powderhorn skiers are also afforded some of skiing's more interesting and expansive views; because the mesa rises so dramatically from the valley below, the view is a mosaic of snowy mountain meadows, deep forests, and far-off canyonlands and arid desert.

Powderhorn's four lifts service 240 acres of trails and a 1,650-foot vertical drop. Terrain is 20% beginner, 60% intermediate, and 20% advanced. Lessons and rental equipment are available, as is limited on-site lodging, though there are plans for expansion. For information, phone (303) 242-5637. For lodging reservations, phone (800) 876-9337. For a recorded **snow report,** phone 242-SNOW.

Information

For maps and complete information on Grand Mesa and Grand Mesa National Forest, stop by the Grand Junction district office of the Forest Service at 764 Horizon Dr., Grand Junction, or phone (303) 242-8211. Information is also available from the Grand Mesa National Forest Headquarters, 2250 Hwy. 50, Delta, CO 81416, tel. 874-7691.

Cedaredge

Cedaredge (pop. 1,200; elev. 6,100 feet) is a robust and colorful small town between the lower slopes of Grand Mesa's south side and the flatlands of the Uncompahgre and Gunnison river valleys. Backed up against the mesa, Cedaredge offers excellent views of the sprawling valleys and orchards and, on clear days, the San Juan Mountains far to the south.

You'll find a nice city park right downtown on Main St./CO 65, with picnic facilities, shade trees, and tennis courts.

COLORADO 133

Colorado Hwy. 133 winds northeast from Hotchkiss along the North Fork of the Gunnison River, past Paonia Reservoir, over McClure Pass (elev. 8,755 feet), and then through the Crystal River Valley past Redstone and on to Carbondale. Weather permitting, this is the best and shortest route between much of Southwestern Colorado and Denver, bypassing the Grand Junction-to-Glenwood Springs stretch of I-70 and cutting an hour or more off the trip. Highway 133 is also the best route connecting Telluride and the ski areas of Central Colorado, and during the winter the you'll see a lot of ski-racked Subarus and Jeeps buzzing back and forth along the highway.

The first third of the way is mostly orchard and ranching country. The open, rolling landscapes are dominated by fertile orchards, and the fields are dotted with grazing cattle. Elk also graze throughout this area and are commonly seen from the roadway. At Paonia Reservoir, the road doglegs due north and lifts up over McClure Pass, where there are trailheads of some excellent cross-country skiing trails. The highway then drops down over the back side of the pass and through the beautiful White River National Forest and the Crystal River Valley, the Crystal River ribboning through the firs and gleaming argentine at roadside.

Paonia

Paonia (pop. 1,670; elev. 5,675 feet) was founded in 1882 and was named for the abundance of flowers in the area. The name is a bastardization of "peonie," probably resulting from misread handwriting. The major industry is agriculture, the area producing excellent peaches, apples, cherries, and other fruits, and there are also several mines nearby.

Paonia is also the rather unlikely site of the offices of one of the West's boldest, angriest, and most progressive and intelligent environmental newspapers, *High Country News*. Published out of an old one-story storefront building on Main St., the News, whose motto is, "A Paper for People Who Care about the West," is supported almost solely by subscriptions and grants, including from the Grateful Dead's Rex Foundation. This allows the paper the freedom to confront sensitive issues head-on without fear of advertisers pulling their ads. The result is a scrupulous press that does thorough investigative pieces on subjects ranging from overgrazing on New Mexico public lands to the official federal stand on grizzly bears in Yellowstone Park, and on all aspects of the West's often-destructive industries—mining, drilling, logging, and the military-industrial complex. For subscription and other information, write Box 1090, Paonia, CO 91428, or phone (303) 527-4898.

If you're looking for a good place to eat in Paonia, try **La Casa** on Main St., where you can get Mexican and Italian food, as well as sandwiches, burgers, and salads for $5-8. Lodging is available at the **Redwood Arms Motel,** just west of town on CO 133, tel. 527-4148.

For more information on Paonia, write the **Paonia Chamber of Commerce,** Box 366, Paonia CO 81428, or phone 527-3885. There's also a tourist information booth on CO 65 at the turnoff to town.

Yule Marble Quarries

This is a National Historic Site where some of the world's purest marble was mined. First dis-

covered in 1870, the marble from this area has been used in government buildings around the country, including the Denver capitol. In addition, deposits here provided the largest single piece of marble ever quarried in the world: the 100-ton brick used for the Tomb of the Unknown Soldier in Arlington National Cemetery in Washington, D.C. Marble from the Yule quarries was also used in the construction of the Lincoln Memorial.

Though the quarries have been inactive for years, the site is open to the public. Wander around the old mill and quarries, view huge slabs of flawless marble that once were used in mill buildings, hike along Yule Creek, where crystal-clear water polishes the marble's swirling veins and faded pastels. But be careful: Some of the old pits are deep, so use caution when exploring and keep an eye on kids.

The Yule marble mill and quarries are accessible only by foot or 4WD vehicle. Turn south from CO 133 onto County Rd. 3 (the turnoff is marked), and continue two miles to the town of Marble. From there it's about four miles to the quarries. You can arrange 4WD tours to the Yule quarries through **Crystal River Jeep Tours,** 116 Main St., Redstone, tel. (303) 963-1991.

Redstone

Redstone, a tiny resort community on the banks of the Crystal River, dates from the turn of the century, when coal baron John Cleveland Osgood (cousin of Grover Cleveland) built a village here comprised of several small cottages and one magnificent "castle." Osgood, founder and director of the Colorado Fuel and Iron Company, was at one time one of the country's most successful industrialists, his peers (and houseguests) including John D. Rockefeller and Theodore Roosevelt. Osgood was reportedly worth some $40 million.

The town of Redstone was built as a model industrial community. Osgood built the cottages to house the families of his employees who worked in the nearby coal mines and the large Redstone Inn for "bachelors and guests." He built the 42-room, 16-bedroom Cleveholm Manor for himself, decorating it with the finest furnishings from around the world—Tiffany chandeliers, Persian rugs, and Italian oil paintings, as well as lots of goldleaf and marble. Osgood and Roosevelt are said to have sat on the front porch shooting deer that the gamekeeper released on the lawn.

John Cleveland Osgood

Today, Redstone consists of a single narrow road paralleling the highway across the Crystal River. A handful of vacation homes and several gift shops, mostly specializing in antiques, dolls, woodcarvings, and glass can be found there; also some vacation lodges, a general store, and a small park and playground.

Redstone Castle (the old Cleveholm Manor) is open for tours by advance reservation. For information, stop in at the Redstone Country Store, or phone (303) 963-3408. The castle has also recently opened as a bed and breakfast and is reserved for groups on weekends. For rates and reservations, phone 963-3463.

The **Redstone Inn** is the lodge built to accommodate Osgood's bachelor workers and is on the National Register of Historic Places..Though not as opulent or huge as the Castle, the inn is still impressive in its grandeur and elegance. If you're looking for a great place to hole up away from daily life's hustle and bustle, you'd be hard-pressed to find a better spot (doubles start at about $70; slightly less for shared bath). The Inn also serves excellent dinners, and is famous for its Sunday brunch. Even if you're just passing through, take a few minutes to look around and maybe have a Bloody Mary in the bar, which is decorated with original Victorian furnishings. For more information and reservations, phone 963-2526.

ASPEN

If there is an Avalon of Colorado, it is Aspen, a place where myth and reality circle round each other like freewheeling falcons under a cobalt sky. And this is the town's real charm—the way it exists as though dismembered from the rest of the world, and how in a strange way it doesn't much matter what's real and what isn't. Though you might feel more grounded after having visited, it's due not as much to the town itself but to the perspective it provides. Like Hemingway said of journalism: Aspen is good for you, if you get out in time.

Of course some people stay longer than others. Though if you plan to stay, you need nearly to be independently wealthy. In the first quarter of 1990, the average price of a home was $1.16 million. In the middle of the same year, the cheapest house on the market was priced at $365,000; the house was under 1,000 square feet.

Which, of course, is why Aspen is almost synonymous with celebrity: Don Henley, Glenn Frey, Goldie Hawn, Jack Nicholson, Hunter Thompson, and John Denver are but a few who either live in the area or spend time here.

And it's not just housing. Walk around the downtown mall. You can almost smell the money. The boutiques and specialty shops aren't here for working people, who are, however, free to window shop and imagine a lifestyle they'll never experience.

What is there, then, for the untitled, the *unentitled?* Just this: Some of the most magnificent scenery and greatest recreational opportunities on the planet. Though best known as a ski resort—in fact, Aspen is probably the country's quintessential ski town—the area offers untold riches for hikers, mountain bikers, anglers, and anyone else willing to explore a bit. White River National Forest literally surrounds Aspen, its woods, streams, lakes, towering peaks, and old logging roads inviting endless hours of exploration, whether you go with a group or prefer the meditative nature of solitude.

Located in a winter-locked box canyon on the Roaring Fork River, Aspen traces its history, as do many Colorado mountain towns, to late-19th-century mining, and the town's homes and other buildings reflect that. Cozy Victorian homes—most of them tastefully remodeled and impressive—line the town's side streets. The Jerome Hotel, at one time one of the most elegant lodges in the west and still defined by glorious opulence, stands sentrylike on Main St., its solid, red-brick sides providing constancy to the pulsing, dynamic community that surrounds it.

Over the last half century, Aspen has earned a reputation as a center of sophistication and

downtown Aspen and
Aspen Mountain

STEPHEN METZGER

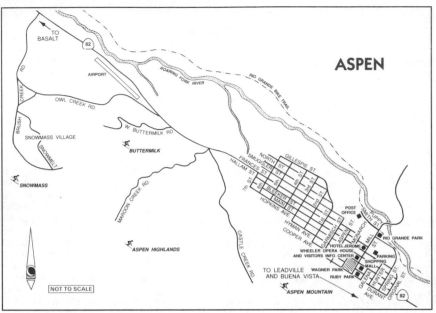

© MOON PUBLICATIONS, INC.

progressive cultural education. A number of institutes, arts centers, and annual festivals—music, film, food and wine—bring famous writers and directors, professors and lecturers, chefs and winemakers to town every summer. In addition, the large number of well-known artists, musicians, and actors who live permanently or part time in or near Aspen guarantee the area will remain a cultural mecca, if an overpriced one, well into the future.

HISTORY

The first mines were staked in the Roaring Fork Valley in the summer of 1879, when prospectors seeking silver arrived from Leadville by way of Independence Pass. By fall of that year, word was out that these mines, at the bases of Smuggler and Aspen mountains, were producing respectable amounts of ore. The valley's first community, originally called Ute City, was established by Midwesterner Henry Gillespie, who had stopped in Leadville en route to the valley just long enough to purchase rights to the mines from the original prospectors. Gillespie didn't

stay long, deciding to go to Washington, D.C. to try to raise money and establish postal service for his camp. In February 1880, B. Clark Wheeler arrived in Ute City, having skied into the valley on "Norwegian snowshoes," and, in Gillespie's absence, changed the name of the camp to Aspen.

That summer, great numbers of miners descended on the Roaring Fork Valley camps, and with them came merchants and others opening shops and services. It was reportedly a rowdy time, the lawless camp attracting men with little regard for social convention or propriety. When winter rolled around, though, and temperatures and snow fell, all but a handful hit the road for more hospitable climes. The few that stayed established the town's first newspaper, organized a Sabbath School, and sponsored regular dances and shows.

For the next three years, Aspen's ore production was kept to a minimum. The camp's remote location made hauling in equipment and domestic items difficult at best—with the nearest railroad 40 miles east, just about anything shipped into or out of the valley came via burro.

In 1883, Jerome B. Wheeler, a New York

businessman vacationing in Manitou Springs, arrived in Aspen and immediately saw its investment potential. Wheeler (who was not related to B. Clark Wheeler) bought controlling interest in several local mines, built the town's first bank, and resurrected an abandoned smelter, which allowed for greatly increased ore production. Shortly after Wheeler's arrival, the little town's annual silver production was $1.25 million.

When the Denver and Rio Grande Railroad arrived in 1887, Aspen's population was approximately 15,000, making it the third-largest town in the state. Local mines, particularly the Molly Gibson, Durant, Midnight, Montezuma, and Smuggler I and II, were producing nearly 100% pure silver, and the value of the area's annual output had increased to $6 million. In addition, the town had earned an international reputation for free-spending wild times and wilder women. Jerome Wheeler opened the Jerome Hotel and the Wheeler Opera House in 1889 at the pinnacle of Aspen's prosperity.

Aspen's boom was destined to be silenced, however. The silver market crashed in 1893, the mines closed down, and folks packed up lock, stock, and barrel, and headed out—some hiked over Independence Pass to Leadville. For the next half decade, Aspen was little more than a handful of crumbling shacks and hardy holdouts hoping good times would return. In the early 1930s, Aspen's population was approximately 250.

Within a few years, however, the first seeds of the valley's second growth spurt were beginning to be sown. In the summer of 1936, American bobsled racer Billy Fiske and his partner Ted Ryan created the Highland-Bavarian Corporation, with plans to develop the area into the kind of ski area the two had seen in Europe. They built the valley's first inn, the Highland Bavarian Lodge, and hired Andre Roche, a Swiss mountaineer, to survey the mountains for possible ski runs. By 1939, Fiske, Ryan, and Roche had organized the town's first ski club, cut the first trail on Aspen Mountain, and hosted the Rocky Mountain Ski Racing Championships. In 1941, Aspen was the site of the U.S. Nationals.

Throughout the 1940s, Aspen Mountain continued to host races, and its reputation as an excellent training mountain spread throughout the country. The summer of 1949 saw the founding of the Aspen Institute for Humanistic Studies, the town's first of many forays into the cultural arena. The following winter, Aspen Mountain was the first American site of the World Alpine Ski Championships. The little community was now on the international map.

In 1958, the Aspen Skiing Corporation expanded, opening Buttermilk Mountain just south of Aspen. Buttermilk, with gentler slopes than Aspen Mountain, was developed primarily as a teaching and beginner-to-intermediate area. Aspen Highlands opened the same winter, and Snowmass Ski Area opened 10 seasons later, in the winter of 1967-68.

MUSEUMS AND "CULCHA"

Since 1949, when Aspen developer Walter Paepcke organized an international celebration in honor of Johann Wolfgang von Goethe's 200th birthday, Aspen has been a center for a wide range of cultural and educational events and permanent institutes, from music and film festivals to various seminars, workshops, and conferences. June through September, the tenor of the town is decidedly intellectual, approaching highbrow, as well-known professors, critics, writers, and artists convene in Aspen to share ideas and to explore the parameters of their disciplines and media. In addition, there are enough museums and galleries, many with a Native American and Southwestern flavor, to keep you occupied for days on end.

Wheeler-Stallard House Museum
Located in the restored private residence of Aspen pioneer Jerome B. Wheeler, this museum displays furniture, clothing, toys, and other period pieces collected by the Aspen Historical Society. Docent-led tours provide insights into Wheeler's life, public as well as private, and offer a keen sense of life in the Roaring Fork Valley before it became a winter playground for the rich and famous. You can also arrange guided walking tours of historic Aspen or pick up a map and take a self-guided tour. The Aspen Historical Society can also recommend and direct you to tours of nearby ghost towns, including Ashcroft and Independence.

The Wheeler-Stallard House Museum is located at 620 W. Bleeker St.; it's open daily 1-4 p.m. mid-June through Sept., and during the ski season (mid-Dec. through mid-April). Small admission fee. For more information, phone (303) 925-3721.

Aspen Art Museum

Located along the Roaring Fork River and the Rio Grande hiking and biking trail, the Aspen Art Museum displays rotating exhibits by well-known artists from around the country, as well as the work of local artists, many of whom themselves are highly respected and widely acclaimed. A variety of media is represented, from architecture and design art to sculpture and paintings.

With its creekside location and adjacent Rio Grande Park, the museum provides an ideal picnic location and in addition offers a complimentary wine-and-cheese reception and gallery tour each Thursday evening at 5:30. The museum, located at 590 N. Mill, is open Tues.-Sun. noon-6 p.m., Thurs. till 8 p.m. Small admission fee; free Thursdays. For more information, phone (303) 925-8050.

Institutes And Galleries

In addition to these museums, the Aspen area is home to several academic and environmental institutes, arts centers that are open to the public, and a score or more of commercial galleries. The **Rocky Mountain Institute** is an experiment in environmentally responsible architecture and lifestyles. The 4,000-square-foot center, entirely solar heated, displays techniques in conserving energy and water. The center is located in Snowmass at 1739 Snowmass Road. For information on tours, phone (303) 927-3851. The **Aspen Center for Environmental Studies,** located along the Roaring Fork River behind the post office, includes a 25-acre wildlife sanctuary and a bird-rehabilitation center, both open to the public. Phone 925-5756 for information and hours. The **Anderson Ranch Arts Center,** at 5263 Owl Creek Rd. in Snowmass Village, displays work of visiting photographers, painters, woodworkers, and other artists and also offers workshops in various media. An example of the caliber of talent here was a recent "Winter Landscapes" workshop taught by Galen Rowell and Robert Glenn Ketchum. For information on touring the center, or on upcoming workshops, phone 923-3181.

Commercial galleries in Aspen and Snowmass range from shops specializing in prehistoric Native American art to places displaying campy art deco and art nouveau, with everything imaginable in between—large-format photography, Southwestern sculpture, 19th-century watercolors, and prints and originals by such names as Picasso, Renoir, Matisse, and Miró.

DOWNHILL SKIING

First, a clarification: there is no *one* Aspen. "Aspen" is actually four separate mountains, three of which—Aspen Mountain, Buttermilk, and Snowmass—are owned by the Aspen Skiing Company. The fourth, Aspen Highlands, is independently owned. To further complicate things, three of the ski areas—Aspen Mountain, Aspen Highlands, and Buttermilk—are within two miles of the *town* of Aspen. The fourth, Snowmass, is about 12 miles northwest of Aspen at Snowmass Village, not to be confused with the tiny *town* of Snowmass, about halfway back to Carbondale. Got that? Now, the ski areas, one at a time.

Aspen Mountain

First off, Aspen's terrain is designated 30% expert, 35% advanced, 35% intermediate, and 0% (!) beginner. That's not to say it should be avoided by all but the most advanced skiers, but this *is* where you'll see the polish, the finesse, the graceful speed—skiers who look like they were born on the mountain (indeed, many virtually were). Rated the third best American ski resort by a 1991 *Ski* magazine readers' poll, Aspen Mountain is truly one resort that every skier should hit at least once.

As with many European ski resorts, Aspen Mountain's base—the gondola, the lift ticket window, the ski school—is right in town. This is why you see skiers walking down sidewalks with skis ashoulder, and why half of those not carrying skis *are* wearing ski clothing (whether they've been skiing or not). It also creates a problem, though: parking. The relatively few on-street spaces in town are limited to 90 minutes and are closely monitored. Your best bet is to park in the newly built parking garage next to the Aspen Resort Chamber (two blocks north of Main St. off of Mill) and then take a free bus to the lifts.

Assuming your first ascent of Aspen Mountain is via gondola (recommended), you'll probably be surprised at how far back, and up, the lift takes you. It seems never to end. In fact, Aspen Mountain's 625 skiable acres are disproportionately lanky compared to most resorts' layouts, and most of the 75 trails are long, narrow, and steep—covering a 3,267-foot vertical drop. In addition to the gondola, Aspen Mountain offers seven other lifts designed to connect the different runs on the top half and lower north side of the mountain.

Buttermilk Mountain
Designed as Aspen's teaching mountain, Buttermilk is divided into three distinct, lift-connected sections. Offering sharp contrast to Aspen Mountain's advanced- and expert-oriented terrain, Buttermilk is geared almost entirely toward beginning and intermediate skiers. Six lifts service 410 acres and 45 trails rated 35% beginner, 39% intermediate, and 26% advanced.

Buttermilk is also much better suited to families than is Aspen Mountain, with lots of wide-open, treeless runs ideal for group cruising, or, after a decent dump, practicing those figure-8s. Three-pinners not up to Aspen Mountain can tune their chops on Buttermilk's gentler slopes and take Telemark lessons through the area's ski school.

Snowmass
The Roaring Fork Valley's newest ski area, Snowmass is located 12 miles "down valley" from the town of Aspen. Like Buttermilk, Snowmass is best suited to intermediate skiers and families—the mountain's skiable acres are rated 9% beginner, 51% intermediate, and 40% advanced and expert. In fact, *Snow Country* magazine's Resort Editor Abby Rand described Snowmass as "the intermediate's paradise" in the January/February 1991 issue. Sixteen lifts service 2,099 acres of skiable terrain with a 3,615-foot vertical drop.

In addition, things are a little more laid-back here than they are in town, and Snowmass attracts folks not interested in the pretensions and celebrity of Aspen. And that's a lot of the area's skiers: in the winter of 1988-89, 50% of the Aspen area's skier-days were spent at Snowmass.

Rated 19th among U.S. ski areas by a *Snow Country* reader survey, Snowmass is popular for its long runs, one of which is over four miles, as well as for its child care facilities and large number of ski-in/ski-out lodges and condominiums.

Aspen Highlands
The only one of the four Aspen-area ski resorts not owned by the Aspen Skiing Company, Aspen Highlands also has the longest vertical drop (3,800 feet), and the most even distribution of terrain: 48% intermediate, 23% beginner, 29% advanced and expert.

Aspen Highlands is on Maroon Creek Rd. just north of the town of Aspen and the Castle Creek bridge. Situated "upvalley," Aspen Highlands generally gets plenty of snow (an average of 300 inches), and though its snowmaking capabilities are minimal, during seasons of limited snowfall its slopes are often in better shape than those at Snowmass or Buttermilk. Aspen Highlands has 11 lifts and 55 trails on 552 acres of skiable terrain.

Alpine Skiing Information
For complete information on Aspen Mountain, Buttermilk, or Snowmass, write the **Aspen Skiing Company,** Box 1248, Aspen, CO 81612, or phone (303) 925-4444 or (800) 825-6200. For **ski-school information,** phone 925-1220. For the company's **snow report,** phone 925-1221.

For complete information on **Aspen Highlands,** write Box T, Aspen, CO 81612, or phone 925-5300.

CROSS-COUNTRY SKIING

Though Aspen is better known as a mecca of downhill skiing and skiers, the area also offers excellent opportunities for the Nordic skier, with miles and miles of groomed trails and vast unbroken forests and meadows where you can cut your own path. The **Aspen/Snowmass Nordic Trail System** maintains 80 km of trails between the town of Aspen and Snowmass Village. Trailheads are located throughout the southern Roaring Fork Valley, including those at the Aspen Club, Aspen High School, the Aspen Cross-Country Center (22475 West CO 82), and the Snowmass Club Touring Center. Free transportation to the trailheads is available on the Roaring Fork Transit Agency's buses. You can get detailed maps of the trail system from the visitor center in the Wheeler Opera House, 328 E. Hyman, or by writing Box 10815, Aspen, CO 81612, or calling (303) 925-2145. Contact the Snowmass Touring Club at 02329 Club Circle, Snowmass Village, CO 81615, tel. 923-3148.

Located 12 miles west of Aspen on Maroon Creek Rd., the **Ashcraft Ski Touring Center** has 30 km of groomed trails in the gorgeous Castle Creek Valley. After a day on the trails, return to the center's **Pine Creek Cookhouse,** where you can get a fixed-price gourmet dinner or take a sleigh ride before skiing back to your car. For complete information (ski trails, dinner, sleigh rides), phone 925-1044.

Skiers looking for the ultimate cross-country experience can choose from two of the county's best backcountry trail systems. With difficult trails at high elevations, these systems are not for beginners. Skiers must carry heavy packs and be accomplished skiers and physically fit athletes.

The **Tenth Mountain Trail Association Hut System** offers European-style hut-to-hut skiing on 300 miles of trails stretching from Aspen to Vail and throughout much of the White River National Forest. On-trail accommodations are provided at 12 huts and lodges located three to eight miles apart. The association owns eight rustic huts and maintains four privately owned lodges. Reservations are generally required months in advance. (For a complete description, see "Winter Sports" under "Vail and Beaver Creek" in the Northwestern Colorado chapter.) For information, write 1280 Ute Ave., Aspen, CO 81611, tel. 925-5775.

The United States Ski Association operates the **Alfred A. Braun Hut System,** the trailhead of which is located on Maroon Creek Rd. near Ashcroft. Each of the six huts can accommodate up to 18 skiers (or hikers—the center is open year-round), with a minimum of four per hut. For information or reservations, write Box 7937, Aspen, CO 81612, tel. 925-7345.

For information on cross-country skiing in the surrounding White River National Forest, stop in at the district office at 806 W. Hallam St., Aspen, or phone 925-3345. You can also get information at any of the town's retail shops, including **Ute Mountaineer,** 308 S. Mill, tel. 925-2848, and **The Hub of Aspen,** 315 E. Hyman, tel. 925-7970. For guide service, contact **Elk Mountain Guides,** tel. 923-6131,

which offers tours of the Tenth Mountain Trail Association and the Alfred A. Braun huts and trails, as well as other half-, full-, and multi-day trips into the backcountry.

OTHER WINTER SPORTS

Snowmobiling

The **T-Lazy-7 Ranch** has become almost an institution in Aspen, with visitors returning year after year. The ranch offers snowmobile tours up into the Maroon Bells backcountry, as well as rides to ghost towns and historic mining camps. You can also take a ride up the back side of Aspen Mountain to meet skiing friends for lunch at the top of the gondola. The T-Lazy-7 also offers sleigh rides and, in the summer, stagecoach rides. For more information, phone (303) 925-4614 or 925-7040.

You can also rent snowmobiles or join tours (two-hour or half-day) at **Western Adventures** north of Aspen at Woody Creek. For information, phone 923-3337.

Skating, Dogsledding, And Sleigh Rides

Aspen Ice Gardens is a 16,000-square-foot indoor rink at 233 W. Hyman. Open year-round, except for April and May, the rink offers instruction, rentals, repair, and sales; phone (303) 925-7485.

Dogsledding in Aspen goes back to just after WW II, and **Krabloonik Kennels** carries on the tradition. Krabloonik is owned and operated by Iditarod racer Don MacEachen, who named the kennels after the first lead dog he ever raised— Krabloonik means "Big Eyebrows" and is the Eskimo term for "White Man."

Sleds pulled by 13-dog teams take visitors on full- and half-day tours through the Maroon Bells area, beginning at the ranch at 1201 Divide Rd., Snowmass Village, where MacEachen keeps over 300 dogs. Full-day trips include lunch on the trail, and half-day trips include lunch at the center. For information and reservations, phone 923-4342 or 923-3953.

If you're feeling more nostalgic than Yukony, you can also tour the Aspen area by horse-drawn sleigh, with several companies offering tours (over the river and) through the woods, as well as through town. **Aspen Carriage Company,** tel. 927-3334, has sleighs as well as carriages, with scenic and historic tours available. You'll see the rigs parked in town at the corner of Cooper and Galena. **Snowmass Stables,** tel. 923-3075, offers nightly rides to a backwoods cabin, where guests are served dinner and treated to live entertainment. Sleighs depart at 5:30 and 8 p.m. Phone for reservations, as the rides are very popular.

Another long-time favorite for sleigh rides is the **T-Lazy-7 Ranch,** tel. 925-7040 or 925-4614. Offering Maroon Creek Valley rides ranging from daytime scenic tours to evening dinner rides where you grill your own meat and enjoy live music, the T-Lazy-7 has sleighs that accommodate up to 24 people.

You can also take sleigh rides at **Ashcroft Ski Touring Center,** tel. 925-1044 (lunch and dinner rides), and at **Moon Run Ranch,** tel. 923-3244. The latter offers afternoon and evening rides with food and live entertainment; the rides are designed specifically for large groups and are available by reservation only.

WHEN THE SNOW MELTS

Aspen's countenance changes considerably when the lifts shut down, when running shoes and golf spikes replace ski boots as the footwear of choice and aloha shirts replace sweaters and parkas. Still, though, there's a common thread: a youthful vigor and an obsession with the outdoors. Running, rafting, biking, ballooning, hiking, tennis, golf, and all sorts of water sports, from fishing to windsurfing. And for those who get their thrills shopping instead of rock hopping, Aspen's pricy boutiques and specialty shops themselves offer plenty of breathtaking thrills (like coats that cost as much as Jeep Cherokees).

Hiking
Aspen locals like to say, "You come here for the winter, but you stay for the summer," and indeed, many of Aspen's year-round citizens originally came with plans to spend a season ski bumming and then return to more serious pursuits when the resorts closed down. And the hiking in the area is without doubt one of the reasons folks stick around.

Aspen is literally surrounded by the White River National Forest, which comprises a total of 2,270,700 acres and contains seven wilderness areas, including the Maroon Bells-Snowmass, Collegiate Peaks, and Hunter-Frying Pan regions near the Roaring Fork Valley. This means there's no shortage of excellent hiking in the area—from short nature walks to serious backcountry expeditions.

One of the area's easiest and more popular hikes is the **Rio Grande Trail,** which begins where Mill St. crosses the Roaring Fork River. The two-mile trail continues northwest along Cemetery Lane and the river, offering a peaceful stroll and good views of the valley. It's also a popular mountain-bike trail.

The **Braille Trail** is a quarter-mile nature walk located on the Roaring Fork River east of Aspen. Blind walkers follow a nylon rope to some two dozen stations with braille as well as printed-text explanations. The trailhead and parking lot are located on the south side of CO 82 about 10 miles east of Aspen. For something a bit more demanding, try the five-mile **Sunnyside Trail,** which begins near the Slaughterhouse Bridge off the Rio Grande Trail. The 2,000-foot vertical rise (to almost 10,000 feet) is guaranteed to give the old ticker a workout, while affording views of spectacular scenery. And speaking of which: the 1 1/2-mile-long **Maroon Lake Scenic Trail** follows Maroon Creek to Maroon Lake to a view of Maroon Bells (whew!) and some scenery that will take your breath away. Take Maroon Creek Rd. about eight miles west of CO 82 (summertime day-trippers will have to take the shuttle, as the road is closed except to travelers heading into the campgrounds or lodges).

Other nearby trails include the Ute Trail, American Lake Trail, and Hunter Valley Trail. For complete information on these and other trails, see *Aspen-Snowmass Trails: A Hiking Trail Guide,* by Warren Ohlrich, available in local bookstores and outdoors shops. For information and maps of White River National Forest, stop by the district office at 806 W. Hallam, or phone (303) 925-3445. You can also get maps, as well as gear and equipment, at **Ute Mountaineer,** 308 S. Mill, tel. 925-2849, **Ute Alpinist,** 605 E. Durant, tel. 925-2489, and **Aspen Sports,** 408 E. Cooper, tel. 925-6331, and in the Snowmass Center, tel. 923-3566.

Elk Mountain Guides, tel. 923-6131, and **Aspen Alpine Guides,** tel. 925-6680, are both licensed outfitters offering guided day hikes and backpacking trips into the Aspen-area backcountry.

Cycling

Not surprisingly, cycling is extremely popular in the Aspen area, and mountain biking especially has caught on big in recent years. Road bikers can take any number of local passes and valley drives, although you need to exercise extreme caution: Not only are many of these roads very narrow, some with steep drop-offs, but you've also got to watch out for tourists more interested in sightseeing than bike-rider seeing.

Roadsters looking for a real workout, with an equally rewarding view, can head up Independence Pass east of Aspen. The 20-mile ride from town to the summit gains 4,000 feet in altitude, and there are excellent photo ops along the way, not only of the valley east of the pass (from the top), but of the tumbling Roaring Fork River (from just a few miles east of Aspen). Castle Creek Rd. to Ashcroft and Maroon Creek Rd. to the Maroon Lake trailhead are shorter and less demanding—each is about 10 miles and gains only 1,500 feet. The Maroon Creek Rd. ride can be especially nice, as it's closed during the summer except to shuttle buses and travelers heading to the campgrounds and lodges, and the lack of traffic is a refreshing respite from the hustle and bustle of town.

Mountain bikers, who have gradually begun to eclipse road bikers in the area, have far more opportunities than their skinny-tire predecessors. First of all, White River National Forest, which surrounds Aspen, is full of old logging and mining roads, fire trails, and other areas to explore. In addition, the ski areas themselves are beginning to solicit mountain bikers, with access roads and ski runs open for fat-tire exploration, expedition, and exhibition.

One of the more popular is the **Richmond Ridge Trail,** which is accessible either from the gondola at Aspen Mountain or via Aspen Mountain access roads (including Summer Road). Other good rides include the **Rio Grande Trail,** beginning near the post office on Puppy Smith St., **Owl Creek Trail,** which connects Aspen and Snowmass Village on the west side of CO 82, and the tour north along the Roaring Fork from Aspen to Woody Creek.

For more information on cycling in the Aspen area, stop in at any of the excellent shops, including **Aspen Velo Bike Shop,** 465 N. Mill, tel. (303) 925-1495; **Aspen Sports,** 408 E.

Cooper, tel. 925-6331, and in Snowmass Center, tel. 923-3566; **The Hub of Aspen,** 315 E. Hyman, tel. 925-7970; or the **Sport Stalker,** 204 S. Galena, tel. 925-9237.

To arrange guided tours, all equipment and transportation provided, contact **Timberline Bicycle Tours,** tel. 925-9237, **Aspen Velo,** tel. 925-1495, **Blazing Paddles,** tel. 923-4544, or **Elk Mountain Guides,** tel. 923-6131.

Golf

What better way to spend a warm summer afternoon in the Roaring Fork Valley than strolling about the links, taking in the great views and the crisp mountain air, and feeling the warmth of the high-altitude sun? Of course, the summer afternoon won't be all you'll be spending: Golf is a high-end sport, Aspen's a high-end resort town, and when you put the two together the results are predictable: high-end greens fees.

Then again, you probably didn't come to Aspen to cut corners. You came to enjoy yourself. So swing away.

The **Aspen Golf Course** is a 7,000-yard-plus, 18-hole course located across CO 82 from the turnoff to Maroon Bells. The municipal course, known for its water hazards, offers a number of discounts (twilight play, multi-day passes, etc.). For tee times and information, phone (303) 925-2145.

The **Snowmass Golf Club Course** is geared toward guests of the Snowmass Lodge but is open to the public on a space-available basis. Designed by Arnold Palmer and Ed Seay, the 18-hole course is part of the large recreation facility that also includes tennis, racquetball, and squash courts, as well as a gym and athletic club with all the luxuries you'd expect in Aspen. Phone the pro shop at 923-3148 for tee times and information.

Tennis

Several private tennis court complexes serve the Aspen-Snowmass area, including the **Aspen Club,** tel. (303) 914-8900, and the **Snowmass Club,** tel. 923-5600. In addition, the area offers a handful of public courts, though you'll still have to pay $4-5 per hour to use them. You'll find public courts on Maroon Creek Rd. at Iselin Park and at Aspen Highlands Ski Area, as well as at Aspen Meadows, 25 Meadows Road.

rainbow trout

BOB RACE

Fishing

Aspen's Roaring Fork Valley is both home to and surrounded by better trout fishing than many people realize. In addition to the two stretches of specially restricted Gold Medal streams, several other rivers and lakes in the Aspen area also offer good fishing—for rainbow, brown, cutthroat, and brook trout, as well as hybrids.

The **Roaring Fork River** flows through the town of Aspen and down the valley to its confluence with the Colorado at Glenwood Springs. The river has a fair amount of public access (respect private property) and, though it gets quite a bit of traffic, can pay off for the patient and savvy angler. The **Frying Pan River,** which is located northeast of Aspen and runs through Ruedi Reservoir to Basalt, is famous for its BIG fish and accessible water. The stretch west of the reservoir is particularly good, with fish topping eight pounds taken regularly. Other streams worth checking out are **Maroon Creek** and **Castle Creek. Important:** Stretches of both the Roaring Fork and the Frying Pan are governed by special regulations, with specific size limits, bait restrictions, and catch-and-release rules. Regulations are available at local sporting-goods stores or from the **Colorado Division of Wildlife,** 6060 Broadway, Denver, CO 80216, tel. (303) 297-1192.

Several lakes in the area can also provide excellent fishing. In addition to **Ruedi Reservoir** east of Basalt, several smaller, tougher-to-get-to high-country lakes can be rewarding. The best sources for information on where to go when are the local shops, many of which offer guide services as well as top-quality instruction and equipment. Among the outfits with good reputations are **Taylor Creek,** 555 E. Durant, tel. 920-1128 (or 927-4374 for the store in Basalt), **Aspen Rod and Gun Company,** 519 E. Cooper, tel. 920-2140, **Aspen Trout Guides and Outfitters,** 614 E. Durant, tel. 928-1050; and **Frying Pan Anglers,** 302 Midland (Basalt), tel. 927-3441.

Camping

Aspen is in the heart of the White River National Forest and literally surrounded by excellent Forest Service campgrounds. And considering how packed the town and valley can get, the campgrounds tend to stay relatively uncrowded. Maybe picnic tables, sooty barbecue grills, and pit toilets are beneath the dignity of the monied noblesse, but I've driven through town on Friday afternoons when the streets were jammed with tourists and plenty of sites were available at nearby campgrounds, particularly those east of town along the upper Roaring Fork.

The following Forest Service campgrounds are located on CO 82 and the Roaring Fork River between Aspen and Independence Pass; all are quite nice: **Difficult** (47 sites, five miles from Aspen); **Weller** (11 sites, nine miles from Aspen); **Lincoln Gulch** (seven sites, 11 miles from Aspen); and **Lostman** (nine sites, 15 miles from Aspen). In addition, there are four campgrounds on Maroon Creek Rd.: **Silver Bar** (four sites, no trailers); **Silver Bell** (four sites, no trailers); **Silver Queen** (six sites); and **Maroon Lake** (44 sites).

For complete information on the Forest Service campgrounds in the Aspen area, stop by the Aspen Ranger District Office at 806 W. Hallam, or phone (303) 925-3445. For 24-hour recorded information, phone 920-1664.

River Running And Windsurfing

With so many rivers and streams in the area, it will come as no surprise that kayaking and rafting are very popular and that several outfitters capitalize on the quality water by offering a full range of trips. Among the popular nearby rivers are the **Roaring Fork, Colorado, Arkansas** (over Independence Pass from Aspen), and **Crystal** (west of Aspen via CO 133). **Caution:** In the spring and early summer, these rivers swell with snowmelt, and their capriciousness is the stuff of legends. Scores of people, including experienced river rats, have been killed. Check with local authorities, and don't get in the water if you don't know what you're doing.

For guided raft tours, contact **Aspen White-water,** tel. (800) 873-8008; **Blazing Paddles/Snowmass Whitewater,** tel. (303) 925-5651 or 923-4544 (the Snowmass number); **Colorado Rift-Raft,** tel. 925-5405 or 923-2220 (Snowmass); or **River Rats,** tel. 925-7648.

Windsurfing and skiing seem to go hand in hand somehow—get a group of skiers together, and it's very likely at least a couple of them will talk about spending the "off season" boardsailing. And though Aspen doesn't offer the thrills of the Columbia River or the Hawaiian Islands, Aspenites do find places to catch the wind. **Ruedi Reservoir** (east of Basalt) and **Twin Lakes** (east of Aspen via Independence Pass) are among the popular spots.

Horseback Riding

A dozen or so outfitters offer rides into the Aspen mountains and Roaring Fork-area backcountry. You can either rent your own animal and explore the areas on your own, or take guided tours, which range from short, two-hour trips and dinner rides with chow on the trail to multi-day pack trips into wilderness areas. The best-known is probably the **T-Lazy-7 Ranch,** whose Maroon Creek Rd. location provides excellent access to the Maroon Bells valley; for information and reservations, phone (303) 925-7040. You can also rent horses and book tours through **Moon Run Ranch,** tel. 923-4945; **Snowmass Stables,** tel. 923-3075; **Pioneer Springs Ranch,** tel. 923-4252, and **Diamond J Ranch,** tel. 927-3222 (located on the Upper Frying Pan River above Ruedi Reservoir).

Ballooning

The Roaring Fork Valley sprawls lush and rolling at the base of the towering Elk Mountains and I imagine is rather breathtaking from the air. A balloon ride offers the opportunity to see the landscape from an eagle's perspective without the in-your-face roar of an airplane engine (though the flatulent hot-air balloons themselves get awfully loud). **Adventures Aloft,** tel. (303) 925-9497, **Aspen Balloon Adventures,** tel. 923-5749, and **Unicorn Balloon Company,** tel. 925-5752, all offer tours of the area's skies, with a variety of incentives to offset the price ($150-200 per person), including transportation, food, champagne, and video filming.

Recreation Information

The Aspen Visitors Center in the Wheeler Opera House at 328 E. Hyman has walls of brochures, fliers, pamphlets, and other information on the area's vast recreational opportunities. Warren Ohlrich's *Aspen-Snowmass Guide to Outdoor Activities* is an excellent book of tips on everything from golf to ice climbing, running trails to snowshoeing, as well as maps and phone numbers for further information. The book is available at Aspen-area bookstores.

ACCOMMODATIONS

As you've probably heard, it's not cheap to stay in Aspen. And as in most of Colorado's resort towns, rates for accommodations fluctuate with the season. High season is mid-December until just after the first of the year. During low season—April, May, and September through November—there's not a whole lot going on in town. It's too warm for snow and most people consider it too cold to hike, mountain bike, and otherwise explore the outdoors. Rates also go up around holidays and three-day weekends.

One of the easiest ways to book a room is through **Aspen Central Reservations,** which handles the full range of accommodations in town. Phone them at (303) 925-9000 or (800) 262-7736. You can also stop in at their offices at 425 Rio Grande Place.

If you're looking for cheap, basic, bargain-basement digs, you're better off staying in Glenwood Springs, 40 miles back down the canyon, where you can get a room for $20-30. In Aspen, a room is going to run you a minimum of $75 a night, and you won't be able to find a whole lot in that range.

Ski Lodges

Staying in a ski lodge can be a relatively inexpensive way to go, and most of them make up in cozy charm what they lack in luxury. The **Heatherbed Lodge,** tel. (303) 925-7077 for information, or (800) 356-6782 for reservations, is a funky old '50s-style ski lodge located directly across the road from the parking to Aspen Highlands and nestled down in the pines along Maroon Creek. The Heatherbed has rooms starting at $90, which includes breakfast and after-ski chili. Located in downtown Aspen

Aspen's Hotel Jerome

just a hundred yards from the lifts of Aspen Mountain, **Skier's Chalet,** 203 Gilbert, tel. 920-2037, has rooms running about $50-120. Also located right downtown is the **Aspen Manor Lodge,** 411 S. Monarch, tel. 925-3001, where rates range from about $110 to $125. The **Alpine Lodge,** 1240 East CO 82, tel. 925-7351, has small but comfortable rooms located within walking distance of the lifts. With rates running about $40-100, the Alpine offers among the least expensive digs in town—and so it's often booked *way* in advance.

Hotels

The hotel for the ultimate Aspen experience is without doubt the **Hotel Jerome,** 330 E. Main, tel. (303) 920-1000. Built in 1889, this gorgeous building has been completely restored and is worth a look around even if you don't plan to stay. The lobby is furnished with plush Victorian-era chairs and sofas, and the bar is a classic place where hip Aspenites rub elbows. Rates at the Hotel Jerome, which has over 90 rooms (about two-thirds of which have been added to the original building), range from about $160 to $650.

Aspen's newest and probably most upscale hotel is the **Little Nell,** 675 E. Durant, tel. 920-4600. Located at the base of Aspen Mountain's gondola and offering unabashed opulence and every possible amenity, the hotel has rooms, suites, and "executive apartments." Cheap rooms in the off-season start at about $170.

Other classic Aspen hotels include the **Hotel Lenato,** 200 S. Aspen, tel. 925-6246; **Independence Square Hotel,** 404 S. Galena, tel. 920-2313; and **Hotel Aspen,** 110 W. Main, tel. 925-3441.

Bed And Breakfasts

The Roaring Fork Valley has a number of bed and breakfast inns that have earned reputations for offering a combination of quiet charm and Aspen luxury. One of the larger and better known is the **Molly Gibson Lodge,** 101 W. Main, tel. (303) 925-2580. The 50 units vary from hotel-type rooms to suites with kitchens; almost half have fireplaces; two Jacuzzis and two heated outdoor pools. Doubles start at about $50 and go to $220. The smaller and recently renovated **Mountain House Bed and Breakfast,** 905 E. Hopkins, tel. 920-2550, has a solarium and hot tub; rooms run about $120-200.

The **Sardy House,** 128 E. Main, tel. 920-2525, is a longtime Aspen favorite famous for its gourmet breakfasts, high-class decor, and overall elegance. Rooms start at about $250.

Camping And RVing

In addition to the many Forest Service campgrounds near Aspen (see "Camping" above), the Roaring Fork area offers a handful of privately run, RV-oriented campgrounds, though none in the immediate Aspen vicinity. The closest is the **KOA** just west of Basalt; for reservations or information, phone (303) 927-3532.

FOOD

There's no shortage of excellent restaurants in Aspen, and many have become little institutions of their own—places to see and be seen, and to catch up on all the important local skinny. Thankfully, many of Aspen's restaurants post their menus on the door or an outside window, providing not only a sense of the type of food and specials but of prices as well. An enjoyable way to spend part of an evening in Aspen, no matter what the season, is strolling about the downtown area "researching" the different dinner houses.

Start Me Up

One of the best ways to get your morning off to an optimistic start is over a cappuccino and croissant at **Pour La France,** 411 E. Main, tel. (303) 920-1150. A favorite of locals looking for a quick caffeine fix, or just wanting to linger leisurely over the morning paper, this little European-style café serves a variety of pastries and coffees—croissants and bran muffins, teas, espressos, and decaf. If you're looking for something more stick-to-your-ribsable, a couple of local favorites are **Poppycock's,** 609 E. Cooper, tel. 925-1245, and **Hickory House,** 730 W. Main, tel. 925-2313.

Dinner Restaurants

Anyone who's spent much time in ski towns knows that Mexican restaurants are always very popular, not only for their food, but for their casually festive ambience—rehash the day over a plate of nachos with margaritas or Dos Equis.

As perhaps America's definitive ski town, Aspen claims at least three first-rate Mexican restaurants, all with excellent reputations and popular with locals and tourists alike. The **Cantina,** 411 E. Main, tel. (303) 925-3663, offers a comfortable, laid-back atmosphere and huge windows looking out on Main Street. The relatively new **Flying Dog Brew Pub,** 424 E. Cooper, tel. 925-7464, serves burgers, seafood, and Mexican dishes. **La Cocina,** 308 E. Hopkins, tel. 925-9714, specializes in New Mexican food, including blue-corn tortilla dishes.

Other distinctive and highly recommended Aspen-area restaurants include **Little Annie's,** 517 E. Hyman, tel. 925-1098, for reasonably priced burgers, salads, ribs, etc.; **Asia,** 132 W. Main, tel. 925-5433, which serves excellent Chinese food in a classic Aspen Victorian (also delivers); **Pine Creek Cookhouse,** Ashcroft Touring Center, tel. 925-1044, serving gourmet meals to diners who (in winter) arrive after a cross-country ski trek or sleigh ride; the **Stewpot,** in Snowmass Village, tel. 923-2263, where you can fill up on homemade bread and excellent beef stew for under $10; **Krabloonik,** also in Snowmass, tel. 923-3953, a restaurant-cum-Yukon-style dog kennel (the owner keeps 300 dogs and regularly competes in the Iditarod) specializing in wild game (moose, boar, and elk).

Picnic Fixin's

The small **City Market** on E. Cooper is Aspen's grocery store and a sort of social hub as well. The store has neither a salad bar nor deli (unlike most City Markets), but you can pick up sandwich makings and other picnic supplies. If you're staying in a place with a kitchen you might also shop here to save some money on meals.

ENTERTAINMENT

Aspen is at once both a rowdy and a sophisticated town, and the entertainment options here run the gamut from smoky pool saloons to opera. If you're looking to tear things up a bit, try the **Cooper Street Pier,** 508 E. Cooper, tel. (303) 925-7758, an often-raucous local watering hole. The **Wheeler Opera House** books a wide range of live music, often big-name acts passing through town on otherwise big-venue tours; past acts have included Bonnie Raitt and Lyle Lovett. Phone the ticket office at 925-2750.

The bar at the **Hotel Jerome,** 330 E. Main, tel. 920-1000, is worth stopping by, not only for its elegant Victorian decor but also to check the pulse of high-end Aspen society. The **Woody Creek Tavern,** about 10 miles north of Aspen in Woody Creek, is a great place to go for a burger and a beer. Neighbors Hunter Thompson and Don Henley stop in from time to time when in town.

CALENDAR

Detailing Aspen's myriad cultural and recreational annual events is far beyond the scope of this book—the town's world-famous affairs virtually merit a book of their own. To find out what's going on, phone or write the **Aspen Chamber Resort Association,** 425 Rio Grande Place, Aspen, CO 81611, tel. (303) 925-1940, (800) 421-7145 (in Colorado), or (800) 262-7736 (outside Colorado). You can also phone the **Aspen Visitors Center** at 925-5656. Once you're here, read the *Aspen Times,* one of the best small-town papers in the country, for complete listings of what's happening and numbers of whom to contact for more information.

Annual Highlights
Among the highlights of Aspen's annual events: **Wintersköl,** a crazy winter fair featuring everything from a canine fashion show to ski competition to a pancake breakfast; **Aspen-Snowmass Food and Wine Classic,** with chefs, winemakers, and food writers from around the world (early June); **Aspen Music Festival,** outside concerts ranging from chamber music to jazz (late June through August); **Snowmass Hot-Air Balloon Festival** (late June); **Aspen Writer's Conference** (mid-July); and the **Aspen Film Festival** (late September).

SHOPPING

Confirmed shoppers will be in hog heaven in Aspen. Though nothing's cheap here—you'll find "sales" but not many bargains—there are oodles of shops to wander around in. Lots of jewelry stores, with emphases on the Southwest and Native Americana; gift shops, specializing in bath oils, kitchenry, and woodcarvings; boutiques, ranging from lingerie to fur; and a T-shirt or sports-apparel shop around every corner.

Part of the fun of Aspen, of course, is simply exploring aimlessly, wandering from one shop to the next. A handful, though, are specifically worth checking out. One of my favorites is **Great Stuff,** which specializes in "vintage sports collectibles and historical memorabilia." Guaranteed to make any sports fan drool, Great Stuff sells jerseys, cleats, helmets, bats, hockey sticks, footballs, baseballs, basketballs—all worn and signed by famous athletes, from Joe Namath to Hank Aaron, Kareem Abdul-Jabbar to Mickey Mantle. In September 1991, Great Stuff owner Mark Friedland attended San Francisco's "Treasures of the Diamond" auction and

bought Lou Gehrig's road jersey and a signed bat, both from 1938. Friedland paid $52,250 for the bat and—you ready for this?—$220,000 for the jersey. The little store also carries autographed photos of celebrities—the Rolling Stones, the Beatles, Marilyn Monroe. A particularly intriguing piece was Don Drysdale's original major league contract with his agent, who retained rights to "exploit" the Dodger pitcher. Prices start at about $75 (baseball signed by Mickey Mantle) and skyrocket from there (signed jerseys worn in playoff games begin at about $4,500). Great Stuff is located at 402 S. Galena; phone (303) 920-BATS.

Another intriguing little shop is **Curious George,** 410 E. Hyman, which specializes in collectible Western Americana. Lots of ceremonial Native American clothing—beaded moccasins and leggings—as well as frontier firearms—1880s Colts and Winchesters; when I stopped by, there was even a matching pair of 18th-century dueling pistols, the same model that Alexander Hamilton and Aaron Burr used.

SERVICES

The main offices of the Aspen **Police Department** and the **Pitkin County Sheriff** are at 506 E. Main Street. Phone the police at (303) 920-5400 and the sheriff at 920-5300. Phone the Colorado **State Patrol** at 945-6198 (Glenwood Springs). The full-service **Aspen Valley Hospital** is located at 200 Castle Creek Rd., Aspen; phone 925-1120.

Aspen's two **post offices** are in town at 235 Puppy Smith, tel. 925-7523, and in Snowmass Village at 1106 Kearns Rd., tel. 923-4266.

Just Kiddin'
Aspen-area kids' programs range from day care to week-long race camps. Snowmass has **Snow Cubs Play School** for children 18 months to four years, and **Big Burn Bears' Pre-School** (ski instruction) for kids four through kindergarten, as well as evening child care for children of night skiers; phone (303) 923-1220. At Buttermilk, kids three to six can play inside or take ski lessons through **Powder Pandas;** phone 925-6336 or 923-3959. Aspen Highlands' **Snowbunnies** offers both day care and lessons; phone 923-4620.

Aspen's Wheeler Opera House and Visitor Information Center

STEPHEN METZGER

Babysitting services not affiliated with the ski resorts include **Super Sitters, Inc.,** tel. 923-6080, and **Georget's Babysitting,** tel. 923-2988.

Recycling

The following **Pitkin County Drop-Off Sites** take aluminum, glass, newspaper, plastic, and tin and steel cans: the county landfill, Aspen High School, Woody Creek Tavern, Basalt Library, and the Conoco Station in Old Snowmass. You can also recycle aluminum at the City Market at 711 E. Cooper.

INFORMATION

A branch of the **Aspen Chamber Resort Association** is located right downtown in the Wheeler Opera House, 328 E. Hyman (corner of Mill). You'll find staff to answer questions, as well as scores of brochures and other publications promoting just about everything there is to do in the area—snowmobiling to trout fishing. Parking in the area can be tough, but directly in front of the building are several 15-minute spaces reserved for center visitors. Phone the visitor center at (303) 925-5656. The chamber's main offices are located at 425 Rio Grande Place; phone 925-1940. For **Aspen Central Reservations,** phone (800)-26-ASPEN.

The **Pitkin County Public Library** is located at 120 E. Main St.; hours are Mon.-Thurs. 10 a.m.-9 p.m., Fri. and Sat. 10 a.m-6 p.m., and Sun. noon-6 p.m. Phone 925-7124. The **Basalt Regional Library** is also located in Aspen, at 99 Midland Ave.; phone 927-4311.

For **road and weather information** phone 945-2221 (Glenwood Springs).

Bookstores

Aspen, which claims one of the most educated citizenries in the country, isn't real big on bookstores. One would expect, as in Boulder, several nooked and crannied holes-in-the-wall with easy chairs for customers, shelves spilling over into disarray, and shopkeepers more interested in reading George Eliot or Joseph Conrad than in designing window displays. But Boulder this is not.

Nonetheless, Aspen does have a couple of bookstores worth checking out. The best is **Explorer, Bookseller and Coffee Shop** at 221 E. Main. Located in an old Aspen Victorian, the shop has devoted each room to a category. What must have been a parlor or sitting room at one time is now the literature room; another room is for kids' books (very possibly at one time a child's room). Upstairs, you'll find a coffee shop . . . and more book rooms. In fact, the tables are scattered throughout the upstairs rooms, and you can sit over coffee and pastry in, for example, the "Travel Room."

Up the hill on the mall is **Unicorn Books From Aspen.** Very big on travel, outdoor recreation, and Colorado, especially with a local angle, Unicorn also carries kids' books, self-help, and reference, as well as magazines. The store is located at 400 E. Cooper, tel. (303) 925-7500. **Aspen Bookstore,** located at the Little Nell Hotel at the base of Aspen Mountain, also carries travel, Colorado, self-help, and magazines, as well as a decent selection of over-sized art books; phone 925-7427. **Timberline Books** is at 425 E. Hyman, tel. 925-2719.

Forest Service Information

For information on White River National Forest, stop in at the **Aspen District Office** at 806 W. Hallam, tel. (303) 925-3445. You can also write or visit the main offices at 9th and Grand, Box 948, Glenwood Springs, CO 81602, or phone 945-2421.

TRANSPORTATION

Getting There

The most Aspeny way to get to Aspen, of course, is to fly into the jet airport just north of town. **Continental Express** offers daily flights from Denver, as does **United Express** (operated by Aspen Airways), which also has nonstop service to Los Angeles, Dallas, Phoenix, and Chicago throughout the ski season. Phone Continental at (303) 925-4350 or (800) 525-0280 and United at 925-3400 or (800) 241-6522.

For the unwashed, Aspen is also accessible by car. The most direct route from Denver is via I-70 to Frisco, south on CO 91 to Leadville, south on Hwy. 24 from Leadville to the CO 82 junction, then west on CO 82 over Independence Pass. This is not only the most direct route, but it offers absolutely spectacular views and relatively little traffic. However, Independence Pass is closed in the winter, and if you're coming to ski, the only way to get to Aspen is via I-70 to Glenwood Springs then 82 south to Aspen (40 miles).

Amtrak has passenger service to Glenwood Springs, where you can either rent a car or hop a Roaring Forks Transit Agency bus. Phone the Glenwood Springs depot at 945-9563 or the central reservations office at (800) 872-7245.

Getting Around

Roaring Fork Transit Agency offers free "City Route" buses around town, and during the ski season also runs buses from the town of Aspen to Aspen Highlands, Buttermilk, and Snowmass, as well as to the cross-country centers. Pick up shuttles at the Ruby Park Bus Station and at the shuttle stops throughout town. RFTA buses also service most of the Roaring Fork Valley, with routes extending north to Glenwood Springs—fee charged for non-City Route rides. Buses depart from the Ruby Park bus station (on Durant between Galena and Mill) to the different ski areas. For information on schedules and fares, phone (303) 925-8484.

Aspen Limousine and Bus Service, tel. 925-9400 or (800) 222-2112, runs daily trips to Glenwood Springs, Vail, and Denver, and **High Mountain Taxi and Limousine,** tel. 925-TAXI, offers taxi and van shuttle service throughout the area. **Mountain Express Rent-A-Car, Inc.,** tel. 925-2880 or (800) 525-2880, specializes in 4WD skier vehicles.

LEADVILLE

The highest incorporated town in the United States, Leadville (pop. 3,900; elev. 10,152 feet) lies in a broad mountain valley at the base of Colorado's two tallest peaks, Mts. Elbert (elev. 14,433 feet) and Massive (elev. 14,421 feet). Once the state's second-largest community, Leadville claims a history firmly rooted in mining. Its stories were written by some of the West's most colorful characters, and its mines yielded some of the world's greatest fortunes—some wisely invested, some squandered.

Though modern Leadville is tame in comparison to the wild days of the late 19th century, when its muddy streets were packed with prospectors and prostitutes, the town still offers excellent views into the past. Tourists can visit a wide range of museums, from the spanking new National Mining Hall of Fame and Museum to the Tabor House (home of one of the state's most famous millionaires and philanderers) and the Matchless Mine (where Tabor made part of his $12 million). In fact, the town is virtually a museum in itself. Stroll the sidewalks of Leadville's main street (Harrison Ave.), wander into the old Tabor Opera House, and hike up the little side streets, all the while taking in that thin 10,000-foot air and the indescribably beautiful scenery—there's not much better place to get a feel for what it must have been like to live in a wild western mining town during the burlesque of Colorado's most important decade.

HISTORY

The story of Leadville is one of the most fascinating in the state, if not the country, as well as one of the most important in the tapestry of world mining history. It's a story of gold and silver, of rowdy miners determined to strike it rich, of lusty saloons and busy brothels, gambling halls and opera houses, and huge fortunes won and lost, and sometimes won and lost again.

Gold was first discovered in the Leadville area in the spring of 1860, and by that summer, Oro City, as the camp was called, had a population of 5,000. The gold proved particularly difficult to extract, however, and within a couple of years most of the miners had lit out for more promising lodes and the camp was all but abandoned. In 1875, "Uncle Billy" Stevens and his partner, metallurgist A.B. Wood, explored some of the deserted mines and, finding traces of silver, staked new claims. Word soon got out, and Oro City experienced a second rush, though this one on a much smaller scale. When Leadville was incorporated in 1878, postmaster H.A.W. Tabor estimated the population at about 200 people.

Tabor had been part of the Pikes Peak gold rush in 1859, having arrived in Colorado from Vermont with his wife, Augusta, and their son. A stonecutter by trade, Tabor had had little luck in the Colorado gold and silver fields and by the late 1870s had pretty much given up on ever finding the big one. In addition to acting as postmaster, Tabor worked as a storekeeper as well.

"Hey, Look Vat Ve Found!"

One day, two German shoemakers, George Hook and Auguste Rische, whom Tabor had grubstaked for partial interest in any ore they discovered, helped themselves to a jug of the

Horace A. Tabor

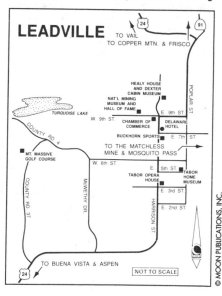

Augusta L. Tabor

halls where the mine owners played for huge stakes, and a general sense of silver-induced frenzy. Mines, and anything remotely resembling one, including simple holes in the ground, were sold and resold at huge profits, often over the course of a single day. One winter a grave-digger hit a silver vein while preparing to bury a body, and the cemetery was immediately staked out—the dead man was left in a snowbank, frozen stiff, until spring.

Meanwhile Tabor had become very much a public figure. He was elected lieutenant-governor, built opera houses in both Leadville and Denver, and served for a brief period as a U.S. senator, filling in between Senator Henry M. Teller's appointment as Secretary of the Interior and the election of a new senator 30 days later. Tabor also divorced his wife, Augusta, and in 1883 married Elizabeth McCourt Doe, a Leadville woman with whom he had apparently been trysting for some time.

Leadville and Tabor went into the skids at the same time, and for the same reason: the devaluation of silver. In 1893, panicking investors sold interest in their mines, banks went under, and Tabor's empire crumbled. He died in 1899, the course of his life having run full circle—he was nearly broke his last years, and working

storekeeper's booze and climbed up a hill and started digging. What they drunkenly happened upon, almost immediately, was what would later be known as the Little Pittsburg at the point where it came closest to the earth's surface. Almost overnight, Tabor's fortunes from the mine totaled $500,000; within a year he had sold his interest in it for $1 million and invested his profits in other lodes. One of them turned out to have been "salted," although digging on the site led to the discovery of the huge Crysolite lode. More important was Tabor's investment in the famous Matchless Mine, which would result in his becoming the district's first multimillionaire; his empire would eventually be worth $12 million. The great productivity of the Matchless also led to Leadville's being overrun, again, by prospectors, and by 1880, the town's population had surged to between 25,000 and 60,000, the figure officially given by the Leadville *Chronicle*.

During the early 1880s, Leadville was a rambunctious town with three breweries, brass bands playing every night along State St., drunken women driving carriages and "smoking long black cigars," fights, vigilantes, rowdy gambling as a civil servant, as the postmaster in Denver. His last words to "Baby Doe," as his second wife came to be known, were "Hang on to the Matchless."

One of the strangest chapters in Leadville history was written in the early winter of 1895, when local merchants organized a "Crystal Carnival." According to the WPA guide to Colorado, they built a "castellated structure of Norman design [that] covered five acres." Its ice walls were eight feet thick and 50 feet high and enclosed a "ballroom, a skating rink, a restaurant, peep shows, and curio shops. Frozen into the walls were specimens of ore, produce, and meat; ice and snow statues graced the interior. The palace, visited by thousands, remained open until July 4, 1896, before it melted away."

"Baby Doe" Tabor went on to become one of Leadville's most well-known citizens, albeit a reclusive and, some say, insane one. Though there were occasional reported sightings of her, she spent over three decades alone in a tiny cabin beside the mine. She was found in 1935, lying on the floor, frozen to death.

Throughout the first quarter of the 20th century, Leadville continued to produce ore, though in no way approaching the amounts of its heyday. In addition to gold and silver, lead, zinc, manganese, and molybdenum were taken from the district's mines. During Prohibition, moonshiners set up shop in the old shafts, and "Leadville Moon" earned a reputation as one of the best whiskeys in the West.

MUSEUMS

Leadville probably has more museums per square foot, and certainly per capita, than any other town in Colorado. And, with the exception of the Matchless, they are all within an easy walk of the center of town.

Historic Slide Show

Presented by the Leadville Chamber of Commerce, "The Earth Runs Silver—Early Leadville," is a six-projector slide show offering a dramatized glimpse of the area's history, from the gold and silver rushes of the late 19th century to modern restoration and tourism.

Showings daily 10 a.m.-5:30 p.m., June through mid-Oct., and 11 a.m.-5 p.m. in May. Screenings are in the Arts and Humanities building in the church next to the chamber of commerce, 809 Harrison. Admission is $3.50 for adults—discounts for seniors and kids. For more information, phone (719) 486-3900.

National Mining Hall Of Fame And Museum

Examining every aspect of U.S. mining, as well as bits and pieces from around the world, this fascinating museum displays a wide range of exhibits. Highlights include a state-by-state explanation of Western states' ores, production rates, and mining methods, as well as important tools and equipment. There are also dioramas showing different extraction techniques

downtown Leadville

STEPHEN METZGER

*interior of the
Tabor Home*

STEPHEN METZGER

and surveying methods, a reproduction of a cableway system near Bordeaux, France, and a display of Egyptian mining techniques. The Hall of Fame, in the same building, features plaques dedicated to various pioneers of the industry.

The museum is located at 120 W. 9th St. and is open daily 9 a.m.-5 p.m. (with limited winter hours). Admission is $2 for adults. For more information, phone (719) 486-1229.

Matchless Mine And Baby Doe's Cabin

Located up on the hill away from the T-shirt and souvenir shops of Harrison St., this is an excellent place to get a sense not only of the famous mine but of how Baby Doe spent the second half of her life. Guided tours take you into the mine's entrance, where original heavy equipment is still in place. In addition, there's a good display of miners' tools, forged in the blacksmith shop on-site, as it was too expensive to ship them from Denver. The rickety one-room cabin, where Baby Doe was found frozen to death in 1935, still contains her meager furnishings, and the walls have been hung with the last known photos of her.

The mine and cabin are open daily 9 a.m.-5 p.m., Memorial Day through Labor Day. Admission is $2 for adults. To get there, take 7th St. two miles east from downtown. For more information, phone (719) 486-0371.

Tabor Home

The residence of H.A.W. and Augusta Tabor from 1877, when Tabor had it built, until 1881 when he dumped his devoted first wife, this small, modest house provides excellent contrast with Tabor's later empire. A self-guided tour takes you through the tiny rooms, packed with Victorian furnishings, photo albums, dolls, and lamps, many of which belonged to the Tabors. A small gift shop sells books detailing Leadville's, and the Tabors', colorful past.

The Tabor Home is located one block off Harrison St. at 116 E. 5th. It's open daily 9 a.m.-5 p.m. Memorial Day through Labor Day and 10 a.m.-4 p.m. the rest of the year. For more information, phone (719) 486-0551.

Tabor Opera House

Built in 1879 when Leadville was home to at least 25,000 people, the Tabor Opera House was at one time one of the most elegant buildings in the West. Hosting a wide range of well-known performers, from Harry Houdini and Oscar Wilde to the New York Metropolitan Opera, the Tabor Opera House originally included boutiques, a saloon, and a suite for visiting artists. Private booths were for Tabor and his guests, who entered from the adjacent hotel via a second-floor walkway.

The Tabor Opera House is located downtown at 308 Harrison and is open for self-guided tours Memorial Day through Labor Day 9 a.m.-5:30 p.m.; closed Saturday. For more information, phone the chamber of commerce at (719) 486-3900.

Healy House And Dexter Cabin

Offering docent-led tours of an early Leadville boarding house and a private residence, this museum shows a side of Leadville history apart from that of the ubiquitous H.A.W. Tabor. The Healy House was built in 1878 by successful St. Louis mining engineer August Meyer and his wife Emma. Between 1897 and 1902, the structure served as a boarding house, primarily for area schoolteachers.

The Dexter Cabin was built by James V. Dexter in 1879 as a social club and poker hall. Don't be deceived by the Daniel Booney outer appearance of the cabin; inside it's lavishly furnished, reflecting Dexter's fortune and his passion for quality art and furniture.

The Healy House and Dexter Cabin, located at 912 Harrison, are open Memorial Day through Labor Day 10 a.m.-4:30 p.m. daily. Admission is $2.50 for adults. For information, or to book off-season tours, phone (719) 486-0487.

Heritage House

Offering an in-depth view of Leadville's boom days, the Heritage House Museum and Gallery features mining dioramas, historical photos, Victorian furniture and domestic items, and other late-19th-century artifacts. The art gallery diplays rotating exhibits of Colorado artists and craftsmen. The museum is located at 9th and Harrison and is open 9 a.m.-5 p.m. daily Memorial Day through Labor Day, with limited hours of operation the rest of the year. Admission is $2.50 for adults. For more information, phone (719) 486-1878.

Leadville, Colorado, And Southern Railroad Company

Offering half-day tours of the Leadville mining district, including the molybdenum mine at Climax, this narrow-gauge railroad is the highest in the U.S., leaving from the Leadville depot and twisting and curving and switching back to its 11,120-foot summit. Both morning and afternoon trips are available. Daily tours Memorial Day through Labor Day, weekends only through fall.

Non-reserved seating is available on a space-available basis. For reservations or further information, write Leadville, Colorado, and Southern Railroad Company, 326 E. 7th St., Box 916, Leadville, CO 80461, or phone (719) 486-3936.

Leadville National Fish Hatchery

Established in 1889, the Leadville hatchery raises brook, rainbow, and cutthroat trout for stocking in a wide range of Rocky Mountain waters, including those in national parks and forests and Indian reservations, as well as lakes and streams under state jurisdiction. In addition to viewing hatchery operations, visitors can take a hike on the one-mile nature trail, where local wildflowers, trees, and other flora are identified. There's also a picnic area on the property.

To get to the hatchery, go south from Leadville on Hwy. 24 for about two miles, then west on CO 300 (the turnoff is well marked). For hours and information, phone (719) 486-0189.

PARKS AND RECREATION

Surrounded by sprawling acres of national forest and some of the state's highest and most impressive peaks, Leadville is as rich in outdoor recreation opportunities as it once was in ore. Though the historic district offers excellent insight into the town's past, the surrounding area offers chances to hike, mountain bike, ski, golf, and sightsee in one of Colorado's most scenic areas.

Cycling

Tourers looking for a place to train for high-altitude competition need look no further than the roads and passes of the Leadville area. Excellent-if-grueling rides include the 60-mile Leadville-to-Aspen route, which winds up over Independence Pass (elev. 12,095 feet). The route drops south and down out of Leadville, follows the upper Arkansas River, then lifts west past Twin Lakes and up over the pass. You could also head north out of Leadville on CO 91, which will take you over Fremont Pass (elev. 11,320 feet), past the mines, titanic machinery, tailings, and rusting detritus of Climax, and down into Summit County. The stretch along Ten-Mile Creek is beautiful, and provides access to Summit County's other bike trails, including the path over Vail Pass (see "Cycling" under "Vail and Beaver Creek" in Northwestern Colorado). From Leadville to the junction of I-70 is about 25 miles.

There are also excellent trails for mountain biking in the region, thanks particularly to the plethora of old mining roads spider-legging over hillsides and along ridges. One good ride is up 7th St. into the Fryer Hill and Matchless Mine area. The route, first cut in the late 1870s, eventually takes you up and over Mosquito Pass (elev. 13,186 feet) and then down into South

Park, connecting with CO 9 just north of Fairplay. For maps and information on mountain biking in the Leadville and Lake County area, stop by the chamber of commerce at 809 Harrison, or contact the **Leadville Ranger District Office** of the Forest Service at 2015 N. Poplar, Leadville, CO 80461, tel. (719) 486-0749.

Golfing

Claiming to be North America's highest golf course, **Mount Massive Golf Club** (elev. 9,700 feet), is located about four miles west of town at the foot of the appropriately named Mt. Massive (elev. 14,421 feet). Only nine holes, but some of the prettiest sights you'll ever see from manicured lawns—bear, elk, and cougar (but no lynx) have been spotted from from the course. For tee times and information, phone (719) 486-2176.

Hiking

Hiking in the Lake County area ranges from a short nature trail at the Leadville National Fish Hatchery to serious and physically demanding backcountry excursions, including at least three specific marked routes to the top of **Mt. Elbert,** Colorado's highest peak (elev. 14,443 feet). Elevation gains on Mt. Elbert trails are in the 4,000-5,000-foot range, and the trails are four to six miles long. In addition, the **Colorado Trail** passes just west of Leadville.

The most popular route up Mt. Elbert is the **North Trail,** which begins from Halfmoon Campground (go west on CO 300 two miles south of Leadville, then south on Forest Service Rd. 110 to the campground).

For maps and more information on hiking in the area, stop by the Ranger District Office at 2015 N. Poplar, Leadville, or phone (719) 486-0749. Another excellent source of information is **10th Mountain Sports,** 112 E. 7th St., tel. 486-2202 (the store also carries ski equipment and rents, repairs, and sells mountain bikes). In addition, you can get gear and information from **Buckhorn Sporting Goods,** 616 Harrison, tel. 486-3944.

Fishing

Turquoise Lake, three miles west of Leadville via CO 300, and **Crystal Lakes,** four miles south of town on Hwy. 24, are both stocked regularly. Though fished fairly heavily, the waters produce rainbow, brown, and cutthroat trout, as well as kokanee salmon, in decent numbers and occasionally of respectable size. There is also fishing at the Leadville National Fish Hatchery. Stream fisherpeople might want to try **Halfmoon Creek,** west of Leadville off CO 300.

For licenses and tips on local hot spots, stop in at **Buckhorn Sporting Goods,** 616 Harrison, tel. (719) 486-3944.

Camping

Leadville is surrounded by excellent Forest Service campgrounds, many of which are situated on or near Turquoise Lake. For a complete list, contact the Ranger District Office at 2015 N. Poplar in Leadville, or phone (719) 486-0749 or 486-0752.

To get to the following Turquoise Lake campgrounds, go south from Leadville on Hwy. 24 two miles, then west on County Rd. 37 and watch for the signs. **Baby Doe Campground** has 50 sites, all RV-suitable, on 13 acres. **Belle of Colorado Campground** is also on the lake, though its 19 sites are designated tents only. Other Turquoise Lake campgrounds include **Dexter** (26 sites), **Father Dyer** (26 sites), **May Queen** (34 sites), and **Silver Dollar** (45 sites).

Halfmoon Campground (24 sites, also maintained by the Forest Service) is located on Halfmoon Creek just south of Turquoise Lake.

WINTER SPORTS

Downhill Skiing

One of Colorado's lesser-known downhill resorts, but a favorite of locals, as well as of Denverites wanting to avoid the crowds and pretensions of some of the state's larger resorts, **Ski Cooper** is located just ten miles from Leadville. The mountain has four lifts serving 312 acres, a 1,200-foot vertical drop (11,700-foot top), and excellent views. Terrain is rated 30% beginner, 40% intermediate, and 30% advanced.

Ski Cooper also offers rentals, lessons, and the "Panda Patrol" children's ski school (for ages three to five). In addition, advanced skiers can take the "Chicago Ridge" snowcat tour to some first-rate backcountry skiing, either bowls or trees—half- and full-day tours available.

For more information on **Ski Cooper,** write Box 896, Leadville, CO 80461, or phone (719)

486-3684. For information on snowcat tours, phone 486-2277.

Cross-country Skiing

Plenty of Nordic skiing in the Leadville area, from Turquoise to Twin Lakes. **Ski Cooper** has a Nordic center with 35 km of groomed trails, as well as access to the lifts. Nordic and Telemark lessons and rentals are available. For information, phone (719) 486-2277. There are also cross-country trails at the **Leadville National Fish Hatchery**; phone 486-1089.

At the Leadville/Lake County Chamber of Commerce, 809 Harrison, you can pick up the *Winter Recreation Trails* guide, which lists and describes 27 cross-country trails in the immediate area. You can also get information, as well as gear, from **10th Mountain Sports,** 112 E. 7th St., tel. 486-2202.

Other Winter Activities

Though known to relatively few, the Leadville area is truly a winter wonderland, with plenty to do outside when the mercury falls. Ice fishing is popular, particularly on Turquoise Lake, as is snowmobiling in the high valley's open meadows. You can also take an evening sleigh ride that includes a candlelight dinner (departures from 127 E. 8th Street). For reservations and information, phone (719) 486-2354, ext. 0210.

For more information on the area's winter recreation opportunities, stop by the chamber of commerce at 809 Harrison. For maps and information on skiing or snowmobiling on Forest Service land, contact the Ranger District Office, 2015 N. Poplar, tel. 486-0749.

ACCOMMODATIONS

Leadville offers a wide range of accommodations options, whether you're looking for an intimate bed-and-breakfast hideaway, a historic hotel, or a no-frills motel room, whether you're just passing through or want digs for the season.

The colorful and gingerbready **Mountain Mansion Victorian Bed and Breakfast,** 129 W. 8th, tel. (719) 486-0655, has an array of rates and rooms available. You can get a basic room (about $15-30) or rent the whole house (up to eight bedrooms, about $150-175 a night). Rooms at the inn, which has been recom-

mended by the Denver *Post* and the Dallas *Morning News,* are furnished with Victorian-era antiques—the "Baby Doe Room" has a couch dating to 1842 and an 1870s marble-topped chest of drawers. The inn also hosts cooking, Spanish-language, and start-your-own-bed-and-breakfast seminars.

You can also stay at the historic **Delaware Hotel,** 700 Harrison, tel. 486-1418 or (800) 748-2004. Built in 1888, the hotel was at one time one of the classiest in town; after Leadville's fall from grace, it served as a dry goods store, and has only recently been restored and reopened for lodging. Rooms are reasonably priced and include breakfast.

Motels in Leadville include the **Silver King Motor Inn,** 2020 N. Poplar, tel. 486-2610, where doubles run $40-60, and the **Timberline Motel,** 216 Harrison, tel. 486-1876 (about $35 for two).

In addition to the many Forest Service campgrounds in the Leadville and surrounding areas, the **Leadville RV Corral,** 135 W. 2nd, tel. 486-3111, is located just a block off Harrison St. and has 28 full-service RV sites.

For more information on accommodations in the area, contact the **Leadville-Twin Lakes Lodging Association,** tel. (800) 748-2057.

FOOD

For breakfast, try the **Garden Café,** 115 W. 4th St., tel. (719) 486-9917, specializing in natural and fresh ingredients and homemade dishes (also open for lunch, and for dinner Wed. through Sun.). A favorite for Mexican and New Mexican food is **La Cantina,** a mile south of town on Hwy. 24, tel. 486-9927. La Cantina features homemade tamales and tortillas, as well as stuffed sopaipillas, and the wonderful green chili of the Southwest. For Chinese food, try the **Silver Dollar Saloon,** 315 Harrison, tel. 486-9969, and for good ol' American burgers, check out the **Pastime Saloon,** 120 W. 2nd, tel. 486-9914.

CALENDAR

Leadville's annual calendar isn't exactly packed back-to-back with events, but those that are scheduled tend to be big, rowdy, and well known. On weekends in late June and early

duck

July, the city hosts the **Oro City Festival,** which re-creates Leadville/Oro City's boom days. Visitors can pan for gold, sample frontier "grub," listen to plenty of good old-fashioned mountain music, and just generally cut loose in the manner of the town's founding rowdies, miners, painted ladies, and entrepreneurs. The event is sponsored by Colorado Mountain College (Timberline Campus) and takes place just south of downtown. For information, phone the college at (719) 486-2015, or contact the chamber of commerce.

Another Leadville classic is the **Boom Days** in early August, which includes a parade, food, music, drilling competitions, and the famous **International Pack Burro Race,** in which participants—teams of burros and humans—haul, er, ass to the top of Mosquito Pass.

The **Leadville 100** (mid-August) is America's highest hundred-mile footrace (9,200 to 12,600 feet). Following backroads and trails deep into the woods, the course is famous among distance runners around the world as one of the most grueling.

In late August, the **Mosquito Pass Challenge** pits mountain bikers hub to hub from downtown Leadville to the top of Mosquito Pass.

For more information on Leadville's annual events, contact the chamber of commerce.

SHOPPING

You won't come up empty-handed if you go looking for souvenirs in downtown Leadville. Harrison St. is packed with T-shirt and poster shops, as well as places to pick up everything from postcards to Native American jewelry. Allow yourself time to stroll both sides of the four- or five-block Harrison St. boardwalk.

SERVICES

Offices of the Leadville **Police Department** are located downtown across from the chamber of commerce at 800 Harrison; phone (719) 486-1365. Phone the Lake County **Sheriff** at 486-1249. Leadville's **St. Vincent General Hospital** has 24-hour emergency service and is located at W. 4th and Washington; phone 486-0230. The Leadville **post office** is at 130 W. 5th; phone 486-1667.

Recycling
You can recycle aluminum at the **Safeway** on the north end of town. Otherwise, the closest recycling centers are in Summit County. **Summit Recycling,** 301 8th Ave. in Frisco, will take aluminum, glass, newspapers, and plastics.

INFORMATION

Probably the best place to begin your visit to Leadville is at the **chamber of commerce** at 809 Harrison. Pick up maps, brochures, and other information on things to do and see in the area. You can also purchase tickets for the multimedia historical presentation shown next door (see above). Write the chamber at 809 Harrison, Leadville, CO 80461, or phone (719) 486-3900.

For books, stop in at **The Book Mine,** 502 Harrison, tel. 486-2866, where you'll find a good selection of local, state, and Western history. The Lake County **public library** is located at 1115 Harrison; phone 486-0569.

Tours
For a bird's-eye view of the Leadville mining district, you can take a **Leadville Air Tour** plane ride. Tours include passes over Turquoise Lake, Twin Lakes and Independence Pass, and the Leadville mines, including the Matchless and Climax. Phone (719) 486-2627. **Dee Hive Tours** offers more down-to-earth tours, both historical and scenic. Phone 486-2339.

SOUTH OF LEADVILLE

Highway 24 drops almost due south out of Leadville, slicing through the beautiful Arkansas River Valley and following the tracks of the Denver and Rio Grande Western Railroad. Probably the single best place in the state to see Colorado's wealth of towering peaks, this route affords stunning—somehow humbling, even—views of the majestic Collegiate Range, a north-south formation of "14ers" paralleling the highway from the turnoff to Independence Pass to Salida.

In addition to Mts. Harvard (elev. 14,420 feet), Columbia (elev. 14,073 feet), Yale (elev. 14,196 feet), Princeton (elev. 14,197 feet), and Oxford (elev. 14,153 feet), the range includes at least seven other peaks over 14,000 feet. There are several places to pull your car off the road to take pictures or simply to enjoy the commanding views.

Just north of Salida, Hwy. 24 forks: You can either veer southeast for Salida, then catch Hwy. 50 east for Royal Gorge and Cañon City, or you can continue south on Hwy. 285, which passes through Poncha Springs, climbs up over Poncha Pass (elev. 9,010 feet), and then beelines through the San Luis Valley and Alamosa before dropping down into Santa Fe, New Mexico.

TWIN LAKES AREA

About 12 miles south of Leadville is the junction with CO 82, which connects the Arkansas River Valley with Aspen via Independence Pass (12,095 feet; closed in winter). South of the road are the two Twin Lakes, home to some of the largest trout in the state; patient Mackinaw anglers have taken 30-pounders. For those more interested in fight than weight, Twin Lakes are also regularly stocked with rainbow and cutthroat trout. You'll find several boat ramps, as well as lakeside picnic areas.

If you feel like holing up for a while, the lakes also offer a handful of very nice Forest Service campgrounds, and the area's moderately remote location keeps them from filling up as quickly as do many of the more easily accessible campgrounds. **Lakeview Campground** is located at the east end of the lower lake and has 59 tent and RV sites (flush toilets). Other Twin Lakes campgrounds include **Parry Peak** (26 sites), **Twin Peaks** (37 sites), and **White Star** (64 sites). None of the Twin Lakes Forest Service campgrounds has showers. For information, phone the **Leadville District Office** of San Isabel National Forest at (719) 486-0752 or 486-0749, or the Pueblo headquarters at 545-8737.

Independence Pass between Leadville and Aspen is closed in the winter.

STEPHEN METZGER

*Buena Vista's
Heritage Museum*

The **Twin Lakes Nordic Inn** offers lodging in a restored 19th-century stagecoach stop and brothel—rooms are furnished with feather beds and antiques. The inn also has a restaurant serving German and American food, and a cross-country ski center (rentals available). For reservations and information, write Twin Lakes Nordic Inn, Twin Lakes, CO 81251, or phone 486-1830.

BUENA VISTA

The name of this town is no lie—this area offers some of the prettiest views in the Rockies (those who know Spanish will cringe when they hear the local pronunciation: It's "BYOO-na VIS-ta" here, not "BWAY-na VEES-ta").

Lying in the rich, green Upper Arkansas River Valley, at the confluence of Cottonwood Creek and the Arkansas River, Buena Vista (pop. 2,075; elev. 7,954 feet) is surrounded by massive mountains, affording views that nearly do take your breath away. West of town, Mts. Yale and Princeton rise over 6,000 feet up from the valley floor to their 14,000-foot-plus peaks, providing the town with a constant reminder of nature's power and beauty. And when the sun of a late afternoon washes over the mountains' flanks, and the mist of a distant rainstorm softens their far ridge lines, well, it's almost enough to make a Believer out of you.

Buena Vista was founded in 1879 by silver miners who established it as the seat of Chaffee County the following year when they absconded

with the county records that had been stashed in a brewery in Granite 20 miles upriver. In 1881, an ore-sampling plant and smelter were built in Buena Vista, attracting large numbers of laborers, and through the 1880s the town was notorious throughout the West for its rowdy dance halls, gambling parlors, and brothels.

Today, Buena Vista's fortunes lie in tourism. Billing itself the "Whitewater Capital of Colorado," Buena Vista each summer attracts tens of thousands of visitors who come to sample the wide variety of runnable river water, from long stretches of calm water to nasty narrows and Class III, IV, and V rapids.

Buena Vista Heritage Museum
This four-room historical museum on the east end of Main St. features a variety of displays spanning a range of interests. Railroad buffs will dig the miniature reconstruction of the Upper Arkansas River Valley and the working model of the three railroads that served the area in the late 19th century. One of the rooms is devoted to mining and minerals, while you can also view clothing and domestic utensils from the 1880s through the 1920s, as well as historical photos.

The Buena Vista Heritage Museum is open daily 9 a.m.-5 p.m. Memorial Day through Labor Day. For more information, phone (719) 395-2515 or 395-8458.

City Parks
A shady lawn area on Hwy. 24 behind the chamber of commerce is perfect for picnicking. You'll

also find picnic tables, lawns, and shade trees at the small city park at the corner of Hwy. 24 and Main St.—kids can fish in the small lake.

River Running
This is modern Buena Vista's raison d'être and pretty much defines the town during the summer. Several rafting companies offer a wide range of trips on the Arkansas River, from no-experience-required sightseeing tours to serious trips requiring not only previous experience but top physical ability and strength as well. The following Buena Vista-based outfits are well established and have good reputations: **American Adventure Expeditions,** (719) 395-2409 or (800) 288-2409; **Buffalo Joe River Trips,** tel. 395-8757 or (800) 356-7984; **Noah's Ark,** tel. 395-2158; **Rocky Mountain Tours,** tel. 395-4101 or (800) 551-5140; and **Wilderness Aware,** tel. 395-2112 or (800) 462-7238.

Hiking
You could pretty much head out in any direction from Buena Vista and, being careful to avoid private property, find yourself in primo hiking country. If you feel like gaining some altitude, head west 12 miles on County Rd. 306 from the stoplight in downtown Buena Vista to the Denny Creek trailhead. From there, a four-mile trail leads to the top of Mount Yale (an elevation gain of 4,300 feet).

Another approach to Mount Yale is from just a few miles north; the trail circles south from the trailhead up to a saddle, where you can either turn around or head on up to the peak. It's a four-mile hike to the saddle (elevation gain: 2,600 feet), six to the peak (gain: 4,900 feet). To get to the trailhead, go north three blocks from the light in downtown Buena Vista, and turn left on Crossman (County Rd. 350). Go west two miles, until you reach County Rd. 361, and turn left. After one mile, turn left on County Rd. 365, and look for the trailhead about three miles up the road on the left.

For additional information on hiking in the Buena Vista area, contact the **Salida Ranger District Office** at 325 W. Rainbow Blvd., Salida, or phone (719) 539-3591.

Mountain Biking
Any area with this much excellent hiking will no doubt afford good mountain-biking opportunities as well. For maps and information on logging roads in the area, as well as single-track trails, contact the Salida Ranger District Office (see "Hiking" above). In addition, several of Buena Vista's rafting companies are "crossing over" and offering mountain bike tours, ranging from half- and full-day outings to combination "pedal-and-paddle" trips. Both **American Adventure Expeditions,** tel. (719) 395-2409 or (800) 288-0675 and **Rocky Mountain Tours,** tel. 395-4101 or (800) 551-5140, can arrange guided tours that include meals and bike and helmet rental.

Other Outdoor Activities
Buena Vista's location in the gorgeous Arkansas River Valley makes it ideal for a wide range of other recreational activities, from cross-country skiing and snowmobiling to fishing and jeep touring. For more information contact the Buena Vista Chamber of Commerce, Box P, S. Hwy. 24, Buena Vista, CO 81211.

Accommodations
A small resort town just a few blocks long, with a motel on nearly every one, Buena Vista often fills up in the evenings with visitors and passers-through—especially in the summer, when tourists need dry beds after spending a day on the river, and cross-country travelers need soft beds before heading back out on the trail in the morning. One of the first to fill up is the **Sumac Lodge,** tel. (719) 395-8111, at 428 Hwy. 24 (south end of town). Doubles go for about $32. The **Topaz Lodge,** tel. 395-2427, across the street and a couple of blocks north, has large inexpensive rooms—nothing fancy, but clean and comfortable. A room for two is about $38. The **Blue Sky Inn Bed and Breakfast,** tel. 395-8862, is located just southwest of town right on the Arkansas River—a nice, quiet home in the country. Rooms are reasonably priced.

RVers can camp at the **Mt. Princeton RV Park,** 395-6206, a mile north of town.

Food
You can get good solid Mexican food at **El Duran,** 301 Main St., tel. (719) 395-2120. Dinners run $5-9, but nightly specials, with drinks, go for under $5.

Entertainment
Let's not kid ourselves here. This a town that has a special "Yard of the Month" award given to

(top) downtown Aspen—boots by Tony Lama? (bottom) Denver's Union Station after dark (both photos: Stephen Metzger)

frozen fountain in Redstone (Stephen Metzger)

the homeowner with the best yard—recently given to the owners of a "rich, green manicured lawn [with] several flower gardens . . . included in the back yard."

Nonetheless, this is also a town full of river rats who need to unwind after spending their days guiding tourists downriver in rafts. And there are a couple of bars where you might stumble on some action. The **Blue Parrot** at 304 E. Main is usually packed with locals pounding beers; also on Main, between the highway and the Blue Parrot, the **Lariat** (whose motto is "We sell and service hangovers") seems to cater to more serious drinkers.

For the kids, **Rolling Wheels Skate Center** offers indoor skating and miniature golf.

Services

The offices of the Buena Vista **Police Department** are located at 101 Park Ave.; phone (719) 395-2451 (in emergencies, phone 395-8098). The nearest hospital is the **Heart of the Rockies Regional Medical Center,** 448 E. 1st St., Salida; phone 539-6661. The Buena Vista **post office** is at 100 Park Lane; phone 395-2445.

You can recycle aluminum at the **Circle Super Food Center,** 428 Hwy. 24.

Information

The **Buena Vista Chamber of Commerce** is in the center of town on Hwy. 24 and has lots of information on things do and see in the area, as well as on places to eat and sleep. Stop in for brochures or to ask questions of the staff. Phone the offices at (719) 395-6612.

Another good source for local information is the weekly *Chaffee County Times.* In addition to running local news and listing events, the paper focuses on outdoor sports— watch particularly for discussions of nearby hiking trails. The paper costs 35 cents in racks throughout Chaffee County. For subscription information, phone 395-8621. The Buena Vista **public library** is at 131 Linderman; phone 395-8700.

SALIDA

Salida (pop. 4,870; elev. 7,340 feet) was founded in 1880 as a division point on the Denver and Rio Grande Railroad, although for years prior to that the area had served as a stopping point for travelers passing through the mountains via the Arkansas River Valley. Throughout the late 19th century, Salida, like Buena Vista, its sister town upriver, had a reputation for rowdy, shoot-'em-up streets, and saloons and brothels famous throughout the Rockies. The railroad based its maintenance and repair operations in Salida into the second half of the 20th century.

Mt. Shavano (elev. 14,229 feet), about 14 miles northwest of Salida (pronounced Sa-LIE-da), is the town's dominant landmark and was named for the Ute Chief Shavano. In the spring, the mountain's melting snow is said to take the form of the "Angel of Shavano," who appeared to the Ute chief who was praying for his dying friend, trader Jim Beckwourth, founder of the town of Pueblo.

Today, motels and fast-food joints surround a quiet, narrow-streeted historic downtown area defined in part by antique shops, jewelers, and old taverns. Salida's definition is completed by the focus on the Arkansas River, running along the east side of town, and the many rafting and kayaking companies offering trips to tourists.

Salida Museum

Located adjacent to the chamber of commerce on Hwy. 50/Rainbow Blvd. (west side of town), this small historical museum displays a variety of Native American and pioneer artifacts from the Salida-Arkansas Valley area, with exhibits highlighting the region's mining and railroad histories. The museum is open daily Memorial Day through Labor Day 11 a.m.-7 p.m. For

downtown Salida

KAREN WHITE

more information, phone the Heart of the Rockies chamber of commerce at (719) 539-2068.

Parks

Salida is a true gateway to some of Colorado's best recreation areas and activities. The Arkansas River, one of the best whitewater-rafting streams in the state, flows right through town, south from Leadville then east toward Royal Gorge. To the northwest of town is the Collegiate Range and Colorado's biggest concentration of "14ers"—excellent hiking, climbing, and cross-country skiing. Also, Salida's surrounded on three sides by national forest—Pike to the north and San Isabel to the south and and west. In addition, Gunnison and Rio Grande national forests sprawl through Saguache County to the southwest of Salida, offering more camping areas and backcountry to explore.

City parks include **Riverside Park,** on the Arkansas River downtown at 1st and E. The park has nice lawns and shady cottonwoods and offers good fishing and picnicking, as well as a place to watch rafts go by. There's also a small park with picnic facilities adjacent to the chamber of commerce.

River Running

Like Buena Vista, Salida is a paradise for river rats, offering an exceptional base camp for a range of waters. Brown's Canyon in the Arkansas River Valley to the north is famous for its Class III and IV rapids. To the east, the

kayaker

Arkansas cuts through the mountains at Royal Gorge, sheer cliffs rising 1,200 feet up from the riverbed. Stretching along a 148-mile section of this river is **Arkansas Headwaters State Recreation Area,** which has established a number of campgrounds, kayak and raft put-ins, picnic facilities, and hiking trails for use by the public. You can get a guide and map to the area by writing Box 126, Salida, CO 81201, or by calling (719) 539-7289.

In addition, several private companies offer a range of river trips, with one to suit just about every budget, desire, and ability. **Dvorak's Kayak and Rafting Expeditions** is based in Nathrop (about 18 miles north of Salida) and books half- to 17-day trips not only on the Arkansas but on rivers throughout Colorado, Idaho, New Mexico, and Utah, as well as Hawaii, New Zealand, Australia, and Mexico. Dvorak's also offers fishing, mountain biking, and pack trips. For their catalogue, write 17921-B Hwy. 285, Nathrop, CO 81236, or phone 539-6851 or (800) 824-3795. Other Salida-area-based rafting companies include **Independent Whitewater,** tel. 395-2642 or 539-4057, and **River Runners, Ltd.,** tel. (800) 332-9100 (in CO) or (800) 525-2081 (outside CO). Write 11150 Hwy. 50, Salida, CO 81201 for a brochure.

Hot Springs

Salida Hot Springs, Colorado's largest indoor hot-springs pool, is located next to the chamber of commerce building at Hwy. 50 and Rainbow Boulevard. The pools were built in 1937 by the WPA. You'll find a lap pool, wading pool, and private tubs. Salida Hot Springs is open year-round, but hours vary. For times and information, phone (719) 539-6738.

Mt. Princeton Hot Springs are located between Salida and Buena Vista, five miles west of Nathrop. In off-and-on operation since the late 19th century, the hot springs, lodge, and restaurant are very popular with locals and passers-through alike. In addition to three swimming pools and several private tubs, there are rock-lined pools on Chalk Creek below the lodge. For reservations or information, write 15870 County Rd. 162, Nathrop, CO 81236, or phone 395-2447.

Skiing

Located just west of Monarch Pass, about 15 miles west of Salida on Hwy. 50, **Monarch Ski**

BOB RACE

Area is a low-key, family-oriented alpine resort offering some of the best skiing in the Rockies (see "Monarch Pass" following).

Golf

Salida Municipal Golf Course is a nine-hole course open year-round. For tee times and information, phone (719) 539-6373.

Accommodations

You'll find a "motel row" on Hwy. 50 on the west side of town with plenty of places to choose from, including the **Best Western Colorado Lodge,** 352 W. Rainbow Blvd., tel. (719) 539-2514, where doubles run about $45-65. The **Super 8 Motel,** 525 W. Rainbow Blvd., tel. 539-6689, has an indoor pool and hot tub and very reasonably priced rooms ($25-45). The **Friendship Inn of Salida,** 7545 W. Hwy. 50, tel. 539-6655 or (800) 453-4511, has rooms for two running about $32-55.

There are also a number of motels on the east side of town, including the **Circle R Motel,** 304 E. Rainbow Blvd., tel. 539-6296 ($30-45 for doubles), and the **Days Inn,** 407 E. Hwy. 50, tel. 539-6651 ($35-48).

The **Poor Farm Country Inn,** 8495 County Rd. 160, tel. 539-3818, is a bed and breakfast located in a three-story brick country home built in 1892. Located on the west bank of the Arkansas River, the cozy little lodge offers excellent mountain views and a peaceful escape from the demands of late-20th-century life. Doubles with full breakfast start at about $50.

The **Little River Ranch Motel and RV Campground,** 7870 W. Hwy. 50, tel. 539-7607 or (800) 727-0525, has motel rooms, RV sites, trout ponds and other activities on seven wooded acres along the Little Arkansas River.

Food

A great place to head for a pre-raft-trip breakfast is the **First Street Café,** 137 E. 1st St., tel. (719) 539-4759. Located in the historic downtown section of Salida, the building was constructed in the late 19th century and has served over the years as a boarding house, barber shop, and Ford auto garage. The café today is hipper (less smoky, for example) than most small-town joints and serves several vegetarian specials (stir-fry, etc.) in addition to traditional fare. Very reasonably priced. The First Street Café is also open for lunch and dinner.

Entertainment

Salida's **Powerhouse Players** is a community-theater group presenting melodrama and a variety of other plays, including musical revues, throughout the summer. The 250-seat theater is located along the Arkansas River in old Salida in the Steam Plant, one of the first electrical-generating plants in the country. For information or reservations, phone (719) 539-2455. The **Victoria Hotel and Tavern,** 143 N. F St., books live music (rock, blues, and rhythm and blues) on weekends.

Services

The offices of the Salida **Police Department** and **Chaffee County Sheriff** are located at 217 E. 3rd St.; phone (719) 539-2596. Phone the **State Patrol** at 275-0015 (Cañon City). **Heart of the Rockies Regional Medical Center** is located at 448 E. 1st St.; phone 539-6661. The Salida **post office** is located at the corner of 3rd and D streets.

Recycle aluminum at the **Safeway,** 232 G St., and at **Development Opportunities,** 203 E Street.

Calendar

The **FIBArk Boat Races** in mid-June kick off Salida's summer whitewater season (FIBArk = First in Boats on the Arkansas). In addition to a 26-mile kayak and raft race, the four-day event features footraces, novelty races (bed races, for example), a pancake breakfast, and a parade. A couple of weeks later, the town sponsors an "old-fashioned Fourth of July" with music, street dancing, a chili cook-off, and fireworks. In late summer (beginning early July), the **Aspen-Salida Music Festival** is a series of concerts featuring classical ensembles from the world-famous Aspen concert series.

For more information on these and other Salida events, contact the Heart of the Rockies Chamber of Commerce.

Information

The **Heart of the Rockies Chamber of Commerce** is a good place to get information not only on Salida but on the wealth of recreational opportunities available in the Arkansas River Valley. Offices are located at 406 W. Rainbow Blvd. (Hwy. 50), tel. (719) 539-2068.

For information on camping, hiking, and other national forest activities, contact the **Salida**

Ranger District Office of the Forest Service, 230 W. 16th St., tel. 539-3591.

For **road and weather information,** phone 539-6688 or 275-1637 (Cañon City).

HIGHWAY 50 WEST

Highway 50 continues west from Salida, connecting the Arkansas River Valley with Gunnison and Montrose. In Montrose, the highway doglegs north, joining Hwy. 550 and ribboning up between the Uncompahgre Plateau and Grand Mesa through Delta to Grand Junction. The Salida-to-Gunnison section of Hwy. 50 is particularly scenic, rising up into Gunnison National Forest, lifting over Monarch Pass, then following Tomichi Creek. Along the way are several Forest Service roads—some paved, some gravel—that lead to campgrounds and provide access to backcountry. For information on camping in Gunnison National Forest, contact the main office at 2250 Hwy. 50, Delta, CO 81416, tel. (303) 874-7691, or the Ranger District Office, 216 N. Colorado, Gunnison CO 81230, tel. 641-0471.

Poncha Springs

Ten miles west of Salida, the little junction town of Poncha Springs has a couple of motels and cafés, including the **Poncha Truck Stop,** a classic little coffee shop/diner open at 6 a.m. daily. In addition to excellent breakfasts (burritos, steak and eggs, etc.), the place serves lunch and dinner (Mexican food, steak, and fried chicken), as well as their monstrous "Alaska burger." There's also a small gift shop and bookstore, as well as public showers.

Monarch Pass

Highway 50 crosses over the Continental Divide at Monarch Pass (elev. 11,312 feet). One of the highest and most scenic highway summits in the United States, the pass affords excellent views and photo ops. To the south are the Sangre de Cristo and San Juan mountains, both ranges continuing across the border into northern New Mexico; to the north are the Ruby Mountains and the towering peaks of the Collegiate Range, several over 14,000 feet. In fact, from Monarch Pass you can see at least a dozen of Colorado's "14ers."

If the view from the roadside isn't enough, you can take the **Monarch Aerial Tram** to almost 12,000 feet. At the top is an enclosed observation tower, from which you'll have one of the best views in the Rockies. Maps and telescopes will help you orient yourself and identify distant peaks. The tram is open daily 9 a.m.-4 p.m. mid-May through mid-October. For more information, phone (719) 539-4789.

Monarch Ski Area, one of Colorado's classic off-the-beaten-path ski areas, is a favorite among locals, who are hip to its low-key atmosphere, relatively low prices, and uncrowded slopes. In addition, the resort's 10,800-foot base guarantees that its 350 average inches of snowfall are as fluffy as the downy flake in a Robert Frost poem—the stuff that makes converts out of pagan powder hounds.

With four lifts on 600 acres of terrrain, Monarch's 1,000-foot vertical drop offers good skiing for just about every ability level. The trails are designated 22% beginner, 44% intermediate, and 33% advanced (and, no, I don't know where that last one percent disappeared to . . .). Instruction and rentals are available, and though there is no on-site lodging, you can stay down the road at the **Monarch Lodge,** 539-2581 or (800) 332-3668, where you'll find a full-service restaurant, indoor swimming pool, Jacuzzi, exercise rooms, and many more amenities.

For more information on Monarch Ski Area, phone 539-3573. For snow conditions, phone (800) 228-7943.

GUNNISON AND VICINITY

Gunnison (pop. 5,785; elev. 7,700 feet) is located in the broad Gunnison River Valley about midway between Montrose and Salida. Home of Western State College and a center for some of Colorado's finest recreation, Gunnison is a youthful and outdoor-oriented town whose roots are in ranching and farming.

Seat of Gunnison County, Gunnison has long served as a trade center for many of the smaller communities in the surrounding area. Today, the town's economy relies largely on education and the tourism industry for its stability: Tourism brings in roughly $35 million annually and education $26 million; ranching brings in another $8 million.

Though Gunnison claims that the sun shines almost every day, it still manages to get damn cold in the winter. This is due largely to its valley location: Average temperatures in town are generally at least several degrees lower than in nearby towns such as Crested Butte, which lies at a higher elevation but is nestled against the mountainside. Gunnison has on occasion recorded the coldest temperature in the nation.

History

The first non-native people to explore the Gunnison area were probably those in the Escalante-Dominguez party, who in 1776 followed the Gunnison River west in their search for an overland route connecting the missions of Santa Fe, New Mexico, and Monterey, California. During the early and mid-19th century, the region was trapped and hunted by mountain men who would trade their furs at Taos and Bent's Fort.

On Sept. 6, 1853, Captain John W. Gunnison, a government surveyor, and his party camped along the Gunnison River near present-day Gunnison after having crossed the mountains in search of a transcontinental railroad route. The Gunnison party continued west into Utah, following roughly what is today the route of Hwy. 50. On October 25, while looking for a place to hole up for the approaching winter, the group was attacked by Native Americans, and Gunnison and all but four of his men were killed.

In the early 1860s, prospectors began to arrive in the Gunnison area, and in 1869, the region's Utes were removed to the Los Piños Indian Agency, clearing the valley for white settlement. It wasn't until the mid-1870s, though, that farmers and ranchers moved into the region in significant numbers. In 1874, Dr. Sylvester Richardson, a Denver physician, established the town site and organized the first town company. Gunnison became the official seat of Gunnison County on May 22, 1877.

Meanwhile, local creeks, particularly Tomichi and Quartz, were beginning to produce quality gold and silver in large amounts, and thriving mining camps were springing up in the nearby mountains. Gunnison was a natural supply center. In 1880, the railroad arrived, a godsend not only to miners but to Gunnison Valley ranchers and farmers as well.

In 1909, Gunnison's Colorado State Normal School was founded; in 1915 its name was changed to Western State College. Throughout this century, Gunnison has been a very popular gateway to some of Colorado's best recreation areas. As early as the mid-1900s, the

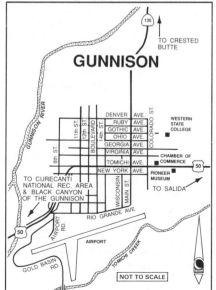

area's waterways—Taylor River and Tomichi and Cebolla creeks—were known for some of the best trout fishing in the Rockies. In 1963, with the opening of Crested Butte Ski Area, Gunnison became a destination for some of the best downhill skiers in the country—today, direct flights from Dallas, Chicago, Atlanta, Houston, and Denver offer easy access to the slopes.

Pioneer Museum

Gunnison's historical museum complex includes a restored turn-of-the-century schoolhouse, the town's first post office, and a railroad depot. There are also displays of railroad artifacts, Native American arrowheads, pioneer farming equipment, and lots of old photos.

The Pioneer Museum is located at S. Adams and E. Hwy. 50 and is open Mon.-Sat. 9 a.m.-5 p.m. and Sun. 1-5 p.m., Memorial Day through Labor Day. For more information, phone (303) 641-9963.

Western State College

Undoubtedly one of the first things you'll notice in Gunnison is the huge "W" on the side of Tenderfoot Mountain on the north side of town. Reportedly the world's largest college emblem, the "W" is made of white-washed flat rocks, carried up the mountain by students and faculty in 1923. Each line of the letter is 16 feet wide and 400 feet long; the overall dimensions are 320 by 420 feet.

For more information on the school's wide range of programs, write Western State College, Gunnison, CO 81230, or phone (303) 943-2119.

PARKS AND RECREATION

Gunnison is surrounded by some of nature's most gorgeous landscapes. Tumbling trout streams, mountain lakes, dense fir woodlands, granite peaks shouldering high above the timberline, broad valleys that come springtime are vibrant with wildflowers and shimmering waves of green—there's enough here to keep the outdoor lover grinning blissfully for a lifetime. In the wintertime, too.

Gunnison's very pleasant **city park** is located on the east side of town on Hwy. 50 and has large lawns, lots of playground equipment, and public restrooms.

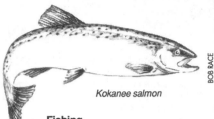

Kokanee salmon

BOB RACE

Fishing

This is one of Gunnison's main draws. In fact, on March 1, 1988, the state record brown trout, weighing 30.5 pounds, was taken from a pond near the East River just north of Gunnison. Though some of the best water in the area flows through private property, there is plenty of excellent easy-to-get-to public-access water in the region. In addition, the area's full of trouty backcountry streams that locals know are well worth the effort to get to.

Some of the best fishing in the area is found at **Blue Mesa Reservoir** about seven miles west of town. The 15-mile-long lake, formed when Blue Mesa Dam was built on the Gunnison River, yields lunker rainbow trout, as well as trophy-size lakes (Mackinaws) and browns. Fishing is best in early spring, shortly after the ice breaks up, and you can troll and jig from boats or work the shoreline, which ranges from rocky cliffs to sandy beach. The reservoir also has a decent population of kokanee salmon—usually caught by trolling. Rent boats at either of the reservoir's two marinas. For more information, see "Curecanti National Recreation Area," following.

Taylor Reservoir, 30 miles northeast of Gunnison at Taylor Park, is another favorite of local lake anglers, who fish for lake, brown, rainbow trout, and kokanee salmon. You can rent boats and pick up fishing supplies and groceries at Taylor Park Boathouse. To get there, take CO 135 north from Gunnison about 10 miles and watch for the turnoff on your right.

The Gunnison area also boasts some of the best stream fishing in the state. The **Taylor River,** above Taylor Reservoir, offers good fly-fishing, while pools below the reservoir are large and deep enough for spinners and other lures. The **East River,** whose headwaters are near Schofield Pass north of Crested Butte, merges with the Taylor at Almont. The East is one of the area's best fly-fishing streams, producing good rainbow, brown, and brook trout (special restrictions apply on some stretches).

The **Gunnison River,** between Blue Mesa Reservoir and Gunnison, and north of town along CO 135, is one of the state's best known and most productive stretches of water. Anglers have been pulling trophy brown and rainbow trout out of holes and riffles here for years, on both flies and lures.

For more information on fishing in the Gunnison area, as well as for licenses and equipment, stop in at **Gene Taylor's Sporting Goods,** 201 W. Tomichi, tel. (303) 641-1845, or **Doug's Sporting Goods,** 111 N. Main, tel. 641-3963. To arrange guided trips, contact **Three Rivers Resort and Outfitting,** Box 339, Almont, CO 81210, tel. 641-1303 or 349-5011 (Crested Butte).

Cycling

Gunnison's proximity to Crested Butte, one of the mountain-bike capitals of the country, guarantees there will be plenty of great rides nearby. Road bikers don't have as many options, though, as there are really only two roads that go anywhere from town: Hwy. 50, with major, high-speed traffic in both directions; and CO 135 to Crested Butte, a *far* better place to take the touring bike for a spin. In fact, a bike path parallels the highway several miles north of town, and though it gets narrow after that, it would still be a rewarding ride.

For more on mountain biking in the area, see "Crested Butte" following.

Golf

The **Dos Rios Golf Course** is an 18-hole course named for the *dos rios* (two rivers) at whose confluence it lies: Comichi Creek and the Taylor River. To get there, take Hwy. 50 two miles west from Gunnison and watch for the sign on your left. For information and tee times, phone (303) 641-1482.

Rafting And Kayaking

With so much river water nearby, the Gunnison area is a natural for whitewater sports. Kayakers, rafters, and canoers enjoy the Gunnison River from Almont to Blue Mesa Reservoir, as well as the Taylor River from Taylor Park Reservoir to Almont. Caution: River water in this area can get awfully fast and brawly during the snowmelt

of late spring. The Taylor, particularly, can get mean and should only be attempted by experienced river rats or with guides.

Companies in the Gunnison area offering guided trips include **Three Rivers Resort and Outfitting,** tel. (303) 641-1303, and **Scenic River Tours,** 703 W. Tomichi, tel. 641-3131.

Camping

At least 30 National Forest and National Recreation Area campgrounds can be found within an hour or so of Gunnison. Gunnison National Forest alone includes a couple of dozen, both north of town in the Taylor Park region and south around Lake City. In addition, Curecanti National Recreation Area, west of Gunnison, offers a dozen or so more.

County Rd. 742, which parallels the Taylor River from Almont to Taylor Park, is virtually lined with Forest Service campgrounds, with at least 10 along this stretch alone. Among them: **Almont Campground,** just south of Almont off CO 135 (10 sites), **Taylor Canyon,** about halfway to Taylor Reservoir (five sites, tents only), and **Lottis Creek,** just below the Taylor Reservoir dam (27 sites). Several other Forest Service campgrounds are located at Taylor Park Reservoir. In addition, you'll find Forest Service campgrounds at the towns of Pitkin and Ohio.

Curecanti National Recreation Area campgrounds include **Cimarron** (22 sites, dump station), **Dry Gulch** (10 sites, pit toilets, no showers), **Elk Creek** (179 sites, flush toilets, dump station, boat ramp and marina, visitor center), and **Lake Fork** (87 sites, dump station, flush toilets, boat ramp and marina, visitor center).

The Forest Service has published a detailed chart and map that lists all the campgrounds in the area and includes information on fees, number of sites, water availability, and fishing and hiking access. Write Gunnison National Forest, Taylor and Cebolla Ranger Districts, 216 N. Colorado, Gunnison, CO 81230, or phone (303) 641-0471. For information on Recreation Area campgrounds, write Curecanti National Recreation Area, 102 Elk Creek, Gunnison, CO 81230, or phone 641-2337.

Sailing And Windsurfing

Though the several dams on the Gunnison River have changed forever this once wild and scenic stream, the trade-off has been an increase in the amount of available recreational activities, including sailing and windsurfing. **Curecanti National Recreation Area,** which flanks the Gunnison River west of town, includes three reservoirs. You'll find boat ramps on Blue Mesa Reservoir, while hand-carried boats only are allowed on Crystal Lake and Morrow Point Reservoir. For maps and information, stop in at any of the three visitors information centers: **Elk Creek** (16 miles west of Gunnison), **Lake Fork** (26 miles west of Gunnison), and **Cimarron** (20 miles east of Montrose).

Skiing

Gunnisonites are fortunate to live close to one of Colorado's best ski resorts, Mt. Crested Butte, just over 30 miles north of town. Offering excellent skiing for all abilities, this out-of-the-way and laidback resort promises an honest good time, relatively uncrowded slopes, and some of the state's most breathtaking scenery. See "Crested Butte," following, for a complete description.

TOURS

Scenic Drives

Gunnison is a wonderful starting point for several of the Rockies' most scenic drives. And if you've got a 4WD rig, you could spend an entire summer exploring little-used high mountain passes. Several unpaved Forest Service roads begin near Taylor Park, affording back-way access to Buena Vista, Salida, and Aspen. One of the most visually arresting drives in the area is up over Kebler Pass and down to CO 133. Though unpaved, this is a well-maintained road, suitable for most vehicles (see "Crested Butte" following).

Another highly recommended drive is the loop over **Cumberland Pass** via Taylor Park. Take CO 135 north to Almont, and turn east on County Rd. 742. At the east end of Taylor Park Reservoir, turn south for Tincup, a mining town dating from 1880 (when it was known as Virginia City). Continue south over Cumberland Pass (elev. 12,000 feet), then down through Pitkin and Ohio, sites of late 1870s silver strikes. Continue to Parlin; then catch Hwy. 50 back to Gunnison.

One of Colorado's most fascinating engineering marvels is located east of Gunnison near Pitkin. **Alpine Tunnel,** a 1,771-foot bore under the Continental Divide, was completed in 1881 by the Denver, South Park, and Pacific Railroad and last used in 1910. Though the tunnel's west entrance has collapsed, you can view the remains of several old buildings, including water tanks and a boarding house, as well as the site of Woodstock, where the telegraph station and coal platform were located. The access road is about two miles north of Pitkin (watch for the sign).

For maps and more information, contact the **Taylor River and Cebolla Ranger District of Gunnison National Forest,** 216 N. Colorado, Gunnison, CO 81230, tel. (303) 641-0471. In addition, the Gunnison Country Chamber of Commerce has published a map and guide to 20 scenic tours in the area. Write Box 36, Gunnison, CO 81230.

Historical Walking Tour

The Gunnison Country Chamber of Commerce has published a map and tour guide to historical Gunnison. Included are residences and commercial buildings dating from the 1880s, as well as several from the turn of the century. The guide, which explains each structure's architectural and historical significance, is available from the chamber.

ACCOMMODATIONS

Gunnison's Hwy. 50 location, its reputation for abundant nearby recreation, and the fact that it's a college town needing digs for parents and visiting professors suggest there'll be plenty of lodging in the area, and there is, most of it reasonably priced. Motels, guest lodges, cabins, bed and breakfasts, in town, in a country meadow, or beside a mountain trout stream—the area should have something to suit your needs.

The Gunnison Country Chamber of Commerce has published an accommodations guide, with descriptions and photos of over 30 places to stay in the area. You can have one sent to you by writing Box 36, Gunnison, CO 81230, or by phoning (800) 274-7580.

Motels And Lodges

The **ABC Motel,** 212 E. Tomichi, tel. (303) 641-2400 or (800) 341-8000, is located near the center of town and has among the least expensive rooms in town, doubles starting at about $28. Two blocks east, **Bennett's Western**

Motel, 403 E. Tomichi, tel. 641-1722, has rooms for two starting at about $38. At the **Friendship Inn,** 400 E. Tomichi, tel. 641-1288, doubles run about $36-60, and you can get rooms with kitchens at the **Mountain View Lodge,** 117 N. Taylor, tel. 561-1799, for around $40.

Two riverside Gunnison-area lodges are the **Lost Canyon Resort,** 8264 CO 135, tel. 641-0181, where cabins start at about $45 a night, and **Three Rivers Resort and Outfitting,** in Almont, tel. 641-1303, where cabins run about $40-80. Three Rivers also has RV and tent sites, as well as a guide service, fly shop, and equipment rentals.

Harmel's Ranch Resort, Box 944, Gunnison, CO 81230, tel. 641-1740, is a classic Rocky Mountain dude ranch located northwest of town on the Taylor River. Harmel's has an excellent reputation, and your stay there can include everything from meals to hayrides and campfire sing-alongs. Doubles start at about $100.

Camping And RVing
In addition to the dozens of National Forest and National Recreation Area campgrounds in the area (see "Camping" above), there are many private campgrounds where you can fetch up for weeks on end. **Sunnyside Campground,** tel. (303) 641-0477, is located 12 miles west of Gunnison on Blue Mesa Reservoir. If you'd rather be streamside, you can get RV and tent sites, as well as cabins, at **Three Rivers Resort and Outfitting,** tel. 641-1303, located 10 miles north of town where the Taylor and East rivers merge to form the headwaters of the Gunnison. A **KOA** campground is located just west of town on the Gunnison River; phone 641-1358.

FOOD

For a small ranching town, Gunnison has a fairly decent number of good, reasonably priced restaurants. That might be due in part to the presence of Western State College: Students get tired of dorm food and Top Ramen and love to go out to eat—on a budget.

For breakfast, try either the **Sidewalk Cafe,** 113 W. Tomichi, tel. (303) 641-4130, serving eggs, pancakes, and other hearty fare, or **Hi-Kountry Kitchen and Bakery,** 302 N. Main, tel. 641-1489,

specializing in pastries, breads, and doughnuts.

Mario's Pizzeria, 213 W. Tomichi, tel. 641-1374, is a local favorite for thick or thin, white- or wheat-crust pizza, as well as pastas and other Italian dinners. Free delivery. For Mexican food, try **Cactus Jack's,** 9th and Rio Grande, tel. 641-2044, and for Chinese, **Hunan Chinese Restaurant,** 405 W. Tomichi, tel. 641-3600, serving several provincial cuisines, including Szechuan, Cantonese, Mandarin. If you're leaning more toward red meat, a big ol' steak, or a slab of prime the size of a Cadillac, it's tough to beat the **Cattlemen Inn,** 301 W. Tomichi, tel. 641-1061.

CALENDAR

The main event on Gunnison's calendar is **Cattlemen's Days** in mid-July, which includes a rodeo, car and livestock shows, a parade, and street barbecues. There's also a parade, barbecues, and fireworks on the Fourth of July.

For complete information on Gunnison's annual events, write the chamber of commerce at Box 36, Gunnison, CO 81230, or phone (303) 641-1501.

SERVICES

The offices of the Gunnison **Police Department** are located at 201 W. Virginia; phone 641-1241. Phone the Gunnison County **Sheriff** at 641-1113 and the **State Patrol** at 641-1242. **Gunnison Valley Hospital** is at 214 E. Denver Ave., tel. 641-1456. The **post office** is at 200 N. Wisconsin, tel. 641-1884.

Recycling
You can recycle aluminum at the **City Market,** 401 W. Georgia, and the **Safeway,** 112 S. Spruce. Gunnison's **Citizens for Recycling** is located at 702 W. Tomichi, where you can drop off aluminum, glass, and plastic; for more information, phone (303) 641-2137.

INFORMATION

The **Gunnison Country Chamber of Commerce,** 500 E. Tomichi, is a good place to begin your visit. Pick up lodging and recreation guides, as well as other brochures, maps, and information. Be sure to get a copy of *River Territory Magazine,* a free tourist-oriented publication with historical articles, profiles of locals, and pieces on exploring the Gunnison-area outdoors. Write the chamber at Box 36, Gunnison, CO 81230, or phone (303) 641-1501.

For information on recreational activities in Gunnison National Forest, stop by the Tomichi District Office at 216 N. Colorado, tel. 641-0471, or the main offices at 2250 Hwy. 50, Delta, CO 81416, tel. 874-7691.

The Book Worm, 211 N. Main, tel. 641-3693, specializes in books on the outdoors, recreation, and wildlife, and also sells maps. **Ann Zegelder Library** (public) is located at 307 N. Wisconsin; phone 641-3485.

For **road and weather information,** phone 641-2896.

TRANSPORTATION

Continental Express, United Express, and **American Airlines** provide passenger service to Gunnison County Airport, with increased flights during the ski season. You can also get here by bus; the terminal for **TNMO Bus Lines,** tel. (303) 641-0060, is located at 303 E. Tomichi #8.

Rent cars in Gunnison from **Budget,** 212 W. Hwy. 50, tel. 641-4403, or **Hertz,** 708 S. 12th, tel. 641-2881. **Colorado Four Seasons Limo,** tel. 641-3322, offers transportation between Gunnison County Airport and Crested Butte Ski Area.

CRESTED BUTTE

A Sunday evening in June, 1991. The sun has just set over Kebler Pass, and the last light of the day is disappearing from the massive flanks of Mt. Crested Butte. I've been eating pasta and drinking red wine at Angello's and watching the Bulls beat the Lakers in the NBA play-offs. I decide to take one more stroll about town. Up Elk Avenue, past Mountain Earth Natural Foods, Oscars, Coal Creek Sports, and Kochevar's, then north on 2nd and back down Maroon. And as I walk past the Union Congregational Church at the corner of 4th, I see a single image that says more about Crested Butte than any collage or long-playing study: There, in the weedy lot in front of the church, are some two dozen mountain bikes—some parked, some sprawled, all muddy, dusty, and well ridden, their riders, obviously, inside. There are fewer than six cars.

Surrounded by jagged mountain peaks and the million-plus-acre Gunnison National Forest, Crested Butte (pop. 1,200; elev. 8,885 feet) is one of Colorado's true gems. A young town with a hundred-year history, Crested Butte is famous for some of the best downhill skiing in the state and is quickly gaining a reputation as its mountain bike capital. Crested Butte is actually two communities: the town of Crested Butte, which was founded in 1880, and the village of *Mt. Crested Butte*, founded nearly a century later, when Mt. Crested Butte Ski Area opened. Separated by a three-mile road and connected by a free shuttle system, Crested Butte and Mt. Crested Butte offer just about everything you could want in a vacation—history, outdoor activities, scenery, a wide range of restaurants and lodging, and friendly, down-to-earth locals.

Crested Butte's mining-era heritage is obvious from first glance: Elk Ave., the town's main drag, is lined with Victorian homes and buildings that once served as saloons, banks, and supply shops. Today, many of them still *are* saloons, banks, and supply shops, though the supplies have changed from pickaxes and gold pans to ski poles and biking shorts. And though many of the buildings have been restored, the town has resisted gentrification, thanks in large part to the locals' respect for their history, as well as the town's off-the-beaten-path location.

History

Crested Butte dates to the early 1880s, when it was a thriving gold camp and supply headquarters for the mines in the nearby mountains, particularly in Washington Gulch, where the boom was launched when prospectors found $350,000 in gold nuggets. In the late 1880s, coal was discovered in the area, providing an economic base that would carry the community into the mid-20th century (unlike most Colorado mining camps, which were all but abandoned when ore prices fell in the 1890s).

In the early 1960s, Mt. Crested Butte Ski Area opened, changing forever the tenor of the town.

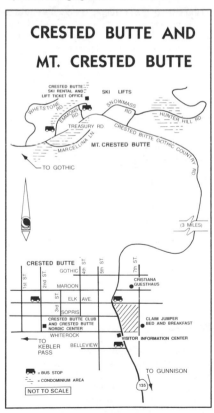

Mount Crested Butte
and Mount Crested
Butte Village

GRAFTON MARSHALL SMITH

At the base of the ski resort, condominiums and hotels sprang up, as did upscale restaurants and after-ski bars and pizza places. Thankfully, the town of Crested Butte was designated a National Historic District in 1974, guaranteeing the preservation of the old buildings, and an architectural review board was established to monitor renovation and new construction.

In the late 1970s and early 1980s, mountain biking came to Crested Butte big-time, and the area's personality shifted again. In fact, by the late 1980s, Crested Butte, along with Durango, was one of the three or four world mountain-bike meccas. In addition to attracting more athletes to the area, both to live and visit, the new sport is contributing greatly to the area's transformation to a year-round resort area. Though winter is still high season out here, summer is not far behind. And it probably won't be too much longer that local lodge owners feel compelled to lower their rates when the lifts shut down.

WINTER SPORTS

During the winter, the town of Crested Butte, the village of Mt. Crested Butte, and Crested Butte Ski Area virtually become one—indeed, they're connected every 15 minutes by free shuttle. And during the winter, just about everything revolves around winter sports: Restaurants and lodges swell with vacationing skiers, students from Western State College in Gunnison cut classes and hit the slopes, and the equipment re-

tail and rental shops do brisk business in boots and bindings, poles and parkas, sweaters and sunscreen. And for good reason: The area claims some of the finest skiing in the Rockies—cross-country and downhill—and some of the prettiest winter scenery this side of the Swiss Alps. In addition, there's a certain sense of abandon here, a nearly palpable feeling of communal *carpe diem,* the result of which is an on-the-edge inventiveness that has spawned sports indigenous only to Crested Butte, like dog fishing and "board joring." Dog fishing came about as a pragmatic solution to the town's notorious dog overpopulation. Though Crested Butte's dog fishermen have now mostly retired, they once trolled in the backs of pickups with fishing poles and Milk Bones, hoping to land lunker Labradors and trophy terriers (on the off-chance a poodle was hooked, it would be ceremoniously tossed back). "Board jorists" ride snowboards, water-ski-like, clinging to ropes pulled by horses galloping across meadows.

Downhill Skiing
Crested Butte might not be as well known as Aspen, as big as Vail, or as easy to get to as Winter Park, but there's no denying the friggin' great snow, the runs that range from long, gentle trails to steep-ass chutes and gnarly bump runs, and one of the friendliest, most kick-back attitudes you'll ever find at a ski resort.

With an average of 229 inches of snow falling annually on Crested Butte's 1,160 acres of ski-able terrain, this mountain guarantees that if any place in the state has snow, it'll be here. In addition, there's a good range of skiing for all ability levels, with 13 lifts providing access to 86 trails. Crested Butte is also upping the extreme-skiing ante, having recently expanded to include 550 acres of ungroomed double-black-diamond terrain, as well as a high-speed quad chair.

Two of Crested Butte's real prides are its ski school, which was chosen by *Rocky Mountain Sports and Fitness Magazine* as the best in the state, and its overall user-friendliness: A recent *Ski* magazine reader poll ranked Crested Butte 10th in the nation in customer service. Additionally, the resort's **Program for the Physically Challenged** caters to disabled skiers, with instructors trained to teach sit and mono-skiing, three- and four-track techniques, as well as to work with blind, deaf, and developmentally disabled skiers. Handicapped skiers can also rent adaptive equipment such as outriggers.

For more information on Mt. Crested Butte Ski Area, phone (303) 349-2222. For ski-school information, call 349-2252. Phone the Program for the Physically Challenged at 349-2296.

Cross-country Skiing

From Telemarking in untracked backcountry bowls to speed skating on groomed track, the Crested Butte area offers plenty of high-quality Nordic skiing. Folks who want to explore the woods have the entire Gunnison National Forest at their ski tips; you can explore old logging and mining roads or take off through the trees. Several of the high mountain passes are ideal for short or extended outings—experienced cross-country. For maps and information, contact the Forest Service District Office, 216 N. Colorado, Gunnison, tel. (303) 641-0471.

You can also get information, as well as equipment, at any of the area's ski shops, including **Paradise Bikes and Skis,** 224 Elk Ave., Crested Butte, tel. 349-6324, and **Gene Taylor's Sporting Goods,** 19 Emmons Loop, at the base of the lifts in Mt. Crested Butte, tel. 349-5386.

The **Crested Butte Nordic Center,** based at 512 2nd St. in downtown Crested Butte, has 30 km of cross-country track and skating lanes. The center offers lessons (private and group) in all types of Nordic skiing, equipment rental,

and guided tours. For information or reservations, phone 349-6201. **Mt. Crested Butte Ski Area** is a favorite among local three-pinners, and its ski school offers lessons and equipment rental; phone 349-2252 for more information.

Other Winter Sports

Though you'll probably want to leave Crested Butte's more innovative winter sports, such as dog fishing and "board joring," to the locals, there are several more conventional winter activities available in the area. **Snowmobile** tours and rentals are offered by a couple of companies. Phone **Action Adventures in Snowmobiling** at (303) 349-6792 or **Burt Rentals and Snowmobile Tours** at 349-7423.

Backcountry powder skiing is available via both helicopter and snowcat at **Irwin Lodge,** tel. 349-5308. With 2,000 skiable acres and a 1,200-foot vertical drop, the lodge offers trips for both intermediate and advanced skiers (also see "Accommodations" following). You can also arrange **sleigh rides** through town and out into the Crested Butte countryside. Phone **Just Horsin' Around** at 349-5765 for reservations and information. There are also two ice rinks in town.

For a complete description of the area's winter activities, contact the Crested Butte-Mt. Crested Butte Chamber of Commerce (see "Information" following).

WHEN THE SNOW MELTS

Mountain Biking

Colorado mountain biking was born in Crested Butte. Following the lead of riders from Marin County, California, Crested Beauties attached motorcycle brakes and multiple gears to old "clunkers" and hit the trails. The first outings were over Pearl Pass to Aspen, but the huge number of old logging and mining roads in the area soon spawned a boom in the sport. Today, Crested Butte is one of the true mountain-bike capitals of the world.

Fat Tire Week each summer draws some of the country's best riders to a wide array of competitions, from serious dual slalom to ski slopes to novelty events like a limbo, a "slow race" (be the *last* one to cross the finish line, without putting your foot down), and mountain-bike polo. The week also provides an opportunity for newcomers to the sport to become better and more knowledgeable riders: Clinics, workshops, and tours are offered daily. (See "Calendar," following, for more information.)

The rest of the summer, too, mountain biking is big in these little communities. Tourists and locals alike explore gravel roads and single-track trails that snake through the valleys and over the ridges of the surrounding mountains. A couple of the classic rides are over **Pearl Pass** to Aspen and **Kebler Pass** to CO 133 near Paonia. Both are steep and demanding, though physical fitness is more important than technical riding ability.

As you'd expect, there are a disproportionate number of bike shops in Crested Butte, all of which are happy to talk bikes and trails. In the town of Crested Butte, stop in at **Paradise Bikes and Skis,** 224 Elk Ave., tel. (303) 349-6342; at Mt. Crested Butte, check out **Crested Butte Sports—Ski and Bike Shop,** in the Evergreen Building at the base of Keystone lift, tel. 349-7516.

Golf

Crested Butte's **Skyland Resort and Country Club** includes a 7,200-yard 18-hole course designed by Robert Trent Jones, Jr. Located on 200 acres at the base of Mt. Crested Butte, Skyland is a full-service resort complex, with tennis courts, private lake, and exercise room, as well as course-side condominiums and homes (also homesites, if you really fall in love with the place).

For tee times and information, phone the pro shop at (303) 349-6131. For accommodations information, phone 349-7541.

River Running

Several rivers in the Crested Butte area offer excellent opportunities for river rats. The lower Taylor River, which flows from Taylor Park Reservoir down through Taylor Canyon to its confluence with the East River at Almont (where the Gunnison River is born), is a kayaker's delight, with rapids ranging from Class II to V. The Gunnison River, slower and broader, is better suited to rafts.

A handful of outfits in the area offer guided tours of local waters, ranging from short float trips to extended backcountry excursions for experienced river runners only. **C B Rafting And Adventures,** 309 Gothic Rd., Crested

Butte, tel. (303) 349-7423, has a full-course menu of tours. The company can also arrange horseback, mountain-biking, and snowmobile tours, as well as sleigh rides and dog sledding.

Horseback Riding

Though the area's chief recreation has taken a decidedly different tack of late, and the saddle of choice has changed from the type found on horses to the type found on mountain bikes, Crested Butte remains the quintessential Western community—ranches sprawl in the surrounding valleys, and horses stand in lots a quarter mile from downtown. And by horseback is still one of the best ways to see the high country—the Elk Mountains, the Sawatch Range, the lush river valleys.

The following are among the stables and outfitters offering horses for rent, as well as guided tours, from half-day rides to multi-day pack trips: **C B Rafting and Adventures,** tel. (303) 349-7423; **Fantasy Ranch,** tel. 349-5425; **Harmel's Ranch Resort,** tel. 641-1740; **Just Horsin' Around,** tel. 349-5765; and **Teocalli Outfitters,** tel. 349-6598.

Ballooning

Big Horn Balloon Company offers balloon tours of the Crested Butte area year-round. Thirty-minute flights start at about $90, and 90-minute flights are $150. Write Box 361, Crested Butte, CO 81224, or phone (303) 349-6335.

Jeep Tours

Located in the heart of high-mountain mining country, with some of Colorado's most spectacular scenery beckoning, Crested Butte is an ideal base from which to explore via 4WD vehicle. In fact, some of the best tours, though they'll take you off the pavement, are perfectly suitable for conventional-traction automobiles (see "Tours" following).

If you are equipped with 4WD, however, you've got substantially more options. Though it's nearly 200 miles from Crested Butte to Aspen by paved road, as the crow flies it's barely 30—just north from town, up over the Elk Mountains, and across the county line. With a 4WD rig, you can at least approximate the general direction of Mr. Crow, by crossing over the mountains at Taylor Pass or Pearl Pass. Topo maps, with 4WD routes indicated, are available at the

Gunnison Office of the Gunnison National Forest, 216 N. Colorado, tel. (303) 641-0471.

Camping

Literally surrounded by Gunnison National Forest, the Crested Butte area offers limitless camping opportunities, whether you hike in to a secluded backcountry spot or set up at one of the many nearby Forest Service campgrounds. **Lost Lake Campground** (10 sites, pit toilets, no drinking water) is located about 15 miles west of Crested Butte just south of Kebler Pass Rd. among some of the area's finest scenery. **Cement Creek Campground** (13 sites, pit toilets) is southeast of Crested Butte via CO 135 and Forest Service Rd. 740.

You'll also find Forest Service campgrounds along the Taylor River and at Taylor Park Reservoir (25-40 miles from Crested Butte), as well as National Park Service and privately owned campgrounds west of Gunnison. For more information on Crested Butte-area Forest Service Campgrounds, phone (303) 641-0471.

Other Summer Activities

If the area's mountain biking, horseback riding, golf, four-wheel-driving, and hot-air ballooning aren't enough for you, there's still more. You'll find excellent **fishing** in nearby lakes and streams, particularly the Taylor, East, and Gunnison rivers, and Taylor Park and Blue Mesa reservoirs. For licenses and information, stop in at **Gene Taylor's Sporting Goods** at the base of the lifts at Mt. Crested Butte, tel. (303) 349-5386. For information on guided fly-fishing trips in the area, try **Coal Creek Sports,** 207 Elk Ave., Crested Butte, tel. 349-6166.

The area is also fraught with excellent hiking opportunities. Serious backpackers have the whole of Gunnison National Forest, including the beautiful Elk Mountains and the mighty Sawatch Range, while nature trailers and day hikers can wander any of the region's shorter and more accessible trails.

Several trails near Cement Creek Campground are perfect for day outings. Go south on CO 135 for seven miles and turn east on Cement Creek Road. You'll also find excellent hiking possibilities west of Crested Butte in the Kebler Pass area; **Lost Lake Campground** is a good base for hikes through aspeny hillsides to views that'll knock your socks off. A good source

for information and equipment is **The Alpiner,** 419 6th St., Crested Butte, tel. 349-5210. You can also get information and maps from the Forest Service District Office in Gunnison.

ACCOMMODATIONS

Accommodations are available in both the town of Crested Butte and the village of Mt. Crested Butte. In the village, slopeside lodges and condos provide the ultimate ski-in/ski-out experience, though regular shuttle service from the smaller and more colorful inns in town makes lodging there nearly as convenient.

Keep in mind that lodging rates in the Crested Butte area, like those at most ski resorts, vary tremendously from summer to winter: rates will be highest during the peak times of the ski season (Christmas vacation, weekends, etc.) and lowest when the lifts shut down. In fact, many of the lodges offer special off-season incentives just to keep their help busy.

COLORADO HISTORICAL SOCIETY

Many Colorado lodges offer rooms with kitchenettes.

For complete information on lodging packages, including air and ground transportation, lift tickets, equipment, and instruction, phone **Mt. Crested Butte Central Reservations** at (800) 544-8448, or write Box A, Crested Butte, CO 81225. You can also get lodging information from the **Crested Butte/Mt. Crested Butte Chamber of Commerce,** Box 1288, Crested Butte, CO 81224, tel. (303) 349-6438.

For condominium information or reservations, phone **Crested Butte Accommodations,** (800) 821-3718. For condominiums and vacation homes, phone **Red Lady Rentals,** 349-5354.

Mt. Crested Butte Lodging

The **Grand Butte Hotel,** tel. (303) 349-2500 or (800) 642-4422, is located 35 yards from the base of the lifts and features 262 rooms, each with whirlpool, wet bar, and other luxuries. Doubles start at around $150 during the ski season. The smaller (27-room) **Nordic Inn,** tel. 349-5542 or (800) 542-SNOW, is 300 yards from the lifts. Doubles during the ski season start at about $60, which includes continental breakfast and après-ski wine and hors d'oeuvres.

The **Crested Butte Lodge,** tel. 349-7555 or (800) 433-5684, is also located in the village and has a large indoor pool, as well as a sauna and outdoor hot tub. For a real winter-wonderland ski vacation, try the **Irwin Lodge,** tel. 349-5308 or (800) 2-IRWIN-2, which during the ski season is accessible only by snowmobile, snowcat, or skis. In addition to offering cozy out-of-the-way lodging and an on-site restaurant, the Irwin also features helicopter and snowcat ski tours on 1,400 acres of terrain (2,100-foot vertical drop). Call for rates and information packages and other activities.

In Town

Located just a couple of blocks from downtown Crested Butte, the **Cristiana Guesthaus Bed and Breakfast,** tel. (303) 349-5326 or (800) 824-7899, is a classic little ski lodge offering very comfortable rooms, a large downstairs lobby with fireplace, and a sauna and outdoor hot tub with a wonderful view of the mountains. Doubles start at about $50.

Billing itself a "unique" bed and breakfast, the **Claim Jumper,** tel. 349-6471, is guilty of nothing but understatement. This place is packed floor to ceiling with one of the strangest assortments of odds and ends you'll ever see. Not only is the lobby full of antiques and parlor games, but each room has a bizarre theme and the decor to match: "Ethyl's Room" has a Shell gasoline pump and a jukebox; "Soda Creek" is dedicated to Coca Cola memorabilia; and the best room of all, the "Sports Fan Attic," is packed with mementos and souvenirs from baseball, football, hockey, and other sports—signed game jerseys worn by Jose Canseco and John Elway, signed baseball cards, and, in a separate room, a *putting green*. Doubles run $75-85 in winter. Phone for reservations or a brochure describing each room in detail.

The least expensive rooms in the area are probably at the two modest motels, the **Old Town Inn,** tel. 349-6184, and **Forest Queen,** tel. 349-5336. Doubles during ski season start at around $55.

FOOD

When the Denver *Post* wrote that Crested Butte "has more fine restaurants per capita than any town in America," the marketing people ate it up (sorry); you'll see the quote all over the area's promotional material. It's not hyperbole, though. There truly are an amazing number of excellent places to eat here—from burger-and-beer joints to upscale, stiff-napkin dining establishments. Some have been around forever; some are brand new; some will probably be gone by the time you read this. At any rate, *salut i force canut.*

Start Me Up

The **Bakery Cafe,** at 3rd and Elk in downtown Crested Butte, tel. (303) 349-7280, opens at 7:30 a.m. daily and is a long-time favorite for breakfast, specializing in fresh baked goods (no preservatives) and gourmet coffees. The Bakery is also open for lunch and dinner, serving pastas, stuffed croissants, and homemade soups and chili.

Dinner Joints

For good Italian food at reasonable prices, try **Angello's,** 501 Elk, tel. (303) 349-5351, serving pizzas, pastas, and antipasto salads. Another favorite is **Rocky Mtn. Steaks** in the Plaza at Mt. Crested Butte. For a slightly more upscale Italian restaurant, try the **Gourmet Noodle,** 411 3rd St., tel. 349-7401; pastas run around $10, and specials (veal, chicken, seafood) are about $12-15.

You'll find two good Mexican restaurants in Crested Butte. **Restaurante Mexicano,** 130 Elk, tel. 349-5494, is the more authentic of the two, while **Donita's,** 330 Elk, tel. 349-6674, a cantina-style restaurant, specializes in atmosphere and can really get to hopping when the lifts shut down.

The same *Post* article that lauded Crested Butte's many excellent restaurants singled out **Soupçon,** 2nd and Elk, tel. 349-5448, as one of the area's best. Specializing in French country cuisine, this restaurant has a rotating menu featuring appetizers such as oysters aioli, shrimp Dijon, and duckling mousse, and seafood, veal, and beef entrees. Ideal for an anniversary or other celebration.

Oscar's Bar and Café, 229 Elk, tel. 349-6107, is a favorite among the after-ski crowd and serves a wide range of lunches and dinners, from huevos rancheros and burgers to pastas and prime rib. Entrees run $6-17. Crested Butte's oldest saloon, the **Wooden Nickel,** 222 Elk, tel. 349-6350, is another restaurant that attracts a rowdy and hungry post-slope crowd (bar opens at 3 p.m.; happy hour is from 4:30-5:30). Dinners include steak, soups and chili, burgers, seafood, and ribs.

ENTERTAINMENT

Crested Butte's a young town, with lots of folks doing some short-term ski and mountain bumming before facing real-world responsibilities—and of course they need places to spend the money they're saving for college. In addition, skiers and other tourists count on at least a certain degree of nightlife as part of their vacation packages. Though this is no Aspen (which is *good* news to most), the area does offer its fair share of places to let off steam.

The Rafters, at Mt. Crested Butte, conveniently located between the bus stop and the base of the Silver Queen lift, is the ski area's main bar and has a classic ski-lodge sun deck. Live music Tues. through Sun. during the ski season, both in the afternoon for the après-skiers, then later, when it's live and louder, rockin' and rowdy—also pool and video games, as well as sandwiches and fajitas for when the munchies kick in.

In Crested Butte, the **Talk of the Town,** at 3rd and Elk, is an unassuming small-town tavern and watering hole that doesn't pretend to be anything but. Shuffleboard, pool, darts, and televisions. **Kochavar's** at 127 Elk, tel. (303) 349-2299, is another local favorite, where music from live bands often spills out onto the streets. The **Wooden Nickel,** 222 Elk, has been in the hangover business (breeding and nursing) since 1929.

CALENDAR

As Crested Butte grows from a winter-only to a year-round resort, more and more events and activities are being scheduled. Throughout the winter, Mt. Crested Butte Ski Area hosts several races and other slope-side fiestas. On opening day of Mt. Crested Butte Ski Area, usually in late November, lift-ticket prices are rolled way back and the hills are alive with the euphoria induced by winter's return. For complete information on winter activities at Mt. Crested Butte Ski Area, write Box A, Mt. Crested Butte, CO 81225, or phone (800) 544-8448.

One of Crested Butte's popular summer events is **Fat Tire Week** in early to mid-July, when the town, already mountain-bike crazy, becomes the hub of the country's mountain-bike activity. Attracting riders from recreational novices to hard-core racers, events include a dual-slalom race on Mt. Crested Butte's ski slopes, a bicycle rodeo, bicycle polo, clinics and workshops, tours of nearby mountain-bike trails, including Pearl Pass, the dirt road to Aspen which gave birth to Colorado mountain biking back in the mid-'70s. For information and registration forms, write Fat Tire Week, Box 782, Crested Butte, CO 81224, or phone (303) 349-6817.

In addition, several other events and programs punctuate the summer in Crested Butte and Mt. Crested Butte, from softball tournaments and "fun runs" to art shows and wildflower festivals. Highlights include Fourth of July festivities (street music, food booths, parade, fireworks); **Aerial Weekend** (hot-air balloon festival; late July); and the **Festival of the Arts** (juried art show, street music, food booths, etc.; early August). For a complete calendar of special events in the Crested Butte area, write the Crested Butte-Mt. Crested Butte Chamber of Commerce, Box 1288, Crested Butte, CO 81224, or phone 349-6438.

SERVICES

Both the offices of the Crested Butte **Police Department** and the Gunnison County **Sheriff's Sub-Station** are at 308 3rd St.; phone (303) 349-5231. Phone the **State Patrol** in Gunnison at 641-6382. The nearest hospital is **Gunnison Valley Hospital,** 214 E. Denver Ave., Gunnison; phone 641-1456. Limited medical facilities are available at **Crested Butte Medical Clinic,** 611 Gothic Rd.; phone 349-6651. The clinic specializes in (appropriately enough) sports injuries and medicine.

The Crested Butte **post office** is at 217 Elk Ave.; phone 349-5568. There's also postal service at Mt. Crested Butte at the 3 Seasons Building, tel. 349-7310.

Recycling

For recyling information in Crested Butte, phone **Sunshine Garbage,** 349-5957. You can also drop off recyclables in Gunnison, at the **Citizens for Recycling** drop-off, 702 W. Tomichi, the **City Market,** 401 W. Georgia, and the **Safeway,** 112 S. Spruce.

Child Care

Mt. Crested Butte Ski Area's **Buttetopia Children's Program** offers a range of supervised activities for kids six months to 12 years. Programs include day care for kids six months to six years (no skiing), beginning group ski instruction for kids three to six, private le·sons for kids two to six, and "Tag-a-Long" lessons for kids 2-12 and their parents—follow the class and learn how to continue instructing your child in technique and chairlift safety. For reservations or more information, phone (303) 349-2259.

TOURS

Though a trip to Crested Butte is a scenic tour unto itself, several roads in the area offer icing on the cake. Of course, you're limited in the winter, when all but the area's main routes are closed, but during the summer, assuming you don't mind getting off the pavement, you can really do some exploring. One of my favorite routes in

the state is **Kebler Pass Rd.,** which lifts up from downtown Crested Butte, winds up over Kebler Pass, past Mt. Baldy, and then drops down to CO 133; there you can either turn north for Redstone and Glenwood Springs or continue west toward Paonia, Delta, and Grand Junction. A wide and well-maintained gravel road, Kebler Pass Rd. features enough vertical rise that you can literally watch the aspens change colors. In the spring, those at lower elevations are green and leafy, while nearer the summit they're still wintry and bare; in the fall, watch them change from green to gold to crimson.

Another interesting drive, and one that's less of a commitment, is the short jaunt to the ghost town of **Gothic,** a Victorian-era silver-mining town with superb views of the East River valley. Gothic, which was pretty much abandoned by the late 1880s, is located about seven miles northeast of Crested Butte; take Forest Service Rd. 327 from Mt. Crested Butte.

Other scenic drives in the area include the Alpine Tunnel tour and the Gunnison, Taylor Park Reservoir, Pitkin, and back to Gunnison loop.

Walking Tour

Crested Butte was designated a National Historic District in 1974, and many of the buildings that line Elk Ave. and some of the side streets date from the late 19th century. A consortium of local businesses has published a map and guide to historical Crested Butte, with over 40 sites, many of which are open today as restaurants, inns, and other small businesses. Full of anecdotal history, the little pamphlet is useful and intriguing whether you just want to know the history of the bar at which you plan to plant yourself or you intend to take the full tour.

INFORMATION

As you approach Crested Butte by car (assuming you come in via CO 135, the main route, and not in the back way, over one of the several unpaved mountain-pass roads), you'll meet almost head-on with a chamber of commerce **visitor information center.** This is a good place to stuff your pockets with brochures on things to do and see while you're in the area, as well as to pick up lodging and dining guides. To stock up before your visit, write **Crested Butte-Mt. Crested Butte Chamber of Commerce,** Box 1288, Crested Butte, CO 81224, or phone (303) 349-6438. For good selections of books on recreation and wildlife in the area, check out **Heg's Place,** tel. 349-5304, in Crested Butte, or stop on your way into town at **The Book Worm,** 211 N. Main (CO 135), Gunnison. The Crested Butte branch of the **Gunnison County Library** is located at 726 Elk Ave., and is open Mon., Wed., and Fri. 1-5 p.m. and Tues. 6-8 p.m.; phone 349-6535.

For information on **Gunnison National Forest,** stop by the ranger station at 216 N. Colorado, Gunnison, or phone 641-0471.

For **road and weather information,** phone 641-2896.

TRANSPORTATION

American Airlines, United Express, Delta, Continental, and **Continental Express** offer regular passenger service to Gunnison, with daily nonstop flights during the ski season from Chicago, Atlanta, and Dallas/Ft. Worth, as well as connecting flights from Denver. Most hotels in Crested Butte offer free airport shuttle service for guests. In addition, you can arrange ground transportation between Gunnison and Crested Butte with **Alpine Express,** tel. (303) 641-5074 or (800) 822-4844, and **Colorado Four Seasons Limo,** tel. 641-3322.

The village of Mt. Crested Butte and the ski area are located three miles from the town of Crested Butte. Free shuttle buses run between the two about every 15 minutes till midnight during ski season.

CURECANTI NATIONAL RECREATION AREA

Paralleling the Gunnison River from Gunnison to Black Canyon of the Gunnison National Monument, Curecanti National Recreation Area includes three reservoirs, 10 separate campgrounds (with over 300 sites), 18 picnic areas, and four visitor centers, as well as marinas, boat ramps, and hiking trails. Extremely popular with anglers—who know the lakes' depths hold lunker rainbow, brown, lake, and brook trout, in addition to kokanee salmon—the area is also excellent for wildlife watching: Ducks and geese and other waterfowl are common in the area, as are bald and golden eagles and great blue herons, and elk, bighorn sheep, and mule deer can be seen in the area in winter.

The three-dam system was designed to provide irrigation water and to generate hydroelectric power. Though the dams' construction met (understandably) with opposition from environmentalists and conservationists, the result has been the development of one of the state's best all-around recreation areas.

Blue Mesa, where you'll find the majority of recreational activities, is the largest of the three lakes and the system's main storage reservoir. Morrow Point and Crystal reservoirs generate power and control water flow through Black Canyon of the Gunnison. Dozens of creeks flow into the three lakes and the stretches of Gunnison between them; the streams flowing into Blue Mesa Reservoir form long arms gouging into the surrounding mesas and plateaus and creating a fjordlike appearance to the waterway.

Camping
The four largest and most developed campgrounds at Curecanti are **Elk Creek, Lake Fork, Stevens Creek,** and **Cimarron.** Other smaller campgrounds, some nestled in the lakes' narrow arms, are better suited for getting away from crowds, and several of the campgrounds offer access to hiking and self-guided interpretive trails. Group camping is available at **East Elk Creek Campground** (by reservation only). To make camping reservations, or for more information on camping at Curecanti National Recreation Area, phone (303) 641-2337.

Fishing
Though rainbow trout are the most commonly caught fish in the park, the waters also hold

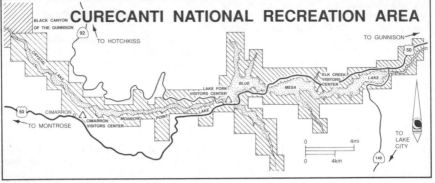

brown, lake (Mackinaw), and brook trout, and kokanee salmon. Fishing is best in spring, shortly after ice-out, and again in the fall, when big browns head up into the tributaries to spawn. Kokanee can be legally snagged beginning in October (check regulations).

The area can be productive from both shore and boat, though the latter is the better way to go, especially if you're looking to hook into one of the monster lake trout, which prefer the cold, deep water (45-70 feet and deeper). Rental boats are available at Elk Creek and Lake Fork.

Water Sports
Blue Mesa Reservoir offers the broadest range of water sports and boating, with waterskiing and windsurfing popular in the summer when the water (and air) warms up. In addition, the lake is large enough—20 miles long, with three separate basins—and contains enough arms and inlets to offer sailors plenty of water to explore. Boating on Crystal and Morrow Point lakes is restricted to hand-carried craft.

Swimming is permitted at Curecanti, but keep in mind that this water's *cold.* Also, remember that swimming is not permitted from docks, launch ramps, and unanchored boats.

Boat Tours
If you want to get out on the water but neither have your own boat nor feel like renting, you can take a tour with an interpreter/naturalist, who discusses the area's geology, history, and

wildlife, as well as the role of the dams in irrigation and power generation. Tours are offered regularly throughout the summer. For information and reservations, phone the Elk Creek Marina at (303) 641-0402.

Winter Sports
Winter activities in Curecanti National Recreation Area include ice fishing, snowmobiling, and cross-country skiing. Be sure to check with rangers to make sure the ice is thick enough (four inches to support an adult, seven to support a snowmobile). The area's nature trails are perfect for Nordic skiing, or you can break your own trail. You'll find a specifically designated beginning cross-country ski trail at the Elk Creek Visitor Center.

Information And Visitor Centers
The **Elk Creek Visitor Center** is the best place to get oriented. In addition to viewing a slide/tape presentation on the area, you can pick up maps and other publications and ask questions of the rangers. There are also visitor information centers at Cimarron, Morrow Point, and Lake Fork. Tours of the Morrow Point dam and powerplant are available in summer. At Cimarron, you can view a restored 19th-century Denver and Rio Grande Railroad engine and cars.

For more information on Curecanti National Recreation Area, write Superintendent, Curecanti National Recreation Area, 102 Elk Creek, Gunnison, CO 81230, or phone (303) 641-2337

BLACK CANYON OF THE GUNNISON NATIONAL MONUMENT

A jagged incision—2,000 feet deep and 53 miles long—in the rocky Gunnison Uplift, Black Canyon of the Gunnison is without doubt one of the Southwest's most startling natural wonders. Named for the gorge's heavy shadows, from walls so steep that little sunlight ever penetrates the canyon's depths, Black Canyon is a haven for hikers, campers, backpackers, and especially rock climbers. Black Canyon of the Gunnison National Monument was established by President Herbert Hoover on March 2, 1933, and encompasses one of the most stunning stretches of the gorge—a 12-mile length of river and sheer canyon wall. It includes two specific scenic drives (one of which, North Rim Rd., is closed in winter). In addition, the monument includes two campgrounds, a handful of nature trails, view points, picnic areas, and a visitor center.

Formed over some two million years by the erosive powers of the Gunnison River, Black Canyon was known 10,000 years ago to nomadic bands of Folsom people, who hunted deer and other game along the gorge's rim. Later, in the 17th, 18th, and 19th centuries, Utes also hunted in the area, chasing deer and buffalo to the canyon's rims, where they'd trap and kill the animals at close range or force them off the cliffs so they'd fall to their deaths.

Members of the Hayden Expedition of 1873-74 were probably the first nonnatives to see the canyon. Then toward the end of the 19th century, a survey crew for the Denver and Rio Grande Railroad proposed diverting water from the Gunnison River west to the Uncompahgre Valley for irrigation. In 1900, surveyors entered the canyon by boat, but their efforts were largely unsuccessful. A year later, a group of explorers and engineers floated the river in a rubber raft and, after nine days and 33 miles, emerged on the far side with the opinion that a tunnel was indeed possible. In late 1904, work was begun, and over four years later, in the summer of 1909, the seven-mile Gunnison Diversion Tunnel was completed.

When visiting Black Canyon, don't miss the visitor center, just inside the National Monument boundary. Here you'll find exhibits on the area's geology, history, flora, and fauna, and you can join regularly scheduled nature walks to the very edge of the canyon's rim, where a ranger discusses the gorge's formation and natural history and will answer questions.

To get to Black Canyon of the Gunnison National Monument, take Hwy. 50 west from Gunnison 60 miles or east from Montrose six miles and turn north on CO 347. During the summer only, you can get to the North Rim by taking CO 92 east from Delta or north from its junction with Hwy. 50, about 30 miles west of Gunnison.

For more information, write Box 1648, Montrose, CO 81402, or phone (303) 249-7036 (main office) or 249-1915 (visitor center).

Camping

Both campgrounds in Black Canyon National Monument are open May through Oct. only. **South Rim Campground** (102 sites), located near the visitor center off CO 347, is the most accessible of the two. During the winter, you can't even get to **North Rim Campground** (13 sites), as the gravel road in from CO 92 is closed.

DELTA

Located at the junction of Hwy. 50 and CO 92, and smack dab in the middle of some of Colorado's richest ranch land, Delta (pop. 3,900; elev. 4,980 feet) is a natural hub for travelers and ranchers alike and is also the headquarters for Grand Mesa, Uncompahgre, and Gunnison national forests. Not exactly a tourist destination in itself, Delta does offer several motels, cafés, and markets for travelers looking to rest for a while or to pull off the road for the night. It's also got a couple of nice city parks.

Billing itself "The City of Murals," Delta displays seven different murals on downtown buildings. The paintings, done by local artists, depict the history, economy, and recreational activities in the area. Examples include a pair of elk in a mountain meadow and a collection of fruit labels used by Delta County growers. Watch for the murals on Main St. (Hwy. 50) as you arrive either from the north or south.

Delta County Historical Museum

A good place to get a sense of Delta's past, this museum displays an array of ranching and farming tools, including harnesses and saddles, as well as dolls and other domestic items and historical photos. Entomologists take note: The museum's butterfly collection includes specimens that are extinct and are the only known surviving examples.

The museum, located at 5th St. and Palmer, is open Mon.-Fri. 1-4 p.m. Memorial Day through Labor Day, and Wed. and Sat. the rest of the year. For information, or to arrange special tours, phone (303) 874-3791.

Delta Dinosaurs

Delta County is the site of several important dinosaur-fossil discoveries. In 1971, paleontologists discovered the humerus of a brachiosaurus, and

in 1979, a nine-foot scapula and a 48-inch-wide vertebra from an ultrasaurus were discovered.

Delta resident Vivian Jones, who has been collecting dinosaur bones and fossils for 40 years, welcomes visitors to her small private museum. Reservations are required. Phone (303) 874-8909.

Ute Council Tree

Included in the book *Famous and Historic Trees of the United States* and recognized as a Colorado Landmark, the Ute Council Tree is an over-200-year-old cottonwood in north Delta. Between 1852 and 1887, Ute Chief Ouray and his wife, Chipeta (the only woman allowed to sit at the tree), met with white settlers in attempts to bring peace to western Colorado. The Ute Council Tree is 85 feet tall and seven in diameter.

To get there, watch for the small sign on Hwy. 50 just north of river bridge.

History As Theater

Thunder Mountain Lives, billed as a "Saga of the Old West," is an outdoor drama production that brings to life the history of Delta and the surrounding area. See and hear the stories of the Southern Utes, Alferd Packard, and Captain John Gunnison, and visit a model of a 19th-century fur-trading post.

Performances run mid-June through Labor Day at Confluence Park, just off Hwy. 50. Tickets are about $10 for adults and $5 for kids (slightly less if bought in advance). For tickets or information, write the Delta Chamber of Commerce, 301 Main St., Delta, CO 81416, or phone (303) 874-8616.

Ute Trail

This four-mile hiking trail, which follows one of the main routes used by Utes for centuries before settlers

Ute Council Tree

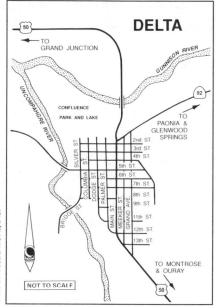

DELTA

TO GRAND JUNCTION

GUNNISON RIVER

UNCOMPAHGRE RIVER

CONFLUENCE PARK AND LAKE

92

TO PAONIA & GLENWOOD SPRINGS

2nd ST.
3rd ST.
4th ST.
5th ST.
6th ST.
7th ST.
8th ST.
9th ST.
11th ST.
12th ST.
13th ST.

SILVER ST
COLUMBIA ST
DODGE ST
PALMER ST
MAIN ST
MEEKER ST
GRAND AVE
BRIDGE ST

TO MONTROSE & OURAY

50

NOT TO SCALE

© MOON PUBLICATIONS, INC.

tel. 874-5787. East of town on Hwy. 92, you'll find the Delta **KOA** campground, tel. 874-3918.

Food

A classic western junction town, Delta offers more than its share of cafés and fast-food restaurants. In addition, you'll find a number of specialty restaurants, including **Daveto's,** 520 Main, tel. (303) 874-8277 (Italian), and **Sun Wah,** 142 Eaton, tel. 874-4884 (Chinese). You'll also find the old standby, **City Market,** at the corner of Main and 6th, for deli food and a salad bar.

Information

The **Delta Chamber of Commerce and Visitors Center,** tel. (303) 874-8616, is right downtown at 3rd and Main. An RV parking lot is located directly behind the building; turn west from Main. For information on camping, fishing, hiking, etc., in any of the surrounding National Forest lands, stop in at the headquarters for the Grand Mesa, Uncompahgre, and Gunnison national forests, located about a mile south of town on Hwy. 50; phone (303) 874-7691.

arrived, takes you from the south rim of the Gunnison Gorge down to the Gunnison River. This is an excellent area to view the geology of the area, as the trail switches back several times in its 1,200-foot descent, displaying sedimentary rocks, as well as metamorphic and igneous formations. In addition, bighorn sheep and river otters (both recently introduced by the Colorado Division of Wildlife) can be seen in the canyon.

To get to the trailhead, where you'll find picnic tables and a parking lot, take CO 92 five miles east to Austin, and go south for three miles on County Rd. 2200. At County Rd. 2450, go east for five miles and watch for the sign to the access road (two miles of dirt; recommended for high-clearance vehicles only).

PRACTICALITIES

Accommodations

The **Sundance Best Western,** tel. (303) 874-9781, on the south end of town at 903 Main (Hwy. 50) has rooms starting at about $40. On the north end of town, just across the Gunnison River, is the **Riverwood Inn and RV Park,**

HIGHWAY 50/550 SOUTH

Highway 50 drops south out of Grand Junction, shooting down between the Uncompahgre Plateau on the west and Grand Mesa on the east. The Gunnison River follows the 40-mile stretch of highway from Grand Junction to Delta, while the Uncompahgre parallels the 48-mile Delta-to-Ridgway stretch. In Montrose, Hwy. 50 doglegs to the east, while 550 continues south.

Just south of Ridgway, the highway begins to lift up into the mountains, and then, suddenly, at Ouray, you're facing an apparently unpassable wall of mountain granite. Don't worry: The road continues. In fact, at Ouray, Hwy. 550 begins a dramatic series of switchbacks up over Red Mountain Pass (elev. 11,008 feet), then drops down again into Silverton before winding back up over Molas Divide (elev. 10,910 feet) and through some of the state's most gorgeous scenery. Fifty miles south of Silverton, Hwy. 550 slips into Durango.

This is one of the Western Slope's most well-traveled roadways. Not only do many motorists take advantage of the quick northern section, which provides the best access between Grand Junction and Telluride, but many drive the southern route for its scenery alone. The Ouray-to-Silverton section, known as the Million Dollar Highway, offers unparalleled views of the Colorado Rockies at their most dramatic.

MONTROSE

The seat of Montrose County, Montrose (pop. 8,884; elev. 5,794 feet) is a small crossroads town in the center of the fertile Uncompahgre Valley on the Rocky Mountain's stark Western Slope. Used during the late-19th century as a supply point for miners working the Uncompahgre River, which flows through the valley, as well as those probing the 14,000-foot San Juan Mountains to the south, Montrose today serves as a hub for ranchers, hunters, and others exploring the vast recreational opportunities afforded by the southwestern Rockies, particularly Black Canyon of the Gunnison National Monument, and the Native American ruins of the Four Corners area.

Just over a mile above sea level, Montrose is blessed with a fairly moderate year-round climate, the town's lowest average temperatures scarcely dropping into the high 30s (in January) and its highs maxing out at about 90° (in July). Average maximum temperature is 63°, and local boosters like to brag about Montrose's 250 or so annual days of sunshine.

History

Like most of the country's most desirable areas, the Uncompahgre Valley was once Native American land. Southern Utes had farmed and hunted in the region for centuries before Europeans arrived, Chief Ouray and his wife Chipeta overseeing local Utes in the fertile river valley in the mid- to late-19th century—until the tribe was "removed" in 1881 by the United States government.

Oliver D. "Pappy" Loutsenhizer was one of the first white settlers in the valley, arriving first in the fall of 1873 with a group of gold-seeking adventurers led by Alferd Packard. Though Loutsenhizer and part of the group eventually turned back (at the urging of Ouray), Packard continued, even as winter temperatures and snow began to fall. Ultimately, Packard was convicted of cannibalizing five members of his splinter group after they became snowbound near Lake City (see "Lake City," under "North of Pagosa Springs" following).

Loutsenhizer returned to the valley several years later and, in 1881, with his friend Joseph Selig, laid out what was to become the town of Montrose—first dubbed "Pomona," after the Roman goddess of fruit, but later renamed after the Duchess of Montrose, a character in a Walter Scott novel. Shortly after its founding, Montrose saw two big changes that would have great effects on its face and character. The first was the railroad, which pushed through in 1882, providing opportunities for local farmers to ship their crops, especially cotton and sugar beets, to destinations throughout the United States. The second was the Gunnison Diversion Tunnel. Begun in 1904 and completed in 1909, the seven-mile passage provided irrigation water from the Gunnison River northeast of town to Uncompahgre Valley farmers whose increasing croplands were requiring more and

Colorado State Prison was Alferd Packard's home for several years after his conviction on charges of culinary impropriety.

COLORADO HISTORICAL SOCIETY

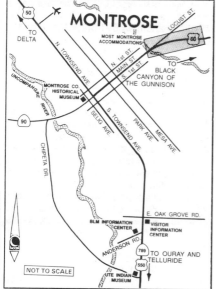

more water. One of Bureau of Reclamation's first projects, the tunnel had a much-celebrated inauguration, with the dedication conducted by President Taft.

Ute Indian Museum And
Ouray Memorial Park

Dedicated in 1956 by the Colorado Historical Society, this small museum sits on land once farmed by the Southern Ute chief Ouray and displays artifacts from the Ute culture as well as dioramas and exhibits describing European exploration of the area, including the Dominguez-Escalante expedition of 1776. In addition to the collections of ceremonial artifacts, some of which once belonged to Ouray himself, the museum and park include a monument to the chief and the grave of his wife, Chipeta, as well as picnic facilities for passers-through.

The museum is located one mile south of the town center on Hwy. 550 and is open Mon.-Sat. 10 a.m.-5 p.m. and Sun. 1-5 p.m., May 15 to Oct. 15. The rest of the year, the museum is open for school groups and pre-arranged tours. Admission is $2 for adults and $1 for kids and seniors. For more information, phone (303) 249-3098, or write 17253 Chipeta Dr., Montrose, CO 81401.

Montrose County Historical Museum

Providing a general history of the Uncompahgre Valley and the Western Slope—from Ute occupation through 20th-century irrigation and development—this museum highlights the late-19th-century pioneer and settler. Especially impressive are the museum's excellent displays of historical photos, particularly of Chief Ouray and his wife, Chipeta, and of the early days of the railroad—as well as the collections of artifacts, including Ute arrowheads and domestic items, from toys to medical equipment to musical instruments. Also of interest are replicas of nearby petroglyphs and a full-size homesteader's cabin with original furnishings. The museum's library includes Montrose newspapers from 1896-1940, photos, and several historical publications.

The Montrose County Historical Museum is open May through Oct. Mon.-Sat. 9 a.m.-5 p.m. and Sun. 1-5 p.m. The museum is located on W. Main St.. For more information, phone (303) 249-2085.

Montrose Children's Museum

Established in 1984, this resource center provides hands-on educational exhibits, summer workshops, and referrals for schools, preschools, and day care, as well for professional services of interest to families both passing through and living in the area. For more information, phone (303) 240-4833.

PARKS AND RECREATION

Golf

Montrose's 18-hole golf course (1350 Birch St., by way of Hillcrest Dr.) is open to the public 7 a.m.-7 p.m. For information and tee times, phone (303) 249-8551.

River Running

Rafting and float trips are also popular on Montrose-area rivers, including the nearby Gunnison and Uncompahgre. Most outfits also book trips to other Colorado waters as well. Go for a half day, or take a three- or four-day excursion. Prices start around $60.

Several Montrose companies offer trips, including **Gunnison River Expeditions,** tel. (303) 249-4441.

ACCOMMODATIONS

Hotels And Motels

Montrose's "Motel Row" is on the east end of town on Main St./Hwy. 50 E, where you'll find a dozen or so places to bed down. There are newer hotel-type lodges, as well as mom-and-pop places. The **Best Western Red Arrow Inn,** 1702 E. Main, tel. (303) 249-9641 or (800) 468-9323, is one of the more fully appointed lodges in town (exercise room, fax and copy services, convention facilities, etc.) and has 60 rooms ranging in price from about $50 to $100. Also on Hwy. 50 E, the **Black Canyon Inn,** 1605 E. Main, tel. 249-3495 or (800) 453-4911, has good clean rooms for about $35-$60. At the **Super 8,** 1705 E. Main, tel. 249-9294, rooms run $30-65; RV and truck parking available.

The **San Juan Inn,** 1480 Hwy. 550 S, tel. 249-6644, is one of the first you'll come to as you approach from the south; rooms for two start at about $35. The indoor pool and Jacuzzi are especially nice after a day on the road.

Camping And RVing

Though it gets a bit cold on the Rockies' Western Slope for winter camping, from late spring to early fall the weather's much more accommodating, and the Montrose area offers a number of campgrounds, both private and government run. The **Hangin' Tree RV Park,** 17250 Hwy. 50, tel. (303) 249-9966 has laundry facilities, showers, and a convenience store, and sites with full hookups for $10-15; open year-round. The Montrose **KOA,** 200 N. Cedar, tel. 249-9177, is open from Memorial Day through Labor Day and has both tent and RV sites, showers, laundry, pool, and small store; rates run about $12-16.

In addition to the campgrounds at Black Canyon of the Gunnison and Curecanti National Recreation Area (see above), you'll find a number of Forest Service campgrounds near Cimarron, in the Uncompahgre National Forest about a half-hour east of Montrose: **Big Cimarron Campground** offers free camping at 16 sites along the Big Cimarron River—no drinking water available; **Beaver Lake Campground** has 16 sites on Beaver Creek; the 60 units at **Silver Jack Campground** on Silver Jack Lake provide access to good boating and fishing on the reservoir, as well as to hiking into the Big

Blue Wilderness Area. To get to all three campgrounds, take Hwy. 50 about 24 miles east of Montrose and then Owl Creek/Cimarron Rd. (dirt) 20 miles south.

FOOD

For a small town, Montrose offers a decent number of non-franchise, non-fast-food restaurants. **The Whole Enchilada,** tel. (303) 249-1881, serves a variety of Mexican and Southwestern dishes, including fajitas, chimichangas, and blue-corn enchiladas. Most dinners are under $10. The Whole Enchilada is located at 44 S. Grand on the corner of Main. If you're more in the mood for a classic steak-and-seafood joint, try the **Backwoods Inn,** 103 Rose Lane, tel. 249-1961. Entrees include prime rib, steaks, lobster, and chicken. Live entertainment Wed. through Sat. evenings.

A favorite among truckers and other passers-through is **Starvin' Arvin's,** tel. (303) 249-7787, on Hwy. 50 on the south side of town, right next door to the San Juan Inn. This moderately priced family-style restaurant serves breakfasts, lunches, and dinners from 6 a.m.-10 p.m. daily. Another favorite is the **Cameo Restaurant,** 613 Main St., tel. 249-5349. For those on the run, **El Sombrero,** tel. 249-0217, offers Mexican take-out Tues. through Sat. 11 a.m.-9 p.m. and Sun. 11 a.m.-10 p.m. For an early-morning caffeine and sugar fix, stop in at **Daylight Donuts,** 219 N. 1st—fresh-baked doughnuts and coffee to get your motor runnin'.

SERVICES

Phone the **Montrose Police Department** at (303) 249-6609 and the **Montrose County Sheriff** at 249-6606. The offices of the **State Patrol** are at 2420 N. Townsend; phone 249-4392. **Montrose Memorial Hospital** is at 800 S. 3rd St.; phone 249-2211. Montrose's main **post office** is at 321 S. 1st Street.

Recycling

Drop off most recyclables at **Montrose Recycle Center,** 1215 N. Townsend. The **City Market,** 128 S. Townsend, and **Safeway,** 1329 S. Townsend, will take aluminum.

Calendar

Montrose is busy with events throughout the year. A few highlights are the **Fourth of July** parade and fireworks display, the **Montrose County Fair** (August), and a number of **Christmas shows and pageants** (December). For a complete listing of annual events, write the Montrose Chamber of Commerce (see "Information" below).

TOURS

The Montrose Chamber of Commerce has delineated several specific scenic day tours from town and has published maps with mileages, average driving times, and other tips. You can drive to Ridgway State Recreation Area, Black Canyon National Monument, Curecanti National Recreation Area, Grand Mesa National Forest (all of which are discussed elsewhere). For maps and information, contact the chamber at 550 N. Townsend, Montrose, CO 81401, or phone (800) 873-0244.

For guided tours, contact **San Juan Mountain Tours,** 2850 Star Ridge Court, Montrose, CO 81401, or phone (303) 249-1535.

INFORMATION

You can obtain further information about the Montrose area by stopping by or writing the **visitor information center,** 2490 S. Townsend, Montrose, CO 81401, or by phoning (303) 249-1726—the visitor center is open seven days a week, May through October only. You can also write the **Montrose County Chamber of Commerce,** 550 N. Townsend, Montrose, CO 81401, tel. 249-5515 or (800) 873-0244—open Mon.-Fri. 8 a.m.-5 p.m. Be sure to ask for the *Montrose Visitors Guide,* which includes a full listing of lodging and restaurants, as well as information sources for various recreational pursuits (hunting to scuba diving).

Montrose's daily newspaper is the independently owned *Montrose Daily Press* (not published weekends or holidays), available for 25 cents in racks around town. For subscription information, write 535 1st St., Montrose, CO 81401, or phone 249-3444.

For **road conditions and weather information,** phone 249-9363 or (800) 821-4765.

TRANSPORTATION

Both **Continental Express,** tel. (303) 249-1399, and **United Express/Aspen Airways,** tel. 249-8455, offer passenger service to Montrose Airport, tel. 249-3203, located on the north end of town, where you can also rent cars. Phone **Budget** at 249-6083, **Hertz** at 249-9447, or **Dollar,** 249-3770.

The Montrose **bus depot** is at 132 N. 1st; phone 249-6673. For taxi service, phone 249-8880.

RIDGWAY

Located at the junction of Hwy. 550 and CO 62, Ridgway (pop. 370; elev. 6,900 feet) marks the point where scenery for southbound travelers begins to get absolutely breathtaking. Telluride-bound travelers will turn west at Ridgway, ascending 8,970-foot Dallas Divide Pass before dropping back down to CO 145 and looping back into the little box canyon from the west. As you rise up out of Ridgway toward the pass, look back over your shoulder to your left at the towering Mt. Sneffels Range, the highest point of which is 14,150-foot Mt. Sneffels.

If you're continuing south from Ridgway, you'll follow the course of the Uncompahgre River for 10 miles before reaching Ouray, a tiny Swiss-like village at the foot of Red Mountain Pass. From Ouray, you'll begin a switchbacky assault on the pass, climbing almost 3,500 feet in about a half dozen miles.

Ridgway dates from 1891, when it was a link on the Rio Grande Southern Railroad's route to Durango (175 miles to the south). Throughout the 20th century, Ridgway has served as a supply center for miners working claims scattered in the San Juan Mountains. In addition, the little town is a natural hub for cattle ranchers in the surrounding valley.

Rail service to Ridgway was halted in 1951, when shipping rates became prohibitively expensive, though the little town still sees plenty of travelers, due in large part to its "gateway" location. In the early 1970s, the movie *True Grit* was filmed in Ridgway.

Ridgway State Recreation Area

This recently opened (1989) recreation area two miles north of Ridgway surrounds a 1,000-acre reservoir on the Uncompahgre River. Though the area is still being developed, current facilities include a campground with almost 200 sites, a boat-launching ramp, picnic facilities, and a visitor center. Plans call for additional campsites, as well as increased fishing and picnic facilities, plus a special area for windsurfing.

For information or to reserve campsites, phone (303) 626-5822.

Food

Passing through Ridgway en route to a day at Telluride? Need a lift? Try **Linda's Bakery,** 520 W. Sherman, tel. (303) 626-5803 (south side of the road). Large coffees, sugary pastries, muffins—to go or eat in the little café. Brought to you by San Juan Mommas, Inc.

For Mexican food, try the **Adobe Inn,** 251 Liddell Dr., tel. 626-5939. Other Ridgway options include the **Sunset,** tel. 626-5494, which features classic American fare for breakfast, lunch, and dinner. At the **Ridgway Mountain Market,** tel. 626-5811, on CO 62, you can build your own sandwich (and pay by the pound), or choose from other deli items, including chicken, ribs, and, well, "everything from wieners to caviar." **The True Grit Cafe,** 123 N. Lena, tel. 626-5739, displays a variety of memorabilia from the film.

Accommodations

Bed-and-breakfast accommodations are available at **Sophie & Annies** (two rooms) at 767 Sherman, tel. 626-3975, and at the **Grey Squirrel Lodge** (three rooms), 151 S. Cora, tel. 626-5324. The **Adobe Inn,** 251 Liddell, tel. 626-5939, is a hostel with three rooms. There's also a **Super 8 Lodge,** at 373 Palomino Trail, tel. 626-5444.

Information

For more information on Ridgway, write the **Ouray County Chamber of Commerce,** Box 145, Ouray, CO 81427, tel. (303) 325-4747 or (800) 228-1876. Be sure to ask for a copy of the *Ouray County Vacation Guide,* a very thorough guide (60 pages) to communities in the area, including lodging, dining, and recreation opportunities. The **Ridgway Visitor Center** is located at 102 Village Square West; phone 626-5868.

OURAY

Nestled in a natural amphitheater in a narrow box canyon and surrounded by peaks that tower 5,000 feet above the valley floor, Ouray (pop. 700; elev. 7,800 feet) is known as the "Little Switzerland of America." Approached from either the north or the south, Ouray will certainly arrest the eye of the motorist. As you enter the valley from the north, the high walls seem to close in on you, and as you pass through the quiet little town—its streets lined with Victorian-era homes and lavish old hotels—you can't help but be struck by the seemingly unpassable pass ahead. All around you the mountains rise: to the west, White House Mountain (elev. 13,493 feet); to the south, Hayden Mountain (elev. 13,100 feet); and to the northwest, Cascade Mountain (elev. 12,100 feet). Ouray (pronounced "you-RAY") seems trivialized by nature.

If you arrive from the south, you'll be switchbacking down Red Mountain Pass and looking at the town almost from straight above. This is when it really seems like a Little Switzerland, the colorful little buildings and green meadows at the base of these towering peaks looking like something right off a calendar or the cover of a travel magazine. The view is breathtaking.

Don't let it take so much of your breath, though, that you forget to keep your eyes on the road. This is a steep sucker, with dramatic horseshoe turns. Look away from the road for too long and you could end up taking the shortcut to town. Instead, take advantage of the turnouts provided for sightseeing and picture taking.

The town takes its name from the Southern Ute Chief Ouray, whose people had been coming to the valley for centuries before the white men came to mine and ranch. The hot mineral waters that bubble up from the ground in several different places were said to have healing powers. Today those same waters soothe the aches of road-weary motorists, as well as hikers, cross-country skiers, horseback riders, and others who enjoy relaxing in the hot mineral waters after a day of recreation. You'll find hot springs at several local lodges as well as the municipal pool and park at the north end of town.

History

Ouray dates from 1875, when prospectors entered the valley and discovered a number of rich silver lodes in the nearby mountains. The town was incorporated in the fall of the next year and named for Chief Ouray, universally praised for his intellect and attempts to bring whites and Native Americans together in harmony. Soon, the Uncompahgre area's first newspaper, the *Ouray Times,* was founded after a wagon train hauled type and presses from Cañon City.

Ouray boomed in the early 1880s but then went temporarily belly up when the silver market crashed in 1893. In 1896, however, carpenter Thomas F. Walsh discovered gold in the Camp Bird silver mine, bought rights to the mine for $20,000, and quickly became one of Colorado's laborer-turned-millionaires. Until 1902, the mine yielded ore worth between $3 and $4 million a year, sometimes matching Walsh's initial investment in a single week. By 1910, the mine had produced $26 million in gold.

Many of the Ouray-area mines are still worked, although as costs of extraction have increased disproportionately to the price of gold, the industry has become less and less important. Instead, Ouray and Ouray County rely on tourism and ranching to keep local economies vital.

ATTRACTIONS

Bachelor-Syracuse Mine

Named for three bachelors and a group of miners from Syracuse, New York, this mine produced $90 million in gold and $8 million in silver, as well as respectable amounts of lead, zinc, and copper. Tours of the mine, which take you 3,350 feet into the side of Gold Hill, offer an excellent sense of Ouray's early (and dangerous!) mining days. Be sure to bring a sweater, as the temperatures inside stay right about 50°.

The Bachelor-Syracuse Mine is open to the public late May through mid-September. Tours are on the hour 9 a.m.-6 p.m. late June through August and 10 a.m.-5 p.m. the rest of the season. Rates are $6.95 for adults, kids and seniors discounted. For an added fee, you can pan for gold and keep what you find. For information or reservations, write Bachelor-Syracuse Mine Tour, County Rd. 14, Drawer 380W, Ouray, CO 81427, or phone (303) 325-4500.

Ouray County Historical Museum

With an emphasis on the area's mining and railroading history, this museum, housed in an old hospital dating from 1887, also features exhibits that highlight contributions of the Southern Utes, ranchers, educators, doctors, and other settlers. The museum is located at the corner of 5th St. and 6th Ave. and is open daily. For exact hours or other information, phone (303) 325-4576.

Walking Tour

Ouray is small enough (downtown is about six by four blocks) that you can easily tour the town by foot in an afternoon—it is hilly, though. The Ouray County Chamber of Commerce has designated a specific walking tour of the National Historic District, with over two dozen buildings of historical significance. Among them: **St. Elmo Hotel,** 426 Main, built in 1898, recently restored, and today operating as a restaurant and inn; the **Western Hotel** (1891), 220 7th Ave., Ouray's original deluxe lodge; and **Wright's Opera House** (1888), fascinating for its Romanesque and Greek Revival architecture. Pick up a map and detailed guide at the visitor center next to Ouray Hot Springs Pool, or write the chamber of commerce, Box 145, Ouray, CO 81427.

Million Dollar Highway

In the early 1880s, Otto Mears built a toll road over Red Mountain Pass to make it easier to get Ouray ore out of the valley; the road greatly increased the efficiency of mining in the Ouray-Silverton-Telluride District. Today, Hwy. 550 from Ouray to Silverton follows the old route much of the way and is known as the Million Dollar Highway. Why? No one seems to be able to say for sure, though there are at least three explanations you'll get, depending on which "expert" you talk to: The road was paved with gold-bearing gravel, the value of which was not discovered until the project was completed; the road was so steep and so precarious that an early traveler was heard to claim, "You couldn't

pay me a million dollars to go back over that pass"; or, the road cost about $1 million to pave in the mid-20th century.

PARKS AND RECREATION

Ouray Hot Springs Pool And Park

Ideal for soaking away a day's hiking or skiing aches, or cooling off after a long day's driving, this municipal facility features hot springs soaking pools as well as cool-water lap and goof-around pools. And the location couldn't be better: Kick back in the 104° water and dig the towering peaks that rise 5,000 feet from the valley floor and box Ouray into the canyon.

If you don't feel like getting wet, there's a spacious grassy lawn, perfect for tossing the Frisbee about, as well as picnic facilities and a playground. The hot springs and park are located right on Hwy. 550 at the north end of town. The pools are open Mon.-Sat. 9 a.m.-9 p.m. and Sun. 9 a.m.-7 p.m. in the summer, Wed.-Mon. noon-9 p.m. in the winter. For more information, phone (303) 325-4638.

Box Canyon Falls And Park

With the waters of Clear Creek crashing nearly 300 feet into the narrow granite-walled Box Canyon, this city-owned park offers spectacular views and hiking trails. In addition, a steel suspension footbridge across the canyon affords a stunning view of the falls and creek. There are also restrooms and picnic facilities.

The falls and park are located just south of town off Hwy. 550 (watch for the signs). Hours are 8 a.m. to dusk mid-May through mid-October. Admission is $1.25 for adults and 75 cents for kids. For more information, phone (303) 325-4464.

Jeep Touring

This is one of the primary reasons folks come to Ouray. Scores of rocky backroads wind into remote canyons, past abandoned mines, through ghosts of old mining camps, and along cliffsides with sheer dropoffs to valley floors thousands of feet below. Trips range from the fairly easy tour to **Yankee Boy Basin** to the more difficult (and dangerous) drive over **Imogene Pass** to Telluride. The Yankee Boy Basin tour begins on Camp Bird Rd. just south of Ouray, follows

Canyon Creek to the Camp Bird Mine (five miles from Ouray), and then veers west toward a series of wildflower-laden valleys at the base of Dallas and Gilpin peaks and Mt. Emma. The Imogene Pass road begins at the Camp Bird Mine and winds up over the 13,509-foot summit, affording views of some of the best scenery in one of most scenic areas of the state.

If you're looking to explore on your own, pick up Forest Service maps at the **Ouray Ranger District Office,** 2505 S. Townsend, Montrose, tel. (303) 249-3711. You'll also find a 4WD map and descriptions of routes in Ouray County's *Vacation Guide.*

San Juan Scenic Jeep Tours, in operation since 1946, offers half- and full-day tours throughout the area. Go on a predesigned tour, or make your own itinerary. Prices start at about $25 for adults for half-day trips. You can also rent vehicles. For reservations or information, write Box 143, Ouray, CO 81427, or phone 325-4444 or 325-4154.

Several other companies in Ouray also offer Jeep rentals and 4WD tours. Among them are **Switzerland of America,** Box 184, Ouray, CO 81427, tel. 325-4484, and **Colorado West,** 332 5th Ave., tel. 325-4014. You can also rent Jeeps at the **KOA** campground north of town.

Hiking

The woods, peaks, and steep canyons of the Ouray area are ideal for exploring by foot, and hikers will find a wide variety of trails. The following are but a sampling of the hikes in the area. The *Ouray County Vacation Guide* describes a dozen or so more, providing lengths and degrees of difficulty. **Lower Cascade Falls Trail** is a short (half mile) but fairly rugged trail that begins at the top of 8th Ave. and takes you down into the canyon to the bottom of Cascade Falls—expect to do some scrambling over boulders, and be careful of slick spots caused by melting snow. For something a little longer, although not as demanding, try the five-mile **Portland Trail,** which begins on the east side of town at Amphitheater Campground in Portland Basin. **Upper Cascade Trail** also begins at Amphitheater Campground and though half as long gains more than twice the altitude (1,500 as opposed to 700 feet). Great views of the valley, as well as of waterfalls on Cascade Creek.

For more information on hiking in the area, stop by the Ouray Visitors Center next to Ouray Hot Springs Pool, or contact **Uncompahgre National Forest,** either at its headquarters at 2250 Hwy. 50, Delta, tel. (303) 874-7691, or at the **Ouray Ranger District Office,** 2505 S. Townsend, Montrose, tel. 249-3711.

Fishing

Ridgway Reservoir at the recently established **Ridgway State Recreation Area,** about 12 miles north of town on Hwy. 550, is regularly stocked with rainbow and brown trout. Fish the 1,000-acre lake either from shore or from a boat; launch your own boat from the six-lane ramp near the main entrance, or rent a boat from **San Juan Skyway Marina** on the lake, tel. (303) 626-5480. You can also fish for trout at the tiny but scenic **Molas Lake** on the Silverton side of Molas Pass, where you'll also find camping and picnicking facilities (fee charged, except for in a very small public area). The **Uncompahgre River** between Ouray and the reservoir is also stocked, though much of the river passes through private property.

For more information on fishing in the Ouray-San Juan-Uncompahgre area, or for licenses or guide service, stop by Telluride's **Olympic Sports,** 150 Colorado Ave., tel. 728-4477, or **Duranglers of Telluride,** 666 W. Colorado Ave., tel. 728-3895. You can also get licenses and information at **Outdoor World,** 1234 Greene St., Silverton, tel. 387-5628.

Cross-country Skiing

The nonprofit Ouray County Nordic Council operates **Red Mountain/Ironton Park Cross-Country Trails,** with several designated routes and loops that wind among eight historic landmarks and sites. There are both beginner and intermediate trails. For information, write Box 468, Ouray, CO 81427.

Other Activities

Though one could devote most of a summer to hiking or Jeep touring in the Ouray area, there are other things to do. One of the best ways to get into the heart of the backcountry is by horseback. **San Juan Mountain Outfitters,** whose stables are located along the Uncompahgre River two miles north of town, offers half- and full-day trips, as well as overnight camp-out rides and full-service hunting pack trips. Reservations required. Write 2882 County Rd. 23, Ridgway, CO 81432, or phone (303) 626-5659.

Ouray Livery Barn has one- and two-hour and half-day rides along some of the nearby area's hiking trails, including Oak Creek and Portland Trail. Located on Main St. in Ouray; phone 325-4606.

San Juan Balloon Adventures offers half- and one-hour balloon tours of the Uncompahgre River Valley, as well as a "Balloon-N-Brunch" flight; soar out to a secluded picnic brunch, sip champagne with your meal, and climb back aboard for the trip home. Reservations required at least 12 hours in advance. Write Box 66, Ridgway, CO 81432, or phone 325-4257 or 626-5495.

ACCOMMODATIONS

Ouray is a wonderful little hideaway town, a perfect place to hole up after a particularly demanding job project or semester of graduate school. Personally, I've always wanted to rent a little room in town, set up my word processor, and write all those scripts I've been telling myself Hollywood is aching to produce. If I ever do set up camp here, however, it's more likely I'll be working on updating this book. Whatever, I couldn't think of a better place.

Ouray offers a variety of accommodation options, with one common denominator: They all tend to fill up. Don't expect to be choosy if you're looking Friday afternoon for digs for Friday night. In fact, you might not be able to find anything at all, at least in the summer, when Southwestern Colorado swells with sightseers and vacationers. Call ahead for a room.

The small **Antlers Motel,** right downtown at 407 Main St., tel. (303) 325-4589, has no-frills doubles starting at about $50. The **Best Western Twin Peaks Motel,** 125 3rd Ave., tel. 325-4427, has a natural hot-springs whirlpool and doubles starting at $72. Both the Antlers and the Twin Peaks are closed in the winter. You'll also find natural outdoor hot tubs at **Box Canyon Lodge and Hot Springs,** 45 3rd Ave., tel. 327-5080; rooms for two run $45-65.

Located in the center of town at 426 Main St., the **St. Elmo Hotel,** tel. 325-4951, was built before the turn of the century and has recently been remodeled into a bed-and-breakfast inn with 11 rooms furnished with Victorian-era antiques. Doubles start at about $55. You can also get bed-and-breakfast accommodations at **Damn Yankees Bed and Breakfast,** 199 6th Ave., tel. 325-4219 or (800) 845-7512.

For more information on lodging in Ouray, write the Ouray Chamber of Commerce, Box 145, Ouray, CO 81427, or phone (303)325-4746 or (800)228-1876.

Camping And RVing
Ouray Rotary Park on Hwy. 550 at the north end of town offers free overnight camping and picnicking. **Amphitheater Campground,** located immediately south of town (east side), is operated by Uncompahgre National Forest and has 30 sites, pit toilets, and no showers. Phone (303) 249-3711.

A **KOA** campground is four miles north of Ouray—110 tent and RV sites, plus a few cabins. Phone 325-4736. You can also camp at **Timber Ridge Motel and Campground,** located just north of town on Hwy. 550. Motel rooms have fireplaces and steam rooms. Phone 325-4523.

FOOD

Ouray has a respectable number of good restaurants, some of which draw folks from throughout the Uncompahgre Valley area. For Mexican food, try the dining room at the **Western Hotel,** 210 7th St., tel. (303) 325-4645. In addition to south-of-the-border favorites, such as enchiladas and chiles rellenos, you can also get buffalo, elk, and venison. Entrees are in the $10-18 range. Another longtime favorite is the **Bon Ton Restaurant,** downstairs in the St. Elmo Hotel at 426 Main, tel. 325-4951. The Bon Ton specializes in Italian food, as well as steaks, seafood, and chicken, with dinners ranging from around $12 to $20. Sunday brunch is served from 10 a.m.-1 p.m. for $6.95. The **Outlaw,** 610 Main, tel. 325-9996, is a classic Western steakhouse that was spotlighted by *National Geographic Traveler* in 1990. You can also get seafood and chicken dinners. Dinners are $10-18.

ENTERTAINMENT AND EVENTS

As the commercial, recreational, and cultural center of Ouray County, Ouray offers lots of goings-on throughout the year, from arts-and-crafts shows to music festivals to the **Jeepers Jamboree.** Highlights include the **Music in Ouray** classical concert series (mid-June); the **Imogene Pass Run** footrace up Imogene Pass, which connects Ouray and Telluride (early Sept.); and the **Octoberfest** (early Oct.). Write the Ouray County Chamber of Commerce (see "Information" following) for a complete calendar of annual and special events.

The **San Juan Odyssey** is a 15-projector, five-screen slide show examining the San Juan Mountains in all their rugged glory. Written and narrated by Ouray mayor and country musician C.W. McCall (remember "Convoy"?), the show, which has been running nightly in summer since 1976, features a soundtrack by the London Symphony. Shows are at 8:30 p.m. in the Opera House at 5th and Main. Admission is $4 for adults, $2 for kids 12 and younger. For information, phone (303) 325-4607.

INFORMATION

If you're passing through, be sure to stop at the tourist **information center** on the north end of town next to Ouray Hot Springs and Pool. If you're planning to visit, write **Ouray County Chamber of Commerce,** Box 145, Ouray, CO 81427, or phone (303) 325-4746 or (800) 228-1876. Be sure to request a copy of the *Ouray County Vacation Guide,* which is full of maps, suggestions for hiking and Jeep-touring trails, and listings of accommodations, restaurants, and other businesses. For information on Uncompahgre National Forest, phone the main office in Delta at 874-7691, or stop by the **Ouray Ranger District Office,** 2505 S. Townsend, Montrose, tel. 249-3711.

You can also get maps (topo, 4WD, hiking, etc.), as well as books on local and regional history at **Big Horn Mercantile,** 609 Main St., tel. 325-4257.

The *Ouray County PlainDealer* newspaper is published weekly and is available in racks and shops throughout the area. For subscription information, write Box 607, Ouray, CO 81427-0607, tel. 325-4412.

SILVERTON

Silverton (pop. 790; elev. 9,300 feet) is the seat of San Juan County and the center of the Las Animas Mining District. Situated in a tiny pocket between Molas and Red Mountain passes, and literally ringed with towering mountain peaks, Silverton began as an isolated mining camp, became a railroad supply center, and between 1880 and 1910 had a reputation as one riproarin' town, where whoring, drinking, and gunfighting went on around the clock.

Known as the "mining town that never quit," Silverton finally shut down its last mine in August, 1991, after a century and a quarter of silver, gold, lead, zinc, and copper production. Eureka, Howardsville, Red Mountain, and other once-thriving mountain communities are accessible by back roads; get information and maps from the Silverton Visitors Center on the west end of town.

Silverton is also known today as the northern terminus of the Durango and Silverton Narrow Gauge Railroad, and for the dozens of gift shops, as well as restaurants and hotels, that occupy 100-year-old buildings. In the summer, passengers take the winding railroad up from Durango, spend a few hours wandering through the shops of Silverton (or spend the night), and then get back on the train for the trip back to Durango (you can also begin the trip in Silverton; see "Attractions" following). The Silverton Gunfighters Association entertains tourists every evening at 5:00 with gunfights in the street.

History

A mining camp dating from 1871, when the first lodes were discovered here, Silverton was originally known as Baker's Park, after Captain Charles Baker, who had explored the area in the early 1860s. According to local legend, the town's name was changed in 1874 when a local mine operator announced, "We may not have gold here, but we have silver by the ton."

downtown Silverton in the late 19th century

COLORADO HISTORICAL SOCIETY

The camp prospered in the late 1870s and early '80s. Several large hotels and other buildings were constructed, among them the Grand Imperial Hotel and the gold-domed courthouse. In 1882, the Denver and Rio Grande Railroad arrived in town, greatly improving accessibility to the little community. During this time, Silverton's Blair St., one block east of Greene, was a hotbed of brothels, saloons, and gambling houses. Madams such as Mamie Murphy, Kate Starr, and Jew Fanny operated 24-hour-a-day "pleasure palaces" that drew huge numbers of miners and other callers from throughout western Colorado. Things got so wild, in fact, that Silverton eventually recruited Bat Masterson from Dodge City to "clean up the town."

Silverton fared better during the silver crash of 1893 than did many of Colorado's ore-dependent towns, its mines continuing to produce an average of $2 million a year. In fact, Silverton prospered well into the next century; the population in 1910 was 2,153, more than twice what it is today. By 1918, over $65 million in silver had been taken from Silverton-area mines.

ATTRACTIONS

Durango And Silverton Narrow Gauge Railroad

Though the vast majority of tourists catch the train at its southern terminus, Durango, you can also begin in Silverton. Options include one-day, roundtrip tours; roundtrip tours with an overnight layover in Durango; one-way trips; and combination bus-train roundtrip tours. Reservations highly recommended. Roundtrip fares are about $40 for adults. Phone the Durango depot at (303) 247-2733, or write Durango And Silverton Narrow Gauge Railroad Company, 479 Main Ave., Durango, CO 81301. Also see "Attractions" under "Durango" following.

San Juan County Museum

Located in the old San Juan County jail, this small museum, operated by the San Juan County Historical Society, is geared mostly toward the area's railroad and mining history. The first floor of the building, constructed in 1902, served as the sheriff's living quarters, while the jail cells, which have not been removed, are on the second floor.

The San Juan County Museum, located on Greene St. between 15th and 16th, is open daily 9 a.m.-5 p.m. Memorial Day through Labor Day, and thereafter daily 10 a.m.-3 p.m. through mid-October. Admission is $1.50 for adults. For information, phone (303) 387-5838.

Historical Walking Tour

Whether you realize it or not, if you're walking around Silverton, you're taking a historical walking tour. You can't help it: Silverton *is* history. The two main north-south streets—Greene and Blair—offer a tour of the town's past, from its most elegant to its most indecorous; while most of the "respectable" businesses were on Greene, Blair was known for its brothels and wild saloons.

The Silverton Chamber of Commerce and the San Juan County Historical Society have printed a map and thorough description of historic Silverton. Included are over 50 structures within a few short blocks of each other. Among the buildings on the tour are the **Grand Imperial Hotel,** 1221 Greene, which was built in 1883;

the **Exchange Livery,** 1244 Greene, built in 1906 (buggies and wagons were stored downstairs, horses upstairs); and **Natalia's,** 1161 Blair, and the **Shady Lady,** 1154 Blair, both of which were popular brothels around the turn of the century.

The map and guide are published in the back pages of the *Silverton-San Juan Vacation Guide,* available at the chamber of commerce visitor center at the town's entrance.

Christ Of The Mines Shrine
Dedicated to Silverton's miners, past and present, this statue of a 12-ton Rio-like Jesus stands arms spread in a stone alcove on the hillside above Silverton. Erected in 1959, the statue, made of Italian marble, is thought to have been the source of several local "miracles," including the fact that no workers were present when a local mine exploded one Sunday night. To get there, take 10th St. west from downtown Silverton.

RECREATION

Hiking
Silverton is surrounded by the San Juan National Forest and is just northwest of 405,000-acre Weminuche Wilderness Area, the state's largest and most visited. This is steep and high country, though, with the Continental Divide passing just a few miles east of town, and hikers should know what they're doing. For topo maps of the area, and for suggestions on hiking, contact the **Animas Ranger District Office** of the Forest Service, 701 Camino Del Rio, Durango, CO 81301, tel. (303) 247-4874. The Silverton Visitors Center also has information and maps, as does **Outdoor World,** 1234 Greene, Silverton, tel. 387-5628.

Though you can get into the backcountry by walking from downtown Silverton, you can also take the Durango-Silverton Railroad. Certain runs stop for backpackers (to let you on or off). For information, phone 387-5416 (Silverton) or 247-2733 (Durango).

Jeep Tours
Like Ouray, Silverton is a four-wheel-driver's paradise, and the old cliff-hanging mining roads are litmus tests for driving skills. One popular

trail is the **Alpine Loop,** which connects Silverton, Lake City, and Ouray and crosses **Engineer Pass** (elev. 12,800 feet) and **Cinnamon Pass** (elev. 12,620 feet). The 65-mile route is designated a **Backcountry Scenic Byway,** and is not one of the more treacherous in the area.

Several companies in the area offer 4WD rentals. Try **Rent-A-Jeep** at the Conoco Station at 864 Greene St., tel. (303) 387-9990, or **Silver Lakes Campground,** just north of town at the junction with CO 110, tel. 387-5721. For guided tours along the Alpine Loop, phone **San Juan Tours** at 387-5565.

Pick up 4WD and topo maps at **Outdoor World,** 1234 Greene, tel. 387-5628.

ACCOMMODATIONS

For such a tourist-oriented town, Silverton has a number of good places to stay at decent rates, from hotels in century-old buildings to modern motels. There's not a whole lot in terms of numbers, though, and you'd be wise to make reservations ahead of time. Remember, too, that things slow down in Silverton considerably during the winter, and some of the lodges are available mid-May through September only.

Hotels And Motels
The **Alma House,** 220 E. 10th., tel. (303) 387-5336, is a small (11-room) inn two blocks from the train depot and one block from Greene. Built in 1902 and empty for years, the old stone hotel has been recently restored. Rooms are $32. Owned and operated by the same couple, the red sandstone **Wyman Hotel,** 1371 Greene, tel. 387-5372, was built in 1902 and is located in the upper-downtown area. Rooms are $53. Smoking is not allowed at either the Alma or the Wyman.

You can also get rooms in the **Alpine House,** 1234 Greene, tel. 387-5628 (about $40 for two), and the **Teller House Hotel,** 1250 Greene, tel. 387-5423, built in 1986 and located upstairs from the French Bakery.

Camping And RVing
Molas Lake Park, tel. (303) 387-5410, five miles south of Silverton on Hwy. 550, is a privately run campground with 60 sites on a 40-acre trout-stocked lake. The area gets a certifiable A+ for

scenery. **Silverton Lakes Campground,** tel. 387-5721, has tent and RV sites right next to town at the junction with CO 110. **South Mineral** Forest Service campground just north of town has 23 sites and flush toilets (no showers). Take Hwy. 550 four miles north, then Forest Service Rd. 585 five miles west. Phone the Durango District Office of San Juan National Forest at 247-4874 for reservations or more information.

FOOD

An excellent place to get started in the morning is at the **French Bakery,** 1250 Greene,. tel. (303) 387-5423. Get standard American fare, as well as fresh-baked goods. The large windows looking out on Greene St. make it an ideal people-watching place. You can also get breakfasts at the **Grand Imperial Hotel,** 1221 Greene, tel. 387-5527, where you can get traditional eggs-and-bacon dishes, as well as fancy pancakes and waffles (topped with berries and whipped cream). Prices run $4-7.

For Mexican food, try **Romero's Restaurant y Cantina,** 1151 Greene, tel. 387-5561. Specializing in margaritas, Romero's also serves menudo (a sure sign the place is authentic!). Dinners are in the $5-7 range.

Another recommended Silverton restaurant is **Handlebars,** 117 E. 13th St., where lunch salads (spinach, pasta, and vegie) are about $5 and soups, burgers, and sandwiches are $5-7. Dinners, which include beef and chicken plates, range $7-15.

ENTERTAINMENT AND EVENTS

Although Silverton is absolutely beautiful during the snowy months, its location and elevation make it less a winter than summer destination. Among the highlights of the summer season are the **Jubilee Folk Festival** (late June); **Fourth of July** (parade, fireworks); **Kendall Mountain Run** (13-mile footrace up Kendall Mountain—4,000-ft. altitude gain, mid-July); and the **Hardrockers Holiday Mining Celebration** (tugs-o'-war, drilling competitions, wheelbarrow races, etc., mid-August); and the **Great Rocky Mountain Brass Band Festival** (mid-August).

For more information on these and other Silverton events, contact the Silverton Chamber of Commerce at (303) 387-5654.

SHOPPING

Though Silverton was at one time defined by miners, saloons, gambling halls, and brothels, today the little town is defined by tourists, restaurants, gift shops, and more gift shops. Like several other Colorado mining-camps-turned-tourist-towns (Cripple Creek, Georgetown), Silverton relies heavily on the out-of-town dollar to keep the head of its struggling economy above water, and its main drag (Greene St.) is virtually lined with gift and souvenir shops. So, if you're looking for something to bring home, look no further. And even if you're not, allow yourself a couple of hours to wander up and down Greene St., and down the side streets. Poke your head into the little specialty shops; you'll find the owners very friendly and laid-back (no high-pressure selling in this low-key little town).

In addition to the shops you'd find in most tourist-oriented towns (Christmas, jewelry, minerals, T-shirts, Native American art), Silverton also has a handful of stores specializing in the area's history.

INFORMATION

You'll want to stop in at the two chamber of commerce visitor centers in Silverton. The main one, at the town's entrance, is stocked with literature on Silverton and the surrounding area, and there are staff members to answer questions—open year-round. The second one, the Blair St. Information Booth, on Blair between 12th and 13th, has brochures and information on local businesses, including the menus of many of Silverton's restaurants. There are also picnic tables and public restrooms—open summer only.

You can get information before your visit by writing the **Silverton Chamber of Commerce,** Box 565, Silverton, CO 81433, or by calling (303) 387-5654. Be sure to get copies of the *Silverton-San Juan Vacation Guide,* which includes coupons good at local gift shops, as well as stories on Silverton's history and suggestions for things to do in the area.

TELLURIDE AND VICINITY

A mining town that has turned world-class resort village, Telluride (pop. 1,300; elev. 8,744 feet) is full of juxtapositions and ironies: Gingerbread Victorian homes stand in the shadows of ultra-modern condominium complexes; grizzled lifetime locals share bar space with Austrian ski racers named Wolfgang, while young WASPy passers-through with wannabe dreadlocks hang out on benches on the sidewalk; chic boutiques, new-age bistros, and Southwestern art galleries line the streets; and, in perhaps the most potentially explosive stand-off of all, developers, no-, and slow-growthers stand poised ready to define the town's future according to their own visions.

Situated at the end of a box canyon deep in the San Juan Mountains, Telluride almost overnight has mushroomed from a sleepy little community with summer music and film festivals and some of the best uncrowded skiing in the country to a hot spot attracting the likes of Tom Cruise and Donald Trump. Which, of course, is why there are such strong feelings among the community. Locals have seen real estate prices skyrocket in recent years (a *modest* restored Victorian in town can fetch anywhere from $500,000 to $1,500,000), and people fear the little town will become another Aspen.

In addition to their ambivalence about the gentrification and possible overdevelopment of the town of Telluride, locals are split over the development of Telluride Village, the new megabucks resort at the base of the ski area. Though the deluxe hotels and other lodging promise to pump big money into the economy, and to provide more jobs for Telluridians trying to eke out a living in the canyon, the new housing is clearly aimed at outside budgets. As Telluride Village began to take shape in the late 1980s, and the cost of living in town zoomed skyward, many local workers were forced to move "down valley," where housing was still affordable. One shop owner told me, "Hell, no one who works in town can afford to live here any more."

Apparently things have slowed down a bit, though, and real estate, for example, has reached a sort of plateau. But as long as the supply of developable land is scarce and de-

mand for it high, you can expect housing to command top dollar. And though Telluride's future hangs uncertain, it's still one of the prettiest and classiest places in Colorado. And on a dark, cold December night with a light snow falling softly on deserted side streets and firelight flickering in windows of century-old Victorians, the place becomes truly magical. If you plan to hit the slopes in the morning, it's easy to think you've found paradise.

HISTORY

Telluride's history dates from 1875, when it served as a supply center for several mines—including the Sheridan, Ajax, and Smuggler—that had been staked in the high mountains just east of the little box canyon. Originally known as Columbia, Telluride took its name from tellurium, a sulphurous compound prevalent in the district and often found in the gold itself. (There's little evidence to support the claim of barstool historians that the name comes from "To Hell You Ride," a saying that apparently once described quite accurately the nature of the trip to the rugged and rowdy little town.)

The Rio Grande Southern Railroad arrived in Telluride in 1890, making the camp far more accessible. Almost overnight, the tents and shacks that had lined Colorado Avenue were replaced by homes, shops, brothels, and hotels. By some estimates, over 5,000 people were living in Telluride in the early 1890s.

The New Sheridan Hotel was constructed between 1890 and 1895 (various sources specify both 1891 and 1895). Typifying the lavishness of Colorado's mining-industry-financed hotels, the New Sheridan offered luxurious accommodations for passers-through, as well as a dining room said to rival that at Denver's Brown Palace. Sarah Bernhardt and Lillian Gish were among the hotel's early guests.

Telluride's boom was short-lived, however. After the silver market crashed in 1893, many of the town's mines shut down, and homes and businesses were abandoned. By the last years of the 19th century, overall productivity had

*downtown Telluride
shortly after a light
January snowfall*

STEPHEN METZGER

greatly decreased and the remaining miners were disgruntled; the euphoria of the early part of the decade had vanished. In 1901, mine owners presented workers with new contracts, and guess what? They stipulated more money to owners and management and less to labor. The union struck, though nonunion miners were brought in, resulting in intense standoffs and violence, with the National Guard being called in during the winter of 1904 to impose peace on the town.

Though a handful of mines remained open through the first part of the 20th century, the Bank of Telluride closed, and all but a few people left town. The population in 1930 was 512. Still, Telluride's contribution to Colorado mining history had been impressive. By 1909, the district had produced more than $60 million in gold, silver, copper, lead, and zinc.

Telluride lay remote and mostly idle for most of the mid-century, though its second boom was on the horizon. As early as 1938, the town was realizing its potential as a winter resort area, although poor snowfalls and WW II combined to discourage the idea's first backers. After the war, however, in 1945, Telluride's first rope tow was built. The lift ran for two seasons, lay inoperative for over a decade, and then was rebuilt in 1958 using an old car engine for power. That winter, season passes sold for $5.

It was still another decade, though, before Telluride would make the transition from a tiny ski area used almost exclusively by locals to one that would ultimately attract some of the best and most sophisticated skiers from around the world. In 1968, in a move that could even-

tually be seen as disconcertingly prophetic, businessman Joe Zoline arrived in Telluride from Beverly Hills with plans to develop a "winter recreation area second to none." Work began almost immediately, and Telluride Ski Area was dedicated in April, 1971.

For the next 15 years or so, although the town was again hitting pay dirt, it enjoyed a relatively downscale and unpretentious elegance, guaranteed by its remote location. Though it had a reputation for some of the best skiing—as well as some of the best music and film festivals—in the state, you had to really *want* to go there: While Denver skiers could get to Winter Park in an hour and a half, Telluride was a six- or seven-hour drive, more if the weather was at all threatening.

Then in the late 1980s, Telluride Regional Airport was built, and it became as easy to get to Telluride as to get to Vail or Aspen. Regular flights were offered from Los Angeles, Phoenix, and Albuquerque, and express jets were flying into Telluride daily from Denver. The face and tenor of the town changed dramatically and permanently. By 1990, local waiters and ski-lift operators were no longer renting cheap rooms in town; there weren't any. By now, property values had skyrocketed, and working people for the most part couldn't afford to live in town. Huge resort complexes—hotels and conference centers—were springing up at Telluride Mountain Village. Movie stars and rock musicians were being seen in shops buying sealskin after-ski boots; realtors found themselves dealing with a whole new breed of buyer, folks who flew into town in their own jets.

Still, though, at least as of last inspection, Telluride has managed to survive the onslaught of outside money. As long as local music promoters continue to book (and sell tickets to) acts like James Taylor, Emmy Lou Harris, and John Prine, and as long as the mountain continues to attract skiers to whom nothing matters but deep snow and steep slopes, the town should retain most of its integrity and charm, and should remain one of Colorado's true treasures.

Historical Walking Tour

The Town of Telluride has published a map and guide to historical Telluride. With over a dozen sites, the tour includes the **San Miguel County Courthouse** (in use since 1887), the **town hall** (built in 1883), the **New Sheridan Hotel** (early 1890s), as well as several private residences dating from before the turn of the century. The map and guide are printed in the vacation guide in *Telluride Magazine*.

PARKS AND RECREATION

This is why folks both live and visit here. Located in one of the prettiest pockets of Colorado's gorgeous San Juan Mountains, Telluride offers a range of activities guaranteed to satisfy even the most demanding outdoor enthusiast. Though best known for its downhill skiing, Telluride is also an excellent base for myriad other recreational pursuits as well, from hiking, horseback riding, and mountain biking to Jeep touring, fishing, and whitewater rafting.

In addition, it's a great place just to experience *being* outdoors. In the fall, when the aspen leaves turn to gold and crimson, there may not be a lovelier place on earth.

Downhill Skiing

Known until recently as a mountain geared mostly toward advanced (and better!) skiers, Telluride has spent the last several summers cutting more trails and opening things up for intermediate and beginning skiers as well. The mountain straddles a high ridge, which provides two separate base areas. Two lifts are based in town and take skiers up the steep face that looks down on Telluride's streets; the main base area is accessible by driving around the ridge to Telluride Mountain Village, where you'll find the ski school, administrative offices, and other base facilities. A free skier shuttle runs regularly between the two areas.

Generally, the advanced and expert skiing is on the town-of-Telluride side. Several of these runs—Spiral Stairs, for example—offer some of the steepest, nastiest lift-serviced skiing in the country. In addition, you'll find excellent bump skiing over here, as well as the best powder—the northern exposure means snow will stay better here longer. Meanwhile, the Telluride Mountain Village side caters more to intermediate and beginning skiers, with lots of long, sweeping runs, perfect for GS-style cruising, in packs or all by your lonesome.

With 10 chairlifts servicing 1,055 acres, Telluride has one of the longest vertical drops in the state: 3,165 feet. In addition, a *Snow Country* magazine reader poll recently ranked its lift lines

Olympic gold medalist Phil Mahre crosses the finish line just ahead of his dual-slalom competitor.

STEPHEN METZGER

Telluride Mountain Village under construction in January 1991

as the state's shortest. The terrain is officially designated 24% beginner, 51% intermediate, and 25% advanced and expert. **Free tours** of the mountain are offered daily at 10 a.m. Look for the guides in the turquoise ski parkas. The Telluride Ski School includes instruction in Tele-marking and snowboarding.

For more information on Telluride Ski Area (ski school, lift tickets, etc.), phone (303) 728-4424. For **snow conditions,** phone 728-3614.

Cross-country Skiing
Nordic skiing in all its forms is very popular in Telluride. Telemarkers, skaters, and tourers all find plenty of action. If you just want to get some fresh air and check out the valley a little bit, try the **Town Park and River Trail,** which is maintained by the city and runs east from town park along the San Juan River. **Telluride Resort Nordic Center** is a full-service center located at Telluride Mountain Village. Sunshine Express lift at the ski area provides access to over 30 km of excellent trails of varying ability levels. You can also arrange guided backcountry tours. Phone (303) 728-4424.

For the more ambitious, **San Juan Hut Systems** offers a series of backcountry cabins linked by cross-country ski trails. The huts are five to six miles apart, and the scenic trails are skiable even for beginning Nordic skiers. For information or reservations, phone 728-6935.

WHEN THE SNOW MELTS

City Parks
Located on the east side of town on the San Juan River, **Telluride Town Park** is perfectly befitting the little community's character and charm. In addition to some two dozen camp-sites (no hookups, small fee), the park has pic-nic facilities, volleyball, basketball, and tennis courts, playground equipment, a skateboard park, and a small lake where kids can catch trout recently arrived from the hatchery. For in-formation or camping reservations, phone (303) 728-3071. **San Miguel County Park** is a very nice little picnic area on the San Miguel River in Placerville, about 15 miles northwest of Tel-luride (no overnight camping).

Cycling
The old mining roads twisting and slicing through-out the San Juan Mountains make Telluride a natural for mountain biking, and the sport has really taken off in recent years. For the ultimate southern Colorado mountain-bike experience, check out **San Juan Hut Systems'** Telluride-to-Moab trip. This 215-mile week-long tour fea-tures stops at six cabins along the way, and all you have to do is ride (you can go with or without a guide). The huts are 35 miles apart and each has 12 padded bunks (with blankets), a propane stove, kitchen utensils, a wood-burning stove,

and firewood. You can also arrange day-trips through San Juan Hut Systems. Guided tours start at about $30 a day. For information or reservations, write Box 1663, Telluride, CO 81435, or phone (303) 728-6935. In town, stop by 224 E. Colorado.

For accessories, tips on biking in the Telluride area, or to rent bikes, stop in at **Paragon Ski and Sports,** 217 W. Colorado, tel. 728-4525, or **Olympic Sports,** 150 W. Colorado, tel. 728-4477.

Guided bicycle tours are available through Paragon Sports and Olympic Sports. Get topo maps of Uncompahgre National Forest from the **Norwood Ranger District Office,** 1760 Grand, Norwood, CO 81423, tel. 327-4261.

Golf

The 18-hole, 7,009-foot **Telluride Golf Course** is located at Telluride Mountain Village, five miles south of town. For information and tee times, phone (303) 728-8000.

Hiking

Hiking is one of the best ways to get out and enjoy Southwestern Colorado, and the Telluride area offers a wide array of trails, from short walks to backcountry excursions. The town's de rigueur outing is to **Bridal Veil Falls.** This two-mile roundtrip walk takes about two hours and is relatively easy (dirt road), leading to the largest waterfall in the state; water cascades off a 425-foot cliff. Begin at Pandora Mill on the east end of town. Total elevation gain is about 1,000 feet. The two-mile **Judd Weibe Trail** begins at the north end of Aspen St., where it crosses Cornet Creek. Allow up to three hours, but expect excellent views. Along the way, you'll also pass the remnants of Telluride's old "pesthouse," where horse-drawn wagons once carried Telluride's contagious to quarantine. Another hike known for its stunning scenery begins in town at Pine St. and climbs two miles and 1,300 feet in elevation through **Bear Creek Canyon** to a multi-tiered waterfall.

For complete information on hiking in the area, pick up a copy of Susan Kees's *Telluride Hiking Guide* (Pruett Publishing Co., Boulder), available in bookstores and some outdoors shops in the area. Get topo maps from the Forest Service District Office in Norwood, tel. (303) 327-4261.

Fishing

Lots of good fishing in Southwestern Colorado, particularly in the San Juan Mountains, and Telluride's as good a place as any to base yourself. Though you won't find the lunker Mackinaw that you might at Blue Mesa or Shadow Mountain Reservoir, there's plenty of good stream fishing, especially for those who'd rather entice a native fish to rise to a hand-tied fly than hook a larger hatchery fish on bait or hardware.

The west fork of the **Dolores River,** which parallels CO 145 south of town, has rainbows, browns, and cutthroats. Fish for rainbows in the faster water and rapids below pools; fish for browns in deeper, slower water. Closer to town, the **San Miguel River** is regularly stocked with pan-size rainbows, as is the little lake at **Town Park,** an excellent spot to give younger kids their first lessons in the sport (fishing here is for kids 12 and younger only).

Popular lakes in the area include **Alta Lake, Priest Lake,** and **Trout Lake,** all accessible via CO 145 south of town; **Woods Lake** is west on CO 145 toward Placerville.

For information, licenses, equipment, and guided fly-fishing trips, stop in at **Olympic Sports,** 150 W. Colorado Ave., tel. (303) 728-4477 or **Telluride Outside,** 666 W. Colorado, 728-3895, the latter also offering a fly-fishing school.

Rafting

Though most Telluride-area streams are too small for rafting, you can book a range of trips on other southwestern Colorado rivers through **Telluride Outside,** 666 W. Colorado, tel. (303) 728-3895.

Four-wheel-drive Tours

Four-wheel-drive rigs and Southwestern Colorado go together like motor scooters and Bangkok. Not only are they ideal for simply getting around in the winter, but in the summer they're the only (well, okay, quickest and easiest . . .) way to some of the region's more secluded and scenic spots.

The mountains around Telluride are interlaced with old mining roads perfect for four-wheeling. And since the roads have already been cut, your contribution to environmental damage is limited. (Do stay on those roads, though: As tempting as it might be to take a

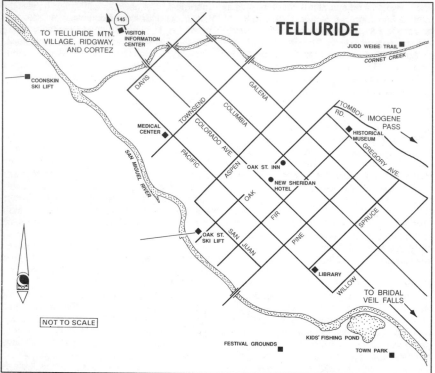

TELLURIDE

TO TELLURIDE MTN. VILLAGE, RIDGWAY, AND CORTEZ

VISITOR INFORMATION CENTER

JUDD WEIBE TRAIL

CORNET CREEK

COONSKIN SKI LIFT

DAVIS

GALENA

TOWNSEND

COLUMBIA

TOMBOY RD.

TO IMOGENE PASS

MEDICAL CENTER

COLORADO AVE.

HISTORICAL MUSEUM

GREGORY AVE.

PACIFIC

ASPEN

OAK ST. INN

NEW SHERIDAN HOTEL

SAN MIGUEL RIVER

OAK

FIR

SPRUCE

OAK ST. SKI LIFT

SAN JUAN

PINE

LIBRARY

WILLOW

TO BRIDAL VEIL FALLS

NOT TO SCALE

KIDS' FISHING POND

FESTIVAL GROUNDS

TOWN PARK

© MOON PUBLICATIONS, INC.

short cut across a high-mountain meadow, keep in mind how vulnerable and fragile these ecosystems are.)

Imogene Pass (elev. 13,509 feet) is the cliff-hanging historical route that connects Telluride and Ouray (about 18 miles). You'll pass both the abandoned Tomboy Mine and the remains of Fort Peabody, which was a guard station during the labor-management conflicts at the turn of the century. For neither the timid nor the amateur back-roadster, the pass is as difficult as it is scenic. Experienced drivers: Take Oak St. north, and turn east onto the Forest Service-maintained pass road.

A much easier and less dangerous 4WD route is **Ophir Pass** (elev. 11,740 feet), an 1881 toll road that connected Telluride and Silverton. Today, it's one of the most popular backcountry scenic routes in the area. Note: This is a one-way road, with traffic moving east to west. Start in Silverton, and go north on Hwy. 550 about five miles; the road is unmarked, but directly across from it is a sign for Red Mountain Summit (five miles). From Silverton to Ophir is about 45 miles.

For information, tours, and 4WD rentals, contact **Telluride Outside,** 666 W. Colorado, tel. (303) 728-3895.

ACCOMMODATIONS

Because of Telluride's remote location, and the fact that it's grown increasingly popular in recent years, especially in winter, lodge owners can pretty much get whatever they want for a room. Though not yet on a par with Aspen, rooms in Telluride are expensive (winter high season is from mid-December till just after the first of the year; summer rates go up during festivals and special events). If you can, plan to come when things are slower. During January, for example, rooms are the least expensive (of the ski season), and the skiing's at its best.

For a complete listing of accommodations available in Telluride, or to make reservations, contact **Telluride Central Reservations** at tel. (303) 728-4431 or (800) 525-3455.

Rooms In Town

For a real taste of Telluride, try the recently re-modeled **New Sheridan Hotel,** tel. (303) 728-4351. Rates for doubles range from about $30 (shared bath, low season) to $150 (private bath, high season, five-day minimum)—quite a jump from the early '70s when a room here ran 80 bucks a month (of course only 500 people lived in Telluride then, and it was sort of an outpost-on-the-frontier resort). The **Victorian Inn,** tel. 728-6601 or (800) 537-2614, though built in 1976, blends in gracefully with the surrounding 19th-century structures and is located within a short walk of Coonskin and Oak Street lifts. Rooms go for about $40-110.

Another distinctly Telluride inn is the **San Sophia,** tel. 728-3001 or (800) 537-4781. This elegant bed and breakfast is located right downtown near the base of the lifts and has doubles starting at about $80. You can also get good, comfortable rooms at comparatively reasonable rates at the **Bear Creek Bed and Breakfast,** tel. 728-6681, and at the **Dahl House Bed and Breakfast,** tel. 728-4158.

Bargains?

You'll probably find the least expensive rooms in town at the **Oak Street Inn,** tel. (303) 728-3383. A member of Youth Hostels of America, this little lodge, located one block off the main drag, offers rooms starting at about $25 (shared bath). Don't expect anything fancy and you won't be disappointed. Discounts offered to AYH members. Showers $3 for non-guests.

Lodging At Telluride Mountain Village

The newly developed Telluride Mountain Village has plenty of lodging in condominium complexes and upscale hotels. Though they don't offer the charm of staying in one of Telluride's historical hotels or refurbished old homes, they do offer convenience and just about every amenity you can imagine, including ski and golf

packages. The newest and fanciest hotel is the **Doral Telluride Resort and Spa,** tel. (303) 728-6800, a 200-room, $60-million number with a huge athletic club, as well as conference and banquet facilities. Rates for rooms range from $150 to $350 a night.

Pennington's Mountain Village Inn, tel. 728-5337, is a smaller and less imposing lodge (12 units) on a grassy knoll; one of the more attractive inns at the village, Pennington's has been the site of many weddings and other gatherings. Doubles start at about $140.

FOOD

Gone Skiing?

Telluride is first and foremost a ski town, and if there's been a good dump during the night, it's not unusual for a restaurant to shut its doors for the day. Don't be surprised when looking for breakfast to find signs on doors that read, "Powder day. Closed. See you this afternoon."

Start Me Up

The **Excelsior Cafe,** right downtown at 200 W. Colorado, tel. (303) 728-4250, serves espressos, cappuccinos, and other coffees guaranteed to put a bite in your morning, as well as pastries and other goodies. Another local favorite is **Gregor's,** 217 E. Colorado, tel. 728-3334, where you can get espressos, regular coffees, pastries, and complete breakfasts. A casual café attracting everyone from white rastas on the road to long-time Telluridians, Gregor's also serves lunch and dinner, with emphasis on health and vegetarian dishes.

Other Telluride Restaurants

The **Roma Bar and Cafe,** 133 E. Colorado, tel. (303) 728-3669, serves excellent Italian food in an anything-but-pretentious atmosphere (listen to the pool balls smacking each other in the next room). Entrees are in the $9-13 range, and you can also order off the appetizer-pizza menu (pizzas start at about $10). The Roma Bar also offers a skier's breakfast special—eggs, toast, and potatoes for around $2. **Floradora,** tel. 728-3888, supposedly named after a couple of Telluride pioneers (Flora and Dora, who worked the Red Light District) serves excellent lunches and dinners at reasonable prices. From burgers

The New Sheridan
Hotel in downtown
Telluride dates from
the early 1890s.

STEPHEN METZGER

to steaks, chicken, and Mexican dishes, with specials daily and a soup du jour. Great bar for munching nachos and watching a game.

Another Telluride favorite is **Eddie's**, 300 W. Colorado, tel. 728-5335. In addition to pizza, either whole or by the slice, Eddie's serves great salads, sandwiches, burgers, and pasta dinners ($5-14). Two relatively new restaurants, **Casa San Miguel,** tel. 728-0171, which serves Tex-Mex, and the **One World Cafe,** tel. 728-5530, have quickly earned solid reputations for good grub. For Asian food, try **Honga's Lotus Petal,** tel. 728-5134.

Grocery Stores

Thankfully, City Market and Safeway haven't arrived in Telluride yet, though there are several small independent grocers. **The Natural Source,** 124 E. Colorado, tel. (303) 728-4833, sells organic produce, bulk foods, vitamins, and other health products. **Rose Food Mart,** 700 W. Colorado, tel. 728-3124, and **Village Market,** 157 S. Fir, tel. 728-4566, both carry meats, produce, and other grocery products, with emphases on natural and health foods.

ENTERTAINMENT

And A Good Saloon In Every Single Town

Sometimes you're in the mood for something smoky, poolly, loud, and local. The **Last Dollar Saloon,** 100 E. Colorado, is it. Put your quarter down on the table, order a draft, and soak in

the local flavor. During the summer the talk is of softball—aging adolescents' tales of catches almost made and hard grounders almost run out—and during the winter it's of skiing—how much snow'll fall tonight, the awesome bumps under Number 9, the new Rossi slalom ski. Just know that you'll have to wash the Marlboro out of your sweater (and hair) in the morning.

For live rock and rhythm and blues, check out **Fly Me To The Moon Saloon,** 132 E. Colorado, tel. (303) 728-6666. You can also sometimes hear live tunes at the bar at **One World Cafe,** 728-5530.

CALENDAR

In addition to Telluride's better-known events— the bluegrass, jazz, and film festivals—the community offers dozens of other intriguing workshops, conferences, bike and foot races, and other festivals. In early June, you can attend the simultaneous **Wine Festival** and **Balloon Rally.** Taste fine wines or sip champagne as the skies fill with colorful hot-air balloons. The world-famous **Telluride Bluegrass and Country Music Festival** is the highlight of the summer. Hotels and campgrounds fill up, and music fills the valley from the stages at Town Park. Wednesday through Friday, lesser-known acts take the stage, while Friday night through Sunday afternoon, players such as Bill Monroe, James Taylor, John Prine, and the Nitty Gritty Dirt Band entertain the crowds. **Talking Gourds** in late June is an annual gathering of poets, storytellers, and performance artists for workshops, readings, and shows. **Fourth of July** has always been a time of festivities and fireworks in Telluride, with much of the action in Town Park.

The **Telluride Jazz Festival** in early August began in the late 1970s and has featured mainstream and experimental artists from around the world, including Herbie Hancock, Branford and Wynton Marsalis, Etta James, and the Neville Brothers. **Wild Mushrooms Telluride** is a three-day celebration of the edible fungus. Included in the late August festival are lectures, workshops, identification hikes, and cooking and tasting events.

Over Labor Day weekend, the **Telluride Film Festival** attracts big- and not-so-big-name directors, writers, and other scholars to retrospectives and national and world premieres. Seminars, featuring directors and actors, take place in Town Park and are free. Finally, the week-long **Telluride Hang Gliding Festival** in mid-September is the longest-running and largest hang-gliding affair in the world. Top flyers sponsor lectures and workshops and compete in the World Hang Gliding Championships.

For festival tickets and information, phone (800) 525-3455.

Western Photo Workshops

Join some of the West's best photographers—Linde Waidhofer, True Redd, Bob Caputo, Bill Ellzey, and others—in a series of workshops designed to improve your artistic vision and technique. Among the workshops offered: composition and design, wildflower shooting, the "Autumn Eye," "Winter in the Rockies," and "Canyon Country." Classes run two to six days and cost $225-950.

For a full brochure, or for more information, write Western Photo Workshops, Box 968, Telluride, CO 81435, or phone (303) 728-3727.

SHOPPING

Although no Aspen, Telluride does claim a number of moderately fancy specialty shops, galleries, and boutiques where without a moviestar income you're not going to be able to do much more than look and hope. In addition, some of the ski shops display duds that are far

more flash than function. Still, isn't that partly what vacation shopping's all about? Who wants to *shop* at a surplus store?

Whether you're looking to buy or simply to ogle, Telluride's galleries are a kick to poke around in. With primarily Native American- and Southwestern-flavored artwork, the shops sell pottery, jewelry, rugs, paintings, prints, and sculpture. Check out **Golden West,** 101 W. Colorado, tel. (303) 728-3664; **Telluride Gallery of Fine Art,** 130 E. Colorado, tel. 728-4242; **Brody Gallery,** 575 W. Colorado, tel. 728-3734; and **Ellison Gallery,** 200 W. Colorado, tel. 728-3980.

If you're looking for souvenirs, you'll find plenty of T-shirt and cap stores on Colorado Avenue.

SERVICES

The offices of the **Telluride Police Department** are in the town hall building at 113 W. Columbia; phone (303) 728-3071. The **Telluride Medical Center** is at 500 W. Pacific; phone 728-3848. The **post office** is at 101 E. Colorado.

Recycling

Drop off most recyclables at the **Telluride Recycling Center,** 237 E. Pacific, or at the transfer station for **United Waste and Recycle,** 330 Colorado Avenue.

INFORMATION

Telluride's **Chamber Resort Association** operates a 24-hour automated **visitor information center** on the west side of town (on your right as you approach). This is an excellent place to pick up brochures and other information on accommodations and things to do in the area. Before your visit, write Box 653, Telluride, CO 81435, or phone (303) 728-6475. For lodging and airline information and reservations, phone (800) 525-3455.

Telluride has two excellent newspapers, the daily *Telluride Times-Journal* and the weekly *Telluride Today*. Check both (25 cents each) for word on local events as well as on matters of interest to the community and visitors alike. Peter Shelton, of nearby Ridgway, named America's Ski Writer of the Year three times, has a regular column in the *Times-Journal*.

Telluride Magazine, published twice a year (summer and winter editions), is rife with information on things to do, and where to eat, stay, and play; it also profiles local celebrities, developers, and developments. Though this is a very commercial and slick publication, heavy on promotional fluff, reading between the lines will teach you a lot about Telluride. It's available at the Chamber Resort Association Center and at most real estate offices in town.

Between The Covers Books And Music, 224 W. Colorado, tel. 728-4504, carries an excellent selection of travel- and Colorado-related publications, with a lot of books of local interest. The **Wilkinson Public Library,** tel. 728-4519 or 728-6613, is located at 134 S. Spruce—closed Sunday and Monday.

For **road and weather conditions,** phone 728-3330.

TRANSPORTATION

Considering its remote, box-canyon location, Telluride's remarkably easy to get into and out of, thanks (or curses, depending on your perspective) largely to the new jet airport in town. **Mesa Airlines,** tel. (800) MESA-AIR, **Skywest,** tel. (800) 453-9417, and **United Express,** tel. (800) 241-6522, offer passenger service to **Telluride Regional Airport.** And once in town, you'll have no trouble at all getting around. You can walk in five minutes from one end of Telluride to the other, and free shuttles run regularly to Telluride Village and the base of the lifts (or you can ski directly from town, with two of the resort's lifts beginning two blocks from the main drag).

Taxis And Local Transportation
Mountain Limo runs free shuttle buses regularly between the town of Telluride and the main ski area/Telluride Village. For routes and

more information, phone (303) 728-4191. **Skip's Taxi,** tel. 278-6667, and **Telluride Transit,** tel. 728-6000, provide local get-around transportation and will meet all flights at the Telluride airport (with 24-hour advance notice). You can also get information on ground transportation by phoning the resort chamber at (800) 525-3455.

HIGHWAY 145 SOUTH TO CORTEZ

One of the most scenic legs of the **San Juan Scenic Byway,** this 80-mile stretch of state highway cuts across San Juan National Forest and drops out of the San Juan Mountains toward the Four Corners area and the Ute Mountain Indian Reservation. About 10 miles out of Telluride, you'll pass through the tiny town of Ophir, a silver camp named for the location of the mines of mythical King Solomon. During the 1870s, the little community boasted some 500 people. Today, it's the starting point for the Ophir Pass road to Silverton.

Lizard Head Pass (elev. 10,222 feet), just a few miles south of Ophir, is named for the 400-foot-high monolith northwest of the highway. Apparently, the needle more closely resembled the head of a lizard before a slab of rock broke off.

Along this route, you'll drive along the east fork of the Dolores River, and pass by several high mountain lakes. The highway also parallels the west fork of the Dolores, a few miles to the west. About five miles north of Rico, you can catch a Forest Service-maintained dirt road that will take you over to and down the west fork, before rejoining CO 145 near the confluence of the two forks, just west of Stoner. From here south, the Dolores runs alongside the highway for 15 miles, past the town of the same name, before feeding into McPhee Reservoir (see "Cortez and Vicinity" following).

CORTEZ AND VICINITY

Seat of Montezuma County, Cortez (pop. 9,000; elev. 6,200 feet) is the closest large town to Mesa Verde National Park. Situated in the heart of the Four Corners area, the community is surrounded by scrubby mesas and canyonlands once home to tens of thousands of Anasazis. Between about A.D. 550 and 1,300, the Anasazi farmed this area, living in elaborate "cities" of stone pueblos, some clinging to cliffsides, some freestanding. The most well known, of course, are the cliff dwellings at Mesa Verde, but this entire area is full of ruins, and the region is remote enough that some of them will probably remain undiscovered forever.

Cortez was first settled by non-natives in 1885, when a group of farmers arrived in the area with plans to irrigate crops with water from the Dolores River. Within a year, the Mitchell Springs Project was pumping water from the river into nearby fields, and in 1887 the town of Cortez was officially founded. The town has served throughout the 20th century as a trading and supply center for local farmers and sheep and cattle ranchers—Ute, Navajo, Hispanic, and white. Recently, tourism has become of more importance, as Cortez capitalizes not only on its proximity to Four Corners-area ruins but to prime recreation areas as well.

SIGHTS

Anasazi Heritage Center

Located 10 miles north of Cortez and three miles west of Dolores, this BLM-operated research and display center includes laboratories, collection areas, a library, theater, museum, and gift shop, as well as a reproduction of an Anasazi dwelling. The center houses nearly two million artifacts and documents, and the museum is highlighted by several hands-on displays: Grind corn like the Anasazi did or examine other seeds under a microscope.

The Anasazi Heritage Center, 27501 CO 184 just west of downtown Dolores, is open daily in the summer 9 a.m.-5 p.m. and 9 a.m.-4 p.m. in the winter. For more information, phone (303) 882-4811. Admission is free.

Lowry Pueblo Ruins

Occupied by some 100 Anasazis between A.D. 800 and 1000, Lowry was restored in the mid-1960s. Lowry Ruins are located nine miles west of Pleasant View off Hwy. 666. Pick up a brochure detailing the self-guiding tour.

Dove Creek

Still farther north on Hwy. 666 is Dove Creek, seat of Dolores County, where many Dust Bowl farmers ended up after fleeing Oklahoma in the 1930s. Zane Grey lived here for a brief period, and his *Riders of the Purple Sage* is supposedly set here.

In the summer of 1990, two University of Colorado hikers who were tracking bighorn sheep in the Dove Creek area stumbled on the virtually untouched ruins of a 1,100-year-old Anasazi village. Mountain Sheep Village, as the site was named, is significant to archaeologists for several reasons, not the least of which is that it is one of the northernmost Anasazi sites ever discovered. The village, which dates from around A.D. 800, probably consisted of around 200 rooms on six acres and housed between 150 and 200 people.

Not much more populated than the abandoned Anasazi site, Dove Creek consists of several small businesses, a couple of gas station/mini-marts, the **Budget Motel,** tel. (303) 667-2234, and the **Country RV Campground and Store,** tel. 677-2850.

PARKS AND RECREATION

Cortez City Park

Located next to the Cortez Visitor and Colorado Welcome centers, this grassy hillside park has very good picnic facilities—plenty of shade—as well as a kids' playground, basketball hoops, and a public swimming pool.

Native American dances are performed free at the Cortez Visitor Center in the park, Tues. and Thurs. evenings at 7 p.m., June-August. For information, phone (303) 565-3414.

McPhee Reservoir

In 1987, when McPhee Dam was completed and McPhee Reservoir filled in, the world lost some of its most gorgeous river and canyon country, as well as some of its most valuable archaeological treasures. The Dolores River was backed up, the canyon flooded, and hundreds of ancient Anasazi ruins, and probably hundreds of thousands of artifacts, now lie deep beneath the surface of the lake, one of the largest in Colorado. Perhaps, though, this is a better place for them. Leaving them undisturbed at the bottom of a reservoir is certainly better than destroying them to build roadways, and maybe more ethical than transplanting them to museum storage rooms. At any rate, as you look out across the water, think about the people who lived in the river valley some 1,100-1,300 years ago, farming beans, corn, and squash, and building intricate stone pueblos. Think about nature's *true* course.

McPhee Reservoir is located about 12 miles north of Cortez via Hwy. 160, CO 145, and a short access road—also via CO 184. The lake offers boating, waterskiing, camping, and fishing (for rainbow trout as well as warm-water fish such as bass and bluegill). Two Forest Service campgrounds, **McPhee** and **House Creek,** offer a combined 133 sites (no showers at either). For information, phone (303) 882-7296; for reservations, phone (800) 283-CAMP.

River Running

The Dolores River is one of western Colorado's premier streams, though McPhee Dam has impacted it in still-untold ways. Stretches are still runable, however, with several Four-Corners-area outfitters offering trips. Among them: **Durango Rivertrippers,** 720 Main, Durango, tel. (303) 259-0289; **Peregrine Outfitters,** also in Durango, tel. 385-7600; and **Wilderness Aware,** tel. (719) 395-2112 (Buena Vista).

PRACTICALITIES

Accommodations

A junction town and base for folks exploring Mesa Verde National Park, Cortez offers plenty of relatively inexpensive lodging, with numerous motels located on the main routes through town (Main St. and Broadway). Among the least expensive digs in the town are the rooms at the **Bel Rau Lodge,** 2040 E. Main, tel. (303) 565-3738. Doubles are about $30. The Cortez **Super 8 Motel,** 505 E. Main, tel. 565-8888, also has rooms for two starting at about $30.

The **Anasazi Motor Inn,** 666 S. Broadway, tel. 565-3773, is one of the nicer lodges in Cortez and has doubles running $40-65. At the **Best Western Sands,** 1120 E. Main, tel. 565-3761, doubles start at $42, and at the **Best Western Turquoise Motor Inn,** 535 E. Main, tel. 565-3778, rooms for two go for $50-65.

You'll also find several RV campgrounds in the Cortez area, including the **Cortez-Mesa Verde KOA,** east of downtown on Hwy. 160, tel. 565-9301, **La Mesa RV Campground,** 2430 E. Main, tel. 565-7156, and the **Lazy-G Campground and Motel,** at the Hwy. 160-CO 145 junction, tel. 565-8577 or (800) 628-2183.

Food

Cortez offers lots of fast-food restaurants and trucker-style cafés. In addition, the town has several longtime favorites that have been feeding locals and passers-through for years. **Stromsted's,** 1020 S. Broadway, tel. (303) 565-1257, is highly regarded for its standard American fare (beef, chicken, seafood), as well as its views from the patio of Mesa Verde; entrees run about $10-18. The **M and M Truckstop and Family Restaurant,** 7006 Hwy. 160, tel. 565-6511, is a classic roadhouse serving good food in the tradition its name implies—open 24 hours a day.

If you've been out in the backcountry living off freeze-dried campfood and just feel like binging, try the **Warsaw Inn Restaurant,** Hwy. 160 E., at the junction with CO 145, tel. 565-8585, where a full-service, all-you-can-eat smorgasbord awaits empty tummies.

Shopping

In the heart of Native American country, Cortez has more than a sampling of Native American gift shops and "trading posts." If you're looking for authentic art—jewelry, sculpture, kachina dolls, etc.—expect to pay for it. The work has gotten very popular in recent years, and gone are the days when you could get a Navajo rug for $50. You'll also find that the prices don't vary a whole lot from one store to the next, though you still should shop and compare. Also, don't fall for the ubiquitous "50% off sale." Seems jewelry is *always* 50% off.

One store worth checking out is **Mesa Verde Pottery and Gallery Southwest,** 27601 Hwy. 160 E., tel. (303) 565-4492. Even if you're not interested in buying, poke your head in and take a look around—in addition to quality art, you'll also find inexpensive souvenirs.

Services

The offices of the **Cortez Police Department** are located at 601 N. Mildred; phone (303) 565-8441. The **Montezuma County Sheriff** is also at 601 N. Mildred; phone 565-8444 (or 565-8441 in emergencies). **Southwest Memorial Hospital** is at 1311 N. Mildred; phone 565-6666. The Cortez

post office is at 35 S. Beech; phone 565-3181.

Information

The **Cortez Visitor Center** and a **Colorado Welcome Center** are housed in an adobe-style building at City Park on Main Street. Stop in for information on lodging, dining, recreation, and sightseeing in Cortez, the Four Corners area, and the rest of Colorado. For information before your visit, write **Cortez Area Chamber of Commerce,** Box 968, Cortez, CO 81321, or phone (303) 565-3414 or (800) 346-6526.

For **road and weather information,** phone 565-4511.

FOUR CORNERS AREA

Four Corners is the only place in the United States where the borders of four different states meet. Colorado, New Mexico, Arizona, and Utah all touch here, and the spot is commemorated by an inlaid slab of concrete and a small visitor center.

This is the heart of Native American country. The Navajo, Ute, and Hopi tribes all lay claim to land nearby—the Navajo and Ute reservations abut here, and the Navajos, particularly, count the country around the Four Corners area among its most sacred. As you drive through, you can see why: It's a haunting and strangely beautiful land, miles and miles of barren plains marked by sudden mesas, red rock, and bizarre sandstone cliffs crumbling and melting away like alien landscapes in a Steven Spielberg film. The hills, dotted with juniper and piñon, roll away like the soft waves of an ocean current to meet the deep sky on a far horizon.

FOUR CORNERS MONUMENT

A stone slab marks the spot where all four states' borders meet, and tourists gather for the requisite photo opportunity (pose on all fours—a foot in Arizona, a foot in Utah, a hand in Colorado, and a hand in New Mexico, and bring a slide of *that* back to show your friends . . .). Native Americans, all of whom are licensed, have booths set up near the parking lot and sell jewelry, pottery, sand paintings, and snacks and

refreshments. Maps, brochures, and drinking water are available at the small visitor center, and there are portable toilets in the parking lot. To get to the monument from Cortez, continue south on Hwy. 160 for about 38 miles and watch for the signs. The monument is open 7 a.m.-8 p.m., and entrance is $1 per vehicle.

HOVENWEEP NATIONAL MONUMENT

Straddling the Colorado-Utah state line, Hovenweep National Monument consists of six individual ruins, although only one of them, Square Tower, is easily and commonly visited. Built by the Anasazi between A.D. 1000 and 1200, the pueblos, like those at Mesa Verde and Chaco Canyon, were abandoned by 1300. The buildings are characterized by tall square, circular, oval, and D-shaped towers, some of them appearing almost medieval.

The ruins at Hovenweep (a Ute word meaning "Deserted Valley") were first photographed in 1874 by William Henry Jackson. The site was explored in 1917-18 by the Smithsonian Institition, which lobbied for its designation as a national monument; it was given that status in 1923.

The headquarters of Hovenweep are at Square Tower Pueblos, across the border in Utah, though you can approach the monument from the Colorado side; neither road in is paved, and though they're well maintained they can get pretty nasty during summer's regular afternoon storms. At headquarters, you can get maps and advice for exploring the other ruins, Holly, Cutthroat Castle, Cajon, Horseshoe, and Hackberry (none of which you can drive to). To get to Hovenweep National Monument from Cortez, go south for three miles on Hwy. 160, and turn west on McElmo Canyon Road. From there, it's 39 miles to the monument (you'll turn north again just over the Utah state line). You can also get there from Pleasant View and Lowry Ruins (see "Sights" under "Cortez and Vicinity" above"). From Pleasant View (20 miles north of Cortez on Hwy. 666), go west 27 miles. The turnoff is well marked.

Hovenweep Campground, which is operated year-round by the National Park Service, has 31 sites and is open on a first-come, first-served basis ($3). For more information on the campground or the monument, write Mesa Verde National Park, CO 81330, or phone (303) 529-4465.

UTE MOUNTAIN TRIBAL PARK

Encompassing 125,000 acres of the Ute Mountain Indian Reservation south of Cortez, this is a sanctuary set aside to preserve the Anasazi ruins of the region. Native Americans lead day-hikes and backcountry overnighters into a gamut of ruins and remains of the ancient culture: cliff dwellings, freestanding pueblos, and petroglyphs.

Be forewarned, though: This may be the most natural and authentic way to see the ruins (no German tour buses), but it's not for lightweights. You'll travel by your own rig over 40 miles of dirt road, hike narrow trails into remote parts of the park, and scramble up primitive ladders to secluded kivas.

Tours usually begin around 8 a.m. June through Oct. and meet at the **Ute Mountain Pottery Plant** 15 miles south of Cortez on Hwy. 666. Be sure to call ahead. Tours are often delayed. For reservations and information, write Ute Mountain Tribal Park, Towaoc, CO 81334, or phone (303) 565-3751, ext. 282, or 565-8548.

MESA VERDE NATIONAL PARK AND VICINITY

Mesa Verde ("Green Table") is an 80-square-mile plateau rising 1,600 feet from the surrounding desert and river valley. As early as A.D. 550, Anasazi were living on the plateau, mainly in the shelter of the many narrow canyons that cleave its top. By 1200, their crude shelters had developed into lavish communities, and multistory pueblos were being built into the cliffsides. By the middle of the 13th century, as many as 5,000 people were living in pueblos scattered about the mesa, and the site was a bustling trade center for other pueblos and communities throughout the Four Corners area. Today, the ruins at Mesa Verde National Park are some of the world's largest and best-preserved testaments to ancient civilization.

The first whites to see the cliff dwellings at Mesa Verde were probably members of an 1874 U.S. Geological and Geographic Survey party. Among them was photographer William Henry Jackson, who took the first photos of the ruins. Six years later, New York journalist Virginia Donaghe McClurg explored the mesa, discovering still more ruins, among them one she called "Brownstone Front," which is today known as Balcony House.

The mesa's main ruins were discovered quite by accident, however. On Dec. 18, 1888, Mancos Valley ranchers Richard Wetherill and Charlie Mason were riding across the mesa in search of stray cattle. As they peered over a canyon rim, they were shocked to see the ruins of Cliff Palace—several stories high with 200 rooms and 23 kivas. They scrambled down into the canyon and explored the ruin, taking with them bits of pottery and other artifacts, then returned to the top of the mesa, where they split up to look for more ruins. Wetherill soon discovered Spruce Tree House near where the museum now stands. The next day they stumbled upon Square Tower House.

Wetherill would eventually become so fascinated with the Mesa Verde ruins that he would devote his life to them. He and his family collected thousands of artifacts, most of which they sold to the Colorado State Historical Society and the C.D. Hazard and Jay Smith Exploring Company, which displayed them at the 1893 World's Fair in Chicago.

By the turn of the century, Mesa Verde was being deluged with treasure hunters, and the ruins were in danger of being destroyed. In June 1906, Theodore Roosevelt signed a bill creating Mesa Verde National Park.

THE ANASAZI

Two thousand years ago, Native Americans were farming along the banks of the Rio Grande south of present-day Albuquerque. Using techniques that had spread north from Mexico and Central America, the Rio Grande tribes farmed corn, beans, and squash, made baskets, and lived in primitive shelters along the river's shores. So fertile was this land and so successful were these early farmers that scientists believe the area actually experienced overcrowding.

Eventually, some of the people left the river area. By A.D. 550, splinter groups had begun to build pit houses and establish small communities on both sides of the Rio Grande, and others had begun to move north toward the Four Corners area.

Although anthropologists refer also to the early Rio Grande civilizations as Anasazi (Basketmaker period, A.D. 1-750), the term is most often used to describe the people who thrived in the Four Corners area from about A.D. 800-1300. The Anasazi (actually a Navajo word that has various translations, including "Enemies of our Ancestors" and "Ancient Foreigners") were a peaceful people—farmers and potters—and highly religious. Their huge adobe and stone pueblos are thought today to have been culture and trade centers, and evidence suggests they traded with other tribes as far west as the Pacific Ocean and as far south as what is now southern Mexico. Their pueblos, three- and four-story apartment-style buildings—both built into cliffs and freestanding—often contained up to 400 rooms, some of which were living quarters, some of which were used to store grain. Also characteristic of the pueblos were kivas, ceremonial meeting places, built partially underground and round—perhaps symbolic of the womb of Mother Earth. The largest of these Anasazi "cities" exist in ruins at Chaco Canyon National Historic Park about midway between Gallup and Farmington, New Mexico, and at Mesa Verde National Park.

The first evidence of occupation of the Mesa Verde plateau is from the Modified Basketmaker Period (A.D. 550-750). Ruins of their pit houses, as well as their baskets and primitive pottery, have been found in the area. During the Developmental Pueblo Period (A.D. 750-1100) the Anasazi began to reach their full stride. Pit houses had been replaced by larger, family-based dwellings, the classic black-on-white Anasazi pottery was being produced, and there is speculation that water-management systems were being developed. It wasn't until the middle of the Great Pueblo Period (A.D. 1100-1300), though, that they began moving into the alcoves formed by the overhanging cliffs. After living on mesas and in river valleys for some 1200 years, they suddenly began work on the cliff dwellings. For years the commonly held anthropological theory was that the dwellings had been built for protection from enemies. Recent research questions that, however. The Athapascan peoples (Navajos and Apaches) weren't to arrive in the area until later, and the Utes probably after them. The Anasazi don't seem to have *had* any enemies. It could be, too, that they moved into the alcoves to more easily control the temperature of their dwellings. For whatever reason the cliff dwellings at Mesa Verde were built, by the middle of the 13th century, they were home to 5,000 people.

And then they left. Perhaps within the span of a single generation, the pueblos were abandoned.

And just as anthropologists debate the reasons for the dwellings' construction, so do they debate the reasons for their abandonment. One theory holds, however, that the Native Americans simply overfarmed their land and had to seek arable land elsewhere. Other contributing factors may have included a very long drought, as well as, according to Park Superintendent Robert Heyder, a "mini-ice age." These factors and perhaps others, combined with dwindling resources in the late 1200s and possibly the problems that typically attend a city bursting at the seams—overcrowding, disease, unrest, internecine hostilities—most likely led to Mesa Verde's downfall; the civilization simply grew up and passed on.

But where'd they go?

As the Anasazi abandoned their large communities, they dispersed, living in small groups and ending up in different parts of the Southwest. Most likely the pueblo people living in northern New Mexico and Arizona—the Hopi, Zuni, Taos, Acoma, and others—are descendants of the people who once lived at Mesa Verde.

Visiting The Park

A visit to Mesa Verde is a highlight of any trip to the Southwest or to Colorado. Ideally, you'd spend several days here, exploring the ruins and the museum, and hiking about the mesa to get a sense of how its early inhabitants lived. But even if you've got half a day, you can still enjoy and benefit from the park. A couple of the ruins are very easy to get to, and even if you're not up for the short hikes to them, there are viewing platforms (wheelchair-accessible) from which you can see the impressive ruins under 100 yards away. In addition, a short visit to the museum and visitor center offers a fascinating lesson in the archaeology of the area and especially of the culture of the Mesa Verde Anasazi. On display are pottery, baskets, cradle boards, fetishes, and countless other artifacts, as well as exquisitely detailed dioramas suggesting how things at the cliff dwellings must have looked when they were thriving—when hunters were returning with game, farmers were harvesting crops, potters were making jars, and children were playing by the water. Other displays explain in great detail the construction and restoration of the pueblos, as well as the various stages of Anasazi culture.

Ruins Road takes motorists along Chapin Mesa to several of the major sites on two six-mile loops. Along the way are viewing platforms or trailheads to over 40 different pueblo ruins. A separate road leads to Weatherill Mesa, where other sites are located.

One of the largest, best-preserved, and most accessible cliff dwellings is **Spruce Tree House,** just behind the museum at park headquarters. A short walk on a paved pathway will take you down to the canyon floor and the base of the pueblo. The best-known ruin is **Cliff Palace,** on the east wall of Cliff Canyon. A little tougher, the hike to Cliff Palace requires some scrambling over and between huge boulders. Self-guided tours to both Spruce Tree House and Cliff Palace are offered in the summer, with a ranger on duty to answer questions, while ranger-led tours are available the rest of the year. Another popular ruin is **Balcony House,** which is open during the summer for ranger-guided tours.

As you enter the park, you'll get a detailed map of the mesa, with ruins, turnouts, and other points of interest identified. Just beyond the park entrance is a special parking area for trailers—this will save you from hauling your rig up onto the mesa and trying to find a parking place—in addition, trailers are not allowed past Morefield Campground (see below), located six miles past the park entrance. In addition to the campground, **Morefield Village** has a small store, gas station, and ranger station. At **Far View Terrace,** another 10 miles in, there's a lodge (see below), gift shop, cafeteria, and gas station.

Mesa Verde National Park is open year-round, although lodging and gasoline are available in summer only. In addition, some of the ruins are closed in the winter, when snow and wet weather make the trails dangerous. Admission is $5 per vehicle; the pass is good for seven days.

Accommodations

To really appreciate Mesa Verde National Park, you need to spend a night here. You need to remain after the tour buses have departed and the museum doors have closed. You need to watch the sun go down, and to listen to wind whispering through the piñons and canyons and ruins; you need to sense the magic and the spirit of the mesa, intensified by the eerie quiet of the night.

Morefield Campground is a huge area inside the park with 477 sites on 92 acres. The campground is open mid-April through mid-Oct. and has showers, laundry facilities, a grocery store and gift shop, and evening ranger-led campfire talks. For information or reservations, phone (303) 529-4474 (summer) or 529-4421 (winter).

The **Far View Lodge** is a scattering of single-story multiunit structures nestled in the juniper and piñons of the mesa. With private viewing porches that offer stunning panoramas across the mesa and the southwest (clear to New Mexico's Shiprock), the Far View offers one of the state's most unique lodging experiences. The upscale dining room at the lodge serves chicken, seafood, veal, venison, and Mexican specialties (accompanied by Anasazi salad) for $12-18. For information or reservations, phone 529-4421.

Information

For more information on the ruins, the museum, special group programs, etc., write Mesa Verde National Park, CO 81330, or phone (303) 529-4465 or 529-4475.

MANCOS

Mancos (pop. 870; elev. 6,993 feet) is a small ranching and shipping town about eight miles east of Mesa Verde and 30 miles west of Durango. Situated in a lush valley on the Mancos River, this is a laid-back and quiet little town in some of the prettiest country in Colorado. **Free camping** for tenters and RVers is available at **Boyle Park/Mancos Wayside Park** (two-week limit), where there's also a shady playground for kids. You'll also find a tiny pioneer and Native American museum at the **Mesa Verde Inn,** tel. (303) 533-7385.

Echo Basin Dude Ranch And RV Park

Located on a hillside overlooking the Mancos River Valley, this lodge and recreational paradise offers just about everything you could imagine in an absolutely beautiful setting. Stay in a log cabin, haul your RV in, or set up your tent beside one of the property's two lakes. Fish, ride horses, play tennis, croquet, and basketball; in the winter, go cross-country skiing, snowmobiling, sledding, or ice fishing.

Rates are quite reasonable: Cabins are about $120 a night for two, with three meals included, and RV sites are $6. For information or reservations, write 11033 N. 23rd Ave., Phoenix, AZ 85029, or phone (800) 426-1890.

DURANGO

The largest town in the Four Corners area of Colorado, Durango (pop. 12,400; elev. 6,512 feet) offers excellent access to that area's many attractions—historical, cultural, recreational. Situated between the southern border of the two-million-acre San Juan National Forest and the northern reaches of the Southwest's stark canyon country, the little community reflects all the vitality, contrast, and diversity of the surrounding geography.

Durango is a youthful and outdoor-oriented town, graced with a wonderful climate and crisp mountain sunshine. During the summer, the otherwise slow-paced town swells with tourists, many of whom come to ride the famous Durango and Silverton Narrow Gauge Railroad and to visit the Anasazi cliff dwellings at nearby Mesa Verde National Park. On those afternoons, the streets are lined with motorhomes; the gift shops, boutiques, and Native American galleries are packed with shoppers; and the town's many restaurants and taverns are crammed with locals and passers-through alike, all enjoying a good time in this fun-loving little community.

History

In the mid-1870s, Animas City, two miles north of present-day Durango, was a thriving town with some 2,000 people and its own newspaper. When the Denver and Rio Grande Railroad pushed through, in 1880, it bypassed Animas City and built its own town. Almost immediately, most Animas City residents transplanted themselves south to the new community, Durango, named by a railroad stockholder who had recently returned from Mexico. By late 1880, Durango was home to about 2,500 people, and 500 buildings had been erected.

With a reputation for being a rowdy, shoot-'em-up town in its early days, Durango and the surrounding area was frequented by ranchers and rustlers, miners and claim jumpers, as well as railroad workers and vigilantes attempting to maintain some semblance of order. Between 1880 and the turn of the century, Durango served as a supply center for the mines in the region and also as an ore-processing center.

By the early 20th century, though, as the mining industry throughout the state began to see the full and long-term effects of the silver crash of 1893, Durango followed suit. Its boom days over, Durango became a quiet little shipping center for farmers and ranchers in the Animas River Valley and in the mesa country to the west.

Then things began to pick up again. As more and more people became interested in the cliff dwellings at Mesa Verde National Park and other Four Corners-area sites, and as roads made getting to them easier, Durango became a natural base camp for tourists. In addition, more and more travelers began to take advantage of Southwestern Colorado's myriad recreation activities, from fishing to snow skiing. Finally, in the early 1980s, the Durango and Silverton Narrow Gauge Railroad began to attract railroad buffs and other tourists from around the country.

So today Durango is experiencing another boom. During the summer, the little town's streets are packed with motor homes, its sidewalks lined with shoppers looking for Native American jewelry and railroad memorabilia, and outdoor enthusiasts waiting for their shuttles to the river.

ATTRACTIONS

Durango And Silverton Narrow Gauge Railroad

In continuous operation since 1882, the 45-mile railway was for many years the main connection between Durango and Silverton, supplying miners and transporting ore down out of the high country. Today, coal-burning trains take 200,000 people per season (May through Oct.) through the lush Animas River Valley and the gorgeous San Juan National Forest to Silverton. The trip takes eight hours roundtrip (three each way, plus a two-hour layover), although you can also arrange overnight lodging in Silverton or go one direction by bus (six hours is a *long* time to be on a loud, slow-moving, ash-spewing train no matter how gorgeous the scenery or authentic the experience).

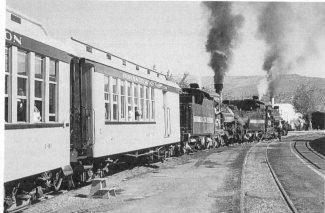

A Durango and
Silverton Narrow
Gauge Railroad train
heads out of town.

STEPHEN METZGER

Trains depart twice daily from the depot at 479 Main Ave. in downtown Durango (8:30 a.m. and 9:30 a.m.) and return about 5:15 p.m. and 6:15 p.m. Fares in 1993 were $37.50 for adults ($18.65 for kids 5-11; no charge for a kid under five sitting on an adult's lap).

This is Durango's primary summer draw, and reservations are very highly recommended (the main office suggests booking your trip at least 30 days in advance). However, if you're lucky, you can sometimes get last-minute tickets. For reservations and information, write Durango and Silverton Narrow Gauge Railroad Company, 479 Main Ave., Durango, CO 81310, or phone (303) 247-2733.

Animas Museum
This small museum located at Durango's north end displays a wide array of historical artifacts from the area, from Anasazi pottery to early ranching gear to domestic items, as well as historical photos. The museum also has a small gift store.

The Animas Museum, located at 31st St. and W. 2nd Ave., is open weekdays 10 a.m.-6 p.m. and weekends 11 a.m.-4 p.m., May through September. For more information, phone (303) 259-2402.

Southern Ute Indian Cultural Center
Located on the Southern Ute Reservation in Ignacio, about 25 miles southeast of Durango, this museum emphasizes the history and culture of the Utes and also displays a variety of Anasazi artifacts, including pottery from nearby

ruins. Among the highlights of the museum's exhibits are elaborate 19th-century Ute bead leatherwork. An adjoining gift shop sells authentic arts and crafts. The museum is open Mon.-Sat. 9 a.m.-6 p.m. and Sun. 10 a.m.-3 p.m. For more information, phone (303) 563-4531.

PARKS AND RECREATION

City Park
You'll find a very nice city park on the Animas River, where you can picnic and let the kids play on the swings and slides while river rafters go by just yards away on the other side of the cottonwoods. Go west from Hwy. 550 at the Holiday Inn, and turn right when you get across the river. Kayakers can also put in here.

Vallecito Reservoir
Located about 20 miles northeast of Durango, this reservoir, which was originally built to store irrigation water, offers a wide range of recreational pursuits. A favorite among local lake anglers, the reservoir has over 22 miles of accessible shoreline, as well as five marinas, where you can rent fishing boats, sailboats, and canoes. The waters hold brown, rainbow, and cutthroat trout, plus kokanee salmon, northern pike, and walleye.

Vallecito Reservoir also offers excellent hiking, with trailheads leading into the Weminuche Wilderness Area. In addition, there are several Forest Service and private campgrounds. **The Wit's End Guest Ranch and Resort** at the

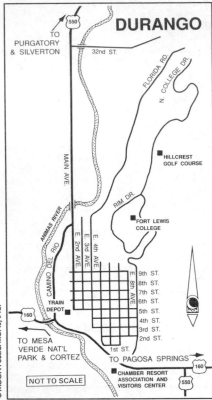

DURANGO

TO PURGATORY & SILVERTON

32nd ST.

FLORIDA RD.

N. COLLEGE DR.

HILLCREST GOLF COURSE

RIM DR.

MAIN AVE.

ANIMAS RIVER

CAMINO DEL RIO

FORT LEWIS COLLEGE

E. 2nd AVE.
E. 3rd AVE.
E. 4th AVE.

E. 9th ST.
8th ST.
7th ST.
6th ST.
5th ST.
4th ST.
3rd ST.
2nd ST.

E. 8th AVE.

160

TRAIN DEPOT

TO MESA VERDE NAT'L PARK & CORTEZ

1st ST.

TO PAGOSA SPRINGS

160

© MOON PUBLICATIONS, INC.

NOT TO SCALE

CHAMBER RESORT ASSOCIATION AND VISITORS CENTER

550

lake offers lodging in "luxury log cabins" and a main lodge built in 1370. In addition, there's a dining room and tavern, with mirrors from the 1853 World Exposition. Summer guests can fish, hike, swim, and go horseback riding; winter guests can go snowmobiling, cross-country skiing, ice fishing, and showshoeing. For reservations or information, write The Wit's End, 254 County Rd. 500, Vallecito Lake, CO 81122, or phone (303) 884-4113.

For more information on Vallecito Reservoir, phone the **Vallecito Lake Chamber of Commerce** at 884-9782, or write Box 804, Bayfield, CO 81122.

Hot Springs

Looking for a place to soak away the aches after a day of skiing, mountain biking, or scrambling around the ruins at Mesa Verde? Try **Trimble Hot Springs,** where you can relax in a private tub, swim laps in the Olympic-size swimming pool, or, if you're really hurtin', treat yourself to a massage. There's also a picnic area.

Trimble Hot Springs is located six miles north of Durango on Hwy. 550. For information, phone (303) 247-0111.

River Running

Next to the narrow-gauge railroad, this is probably Durango's main tourist attraction, with numerous companies offering trips on the Animas and other nearby rivers. Booking a trip is easy. You'll find temporary booths set up along Main Ave. near the train depot, as well as flyers and posters tacked to telephone poles and taped to windows. You can also book river trips through most of the local sporting-goods stores.

The following companies offer a wide range of trips—half day and full day, in canoes, kayaks, and rafts, on the Animas, Piedras, and Dolores rivers: **Durango Rivertrippers,** tel. (303) 259-0289; **Flexible Flyers Rafting,** tel. 247-4628; **Mountain Waters Rafting, Inc.,** tel. 259-4191; **Peregrine River Outfitters,** tel. 385-7600; and **Rivers West Adventures,** tel. 259-5077.

Cycling

Both touring and mountain biking are very big in Durango, as you'll quickly notice: Lycra-thighed riders pump lightweight racing bikes along roadsides, and it seems every porch has a muddy mountain bike locked to its railing. In fact, as one of Colorado's mountain-biking meccas, Durango is second only to Crested Butte. In addition, Durango is home to Ned Overend, one of the country's premier riders/racers.

Among the trails locals recommend are the **Colorado Trail, Hermosa Creek Trail,** and **La Plata Canyon Road.** The truly adventurous can drive 28 miles north to **Purgatory Ski Area,** tel. (303) 247-9000, haul their bikes to the top of the mountain via chairlift, and ride down on the ski trails.

For maps and information on mountain biking in the surrounding San Juan National Forest, stop by the **Animas Ranger District Office,** 710 Camino Del Rio #301, or phone 247-4874. You can also get maps, information, and expert advice from most Durango-area cycling shops, including **Durango Cyclery,** 143 E. 13th

St., tel. 247-0747; the **Outdoorsman,** 949 Main Ave., tel. 247-4066; and **Hassle Free Sports,** 2615 Main Ave., tel. 259-3874—Hassle Free also rents bikes.

To arrange tours, contact **Mountain Bike Specialists,** 949 Main Ave., tel. 247-4066.

Hiking

From Durango you can head out into the woods for a full gamut of hiking experiences. Wander along the river for a couple of miles, taking in the scenery and the mountain air; hike up into the La Plata Mountains and the San Juan National Forest; or tackle part of the 469-mile Colorado Trail, whose southwestern trailhead is just outside town. A good mid-range hike is the six-mile **Red Creek Trail,** which winds through aspens to the top of Missionary Ridge and affords excellent views of the valley below. To get to the trailhead, go northeast on E. 3rd Ave. for 10 miles, turn left at the sign for Colvig Silver Camps, and continue for two more miles. You'll also find excellent hiking trails at Vallecito Reservoir, including several into the Weminuche Wilderness Area.

For more information on hiking and backpacking in the Durango area, stop by **Backcountry Experience,** 780 Main, tel. (303) 247-5830, where you'll find an excellent selection of maps and books, as well as equipment and clothing (rentals available). You can also get maps and information from the **Animas Ranger District Office** of San Juan National Forest, 701 Camino Del Rio, tel. 247-4874.

Fishing

One of the most popular Durango-area fishing spots is **Vallecito Reservoir,** 18 miles northeast of town. Fish along the 22 accessible miles of shoreline or take a boat out into deeper waters and troll for lunker rainbow, brown, cutthroat trout, northern pike, walleye, and kokanee salmon. Boat rentals are available at the lake.

Stream anglers can work the Animas River. Though you can catch trout within the city limits, you're better off heading north or south where there's less traffic. Locals recommend the **Devils Falls** area near the Takoma Power Plant, about 20 miles north of town via Hwy. 550.

For gear, licenses, and information, stop by **Duranglers Flies and Supplies,** 801-B Main, tel. (303) 385-4081, or **Gardenswartz,** 863 Main, tel. 247-2660.

Camping

With San Juan National Forest sprawling to the north, Durango offers plenty of camping possibilities. The largest concentration of campgrounds is in the Vallecito Reservoir area, about 20 miles northeast of town. You'll find over a half-dozen different areas with over 200 sites. The largest is **Vallecito Camgpground,** with 88 sites (pit toilets, no showers). The smaller and more private **Pine Point Campground,** also at Vallecito Reservoir, has 30 sites (pit toilets, no showers). For information on these and other Vallecito Reservoir campgrounds, phone the **Pine Ranger District Office** in Bayfield at (303) 884-2512. For campsite reservations, phone (800) 283-CAMP.

You'll also find several Forest Service campgrounds at the Haviland Lake area about 20 miles north of Durango on Hwy. 550. **Haviland Lake Campground** has 45 sites on 20 acres (pit toilets, no showers). In addition, there are several Forest Service campgrounds just off Hwy. 160 between Durango and Mancos, including **Target Tree,** where you'll find over 40 nicely secluded sites. Phone the **Animas Ranger District Office** at 247-4874 for more information.

Golf

Durango's public course is the 18-hole **Hillcrest Golf Course** on the Fort Lewis College Mesa overlooking town. Phone (303) 247-1499 for information and tee times. The public can also play the private **Tamarron Resort Golf Course,** though Tamarron guests are given priority. Phone 259-2000, ext. 2000.

WINTER SPORTS

Downhill Skiing

Though not the best-known resort in the Rockies, **Purgatory Ski Area,** located about 30 miles north of Durango on Hwy. 550, has its devoted fans—folks who care more about amount and quality of snow than about flash and fashion. With nine lifts on 630 acres and a vertical drop of nearly 2,000 feet, Purgatory offers good skiing for all ability levels; its terrain is ideally diversified, rated 20% beginner, 50% intermediate, and 30% advanced.

Though Purgatory is primarily a day-use area, in recent years the resort has developed its base facilities. There's a shopping area, several restaurants, and on-site accommodations. Shuttles run regularly between Durango and the lifts (phone 303-259-5438 for rates and schedule). Rentals and instruction are available.

For more information on Purgatory Ski Area, phone 247-9000 or (800) 525-8855.

Cross-country Skiing

The lush valleys and deep forests of San Juan National Forest north of Durango offer some of the best Nordic skiing in Colorado. Check out the trails in the **Haviland Lake** area (beginning at Haviland Campground, about 18 miles north of Durango) and at **Molas Pass,** about 35 miles north of town. Both afford perfect opportunities for heading off into the quiet white backcountry—the views in the Molas Pass area are particularly exquisite. Plenty of places to pull off the road and park.

For groomed trails, check out **Purgatory Ski Touring Center,** at the Purgatory Ski Area 30 miles north of Durango on Hwy. 550. The center offers 15 km of trails, as well as rentals and instruction (in Telemarking and touring). For more information on the Purgatory Ski Touring Center, phone (303) 247-9000.

For more information on cross-country skiing in the area, as well as for rentals, contact **Hassle Free Sports,** 2615 Main Ave., Durango, tel. 259-3874. You can also get information from the Animas Ranger District Office of the Forest Service, 701 Camino Del Rio #310, Durango, CO 81301, tel. 247-4874.

TOUR

San Juan Skyway

Durango is an ideal starting point for the 236-mile San Juan Skyway, mile by mile one of the most scenic drives in the country. From Durango, the route heads due north on Hwy. 550, winds up over Molas Pass (elev. 10,910 feet), drops down into Silverton, rises on the Million Dollar Highway again over Red Mountain Pass (elev. 11,008 feet), then falls dramatically down a series of switchbacks into Ouray. From Ouray, continue north to Ridgway, where you turn west on CO 62, which lifts gently over Dallas Divide (elev. 8,970 feet) and provides excellent views of the Mt. Sneffels Range. On the back side of Dallas Divide, CO 62 tees into CO 145; here, turn southeast for Telluride. From Telluride, continue south over Lizard Head Pass (elev. 10,222 feet), and then head toward the Four Corners area and Cortez. In Cortez, catch Hwy. 160 east back to Durango.

Note: The entire loop can be driven in a day—a long day—when the weather's good. However, there are enough interesting diversions along the way that you could easily take three or more days. (All the points of interest on the San Juan Skyway are covered in detail elsewhere in this book.)

ACCOMMODATIONS

Durango's got a wide range of accommodation options, from private RV parks and budget motels to condos, bed and breakfasts, guest ranches and private cabins, as well as a number of restored historic hotels. In fact, if you drive in from the north on Hwy. 550, you'll probably think Durango is nothing *but* lodging: It seems two of every three buildings along there are motels. Be forewarned, though: Durango fills up during the high season (July and August), and if you show up without reservations you may find yourself scrambling to get a room. In addition, though many of the motels advertise budget rates, you might be surprised at what they are. In Durango in summer, "budget" generally means starting at around $40 for a double.

You've even got a range of choices (read *prices*) should you want to set up camp as close as possible to the train depot. Four accommodation options are within one block: the Durango Youth Hostel, the Durango Lodge, the Rio Grande Inn Best Western, and the General Palmer Hotel.

Prices below reflect the range you'll find for each property. Generally high seasons are summer (June, July, and August) and Christmas holiday (Dec. 24-Jan. 1). You'll find lower prices the rest of the year.

For more information on lodging in Durango, or for assistance booking a room, phone **Durango Area Chamber Resort Association** at (800) 525-8855.

Historic Hotels

The elegant **General Palmer Hotel,** tel. (303) 523-3358 or (800) 247-4747, offers convenience (one block from the train depot) and class, with doubles ranging about $65-145. A few blocks north, the **Strater Hotel,** tel. 247-4431 or (800) 247-4431, has doubles running about $60-100. A couple of bonuses here: The **Diamond Circle Theater** and the **Diamond Belle Saloon** adjoining the lobby, where the bartender and waitresses dress in Gay Nineties garb, garters and all, and you can drink a draft by the window or bellied up to the bar and imagine you're a miner or railroad worker from Durango's early days.

The **Jarvis Suite Hotel,** tel. 259-6190, was built in the early 1890s and housed a variety of businesses, including a cobbler, a printer, and a tailor. From 1910 to 1915, Durango's first theater operated on the first floor of the building. The building was remodeled in 1984, and today features 22 suites, each with a fully equipped kitchen. Doubles run about $70-120; ski packages are available in winter.

Motels

Highway 550 on the north end of town is virtually lined with motels, and rates don't vary a whole lot, generally running $40-60 for doubles. Among the least expensive rooms on the strip are those at the **National 9 Sunset,** 2855 N. Main, tel. (303) 247-2653, where doubles run about $30-40. The **Comfort Inn,** 2930 N. Main, tel. 259-5373, has rooms for two starting at about $50.

Youth Hostel

The least expensive rooms in town are probably at the **Durango Youth Hostel,** 543 E. 2nd Ave., right across from the train depot, tel. (303) 247-9905. For $9, you can get a bunk in a shared room.

Camping And RVing

At the southern border of San Juan National Forest, Durango offers lots of good Forest Service camping. In addition, there are dozens of private campgrounds in the area, many of which flank the highway between Cortez and Durango. Durango's **East Piñon Acres KOA,** tel. (303) 247-0783, is located just east of town on Hwy. 160 heading toward Pagosa Springs. North of town (15 miles) is **Ponderosa KOA,** tel. 247-4499.

FOOD

Start Me Up

A very reasonably priced and popular breakfast spot is **Mr. Rosewaters,** 522 Main (across from the train depot), tel. 247-8788, specializing in healthful meals for folks heading out adventuring (they also sell excellent lunches, including box lunches for train customers).

Farquahrt's on Main serves Bloody Marys for $1 on Saturday mornings.

Other Durango Restaurants

Another restaurant specializing in healthful meals, including bread (and beer) baked (and brewed) on-site, is **Carver's Bakery and Brew Pub,** 1022 Main, tel. (303) 259-2545, offering vegie specials (salads, stews, and stir-fry), with delicious black-bean dishes, as well as beef and chicken plates. Dinners run $3-7. Carver's is also open for breakfast, featuring espresso drinks and fresh, home-baked 100% organic whole-wheat bread. Informal live music by local musicians.

If your tastes, or mood, run more to pizza, try Farquahrt's downtown, a local favorite for a variety of pizzas and Italian dishes, as well as Mexican food. A classic, saloon-style restaurant, the place is loud, smoky, and full of local color. Dinners run $5-7, and the restaurant regularly features live music (blues and rock 'n' roll), with open-stage jams every Sunday night.

If you step off the train feeling famished and flush, try **The Palace Grill,** tel. 247-2018, one of Durango's best and best-known high-end restaurants. Beef, seafood, and poultry are grilled over mesquite and hardwoods; entrees run $12-18.

Something Sweet

Heart's Delight, located right next to the train depot, sells excellent ice cream and frozen yogurt, as well as sandwiches. The outdoor tables are perfect for waiting for train time, or for a cool treat at the end of a summer day. There are also a handful of places downtown that sell homemade candies and fudge.

ENTERTAINMENT

Durango's a hoppin' little town, especially during the summer when its motels are booked with railroaders and river rats, and locals are looking for places to unwind after a day on their mountain bikes. A continually popular tourist attraction, the **Bar-D Wranglers** offer up a combo plate of live country-and-western music and chuckwagon suppers Memorial Day through Labor Day. A Durango institution for nearly a quarter century, the Wranglers serve a dinner of barbecued beef, baked pototoes, beans, and biscuits nightly at 7:30, "rain or shine." Get there early and explore the Wranglers' "spread"— blacksmith shop, record store (buy Wranglers' records, tapes, and CDs), and other gift shops. Tickets are $11 (dinner and show). Reservations required. Phone (303) 247-5753. To get there, go north about seven miles from downtown to Trimble Ln./County Rd. 252, where you'll turn right. Cross the railroad tracks and the Animas River, and then continue north on County Rd. 250.

The **Durango Jamboree** is a musical variety stage show performed twice a night Tues. through Sun., Memorial Day through October. The jamboree offers country-and-western, bluegrass, and country gospel. Admission is $10 for adults. Reservations recommended. Phone 259-1290. Shows are at 6 p.m. and 8 p.m.

If you're looking for live music in Durango, you don't have to look far, with several local watering holes offering up a variety of music. **Farquahrt's,** 725 Main, tel. 247-5440, regularly books live rock and blues bands; check out Sunday nights' live jams. **Carver's,** 1022 Main, tel. 259-2545, hosts very informal concerts beginning in the early evenings. For live jazz, check out **Bourbon Street,** 7th and Main, tel. 259-2988.

Watch the Durango *Herald* for current listings of who's playing where and what else is going on around town.

SHOPPING

Be sure to allow yourself at least a couple of hours to wander around the shops of Durango's downtown area, where you'll find a variety of galleries and gift shops, many of which specialize in Native American jewelry, pottery, sculpture, and prints. Among the galleries worth checking out are **Toh-Atin,** 145 W. 9th St., tel. (303) 247-8277, where you'll find an excellent selection of Navajo rugs, and **Gallery Ultima,** specializing in contemporary Southwestern art. The **Thompson River Trade Company,** 140 W. 8th St., tel. 247-5681, specializes in pre-1940 Native American baskets, weavings, pottery, and other artifacts.

You'll find several sporting-goods stores— whose emphases are on adventure and backcountry outings—as well as 21 factory outlet stores, including London Fog and Benetton. In addition, there are several boutiques, emphasizing upscale Southwestern styles, and souvenir shops, including several at the train depot, as well as the requisite T-shirt emporiums.

On the east end of town on Hwy. 160, the Durango Mall has a JCPenney, Sears, and other standard mall shops.

CALENDAR

Durango's calendar is practically fully booked, especially during the summer when the town's full of tourists. Your best sources for details on upcoming events are Durango *Magazine* and *Southwest Summer,* both of which are promotional publications with complete listings. Pick up copies at the Resort Chamber office. In addition, watch the Durango *Herald* and its regular supplements.

Among the highlights of Durango's annual events: the **Iron Horse Bicycle Classic,** which attracts some 1,500 riders in a Memorial Day weekend race against a Durango and Silverton Narrow Gauge locomotive to Silverton (47 miles); **Whitewater Races,** a series of races and seminars on the Animas River, attracting some of the country's best-known river runners (early June); **Fiesta Days,** three days celebrating Durango's heritage, with a parade, music, and rodeo (late June); the **Durango Cowboy Gathering,** a three-day festival with musicians, storytellers, and cowboy poets (early October); and **Colorfest,** a multi-event "celebration of color, culture, and adventure" (Sept. through Oct.).

Since 1976, a highlight of Durango's winter has been the annual **Snowdown,** in late January. This five-day celebration includes over 60 different events, from snowsculpting to ski golf and softball, with lots of live music and good eats for competitors and spectators alike. For information on these and other events, contact the **Durango Chamber Resort Association** at (303) 247-0312 or (800) 525-8855.

SERVICES

The offices of the **Durango Police Department** are at 990 E. 2nd Ave.; phone (303) 247-3232. The **La Plata County Sheriff** is at 742 Turner; phone 247-1155. Phone the **State Patrol** at 247-4722. Durango's **Mercy Medical Center** is at 375 E. Park Ave., tel. 247-4311. The main **post office** is at 222 W. 8th, tel. 247-3434.

Recycling
The City of Durango has its own recycling program, with several drop-off sites where you can leave aluminum, glass, newspaper, and tin cans. The most convenient is the **City Market,** 3130 N. Main. For information on recycling in Durango, or for a listing of other drop-off sites, phone (303) 247-5622.

INFORMATION

The office of the **Durango Chamber Resort Association** is an excellent source for brochures, dining and lodging guides, and complete lists of Durango-area services. Stop by 111 S. Camino Del Rio. Before your visit, write Box 2587, Durango, CO 81302, or phone (303) 247-0312 or (800) 525-8855. The Durango **public library** is at 1188 E. 2nd Ave., tel. 247-2492.

The independently published *Durango Herald* is published Sun. through Fri. and is available in racks around town for a quarter.

Bookstores
Durango has three exceptional bookstores always well stocked with books on the Southwest. **The Bookcase,** 601 E. 2nd. Ave., tel. (303) 247-3776, features collectors' and first editions, including some rare enough to be locked away in glass cases. The shop also carries used paperbacks and new books on Colorado and the Southwest, particularly the Four Corners area. **The Southwest Book Trader,** 175 E. 5th., tel. 247-8479, has an excellent selection of books on Colorado and the Southwest, though you might have to dig around, as the little shop is wonderfully cluttered, with books piled on the floor, in every corner, and spilling out into aisles. **Maria's Bookshop,** 928 Main, tel. 247-1438, specializes in books on the Southwest and Native Americana and also sells Navajo rugs and topographical maps of the area. There's also a **Waldenbooks** next to the train depot.

TRANSPORTATION

The **Durango-La Plata County Airport** is located 14 miles east of Durango off CO 172. Passenger service is provided by **America West, United Express, Continental Express,** and **Mesa Airlines.** Durango's **Greyhound bus depot** is at 275 E. 8th Ave., tel. (303) 247-2755.

The **Durango Lift** is the town's public transportation system. Buses run regularly through town year-round, as well as to Purgatory Ski Area during the ski season. For routes and information, phone 247-5438. For 24-hour taxi service in Durango, phone **Durango Transportation, Inc.** at 259-4818.

PAGOSA SPRINGS AND VICINITY

Pagosa Springs is a combination Old West town and soon-to-be booming resort town. You'll probably be surprised at the huge number of real estate and land-sale offices, particularly on the west side of town. The **Fairfield Pagosa Resort,** also on the west side, is a deluxe spread, with gorgeous executive-style homes right on the golf course.

Named for the nearby hot mineral springs (Pagosa is Ute for "Healing Waters"), which average 153°, Pagosa Springs was the focus of a centuries-long dispute between Navajos and Utes. According to the WPA guide to Colorado, in 1866 the two tribes agreed to a final one-on-one duel over the springs' rightful ownership. The Utes chose as their representative Albert Henry Pfieffer, a Scotsman who had worked alongside Kit Carson and who had served as a U.S. Indian agent in New Mexico, where Pfieffer's Spanish wife had been killed by natives. Pfieffer chose Bowie knives for the duel. Apparently, the two men rushed at each other, and Pfieffer flung his knife at his Navajo rival, killing him, and the Utes took undisputed possession of the springs.

Of course, Native American possession of anything of value was not part of the Great European Plan, and Pagosa Springs was no exception. By 1880, a one-square-mile area surrounding the springs had been claimed by the U.S. government, and a townsite was platted that year.

Throughout the early 20th century, local boosters tried to promote Pagosa Springs as a resort spa, although they were largely unsuccessful. Only in the last decade or so has the area begun to see growth and development to any significant degree.

ATTRACTIONS

Chimney Rock Anasazi Ruins

An "outlier" community of the Chaco Canyon pueblos and cultural center, the Chimney Rock site is a fascinating thread in the Anasazi tapestry of the Southwest—a tapestry that includes not only Chaco, but Aztec, Bandelier (all three in New Mexico), Mesa Verde, and literally thousands of other ruins.

Chimney Rock was named for the twin spires that stand guard over the ruins, which during the 11th century were home to as many as 2,000 people. Recent archaeological research suggests that the Chimney Rock site was very likely of great religious significance, and one theory is that the inhabitants of this remote outpost were priests sent north from Chaco. Other anthropologists suggest the community was a trading and shipping center, and that timbers from the northern forests were harvested here and shipped south for pueblo construction in the barren area around Chaco.

Encompassing six square miles, the Chimney Rock site includes dozens of structures, many of which have been partially restored. Homes, ceremonial kivas, and storage rooms are scattered about the pueblo. Walking among these isolated ruins is a powerful spiritual experience that can help you ask questions to better understand your earth, your self, your ancestors, and your gods.

Touring Chimney Rock is possible only with Forest Service guides. Groups of 30 (maximum) leave from the Chimney Rock entrance 20 miles west of Pagosa Springs via Hwy. 160 and CO 151. Tours are free, reservations required. For information or reservations, contact the **Pagosa Springs Ranger District** of San Juan National Forest, Box 310, Pagosa Springs, CO 81147, tel. (303) 264-2268, or the **Pagosa Springs Chamber of Commerce,** tel. 246-2360.

San Juan Historical Museum

This small museum features most of the requisite historical-society-type displays, focusing on the Pagosa Springs area's Anglo settlement. Lots of ranching and farming artifacts, as well as early domestic items: a horsehide coat, a turn-of-the-century loom, early dentists' equipment. Admission is $1 for adults and 50 cents for kids.

The museum, located on the east side of town at Pagosa and 1st, is open Tues. through Sat. 11 a.m.-5 p.m. Memorial Day through Labor Day. For hours and more information, phone (303) 264-4424.

PARKS AND RECREATION

City Park
You'll find a very nice city park along the San Juan River next to Pagosa Springs visitor center. There's a lawn, playground equipment, picnic tables, and restrooms.

Hot Springs
The mineral-water tubs at the **Best Western Oak Ridge Mineral Spring Inn**, tel. (303) 264-4173, and at the **Spa Motel**, tel. 264-5910 are open to the public (small fees for non-guests). Both are located right down on the river near the Pagosa Springs visitor center.

Golf
The **Fairfield Pagosa Resort** has both a nine- and an 18-hole course. The wide-open terrain offers excellent views of the mountains to the north and east and of rolling hills and canyons to the south and west. For information, phone (303) 731-4141 or (800) 523-7704.

Fishing
Plenty of good fishing opportunities in the Pagosa Springs area, whether you like to stalk native rainbows with #18 flies or prefer to sit in a lawn chair and tip brews with a bell on your rod. Stream anglers can pull decent rainbows out of both the **East** and **West Forks** of the **San Juan River;** the confluence of the two forks is 10 miles north of Pagosa Springs. From town, the San Juan flows southwest, eventually dumping into **Navajo Reservoir,** which straddles the Colorado-New Mexico state line. Another popular trout stream is the **Piedra River,** which drops down out of the Weminuche Wilderness Area about 20 miles west of Pagosa Springs.

Lake anglers often do well at **Capote Lake,** 16 miles west of Pagosa Springs at the junction of Hwy. 160 and CO 151 (boat rentals available), and at **Echo Lake,** five miles south of town via Hwy. 84. For more information on fishing in the area, stop by **Duranglers Flies and Supplies,** 801-B Main Ave., Durango, tel. (303) 385-4081, or **Gardenswartz Sporting Goods,** 863 Main Ave., Durango, tel. 247-2660.

Arrange guided river trips from Pagosa Springs through **Colorado Fishing Adventures** at Fairfield Pagosa Resort, tel. 731-4141, ext. 2086, or **Sundowner Outfitters,** 264-2869.

Camping
Pagosa Springs is literally surrounded by San Juan National Forest, so the camping opportunities in the area are virtually limitless. In addition to the primitive camping allowed by the Forest Service, you can head out in just about any direction and arrive at a designated Forest Service campground. To the northeast are **Wolf Creek** and **West Fork** campgrounds (75 sites total); take Hwy. 160 13 miles to Forest Service Rd. 684. To the south is **Blanco Campground** (18 sites on eight acres, no water); take Hwy. 84 13 miles to Forest Service Rd. 656. To the west is **Cimarrona Campground** (21 sites on six acres); take Hwy. 160 two miles to Forest Service Rd. 631, and then follow 631 for 22 miles to Forest Service Rd. 640.

For more information on these and other Pagosa Springs-area Forest Service campgrounds, contact the **Pagosa Springs Ranger District** office, Box 310, Pagosa Springs, CO 81147, or phone (303) 264-2268.

Skiing
Wolf Creek Pass Ski Area is one of Colorado's little-known gems. Averaging well over 400 annual inches (!) of the Rockies' finest powder, Wolf Creek is a favorite of some of the sport's most discriminating connoisseurs.

Wolf Creek's six lifts service 700 acres and a nearly 1,500-foot vertical drop, and the area's terrain is about as well divided as you could hope for—20% beginner, 50% intermediate, and 30% advanced. The 10,350-foot base guarantees that all that snow will be nothing but the lightest, fluffiest, most skiable *powder* imaginable.

There are no overnight facilities at Wolf Creek, though there is a restaurant, cafeteria, and the proverbial bar for that post-ski nip. For more information, phone (303) 731-5605.

Cross-country Skiing
Pagosa Pines Touring Center is located west of town at the Fairfield Pagosa Resort. With 12 km of groomed trails winding about the resort's two golf courses, the area offers instruction and rental equipment. For information on rates and hours of operation, phone (303) 731-4755.

The Wolf Creek Pass area is very popular among Nordic skiers who prefer to cut their own trails through the fluff; the views from up here are exceptional. For maps and information on cross-country skiing in the San Juan National Forest, phone the **Pagosa Ranger District Office** at 264-2268. You can also get information and maps, as well as rental equipment, from **The Ski and Bow Rack,** at the east end of Pagosa Springs, tel. 264-2370.

PRACTICALITIES

Accommodations
If you're gonna be staying here, you might as well take advantage of the hot springs. The **Spa Motel,** tel. (303) 264-5910, and the **Best Western Oak Ridge Mineral Spring Inn,** tel. 264-4173, both offer free mineral-water hot tubbing for guests, and rooms are reasonably priced (about $35 for two at the Spa, $50 at the Oak Ridge). Both are conveniently located right in town across from the visitor center.

Food
A Pagosa Springs tradition, the **Elkhorn Cafe,** 438 Main, tel. (303) 264-2146, has a reputation for some of the best Mexican food in the area, as well as hearty American fare—located in the center of the downtown area. For a carb fix, try **Amore's House of Pasta,** 121 Pagosa St., tel. 264-2822, offering standard choices plus vegetarian and low-cholesterol dishes. For beef, try the **Branding Iron Barbecue,** three miles east of town on Hwy. 160, tel. 264-4268, which specializes in ribs, links, and chicken.

Information
Pagosa Springs' brand new **visitor center** building is located in the center of town on the river (watch for the signs). Lots of brochures and maps, particularly on recreation in southern Colorado, as well as information on lodging and real estate. To have information on the area sent to you, phone the chamber at (303) 264-2360 or (800) 252-2204.

Moonlight Books, located right downtown, tel. 264-5666, has a good selection of books of local and regional interest.

NORTH OF PAGOSA SPRINGS

Highway 160 lifts northeast out of Pagosa Springs into San Juan National Forest, crosses the Continental Divide into Rio Grande National Forest at Wolf Creek Pass (elev. 10,850 feet) and then drops down west of Del Norte Peak (elev. 12,400 feet) on its way toward the San Luis Valley. Without doubt one of the prettiest 45-mile stretches of highway in the country, the route offers views guaranteed to take your breath. The first time I drove along here I was returning to California after spending a summer in New Mexico. The lush green forests, the massive peaks, the sprawling lonesomeness of the countryside had me convinced I'd found paradise on earth. I'm not sure I hadn't.

DEL NORTE

Situated on the far west side of the San Luis Valley, Del Norte (pop. 1,700; elev. 7,874 feet) is the seat of Rio Grande County. The town was founded in 1860 and in its early days was a supply center for miners working the San Juan district to the west. Apparently those early days were rowdy ones, and a vigilante group was organized to try to bring peace to the community. A ragtag group, the vigilantes succeeded in doing more harm than good, one night shooting up much of tho town, including each other—vigilante activity decreased substantially thereafter.

Rio Grande County Museum

Devoted to the multicultural heritage of the area, this small museum features exhibits highlighting the contributions of prehistoric peoples, early Spanish explorers, and Anglo trappers, miners, and farmers. The museum, located at 580 Oak St., is open daily 10 a.m.-5 p.m. June through Aug., and 11 a.m.-4 p.m. Sept. through mid-Dec. and Feb. through May. Small admission fee. For more information, phone (719) 697-2847.

HIGHWAY 149 NORTH

Colorado 149 tees into Hwy. 160 about 15 miles west of Del Norte, winds north through Creede, crosses the Continental Divide at Spring Creek Pass (elev. 10,901 feet), rises again over Slumgullion Pass (elev. 11,361 feet), drops down into Lake City, and then connects up with Hwy. 50 about 10 miles west of Gunnison. Hardly one of the better-traveled routes in Colorado, it nonetheless offers the adventurous traveler a unique perspective on the state, including glimpses of one of the strangest chapters in western history. Also, the route provides a gateway to some of Colorado's most scenic recreation areas. Side trips to excellent fishing, skiing, and 4WD areas begin along here.

In addition, the scenery along here is downright gorgeous. In fact, the 75-mile stretch from South Fork to Lake City has been designated the "Silver Thread Scenic Byway" by the Forest Service. From the upper Rio Grande that parallels the roadside to waterfalls in distant canyons, from high mountain lakes to ghost towns, the scenery here is ever changing and uniquely Colorado.

CREEDE

Seat of Mineral County, Creede (pop. 610; elev. 8,852 feet) dates from 1890, when Nicholas C. Creede discovered silver and staked out the Holy Moses mine. In 1893, the population of Creede was 8,000, and the community had earned a reputation as one of Colorado's rowdiest mining camps. Gunfights were commonplace, and saloons, gambling houses, and brothels operated round the clock. One of Creede's early entrepreneurs was Bob Ford, who killed Jesse James (shot him in the back); Ford was murdered in Creede in 1892.

Creede's first newspaper, *The Candle,* was published by Cy Warman, whose versified de-

KAREN WHITE

Nicholas C. Creede

scription of the town became as well known in the mining camps and as oft recited as the poetry of Robert Service:

. . . the cliffs are solid silver,
With wond'rous wealth untold,
And the beds of running rivers
Are lined with the purest gold
While the world is filled with sorrow,
And hearts must break and bleed—
It's day all day in daytime,
And there is no night in Creede.

Creede has faced more than its share of setbacks over the years. In addition to being pummeled by the crash of the silver market in 1893, Creede has four times been all or nearly destroyed by fire, most recently in 1936. The small number of folks who make their home here today, though, are a hardy lot, with much in common with the miners who first settled the town. They appreciate the rugged scenery and the independence guaranteed by their remote location.

Visitors to Creede will find shops and restaurants along the several-block main drag, Creede Ave., which dates from the town's glory days. Creede's tourism, though, is oriented almost entirely toward summer, when folks flock to town to see the famous Creede Repertory Theater, and many of the town's businesses shut down for the winter.

Creede Repertory Theater
Offering talented and well-known actors a summer in one of the Rocky Mountains' prettiest pockets, this little theater group presents highly polished productions that have been favorably reviewed by newspapers throughout the country. Established in 1966, the nonprofit company has been steadily growing in quality and reputation for over a quarter century, and many playgoers are long-time "regulars." Plays, a different one each night of the week, are performed downtown in the Creede Opera House. They range from modern classics (Synge's *Playboy of the Western World*) to adaptations for kids. Tickets are about $10. Advance reservations highly recommended.

For tickets and information, write Creede Repertory Theater, Box 269, Creede, CO 81130, or phone (719) 658-2540.

Creede Underground Mining Museum
Operated in 23,000 square feet of tunnels, rooms, and bays, this museum displays artifacts and historical photos from the mining camp's heyday. On exhibit are the town's first fire truck (hand pulled), a horse-drawn hearse, and mining tools and equipment. The museum, located at 6th and San Luis, is open daily, with tour times varying according to season. For information, write Box 608, Creede, CO 81130, or phone (719) 658-0406 or (800) 327-2102.

Practicalities
Lodging is available in Creede at the rustic **Creede Hotel** (built in 1890), tel. (719) 658-2608, as are breakfast, lunch, and dinner (rotating dinner menu). About 20 miles south of Creede on CO 149 is the **Bristol Inn,** tel. 658-2455, which locals recommend for dinner and Sunday brunch (the restaurant's closed in the winter).

Information
For more information on the Creede area, write the **Creede-Mineral County Chamber of**

Commerce, Box 580, Creede, CO 81130, or phone (719) 658-2374. For information on Rio Grande National Forest, phone the **Creede Ranger District Office** at 658-2556.

LAKE CITY

Sandwiched between Uncompahgre and Rio Grande national forests, Lake City (pop. 206; elev. 8,671 feet) is an 1870s-era mining town with a unique history. First of all, the community seems to have been fortunate enough to avoid the traditional trappings of the other mountain mining camps—brothels, gunfights, gambling, and other assorted manifestations of lawlessness. In fact, by 1877, the town was defined largely by its healthy religious community, with its flocks divided into four churches—Presbyterian, Baptist, Episcopalian, and Catholic. Susan B. Anthony passed through the area on Sept. 20, 1887, speaking for two hours on the suffrage movement.

History remembers lurid excess more than righteousness, though, malevolence more than virtue. And Lake City remembers Alferd Packer, cannibal.

Though Packer's tale has been mythologized over the last century, and historians will probably never fully untangle fact from fiction, a basic story has emerged. Packer had been part of a party of prospectors that stopped at a Ute camp near present-day Delta as the winter of 1874 set in. Chief Ouray, sensing the risk of heading into the mountains, encouraged them to turn back. But men are often blinded by the glare of gold and silver, and Packer and five others didn't listen to the chief. Instead they continued into the mountains. Come spring, Packer alone came down out of the mountains; he claimed he had gone lame and his fellows had deserted him. He had, he said, survived on roots and small game. When offered food, he turned it down; he wanted whiskey instead. He also claimed he was broke, but days later appeared drunk at a gambling hall; some say he was taking money out of several different wallets.

Shortly after a Ute stumbled upon strips of human flesh about five miles from Lake City, a photographer from *Harper's Weekly* discovered in the same area the remains of five men. Their skulls had been crushed and strips of flesh had been torn from their bodies.

Packer maintained his innocence, claiming the men had gone insane and that he had killed one of them, but in self defense. He was arrested, but escaped shortly thereafter and evaded the law for nine years—until 1883, when he was captured in Wyoming. On April 13, Packer was tried in Lake City and sentenced to hang. However, he got off on a technicality and was instead convicted of manslaughter. He was paroled in 1906 and died of natural causes a year later.

The site where the bodies were found, on the northeast side of Lake San Cristobal, is now known as Cannibal Plateau. Colorado remembers Packer himself in strange ways: Lake City hosts an annual Alferd Packer Jeep Tour and Barbecue, and the cafeteria in the student union at the University of Colorado (Boulder) is the Alferd Packer Memorial Grill.

Lake City, meanwhile, has seen a recent rise in tourism. Though too remote to attract many winter visitors, summer sees the little town swell with passers-through, many of whom take advantage of the great recreational opportunities the area affords.

Summer Activities

Fishing is one of the Lake City area's primary draws, with nearby **Lake San Cristobal,** the state's second-largest natural body of water, known for its rainbow and brown trout. Try a Mepps, Kastmaster, or a red-and-white spoon for rainbows; browns, typically voracious and greedy, can often be taken with Rapalas and other lures that look like small bait fish. Of course, some diehards never give up their salmon eggs. Just below the lake, the **Lake Fork** of the Gunnison River offers good dry-fly fishing, with some decent holes right in town. Both the lake and the river are stocked regularly.

Another popular diversion in the area is four-wheeling, with one of the state's best loops beginning just outside town. The 49-mile **Engineer Pass/Cinnamon Pass Loop** takes you west from Lake City through Henson Creek Canyon and over Engineer Pass (elev. 12,810 feet). Once over the pass, you can either continue on to Silverton or Ouray or circle back to Lake City via Cinnamon Pass (elev. 12,620 feet). Between Lake City and Engineer Pass, you'll travel through several ghost towns, including **Capital City, Engineer City,** and **Rose's Cabin.**

The Lake City area also offers excellent **hiking and climbing** opportunities. **Uncompahgre Peak** is the state's sixth-highest mountain and one of the least technical "14ers." The daylong roundtrip hike gains 5,000 feet in elevation. In addition, the surrounding San Juan National Forest offers unlimited backcountry hikes.

Forest Service camping is available at **Slumgullion Pass Campground,** about nine miles south on CO 149 (21 sites on seven acres, no showers). **River Fork Camper Park,** tel. (303) 944-2389, offers RV and tent camping along the Lake Fork of the Gunnison River. Located right in town.

Winter Activities

Though winter doesn't see the tourists in the Lake City area that summer does, some still like to get out and explore the area. Cross-country skiers can head out in virtually any direction and find the soft peace and winter quiet that a snowfall in the Rockies ensures. Those who prefer thrills and speed over peace and quiet take to the old 4WD roads on snowmobiles.

Information

For more information on Lake City, write the **Lake City Chamber of Commerce,** Box 430, Lake City, CO 81235, or phone (303) 944-2527.

For tips and information on recreation, stop by **The Sportsman,** in town on CO 149 S, tel. 944-2526. You can get information on camping in San Juan National Forest from the **Creede Ranger District Office,** tel. 658-2556.

STEPHEN METZGER

SUMMIT COUNTY

This is one of Colorado's best and most popular year-round playgrounds. Located just 70 miles west of Denver via I-70, Summit County, 80% of which is within the borders of Arapaho National Forest, offers more recreational opportunities per square foot than any other area in the state, perhaps the country. Skiing, cycling, hiking, off-road touring, and water sports from fishing to windsurfing combine to draw some three million visitors a year.

Situated just west of the Continental Divide in the high mountains of the Gore and Tenmile ranges, Summit County is an outdoor lover's Garden of Eden, with the Snake and Blue rivers, as well as Tenmile Creek, all tumbling through steep canyons and lush mountain valleys; Dillon Reservoir sprawls as the county's centerpiece. With many of the surrounding peaks topping 13,000 feet, and the towns themselves nestled in 9,000-foot-high valleys, this is about as close to the Rockies' soul as one can get.

During the winter, Summit County, whose full-time population is about 8,000, swells with winter sports enthusiasts from around the world. Skiers flock to the slopes of four of the state's best ski areas: Arapahoe Basin, Breckenridge, Copper Mountain, and Keystone. The funky little streets of Frisco and Breckenridge—mining towns rich in

---

SUMMIT COUNTY HIGHLIGHTS

skiing: Arapahoe Basin, Keystone, Copper Mountain, Breckenridge

fishing: Dillon Reservoir, Green Mountain Reservoir, Blue River, Tenmile Creek

whitewater rafting: Blue River, plus access to nearby Arkansas and Colorado rivers

bicycling: Blue River Bikeway, Tenmile Canyon National Recreation Trail, Vail Pass Bikeway

also: summer chairlift rides at Breckenridge and Copper Mountain, sleigh rides, snow tubing, museums, golf, hiking, horseback riding, jeep tours, historical tours, ballooning in Dillon, shopping, Breckenridge's Ullr Fest, Copper Mountain's West Fest

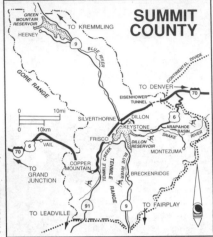

SUMMIT COUNTY

© MOON PUBLICATIONS, INC.

crunching the dry snow. More skiers visit Summit County per year than Aspen and Vail combined.

When the snow disappears from the mountainsides and the ski lifts shut down, Summit County turns its attention to warm-weather recreation. Sails appear on Dillon Reservoir. Bicycles come out of storage, then are tuned and readied for the nearly 50 miles of paved bike paths and hundreds of miles of backcountry trails. Golf clubs are dusted off, tennis nets unfurled and strung across courts, softball gloves oiled for another season.

All of which means you won't have any trouble occupying yourself during your visit to Summit County. And on the off chance that occupying yourself isn't what you had in mind, this is one of the best places in Colorado to simply relax. The mountain sunshine, the scent of pines, the sound of water gently lapping against the shore—Summit County is the best prescription you'll find for urban anxiety, whether you're just passing through or you're here for the long haul.

history—are full of shoppers and après-skiers, bundled up against the cold, their ski boots

INTRODUCTION

HISTORY

Summit County's history dates from summer 1859, when prospectors discovered gold on the Blue River and built a blockhouse near what is now **Breckenridge** as protection from the Utes, who had long claimed this land for their own. Word of the strike soon got out, and when the snows melted the following year, hordes of miners descended on the valley from Denver. Before long, a substantial mining camp had sprung up, with several other smaller ones in the surrounding area. Because the camps were so isolated, the miners sought to be assigned their own post office, and in a political move named their community for Vice President John C. Breckinridge. The town was then granted mail service. When the Civil War broke out and Breckinridge sided with the South, angry citizens changed the spelling of the town's name to Breckenridge.

Silverthorne was founded in 1881, when Judge Marshal Silverthorne purchased 160 acres of land from the U.S. government. Within

a couple of years, the savvy Silverthorne, who ran the Silverthorne Hotel in Breckenridge, had discovered an efficient way to extract gold from the Blue River. He eventually got a patent for the Silverthorne Placer.

Dillon was founded around the same time as Silverthorne, although the present-day town is actually Dillon number three. The town was originally built east of the Snake River; when the railroad arrived, it was moved across the Blue River to be closer to the depot. The new little town did quite well, supporting two newspapers, four saloons, and a couple of general stores. In the early 20th century, local skiers built a ski run above the town, which in 1919 was the site of a world-record-setting ski jump: 213 feet.

In the late 1950s, though, in response to Denver's water shortage, the Blue River was dammed to form Dillon Reservoir. Old Dillon and the ski hill were submerged deep beneath the lake. Dillon was moved to its present site in 1961.

Though miners had used snow skis to get around as early as the 1880s, and turn-of-the-century Summit Countians had begun to use

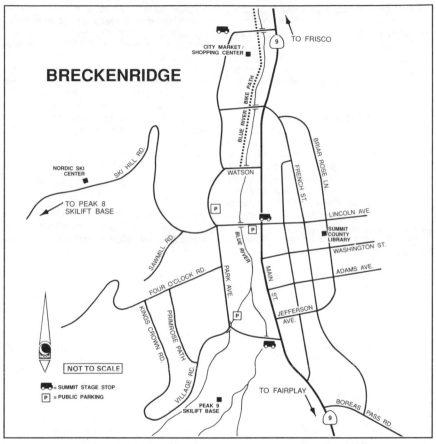

skis for recreation, it wasn't until the late 1940s that skiing really began to take off in the area. That was the year Arapahoe Basin opened, and a number of lodges and inns were built in the Dillon-Keystone area, turning the county into a prototypical ski resort. By the mid-1960s, the nation had caught "ski fever," and Summit County was in the perfect position to take advantage of it. By the winter of 1972-73, all four of Summit County's ski areas were open for business and attracting skiers from all over the world. That winter also saw the completion of the first bore of Eisenhower Tunnel through Loveland Pass, making for a safer and faster drive from Denver (see the "Eisenhower Memorial Tunnel" special topic).

The 1970s and '80s witnessed huge improvements at the ski areas, not only in additional acres and increased numbers of lifts, but in technology (better, faster, and safer lifts), instructional methods, shuttle services, lodging facilities, and on-mountain amenities. Also during the '70s and '80s, Summit County began to develop into a four-season resort area, with summer visitors flocking to the area to golf, mountain bike, whitewater raft, and hike the back trails of Arapaho National Forest.

Today, Summit County offers many chances to view its history. The Summit County Historical Society sponsors walking tours of Breckenridge Historical District, as well as tours to mining towns; Frisco Historic Park displays buildings from that town's heyday. And if that's not enough, just take a gander at the tailings along the Blue River between Frisco and Breckenridge. Unfortunately, mining leaves ugly scars, and the county hasn't wholly escaped the fate that has befallen so many other Colorado mining regions.

BRECKENRIDGE

Breckenridge (pop. 1,200; elev. 9,500 feet) is both the oldest and the largest community in Summit County. Located in the Blue River Valley at the base of the massive Tenmile range, Breckenridge is a ski town in the truest sense of the term, with the three-mountain Breckenridge Ski Resort dropping nearly down to the little town's ski-shop-lined Main Street.

Dating from the mid-19th century, when it was a roaring mining camp, Breckenridge is a National Historic District, and many of its Victorians have been gorgeously restored, today housing bed and breakfasts, restaurants, and retail shops. In contrast, several deluxe hotels, convention centers, and condominium complexes are scattered on the hills between Main St. and the ski area.

One of the oldest continually occupied mining towns in the state, Breckenridge still has a bit of a frontier feel to it. It's a young and vital town that can still get awfully rowdy on Saturday nights when the bars are packed with ski resort employees and miners down out of the mountains spending their paychecks.

During the summer, downtown Breckenridge becomes a shopping mecca, its sidewalks packed with visitors exploring the scores of gift and souvenir stores, boutiques, and T-shirt shops. Many of the restaurants feature patio seating, and you can sit and enjoy a salad and a lemonade, or a burger and a beer, in the crisp thin-air sunshine.

FRISCO

Located at the junction of I-70 and CO 9 in the center of Summit County, Frisco (pop. 1,320; elev. 9,000 feet) offers excellent access to the county's skiing and other recreational sports. A late-19th-century mining town, Frisco today is an unpretentious little community defined by friendly people who seem somehow less caught up in the glamour of the ski industry, though the town's economy is still largely dependent on winter tourists.

The town's quiet main drag has a handful of restaurants, older motels, and sports and gift stores. The back streets south of Main are lined with old homes and cabins, some converted to bed and breakfasts; larger vacation-type homes and complexes are scattered in the woods just north of Main. Not far from the downtown area, Frisco loses some of its intimacy and charm, the highway both north and south lined with fast-food restaurants, gas stations, and malls (with a Wal-Mart, a Safeway, and other modern conveniences).

DILLON

On the shore of Summit County's centerpiece, Dillon Reservoir, Dillon is a blend of backwoods cabins, modern vacation homes, and deluxe hotels and condo complexes. Its streets winding through the pines and down by the lake, Dillon is without a real "downtown," though the Dillon Mall is home to several restaurants, business offices, ski shops, and other retailers.

© MOON PUBLICATIONS, INC.

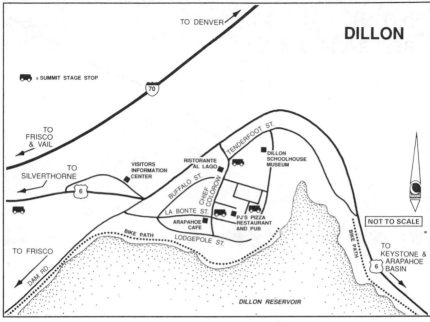

Dillon has been a popular resort community since the 1940s, when Arapahoe Basin skiers built log cabins in the area and the first restaurants and lodges opened. Today, the community offers some of the most upscale lodging in the county. During the summer, Dillon is very popular with sailors, anglers, and other water-sports enthusiasts, who can lodge within yards of the lakeshore.

SILVERTHORNE

Silverthorne lies at the junction of I-70, Hwy. 6, and CO 9, and though it dates from the 1860s, the town has the feel of the popular tourist stop that it is. Silverthorne sees millions of travelers annually, many of whom stop to take advantage of the chain motels and hotels, fast-food outlets, gas stations, recreation-equipment-rental outfits, and the huge Silverthorne Factory Stores mall. To get a sense of less-traveled Silverthorne, take a drive north on CO 9; this is the gateway to the Blue River Valley and Eagles Nest Wilderness Area. Hidden in the pines di-

rectly west of the central shopping areas, on the hillside overlooking I-70 and the lake, are a number of condominium complexes and deluxe vacation homes.

COPPER MOUNTAIN

Copper Mountain is a self-contained resort community, with several high-rise condominium complexes and lodges, as well as a central plaza area where you'll find a conference center, ski shops, boutiques, and restaurants. Many Copper employees live in on-site resort-owned housing.

Copper Mountain first opened in the winter of 1972-73 and revolves primarily around snow skiing. During the winter, the place bustles with skiers in for the day from Denver as well as Texans, New Yorkers, and Europeans here to hit the slopes for a week or more. In the summer, things die down considerably, though the resort also offers a variety of recreation, including golf at Copper Creek Golf Club, as well as tennis, fishing, and whitewater rafting.

KEYSTONE

Like Copper, Keystone is a self-contained vacation resort area devoted largely to skiing. Located in the lush Snake River Valley above Dillon Reservoir, Keystone is surrounded by massive mountains, many of which rise to over 13,000 feet. Keystone first opened for skiing in the winter of 1969-70.

Tucked away among thick pine forests, Keystone is comprised of condominium complexes, the Keystone Conference Center, and a small village with ski stores, gift shops, and restaurants. To keep the cash flow at least moderate between ski seasons, Keystone offers a wide range of summer activities, including gondola rides, horseback riding, and golf. The resort also hosts the annual Keystone Music Festival with classical and pop concerts by the National Repertory Theater and the Summit Brass.

MONTEZUMA

The highest occupied community in the United States (elev. 10,268 feet), Montezuma is a tiny town isolated just off the Continental Divide east of Keystone. Dating from the late 1800s, Montezuma has yet to be taken over by T-shirt and souvenir shops, unlike other 19th-century silver-mining towns like Cripple Creek and Central

City. A small handful of hardy Summit Countians call Montezuma home. To get there take Montezuma Rd. off Hwy. 6 just east of Keystone.

HEENEY

Heeney is the northernmost community in Summit County. Located on Green Mountain Reservoir off CO 9, the town is small enough and far enough away from the ski resorts that it doesn't take itself too seriously. To wit: Each June, the town sponsors the Heeney Tick Festival, which, according to one story, began when a popular Heeneyite recovered from a tick-bite related sick spell. The highlight of the festival, which also features a dance and kids' programs, is the parade down Main St., with "tick-sized floats."

MUSEUMS

Summit County is much richer in history than it is in museums, although the Summit Historical Society, with local dynamo Rebecca Waugh at the helm, has recently increased efforts to bring history to the public. The **Dillon Schoolhouse Museum,** a 19th-century one-room schoolhouse, displays early educational supplies, desks, readers, and musical instruments.

The museum is located at 403 La Bonte St., Dillon, and is open late May-early Sept., Wed.-Sat. 11 a.m.-4 p.m.

Also administered by the Summit Historical Society is the **Montezuma Schoolhouse Museum,** isolated in the deep woods east of Keystone at the old Montezuma mining camp. A visit here is an excellent way to learn about mining and the early settling of Summit County. The Montezuma Schoolhouse Museum is open Saturdays only from early July through mid-August. To get there, take Hwy. 6 past Keystone to Montezuma Rd., and continue about five miles to the town of Montezuma. Admission to both museums is by donation. For more information on either, phone (303) 453-9022.

Frisco Historic Park

This collection of seven buildings from late-19th-century Frisco will give you a good idea of what the town was like as a logging and mining center. Included are a one-room schoolhouse, a jail, a ranch house, and a chapel. The museum also displays historical photos, clothing, and other artifacts from the period.

Frisco Historic Park, located at the corner of Main and 2nd, is open Tues.-Sat. 11 a.m.-4 p.m. (through Sun., Memorial Day through Labor Day). Admission is free. For more information, phone (303) 668-3428.

PARKS AND RECREATION

Okay, museums are all fine and well, but you can't fool me. You didn't come to Summit County to brush up on your history. You came to play. Though one of the side benefits of this playground is its marvelous sense of history, its main draw is recreation. And though Summit County's begun to sell itself this past decade as a year-round resort, the area's really about skiing. When the first downy flakes of the white stuff begin to swirl from a dark autumn sky, Summit County turns its attention to the slopes.

For complete information on the wide range of recreational possibilities in Summit County, contact the Forest Service office at 135 CO 9 in Silverthorne, tel. (303) 468-5400, and ask for their *Recreation Opportunity Guide.*

SKIING

Four of Colorado's best ski areas are concentrated within the borders of relatively tiny Summit County. With a total of nearly 60 lifts servicing almost 300 marked trails on 4,000 acres of skiable terrain, Arapahoe Basin, Breckenridge, Copper Mountain, and Keystone combine to offer some of the finest skiing in the country.

No matter what your level—whether you're a first-time beginner or a retiring weideler, bump basher, powder hound, or chute shredder—you're bound to find something in Summit County to your liking.

Skiers pause to take in the view at Keystone.

STEPHEN METZGER

Avoiding The Crowds

And, unfortunately, sometimes it seems as though *everyone* is here. Not only are these some of the best ski areas in the state, but they're also about the most accessible—just 70 miles from Denver, with shuttles running back and forth about every 10 minutes. So the slopes can get crowded.

And so can the roads.

Not only does I-70 bottleneck between the resorts and Denver on Friday and Sunday afternoons, but some of the smaller access roads can also grind to standstills. Hints to avoid crowds: unfortunately, no profound secrets here. In fact, most folks know exactly how to avoid crowded slopes—it's just that their jobs won't let them. If yours does, try this: don't ski weekends, especially long ones; don't ski during Christmas vacation (approximately Dec. 26-Jan. 2 or 3). If you have no choice but to ski during those crowded times, get up early, get to the parking lot early, buy your ticket early, start skiing early, break for lunch early, quit early. Then get to bed early and do it again.

Also, don't forget about late-season skiing. Arapahoe Basin regularly stays open until June, and then it might only close due to lack of customers. Just because your friends are calling you to play tennis or to chase trout, don't think the ski season's over. Indeed, you could very easily head up to the Basin one fine spring day and look around you and find that you *are* the lift line, that you're the only one on the entire lift, or that you've got a whole mile-and-a-half run all to

your lonesome. Ain't nobody but you and the mountain; that's one of the greatest feelings in the world.

Lift Tickets

As lift-ticket prices approach and in some cases surpass the $40 mark, a day's skiing takes a bigger and bigger chunk of your life's savings. And unless you're Donald Trump or Michael Jackson, you'll probably want to keep an eye out for ways to trim the cost. You won't be able to save a whole lot, but if you play your cards right, you will find breaks here and there. First of all, most of the resorts offer multiday discounts, and you can buy tickets that are good at all four resorts. Second, many of the retailers in the area—from grocery stores to ski-rental outlets—offer discounts. Watch the local papers, coupon booklets, and advertising. Three bucks saved on a lift ticket will almost buy you a beer at the end of the day. For more information on multiday tickets and discounts, call **Ski the Summit,** at (303) 468-6607.

Arapahoe Basin

Look at these terrain statistics: 40% advanced, 50% intermediate, 10% beginner. That should tell you that A-Basin is one demanding ski area. Steep, challenging, unforgiving—where some of the toughest skiers in the area fine-tune their chops. Skiers who don't care that this is the smallest ski area in Summit County know it's the best, and a lot of them wouldn't ski anywhere else.

Arapahoe Basin first opened shortly after WW II, when members of the U.S. Army's 10th Mountain Division improvised a cable ski lift using old mining equipment. The resort stayed small and low-key, even as many of the state's other ski areas were being developed into major destination resorts. In the late 1970s, A-Basin was bought by Keystone, the owners of which invested money in upgrading the Basin. Still, though, it remains refreshingly unglitzy. This is in part because it's the least accessible of the four Summit County ski areas. It sits high on the west side of Loveland Pass, and Denver skiers must either drive through Eisenhower Tunnel to Dillon and then turn around and go east again via Hwy. 6, or they must drive over the top of the pass, a harrowing if awesomely scenic road, and drop down to the base of the lifts.

Today, A-Basin has five lifts servicing 30 trails on 350 mostly above-timberline acres. Its 360-inch average snowfall, coupled with its 10,780-foot *base,* ensures that it regularly stays open until June, oftentimes longer. The same lift ticket is good at both Keystone and A-Basin, and shuttles run every 20 minutes between the two (there are no accommodations at Arapahoe), though again beginners would be better off heading elsewhere and mastering at least a decent christy turn before risking frustration here. Those whose goal is to sample the range of American skiing owe it to themselves to try the Basin, where you're as close to the top of the world as any chairlift will take you.

For more information on Arapahoe Basin, phone the resort at (303) 468-0718, or write Keystone Resort, Box 38, Keystone, CO 80435, tel. 468-2316.

Keystone

In contrast to Arapahoe Basin, Keystone is an area ideally suited to beginners and intermediate skiers. Excluding the North Peak area (see below), Keystone's terrain is 20% beginner, 65% intermediate, and 15% advanced.

Keystone is the epitome of a user-friendly resort. Among its attractions: well-groomed slopes ideal for effortless cruising, high-tech lifts and equipment, exceptional instructional programs, convenient accommodations and facilities, and night skiing—lifts run for 13 hours.

Keystone's back side, the North Peak area, significantly increased the resort's advanced skiing; North Peak is 29% intermediate and 71% advanced. Combined, the two areas' 15 lifts service nearly 800 acres (snowmaking on 600), with 51 marked trails. The longest run is three miles.

To get there, take Hwy. 6 east from Dillon and watch for the signs.

For more information on skiing Keystone, contact the resort at Box 38, Keystone, CO 80435, tel. (303) 468-2316.

Copper Mountain

Copper Mountain first opened in the winter of 1972-73 as a completely self-contained resort community. The second-largest ski resort in Summit County, Copper Mountain leases from the Forest Service three separate mountains, which naturally divide the resort's terrain fairly evenly among ski abilities (25% beginner, 40% intermediate, 35% advanced). In all, there are 1,200 acres serviced by 20 lifts, including two quads and six triple chairs.

EISENHOWER MEMORIAL TUNNEL

First open to traffic in the spring of 1973 and completed in 1979, when the second bore was punched through, Eisenhower Memorial Tunnel cost just under $300 million and tremendously increased the accessibility of Colorado's ski resorts. The new route cut as much as an hour off the drive from Denver to the lifts at Vail, Copper Mountain, Breckenridge, and the others. In fact, the new tunnel so dramatically opened up the mountain resorts to motorists (its first year 4.6 million cars passed through) that within 10 years of its completion it was already being viewed as inadequate, and the highway department was bemoaning that the tunnel's four lanes weren't six. State highway officials estimate that by the turn of the century the tunnel will see some 10 million cars a year, far more than it was designed to, or is able to, accommodate.

In addition to the snags on the back sides of the two major summer holidays (Memorial and Labor days), Eisenhower and I-70 also get snarled on winter weekends, especially the three- and four-day presidents' celebrations in February.

For road conditions in the Eisenhower Tunnel area, phone (303) 639-1111.

Because of the wide range of excellent skiing, as well as the resort's wonderful accessibility (it's just yards from I-70 on the east side of Vail Pass), it's a favorite of Denver day-trippers. Its range of fine skiing also makes it attractive to families and other groups within which ability levels vary. Groups can ski together awhile, then head off for terrain suited to their individual abilities, then meet again for lunch or to show off for each other before retiring at day's end for a beer.

Another one of Copper's advantages is its self-containment. There's plenty of on-site lodging, shopping, and dining, and it's a great place to hole up for a week doing nothing but skiing—you can be out your door and on the slopes in minutes.

For more information on skiing or accommodations at Copper Mountain, write Copper Mountain Resort Association, Box 3001, Copper Mountain, CO 80433, tel. (303) 968-2882 or (800) I-LUV-FUN.

Breckenridge

With 1,600 skiable acres, Breckenridge is Summit County's largest ski area. Sixteen lifts service 112 designated trails, the longest of which is three miles. Like Copper Mountain, Breckenridge offers a roughly even mix of beginning, intermediate, and advanced skiing, though recent expansion has made the area more attractive to better skiers (the actual breakdown is 20% beginner, 31% intermediate, and 49% advanced). Also like Copper, Breckenridge sprawls over three separate mountains—Peaks 8, 9, and 10. Beginning and low-intermediate skiers have the lower parts of Peaks 8 and 9 to roam, while advanced skiers claim the back sides of peaks 8 and 10, which are also good places to avoid crowds. The two base areas provide access to all three mountains.

One of Breckenridge's real pluses is its open-mindedness and the resulting on-mountain eclecticness. One of the first ski areas in the state to okay snowboarding—skiing's Eddie Haskell of a little cousin—then actively to court the wild snow surfers, Breckenridge hosts the World Snowboard Championships every January. The resort is also popular with Telemarkers.

Something else that distinguishes Breckenridge from Copper, Keystone, and A-Basin is that here the town and the ski resort are more closely linked—in fact, the town and the ski area are virtually one and the same. Much like Telluride and Aspen, Breckenridge is a ski town in the truest and most aesthetically pleasing sense. Though Breckenridge claims its share of condos and fancy modern motels, the town is much more defined by its Victorian-lined main streets, its tiny shops, and its laid-back locals—young, unpretentious, and completely ski oriented. After a good dump, the little town's streets are all but deserted, as just about everyone's "gone skiin'."

For more information on skiing and accommodations in Breckenridge, contact **Breckenridge Ski Corporation,** Box 1058, Breckenridge, CO 80424, tel. (303) 453-2368, or **Breckenridge Resort Chamber,** Box 1909, Breckenridge, CO 80424, tel. (800) 221-1091 or (800) 822-5381 (in Colorado).

Cross-country Skiing

Take a look at the racks atop cars coming into Summit County from Denver, as well as those on local rigs, and you'll see that cross-country skiing is, if not as popular as downhill, certainly the passion of *many* people. In fact, Summit County skinny skiers have even more to choose from than Alpiners do: everything from quiet, ungroomed lakeside trails to groomed skating tracks to the lift-serviced runs of the resorts themselves, where three-pinners practice Tele turns on the same slopes as downhillers.

Frisco Nordic Center, 1121 N. Summit Blvd., Frisco, tel. (303) 668-0866, offers nearly 40 km of trails (one-way loops) in the woods near Dillon Reservoir. Lessons and rentals are available. **Copper Mountain/Trak Cross-Country Resort,** Box 3001, Copper Mountain, CO 80443, tel. 968-2882, ext. 6342, has 25 km of groomed track and skate lanes. A favorite among intermediate and advanced Nordic skiers, this center also offers access to Copper Mountain's lifts, as well as a variety of special programs, including races, moonlight tours, and Telemark, waxing, and snow-safety workshops. **Breckenridge Nordic Ski Center,** Box 1776, Breckenridge, CO 80424, tel. 453-6855, has 30 km, rentals, and lessons (located a mile west of town on Ski Hill Road). Cruise the Keystone area at **Keystone Cross-Country Center,** Box 38, Keystone, CO 80435, tel. 468-4275, where 30 km meander among the backcountry lodges, creek, and valley.

In addition, the county has many easily accessible trails ideally suited to cross-country skiers, including some of the bike paths and areas around Dillon Reservoir. Parts of the 15-mile bike path paralleling CO 9 between Frisco and Breckenridge are perfect for easy-access sliding, as are some of the Forest Service campgrounds on the lake (roads and weather permitting).

For further information on Nordic skiing, contact the Dillon District office of **Arapaho National Forest,** 135 CO 9, Silverthorne, CO 80498, tel. 468-5400. You can also get information from the retail ski shops in the area, including **Peak Performance,** 309 S. Main, Breckenridge, tel. 453-4463, and **Breckenridge Ski Shop,** 117 S. Main, tel. 453-2455. In Silverthorne, stop in at **Wildernessports,** 171 Blue River Parkway, tel. 468-8519, and in Frisco, try **Antler's Ski and Sport Shop,** 908 N. Summit, tel. 668-3152.

Helicopter Skiing

Helicopters provide expensive but quick and effortless access to untracked bowls high on backcountry mountainsides, offering advanced and expert skiers the experience of a lifetime. Frisco-based **Colorado Heli-Ski** offers a range of guided tours, including single-run flights and full-day multirun excursions that include lunch. Rates run from about $75 (one run, allow two hours) to $400 (six hours of runs, with lunch and instruction). The company also offers scenic flights and charters. For more information or to make reservations, phone (303) 668-5600.

Helicopter skiing is also offered by **Montezuma Helicopter,** an affiliate of the **United States Backcountry Association,** 5435 Summit County Rd. 5, Montezuma, tel. 468-5378.

OTHER WINTER ACTIVITIES

Snowmobiling

Though controversial by definition (the machines are loud, exhausty, and fossil-fuel gobbling), this sport has its fans, with several outfits in the county providing a range of services and activities. **Tiger Run Resort,** Box 1418, Breckenridge, CO 80424, tel. (303) 453-2231, has 150 snowmobiles for rent (as well as boots and snowsuits). Tiger Run is located four miles north of Breckenridge on CO 9. You can also rent snowmobiles at **Summit Adventure Park** at Farmers Korner between Frisco and Breckenridge; phone 453-0353. **Kingdom of Broke 'n' Rich Snow Company,** at the south end of Breckenridge, tel. 453-2333, has a snowmobile track and equipment rentals.

Ice Skating

Summit County probably has more ice-skating rinks than any similar-size area west of New York and south of the Canadian border. One of the most popular is **Keystone Lake** in Keystone Village, open daily 10 a.m. to 10 p.m. Rental skates available. Phone Keystone Resort at (303) 468-2316 for more information.

base of lifts at Copper Mountain

Ice skating is also available on Maggie Pond in Breckenridge (next to the Bell Tower Mall) and on West Lake in Copper Mountain.

Over The River And Through The Woods

A number of Summit County outfits offer day and evening sleigh rides, from short jaunts to dinner rides that might include buffalo soup or baked salmon. Copper Mountain's **Dining in the Woods** sleigh leaves the central plaza Wed.-Sun. evenings at 6 p.m. for an elegant meal in a miners' tent. Fixed price (about $35); menu changes nightly. Phone (303) 968-2882, ext. 6320 for reservations. **Alpine Adventures, Inc.** has 16-passenger "Dinner on the Trail" sleighs that leave at 5:30 p.m. and 8 p.m. nightly from **Summit Adventure Park** at Farmers Korner. Write Box 2620-B, Breckenridge, CO 80424, or phone 453-0111. Sleigh-ride dinners are also offered by **Tenderfoot Tours,** Box 2882, 149 Tenderfoot St., Dillon, CO 80435, tel. 468-5000.

Totally Tubular

In this world of high-tech, high-cost diversions and "adventure travel," it's often easy to forget the simple pleasures: snow tubing, for example. Simply speaking, tubing can be a *gas.* Bundle up, find yourself an inner tube and a hill, and let yourself be nine years old again. Guaranteed to cure what ails you; there's no room for depression, domestic squabbling, or existential angst on a tubing hill. And nothing tastes quite so good as a hot chocolate or brandy afterward.

If you truly can't find a tubing hill on your own, check out **Summit Adventure Park,** at Farmers Korner between Frisco and Breckenridge, tel. (303) 453-0353. Rentals available.

WHEN THE SNOW MELTS

Though Summit boosters have been very successful changing the area's image from that of a cluster of ski towns to a year-round resort, Summit County remains predominantly winter oriented. So far. But each summer, more and more tourists are drawn to the area for its myriad recreational opportunities—from cycling to windsurfing, fishing to horseback riding.

Cycling

Anyone skeptical that this is the sport of the '90s, and that Summit County is one of the premier biking areas in the country, need only take a look around. Miles and miles of bicycle paths connect the various communities; not only are they ideal for exploring, but they make commuting easy for locals. Come spring, don't be surprised to see a mountain biker on Main St. in Breckenridge with a pair of skis under his arm or bungie-corded to his top bar.

Among the excellent paved bike paths in the area are the **Blue River Bikeway,** which connects Breckenridge and Frisco and winds in and out of meadows and forests of sweet-smelling pines; **Tenmile Canyon National Recreation Trail** between Copper Mountain and Frisco; and **Vail Pass Bikeway,** a 20-mile route up over the 10,600-foot pass that drops down into Vail Village—excellent scenery en route.

For more serious touring, you can head off in just about any direction, though traffic will of course be heavier on some routes. Colorado 9 north along the Blue River is a moderate ride, with rises but no significant hills. At the other end of the range, Hwy. 6 east passes A-Basin and climbs over the grueling **Loveland Pass** (11,990 feet). Even Ah-nold or Bo might huff and puff a bit.

The county is also rife with mountain-bike trails, with several designated paths over nearby mountain passes, including **Boreas, Georgia,** and **Webster** passes. Your best source for information on mountain biking in the area is the Dillon District Office of **Arapaho National Forest,** 135 Hwy. 9, Silverthorne, tel. (303) 468-5400. The Forest Service, in conjunction with the county, has published an excellent map that shows the various trails in the area, and also provides mileage, difficulty ratings, safety and camping information, and recommended tours. The maps are available free at the Forest Service office and at most bike shops in the area.

Fat Tire Tours, 303 South Main St., Breckenridge, tel. 453-1872, offers a variety of guided mountain-bike tours for all ability and fitness levels: ghost-town, moonlight, bed-and-breakfast, fall foliage, and "singles" tours. You can also arrange trips through **Kodi Mountain Bike Rentals,** Box 1215, Breckenridge, CO 80424, tel. 453-2194 or (800) 525-9624. If you're more interested in the ride down than the one up, the **Montezuma Helicopter,** through **United States Backcountry Association,** will haul you and your bike to some remote mountaintop. For more information, phone 468-5378.

Golf

Golf is another exceptionally popular summer activity in Summit County, and some of the ski resorts, specifically Keystone and Copper Mountain, promote golf-and-lodging packages with the same enthusiasm with which they promote skiing plans during the winter. The public **Breckenridge Golf Course** is owned and operated by the town of Breckenridge. Designed by Jack Nicklaus, the 18-hole course, located at 200 Clubhouse Dr., offers a wonderful natural setting in the Blue River Valley just north of town. Phone (303) 453-5544 for tee times and information. **Copper Creek Golf Club** at Copper Mountain, another lush 18-hole course with excellent views, claims to be the highest-elevation PGA course in the country. Phone 968-2339.

Keystone Ranch Golf Course at Keystone Resort offers a blend of the old and the new: the 18-hole course is not yet a teenager, but the clubhouse dates from the 1930s. It's reserved for Keystone guests, except on a space-available basis. Phone the golf course at 468-4250 or Keystone Resort at 468-2316. The nine-hole **Eagles Nest Golf Course** is located in north Silverthorne off Hwy. 9. Phone 468-0681.

Hiking

Summit County abounds in hiking trails, from half-mile walks to scenic overlooks to ten-mile (and longer), full-day wilderness excursions. The Forest Service, in conjunction with several local businesses, publishes an excellent *Summer Trailhead Guide,* which discusses a dozen trails of varying lengths and difficulty levels. The guide also includes recommendations for specific topo maps and provides a day-pack checklist and suggestions for environmental responsibility.

Here is a small sampling of Forest Service-suggested hikes: **Tenderfoot Mountain** is an easy mile-and-a-quarter hike that offers views of Dillon Reservoir and the Gore and Tenmile mountain ranges. Turn north from the stoplight on Hwy. 6 in Dillon, and turn immediately right onto the frontage road, which you'll follow to the trailhead. **Gold Hill Trail** is a popular three-mile hike that begins five miles south of Frisco on Hwy. 9. Ranked "more difficult," Gold Hill is part of the Colorado Trail and joins up with **Peaks Trail** three miles south of Frisco. **Wheeler National Recreation Trail** is an 11-mile hike, also ranked "more difficult," linking Breckenridge and Copper Mountain. The trail crosses the Tenmile Range through Breckenridge ski area, and offers views of the Tenmile, Gore, Sawatch, and Flat Top ranges. There are also lots of excellent hiking trails in the **Eagles Nest Wilderness Area** north of Silverthorne. The **Forest Service** can provide complete information.

Fishing

There's a lot of water in Summit County, most obviously the sprawling arms and main body of Dillon Reservoir. In addition, there are many streams and rivers, with lots of accessible shoreline. Also, Green Mountain Reservoir north of Dillon midway to Kremmling offers lots of fishing opportunities for both the shore and boat angler. Among the fish you'll find in the county's various waters are brook, brown, rainbow, and lake trout, and kokanee salmon.

Summit County waters are so accessible, though, that they see an awful lot of traffic, and you've got to be pretty persistent and trout-savvy to hook into big fish. Remember, too, that some of the streams have special restrictions; make sure you read and understand all regulations before making that first cast.

Dillon Reservoir offers decent fishing year-round (ice fishing in the winter) for trout and kokanee salmon. Boats are ideal, though fishing from the shore can be successful as well. **Green Mountain Reservoir** is also open year-round, with the narrower Blue River Channel stretches, as well as the area between the town of Heeney and the dam, offering the best bets.

The **Blue River** north of Silverthorne is a Gold Medal Water-designated trout stream with some excellent catch-and-release-only sections (fly fishing only). **Tenmile Creek** between Frisco and Copper Mountain can also be good.

An excellent source of information is *Fish The Summit,* a map and guide that discusses the Summit's various streams and lakes in detail, offering a season-by-season series of tips on lures, bait, and hot spots. The guide also identifies the individual species of fish (with both drawings ánd text), discusses stream restrictions, and provides a list of fishing-license agents. The map and guide is available at most tourist and chamber of commerce offices or by writing New Sensations, Box 36203, Denver, CO 80236, tel. (303) 987-9330.

A number of outfitters in the county provide guided fishing trips. The following companies offer half- and full-day trips, as well as instructions and rental equipment: **Columbine Outfitters,** 502 Main St., Frisco, tel. 668-3704; **Mountain Angler,** 311 Main St., Breckenridge, tel. 453-HOOK—specializing in catch-and-release fly fishing on private waters; and **Summit Guides,** 110 Ski Hill Rd., Breckenridge, tel. 453-1430.

The Gore Range Anglers chapter of Trout Unlimited meets the last Thursday of each month at the Best Western Inn in Frisco.

Whitewater Rafting

Though there's not a whole lot of whitewater in Summit County, there's plenty nearby, and a number of companies offer half- and full-day trips on the county's Blue River, as well as on the Arkansas and Colorado. Contact **Performance Tours Rafting,** tel. (303) 343-0661 or (800) 328-7238; **Tiger Run Resort,** 128 S. Main St., Breckenridge, tel. 453-2231; or **Kodi Whitewater Rafting Tours,** Box 1215, Breckenridge, CO 80424, tel. 453-2194.

Boating, Sailing, And Windsurfing

Dillon Reservoir and Green Mountain Reservoir are exceptionally popular for most water sports (though the water's *awfully* cold for swimming). There are several public boat launches around Dillon Reservoir, and the shore is generally gently sloped for easy put-ins. In addition, a handful of marinas rent sailboats, paddleboats, and fishing boats. In Dillon, check out Dillon Yacht Basin, on E. Lodgepole, tel. (303) 468-2396. In Frisco, you can rent canoes and motorboats at Osprey Adventures, 810 Main St., tel. 668-5573, which also offers guided canoe tours.

Ballooning

To see Summit County Frank Morgan-style, from the basket of a hot-air balloon, contact the Dillon office of **Balloon America,** tel. (303) 468-2473.

Horseback Rides

This is superb country to explore by horseback, and a number of pack companies in the area offer a range of trips. **Alpine Adventures,** Box 2620-B, Breckenridge, CO 80424, tel. (303) 468-9297, offers short trail rides as well as overnight pack trips to the Montezuma Mining District and into Arapaho National Forest; meals and a sleeping bag provided. **Eagles Nest Equestrian Center,** Box 495, Silverthorne, CO 80498, tel. 468-0677, also offers a full range of trips, specializing in extended backcountry tours and fall hunts. You can also arrange rides, from one hour to a full day, through **Tenderfoot Tours,** Box 2882, Dillon, CO 80435, tel. 468-5000, and **Breckenridge Stables,** Box 1816, Breckenridge, CO 80424, tel. 453-4438, which specializes in large groups and short rides that include meals.

Chairlift Rides

Breckenridge and Copper Mountain both offer off-season chairlift rides for sightseers, while you can ride Keystone's gondola. At the top, grab something to eat while you take in the panoramas, and then either ride or hike back down. Lifts are usually open from late spring through September. For more information, phone **Breckenridge Ski Area,** tel. (303) 453-2368; **Copper Mountain Resort,** tel. 968-2318; or **Keystone Resort,** tel. 468-2316.

Jeep Tours

The old mining roads and high mountain passes in Summit County make the area a natural for exploring with an off-road vehicle. From ghosts of old mining towns to high lakes, some of Summit's most interesting areas are accessible only by 4WD. For maps and information, stop by the Forest Service, 135 Hwy. 9 in Silverthorne. **Tiger Run Resort,** tel. (303) 453-2231, and **Tenderfoot Tours,** tel. 468-5000, can arrange jeep tours of the backcountry.

Historical Tours

The Summit County Historical Society has designed a number of guided and self-guided tours of the area, including Breckenridge and local ghost and mining towns. Guided tours of the Breckenridge Historic District are offered Wed.-Sat. at 10 a.m. (summers)—a ghost is said to haunt the bathroom of the Brown Hotel. The society also sponsors tours to Washington Gold Mine and the Carter House Museum. Meet at the Breckenridge Activities Center, 201 S. Main Street. For starting times and more information, phone (303) 453-5579.

Take Me Out To The Ball Game
One of the most relaxing ways to spend a summer evening or Saturday afternoon is by watching a local slow-pitch softball game. Spirits are high as teams representing local pizza parlors, construction companies, and ski shops vie for Summit County trophies. Watch excellent athletes (many of the best skiers in the area) drive ground balls up the middle or line deep ropes into the gaps. The Breckenridge fields are located just north of town; turn down behind the City Market and continue north.

PRACTICALITIES

You'll find a huge range of accommodations in Summit County, from small mom-and-pop motels to luxurious condominium complexes and convention centers—each year fewer and fewer of the former and more and more of the latter. You can also rent individual homes, some sprawling and estatelike, others smaller and more budget oriented. Generally, if you're looking for cheap digs, you'll be least disappointed in Frisco and Silverthorne, both virtually lakeside to Dillon Reservoir, whereas if you're more interested in being pampered, you might want to check out the condos and hotels in Breckenridge, Dillon, Keystone, or Copper Mountain. Between the two extremes are a handful of highway-side franchise inns both in Frisco and Dillon. Most of the lodges offer free shuttle service to the ski areas, as well as package deals that include lift tickets, equipment rentals, and transportation.

When it comes to lodging (and what you'll pay), though, the main consideration here, as in most resort towns, is season: most places adjust their rates to the ol' law of supply and demand—when the snow comes down, prices go up. High-season prices here generally revolve around the ski resorts and holidays. Rates will be highest between Christmas and the end of New Year's weekend. They'll also be high in February, around the time of Washington's and Lincoln's birthdays (often shoved together and celebrated jointly in ski country to allow schoolkids a whole week off). Predictably, rates will be lower once the snow melts, especially in late spring before the weather warms up enough to allow for swimming, sailing, and shirt-sleeved bike riding and hiking, and in the fall, when it cools off again and before the clearcuts on the mountainsides are snow covered and the engines of the chairlifts get fired up again.

The other thing to keep in mind here is that even though rates go up significantly when the skiing gets good, people still clamor to pay them. Don't even think of trying without reservations to find a room in this part of the country when the skiing's good. Book a room at least a month before you plan to come. Or better yet, two months. Or six. A year if you can. (The only way you might find a room at the last minute during high season is by calling to see if there have been any cancellations.)

Summit County Lodging Information
For complete information on accommodations in Summit County, write the **Summit County Chamber of Commerce,** Box 214, Frisco, CO 80443, or phone (303) 668-0376. You can also get lodging information from the following ski resorts: **Breckenridge,** tel. (800) 822-5381 in Colorado, or (800) 221-1091 outside Colorado; **Copper Mountain,** tel. (800) I-LUV-FUN (it wasn't my idea . . .); and **Keystone,** tel. (800) 222-0188 for condos, (800) 541-0346 for the lodge. You can also book vacation rentals, summer or winter, through **Summit County Central Reservations,** Box 446, Dillon, CO 80435, tel. (800) 365-6365; or **High Country Travel And Tours,** tel. 468-1080, (800) 999-0823 in Colorado, or (800) 367-1654.

MOTELS AND HOTELS

Most of the smaller motels and hotels are in Frisco and Silverthorne, each within a short drive of all of the Summit County ski areas, as well as Vail and Beaver Creek. They're also right in the heart of most of the summer resort activity—sailing, cycling, hiking, rafting, and golfing.

Frisco

Rooms at the **Holiday Inn,** tel. (303) 668-5000 or (800) 782-7669, start at about $50. The indoor Jacuzzi and pool, shuttle service, on-site ski shop (rentals, repairs, and sales) and convenient location (just off I-70 at Exit 203) make this a natural for skiers. The **Frisco Lodge,** 321 Main St., tel. 668-0195, probably has the cheapest rooms in town, bare-boned but comfortable. At the **Snowshoe Motel,** 521 Main, tel. 668-3444, doubles run about $30-60. The **Sky-Vue Motel** is at 305 S. Second, tel. 668-3311; rooms for two are $35-70.

Silverthorne

In Silverthorne, you can get doubles at the **Wildernest,** 204 Wildernest Rd., tel. (303) 468-6291, for $40-85 (condos for two at the Wildernest run $50-135). The **Summit Inn and Conference Center,** tel. 468-6200, has rooms running $60-150, and at the **Days Inn,** tel. 468-8661, doubles are $60-110—both are right off I-70 on Silverthorne Lane.

Dillon

Dillon couldn't stay forever young, and the community's growth over the last decade or so has been phenomenal—the times they have a-changed. Most of its lodging is in condominiums and luxury hotels, though there are in fact a few relatively inexpensive inns. The **Super 8 Motel,** 808 Little Beaver Trail, tel. (303) 468-8888 or (800) 843-1991, has rooms for $40-65. At the **Best Western Lake Dillon Lodge,** tel. 668-5094 or (800) 727-0607, you can get doubles for about $80-160—on-premises ski shop, free ski shuttle, indoor pool, and Jacuzzi.

CONDOMINIUMS AND MORE EXPENSIVE HOTELS

Breckenridge

The Village at Breckenridge Resort is a sprawling complex (actually encompassing three separate lodges) with over 400 rooms, ranging from studios to penthouse suites. Though prices range as well, this is generally for the expense-account crowd, those who've saved for the Big Splurge, and the fortunate (?) few who never have to ask, "How much?" Amenities include the standard exercise room, spa, and pool, as well as kitchens. Base, I mean *base,* prices start at about $80 for a double in low season, but you should expect to pay a lot more—like maybe $150. Cream-of-the-crop suites are over $400 a night for two. Phone (303) 453-2000 or (800) 321-8552.

Among other Breckenridge luxury accommodations: the **Breckenridge Hilton,** tel. 453-4500 or (800) 321-8444, $80-200; the **Beaver Run Resort,** tel. 453-6000 or (800) 525-2253, $70-300; and the **River Mountain Lodge,** tel. 453-4711, $60-450.

Copper Mountain

The base of Copper Mountain is dotted with condominiums and lodges, many of which offer to-your-doorstep skiing, and all of which are steps away from a shuttle-bus stop. Copper's **Club Med** (the first in the United States), tel. (303) 968-2121, is near the central plaza right at the base of the lifts. For rates and a full listing of accommodations and ski and summer-vacation packages, write **Copper Mountain Resort Lodging Services,** Box 3001, Copper Mountain, CO 80443; or phone (800) 458-8386, ext. 1; locally, phone 968-2882.

Dillon

Dillon offers about two dozen hotels and condominium complexes, many of which are right on or overlook the lake. Among them: **Summit Yacht Club,** tel. (303) 468-2703; **Lake Dillon Condotel,** tel. 468-2409 or (800) 323-7892; and **The Spinnaker at Lake Dillon,** tel. 468-8001. For more information on lodging in Dillon, write Town of Dillon, Box 8, Dillon, CO 80435, or phone 468-2403, or 629-6342 from Denver.

Keystone

Like Copper Mountain, Keystone is a small village of condominium complexes, restaurants, ski shops, and boutiques built to accommodate the ski crowd but which in recent years has begun (successfully) to woo summer vacationers as well. Three basic options here: the lodge at the resort, the Ski Tip Lodge (see below), or one of the many condo complexes (some 800 suites total). Either way you can book rooms by the night or buy full-bore ski-golf-ride-sail-fish-bike-eat-drink-and-be-merry packages. Five-night ski packages at the **Keystone Lodge** or a nearby condo begin at around $300 per person, and include four days' skiing at Keystone and/or Arapahoe Basin. One-night's-lodging/one-day's-skiing packages start at about $60. For more information, write **Keystone Resort,** Box 38, Keystone, CO 80435, or phone (800) 541-0346 (the lodge) or (800) 222-0188 (condos); from Denver phone (303) 534-4806 (the lodge) or 534-7712 (condos).

BED AND BREAKFASTS

Gaining in popularity recently, bed and breakfasts offer a wider range of prices (and comfort levels) than one might imagine. The **Summit County Bed and Breakfast Association** includes some 20 members in the area. For a complete listing, write the Summit County Chamber of Commerce (see "Information" following).

Of the two dozen bed and breakfasts in the county, one of the most comfortable and down to earth is the **Twilight Inn,** 308 Main St., Frisco, tel. (303) 668-5009, which owes its charm partly to its father-and-son team of innkeepers, Bjorn and Eric (two of the mellowest and most lovable Labrador retrievers in snow country). The Twilight has 12 rooms, some with private baths, some with shared baths (not to worry: the bathrooms for those rooms are huge).

If you're looking to get away from the hustle and bustle of the Frisco-Dillon-Silverthorne-Keystone area, a couple of wonderful lodges back in the woods offer the perfect escape.

Keystone's **Ski Tip Lodge** was built in the 1940s as Colorado's first ski lodge. Set back among the pines, the inn was sold to Keystone in the early 1980s, and it's still a far cry from the more conventional condos at the resort. Fourteen rustic rooms are decorated with antiques and have neither phones nor televisions, and the old stone fireplace and relative isolation (shuttles to Keystone every half-hour in winter) provide the sense that your're an original guest and that your baggy wool ski pants are drying by the fireside for tomorrows's weideling at Arapahoe Basin. For reservations and more information, phone 468-4202.

About three miles deeper into the woods, the **Paradox Lodge,** tel. 468-9445, offers rooms in the main inn or in one of the self-contained cabins on the property. The seclusion of the Paradox (its original owners were two doctors . . .), and the

fact that the rooms don't have phones, makes it the perfect place to lose yourself after a particularly grueling project at the office or semester of school. For more information, write Paradox Lodge, 35 Montezuma Rd., Dillon, CO 80435.

In Breckenridge, the **Williams House,** tel. 453-2975, is a much smaller bed and breakfast, the owners having just completed a third room. With an excellent location, especially in winter, when you're just a few blocks from Breckenridge skiing, this inn also offers a real sense of history (the house was built in the mid-1880s). Rooms start at about $50 a night, though they go up to $100 during the ski season.

VACATION HOMES

Generally at the high end of vacation accommodations options, individual homes offer privacy and oftentimes the size needed to accommodate large groups, and they sometimes offer better long-term rates. To rent from owners, look in the "Vacation Homes" section of the *Denver Post's* classified ads. In addition, **Americana Resort Properties,** tel. (800) 367-0458 or (303) 468-0485, **Columbine Rentals,** tel. (800) 289-7666 or 468-0611, **Executive Resorts Rentals,** tel. (800) 662-5368 or 453-4422, and **White Cloud Lodging Co.,** tel. (800) 345-0593 or 453-1018, can all arrange lodging at individual homes in Summit County.

CAMPING AND RVING

Summit County is entirely contained within the borders of Arapaho National Forest, so summer visitors will find a variety of Forest Service-maintained campgrounds within short drives of Breckenridge, Copper Mountain, Dillon, and Keystone, including several at Dillon Reservoir. Be forewarned, though: those on the lake (Heaton Bay, Peak One, Pine Grove, and Prospector campgrounds—over 300 sites total), though very nice, fill up quickly when the weather's warm. Don't expect to get a site without reservations. Some areas are designated hike-in and bike-in only.

Several campgrounds in the north arm of Summit County offer less developed but also somewhat less crowded facilities. Take CO 9 north from Silverthorne. The road winds through the beautiful Blue River Valley past Green Mountain Reservoir to Kremmling, with several campgrounds on the way. **Blue River Campground** is about five miles north of Silverthorne on CO 9 (well water and pit toilets only).

Cow Creek Campground offers free camping on the east shore of Green Mountain Reservoir just off CO 9. Another fairly primitive area (pit toilets), this campground has zippo in terms of shade, but the lack of trees makes for good winds, and the spot is very popular with boardsailers. Not much shade at **Prairie Point Campground**, either, at the south end of Green Mountain Reservoir, though the views, particularly of the massive Gore Range, make for a fair trade.

For information on camping in the area, or to make reservations, stop in at the Forest Service district office at 191 Blue River Parkway, Silverthorne, tel. 468-5400.

Tiger Run RV Resort, tel. 453-9690, on the Blue River between Frisco and Breckenridge, is the only RV park in the county, and, in true Summit County style, it's actually a full-fledged resort, with tennis courts, pool, hot tub, etc. Write Box 815, Breckenridge, CO 80424.

FOOD

Start Me Up

A veritable Summit County institution, established in the early 1940s when skiers would stop en route to a day at Arapahoe Basin, the **Arapahoe Cafe** in Dillon at the corner of Chief Colorow and La Bonte, tel. (303) 468-0873, serves a breakfast guaranteed to kick your morning in the backside. Try the "Hans and Franz (we-just-want-to-pump-you-up) Power Breakfast" of steak, eggs, home fries, and toast ($6.95). The Arapahoe is also open for lunch and dinner, serving burgers, soups, salads, and other hearty fare.

Another favorite breakfast-and-lunch spot is the tiny, dinerlike (only a half dozen tables and the counter) **Alice's Restaurant** in the cluster of buildings just lakeside of the Dillon Mall. Opening at 6 a.m., Alice's serves standard American breakfasts, and sandwiches, burgers, burritos (excellent!), homemade soup, and salads for lunch ($4-6).

In Breckenridge, try the hearty ante-ski breakfasts at the **Prospector,** 130 S. Main, and the **Gold Pan,** 105 N. Main (see below). For pastries and coffee, try **Alpentop Gourmet Bakery,** at Keystone Plaza in Dillon, tel. 468-2774, or **Go-betweens Deli and Bakery,** Park Ave. and 4 O'clock Rd. in Breckenridge, tel. 453-5855. There's a **Daylight Doughnuts** at 807 Summit Blvd. in Frisco.

Inexpensive To Moderate

The **Moose Jaw,** in downtown Frisco at 208 Main, tel. (303) 668-3931, is a classic little diner and bar for the pool/softball/country-music, just-finished-framing-a-house-up-in-Breck set. Originally built in the '50s as a bunkhouse for Dillon Dam workers, the structure was cut in half in 1961 and moved to its present site, where it initially served as a grocery store. Today, a burger with a basket of fries will run you $4-6, or you can get a fish sandwich or a bowl of chili and fries for about the same price.

One of the best places to go for a hot lunch on a cold day is **The Prospector Restaurant,** 130 S. Main St., Breckenridge, tel. 453-6858. Hide yourself in a cozy booth and enjoy a burger, omelette, or bowl of hot soup for $4-6. The Prospector also serves excellent breakfasts and dinners.

Another Summit County institution is the **Gold Pan Restaurant and Bar,** 103 N. Main St., Breckenridge, tel. 453-5499. Located in a building dating from the 1880s that has housed over the years a dry goods store, a bowling alley, and a gas station, the Gold Pan claims to hold the longest continually operating liquor license west of the Mississippi. The Gold Pan Bar is a long-time favorite of locals of all stripes, from Glen Plake Wannabes to miners who look more like Hank Williams, Jr., than ol' Hank does himself. The restaurant tends to cater to a slightly more civil crowd, après-skiers who munch on Mexican food (try the nachos) or the famous Gold Pan burgers. Dinners run $3-7.

A newcomer to Breckenridge, but an immediately successful one, is the **Breckenridge Brewery and Pub** at the south end of town at 600 Main St., tel. 453-1550. Offering a half dozen or so different house beers (ranging from their Avalanche Ale—"it can overtake you before you know it"—to an oatmeal stout), the pub also serves a variety of traditional pub grub—

shepherd's pie, fish and chips, burgers, sandwiches, and salads. Lunches run about $6-11, and pints of beer are $2. Home-brewed ginger ale and root beer are also available. Look for Breckenridge beer in local liquor stores.

One of Summit County's better and more reasonably priced Chinese restaurants is **Szechuan Taste,** 310 Main St., Frisco, tel. 668-5685. Specials (duck and seafood) run $11-13, but you can also get good-sized vegetable, beef, and noodle dishes for $6-9.

A Dillon favorite is **P.J.'s Restaurant and Pub,** 109 Dillon Mall, tel. 468-2006, serving pizza, pastas, and chili, and beer by the pitcher (with takeout and delivery).

Expensive

Summit County's not hurting for high-end white-linen-and-silver restaurants, and if you're looking to relax with a good meal and a special bottle of wine, you've got several choices. A consistently strong contender for local favorite is the **Blue Spruce Inn,** 120 W. Main, Frisco, tel. (303) 668-5900, which serves beef, veal, and seafood dishes ranging from $14 to $25 (steak and lobster). For Italian food, it's hard to beat **Ristorante Al Lago,** 240 Chief Colorow, Dillon, tel. 468-6111. Veal, chicken, seafood, and pasta dinners run $12-20. Another Dillon favorite is **Pug Ryan's Prime Rib and Seafood House,** 101 Dillon Mall, tel. 453-0063, where steaks, prime rib, chicken, and fish dinners run $12-25 (there's also a Pug Ryan's in Breckenridge at 208 N. Main).

Among the better upscale Breckenridge restaurants are the **Briar Rose,** 109 E. Lincoln, tel. 453-9948, specializing in exotic game dishes (elk, venison), beef, and seafood, and **Weber's Restaurant,** 200 N. Main, tel. 453-9464, serving authentic German dinners and desserts.

ENTERTAINMENT

When ski season's in full swing and Summit County's swollen with skiers of every hue—honeymooners from Houston, families from Fargo, and countless college students here between (or instead of) semesters—there's a lot going on, and you'd be hard-pressed not to find something to do when you pull your ski boots off. Most of the ski-area bars feature live music,

and there's a huge range of clubs and nighteries around the county. Summer's a bit slower, though, and spring and fall slower still.

For current information on what's happening where, check out the local papers. The *Summit County Journal* and the *Summit Sentinel* provide up-to-date information on everything from reggae concerts to dinner theater, gallery openings to pool tournaments. Both papers are available in racks around town.

Though you'll find live music and other entertainment throughout the county, the largest cluster is in Breckenridge, and come nightfall, locals as well as visiting skiers often head into "Breck" where a dozen or so clubs are within walking distance of each other. **Eric's Underworld,** downstairs in the Georgian Square, tel. (303) 543-0999, **Shamus O'Toole's,** 115 S. Ridge St., tel. 453-2004, and **JohSha's,** 500 Park Ave., tel. 453-4146, regularly feature dance music—from reggae to Cajun to experimental and progressive rock. **The Gold Pan,** 105 N. Main St., tel. 453-5499, books live music "when we feel like it," generally softer rock, in the Kenny Rankin-James Taylor-Jackson Browne mode.

Another place worth checking out is **Jake T. Pounder's,** tel. 453-2000, "the only bar in Breckenridge owned by a dog."

Other Summit County Entertainment

In Keystone, several clubs offer live and dance music, including the **Snake River Saloon,** tel. (303) 468-2788, and **Bandito's,** tel. 468-0404, on Hwy. 6, and, in Keystone Village, the **Last Chance Saloon,** tel. 468-9501.

A tradition in Summit County, the **Old Dillon Inn,** tel. 468-2791, 321 Blue River Parkway in Silverthorne, books country and country rock, for those whose tastes run to Merle Haggard and Marshall Tucker. Up in Dillon, **Pug Ryan's,** tel. 468-2145, also books live music.

CALENDAR

Summit County's annual events range from ice sculpture and snowboard competition to sailing regattas, horse and bike races, and a wide range of concerts. The winter biggy is Breckenridge's **Ullr Fest** in mid-January, honoring the Norse god Ullr, Thor's son. According to a slightly revisionist version of the legend, the mighty Thor and his gorgeous wife Sif had no time for Ullr, and so out of boredom, the kid hit the road. And where do you think he ended up? Why, Breckenridge, of course, where he fell in love with the beautiful Blue River Valley.

The week-long party commences with the International Snow Sculpting Competition (in town on Main St.), and includes a variety of skiing competitions (aerials, moguls, ballet), a parade, and the "Mr. and Mrs. Ullr Beauty Pageant and Dance." In March, Breckenridge hosts the increasingly popular **Snowboard Race Series.**

At the other end of the scale is the **Bach, Beethoven, and Breckenridge** concert series in July. Not limited to the two Big B's of classical music, performances also include the works of other major and minor composers, from Copland to Wagner. The month-long season also includes workshops—on music theory, education, and individual instruments. For more information, write Box 1254, Breckenridge, CO 80424, or phone (303) 453-9142.

A variety of festivities and events punctuate the Fourth of July weekend throughout Summit County, including fireworks, food booths, and concerts. The route of mid-July's **Montezuma's Revenge Mountain Bike Race** crosses the Continental Divide seven times in the course of 200 miles. Over Labor Day weekend, Copper Mountain hosts the **West-Fest,** which focuses on the art and culture of the western and southwestern United States. Lots of Native American art and jewelry, as well as music and food. Phone (800) 458-8386 for more information. Also in September is Breckenridge's **Fall Classic Mountain Bike Race,** which attracts the best riders in the country.

For complete listings of the county's myriad events, contact the Summit County Chamber of Commerce. Also, watch the *Summit Daily News,* the *Summit Sentinel,* and the *Summit County Journal.*

SHOPPING

A favorite recreational activity among visitors to Summit County, shopping knows no bounds here in what would seem to be an unlikely place to find everything from Native American pottery to bargains on lingerie, from Christmas ornaments to T-shirts (Breckenridge must have the highest number of T-shirt shops per capita in the country). In Frisco, be sure to check out **Peddlar's Barn,** on Main St. across from the Twilight Inn. This place carries a bizarre collection of odds and ends, from first-edition Hardy Boys books to vintage snow skis (from the 1920s and '30s). Look for the locomotive in the window.

Silverthorne Factory Outlets

A seemingly unlikely spot for a factory outlet mall, the Silverthorne site is nonetheless extremely popular. For those who'd rather shop than ski or mountain bike, there's Van Heusen, Bass shoes, Evan-Picone, American Tourister, Liz Claiborne, plus socks, underwear, ribbons, toys, wallets, fragrances and bath oils, and jewelry (there's even a real estate office). Take the Silverthorne exit from I-70 and follow the signs; keep a leash on your credit card.

SERVICES

The **Breckenridge Police Department** is located at 150 Ski Hill Rd.; phone (303) 453-2941. Phone the **Dillon Police** at 468-6078. The offices of the **Summit County Sheriff** are in Breckenridge at 501 N. Park; phone 453-2232.

Summit Medical Center in Frisco is open weekdays 9 a.m.-5 p.m (plus 24-hour emergency care). The clinic is located at the corner of Hwy. 9 and School Rd.; phone 668-3300 or (800) 843-0953. The **Breckenridge Medical Center** is located at 535 S. Park St.; phone 453-9000.

Post offices are located at the following addresses: Breckenridge, 300 S. Ridge Rd., tel. 453-2310; Dillon, 224 Dillon Mall, tel. 468-2501; Frisco, 400 Granite, tel. 668-5505; and Silverthorne, 390 N. Brian Ave., tel. 468-8112.

Recycling

The **Summit Recycling Project** has two drop-off spots, both of which will take most recyclables: 301 8th Ave., Frisco, and on Summit Ln., Breckenridge.

Child Care

Breckenridge, Copper Mountain, and Keystone ski areas all have children's centers, providing day care for kids two months to five years old, with snow and ski programs for kids three and older. Reservations are required at all three. Phone Copper Mountain's **Belly Button Bakery** at (800) 458-8386, ext. 5; **Breckenridge Children's Center** at (303) 453-2368; and **Keystone's Children's Center** at 468-4182.

INFORMATION

One of the best places to begin your visit to the area is the **Summit County Chamber of Commerce** in Frisco at the east end of Main St. between Dillon Reservoir and CO 9. Pick up maps, brochures, and tips on everything from lodging to cycling, fishing, rafting, and after-hours entertainment. Write the chamber at Box 214, Frisco, CO 80443, or phone (303) 668-0376.

The chamber also operates a tourist information center just off Hwy. 6 between Silverthorne and Dillon with lots of information on places to stay and eat, and things to do and buy, tel. 668-5800. Watch for the road signs. The Breckenridge Resort Chamber operates the **Breckenridge Information Center** out of their offices at 309 N. Main.

The toll-free number for **Summit County Reservations** is (800) 365-6365. For **ski information** (transportation, lodging, ski school, lift tickets, etc.) in Summit County, write **Ski the Summit,** Box 267, Dillon, CO 80435, or phone 468-6607. You can make lodging reservations by calling the following numbers: (800) 221-1091 (Breckenridge); (800) 458-8386 (Copper Mountain); and (800) 222-0188 (Keystone/Arapahoe Basin).

You can also get more information from the **Breckenridge Resort Chamber,** Box 1909, Breckenridge, CO 80424, tel. 453-6018, and the **Town of Dillon,** Box 8, Dillon, CO 80435, tel. 468-2403.

Libraries And Bookstores

The main branch of the Summit County **public library** is in Frisco at 43 Mt. Royal Dr.; phone (303) 668-5555. The north branch is at the town hall in Silverthorne, tel. 468-5887, and the south branch is in Breckenridge at 103 S. Harris, tel. 453-6098.

Write the **Summit County Historical Society** at Box 747, Dillon, CO 80435, tel. 468-6079. Offices are located at 104 N. Harris, Breckenridge, tel. 453-9022 and 403 La Bonte, Dillon.

The **Book Nook,** 120 Dillon Mall, tel. 468-5446, is a cozy little store whose friendly owners are full of tips on the area. In Frisco, stop in at **Daily Planet,** 120 N. 3rd., tel. 668-5015. **Mountain Pride Books** is located at 555 S. Columbine in Breckenridge, tel. 453-2444.

Forest Service Information

For maps and information on camping, hiking, mountain biking, Jeep touring, and backcountry skiing in Summit County, contact the Silverthorne district office of **Arapaho National Forest,** 191 Blue River Parkway, tel. (303) 468-5400.

Ski Reports And Weather Conditions

Remember when calling ski resorts for their snow conditions that they're in business to make money, and their reports are often optimistic and overly enthusiastic. Sometimes you're better off stopping by a local ski shop.

For information from the resorts, phone (303) 345-6118, Breckenridge; tel. 968-2100, Copper Mountain; and tel. 468-4111, Keystone and Arapahoe Basin. For the latest in **road and weather conditions** in Summit County, phone 453-1090.

Newspapers

In addition to the several locally published commercial guides to Summit County, check out the *Summit County Journal* and the *Summit Sentinel,* available in racks throughout the area. Both list upcoming events and run stories spotlighting local celebrities, as well as pieces on local political maneuvering.

Further Reading

Janet Marie Clawson's *Echoes of the Past: Copper Mountain Colorado* (published by Copper Mountain Resort, 1986) is a thoroughly researched narrative history of the old mining-camp-turned-resort, and except for the last few pages is mostly free of PR-type promotion for the ski area.

An excellent account of the history of Frisco and the area is *Frisco! A Colorful Colorado Community* (it's livelier than the title would suggest!), by local writer Mary Ellen Gilliland and published by the Frisco Historical Society. After a brief discussion of the area's natives (the Utes), Gilliland chronicles the town's development and discusses its major players.

TRANSPORTATION

Summit County's very easy to get to and around in. Only 70 miles from Denver via the I-70 autostrada, the area is serviced by a number of independent shuttle services, and many of the hotels offer free transportation from Denver's Stapleton Airport (serviced by most major domestic airlines). You can also fly into Stapleton and rent a car for the short drive up over Loveland Pass.

Buses And Shuttles

The **Resort Express,** Denver's airport shuttle, offers buses hourly during the ski season and every hour and a half the rest of the year. Cost is about $60 (roundtrip), and reservations are required. Phone (303) 468-7600 or (800) 334-7433, or write Box 1429, Silverthorne, CO 80498. The main office is at 273 Warren Ave. in Silverthorne. Denver-to-Summit County shuttle service is also provided by **The Skiers' Connection,** tel. 668-0200 or (800) 824-1104. During the ski season, buses leave on the hour from Stapleton Airport 8 a.m.-11 p.m. and from Breckenridge 5 a.m.-8 p.m. (during the summer, buses run every other hour). Roundtrip fare is about $45.

In addition, free shuttle service is offered within the county by the **Summit Stage.** Bus routes link Breckenridge, Frisco, Copper Mountain, Dillon, Silverthorne, and Keystone (no service to Arapahoe Basin). For route schedules and more information, phone 453-1241 or 453-1339. The **Breckenridge Free Shuttle and Town Trolley** provides service through town and up to the ski resort (both base areas).

For schedule information, phone 453-2368. The **Frisco Flyer** has routes throughout Frisco, from the Safeway at I-70 and CO 9 up into town on Main and back through into the condos and vacation homes. Phone 668-5276 for a map and schedule. Keystone offers regular shuttle service between Keystone Ski Area and Arapahoe Basin.

Greyhound-Trailways offers passenger service to Summit County, with a local depot at 1202 N. Summit in Frisco. Phone 668-5703.

Rental Cars

If you're coming into Summit County via Stapleton Airport, you can either rent cars in Denver, where you'll find all the major franchises plus a couple of independents, or take a shuttle to the county and rent a car there. All rental agencies in this neck of the woods provide mountain-ready cars, with snow tires, ski racks, etc., as well as lots of 4WD rigs (significantly more expensive). See the Denver chapter following for rentals at Stapleton.

In Summit County, you can rent from **American International Rent-a-Car,** tel. (303) 968-6719, at the junction of I-70 and CO 9, and from Copper Mountain Resort, tel. 968-6311. You can also rent cars in Frisco from **Alpine Rent-a-Car,** 857 N. Summit Blvd., Frisco, tel. 668-3785, and from **Summit Car Rental,** 325 S. Main, Frisco, tel. 453-4600.

Taxis

Breckenridge-based **Around Town Taxi,** tel. (303) 453-6425, offers 24-hour 4WD taxi service. In Dillon, phone **Summit Taxi Service** at 468-8294.

STEPHEN METZGER

THE DENVER AREA
DENVER

The only Word I had was "Wow!". . .
Here I was in Denver . . . I stumbled
along with the most wicked grin of joy in
the world, among the bums and beat
cowboys of Larimer Street.

—Jack Kerouac, *On the Road*

INTRODUCTION

Situated at the far western edge of North America's Great Plains, and sprawling north, south, east, and west almost up into the foothills of the massive blue Rocky Mountains, Denver (pop. 500,000; elev. 5,280 feet) is the focal point of Colorado's commerce, government, and transportation. It's also a major tourism center, offering not only abundant attractions within the city limits, but also easy access to some of the state's premier playgrounds and historical sites.

A bona fide urban center, with high-rise office buildings lifting steep and glassy off the plain, and downtown professionals marching gray-suited and power-tied through the day, Denver is the American Rockies' largest and busiest city. The population of the surrounding metropolitan area is approaching two million.

All of which runs contrary to the image many people have of Denver: To many it's just a glorified cow town, or simply a cold, wintry stepping-stone to the world-class ski resorts fewer than 100 miles west. And Denverites seem unduly self-conscious of their image, going out of their way to teach outsiders the truth—which is that it's not a cow-town at all (save for a couple of weeks each January, when the world's biggest rodeo comes to town), and it's hardly as cold and wintry as many people think.

To get an idea of how Denver's grown up since the turn of the century when it *was* very much a stock and agriculture center, just take a walk downtown. Many of the high-rises you see (though deplored by many locals because

DENVER AREA HIGHLIGHTS

Denver: state capitol, historic and art museums, botanical gardens, Denver Zoo, recreation areas, hiking, biking, and skiing along the Colorado Urban Trail System, dining, nightlife, Tattered Cover Bookstore, 16th Street Mall, Capitol Hill People's Fair

Boulder: climbing, cycling, and virtually all forms of recreation, people-watching, shopping, nightlife, bookstores and cafés, Colorado Music Festival, Kinetic Sculpture Challenge, Colorado Indian Market

Golden: Coors Brewery, Colorado School of Mines, hiking and biking in Golden Gate Canyon State Park, museums, International Heritage Festival of Folk Arts

Georgetown/Idaho Springs: museums, historic districts, the Georgetown Loop Railroad, skiing, hiking, and camping in Arapaho National Forest, Indian Springs Resort

Central City/Black Hawk: museums, mine tours, shopping, gambling, festivals, Central City Opera

(as anyone who's watched a Broncos' home game knows . . .). And anyone visiting town between October and April would be well advised to bring hat, scarf, gloves, thermal underwear, and down jacket (Denver's annual average minimum temperature is 37.2°). But even when it's cold, it's dry, and, as the figures show, it's often sunny (in fact, the city claims to get "more hours of annual sun than San Diego or Miami Beach"). And when it's dry, cold temperatures are a *lot* easier to take than when the barometer falls and there's moisture in the air.

A lot's changed in Denver since Jack Kerouac and Neal Cassady and the gang were raising hell on Larimer St. and trying their damnedest to live life on the stark edges of experience, and most of the old pool halls and flophouses are long gone (much to the chagrin of purists, who deplore the city's gentrification). But it's still a wonderful place, very much tied to the psyche of the American West and its vision of itself. And modern travelers looking for the heart of America must not overlook Denver, a city sprawling at the confluence of two of the country's greatest geological features and offering a history rich with the deepest textures of the American experience.

HISTORY

Though Denver today is Colorado's capital, as well as its largest city, its history is more recent than many of the other cities and towns in the state. And it's much younger, historically, than other parts of the West—particularly the coast and New Mexico, where Spaniards were exploring and beginning to colonize as early as the late 16th century. The first outpost in the Denver area was built in 1832 by fur trader Louis Vasquez, though there were no permanent settlers in the region until 1858. That year William Green Russell discovered small amounts of gold along the South Platte River. When word of his strike spread southeast to Pikes Peak, which wasn't living up to its promises, a handful of hopefuls packed up in search of better prospects. Along what is now W. Evans Ave., the new arrivals built several cabins, which they named Montana City. The gold there soon played out, however, and the group, led by Charles Nichols, moved downstream to the

historical buildings were razed to build them) are as contemporary in design and as elegant as anything you'll see in any other major North American city. And take a look at the people going to work in them. They're young—young and, on the average, very highly educated: 35% of Denver's residents are between the ages of 18 and 35, and the city claims its downtown workforce is the highest educated in the country, and that the city overall has the country's second-highest number of college graduates (behind Washington, D.C.). In addition, Denver claims to lead the nation in movie attendance—though I've seen no figures that distinguish between films by Sylvester Stallone and, say, Martin Scorsese or Woody Allen.

And as far as Denver's being cold and wintry—and only a necessary obstacle en route to the ski slopes—consider: According to city statistics, the sun shines on Denver an average of 300 days a year, and less than 15 inches of precipitation fall. Of course, cold winter winds can and do sweep across the plains, whipping icy particles of snow against unprotected cheeks

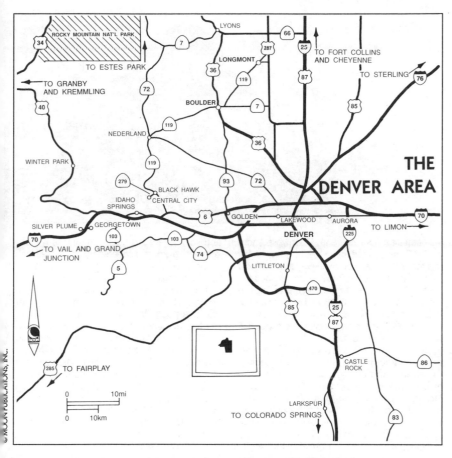

THE DENVER AREA

confluence of the Platte and Cherry Creek, where in the fall of 1858 they drew up plans for their new town, St. Charles City.

Meanwhile, word of gold in the Cherry Creek-South Platte area had reached the East Coast, and optimistic miners were soon rushing west to try to make their fortunes. Also, members of William Russell's party, who had moved back into the mountains, learned that their original find may have been more significant than they first thought; they returned to the Cherry Creek area and built a small settlement, which they named Auraria, across the stream from St. Charles City. Shortly afterward, General William Larimer arrived from Kansas and established

next door to St. Charles City the area's third townsite, which he named Denver City, after General James W. Denver, a former governor of Kansas Territory (of which Colorado was still part). Almost immediately, though, Larimer's party "incorporated" Nichols' camp (some say by force), and once again there were just the two towns, Denver City and Auraria.

Denver's Silver Lining

For the next several years, the two towns grew in size, with saloons, hotels, schools, and churches springing up along the creek. The first edition of the *Rocky Mountain News* was published from its "office" on mid-stream pilings between

The Brown Palace is still one of the state's grand hotels.

COLORADO HISTORICAL SOCIETY

the camps on April 23, 1859. Meanwhile, more gold strikes occurred in the area—some highly exaggerated—many of which played out almost as soon as word of their existence reached the public. Still, prospectors continued to flock to the area, and on April 3, 1860, Denver and Auraria were consolidated; in January, 1861, when the new town held its first election, the population was approximately 6,000.

Over the next 20 years, gold fell off in Denver, and with it so did the infant city's economy. Prices fell, and discouraged miners left for greener pastures. In the early 1880s, however, focus on Colorado's ore changed from gold to silver. Prospectors in the mountains west of Denver discovered immensely lucrative lodes, particularly at Cripple Creek, Leadville, Aspen, and Georgetown. Almost overnight, Denver's future again looked bright. Between 1880 and 1890, Denver's population tripled; banks, machine shops, smelters, and other businesses sprouted up downtown; and boutiques and other retail shops opened on Lawrence Street. By the end of the decade, Denver was producing more mining machinery than any other city in the world. In addition, Denver was becoming somewhat of a social hub, as miners who had made their fortunes in the nearby mountains moved to the city and built elaborate houses and threw lavish parties. Among the silver barons who brought their prosperity and high living to Denver was Horace Tabor, who opened the Tabor Opera House (located on 16th St. where the Tabor Center now stands) in 1881

and soon afterward built a magnificent mansion whose grounds covered an entire city block on Capitol Hill (see "History" under "Leadville" in the Southwestern Colorado chapter).

The 1890s saw a depression in Denver's economy, brought on by a sudden drop in silver prices, although by the turn of the century the city was already well on the road to recovery. Throughout the early 1900s, Denver continued to grow, with great improvements in roadways, schools, and parks, although the massive Rocky Mountains pretty much kept the city isolated from the rapidly developing cities on the West Coast, Los Angeles and San Francisco in particular. In 1928, however, Moffat Tunnel was blasted through the Rockies, providing a direct railway to the coast, and Denver was finally a part of the burgeoning national village.

Modern Times

Still, though, Denver retained its image as a Wild West frontier town, and its location in America's heartland as well as the fact that it had become a veritable hub for an expanding national highway and railway system, ensured lots of short- and long-term visitors—from the upper crust to the down and out. In fact, until the city's "urbanization" in the late 1970s and early '80s, Denver still boasted (or bemoaned, depending on your perspective) many of the things that attracted the Kerouac gang in the '50s: pool halls, saloons, flophouses, and more than its share of folks who had slipped through the cracks in the American Dream.

In the early 1980s, natural resources again changed the face of Denver—this time in the form of oil and coal, which brought new revenues to the city. Although preservationists argued for the restoration of Denver's historic buildings, many—including the Tabor Opera House, of course—were razed and replaced with shopping centers, office buildings, and hotels. Though costing Denver much of its unique architectural heritage, this resulted in a very attractive and contemporary city, thoroughly modern in every sense of the word.

MUSEUMS AND OTHER SIGHTS

A United States mint, a children's museum, and museums of history, art, natural history, transportation, and firefighting—many of which are right downtown—will keep museophiles entertained for days. Spend a morning learning about the history of the state; break for lunch; then take in prehistoric, Native American, modern, and postmodern art in the afternoon. Or head out to the transportation museum, and (appropriately enough) take a trolley along the Platte River to Denver's Children's Museum.

Colorado History Museum
Without doubt one of the best places to begin your exploration of Denver, particularly if your knowledge of the state's and city's history is at all sketchy, this beautifully designed and impressively laid-out museum provides the opportunity to wander among a huge assortment of ex-

hibits. Start at the Colorado time line, a multidimensional and multimedia display that explains the history of the state from just before the Louisiana Purchase of 1803. You'll also want to check out the re-created machine shop, the displays of the various mining techniques used in Colorado's past, and the beautiful textile exhibit with Native American rugs, mostly from the Rio Grande Valley, from the mid-19th through the late-20th century. The museum also features lots of Plains and Ute Native American clothing (take a look at the beaded leggings), a Conestoga-style wagon built in 1824, and a 100-Mile Fritchle Electric Car (which could go 100 miles between battery chargings) built in 1910—displayed with the car are the original owner's manual, the purchase deed, and various advertisements for the early autos, manufactured in Denver between 1904 and 1917. The museum is located downtown at the corner of 13th and Broadway and is open Mon.-Sat. 10 a.m.-4:30 p.m. and Sun. noon-4:30 p.m. For more information, phone (303) 866-3682.

State Capitol
On July 5, 1886, almost 10 years after Colorado achieved statehood, and after the territorial government had been moved first from Colorado City and then from Golden City, excavation was begun on the state capitol building. Built on 10 acres of land donated by Henry C. Brown—who retained much of the surrounding property and grew rich by developing it for settlers and merchants who wanted to be near the state's new headquarters—the capitol took

mid-19th-century storekeepers

The capitol building is a short walk from downtown.

22 years to complete, though 160 rooms were in use for the last 12 years of construction. In an attempt to represent Colorado in the building, designers worked primarily with materials from the state: The outer walls are of granite from the Gunnison area; the marble floors are from Marble; and the interior walls are wainscotted with rose onyx from Buelah (whose resources were exhausted by the shipments to Denver).

Particularly impressive are the building's gold-plated outer dome, the gorgeous stained-glass and hand-carved white oak throughout the building, and the monstrous chandeliers—the one in the original Supreme Court chambers weighs a ton and was originally lighted with gas, as the engineers didn't trust the newly discovered electricity.

The Colorado State Capitol is located at Colfax and Broadway. Free 30-minute tours, which end at the rotunda and provide wonderful views of both downtown and the distant mountains, are offered weekdays from 9 a.m-3:30 p.m. (on the half-hour). For more information, phone (303) 866-2604.

Denver Museum Of Natural History

Ideally, you'd allow yourself at least an entire day to wander around this place and see everything, and one could easily spend more than that here. The seventh-largest museum in the United States, this is a beautifully and intelligently designed multistory complex of exhibits that will delight visitors of all ages. A sampling: Dinosaur fossils and skeletons (including the stegosaurus, Colorado's state fossil), skeletons from La Brea Tar Pits (a saber-toothed tiger, dire wolf, and ground sloth); a display of the world's minerals; a small Egyptology exhibit, with a mummy, a casket, and an illustrated explanation of the mummification process; a "Development of Man" display, beginning with a facsimile of the remains of "Lucy," who, named for the Beatles' song *Lucy in the Sky with Diamonds,* is probably 3.2 million years old; and exhibits of whales of the world, fishes of Colorado, and, well, you get the picture.

Don't miss the museum's **IMAX Theater,** the world's largest motion picture system. Films are projected onto a four-story-tall screen, and the wide-angle photography is absolutely stunning. Shows are also regularly offered at the museum's **Charles C. Gates Planetarium.** Separate admission prices are charged for the museum, theater, and planetarium. An excellent gift shop is in the museum's lobby. The Denver Historical Museum is located at 2001 Colorado Blvd.; phone (303) 322-7009 for more information.

United States Mint

Free guided tours of this penny-printing press explain the history of the mint (next to Fort Knox, the second largest gold depository in the U.S.) and the process of making coins. During the height of the tourist season in summer, you'll want to get here early to beat the crowds; otherwise, expect to stand in line for up to a half-hour (sometimes more). You can avoid the crowd (and the tour) by going to the gift store entrance around back—pick up freshly minted commemorative coins for your collection. The mint is open Mon. through Fri. 8 a.m.-3 p.m. (8:30 a.m.-3 p.m. in winter). It's located right behind the city and county building at W. Colfax and Cherokee, tel. (303) 844-3582.

Children's Museum Of Denver

My friend Kristin, who knows kids as well as anyone I know, gives this museum a big A+. "Fantastic," she says. "A *perfect* place to take kids." With regularly changing exhibits, the mu-

seum offers dozens of hands-on experiences. Kristin continues: "A media display allows kids to videotape each other in a miniature newscasting room complete with weather station, news desk, viewing booth, and kid-size video recorders and monitors." In an Indians of the American Northwest display kids can also create their own totem poles, and there are "classes" on such things as recycling and candy making. And if that's not enough to wear the little ones out, there's a park outside with all kinds of equipment to climb around on *and* a trolley that'll take the clan two-miles along the South Platte to the Transportation

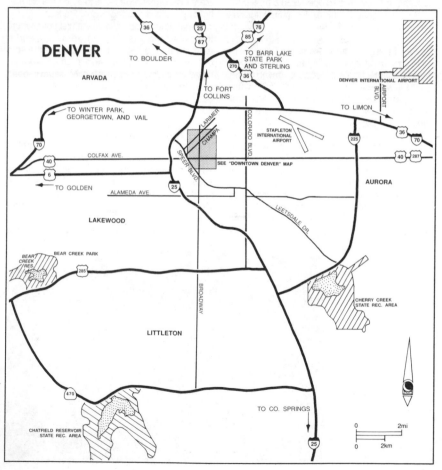

Museum (the trolley costs $2 for adults and $1 for seniors and kids and takes about 25 minutes). Special days at the museum are Cinco de Mayo (May 5, Mexican Independence Day), Disney Days (late June), Young People's Mini Prix (mid-August), Big Shoes to Fill Career Day (late September), and Trick or Treat Street (you guessed it, late October).

The Denver Children's Museum is located just off I-25 (take Exit 211) across from Mile-High Stadium at 2121 Crescent Drive. Admission is $4 kids, $3 adults, age two and under free. Hours are Tues.-Sun. 10 a.m.-5 p.m. Fridays the museum is also open 5:30 p.m.-8 p.m. for "Friday Night Live" (free). For more information, phone (303) 433-7444.

Denver Firefighters Museum

An unassuming little building at 1326 Tremont, this is Denver's original firehouse, dating to the mid-19th century. Though the old uniforms, fire carts and trucks, nets (used in drills only, never in real fires), switchboards, and bells are all interesting, the bonus of this museum is tour guide Mary Felix, whose animated story-telling turns the little museum into theater. With a wink and an "I-don't-tell-everyone-this-Honey," the grandmotherly woman launches into the story of Chief Healy, who held the reins from just after the turn of the century until 1945. "The story goes that Ol' Chief Healy had but two questions for new recruits, and a yes answer to either one disqualified him. The first was 'Would you take a drink?' and the second was 'Would you step out on your wife?' If a potential firefighter answered yes to either question, why the chief felt he wasn't man enough to be a firefighter." Mary pauses, grins, and winks again. "Good thing times have changed, isn't it, Honey?"

Mary also delights in telling about how dalmatians came to be used—to keep the horses clipping along en route to the fire, the dogs nipped at their hooves; then once they got there, the dogs led them away from the fire and kept them waiting until it was time to return to the stables, located in the back of the fire house. Mary also encourages kids to try on the old firefighting uniforms at the end of the tour.

Today, the museum is on the first floor, where the carts (and later, trucks) were kept, and a restaurant (see "Food" following) is on the second, where the men's living quarters were located. The Denver Firefighters Museum is open Mon. through Fri., 11 a.m.-2 p.m. Admission is $2. Phone (303) 892-1100 for more information.

Molly Brown House Museum

Though most people remember Debbie Reynolds and the 1960s Walt Disney movie when they hear of "The Unsinkable Molly Brown," there really was such a woman. And what a woman she was—part redheaded Irish-Catholic pioneer, part early women's rights activist, rabble-rouser, and all-around bon vivant. Born in 1867 in Hannibal, Missouri, Molly (née

the Molly Brown
House and Museum

STEPHEN METZGER

Margaret Tobin), moved to Leadville when she was 18 and married J.J. Brown there on Sept. 1, 1886. After their two children were born (Larry in 1887 and Helen in 1889), the family moved to Denver, where in 1909, as a result of the conflict between Molly's love of traveling and J.J.'s commitment to Colorado business, the couple was legally separated.

In 1912, the world learned of Molly. Traveling on the "maiden" voyage of the Titanic, Molly, with her knowledge of seven languages, helped save many of the immigrants and later went on to help the survivors chart new courses for their lives—by organizing and donating money to them.

The Molly Brown House and Museum is an ornate Victorian mansion built in 1889 and purchased by the Browns in 1894. It has been completely restored (having been used for many purposes over the years, including a men's boarding house), and the furniture is either original (such as the horsehair sofa) or replicated (such as the piano). Particularly impressive is the gilt-relief wallpaper throughout the house, lending the walls a look that's part European parlor, part Las Vegas brothel.

The Molly Brown House is located at 1340 Pennsylvania (between 13th and 14th streets). Note: No off-street parking is available, and you're probably better off walking from downtown than driving the few blocks and trying to park. Tours (by docents dressed in Victorian garb) are offered year-round. Museum hours are: June-Aug., Mon. through Sat. 10 a.m.-4 p.m. and Sun. noon-4 p.m.; April, May, and Sept., same hours as above except closed Mondays; Oct.-March, Tues. through Sat. 10 a.m.-3 p.m. and Sun. noon-3 p.m. For more information, phone (303) 832-4092.

Black American West Museum And Heritage Center

Though naturally overlooked in the whitewashed histories of the country, blacks played an important role opening up the West. In fact, according to documentation at this unique museum, roughly a third of the West's cowboys were black, as were many pioneer doctors, politicians, and teachers. Fortunately, historians are beginning to realize their vast contributions to American history, and textbooks are slowly beginning to reflect the truth. Maybe someday, museums like this one—situated in one of Denver's poor, black neighborhoods, well away from the polish and gentrification of downtown—won't seem such anomalies, and the history of black America will be fully integrated into our museums, books, and consciousnesses.

The museum is located at 3091 California Street. Hours are Wed. through Fri. 10 a.m.-2 p.m., Sat. noon.-5 p.m., and Sun. 2-5 p.m. Phone (303) 292-2566.

Forney Transportation Museum

Located in an old brick warehouse on the Platte River west of downtown, this museum houses a gigantic array of vintage automobiles, railroad cars, sleighs, carriages, and just about anything else that once carried human beings (or cargo) from one place to another. Among the cars: an 1898 Renault Opera Coupe, a 1915 Hudson, 1919 Fiat limousine, and 1924 Moon sedan (the cars were built between 1906 and 1929), and scores more—from 1930s roadsters to a 1970 limited-edition Ford Mustang. An eccentric and eclectic museum, the Forney offers a chance to wander around—even to get lost—in the maze of half-completed exhibits, storerooms, and the weedy, overgrown yard full of rusted train engines, passenger cars, and careening sailing ships, their paint faded and chipped; one room, and I'm not sure how it fits into the general theme, is full of mounted game fish in glass cases, all of apparently near-record size. A small gift shop sells posters, postcards, model airplanes, and other souvenirs. The Forney Transportation Museum is located at 1416 Platte. From downtown, take 15th St. west, and turn left on Platte. The museum is open Mon. through Sat. 10 a.m.-5 p.m. and Sun. 11 a.m.-5:00 p.m.

ART MUSEUMS

Denver Art Museum

This modern six-story facility right downtown offers the visitor a mind-boggling array of art and information about the countries and societies where the works originated. One of the true beauties of this museum is that the exhibits are arranged to demonstrate the distinct links between the various cultures and societies. Just a preview of what you'll find: African masks, sculpture, and beaded belts and necklaces, along with Northwest Native American

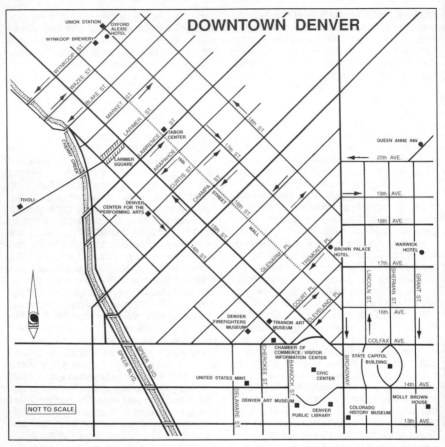

totems, gigantic carved masks, and rattles, and South Pacific ceremonial staffs, masks, and clothing (pieces range from prehistoric to mid-20th century); Spanish colonial paintings and sculpture, including a beautiful collection of Santos (carved cottonwood or pine figures, usually of Christ on the cross or the Madonna), a recreated 17th-century New Mexican church; European and Mediterranean art, Egyptian caskets, Greek statues, and Roman urns; modern pieces by Picasso, Juan Gris, Georges Braque, Matisse, and Breton; and art from the United States and the American West, with pieces by Frederic Remington, Winslow Homer, Thomas Hart Benton, and E. Irving

Crouse and Joseph Sharp, two of the founders of the early-20th-century Taos artists' colony.

The Denver Art Museum is located at 100 W. 14th Ave. (near the corner of Broadway) and is open Tues. through Sat. 10 a.m.-5 p.m. and Sun. noon-5 p.m. (admission is free on Saturday). The museum also has a classy gift shop, with an especially fine selection of books. For more information, phone (303) 640-2793.

Museum Of Western Art

Located downtown right across from the Brown Palace, this small museum features three stories of the art of western America. Included are bronzes and paintings by Frederic Remington (one of the most remarkable is the sculpture *Coming Through the Rye,* four wild horsemen, pistols waving madly), Charles Russell oils, Georgia O'Keeffe's *Cow Skull on Red* (1931), Grant Wood's *Spring Flowers* (1932), and Norman Rockwell's *Gary Cooper as Texan* (1930). The museum also shows works by Ernest L. Blumenschein and E. Irving Crouse (for information on these Taos painters, please refer to Moon Publications' wonderfully illuminating *New Mexico Handbook),* and also offers an interesting perspective on westward expansion and the death of the frontier. A highlight is a letter from Charles Russell, dated May 4, 1914, which is illustrated with a cartoon of people at an art gallery. Russell writes: "Was shure good to here from you London is a sisobol camp."

The museum also has a small gift shop with jewelry, rugs, pottery, and postcards, as well as a bookstore with coffee-table-size art books and books on the American West, including some rare books and some signed by the authors.

The Museum of Western Art is located at 1727 Tremont Place and is open Tues. through Sat. 10 a.m.-4:30 p.m. For more information, phone (303) 296-1880.

Trianon Museum And Art Gallery

Half a block from the Denver Firefighters Museum, this is a classic example of the adage, "Don't judge a book by its cover." From the outside this little place looks all but abandoned, save for the small awning out front. But step inside, and you're in a world of stunningly beautiful antique vases, furniture, silver, china, Oriental screens, and much more, all arranged—some might say cluttered—into two small rooms. Betty Metzger (no direct relation) gives tours as minutely detailed as the pieces she shows. Among the works are Louis XVI service plates, a silver tray once owned by Czar Peter the Great, and a 60-key Steinway piano from the early 18th century. In addition, there's an antique gun collection dating to the 16th century, as well as a late-19th-century Gatling gun and a 12-pound mountain howitzer. The Trianon is located at the corner of 13th St. and Tremont and is open Mon. through Sat. 10 a.m. to 4 p.m. Admission is $1. Some art, antiques, and prints for sale. For more information, phone (303) 623-0739.

PARKS AND RECREATION AREAS

With Denver's youthful and outdoor-oriented population, an abundance of parks should come as no surprise. In fact, there's more than an abundance: There are over 200 parks in the metro area, and Denverites take full advantage of them—for cycling, picnicking, swimming, tennis, or just sprawling on a lawn and napping. For a complete listing of city parks, contact the Denver Parks and Recreation Department, (303) 575-3043.

City Park

When this park was first established, in 1881, it was a good horse-and-buggy day-trip from Denver out to the lawns and lakes. Since then, the city has grown up around it, and though still a bit of a drive from downtown, the facility is a city park in the truest sense of the word. In addition to the spacious lawns perfect for picnicking, the small lakes where you can rent rowboats, and the rose gardens (the place makes you feel like you're living in a Matisse painting), the park also contains the **Denver Zoo,** the **Natural History Museum,** and a golf course (see below). You could spend an entire day here, maybe even a weekend, and still not see everything. To get to the park from downtown, take Colorado Blvd. to 17th Street.

Denver Zoo

Now I'll admit to being somewhat of a cynic when it comes to zoos—the sight of sickly looking animals baking under a too-hot sun in too-small cages doesn't do a whole lot for me. But some zoos seem to respect the animals more than others, and as zoos go, Denver's is all right. In fact, it's a participant in the North American Species Survival Program, which attempts to keep the bloodlines of different species thriving and to educate the public about the plight of nonhuman animals. The Denver Zoo draws special attention to endangered species (officially recognized and otherwise), and among the gift shop's more popular T-shirts are the ones with the logo "Extinction is Forever."

If you're not up for wandering footloose around the 76-acre compound, viewing the lions, and tigers, and bears (oh, my!), hop on the "Zooliner," a train that routes nonstop through the zoo complete with a "safari lecture." If you're interested in pinipeds, stop by the seal and sea lion exhibit, where regular feedings and shows are scheduled.

Snack huts are scattered around the complex, though the many lawns make ideal picnic areas, as do the lawns at the City Park, just outside the gate. (By the way, full literary pun awards go to the snack shack "Ice Cream Station Zebra.")

The Denver Zoo is located at E. 23rd and Steel streets (on weekends, a shuttle runs between the zoo and the Natural History Museum, and concerts are scheduled throughout the summer). For more information, phone (303) 331-4110.

Denver Botanic Gardens

If you've been pounding the pavement of downtown Denver, taking in the sights and sounds of the city, chances are you're starting to feel the effects: The noise and crowds have gone from attractive novelties to overbearing encroachments on your senses. If this is the case, one of the best places in town to restore your sanity is the Botanic Gardens, where you'll find acres of gardens, from gorgeous spreads of wildflowers and native grasses to plots of domesticated perennials, vegetables, and a water garden with a dozen or more different types of water lilies. With paved sidewalks wandering among the various gardens, benches, and gazebos, and arboretums for shade, the Botanic Gardens—still in the heart of the city—is one of the best places to come for a change of pace. (In addition, people planning to do a little landscaping of their own might want to wander around simply gathering ideas and inspiration; pamphlets and fliers explaining the different plants are available in racks throughout.) There's also a gift shop and huge library. In the summer, the gardens feature a series of evening concerts.

Denver's Botanic Gardens are open daily 9 a.m.-4:45 p.m. To get there from downtown, take 14th St. to York. The gardens are located at 1005 York. For more information, phone (303) 331-4010. For information on the concert series, phone 744-9999.

Bear Creek Lake State Park

Operated by the City of Lakewood Parks and Recreation Department, this small park (just

short of 3,000 acres) also contains the two smaller Soda Lakes and offers many different recreation opportunities—from windsurfing and fishing to picnicking, overnight camping, horseback riding, and birdwatching (waterfowl and birds of prey). You can rent sailboards, paddleboats, canoes, and sailboats. The best way to get there is to take Kipling Ave. to Morrison Rd. and go west. Entrance fee is $2 per car. For more information, phone (303) 987-7880 or 987-7800.

Cherry Creek Lake State Recreation Area

Offering easy-access relief from the strip malls, townhouses, and high-rise office buildings of surrounding Aurora, this multi-purpose recreation area is popular among Denverites looking to cool off on hot summer days. Lately, the lake has become especially popular with jet-skiers, who jam around the lake, much to the chagrin of some of the other folks—waterskiers, windsurfers, fishermen, picnickers, cyclists, and campers. In the winter, the lake is open for ice fishing, skating, and boating, as well as cross-country skiing and snowmobiling (over 1.5 million visitors a year).

Built between 1946 and 1950 as a flood-control project, Cherry Creek Dam is nearly 1,500 feet long and 150 feet high; the lake is 3^1/2 miles long. Public recreation facilities include bicycle and jet-ski rental, campgrounds and picnic areas, a golf course, riding stables, nature trails, and fishing areas, with some especially designated for use by disabled persons.

For general information on Cherry Creek Lake State Recreation Area, phone (303) 690-1166, or write 4201 S. Parker Rd., Aurora, CO 80014. For information on horseback riding, phone 690-8235; for information on nature walks, picnicking (to reserve sites), and special events, phone 690-1211.

To get to the lake from downtown, take Leetsdale to Parker Rd.; from I-225, take the Parker Rd. Exit. The gates are well marked.

Chatfield Lake State Recreation Area

Quite a bit nicer than Cherry Creek Lake (you can't see high-rises from the shores), Chatfield isn't quite as accessible from downtown. But it's worth the drive, especially for nature lovers. In addition to a blue heron reserve at the lake, the area has a nicely presented visitors center with the skull of a mammoth found during dam excavation, and a United States Army Corps of Engineers exhibit of rivers, flooding, and damming. Excellent historical photos of 19th-century floods. The lake has several marinas and campgrounds, as well as riding stables, bike trails and hiking paths. In the winter, Denverites go with the floe (sorry . . .) and head to Chatfield for ice fishing and cross-country skiing.

The Army Corps of Engineers offers free hour-and-a-half tours of Chatfield Dam on Sat. mornings from late May through August. Call (303) 979-4120 for information about tours, or 791-7276 for information about the recreation area.

SPORTS AND OUTDOOR ACTIVITIES

Skiing

Skiing, of course, is the sport most people associate with Denver. And with good reason—the city's the gateway to a concentration of ski resorts that offers some of the finest runs, conditions, and facilities the sport has to offer. Not only are there huge destination resort complexes—Vail, Aspen, Breckenridge, and others—within easy drives of Stapleton Airport, but several other smaller resorts—Arapahoe Basin, for example—offer world-class skiing in less crowded (as well as less pretentious) areas, also within easy reach of the metropolitan area.

From Denver, it's very easy to get to the slopes. Whether your destination is Winter Park, Copper Mountain, or Vail, you can drive your own car, rent one, or take a shuttle, and be buckling your boots in under two hours (weather permitting). For more information on the ski areas, as well as on transportation to them, refer to the specific chapters. **People's Choice Transportation** is based at Stapleton and offers rides to the ski areas; phone (303) 659-7780 or (800) 777-2388.

For an only-in-Denver ski experience, take a ride on the **Rio Grande Ski Train.** Departing from Union Station on weekends at 7:15 a.m., Dec. through April, the train takes you up out of the city, northwest into the mountains, through Moffat Tunnel (completed in 1928), and eventually deposits you at the base of **Winter Park Ski Resort.** The train leaves the ski area in late afternoon, and will have you back at Union Station (conveniently located across the street from the Wynkoop Brewery) by early evening (it's a two-hour trip). Coach tickets are $25 roundtrip; first-class tickets are $40.

For more information on the Ski Train, write 555 17th St. #2400, Denver, CO 80202, or phone 296-I-SKI.

Cycling

Bicycling is so popular in Denver that speed limits are enforced in the city parks. In addition, the city offers a huge network of bike paths that can take the adventurous cyclist into most areas of the metro Denver area. From downtown, a bike path follows Speer out to Cherry Creek Shopping Center. The outlying areas offer limitless cycling, and some Colorado bikers "collect" passes: Berthoud (elev. 11,315 feet), Loveland (elev. 11,992 feet), Independence (elev. 12,095 feet), and others.

The **Denver Bicycle Touring Club** offers regular rides at all levels of interest and ability, and also publishes maps and a newsletter (with complete listings of events and rides). For information, write Box 8973, Denver, CO 80201, or phone (303) 798-3713. You can also call their number for information on current ride schedules and meeting places, as well as for names and numbers of ride leaders.

Golf

There are so many public golf courses in the Denver metro area that you could almost play a different course every day for a month without walking (or driving) the same fairway. Ranging from plain and pleby to elaborate and aristocratic, Denver's courses offer something for just about every level of skill and dedication, whether you go in for caddies and carts, plaids and spikes, or you prefer to sling your clubs over your shoulder, scoot on out to the course on your motorcyle, and hoof it from tee to tee in jeans and sneakers.

One of the area's most popular courses is **Arrowhead Golf Club,** located in Roxborough State Park, 45 minutes southwest of Denver (south of Chatfield Dam). Designed by Robert Trent Jones, Jr., Arrowhead is famous for its views and setting, as well as the challenge it provides golfers of all abilities. For information and tee times, phone (303) 973-9614.

City Park Golf Course, E. 25th Ave. and York, is an ideal family course, especially for the family whose members don't all share the same enthusiasm for the sport—also located at the park are tennis courts, the Denver Zoo, the Museum of Natural History, and 134 acres of sprawling lawns. For more information, phone 295-2095.

Other popular Denver-area courses: **Hyland Hills** in Westminster, tel. 428-6526; **Meadow Hills** in Aurora, tel. 690-2500; **Riverdale** in Brighton, tel. 659-6700; and **Welshire** in Denver at the corner of Hampden and Colorado boulevards, tel. 757-1352.

The **Colorado Golf Resort Association,** located at 1407 Larimer Square, has golf-oriented visitor and convention information and can arrange accommodations-and-greens-fees packages. Phone 973-4076.

For information on the courses owned and operated by the Denver Parks and Recreation Department, phone 575-3155.

Colorado Urban Trail System

The Colorado State Trails Program, a division of the state Parks and Outdoor Recreation Department, has organized a series of nearly 100 hiking, cycling, horseback riding, and cross-country ski trails throughout the Denver metro area, from Golden to Aurora to Roxborough State Park. You can get maps, which designate degrees of difficulty and facilities (restrooms, picnic tables, shelters, etc.), by writing the Colorado Division of Parks and Outdoor Recreation, 1313 Sherman St. #618, Denver, CO 80203, or by phoning (303) 866-3437.

Kayak Course

Unbeknownst even to many Denverites, the city has its own kayak course, at the confluence of Cherry Creek and the South Platte near the Forney Transportation Museum.

Amusement Centers And Parks

Denver offers a handful of amusement parks, for those whose diversions need direction. The **Celebrity Sports Center,** 888 S. Colorado Blvd., is a 150,000-square-foot facility featuring everything from bowling, swimming, and water slides to video arcades, bumper cars, and pinball machines. The complex is open weekdays till midnight and Fri. and Sat. till 2 a.m. Free child care. Phone (303) 757-3321.

Elitch Gardens and Amusement Park is sort of a Rocky Mountain version of Coney Island, with roller coaster and gondola rides, miniature golf, musical revues, and islands of flowers, as well as fast food at every turn. Dating to the early part of the century, Elitch's is a veritable Denver institution, and was home for years to one of the country's original summer stock theaters. Elitch's is located at 4620 W. 38th St., and is open daily June through Labor Day (and weekends in May). Phone 455-4771.

If you drove into Denver from the west, chances are you noticed **Lakeside Amusement Park** just before you got into town. Like Elitch's, Lakeside is a classic amusement park, evoking a simpler and more innocent America. Get your thrills on the roller coaster, speedboat rides on the lake, or any number of other rides; there are also rides for the less adventurous, and those whose stomachs insist they stay in tamer territory (see you there . . .).

Major League Baseball

On July 5, 1991, less than a year after Colorado voters approved the construction of a new baseball stadium, Denver was awarded a National League Baseball team. Though games will not be played in the new stadium until the 1995 season, the Colorado Rockies began playing on April 9, 1993, in Mile High Stadium, home of the Denver Broncos, and will play their first two seasons there, after which the new Coors Stadium, to be located in lower downtown Denver, will be completed.

Admission to Colorado Rockies' games ranges from $1-16, and the season runs from early April through late September. For tickets or more information, phone (303) ROCKIES. You can also arrange ticket-hotel-rental-car packages through the Denver Metro Convention and Visitors Bureau; phone (303) 892-1112.

COMMERCIAL ATTRACTIONS

Tattered Cover Bookstore

Bibliophiles'll go nuts here, for this is one of the west's truly great bookstores: three floors of floor-to-ceiling books on everything you can imagine, as well as chairs and tables and a wonderfully friendly and knowledgeable staff that encourages you to hang around and read.

downtown Denver from the capitol building

A bonus: The Tattered Cover will validate your parking in the adjacent garage for up to an hour and a half. A warning: It's *very* difficult to leave the Tattered Cover empty-handed; I ran into one couple looking for a book about Santa Fe and who left, happily, with $100 worth of books on everything from modern poetry to bed and breakfasts of the West. I dragged myself away with a mere $50 purchase—mostly on Colorado history. The Tattered Cover is located at 2955 E. 1st Ave.; phone 322-7727 or (800) 833-9327.

Gart Brothers

Denver has more sporting goods stores per capita than any other city in the world, thanks in large part to Gart Brothers. With stores throughout the Denver area, Gart's offers multistory sports emporiums with gigantic selections in golf, skiing, bow hunting, roller blading, and everything else you can imagine. With entire floors and rooms devoted to single sports, some Gart stores are so huge that directional signs are provided to help you find your way around. Anyone with even the slightest interest in sports owes it to herself to stop by a Gart's. The Gart's closest to downtown is at 10th and Broadway.

Wynkoop Brewery

This pub and brewery located at the west end of 17th St., across from Union Station, offers not only excellent food and beer, but free tours of the brewing facility (Saturday afternoons). See how quality, microbrewery beer is made, and sample the goods. (For more information, see "Food" following.)

TOURS

Best Mountain Tours by Mountain Men, tel. (303) 750-5200, offers half- and full-day historic and scenic tours, as well as ski charters. Write 3003 S. Macon Circle, Aurora, CO 80014. **Discover Colorado Tours,** tel. 277-0129, also offers scenic and historic tours, specializing in off-road trips, with full-day, half-day, and campfire tours. Write Box 205, Golden, CO 80402. **Denver Mobility, Inc.,** tel. 629-6175, provides tours, charters, and ski trips, with vans available for disabled persons. Write 3650 Chestnut Place, Denver, CO 80216. **British Double Decker,** tel. 892-1800, has a fleet of 10 buses available for sporting events, conventions, etc.

ACCOMMODATIONS

Although you can find motels throughout the Denver metropolitan area, particularly at major artery junctions and interstate off-ramps, the city's accommodations are primarily concentrated in three areas: downtown, near the airport, and in the southeastern region. If you can afford to, the best area to stay is downtown, where a good number of Denver's main attractions are within walking distance—the 16th Street Mall, the capitol building, several excellent museums and historical landmarks, and some of the city's best restaurants are concentrated within an area not much bigger than a couple of square miles. And the best way to see them is by walking tour.

The **Denver Metro Convention and Visitors Bureau** offers three separate packages that can save you money on accommodations and facilitate your stay. The **Denver Ski Lift** arranges day-trip skiing to 10 different resorts; **Mile High Adventure Club** arranges summer day-trips; and **Mile High Lights** arranges accommodations in conjunction with tickets to shows and events. Phone (800) 489-4888.

Downtown

Denver's oldest and most elegant downtown hotel is the **Brown Palace,** tel. (303) 297-3111, (800) 321-2599, or (800) 228-2917 in Denver. Completed in 1892 and designed in Italian Renaissance style, this grande dame of Denver's hotels is worth a visit just to have a look around—even if you're staying somewhere a bit less ostentatious. Management has actually printed up a descriptive walking-tour guide (available at the registration desk) that provides information on design, construction materials, former guests, and furnishings. Rooms start at about $160 a night and go up to over $675.

Another of downtown's nicer and more elegant hotels is the **Oxford Alexis Hotel,** tel. 628-5400. This European-style hotel at the corner of 17th St. and Wazee offers luxurious rooms and all the pampering you can take—including a health club, complimentary limousine service downtown (although it's only about four blocks to the north end of the 16th Street Mall, a perfectly splendid walk), and hosts who take the time to know their guests almost as family. Rates start at $120 for a double.

The **Warwick,** tel. 861-2000, at the corner of 17th and Grant, is a classically styled high-rise offering complimentary downtown transportation, athletic facilities, and a rooftop pool looking out over the modern, glassy high-rises of the city. Rooms start at about $135. Just three blocks away, at 401 17th St., the **Comfort Inn,** tel. 296-0400, has high-rise rooms overlooking the city—the corner rooms are especially impressive, with wraparound floor-to-ceiling windows for excellent views of the downtown area. Doubles run about $70.

Other conveniently located downtown hotels include the **Westin,** tel. 572-9100 or (800) 228-3000, the **Radisson,** tel. 893-3333, and the **Holiday Inn,** tel. 573-1450 or (800) 423-5128.

The South End

You'll see it from a distance—the black tower that stands apart from the other muted southern Denver high-rises and penetrates the sky has an almost otherworldly feel to it. But step inside **Loews Giorgio Hotel,** tel. (303) 782-9300, and the change is as dramatic as the tower itself. Suddenly you feel like you're in Milan and that La Scala or DaVinci's *Last Supper* is just a short cab ride away. Indeed, this Italian-style hotel is one of Denver's real luxuries, and though located a bit south of downtown still affords easy access to most of the city's attractions. An added bonus is that you don't have to pay for parking here—unless you opt for valet—while you usually do downtown, where parking alone can add a sizable sum to your bill. Rooms at the Giorgio start at about $135. To get there, take the Colorado Blvd. Exit from I-25, go south to Mississippi, and turn left.

Other, more moderate lodging at the south end of town (still at the junction of Colorado and I-25) includes the **Belcaro Motel,** tel. 756-3671, **Days Inn,** tel. 691-2223 or (800) 325-2525, the **Landmark Best Western,** tel. 388-5561, and **La Quinta,** tel. 578-8886 or (800) 531-9500.

Also on the south side of town (in Englewood, near the junction of I-25 and Hwy. 88: **Days Inn,** tel. 790-8220 or (800) 325-2525, **Hampton Inn,** tel. 792-9999 or (800) 426-7866, and **Radisson,** tel. 799-6200.

At The Airport

If you're looking only for a place to crash between flights and don't want to head into town, you've got several choices, all typical of airport-type hotels. **The Registry Hotel,** tel. (303) 321-3333 or (800) 247-9810, the **Sheraton,** tel. 333-7711 or (800) 325-3535, the **Stapleton Plaza Hotel,** tel. 321-3500 or (800) 950-6070, and the **Stouffer Hotel,** tel. 399-7500 or (800) HOTELS1 are all located directly across Quebec St. from Stapleton. As do many airport hotels in other large cities, these cater to groups, conventioneers, and seminarees, and the lone gypsy traveler (or travel writer) can't help but feel a bit out of place.

Other airport hotels include the **Courtyard Marriott,** tel. 333-3303 or (800) 321-2211, and the **Regal 8,** tel. 371-0740 or (800) 851-8888, the latter located two miles from the airport at I-70 and Peoria but with some of the least expensive rooms in the area.

Note: As discussed elsewhere, Stapleton Airport is not long for this world: By 1994, the new airport northeast of town should be operative. New editions of *Colorado Handbook* will attempt to keep you as up to date as possible on both the airport and airport lodging. The **Denver Convention and Visitors Bureau** will also gladly fill you in on the latest developments; contact them at 892-1112.

For current **information** on airport traffic conditions, tune your radio to AM 530.

West Of Town
As you head into Denver on I-70 from the west, you'll find another cluster of motels and hotels to choose from: Among them: a **Regal 8,** tel. (303) 455-8888 or (800) 851-8888; a **Howard Johnson,** tel. 433-8441, I-70 at Exit 272/Federal north; and a **Motel 6,** tel. 232-4924, at Exit 266.

Bed And Breakfast
The **Queen Anne Inn,** tel. (303) 296-6666 is located just east of downtown at 2147 Tremont. Constructed in 1879, the building is on the National Register of Historic Places and was beautifully restored and decorated by proprietors Chuck and Anne Hillestad, who court honeymooners and often hold weddings on the premises. The Queen Anne has been touted in dozens of national publications and was recently named Denver's best bed and breakfast by *Westword*. Its residential neighborhood is within easy walking distance of most downtown attractions and restaurants. To get to the Queen Anne from I-25, take the Colfax Exit, and follow Colfax past the capitol to Logan; go left on Logan until it tees into a small park (you'll be looking straight across at the Queen Anne); go left, and then veer right onto Tremont.

Hostels
Generally the least expensive way to travel, and one of the best ways to meet fellow travelers, hosteling can be a real adventure, though it's not for everyone. The typical dorm-style accommodations, the chore(s) you'll be asked to do to offset the exceptionally low rates, and the socializing demanded by the lack of privacy can either suit your needs and moods or not. If this is the kind of digs you prefer, or upon which your budget insists, the city offers the **Denver International Youth Hostel,** tel. (303) 832-9996, at 630 E. 6th Avenue. For more information on hosteling in the Rocky Mountain area, write **American Youth Hostels, Inc.,** Rocky Mountain Division, Box 2730, Boulder, CO 80306.

The downtown **YMCA,** tel. 861-8300, located at 25 E. 6th St., a block from the capitol, also has inexpensive rooms.

Camping And RVing
Of course the mountains west of Denver are full of campgrounds, both privately owned and government run, and there are hundreds of thousands of acres of national forest and wilderness areas within a short drive of the city (see individual chapters). If you're heading into Denver and just need a place to pull off the road, you've got several options, including **Chief Hosa Campground,** tel. (303) 526-0364, west of town just off I-70 at Exit 253, and **Denver-North Campground,** tel. 452-4120, north of town at Exit 229 (Broomfield) off I-25.

FOOD

Start Me Up
One of the best places to face the morning in Denver is at **The Market,** on Larimer Square at 1445 Larimer, tel. (303) 534-5140. Grab a newspaper and get in line at the espresso bar for a latte, cappuccino, or house coffee and a croissant or fresh-baked muffin. Open at 6:45 on weekday mornings, 8:30 on Sat. (this is where many local cyclists get their caffeine jolts before their rides, and their juices afterward) and till midnight on Fri. and Saturday. The Market also sells gourmet groceries, deli sandwiches, and desserts (try a creampuff or truffle). Seating available both inside and on the sidewalk outside, weather permitting.

If you're in the mood for something heartier, you might try the **Delectable Egg,** 1642 Market (between 16th and 17th streets), tel. 572-8146. Open at 6:30 weekday mornings and 7 a.m. on Sat., the Egg serves daily specials for around $5 in a large airy, woody, and ceiling-fanned dining room.

Dozens, 236 W. 13th, tel. 572-0066, is a veritable downtown institution. Located in a restored Victorian, the restaurant is walking distance from downtown businesses and many of the local tourist attractions. That fact, along with its reputation for excellent food at reasonable prices, ensures its popularity with locals and out-of-towners alike.

Inexpensive

Perennially voted "best deli" by *Westword*, **Goldie's Deli** on the 16th Street Mall at Glenarm serves every kind of deli sandwich you could imagine and some you probably never could—also breakfast burritos and other specials to jumpstart your day. Noisy, crowded, hectic—in short, a deli made to order. Try the "Turkey Jive" on light rye, grab a table on the mall and watch the world go by. Or pick up an ice cream cone or bag of popcorn and continue your stroll.

Another local favorite—and another restaurant regularly recognized by *Westword*'s "Best of Denver"—is the **Blue Bonnet Café**, at 457 S. Broadway, tel. (303) 778-0147. Nothing fancy here—in fact the rather tacky decor goes hand in hand with the run-down look of the building's exterior, not to mention the boarded-up buildings nearby—but if it's good cheap food you're after, look no further. Be prepared to wait, though: The Blue Bonnet's no secret. But even the waiting here's part of the picture—try one of the half dozen or so types of margaritas, by the glass or by the pitcher, on which the Blue Bonnet prides itself. Dinner combos run $4-6, specials $6-8; à la carte tacos, burritos, enchiladas, and tamales are $1.50-3.

Right up there with the Blue Bonnet, and even more authentic (no Anglo "hosts" here), is **Las Delicias**, tel. 839-5675, at the corner of E. 19th and Pennsylvania. With the television in the lobby tuned to a Spanish-language station and the waitresses, busboys, and cooks rarely breaking into English, this is the *cosa real* (real thing). And the prices are unbeatable: Dinners run $3-8, with most right around $4. The tamale plate (three tamales), for example, is $3.30, the three-chicken-enchilada dinner is $3.50, and a bowl of menudo is $3.75. All of Las Delicias' food is available for carry-out (including the green chile stew, at $2.90 a pint). In addition to the restaurant on 19th, **Las Delicias II** is located at 50 E. Del Norte, tel. 430-0422. Hours at both restaurants are Mon. through Sat. 8 a.m.-9 p.m. and Sun. 9 a.m.-9 p.m.

The **Old Number One Firehouse Restaurant**, tel. 892-1100 above the Firefighters Museum at 1326 Tremont (see "Museums and Other Sights" above) serves sandwiches and specials for $3-5. More interesting as a continuation of the museum than as a restaurant, the Firehouse occupies the firefighters' old quarters, and the men's room (I can't speak for the women's) is worth a visit whether you need to head back that way or not—inside are the firefighters' wooden lockers and pedestal washbasins.

Although a chain/franchise restaurant (which will usually have the same effect on me as a silver cross does on Dracula), **The Old Spaghetti Factory**, corner of 18th and Lawrence, tel. 295-1864, offers excellent food at bargain prices. Spaghetti, fettuccine, and tortellini dinners (with salad and French bread) run $4-7, and the atmosphere is great to boot—crowded and rowdy, with Victorian-style velvet couches (in the waiting lobby) and fringed chandeliers. Spumoni is included in the price.

The Spaghetti Factory is open for lunch Mon. through Fri. 11:30 a.m.-2 p.m., and for dinner Mon. through Thurs. 5-10 p.m., Fri. and Sat. 5-11 p.m., and Sun. 4-10 p.m.

Moderate

Here's the guidebook writer's dilemma: His mission, should he choose to accept it, is to ferret out all the best restaurants in a given area and to recommend them to you, dear reader. Yet there's a problem. Sometimes he finds one so good, and so reasonably priced, that he hates to leave; he'd just as soon eat every meal there, to hell with the rest of them. Such is the case with **Wynkoop's Brew Pub**, tel. (303) 297-1900. In fact, were it not for a gargantuan amount of self-discipline, yours truly could easily have spent his every afternoon in Denver tasting the different beers (brewed on the premises!), trying the various lunch specials, and lounging through happy hours (when pints are $1.50), until not much was left to do but call a cab and head back to the hotel for a nice long nap. Fortunately, self-discipline won out. Most of the time.

At any rate, no trip to Denver is complete without a stop at Wynkoop's Brew Pub, at the corner of 18th and Wynkoop. Whether you stop in to taste the half dozen or so beers the day presents, or you're more interested in pub chow, this place is a must. The beers vary from week to week (unlike Coors, which varies from weak to weaker), and, particularly, from season to season, but they'll usually range from a light ale to a dark stout or porter. Lunch specials include salads, soups (including the Gorgonzola Ale, made with cheese and beer, natch!), sandwiches, the Ploughman's Platter (buffalo and veal bratwurst, cheeses, eggs, onions, beer mustard, and fresh fruit chutney), as well as Shepherd's Pie, bangers and mashers, bockwurst, and Italian sausage—all lunches range from $5-7. For dinner, try grilled game hen, curried coconut chicken, trout or shark—running from about $8 to $12. Whatever your preference, whether it's bangers or bratwurst, be sure to wash it down with a Wynkoop's beer (assuming you're of age). It'd be sacrilege to drink anything else—I actually witnessed an otherwise intelligent-appearing gentleman order a Miller Lite, *and drink it*. Wynkoop's has also recently added 40 deluxe pool tables upstairs and a cabaret theater downstairs. (Wynkoop's also offers tours of the brewery; see "Commercial Attractions," above.)

One of the best places downtown to see and be seen, as well as to get decent grub at reasonable prices, is the **Paramount Café,** tel. 893-2000. This little bar and café, with plenty of outside tables for watching 16th St. strollers, serves fajitas, cajun chicken, meatloaf and albacore sandwiches, Tex-Mex specialties ($5-8), and a variety of appetizers, ranging from wontons to potato skins ($3-4). Daily specials are $4-6.

If you like raw fish, try **Han Sushi,** "downtown's only sushi bar," located in Writers Square. Combo dishes run $7-14. Other popular Japanese and sushi restaurants: **Sushi Heights,** 2301 E. Colfax, **Mori Japanese Restaurant,** 2019 Market, and **Toshi's,** 299 Detroit. The **Panda Café,** 1098 S. Federal, and **Tommy's,** 3410 E. Colfax, are two of the city's favorite Chinese restaurants.

Expensive

For authentic Russian food, try the **Little Russian Café,** tel. 595-8600, in Larimer Square. Dinners run $10-16 and include a complimentary shot of vodka. Indoor and patio seating.

A favorite for fish and other seafood is **McCormick's,** tel. 825-1107, a classic fish house and oyster bar located on the corner of 17th and Wazee (right next door to the Oxford Alexis Hotel). The huge menu regularly features fresh swordfish, salmon, and crab, as well as bouillabaisse and Bluepoint oysters.

High-end Denver Classics

Cliff Young's is one of those institutions that regularly surpasses even the mile-high expectations it engenders—perfect for no-holds-barred special occasions. Of course, the place ain't cheap, but that's not what you go here for. Try the rack of lamb (about $30). Reservations recommended. Phone (303) 831-8900.

Another Denver restaurant with a reputation for excellent food and atmosphere (very formal), is the **Zenith, an American Grill,** 1750 Lawrence, tel. 820-2800. Again, prices run high, but the "dining experience" is said to be worth the cost.

Claiming to be Denver's oldest restaurant, and having served over the years countless luminaries—from Teddy Roosevelt to Ernest Hemingway—**The Buckhorn Exhange,** 10th Ave. and Osage, tel. 534-9505, is yet another Denver tradition. Specialties include buffalo, elk, alligator, and Rocky Mountain Oysters. Live folk music Fri. and Sat. nights.

Health Food/Vegetarian

A popular and centrally located vegetarian restaurant, **Greens,** 320 E. Colfax, tel. (303) 831-1315, is regularly singled out by the local press for its devotion to healthful meals. Open for dinner Wed. through Sat. 6-9 p.m., lunch Mon. through Fri. 11:30 a.m.-2:30 p.m., and breakfast weekends 9 a.m.-2:30 p.m. Greens is located just up the street from the capitol.

ENTERTAINMENT

At **El Chapultepec,** at the corner of 20th Street and Market, the motto is "hot burritos and cool jazz nightly." A small, neighborhood bar that's grown popular with folks from throughout the Denver area (and beyond!), El Chapultepec features formica tabletops, Naugahyde bar stools, a smoky air (even with the doors open to the cool night), and, despite that motto, some of the hottest jazz in town. No cover charged. (On Fri. and Sat. nights, it's often standing room only, but you can have Mexican food delivered to wherever you're standing . . .) A real bonus here is that big-name talents playing other venues in town often drop in unannounced to jam.

Rock 'n' rollers have dozens of places in the city to choose from, including everything from

WHERE TO FIND LIVE MUSIC
IN THE DENVER AREA

As a breeding ground for new music, Denver has yet to, well, really score. The city has its share of rock 'n' roll interlopers, but most have just flitted through Denver stopping only long enough to pick up their bags at the airport before heading to the mountains.

When it comes to music, Denver is no New York or Los Angeles—or even a Minneapolis, Austin, or Nashville. Local musicians, however, have a one-word reply to that statement: yet.

First, those that perform take little for granted. They work hard. Second, the clubs fill up, depending on the act, but are rarely packed. Even touring national club acts can be studied from close range. And third, the cover charges are nominal—$5 or so on the weekends for local favorites, less earlier in the week. Even better, many shows start by 9:30 p.m. or so, which means it's possible to take in a couple of bands before midnight (which also means that Denver is not a late-night town . . .).

At a host of fun and funky clubs you'll discover a wonderful assortment of people out absorbing a wide range of live music. And new clubs pop up out of nowhere every month or so and can just as easily disappear into the twilight zone. There are, however, two methods for finding what's on tap each week.

Method #1: Look for a telephone or light pole along E. 13th Ave. on Capitol Hill. That's the sprawling central neighborhood east of the capitol. Hardworking bands that want to publicize a gig decorate the poles with announcements on a weekly basis. Of course, the flyers will give you no idea of what the bands might sound like.

Which leads to Method #2: Walk into the mecca known as **Wax Trax** (the music store on the corner of E. 13th Ave. and Washington), and try to get the attention of the friendly clerks behind the counter. As you point astutely to the stack of flyers on the counter in front of you, ask for a recommendation and casually mention what kind of music you like. Chances are good at least one band playing is worth a listen.

As a backstop, check the pages of *Westword*, which is distributed on Tuesdays and widely available in restaurants, clubs, bookstores, and record shops. Just about every local show is listed. Again, the question comes: But what do they sound like? If you're intent on knowing beforehand, none of the major club operators will refuse a few questions

over the phone. And beyond that, there's always that one far-out rock 'n' roll possibility: Take a chance.

Though Denver rockers mourned the closing last year of one of the city's premier night spots, The Garage, the slack was quickly taken up by **South Seven,** Denver's newest and hippest club. With live alternative and hard rock 'n' roll Wednesday, Friday, and Saturday nights, South Seven does its best imitation of a Seattle night spot, attracting late-night hardcores and the area's best bands. Cover charge is usually around $5. South Seven is located at 7 S. Broadway. For information, phone (303)744-0513.

Herman's Hideaway, 1578 Broadway, tel. 778-9916, started as a funky neighborhood bar, and though it's expanded twice in recent years, the atmosphere is still down-home casual and friendly. Watch for special showcase nights when bands are whisked off after only 45 minutes or so, providing the kind of evening when boredom doesn't stand a chance. Herman's is located a couple of miles south of where Broadway passes under I-25.

Back downtown, **The Mercury Cafe,** 2199 California, tel. 294-9281, is a multipurpose facility with a main music room, restaurant, and theater. It's possible to eat an exquisite and healthful meal, watch some drama, and then head upstairs for some music, which, slightly more eclectic than at Herman's and The Garage, often includes acoustic sets, jazz, experimental music, and a lot of rock 'n' roll.

For a truly tough and gritty edge, **The Broadway,** 1082 Broadway, tel. 860-7558, offers a steady stream of metal and headbanging, with the occasional alternative rock thrown in. It's usually so loud you can stand in the street, or just inside the doorway, and decide whether it's your bag or not.

In Boulder, **J.J. McCabe's,** 945 Walnut, tel. 449-4130, has been a stalwart college hangout for years. The stage is kind of an afterthought, but that hasn't bothered the throngs that pack this club for local favorites many nights a week. Also in Boulder, on The Hill, the subterranean **Ground Zero,** 1130 College, tel. 444-5333, books a variety of national touring acts and locals too. The tables are rickety, and over-21 drinkers are corralled into a screwy area off to the side of the stage. But the sound is excellent, and the quirky place has often been whipped into a wonderful frenzy by hardworking bands.

For jazz, don't overlook the tiny club in lower downtown known as **El Chapultapec,** 1962 Market, tel. 295-9126. Hint: Go early in the week. Sometimes that jazz can be just as good, and you can actually find an open booth or bar stool. Nearby, the **Jazzworks,** in the basement of the Wynkoop Brewing Co. at 1634 18th St., tel. 297-0920, offers a full slate of wide-ranging jazz styles. If they're not pouring the homemade beer downstairs, buy your own upstairs and carry it in. Nobody will mind.

If you're coming into town from the mountains, always keep in mind the **Little Bear,** 28075 CO 74, tel. 674-9991. Smack in downtown Evergreen in the foothills south of Denver, the Little Bear offers a true roadhouse feel and romps with friendly enthusiasm on Sunday afternoons, not to mention Friday nights—check out the bra collection on the wall. The emphasis here is on blues and rock, and the last time somebody whispered alternative music he was thrown out

on his ear and accused of being a communist.

And if you're in Denver during the summer, don't miss a chance to watch an outdoor show at **Red Rocks,** a natural amphitheater in the rust-red cliff outcroppings just west of downtown Denver. When the moon rises over the city lights, and you're listening to a band and gazing up at the giant rocks, everybody's a music fan. And it doesn't matter where you're from.

—Mark Stevens

Mark Stevens currently reports for the Denver Post *and writes a music column in the monthly Denver entertainment magazine* Icon. *He has been a staff producer for the* MacNeil/Lehrer News Hour *and a staff reporter for the* Rocky Mountain News *and the* Christian Science Monitor.

---

outdoor, concert-sized venues such as Red Rocks (see below) to small clubs where you might be closer to the stage (and sound system) than to your partner across the table.

One of the more popular hanging-out spots among the younger crowd is **Wynkoop's Brew Pub.** Friday and Saturday nights the full-circle bar is jampacked with people sampling Wynkoop's excellent beers, brewed on the premises.

An only-in-Denver opportunity is "jazz at the art museum" on Wednesday afternoons. Described by one local as "art, jazz, and yuppies," this has been a popular singles scene, particularly among the young downtown set. See "Denver Art Museum," under "Art Museums" above.

The **Comedy Works,** tel. (303) 595-3637, also located right downtown (1226 15th St., in Larimer Square), features local and comedy-circuit comics most nights of the week. Two shows Fri. and Sat. nights, with an $8 cover—slightly less weeknights. A recorded message will give you showtimes.

For the inside scoop on Denver's nightclub and music scene, see the accompanying special topic by Denver music critic Mark Stevens.

Concert Venues
Among Denver's places to see acts big enough to draw huge crowds is **Red Rocks,** tel. (303) 572-4704, a gorgeous natural amphitheater in

the hills on the city's west side. Recent acts have included Rickie Lee Jones, Lyle Lovett, and Jimmy Cliff. **Fiddler's Green,** tel. 741-5000, also features outdoor concerts ranging from country (the Judds) and folk (Peter, Paul, and Mary, Garrison Keillor) to rock (Joe Cocker, Santana), jazz (Kenny G), and classical (local and national orchestras and symphonies).

The renovated **Paramount Theatre,** downtown at Glenarm and 16th, tel. 623-0106, is historical, plush, and evocative of the early 20th century; the Paramount books a wide range of acts and activities—from rock to theater to body-building contests. **Elitch's Gardens and Amusement Park,** tel. 455-4771, also known for its roller coaster and other rides, as well as its perennial county-fair atmosphere, books live music throughout the summer. Often country-flavored, acts have included Emmylou Harris, Riders in the Sky, and Air Supply.

Denver Performing Arts Complex
This center, located downtown at 14th and Curtis, is the home of many of Denver's entertainment and cultural events, shows, and troupes, including the Denver Symphony Orchestra, the Colorado Ballet, and the Denver Theater Company, which each season produces 12 plays on the center's four stages. For tickets, phone (303) 893-4100; for information, free tours, and season brochures, phone 893-4000.

THE CAPITOL HILL PEOPLE'S FAIR

In the first weekend of June over 250,000 people swarm through scores of colorful booths at Civic Center Park, the stretch of lawn between the gold-domed capitol and the majestic Greco-Roman-style courthouse in downtown Denver. An arts-and-crafts fair on a grand and multicultural scale, the Capitol Hill People's Fair offers a perfect opportunity to examine everything from ceramics and paintings to bamboo art and African masks. In addition, you can find a booth representing almost any political, philosophical, or religious viewpoint. You can have your fortune told by tarot-card readers, then walk a few feet to Rocky Mountain Skeptics and learn that it's all bunk anyway. From the Caleb Campaign learn that Jesus loves you, and then talk to an American Atheist and find He doesn't even exist. You can talk to right-wingers and socialists, yoga teachers and chess experts.

If all that philosophical discussion makes you weary, you might want to relax and enjoy some entertainment. A variety of music, from heavy metal and modern jazz to country and classical, is offered on the five different stages. In addition, there are dance performances, ballet to break dancing, while clowns juggle machetes, torches, and even watermelons.

And then there are the food booths, where you'll find every imaginable food type and cuisine—Chinese, Japanese, Greek, Turkish, Mexican, Indonesian, and more, not to mention good old-fashioned hamburgers, hot dogs, and popcorn.

Attending the People's Fair is an act of bravery because you never know what Colorado's temperamental Mother Nature might do—despite the meteorologist's predictions. You might enjoy several hours of sunshine, only to be bombarded by rain, hail, and gusty winds. In anticipation of such outbursts, the booths are all covered by canopies, and it's not uncommon to make new friends while weathering a storm. If bad weather's expected, the event's organizers move the fair to the second weekend in June. The fair opens at 10 a.m. and closes at 7 p.m. on Sat. and 6 p.m. on Sunday.

For more information on the Capitol Hill People's Fair, contact CHUN (Capitol Hill United Neighborhoods) at (303) 388-2716.

—Thomas Owen Meinen

Thomas Owen Meinen is a freelance writer in Denver, where he has won public-speaking awards. He has degrees in German and English from California State University, Chico.

CALENDAR

Denver's a big city, the biggest for over 600 miles in any direction, and there's something going on almost every day, evening, and weekend—from arts-and-crafts fairs to auto races, from music festivals (*lots* of music in this town) to golf tournaments. The new year kicks off in mid-January with the two-week **National Western Stock Show and Rodeo,** the largest such show on the planet. In addition to pro and amateur rodeos and livestock competitions, you can watch the city transmogrify into a shit-kickin' cow town with Ralph Lauren and Obsession stepping aside for Wrangler and *eau de chevaux.* If you plan to be in Denver during the festivities, whether you're ridin' and ropin' or just watching from the rails, be sure to make hotel reservations well in advance. For schedule and ticket information, phone (303) 297-1166.

Denver's annual two-day **Cinco de Mayo** party takes place on the 16th Street Mall and includes music, dancing, arts and crafts, and food—in a salute to Denver's Chicano heritage and to Mexican independence. For more information, phone 534-6161.

Also in May, things get crazy for a couple of days at the Civic Center Park during the annual **Capitol Hill People's Fair.** Join the more than 100,000 revelers, politicos, and New-Agers, and check out everything from the latest in low-impact high technology to non-competitive games, from herbal teas to current political agendas. Virtually nonstop live music. Phone 388-2716. (See accompanying special topic.)

Another folky favorite is the **Colorado Renaissance Festival,** in Larkspur, south of Denver, on weekends in June and early July. Paint your face, don a beret and plume, or squeeze into your favorite pair of tights, and get thee to the funnery. Once inside the grounds, located hillside amid pine and scrub oak, you can forget the travails that the centuries since Elizabeth I hath wrought. Listen to buxom wenches tell bawdy tales; toss overripe fruit at shackled heads; gnaw on a fresh-fired turkey drumstick and wash it down with a pint of mead; listen to the sweet melodies of zithers and lutes; and sample the wares—glassware, hats, and jewelry of local artisans. Phone 756-1501 for exact dates and more information.

As is true throughout the state, the Fourth of July offers a wide array of activities, highlighted by the fireworks at Mile-High Stadium. Take in the evening's Zephyr (Denver's Triple-A baseball team) game, and stick around for the fireworks afterward. For ticket information, phone 433-8645.

For current information on annual events in Denver, contact the **Denver Metro Convention and Visitors Bureau** at (303) 892-1112. The staff publishes an exhaustive Denver events guide, which they'll gladly send you. Watch also the entertainment sections of the *Denver Post,* the *Rocky Mountain News,* and *Westword,* as well as *Icon.* You'll also find more information on events in the area in the Golden, Boulder, and Colorado Springs chapters of this book.

SHOPPING

Downtown Denver is rife with shopping malls, plazas, squares, and "centers." In fact, there are so many so close to one another that sometimes you don't realize you've passed from one to the next.

16th Street Mall
Even if you're the type whose blood runs cold at the very sound of the word "mall" and you find yourself looking for a tavern to duck into whenever shops and boutiques have the nerve to enter your line of vision, you won't mind Denver's 16th Street Mall. In fact, you'll probably enjoy it. Here, strolling, people watching, window-shopping, or stopping for junk food or a cup of coffee is much more important than *buying things.* You'll be endlessly entertained by street vendors ("Get your ice cold lemonade"), jugglers, flirting teenagers, and local business people talking about the Broncos or stocks and commodities. And if you do want to do some shopping, there's every kind of store imaginable—from Walgreen's and Woolworth's to Wilson's Suede and Leather, from the Banana Republic and Eddie Bauer to bookstores, T-shirt shops, and jewelers.

The **Tabor Center** at the mall's north end is where you'll find most of the upscale stores, including Brooks Brothers (suits and menswear), Crabtree and Evelyn (soaps, lotions, and cosmetics), Johnston and Murphy (shoes), Keepsakes (foofoo throw rugs, scents, lamps, etc.), and Pollyanna (fine lingerie). In addition, check out the Lawrence Street Bridge Market on the third floor (be sure to take the glass elevator near the fountain). This is an almost European-style potpourri of assorted cart vendors and booths—selling everything from hats and jewelry to kites and rubber stamps. On the bottom floor of Tabor Center, you'll find The Sharper Image—an amazing

mural at 14th and Champa, downtown Denver

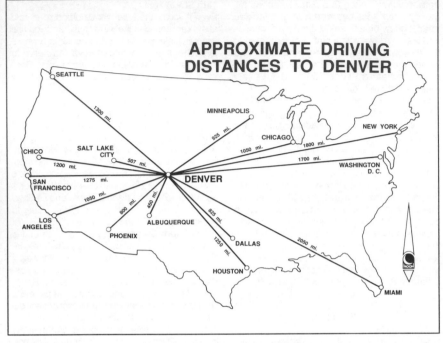

APPROXIMATE DRIVING DISTANCES TO DENVER

SEATTLE
MINNEAPOLIS
CHICAGO
NEW YORK
CHICO
SALT LAKE CITY
WASHINGTON D.C.
SAN FRANCISCO
DENVER
LOS ANGELES
ALBUQUERQUE
PHOENIX
DALLAS
HOUSTON
MIAMI

1300 mi.
925 mi.
1050 mi.
1800 mi.
1700 mi.
507 mi.
1200 mi.
1275 mi.
1050 mi.
800 mi.
450 mi.
825 mi.
1250 mi.
2050 mi.

© MOON PUBLICATIONS, INC.

array of high-tech toys and equipment, much of it on working display for passers-by. A few shops toward 17th St., Watson's Soda Fountain is open long after most everything else around is closed (till 11 p.m. Mon. through Thurs., till midnight Fri. and Sat., and till 9 p.m. Sun.) and in addition to grabbing a malt, a hot dog, or a bag of popcorn, you can pick up convenience items, soft drinks, liquor, prescriptions (the pharmacy is open Mon. through Fri. 9 a.m.-5 p.m.), and snacks.

Free shuttle buses run every few minutes from one end of the mall to the next with stops at each block.

Still More Downtown Shopping
In addition to the 16th Street Mall, **Larimer Square,** at Larimer and 15th, has a number of shops and boutiques, including **Boutique International,** a classy shop with everything from hats (men's and women's) to paperweights, wooden soldiers, and beer steins. Across 15th St. from Larimer Square, Writers Square also has a number of interesting shops, boutiques,

and cafés, including **The Creative Cook** (upscale kitchenware), **Colorado Peddler** (quality—mostly—Colorado gifts and souvenirs, prints, dolls, pottery, etc.), a **Benetton, Merle Norman,** and **Aspen Leaf** (men's and women's sports and dress wear). If you're looking to send word of your travels to folks back home, be sure to check out **Avant-Card,** which, as its name suggests, has an excellent selection of greeting cards—innovative and provocative (postcards, as well). Across 16th St. is the Tabor Center, and you're back at **16th Street Mall.**

Another of Denver's popular malls is **Tivoli,** built in the historic Tivoli brewery, which dates to 1864 and under several different names and owners brewed beer here until 1969. Today, Tivoli is a six-story shopping center with several restaurants, a cinema complex with 12 screens, and a variety of different shops and boutiques. The entire facility is worth exploring—the many nooks and crannies of the old brewery, as well as the historic photos, will keep you poking around for hours.

DENVER'S BEST BOOK AND RECORD STORES

If you want to go shopping and feel like you're right at home—if home is just about anywhere in the U.S.—head for the mall. Denver has an ample supply, and they're all in the obvious locations—stuck by interstates or in the heart of suburbia. There's even one mini-version (the Tabor Center) smack downtown, where the outside is beautiful, the atrium stunning, and the products la-de-da.

But if you've got records or books on the mind, a couple of Denver landmarks ought to be on your itinerary. Both pass a few simple tests of retail success: They stock everything (or try to); they don't let on that they stock everything; and they'll help you find anything if that anything is available.

For music, it's **Wax Trax.**

For books, it's the **Tattered Cover.**

Gaping up at the volume of books in "TC" is the equivalent of staring up at the skyscrapers in New York. You may as well tattoo "tourist" on your forehead.

The Tattered Cover is a retail curiosity, breathtaking for sheer size yet still somehow understated. There are 400,000 volumes (150,000 titles) tucked into dozens of nooks and crannies throughout the four-floor building. The local mall bookstore might have one book on woodworking, but how about choosing from among fifteen? Need a mystery? How 'bout a mystery bookstore within a bookstore?

In 1974, three people managed the Tattered Cover, then located a few blocks from its present site in the Cherry Creek shopping district. One of those people was Joyce Meskis, who owns the operation and can still be found digging in the stacks, unassumingly helping customers. Denver book lovers quickly spread the word about the endless racks of books, friendly service, and low-key, almost library-like style. Comfy chairs? You mean you can actually sit down and read a book? For an hour or so and nobody will bother you? Come on . . .

After an interim stop in a nearby space to accommodate the burgeoning racks, the Tattered Cover is now in its third location. The exterior is cool and indifferent, smack across the street from Denver's snobbiest mall, the Cherry Creek Mall. The interior is warm, inviting. But again, it's about to burst at the seams. The store now has 300 employees. That's not customers per day. That's employees.

But this isn't a warehouse—it's a group of bookstores within one. You walk in for a cookbook or a magazine and find yourself browsing through the computer manuals and travel guides, suddenly thinking about a new hobby, wondering about climbing a mountain, or thinking about what modern American literature has really managed to say about modern American life.

The Tattered Cover is located at 2955 E. 1st Avenue. Hours are Mon.-Fri. 9:30 a.m.-9 p.m., Sat. 9:30 a.m.-6 p.m., and Sunday noon-5 p.m. For more information, phone (303) 322-7727.

Like the Tattered Cover, **Wax Trax** is several stores in one. Five, really. The original, on the corner of E. 13th Ave. and Washington, is for rock 'n' roll and vinyl. Yes, vinyl. The owners have vowed to stick with the format until the last independent label or underground band stops pressing music into real, live black grooves.

Their vinyl supply is still fairly plump. But when it does buckle to CD mania, it's hard to imagine a Wax Trax that wouldn't buy from offbeat labels, keep a wide variety of music in stock, and help guide the customer with quirky descriptions on the dividers, which are part of the kick here. Scrawled mini-descriptions are tagged onto the top in Magic Marker: "silly goofy pop from Hoboken, New Joisey," "Jesus & Mary Chain Velvet Underground Type Fuzzy Guitar Psych," "kinda skewed folkish pop."

Then there are four more stores, but don't try to keep track. Just head west for the first three, and then across the street for the fourth. The CD shop is on the next street—again, many alternatives, as well as a strong rap and soul section (look for rare issues and expensive imports underneath the front counter). Next door is Across the Trax, where you can rent offbeat videos and buy T-shirts, buttons, and postcards. Next door to that is where you'll find a huge selection of new and used 45s, as well as country, blues, and jazz, plus international music and reissued compilations of oldies. Then watch the traffic as you cross the street to the used store—CDs, 45s, LPs, and even eight-track tapes.

Wax Trax is (are?) located on the 600 block of E. 13th Ave. Hours are Mon.-Sat. 10 a.m. to 8 p.m. and Sun. 11 a.m.-5 p.m. For more information, phone 831-7246.

Note: If you really want to blow the afternoon, Wax Trax and the Tattered Cover are just a few miles apart. You might waste 15 minutes getting from one to the other. And then you could count on a couple of weeks at home where all you'd do is sit around, listen to music . . . and read.

—Mark Stevens

Tivoli's hours are Mon. through Sat. 10 a.m.-9 p.m. and Sun. noon-5 p.m. Some of the restaurants stay open later. Tivoli is located at the corner of 9th and Larimer. You'll see its seven-story tower from several blocks away.

Cherry Street Mall

This is Denver's most upscale shopping complex. Stores include Abercrombie and Fitch, Liz Claiborne, Sak's Fifth Avenue, and Neiman-Marcus, as well as the other mall-standard shoe, jewelry, cookie, and frozen-yogurt shops (over 100 stores in all). The Cherry Creek Mall is located at 3000 1st Avenue.

SERVICES

The central information number for the Denver **Police Department** is (303) 575-3127 (in emergencies dial 9-1-1). The number for the **sheriff's office** is 375-3451. For general information at the City and County of Denver, phone 575-2790. To report accidents and emergencies to the **Colorado State Patrol**, or for nonemergencies, phone 239-4501.

For medical care, dial 9-1-1 in emergencies. Denver's **University Hospital** is located at 4200 E. 9th Ave. at the corner of Colorado; phone 270-8901 in emergencies or 399-1211 for general information. **AMI St. Luke's Hospital** is at 601 E. 19th; phone 629-2111 in emergencies or 839-1000 for general information.

The main branch of the Denver **post office** is located at 1823 Stout; phone 297-6168. Two **post offices** are located downtown. One is in the basement of the May D and F Building at the corner of 16th and Tremont, and the other is on the first floor of Tabor Center underneath the Westin Hotel at 16th and Lawrence. For zip code information, phone 297-6000.

Recycling

The best places to drop off recyclables in Denver are the **King Soopers** grocery stores, which all take aluminum, glass, newspapers, and plastic bottles. There are over two dozen stores in the Denver metropolitan area. **Albertsons** and **Safeway** stores will take aluminum.

For information, phone the **City of Denver Recycling Hotline,** (303) 640-1675.

Child Care

Summer Fun Day Camp, tel. (303) 232-9191, provides entertainment for visiting kids, including trips to Elitch's amusement park and other kids' favorites. **Mile High Child Care Association,** tel. 388-5700, has locations throughout the metro Denver area, with its main office at 1510 High Street. **Mile High United Way Child Care Resource and Referral Service** can provide information on thousands of day-care centers in the Denver area; phone 433-8900.

INFORMATION

All within a few blocks of each other are several good sources of different kinds of information. On the triangle formed by Colfax, Court, and 14th streets is the **Denver Metro Convention and Visitors Bureau,** where you'll find an office staffed with helpful and knowledgeable people, as well as brochures on everything from the city's museums and accommodations to parks, events, and galleries. Their mailing address is 225 W. Colfax, Denver, CO 80202; they can be reached by phone at (303) 892-1112. Hours are Mon. through Fri. 8:30 a.m.-5 p.m. and Sat. 9 a.m.-5 p.m. (winter hours are Mon. through Fri. 8 a.m.-5 p.m. and Sat. 9 a.m.-1 p.m.)

Just a few blocks north, on the the 17th floor of the World Trade Center on the 16th Street Mall is **Colorado Tourism Board**; phone them at 592-5510. Two blocks south of the Convention and Visitors Bureau, at the corner of Broadway and 13th, you'll find the **Denver Public Library,** whose hours are Mon. through Wed. 10 a.m.-9 p.m., Thurs. through Sat. 10 a.m.-5:30 p.m., and Sun. 1-5 p.m. For more information, phone the library at 640-8845; the number for the children's library is 640-8820. (There are over 20 branches of the Denver public library; the downtown branch can provide addresses, phone numbers, and hours of the others.)

For **road conditions,** phone 639-1111 (Denver and the west) or 639-1234 (I-25).

Bookstores

In addition to the **Tattered Cover** (see "Commercial Attractions" above), which has one of the West's best selections of books, including huge travel and Colorado sections, with lots of special-interest works, dozens of other bookstores are scattered throughout the city. On the 16th Street Mall, you'll find several chain stores (B. Dalton, Waldenbooks), as well as a handful of small newsstands with tourist publications, Denver and Colorado magazines, and guidebooks.

The **Radical Information Project Bookstore** tel. (303) 388-1065, 2412 E. Colfax, carries an excellent selection of radically left political books and literature, including T-shirts and bumper stickers. Open afternoons only; call first.

Farmers Market

Each Sat. morning from late June through late October, farmers back their pickups against the curb at 17th and Market streets and sell fresh produce. There's usually live music and an array of T-shirt booths as well. Open from 7 a.m. to 1 p.m.

TRANSPORTATION

Getting There

As we went to press, **Denver International Airport** was nearing completion and was scheduled to open in October, 1993. The new airport, which will replace Stapleton International, will be accessible to I-70 via Peña Expressway.

Meanwhile, operations continue at **Stapleton International Airport,** with service to all major U.S. cities and connecting flights to smaller western towns. Located just north of downtown (about eight miles, or 15 minutes by car). For airport information, phone (800) AIR-2-DEN.

The John Maddens and Erica Jongs among us don't have to fly to get to Denver. The city's Union Station, located downtown at the west end of 17th St., is a stop on **Amtrak**'s major east-west route (between Chicago and Los Angeles). For information, phone (303) 893-3911.

Getting Around

Denver also has an elaborate and much-used bus system (RTD—Regional Transportation District), with service throughout the metro area and to some of the smaller nearby towns, including Boulder. For route and schedule information, phone (303) 778-6000.

The **Cultural Connection Trolley** takes visitors to several of Denver's main attractions, including the Museum of Natural History, the zoo, the state capitol, and the U.S. mint. The trolley runs daily every half hour from 9 a.m. to 6 p.m., and tickets are $1 for an all-day ticket (which will let you ride as many times as you want).

A number of ground transportation companies offer service between downtown and metro-area hotels, as well as to nearby towns and the ski resorts. **Air Transportation Service,** tel. (800) 247-7074 has hourly shuttles from the airport to Vail and Beaver Creek; **The Airporter,** tel. 321-3222, offers departures to downtown every 15 minutes, and to Boulder and southeast Denver on the half-hour; **People's Choice Transportation,** tel. (800) 777-2388, serves the Denver area and the ski areas.

For taxi service in the Denver area, phone **Yellow Cab,** tel. 777-7777, **Metro Taxi Company,** tel. 333-3333, or **Zone Cab,** tel. 444-8888.

You can rent cars in Denver from all the major chain agencies, as well as from **Mountain Express Rent-a-Car,** tel. (800) 525-2880, specializing in 4WD vehicles, and **Metro Rentals, Inc.,** tel. 371-4600, and **Rent-a-Lemon,** tel. 355-3666, both of which offer budget rates.

Once here, you'll find Denver is amazingly easy to get around in. First, you can walk from one end of downtown to the other in about a half-hour—and that includes window-shopping along the way. And if you're not up for walking—if your arms are too loaded with packages or the day has taken its toll on your feet—there's always the **Mall Ride,** a free bus that runs from one end of 16th Street Mall to the other. With buses running every few minutes and taking on and letting off passengers at every block, the system will take you from the capitol to the Tabor Center in a matter of minutes (though you'll have to hoof it a block or so from the capitol to the east end of the mall).

AROUND DENVER

Heading South

After slicing south through downtown Denver, rising up over railroad tracks and waterways, scooting under overpasses, and passing within yards of the Broncos' Mile-High Stadium, I-25 (which at peak hours is often commuter-crowded) routes down through the city's sprawling southern suburbs and finally out onto the rocky plains, always paralleling the massive Front Range, looming just to the west. The 70 miles between Denver and Colorado Springs don't offer a whole lot in terms of scenery and diversions—save for the Rockies' forested shoulders and towering peaks to the west—although the trip is quick and easy; it's not unusual for folks in Colorado Springs to run up to Denver for a day of shopping, or even to meet friends for lunch.

Just south of Denver proper, Littleton, seat of Arapahoe County and once a thriving farming community, shows the effects of urban sprawl, with little to distinguish it from southern Denver—strip malls, office buildings, and quiet, whitewashed suburban housing developments, with nice lawns and fences. Nearly halfway to Colorado Springs is the little town of Castle Rock (pop. 3,900; elev. 6,000 feet), named for the stone outcropping appearing very much like some medieval European castle. Over the centuries, the "castle" has served as a landmark for travelers—Native Americans, traders, miners, pioneers, and early settlers. Modern travelers now have another landmark, the recently opened **Larkspur Factory Shops**. Take the Meadows Parkway Exchange from I-25.

About 10 miles south of Castle Rock is the turnoff to Larkspur, a tiny little community where the plains begin to green and gently roll as they rise up to meet the steep eastern wall of the Rockies. Although not a year-round tourist destination, for a month or so every summer Lark-

spur is extremely popular among faire travelers and pilgrims, who don leotards and feathered caps and spend the day here (see "Colorado Renaissance Festival" under "Calendar" above).

You'll find a **KOA** campground between Castle Rock and Larkspur—open May through October. Take Exit 174/Tomah Rd.

Heading West

As you head west out of Denver on I-70 toward Dillon and Summit County, a number of interesting stops could stretch the 70-mile drive into a full-day (or longer) excursion. From the museums and brewery tour in Golden to the old mining towns of Idaho Springs and Georgetown, from Buffalo Bill's grave and museum to the handful of National Forest picnic areas, there are seemingly countless diversions. In fact, one of the best and most fascinating is the pure and simple scenic wonder: As you barrel up out of the Denver flats and into the high country of the western slope—where pine and fir encircle mountain meadows and aspen and spruce mingle on ridgetops—the vistas and panoramas get downright *serious*. Take the time to pull over at the turnouts along the way: Geology buffs will appreciate the little exhibit at Exit 258, where you can examine closely the layers of rock that were cut away to build the interstate; near Genesee, you might get lucky and see a herd of buffalo; and if you look really closely, up on the hill to the south just west of Exit 256, you can see the futuristic house that Woody Allen used in *Sleeper* (don't get too excited: The orgasmatron's long gone . . .).

Just off the freeway, at Exit 253, **Chief Hosa,** tel. (303) 526-0364, is a pleasant little campground with RV and tent sites nestled in the pines. Not the type of place you'd want to spend your two-week vacation, but ideal for short-term, we'll-be-moving-on-in-the-morning camping.

GOLDEN

Probably best known for the massive Coors brewery, which attracts nearly 400,000 visitors a year, Golden (pop. 15,000, elev. 5,680 feet) is a compact and isolated little town in Clear Creek Canyon in the rocky foothills about a half-hour drive west of Denver. Seat of Jefferson County, Golden is also home to the Colorado School of Mines, the Colorado Railroad Museum, the Buffalo Bill Museum and gravesite, and several other small museums and parks. Central Golden is an Old-Westy little downtown area, with gift shops, taverns, and western-wear stores.

HISTORY

Though officially founded in the summer of 1859 by a group of Bostonians in search of gold, the little camp on Clear Creek had been a popular stopover for miners heading west for some time, and at least one settler, farmer David Wall, had been calling the place home for over a year. In fact, during the spring of '59, Wall made over $2,000 selling produce to the hordes of miners flocking to the canyon to make their fortunes off the area's fabulous lodes.

On June 12 of that year, Bostonian George West and crew, calling themselves the Boston Company, built the area's first frame house and dubbed the then-thriving camp Golden City, apparently after miner-cum-merchant Thomas Golden. The group also built a bridge across Clear Creek (at what is now Washington St.), charging tolls to the increasing numbers—from the nearby towns of Black Hawk, Central City, Silver Plume, and Georgetown—dependent on Golden for trade. It was about this time that journalist Horace Greeley rode a rented mule up into Clear Creek Canyon, was mightily impressed by the mines and bustling enterprises, and returned to the east coast to write, "Go West, young man, and grow with the country."

By the early 1860s, Golden City had some 800 year-round residents, as well as saloons, stores, hotels, and a school, and from 1862 to 1867, the town was the capital of Colorado Territory. In 1872, the word "City" was officially dropped from the town's name.

The 1870s saw the arrival of three important contributors to the development of Golden: the Colorado School of Mines, the railroad, and the Coors-Schueler Brewery. Though originally founded in 1869, the Colorado School of Mines, first called Jarvis College and headed by a missionary bishop of the Church of Colorado, opened its doors to students in 1871, offering degrees in assaying and chemical ore testing. With a 25 acre campus, the school is still home to three of the town's earliest buildings, constructed between 1880 and 1890. Colorado's first railroad—the Colorado Central—began operation in late 1870, and by the early part of the decade had a line to Golden. In fact, within a few short years, Golden had become the site of the company's headquarters as well as its western terminus, supplying other nearby camps and towns. Golden's heyday as a railroad center was short-lived, however, as by the early 1880s the headquarters had been moved to Denver.

The Coors-Schueler brewery was built in 1873 by Adolph Herman Joseph Coors and by the turn of the century was producing 500,000 barrels of beer a year. Prohibition (1919-1933)

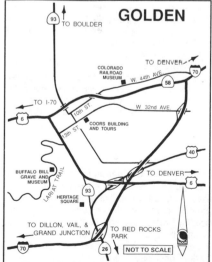

ROCKY FLATS

For all its pristine tourist-brochure images, Colorado has its share of environmental headaches. A persistent brown cloud of pollution gas—an inversion layer made up largely of automobile exhaust and wood-burning-stove smoke—has plagued Denver and other Front Range cities for decades. Many mountain towns have had to battle for breathable wintertime air. And the tailings from old mines will keep environmental cleanup specialists occupied well beyond the turn of the century.

But nothing has prompted prolonged controversy like the existence of Rocky Flats, a plutonium trigger manufacturing complex 17 miles northeast of Denver. Part of the national nuclear weapons production complex, Rocky Flats occupies a grassy plateau between Golden and Boulder. Some of Rocky Flats' taller buildings and towers are visible from downtown Denver on clear days. But even when it's cloudy, political battles over the safety and necessity of the operation have never let "The Flats" stray far from the public eye. Years of urban sprawl have made Rocky Flats a next-door neighbor to tens of thousands and have placed the plant squarely in the pincers of protest.

Over the decades, opponents to The Flats have sprouted with all manner of personal and political motivations. Former workers—and sometimes their widows—have claimed unsafe work conditions led to disease and death. County health officers have sounded alarms, having found dangerous levels of radioactivity in water and topsoil around the plant. And peace groups, notably Greenpeace and the American Friends Service Committee, have used The Flats as a rallying point for protest against the U.S. military-industrial complex.

In 1978, a year after what plant officials described as a "minor" release of plutonium into the atmosphere, a former Colorado Health Department Director said publicly what many had long believed: "The plutonium mission of Rocky Flats ought to be phased out, it's just not sufficiently safe to be that close to Denver," he said.

Through the 1970s and 1980s, pinning down reliable facts about the plant's operation made debate tricky. How safe were containers used to ship materials? Were nearby levels of radiation normal? Why were many farm animals being born with deformities? If the Federal Housing Authority was getting nervous about extending mortgage assistance to nearby subdivisions, why shouldn't other residents be worried?

As the chairwoman of the state's public watchdog group said in 1978: "There are storehouses of questions and only tiny envelopes with a few answers."

Rocky Flats hung tough through the 1980s as Congress and President Reagan pumped ample resources into the defense budget. But in late 1989, the lid of secrecy began to lift. Beset by safety and environmental problems—including designation as a federal Superfund site—the plant's plutonium operations shut down. In 1990, President Bush's energy secretary proposed moving the nuclear aspects of the plant's business.

But plant managers—both government officials and EG&G, The Flats' current operators—have mounted a public relations blitz to highlight the plant's economic advantages, among them a payroll of more than 7,000. With the Cold War on a "deep thaw" cycle, plant officials even offered select tours of Building 559, the heartbeat of the plant.

Suddenly Rocky Flats wanted to be seen as a corporate good-citizen. It admitted mistakes, found money to provide scholarships, and even sent a team of local high schoolers to participate in the National Science Bowl.

Eager to survive, its managers have floated the idea that "The Flats" could be used to dismantle the bombs it helped create. As the debate continued—and as clean-up alone looked like plenty of work through the year 2000—few were betting against the ability of Rocky Flats to find a way to thrive.

—Mark Stevens

---

definitely put a damper on the outfit, although management was savvy enough to move into the production of non-alcoholic commodities—"near beer," malted milk, and other milk by-products. By Prohibition's end, the brewery was able to again produce beer, unlike the vast majority of the nation's breweries, permanently shut down by the Constitution's ill-fated 18th Amendment.

ATTRACTIONS

Coors Brewery

Tours of the Coors brewery—the largest single brewery in the world—are the reason most visitors come to Golden, and indeed, summer days the town is packed with people who've come

STEPHEN METZGER

Welcome to Coors Country.

to pay their respects to the great "Colorado Kool-Aid" and to see how it's made. The tour's free, too. And at the end—assuming you're of age—you can even sample a couple of glasses of Coors' products: Coors, Coors Lite, the "Silver Bullet," etc. And then there's the gift shop (it's no accident that the gift shop is *after* the free sampling), where you can buy Coors T-shirts, steins, Frisbees, and all kinds of other knickknacks with the Coors logo.

And the tour itself is interesting—considering how little one can say about the remarkably simple process of making beer, which explains in part why the half-hour tour is disproportionately more promotional than informational. To be fair, the packaging part of the tour *is* interesting: Here you can view cans of beer hustling down conveyer belts to be put into six-packs, twelve-packs, and case cartons.

Suggestion: If you're interested in real beer—in seeing how the "little guy" makes a good wheat beer, pale ale, or lager—go instead to one (or more) of Colorado's several microbreweries—in Denver, Boulder, Fort Collins, Breckenridge, and Telluride (see individual chapters).

In addition to tours of the brewery, Coors offers brief tours of Golden, with buses routing their ways through town, picking up tourists from parking lots, while drivers point out important historical landmarks before delivering passengers to the brewery's doors.

Tours of the Coors brewery are offered Mon. through Sat. 10 a.m.-5 p.m. (June through Aug.) and 10 a.m.-4 p.m. (Sept. through May). To get to Golden from Denver, take Hwy. 70 west and then CO 58 north; you can also take Hwy. 6 (6th Ave.) directly west out of Denver. A shuttle bus will take you to the brewery from the parking lot at 13th and Ford. For more information, phone (303) 277-BEER.

Colorado Railroad Museum
This is an absolute must for train buffs, from old-timers who recall the train in its glory days to those whose childhoods were spent assembling model trains and villages. Nothing fancy or high-tech here (as it should be—in fact, the yard is overgrown with weeds and truly invokes ghosts of a bygone era), but the museum does have plenty to recall the railroad and to teach about its past. From historical photos and original ledgers and records to a model train with an impeccably detailed miniature town of Golden (cars, people, the courthouse, even a baseball game in progress); from switch lamps, uniforms, and silver from dining cars to the cars and locomotives themselves, this is a wonderful testament to the railroad, as well as a lesson in Colorado's (and the west's) history. The gift shop, in addition to selling mugs and other souvenirs, has an excellent selection of books on the railroad and on Colorado history, as well as authentic historical papers (original schedules, announcements, records, etc.).

The Colorado Railroad Museum is open daily from 9 a.m.-5 p.m. (till 6 p.m. during the summer). To get there from Denver, take I-70 west to Highway 58, and follow the signs (take Exit 265).

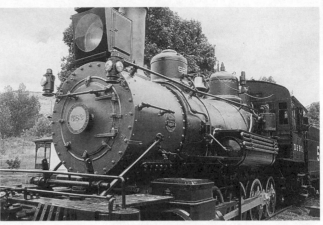

*locomotive in the yard
of the Colorado
Railroad Museum*

STEPHEN METZGER

If you're heading east on I-70, take Exit 266. For more information, phone (303) 279-4591.

Colorado School Of Mines

First open to students in 1871, this is the largest and most important school of mineral engineering in the United States. The college's **Geology Museum,** open daily from 8:30 a.m.-4:30 p.m., displays gems, ore, and minerals from around the world, including pieces from Golden's 19th-century mining boom. Located at the corner of 16th and Maple; phone (303) 273-3823.

The School of Mines is also home to the **National Earthquake Information Center,** recording continental drift and other geological activity from around the world. The center's 24-hour-a-day Earthquake Early Alerting Service determines the location and magnitude of temblors around the world (roughly 12,000 a year) and disseminates relevant information to authorities. The center is also responsible for publishing data on seismic activity. Free 30- to 45-minute tours available by appointment (weekdays between 9 and 11 a.m. and 1 and 3 p.m.); phone 236-1500.

For general information on the Colorado School of Mines, phone 273-3300.

DAR Pioneer Museum

Exhibiting local pioneer artifacts from the mid-19th century to the 1930s, this small museum at 911 10th St. displays a wide variety of local and American historical artifacts—in addition to individual rooms (kid's nursery, lady's boudoir,

etc.), you'll see an eclectic collection of domestic items and historical military gear (Civil War bayonets and uniforms). For hours and information, phone (303) 279-3331.

Astor House Hotel Museum

Built in 1867 of local stone, this hotel at the corner of 12th and Arapahoe has been restored and decorated with authentic Victorian furnishings and is now on the National Register of Historic Places. For information, phone (303) 278-3557.

Rocky Mountain Quilt Museum

Located at 1111 Washington Ave. in Golden (temporarily—the board of directors is looking for a larger space), this museum displays over 100 antique and contemporary quilts and attempts to keep alive this American tradition. Nonagenerian Eugiana Mitchell, the museum's primary donor, has taught quilting in the Rockies for over 30 years and continues teaching classes at the museum.

For hours or more information, write Box 365, Golden, CO 80402.

Buffalo Bill's Grave And Museum

Even those not particularly interested in Buffalo Bill, or who feel the hunter, guide, and entrepreneur did as much to make a circus of the West as he did to open it up, will enjoy the drive up Lookout Mountain to his grave and the memorial museum. First of all, just the drive up is quite impressive, with a view from the top of Golden and of Denver in the distance. Second, you'll be surprised how quickly you'll have risen up out of the scrubby foothill fauna and into the fresh-smelling pines.

The grave itself is small and unimposing, though the location is spectacular, and you can easily understand why the outdoorsman would want to be buried here—especially before the view was dominated by the gigantic Coors brewery, only partially obstructed by electrical wires and radio antennae. A small museum displays Cody's saddle, western rifles, Sitting Bull's bows and arrows, supposedly from the Battle of the Little Big Horn, lots of Plains Native American clothing and gear, and, appropriately enough, barbed wire (one of the great contributors to the conquering of the West) from throughout the area.

In addition, there's a small souvenir and curio shop and a snack bar, with homemade fudge. A picnic area, with barbecue pits and restrooms, is located near the parking lot. The museum is open daily 9 a.m.-5 p.m., May through Oct., and 9 a.m.-4 p.m. Nov. through April. To get there, take 19th Ave. out of Golden, or Exit 256 from I-70. For more information on the Buffalo Bill Museum, phone (303) 526-0747.

PARKS AND RECREATION

Golden Gate Canyon State Park
This 8,500-acre park about 15 minutes northwest of Golden offers hiking, fishing, horseback riding, camping (both backcountry and in campgrounds), cross-country skiing, and year-round sightseeing—from fields of wildflowers to deep, pine-forested hillsides and steep, rocky cliffs. Orient yourself at the visitor center, where you'll find exhibits of the park's flora and fauna, as well as naturalists and rangers to answer your questions and suggest the best ways to enjoy the park.

To get to the Golden Gate Canyon State Park, take Washington Ave. north to Golden Gate Canyon Rd. and turn left (west). From there it's about a 15-mile drive to the park's entrance. For more information, write Route 6, Box 280, Golden, CO 80403, or phone (303) 592-1502.

Golf
Golden's **Applewood Golf Course** is an 18-hole public facility located just east of town at 14001 W. 32nd Ave. Phone (303) 279-3003 for tee times and information.

Hiking
In addition to the 50-plus miles of marked trails meandering through Golden Gate Canyon State Park, **Jefferson County Open Space** also has its own 14,000-acre park system, with nearly 100 city-, county-, and recreation-district-managed parks, many with excellent hiking and sightseeing possibilities. Check out **Apex Trail,** which takes hikers from Heritage Square in Golden to the **Jefferson County Nature Center** on Lookout Mountain, and from there to **Beaver Brook Trail.** You can also get to Beaver Brook Trail from a trailhead and parking lot a few miles up 19th Ave. en route to the Buffalo Bill Museum (watch for the sign and small parking lot). Up there, chances are good you'll get to see a hang glider or two, as this is a popular launching site for these crazy sky pilots.

For maps and more information on hiking in the Golden area, phone the administrative offices of Jefferson County Open Space at (303) 278-5925.

TOURS

In addition to the tours of the Coors Brewery (see above), the Historical Preservation Board of Golden has designed a self-guided walking tour of historic Golden, specifically the town's Twelfth Street District, which is on the National Register of Historic Places. Included on the tour are the Astor House Hotel Museum (see above) and many residences dating from the 1860s, as well as Colorado's original National Guard Armory (1913), the largest cobblestone building in the country (made from 3,300 wagonloads of stone from Clear Creek).

ACCOMMODATIONS

Golden's accommodations range from state park campgrounds to mom-and-pop-type motels and chain hotels. The recently opened **Table Mountain Inn,** tel. (303) 277-9898, is located in downtown Golden and offers comfortable accommodations in a Southwestern setting. Also downtown is the **Williamsburg Inn,** tel. 279-7673. For bed-and-breakfast accommodations, try the **Jameson Inn,** tel. 278-0351, in a historic Golden home. The **Golden**

Motel, tel. 279-5581, 24th and Ford also has reasonably priced rooms, some with kitchenettes. All of the above are within walking distance of the Coors Brewery and the Colorado School of Mines. You'll also find in Golden a **Holiday Inn,** tel. 279-7611, **Days Inn,** tel. 277-0200, **La Quinta Motor Inn,** tel. 279-5565, and the **Denver Marriott West,** tel. 279-9100.

Golden Gate Canyon State Park (see above), about 20 minutes from downtown Golden, offers RV and tent sites, with laundry facilities and showers. Phone 592-1502. **Clear Creek Campground,** tel. 278-1437, just west of town (take 10th St. from Washington), also has tent and RV sites, showers, and a dump station. Showers at the campground are open to the public (at $1.50 pp). **Scenic Rock RV Park** is a upscale campground located five minutes west of Golden at 17700 W. Colfax; phone 279-1625.

FOOD

From Old-West saloon-style diners to Mexican restaurants to fast-food franchises, Golden's got something for just about every appetite and budget. **Kenrow's,** 718 12th St., tel. (303) 279-5164, is a great place to grab lunch after a morning of poking around Golden. The restaurant serves deli and hot sandwiches, salads, Mexican food, pizzas, burgers, and for the hungrier, steaks and seafood dinners. Or check out the **Briarwood Inn,** tel. 279-3121, for fine dining and the **Mesa Bar and Grill,** tel. 277-9898, at the Table Mountain Inn for Southwestern fare. The **Golden Eagle,** 279-5257, serves burgers, steaks, and Mexican food, while the **Golden Ram** (located above Foss Drug), tel. 279-6011, is a local favorite for a casual breakfast or lunch. Fast-food freaks can satisfy their cravings at Wendy's, Dairy Queen, and others.

ENTERTAINMENT

Visitors to the **Heritage Square Music House** can see post-Civil War musicals and comedies performed by local actors and musicians. The Victorian setting adds authenticity to the experience. For information and reservations, phone

(303) 279-7800. If cummerbunds and melodrama aren't your style, then the **Buffalo Rose,** tel. 279-5190, might be. Located downtown at 1119 Washington, this little bar features live music Thurs. through Sat. nights (sometimes other nights), with local and touring acts, some surprisingly well known: Rick Derringer, Edgar Winter, Charlie Musselwhite, and Delbert McClinton have all played the Rose. Across the street, **Kenrow's,** tel. 279-5164, also features live music on weekend nights (and pool tournaments Mondays).

Foothills Art Center, at 15th and Washington in downtown Golden, features art galleries (with rotating exhibits), an Artisans' Showcase (for local artists), and a gift shop. In addition, the center offers workshops, demonstrations, lectures, poetry readings, and concerts, and each year from late November to Christmas the center is the site of the Holiday Art Market.

For current information on Golden entertainment, check the *Rocky Mountain News,* the *Denver Post,* and the local paper, the *Golden Transcript.*

CALENDAR

Golden's annual events calendar is virtually booked solid with a variety of things for both visitors and locals to do—from free concerts in the downtown park to fireworks displays, parades, bike races, and car, gun, flower, and art shows. Among the highlights: **International Heritage Festival of Folk Arts** (mid-June), **Fourth of July fireworks, Buffalo Bill Days** (late July), and the **Oktoberfest** (mid-September). For more information on these and other Golden events and activities, phone the Golden Chamber of Commerce at (303) 279-3113. Also be sure to check the local newspaper, the *Golden Transcript,* for current goings-on.

SHOPPING

Golden is particularly proud of its **Heritage Square,** a re-created late-19th-century Western village with boutiques, gift shops, restaurants, and even an Alpine slide and other rides for the kids. Open daily 10 a.m.-6 p.m. (till 9 p.m. Memorial Day through Labor Day). Phone (303) 279-2789.

Downtown has recently undergone a major make-over, and you'll find there a variety of boutiques, galleries, and specialty shops.

SERVICES

The **Golden Police Department** is located at 911 10th St.; phone (303) 279-3331. Contact the **Jefferson County Sheriff** at 277-0211 and the local offices of the Colorado **State Patrol** at 273-1616. Jefferson County's general hospital, **Lutheran Medical Center,** is located at 8300 W. 38th St., Wheatridge (between Golden and west Denver—take the Wadsworth Blvd. exit from I-70); phone the hospital at 425-4500 (425-2089 in emergencies).

Golden's main **post office** is located at 619 12th St.; phone 278-8537.

Recycling
Drop off aluminum, glass, newspaper, and plastics at **Evergreen Disposal,** 15969 S. Golden Rd., tel. (303) 278-6000.

INFORMATION

For more information on Golden and Jefferson County, write the Golden **Chamber of Commerce,** Box 1035, Golden, CO 80402, tel. (303) 279-3113, or stop by their offices at 611 14th Street. The Jefferson County **public library,** tel. 279-4585, is located at 923 10th St., and the Arthur Lakes Library (largest map collection in the area) is on the campus of the Colorado School of Mines; phone 273-3690.

For **road conditions** in the Golden area, phone 639-1111 (westbound) or 639-1234 (eastbound).

TRANSPORTATION

Golden is about a half-hour by car from Denver. Get there by heading west on either I-70 or Hwy. 6 (W. 6th Ave.). Turnoffs are well marked. You can also get to Golden from Denver by bus (Golden's part of the Denver metro Regional Transportation District); phone (303) 778-6000. **Golden West Shuttle,** tel. 422-1277 provides limousine, taxi, and shuttle service throughout the Golden area.

IDAHO SPRINGS, GEORGETOWN, AND SILVER PLUME

Interstate 70 barrels west past the turnoff to Golden then begins to lift slightly into the sorrel foothills of the Front Range before winding dramatically up into the Rockies' steep and forested canyons, finally rising above the timberline entirely just east of Loveland Pass. From the junction with Highway 6 (to Golden) to the east side of Eisenhower Tunnel, the road snakes its way through Clear Creek Canyon, where the water, particularly during late-spring runoff, roars riotously toward the plains.

Had you found yourself in this part of Colorado between the early 1870s and 1893, when the silver market crashed, you would have witnessed a canyon teeming with miners, merchants, and railroad workers, and your ears would have buzzed with sounds of men building cabins, mills, and smelters, which they either squeezed into the canyon floor or hung hopefully from cliffsides. Three communities that grew out of this mad

rush (which eventually produced more than $90 million in silver, gold, copper, and zinc) are Georgetown, Idaho Springs, and Silver Plume, which today provide both entertaining and educational tableaux of Colorado's past.

HISTORY

Though a handful of small gold claims were staked in Upper Clear Creek Canyon in the late 1850s, by the mid-'60s silver had become the area's most abundant, lucrative, and sought-after ore. Idaho Springs (originally called Jackson's Diggin's, after an early gold miner) was named for the nearby hot springs, which attracted aching and arthritic pioneers. Georgetown was named after George Griffith, another early Clear Creek miner, who had come down from Central City around 1860.

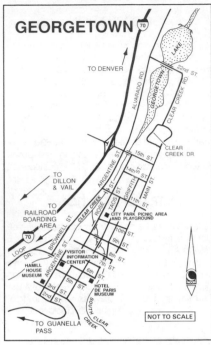

Placer mining was the first method of extracting ore from the canyon, and it wasn't long before the few mines played out. By the 1870s, however, lode mining had been developed, and by the middle of the decade Georgetown, home to some 5,000 people, was the third largest city in Colorado; until silver was discovered in Leadville in 1878, Georgetown was the most important silver camp in the state.

The Colorado Central Railroad reached Georgetown in 1877. With the completion a few years later of the Georgetown Loop Railroad, which connected Georgetown and Silver Plume, two miles upstream, silver could be much more easily transported down out of the canyon. When silver fell off in 1893, though, many of Clear Creek Canyon's residents left for towns whose economies were not strictly dependent on mining. Many of Georgetown's and Idaho Springs' homes and businesses were abandoned.

Still, a few persistent miners stayed, working away in a labyrinth of tunnels beneath the earth's rocky crust, and in 1910 the Argo Tunnel,

connecting Idaho Springs and Central City, was completed. In the 1930s, when gold and silver began once again to command high prices, some of Clear Creek Canyon's mines reopened. Today, Georgetown, Idaho Springs, and Silver Plume rely heavily on tourism to keep their economies stable, as well as on the abundance of nearby recreational opportunities—particularly skiing, cycling, camping, fishing, and hiking.

ATTRACTIONS

Georgetown Historic District

Even if you're just passing through and don't have time for the railroad and mine tours, you'll enjoy a few hours poking around the restored Victorians and gift shops in downtown Georgetown.

Of particular interest in Georgetown is the **Hotel de Paris**. At one time one of the best-known hotels west of the Mississippi—for its elegant design and cuisine, as well as for its controversial builder/owner/proprietor—the Hotel de Paris has been restored with original furnishings that suggest the building's, and area's, colorful past.

Louis du Puy, born the wealthy and titled Adolphus Francis Gerard in Alençon, France, in 1844, came to Georgetown in 1869, was injured in a mining accident in 1873, and bought Georgetown's Delmonico Bakery in 1875; immediately he set about converting it to a hotel to rival those he remembered from his homeland. Known as a fine cook, philosopher, misogynist, and all-around crank, albeit an intelligent and well-educated one, du Puy was rumored to have been a deserter from the French army. As a hotel proprietor, du Puy was constantly angering and amusing the residents of Clear Creek Canyon, for most of whom he had little or no respect—nor did du Puy care much for his guests, and only those who met his capricious demands were permitted to stay; some, upon earning his disfavor, would be ordered to leave mid-stay. When du Puy died in 1900, he willed the hotel to Sophie Galet, about whom history seems to know little, except that she was the widow of a French cabinet maker, worked for du Puy at the hotel, survived him a scant four months, and was buried beside him, as she had requested.

The Hotel de Paris is located at 409 6th St. in Georgetown and is open to visitors daily May-Sept. and Tues.-Sun. noon-4 p.m. the rest of the year. For more information phone (303) 569-2840.

Georgetown Loop Railroad

This six-mile tour takes passengers from Georgetown to Silver Plume (and back) via a narrow-gauge steam train that winds through Clear Creek Canyon, up Devil's Gate High Bridge (100 feet high, 300 feet long). Included on the trip is a stop at the Lebanon Mine and Mill, with an optional added tour.

World famous as an engineering marvel when it was completed in 1884, the railroad was all but forgotten—in fact, the tracks were completely torn up in 1939—from the turn of the century until a hundred years after its inauguration, when the route was restored. Today, roundtrip tours begin from either Silver Plume or Georgetown, with a slide show at the Georgetown depot and a gift shop in Silver Plume. During the summer (Memorial Day through Labor Day), trains run several times a day; the rest of the year weekends only. Adult rates are around $10 (slightly more for the mine tour), with discounts for children 4-15. Reservations recommended.

Note: The Lebanon Mine tour takes you 600 feet underground, and it gets cold and wet. If you plan to include the mine on your trip, bring warm clothes.

To get to the depots, take I-70 Exit 226 (Silver Plume) or 228 (Georgetown). For more information, phone (303) 279-6101 (recording), 670-1686 (reservations), or 569-2403. You can also send away for brochures by writing Box 217, Georgetown, CO 80444.

Phoenix Mine

A small, family-owned mine first worked in the early 1870s, the Phoenix offers guided public tours during which you can experiment with 19th-century mining tools as well as pan for gold (keep what you find). Open Wed. through Mon. 10 a.m. to 6 p.m; group tours by appointment.

Take Exit 239 at Idaho Springs, go one mile west on the frontage road, and take Trail Creek Road.

Hamill House

Built in 1869 by silver baron and politician William Hamill, this restored Victorian home was one of the most elegant in Colorado Territory. With an interior rich with marble, walnut, and glass, as well as gas lighting and central heating, the house is testament to the wealth the Rockies' mines (and miners) brought to their owners.

The Hamill House is located in Georgetown at 305 Argentine St. and is open daily late May through early September, with limited hours the rest of the year. Phone the Georgetown Society at (303) 569-2840 for more information.

Argo Gold Mill

Idaho Springs' Argo Mill was built in 1913 as a processing plant for much of the area's ore,

Kristin would rather pet horses than sightsee, downtown Georgetown.

primarily that brought down from Central City via the 22,000-foot Argo Tunnel. In 1943, the Argo Mine was flooded and the mill shut down; today it is on the National Register of Historic Places and is open to the public for self-guided tours from late May through mid-October. Located at 2350 Riverside Drive. For more information, phone (303) 567-2421.

George Rowe Museum

One of the most prominent buildings in Silver Plume (it's the big boxy number nestled against the hillside; you can see it from the freeway), this was a schoolhouse built just before the turn of the century. In addition to displaying sundry artifacts from Clear Creek's past and a restored school room, the museum sells books about and maps of the area. The museum, located at 95 Main St., Silver Plume, is open daily 10 a.m. to 4 p.m. Memorial Day through Labor Day, and weekends into September. For more information, phone (303) 569-2562.

PARKS AND RECREATION

Georgetown, Idaho Springs, and Silver Plume are surrounded by Roosevelt and Arapaho national forests, whose lands are rife with campgrounds, hiking trails, and streams for fishing. Whether you're a cross-country skier, ice climber, mountain biker, or mule trainer, you'll find lots of area to explore.

An excellent source for maps, advice, and general information is the **Arapaho National Forest Information Center** (Clear Creek Ranger Station), located at the west end of town at the junction of Hwy. 103 and I-70; take Exit 240; phone (303) 567-2901 or 893-1474.

If you're just passing through and looking for a nice place to pull off the road, check out the quiet little creekside picnic area in downtown Idaho Springs at the corner of Colorado Blvd. and 23rd St.—no overnight camping. There's also a very nice city park in Georgetown, about a quarter-mile east of the central historic district, with picnic benches and a playground. In Silver Plume, directly across the street from the George Rowe Museum, you'll find a small kids' playground.

Downhill Skiing

Whoever coined the term "centrally located" could certainly have been referring to the Clear Creek Canyon area and its relation to Colorado's ski areas. Within an easy hour's drive (weather permitting) are some of the finest slopes in the country: Winter Park, Arapahoe Basin, Copper Mountain, Vail, and several others. In addition, the mountain roads provide access to some of the state's finest expert-only off-piste skiing. A favorite is **Loveland Pass,** where you can drive up, hoist your skis ashoulder, hike along the ridge-top, and ski down to a waiting car. When all that's left of the snow are a few scattered patches and the resorts are closed (as late as June for Arapahoe Basin), downhill diehards head to **St. Mary's Glacier,** where you can ski year-round. Take the Fall River Rd. exit from I-70 (two miles west of Idaho Springs). For more information, phone (303) 567-2191.

The nearest lift-serviced downhill skiing is at **Loveland Basin,** a small family-oriented resort 12 miles west of Georgetown near the east entrance to Eisenhower Tunnel. Loveland offers over 800 acres of skiable terrain, equipment rental and sales, a restaurant, and day-care facilities. For more information on Loveland, write Box 899, Georgetown, CO 80444; or phone 569-3203 (from Denver, phone 571-5580).

Cross-country Skiing

Arapaho National Forest provides virtually unlimited cross-country skiing opportunities within a few short miles of these little towns and the interstate connecting them. Again, the ranger station (at I-70 Exit 240) is an excellent source for maps and general information. Write Box 3307, Idaho Springs, CO 80452, or phone (303) 567-2901 or 893-1474.

Cycling

The steep roads leading up into the high country above Clear Creek Canyon are excellent for in-shape riders, and they get surprisingly little auto traffic, considering their proximity to the busy interstate. Colorado touring clubs hold a number of races and rides in the area.

Colorado 103, winding south from Idaho Springs (Exit 240), offers a gently rising ride alongside the rippling waters of Chicago Creek. If you turn onto CO 5 (Mt. Evans Rd.) at the junction (about 14 miles south of Idaho Springs), you'll be in for one doozy of a ride—the road now rises suddenly up toward the treeline, over it, and twists up nearly to the 14,264-foot summit of Mt. Evans. At Summit Lake, you'll find a small picnic area with tables and restrooms.

For information on mountain biking in the area, stop by the Clear Creek ranger station or **Chickenhead Mountain Sports** in Idaho Springs (see "Information" following).

Hiking
The Clear Creek area is surrounded by miles and miles of excellent hiking trails and back-packing wonderlands, much of it within the borders of Arapaho National Forest. Among the better designated trails are **Chicago Lakes Trail,** south of Idaho Springs off CO 5, **Summit Lake Trail,** a 12-mile walk-that-turns-to-climb from Echo Lake Campground to the summit of Mt. Evans, and the **Griffin Monument Trail,** a two-mile hike from downtown Silver Plume to a hillside monument erected to honor a 19th-century English miner.

For more information on hiking in the area, stop in at the Clear Creek Ranger Station or Chickenhead Sports in Idaho Springs (see "Information" following).

Fishing
Though Clear Creek looks awfully trouty from the road, fishing has been all but ruined by the century and a half of mining in the area. Locals like to work Chicago Creek, south of Idaho Springs along CO 103 (respect private property), and the lawnchair crowd competes for the rainbows regularly stocked in the easily accessible Georgetown Lake, at the east end of town.

ACCOMMODATIONS

You'll find a handful of relatively inexpensive motels along Colorado Blvd. on the east end of Idaho Springs. Among the newest and nicest are the **Argo Motor Inn,** tel. (303) 567-4473, and the **H and H Motor Lodge,** tel. 567-2838; doubles at both start at about $30. Just before Colorado Blvd. feeds back onto the freeway, there are a couple of other motels. The **Peoriana Motel,** tel. 567-2021, has doubles in the $25-35 range. Doubles at the **Georgetown**

Motor Inn, tel. 569-3201 run around $50.

Indian Springs Resort, tel. 567-2191, is a hot springs with a long history (claiming visitors including Teddy Roosevelt). Today the spa and resort offers mineral baths, vapor caves, a swimming pool, and the "Club Mud" (a mud puddle supposedly capable of cleansing the skin and soul . . .). You can get a room in either the main lodge (125 years old and quite run-down; no private baths) or in the motel across the street.

Camping And RVing
In the heart of Arapaho National Forest, the Georgetown-Idaho Springs-Silver Plume area is naturally very near to some excellent campgrounds. One particularly nice one is **West Chicago Creek Campground** about nine miles from the west of town just off CO 103 (take Exit 240 from I-70). Go south on 103 for six miles, and then follow the signs up a short dirt road to Chicago Creek. Sites are $7 a night.

You'll also find several campgrounds just west of Idaho Springs near the junction of I-70 and Hwy. 40. At Exit 232, take Hwy. 40 three miles toward Winter Park to the privately owned **Mountain Meadow Campground.** If you'd rather be in the national forest, continue on US 40 for another couple of miles, and almost as soon as you cross back into Arapaho National Forest, you'll find **Mizpah Campground,** where nice shaded sites lie right on Clear Creek—well water and pit toilets; fee is $7 a night. There are also two Forest Service picnic areas nearby (well marked from the highway): **Clear Creek** and **Big Bend,** both piney, shaded and cool.

FOOD

Start Me Up
Marion's of the Rockies, on Colorado Blvd. at the east end of Idaho Springs, serves breakfast specials daily, as well as biscuits and gravy, eggs, pancakes, and waffles, from 6 a.m.—this is where local contractors scarf down big breakfasts before heading out to their job sites. **Mainstreet, A Restaurant,** at 1518 Miner Street, Idaho Springs, is a popular local hangout and down-home kind of place, where waitresses call everyone "Hon." Lots of pancake dishes, including the "Skier's Special" (blueberry), as well as other standard American breakfast fare—

prices range $2-4.50. Mainstreet also serves lunch—sandwiches, burgers, etc.—for $3-6.

Other Restaurants
Some of the best pizza in the Denver area is served up at **Beaujo's Pizza,** 1517 Miner, tel. (303) 567-4376. A favorite among Denver-area pizza aficionados, Beaujo's regularly wins rave reviews from local media and readers' polls. Idaho Springs is also home to an excellent and unpretentious little Chinese restaurant, **Szechwan Fu,** located at 1744 Miner St. toward the middle of town, tel. 567-9378. Though prices here top out at $16-18 for dinner specials and seafood (lobster with hot Szechwan sauce), you can order off the south end of the menu and get a huge and satisfying meal for $5-7. The chow and lo mein noodles are excellent, as are the moo shu vegetables.

In Georgetown, try the **Ram Bar and Restaurant,** 606 6th St., tel. 569-3263. Part Old-West saloon and part family restaurant, the Ram serves good food (burgers, salads, pastas) at very reasonable rates. For Southwestern fare in Georgetown, check out the **Silver Queen Restaurant,** also on 6th St. in Old Georgetown, tel. 568-2961. Lunch specials include Navajo tacos, enchiladas, and Prospector's chili. The **Happy Cooker,** corner of 6th and Taos (across from the Hotel de Paris), tel. 569-3166, is a good choice for a hearty breakfast, lunch, or dinner. Daily specials include waffles, soups, lasagna, and homemade bread.

ENTERTAINMENT

A favorite nightery among locals as well as tipped-off passers-through (particularly skiers heading home to Denver from the ski slopes) is Idaho Springs' **Buffalo Bar,** 1617 Miner, tel. (303) 567-2729. In Georgetown, check out **Marti's Crazy Horse Saloon,** 1211 Argentine Street, tel. 659-2475.

INFORMATION

One of the best sources of information for hikers, backpackers, mountain bikers, climbers, and anyone else interested in the backcountry is **Chickenhead Mountain Sports,** on Miner St. in downtown Idaho Springs. This low-key, funky, but excellently equipped sports store has a wonderful selection of topo and "fat-tire" maps, as well as books and magazines on local recreation—not to mention a friendly and knowledgeable staff.

The **Town of Georgetown Visitor Center** is at 404 6th Street. Stop in for more information on dining, lodging, and exploring the area. Before your visit, write Box 426, Georgetown, CO 80444, or phone (303) 569-2555. You can also get information from the **Georgetown Society,** Box 667, Georgetown, CO 80444, tel. 569-2840, and the **Idaho Springs Visitors Information Center,** Box 97, Idaho Springs, CO 80452, tel. 567-4382 or (800) 658-7785. You can also stop by the center at the intersection of Colorado Blvd. and Miner Street.

WEST OF GEORGETOWN

Loveland Pass
Once featured in *National Geographic* magazine as one of America's most harrowing passes for interstate truckers, Loveland is a twisting, turning, switchbacking son-of-a-bitch that climbs well above the treeline to 11,992 feet (that's over *two miles* high). In the late spring of 1973, Eisenhower Tunnel was opened, so motorists traveling between Denver and Summit County no longer had to go up and over the pass, which of course is especially nasty in winter. And, naturally, the tunnel is still the wisest way to go if your main objective is to get where you're going as quickly (and as safely) as possible. But if you've got an extra half-hour or so (when the road's clear), and if your brakes are good, take the drive up over the pass. The views are astounding, and it's one of the best ways to get a real sense of the real Rockies. When there's snow on the mountainsides, watch for skiers, who drive up the pass, hike along the ridgetop, and ski down (recommended for experts only!). Also see the special topic on Eisenhower Tunnel (Summit County chapter).

BOULDER

The Berkeley of Colorado? The Chamonix of the Rockies? A bastion of upscale fitness freaks, politically progressive intellectuals, New Age tofu heads, and the last remnants of 1960s hippiedom?

Perhaps. Of course it's easy to resort to reductionism when trying to capture the essence of a town and people in a few words. And it's neither possible nor fair to classify Boulder and Boulderites. Sure, *Outside* magazine named it the number-one town in the country for outdoor sports, and the city has a disproportionate amount of open-space-designated land. Granted, the state's number-one academic institution is one of the town's major influences. Yes, you do see more Saab Turbos, BMWs, and Jeep Wagoneers and other Yuppie rigs here than you do anywhere east of Marin County. And, okay, long-haired, barefooted street musicians still strum Dylan tunes on street corners, their guitar cases open for coins, and the city is relatively tolerant of

transients, who hit up passers-by for spare change, while the occasional space case floats by talking to himself, or maybe conducting an orchestra only he can hear.

But still, Boulder is its own town, completely defying classification—in fact, the only generalization one can safely make about the city is that it's diverse, and, for a relatively small town a *long* way from either coast and the cosmopolitan influences there, it's a remarkably tolerant one.

HISTORY

In part because the Boulder area was at one time sacred to several different Native American tribes (predominantly Arapahoe), the line between mythology and history often blurs, creating a folklore that both defines and reflects the town's rare blend of whimsy and stubborn intellectualism. Among the legends of the region is Chief Niwot's (Chief Left Hand) curse, profoundly proximate to the hearts of thousands of transplanted Boulderites who originally came with no intentions to stay but just to vacation or attend the university. According to the curse, anyone who sets eyes on the area will be so drawn to it that she will be unable to leave, leading eventually to the area's overcrowding and self-destruction (some claim the curse has already proved itself prophetic).

White Settlement
Evidently, Chief Niwot's curse is grounded in history and is linked with his first encounter with white settlers.

In 1858, Captain Thomas Aikens was leading a small group of settlers up the South Platte River and, after spotting the area through a telescope from the walls of Fort St. Vrain, described it as "right for gold and the valleys . . . rich for grazing." Shortly thereafter, Aikens led a splinter group from the main wagon train and set up camp at what is today Boulder. Also camped in the area was a group of Southern Arapahoe, led by Chief Niwot. According to the WPA guide to Colorado, when the two men first met, Niwot asked Aikens if he remembered when the stars

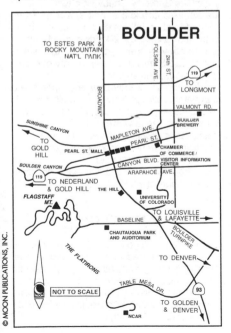

fell. Aikens responded that it was 1832, and Niwot told him he was correct, and that that was the year the whites first came. Then Niwot pointed to a comet in the sky and said its tail pointed "back to when the stars fell as thick as the tears of our women shall fall when you come to drive us away." Three days later, Niwot, after asking the whites to leave (and being rebuffed), came alone to Aikens's camp and told of a dream he had had: Boulder Creek had overflowed, the Arapahoe had been washed away, and the whites were saved. From then on, the natives in the area pretty much left the white settlers to their own devices, watching from woods as the newcomers planted crops, dug irrigation ditches, carved roads, and built structures with corners.

Boulder City

As early as 1859, Boulder City, then part of Nebraska Territory, was being laid out, with the first 4,044 lots selling for $1,000 each. By 1860, the town claimed 324 residents; in 1861, a federal bill put the town officially in Colorado Territory.

During the 1860s, Boulder's survival depended largely on its proximity to both the plains and the mountains, with crops as well as gold contributing to its economy. Still, though, Boulder was more a trading center for goods than a supply source, and the 1860s weren't really the best of times for the town; eventually many of the area's early settlers became discouraged and left. Things began to look up in the early 1870s, however, when the town began to build schools and the track of a couple of railroads (Colorado Central and Boulder Valley) reached town. In 1871, Boulder was incorporated (and "City" dropped from the name), and in 1874, the state legislature approved $15,000 for the construction of the University of Colorado, on the condition that the community match the funds, and work was begun on Old Main, which still stands tall, like the campus patriarch that it is. The first class of freshmen consisted of just 12 students, yet by 1880 the university population was over 3,000.

With the establishment of the university, the school's and the town's history and development became complexly intertwined. At the turn of the century, the campus claimed over 6,000 students, and the university "Hill" was beginning to develop into the colorful blend of small businesses, university-affiliated buildings, and student housing found there today.

It was also around the turn of the century that Boulder was first targeted for its tourism potential. In 1898, the Colorado Chautauqua was built at the base of the Flatirons by a group of Texans looking for a place to escape the heat of the summer lowlands. Included were an auditorium, dining hall, community center, and over 100 cottages. (Chautauqua is still used today for music festivals, conferences, and retreats, and cabins can still be rented by individual parties—see "Accommodations" below).

Postmodern Boulder

At the end of WW II, Boulder's population took a significant leap, as the university attracted students on GI loans. By the late 1960s, Boulder was beginning to establish a reputation as one of the counterculture's strongholds, a sort of geographical, political, and spiritual link between Madison and Berkeley, and the town's nightclubs were hosting some of the best rock and folk bands in the country, thanks primarily to the students. Susan Berman, author of the 1971 book *The Underground Guide to the College of Your Choice,* wrote, "For the most part it looks like Berkeley—heavy hip types, mostly freaks. Lots and lots of hair and beards and fringed leather jackets and old jeans, chicks without bras wearing all kinds of good stuff . . . Chicks are very liberated . . . Entertainment is balling . . . Survival is easy. Plenty of drugs, cohabitation, and smiles."

Well, the times they have a-changed, and survival isn't always easy. The area's desirability and the large number of students who'll work for peanuts keeps wages low; the number of homeless is shocking and sad; Rocky Flats is producing major nuclear weaponry (and waste) just 15 miles down the road.

But Boulder's still a beautiful place, and there are still plenty of smiles.

ATTRACTIONS

Face it. You don't go to Boulder to go to museums. *But,* if you need some time off from mountain biking, hiking, and outdoor sightseeing, or if the afternoon brings with it a storm that makes doing indoor activities more sensible, the town does offer a handful of museums and other attractions worth checking out.

*the University
of Colorado's
ivy-covered
museum*

STEPHEN METZGER

University Of Colorado Museum

With three stories of small rooms—some with revolving exhibits—the CU museum has a good display of Southwestern cultures, with Anasazi pottery, Clovis and Sandia points; one wing is devoted to prehistory, with dinosaur fossils and bones, including the skull of a triceratops, and a display of the evolution of the horse, with the hooves and skull of the tiny Eohippus. Kids will love Discovery Corner ("Please Touch"), which teaches them about X-rays, seashells, and starfish. There's also a gigantic bird exhibit. Hours are Mon. through Fri. 9 a.m.-5 p.m., Sat. 9 a.m.-4 p.m.; and Sun. 10 a.m.-4 p.m. Admission is free. Phone (303) 492-6892 for information. The museum is located on the CU campus just off Broadway. Look for the signs.

Harbeck House

This museum, which occupies an 1899-vintage Victorian home just west of the university, displays items from the town's past—quilts, dolls, China, a huge doll house, and other domestic artifacts. On the second floor is a small gift store specializing in books on Boulder's and the state's history. Hours are Tues. through Sat. noon-4 p.m.; group tours offered by appointment. Admission is $1. The museum is located at the corner of 12th and Euclid. Adjacent to the museum is Beach Park, lawny, shady, and perfect for picnicking. Phone (303) 449-3464 for more information.

Heritage Center

Located in "Old Main," the University of Colorado's first building, this museum contains a variety of artifacts from the area's past, as well as historical photos. Phone (303) 492-6329 for more information.

National Center for Atmospheric Research

Located on a gorgeous 360-acre site in the Boulder foothills just southeast of the Flatirons, the National Center for Atmospheric Research (NCAR) is the world's foremost research center for scientists studying weather—"from the tiniest snowflake to the cataclysm of droughts and hurricanes." Known as Mesa Laboratories, the facility is open to visitors Mon. through Fri. 8 a.m.-5 p.m. and weekends and holidays 9 a.m.-3 p.m. Both guided and self-guided tours are available (a highly detailed map, with explanatory text, makes the self-guided tour informative and rewarding). View the massive supercomputer system and the 30-foot-high portable automated mesonet (PAM), a weather station that measures wind speed and direction, temperature, humidity, and air pressure. Also on display are some absolutely stunning photographs of lightning.

To get to NCAR, take Table Mesa Rd. west from Broadway and follow the signs to the parking lot. Admission is free. For more information, phone (303) 497-1174 (recorded tour information) or 497-1000 (main office).

PARKS AND RECREATION

This is what Boulder's all about. Recently named the country's number-one sports town by *Outside* Magazine, Boulder at times looks like an amusement park for outdoor lovers. No sooner do you cross over into the city limits than the whole landscape comes alive with runners (*not* joggers), cyclists, and overall the most active, healthy-looking people you've seen this side of an Olympic training camp. In fact, many world-class athletes live and train in Boulder. Among them are Norway native Ingrid Kristiansen, who won the 1989 New York Marathon and holds the record for the women's 10,000 meters; and Christian Griffith, a Boulder native and former member of the United States Rock Climbing Team.

And it's not only the people who'll tell you this is one outdoor-oriented town. Pull into any parking lot, or take a look at the cars on the street: skis, bikes, kayaks, sailboards, climbing gear, and every kind of outdoor equipment imaginable is strapped, bungie-corded, or racked atop and stuffed into the backs of 4WD Jeeps, Subarus, and other rigs built for the mountains.

Hiking

Boulderites claim that one of the true beauties of living in the area is the easy access to so many wonderful hiking areas. In fact, many homes in town are literally within a few yards of trailheads leading into some magnificent country.

Boulder's prime close-to-town hiking is in and around **Chautauqua Park** on the southwest side of town. Newcomers to town will be amazed to find such a place exists within the city limits. Located at the base of the Flatirons and reached by taking Baseline Rd. west from town, Chautauqua begins as a sloping meadow, then quickly (within a few hundred yards) gets into some steep, rocky, and piney backcountry that feels miles from nowhere—with several different trails webbing up into the woods. If you'd rather start a bit higher, continue up Baseline (it turns into Flagstaff Mountain Rd.) into the **Boulder Mountain Parks,** where you'll find over 33,000 acres of city open space and 100 miles of trails. In fact, it seems a trailhead awaits around every bend in the road—and there are *lots* of those, as the road switchbacks steeply up the mountainside. In addition to the trailheads, picnic tables are scattered along the road, especially at the top, where you'll find 20 or so, along with grills and a shelter (groups can reserve the facility by calling the city **Parks and Recreation Department** at 303-441-3400). A bonus of hiking on Flagstaff Mountain is the views—you're looking directly down on Boulder, and it's a great way to orient yourself to the city.

There's also a plethora of hiking trails in the lower reaches of **Sunshine Canyon** at the west end of Mapleton, as well as farther on up the road on Bald Mountain. Good hiking trails also begin at NCAR (see "National Center for Atmospheric Research" under "Attractions" above).

Another hike, albeit a much shorter one than most of those in the Chautauqua or Sunshine Canyon area, is one that begins not far above the Pearl Street Mall. Just west of the mall, where Pearl St. joins Canyon Rd., is a small parking lot and trailhead. From there, a short hike takes you up the side of the hill to some redrock outcroppings and an excellent view of Denver and the valley.

When you're ready to head out of town a ways, one of the best places to hike is up by the **Eldora Ski Area.** Take Canyon Rd. up to Nederland, turn south on CO 119, and turn off at the ski area; follow the paved road to the trailhead. Several great hikes wander up into the mountains. You can follow the creek, hike up to **Lost Lake,** or let your soul get lost in the high peaks; whether you just want to get outside and sniff the mountain air or you want to get into serious hiking, this area offers excellent opportunities.

Golden Gate Canyon State Park also offers excellent hiking, as well as fishing and camping. A sprawling park off CO 119 between Nederland and Blackhawk, Golden Gate Canyon offers a wide range of trails—from simple roadside walks, or strolls to nearby lakes, to serious backcountry challenges, with close to 30 campsites accessible only by foot. For more information, phone the park at 592-1502.

This is just a small sampling of available hiking near Boulder; it would take a book-length guide to list everything. Besides, you want to do some exploring on your own, don't you?

For maps and more information on hiking in and around Boulder, stop by the **Boulder Mountain Parks Ranger Cottage** at Chautauqua

Park (south end of parking lot by main entrance at Grant and Baseline), or phone 441-3408. Boulder Mountain Park Trail Maps are $3. You can get information from the **City of Boulder Open Space Operations/Ranger Services** at 1405 S. Foothills Hwy.; phone 494-0436. Open Space Trail maps are $5.

Cycling

One of the first things you'll notice about Boulder is that just about everyone rides—mountain bikes, touring bikes, racing bikes. In fact, according to a recent *Colorado Daily* article, seven out of every 10 Boulderites own cycles. And so of course the area's got miles and miles of bike trails, including a wonderful trail system that will take you just about anywhere and everywhere in the city you want to go. Commuters, students, weekend cyclists and out-of-towners see that the Boulder Bike Path gets lots of use.

More serious riders head out of town, though—up into the canyons or up the switchbacky roads like the one up Flagstaff Mountain. Following are just a few basic suggestions. For more information, contact the **University of Colorado Bike Office**, (303) 492-7384; the **Bike Touring Group of the Colorado Mountain Club**, 449-1135; or most any bike shop in town. The City of Boulder Bicycle Program also has more information on routes, and can provide you with maps, brochures, and safety manuals; phone 441-3216.

East Boulder Trail: This is the longest of the city's off-road trails. Pick it up at the Teller Farm Trailhead on Arapahoe between 75th and 95th streets.

Flagstaff Mountain: If you're really in shape and want to give your legs the ultimate workout, head up Flagstaff Mountain (from Baseline). This is one rude ride, the road rising up by a series of serious switchbacks, but the rewards should be great—not only the knowledge that you did it, but the views of Boulder you'll get along the way (assuming you can keep the sweat from your eyes). The four-mile ride rises 900 feet.

Gold Hill-Nederland Loop: Another serious ride is the loop (or any part thereof) that winds up out of town via Mapleton Rd., up over Bald Mountain, through Gold Hill, down into Nederland, and back to town through Boulder Creek Canyon. (Note: A good portion of this road is not paved—in fact, it's downright rutty—and you'll need fat tires, not to mention legs of iron, to make it the entire way.)

You can also do this loop the opposite direction; many riders head up Boulder Creek Canyon, where a not-so-steep paved path follows CO 119 and the creek up out of town. After a few miles, the pavement ends, then continues as dirt for a bit longer before joining the highway; if you continue on the curvy road, you need not only be in good shape but constantly vigilant for cars, which are known to drive this road faster than they ought.

Boulder-to-Jamestown Loop: This 34-mile roundtrip ride begins at the corner of Broadway and Canyon. Take Broadway eight miles east to Left Hand Canyon Drive. After about six miles, watch for James Canyon Dr., a four-mile stretch that takes you to Jamestown.

Rollins Pass: Originally a section of the Northwestern and Pacific Railway, this route took passengers—en route between Denver and Winter Park—over the Continental Divide from 1903 to 1927, when the Moffat Tunnel was completed. Eventually the tracks were torn out, and today the road is a popular 4WD vehicle pass and one of the premier mountain-bike routes in the state. You can catch the pass at a number of different places (get a map), but the main road runs from Rollins, on CO 72 south of Nederland, over to Winter Park.

For a complete guide to mountain-bike riding in the Boulder area, stop by any bike shop and pick up **Boulder Mountain Biking Map.** Also, watch the *Colorado Daily* (CU's newspaper) for regular articles about mountain biking and recommended trails.

If your derailleur, brakes, or cones need adjusting, stop in at **High Wheeler Bicycles,** tel. 442-5588, on Pearl a half block up from the Pearl Street Mall, where the friendly and helpful crew will loan you tools for repair.

Renting Bikes: Among Boulder's shops that rent bikes are **The High Wheeler,** 1015 Pearl St., tel. 442-5588; **The Spoke,** 1301 Pennsylvania, tel. 442-4086 (also at Table Mesa Center, tel. 497-0977); **Full Cycle,** 1205 13th St.; **Morgul Bismark,** 1221 Pennsylvania, tel. 447-1338; **University Bicycles,** 839 Pearl, tel. 444-4196; **Wheels of Boulder,** 1538 28th St., tel. 444-2415; and **Doc's Ski and Sport** at Table Mesa Center, Table Mesa and Broadway, tel. 499-0963.

Further Reading: If you're serious about biking in the Boulder area, and throughout the state, you ought to pick up a copy of Jean and Hartley Alley's *Colorado Cycling Guide* (Pruett Publishing Company, Boulder, 1990). This exhaustive book examines back-road and main-route tours around Colorado for both weekend cyclists and serious tourers. Included are over 30 different trips, with several variations on each one. Learn how to get from Denver's Stapleton Airport to Boulder, as well as where to ride in Telluride. The authors also include maps, photos, discussions of difficulty, brief histories of several of the towns along the way, suggestions for accommodations, and listings of contacts of interest to Colorado cyclists.

River Running

With Boulder's penchant for outdoor sports, coupled with the many rivers and streams in the area, it should come as no surprise that this town is big on kayaking, rafting, and canoeing. One of the best places to get your feet wet, so to speak, is at the **Boulder Outdoor Center,** tel. (303) 444-8420, at 2510 N. 47th St., between Pearl and Valmont. Offering classes and clinics for all abilities, as well as a variety of trips (including to the Cache La Poudre, the Arkansas, Clear Creek, and Royal Gorge), the Outdoor Center is a highly professional outfit dedicated to river preservation and environmental awareness. The Boulder Outdoor Center also has equipment for rent and sale.

Acquired Taste, tel. 443-4120, and **Boulder Outdoor Center,** tel. 444-8420 are two of Boulder's best-regarded whitewater guide services, offering half-, full-, and multiday trips down the Arkansas, Colorado, and other rivers in the area.

Fishing

The lakes and streams around Boulder, including many operated by the city, offer good fishing for both warm- and cold-water species. **Boulder, Viele,** and **Lagerman** reservoirs are popular for boat and shorefishing, as are **Wonderland** and **Thunderbird** lakes and **Walden** and **Sawhill** ponds, and **Barker Meadow Reservoir** in Nederland. Among the streams attracting trout fishermen are the Middle and South forks of **St. Vrain Creek, Left Hand Creek** between Left Hand Reservoir and Buckingham Park, **North Boulder Creek** between CO 72 and Boulder Falls, **Middle Boulder Creek** from its headwaters to 28th St. (special restrictions within city limits), and **South Boulder Creek** from its headwaters to Baseline Rd. (special restrictions between Walker Ranch and South Boulder Rd.).

You'll also find excellent trout fishing in the streams and lakes of the high country west of town. For more information on fishing in Boulder, phone the Colorado Division of Wildlife, (303) 297-1192; City of Boulder Open Space, 441-3440; or County of Boulder Open Space, 441-3950.

Golf

Boulder's 18-hole **Flatirons Golf Course,** located at 5706 Arapahoe Ave., is among the more popular public links in the area; phone (303) 442-7851 for information and tee times. Five miles north of town on Neva Rd., **Lake Valley Golf Club** is another 18-hole course open to the public; phone 444-2114.

Other courses in the area: in Golden, **Applewood Golf Course,** tel. 279-3003; in Broomfield, **Eagle Golf Club,** tel. 466-3322; and in Longmont, **Haystack Mountain Golf Course,** tel. 530-1400, **Sunset Municipal Golf Course,** tel. 776-3122, and **Twin Peaks Municipal Golf Course** (where you still won't find out who killed Laura Palmer), tel. 772-1722.

COMMERCIAL ATTRACTIONS

Claiming to be the oldest microbrewery in the United States, the **Boulder Brewing Company** began in 1979 as a 1,000-square-foot shed near Longmont. By the early '80s, the beer had achieved an excellent local reputation, and in 1984, the company moved to its present location; with increased capacity and efficiency, the beer could be better marketed and distributed. In 1987, Boulder Beer's porter won a silver medal at the Great American Beer Festival, and its stout took home the gold.

Free tours of the brewery (which include a sampling) are offered at 2 p.m., Mon. through Sat. The brewery also operates a restaurant, open to 10 p.m. for food and till midnight for brews. Take Valmont to 2880 Wilderness Place. For more information, phone (303) 444-8448.

Celestial Seasonings tea makers, 1780 55th St., tel. 581-1202, are based in Boulder and offer tours by appointment.

TOURS

From historical walking tours of specific areas of downtown to Jeep, mining, railroad, brewery, and national park tours, if you're looking to go a-touring, you needn't look far.

Boulder Historical Tours

Every Sunday from early June through Sept., groups meet at the Hotel Boulderado at 10 a.m. and 1 p.m. for tours of Boulder's historical districts. The three different areas (the downtown commercial area, the Whittier neighborhood, and Mapleton Hill) are visited on a rotating basis; tours last about 90 minutes and cost $3 per person (groups of 10 or more should make reservations). Wear good, comfortable walking shoes. Phone (303) 444-5192 for more information.

Scenic And Boulder-area Historical Tours

Doo-dah Detours, tel. (303) 449-0433, offers a variety of tours of the Boulder area, with hotel pick-ups and jaunts to Rocky Mountain National Park, Central City, and other nearby destinations. Doo-dah also offers three-day/two-night camping excursions, as well as seven-day/six-night "safaris, Colorado style." Guides have "BS" degrees.

In addition, **The Boulder Mountain Tour Company,** tel. 444-0645, offers morning, afternoon, and full-day tours to Gold Hill, Red Rocks Park, Rocky Mountain National Park, and sites in the Boulder area. They'll pick up at all Boulder accommodations.

Scenic Drives From Boulder

If you want to see the Boulder area without having to worry about driving and parking, it may help to have a guide, yet being your own guide can be far more rewarding. And since the area abounds in stunning scenery, with scenic drives lasting from 20 minutes to several days in length, you really owe it to yourself to get out and do a little exploring. Following are but a few of the many routes that provide fascinating history and stunning scenery.

One of the more popular day-trips is the Peak to Peak Highway Loop. Start by heading out Canyon Rd. through Boulder Creek Canyon. At Nederland, turn north on CO 72. This road takes you past the old mining town of Ward, along the eastern side of Rocky Mountain National Park (with several access roads to picnic areas and campgrounds along the way), through Allenspark and Ferncliff, Meeker Park, and into Estes Park. In Estes Park, you can either catch Hwy. 34 west into Rocky Mountain National Park, or you can loop back through Lyons and into Boulder via Hwy. 36 east.

A shorter, but more demanding (at least on your car) tour is a mostly dirt road up through the mining town of Gold Hill and back into Boulder via Nederland and Boulder Creek Canyon. Take Mapleton Ave. west out of town into some of Boulder Open Space lands (you'll pass several trailheads leading up into the hills), and follow it up to Bald Mountain and then down into Gold Hill; just west of Gold Hill, you'll come back onto CO 7 (where you'll turn south), which will take you back down to Nederland. Allow at least an hour and a half—more if you want to get out and hike, or wander around Gold Hill or Nederland.

Another popular day excursion is the 80-mile round trip southwest to Black Hawk and Central City. The scenery is stunning along the way, although by the time you get to Central City you'll have met up with hordes of other visitors—mostly tourists taking day jaunts from Denver—and if the point of your trip was to get out and "away from it all," you're probably better off heading elsewhere (on weekends in the summer, traffic can be backed up bumper to bumper a half-mile *outside* Central City, while motorists wait to park). If, on the other hand, you're in the mood for wandering through casinos or going on mine tours, then an afternoon in Central City might be just the ticket.

ACCOMMODATIONS

As you'd figure, Boulder offers a full range of lodging options, from bare-bones budget to outrageous opulence. You can camp, stay in a hostel, check into a motel, or go first class by staying in one of the city's luxury hotels.

Boulder Chautauqua

For no-frills yet uniquely Boulder accommodations, consider a room or cottage at Boulder Chautauqua. Rent by the day, week, month, or season in a quiet, self-contained mini-community at the base of the Flatirons. The two lodges (13

Sunday brunchers at the Chautauqua Dining Hall

and 15 rooms) and the 61 cottages are throwbacks to the turn of the century when the Chautauqua was founded. Maintained by the City of Boulder, the complex features a gorgeous old dining hall, an auditorium, and spacious lawns and hiking areas. Ideal for a quiet getaway or isolated retreat.

Lodge rooms at the Boulder Chautauqua start at about $40 for two, and cottages start at $43 a night (minimum of four consecutive nights for the cottages). For a complete brochure, write Colorado Chautauqua Association, Chautauqua Park, Boulder, CO 80302, or phone (303) 442-3282.

Hotels

Boulder's most elegant hotel is the **Hotel Boulderado,** tel. (303) 442-4344 or (800) 433-4344, made famous in song and story (John Prine sings about the prerestoration days, "at the dark end of the hall"). Built just after the turn of the century and first open for business on New Year's Day, 1909, the hotel was renovated in the 1980s and today has over 100 rooms, plus restaurants and convention facilities, while still retaining its early-20th-century feel. Centrally located, the hotel is within easy walking distance of the Pearl Street Mall, The Hill, and the University of Colorado. Doubles start at about $124.

If you're the *Accidental Tourist* type, and would prefer something a little more conventional and less "Boulder-like," you can go with either of the two Marriotts (the **Residence Inn,**

tel. 449-5545, or the **Courtyard,** tel. 440-4700); a **Holiday Inn,** tel. 443-3322 or (800) HOLIDAY; a **Days Inn,** tel. 499-4422 or (800) 325-2525; or the **Clarion Harvest House,** tel. 443-3850 or (800) 252-7466.

Motels

Boulder has a large number of motels, some located right along the highways, some tucked up in canyons and hidden in trees, others right downtown. The **Silver Saddle Motel,** tel. (303) 442-8022, claims one of the choicest lodging sites in Boulder. Located on the city's west end, right at the entrance to Boulder Creek Canyon, this unassuming little motel has 32 units, some with kitchenettes; fall asleep to the sound of Boulder Creek tumbling by. Rooms for two start at about $40. A few bends downstream, the **Foot of the Mountain Motel,** tel. 442-5688, also offers quiet, perfectly located rooms starting at about $40.

Another lodge with an ideal location is the **Boulder Mountain Lodge,** tel. 444-0882, located in Four-Mile Canyon just north of Boulder Creek Canyon. Offering motel rooms, kitchenettes, bunkhouse rooms, and campsites, with rates ranging from $50 to $85, Boulder Mountain probably has the widest range of accommodations options in the area. The motto of **University Inn,** tel. 442-3830 or (800) 258-7917, is "in the center of things," and that's a pretty decent description of its location. With the university directly to the south and the Pearl Street Mall three blocks to the north, this lodge offers excellent access to libraries, shopping, biking, as well as mingling with locals in their own milieu.

In 1985, a classic downtown Boulder Victorian was restored, and the result is the **Pearl Street Inn,** tel. 444-5584. Located at 1820 Pearl, this elegant inn offers private rooms, a restaurant, and full bar, as well as meeting rooms for up to 30 and banquet facilities for 150.

If you're just passing through and you don't want to get off the beaten track, you've got several options right on Hwy. 36 (28th St. through town). The **Highlander Inn,** 970 28th St., tel. 443-7800 or (800) 525-2149, has rooms starting at $42. Doubles at the **Golden Buff Best Western,** 1725 28th St., tel. 442-7450 or (800) 999-BUFF, start at about $60.

The **Arapahoe Lodge,** 2020 Arapahoe, tel. 449-7550, is one of the most centrally located inns in town—between the university and the Pearl Street Mall. Rooms are nice and reasonably priced.

Hostels
The **Boulder International Youth Hostel,** tel. (303) 442-0522 is located at 1107 12th St. on The Hill just a couple blocks west of campus. The office for **American Youth Hostels, Inc.** is in Boulder at 1058 13th St.; phone 442-1166.

Bed And Breakfast
Located downtown at 2151 Arapahoe, near both the university and the Pearl Street Mall, the **Briar Rose Bed and Breakfast,** tel. (303) 442-3007, has 11 rooms in a secluded old home, and you can either lose yourself in your own privacy or join other guests around the fire or on the sun porch.

Camping And RVing
Boulder is virtually surrounded by campgrounds—or at least national forest lands where you can camp anywhere anyway. In addition, two state parks, **Eldorado Canyon** and **Golden Gate Canyon,** are within short drives of town. And, perhaps most spectacular of all, **Rocky Mountain National Park** is only about 45 minutes away.

Kelly-Dahl Campground is one of many in the nearby Roosevelt National Forest. With 46 units, running water and pit toilets, trailheads leading up onto the Continental Divide, as well as some of the most stunning vistas on the Front Range, this is a choice little campground. Lo-

cated three miles south of Nederland on CO 119—$7 per night. Other Roosevelt National Forest campgrounds include **Camp Dick,** in the Middle St. Vrain Recreation Area; **Olive Ridge,** about 15 miles south of Estes Park on North St. Vrain Creek next to Rocky Mountain National Park; **Peaceful Valley,** on CO 72 southwest of Lyon; and **Rainbow Lakes** and **Pawnee,** north on CO 72 just north of Nederland. For more information on camping in Roosevelt National Forest, stop by the district ranger station in Boulder at 2995 Baseline Rd., Room 16, or phone (303) 444-6001.

Golden Gate Canyon State Park, located just off CO 119 south of Nederland, has camping for all tastes. **Reverend Ridge** has over 100 sites with hookups; **Aspen Meadows** has nearly three dozen tent-only sites; and there are some 30 backcountry sites scattered throughout the park (which features over 50 miles of hiking trails). In addition, the park offers stream and lake fishing (check out the rainbows in the pond near the visitor center—sorry, no fishing allowed there . . .), and stunning Front-Range scenery. For maps and information, phone Golden Gate Canyon State Park at 592-1502.

Rocky Mountain National Park offers thousands of square miles of camping, hiking, and backpacking, with entrances on both the west (Grand Lake) and east (Estes Park) sides. See the section on the park in the North Central Colorado chapter.

Closer to town (five miles up Boulder Creek Canyon), **Boulder Mountain Lodge,** tel. (303) 444-0882, offers creek-side tent and RV sites (in addition to the motel—see above).

A **KOA** campground south of Nederland just off CO 119 (five miles north of Blackhawk) offers standard RV-type camping amenities. Phone 582-9979.

FOOD

Start Me Up
Dot's, tel. (303) 449-1323, at 799 Pearl St. in an old gas station just west of the mall, has the look and feel of a classic greasy-spoon-type dive, yet true to Boulder form, this little place offers its own interpretation of tradition: It specializes in soy and other vegetarian products, including tofu, and chai tea is as popular as the coffee. An

excellent place to see who crawls out of the woodwork on Sat. and Sun. mornings, Dot's serves omelettes, eggs and grits, huevos rancheros, cinnamon rolls and muffins; for lunch try the burrito, stir-fry, or black-bean chili.

Another Boulder breakfast restaurant with an atmosphere all its own is the **Last American Diner,** tel. 447-1997, also known as the LA Diner. With the hostess and waitresses on roller skates, and the jukebox pumping out songs like "Blueberry Hill" and "In the Still of the Night" this retro-diner on Hwy. 36 (28th St.) just north of the corner of Canyon serves standard American fare (you were expecting maybe couscous?) at very reasonable rates. Hours are Mon. through Thurs. 6:30 a.m.-10 p.m., Fri. 6:30 a.m.-3 a.m., Sat. 8 a.m.-3 a.m., and Sun. 8 a.m.-10 p.m.

Inexpensive To Moderate

Pasta fans swear the best pasta in town is at **Pasta Jay's,** tel. (303) 444-5800, at 925 Pearl. Pizzas, pastas, and other Italian specialties (eggplant parmigiana, for example) run $5-8; sandwiches are around $4. When weather permits, sit outside on the patio.

If Jay's is too crowded, try **Old Chicago,** 1102 Pearl on the Pearl Street Mall, tel. 443-5031, which also serves good Italian food—pastas, pizzas, and sandwiches. Old Chicago is especially popular among the younger crowd, who appreciate the restaurant's huge beer selection.

For health and vegetarian food, try **The Harvest Restaurant and Bakery,** 1738 Pearl, tel. 449-6223. This place has Boulder written all over it, from the fried brown rice (it's a main dish) to broccoli and walnut casseroles, scrambled tofu, vegetarian enchiladas, and tempeh burgers. Dinners run about $4-8.

Over on The Hill, **Dino's,** tel. 443-2300, serves Greek and American food, including cheeseburgers for under two bucks (and pitchers of beer for $1.99). From its modest beginnings as a hamburger stand on The Hill in 1972, **Nancy's,** 825 Walnut, tel. 449-8402, has grown into a full-fledged restaurant with an extremely loyal following. Breakfast (omelettes, eggs Benedict, blintzes, etc.) run $3.50-6; lunch (salads, homemade soups, pastas, and vegetable dishes), $6-7; and dinners (steaks, veal, fowl—including quail—pastas, and salads), $7-18.

Another popular restaurant is **Rudi's,** 4720 Table Mesa Dr., tel. 494-5858, which serves a variety of international vegetarian dishes made with local organic produce and range-fed chicken. There doesn't seem to be too much debate about where the best hamburgers in town are. **Tom's Tavern,** 1047 Pearl, tel. 442-9363, serves a variety of burgers and sandwiches ($4-6), with excellent people-watching window booths and tables.

Moderate

Visitors who truly want a taste of Boulder need to hit the **Chautauqua Dining Hall,** tel. (303) 440-3776, in the shadows of the Flatirons at Chautauqua Park. Eat inside in the high-ceilinged dining room, light slanting in onto the polished hardwood floors, or, if you prefer, dine on the porch overlooking the park's lawns, wildflowered meadows, and rocky cliffs. As if that weren't enough, the food perfectly reflects much that is Boulder: For breakfast ($3-7), try a hearty helping of pancakes (blueberry or buttermilk), French toast, or an omelette (yolkless eggs, tofu, and non-dairy soy cheese are available as substitutions); if you prefer something lighter, try the fresh fruit bowl or yogurt and granola. For lunch, the Chautauqua specializes in healthful variations of old favorites—turkey burgers, spinach and pasta salads, quiches, and soups; lunches run $4-7. To get there, take Baseline Rd. toward the Flatirons and watch for the signs to the park. Expect to wait a bit, as the place is popular, but it's difficult to imagine a more pleasant spot to wait for a good meal.

Another place that captures much of the Boulder mystique—and is an extremely popular gathering for locals as well—is **Walnut Brewery,** tel. 447-1345, at 1123 Walnut. Boulder's first brew pub, the Walnut serves beer made on the premises, as well as a wide range of meals, from typical pub fare (fish and chips, bratwurst, burgers) to full-course dinner entrees, pastas, soups, and salads—a favorite is the duck enchiladas. To wash down with the various beers, the Walnut also serves a variety of appetizers, including beer-shrimp boil and crab cakes. Of course the real attraction here is the beer. Ranging from light ales and wheat beers to porters and stouts, the brew ranks right up there with the best from other microbreweries. Try a pint of Buffalo Gold; or get a sampler: Taste six beers for $4.80.

Speaking of beer, Boulder is home not only to a brewpub but a microbrewery as well. The

Boulder Beer tasting room and small restaurant, tel. 444-8448, serves beer-cheese soup, salads, sandwiches, and burgers, Mon. through Fri. from 11 a.m.-11 p.m. Take Valmont Rd. to Wilderness Place and go south; you can't miss the brewery.

The James Pub and Grille, 1922 13th St., tel. 449-1922, is as close as you're going to get to a traditional Irish pub on the Rockies' Front Range. Specializing in corned beef and cabbage, but serving a variety of other Irish dishes as well, The James, just off the Pearl Street Mall, also has an outstanding selection of British-Isles beers on tap. Dinners run $5-14. Friday and Saturday nights, The James hosts live music, usually in the acoustic/folk vein and with an Irish bent, and on Tuesday nights there's an all-out traditional Irish jam, when anywhere from 12 to 45 musicians circle up their chairs and play whatever moves them—if you've got an instrument, join in, or just keep time by tapping a spoon on your glass. Music generally starts around 9 p.m.

Mexican Food

Two places seem regularly to vie for most votes for Boulder's favorite Mexican food. The **Rio Grande Mexican Restaurant,** tel. (303) 444-3690, located just east of the mall at 1709 Pearl St., offers excellent food and service at reasonable prices—dinner plates and combinations run $6-8, and lunch specials are $4-6. A bonus are the 99-cent lunch-special margaritas. (Note: A second Rio Grande Mexican Restaurant is located in Fort Collins, at 150 North College Ave.)

The Rio Grande's competition is just up the street at 1043 Pearl. **Juanita's,** tel. 449-5273, also offers excellent food and service in the same price range, in the same low-key atmosphere. Differences? The Rio Grande doesn't serve chimichangas; Juanita's does. Juanita's doesn't serve 99-cent margaritas; the Rio Grande does. Hell, try them both.

Still another excellent Mexican restaurant is **Pablo's,** tel. 442-7512, combining Mexican and Central American cooking with the Boulder health consciousness (including what they claim is the only no-smoking bar in town). Pablo's uses black instead of the conventional refried beans, and strict vegetarians will delight in the soy cheese. Entrees run $6-10. The restaurant is located at the corner of Baseline and 28th.

For good Mexican food in a more cantina-style setting, try **Jose Muldoon's,** 38th and Arapahoe, tel. 449-4543. Serving Mexican and Southwestern food, Muldoon's prides itself on its chimichangas, cilantro chicken, and fajitas, as well as its happy hours and margaritas (enjoyed during nice weather on the patio). The restaurant is also open for Sunday brunch.

When The Boss Is Buying

The **Flagstaff House,** tel. (303) 442-4640, on Flagstaff Mountain overlooking town, is one of the most famous and elegant restaurants in the entire Boulder-Denver area, popular for high-class special occasions. In addition to the over three dozen main courses offered (including elk, Maine lobster, and pheasant breast), the Flagstaff goes above and beyond the call of duty in presenting a huge array of gourmet side dishes and other treats, from the rattlesnake appetizers to the cappuccino-chocolate-mousse dessert. Those on special diets can call ahead to have the staff cook up custom gourmet meals. Reservations requested. Take Baseline Rd. up past Chautauqua, and watch for the sign on your right.

Outside Town, But Worth The Drive

A half-hour out of Boulder in Nederland, **Neapolitan's,** tel. (303) 258-7313, is a small unassuming Italian restaurant—one of the best in the state. From the homemade rolls and salad dressings to the huge portions of lasagna, vegetarian combos, and other pasta specials, this fare is guaranteed not to disappoint. Complete dinners and pizzas are $5-11. All food can be ordered to go.

Just a few miles up Boulder Creek Canyon is one of Boulder's more popular and, well, unique restaurants. **The Red Lion Inn,** tel. 442-9368, specializes in wild game (elk, caribou, buffalo, pheasant, and others), as well as in presentation (many of the dishes are prepared table-side). Dinners run $10-25, but early-bird (of course, pun intended) specials ($7.95) are offered Mon. through Fri. 5-6:15 p.m., Sat. 4:30-5:45 p.m., and Sun. 4-6:15 p.m.

In Gold Hill about 10 miles west of and 3,200 feet above town is the **Gold Hill Inn,** tel. 443-6461, which is somewhat of an institution. It's been written up in several national magazines and has achieved a reputation for huge and delicious dinners. The menu changes nightly, but entrees may include roast duck, paella, or venison; the price is fixed at $21.

Grocery Stores

Only in Boulder would you find a place like **Alfalfa's.** Located at the corner of Arapahoe and Broadway, this organic-new-age grocery store and deli carries everything from organically grown fruits and vegetables to pet health food and biodegradable paper towels, from dairyless bakery items to "cruelty-free" cosmetics. Alfalfa's also has a fish market and deli, yogurt-and-smoothie bar, flower shop, bookstore, the best selection in town of mineral waters, spritzers, and juices. Alfafa's offers a 5% discount to seniors.

ENTERTAINMENT

Boulder's a college town, which means it's a young town, which means there's usually a lot going on—from poetry readings to head-banging rock 'n' roll, from gallery openings to outdoor jazz. The best sources for what's happening are *The Colorado Daily,* the newspaper of the University of Colorado (available free around town); *Friday,* the supplement to Friday's *Daily Camera* (Boulder's daily newspaper, available in racks around town); *Westword* (Denver's free weekly alternative paper); *Icon,* Denver's free monthly "arts alternative"; as well as the Denver dailies, the *Post* and the *Rocky Mountain News.*

You can count on many clubs in Boulder booking quality acts regularly, and there's certain to be music to suit just about every taste. A favorite is **Tulagi,** on The Hill at 1129 13th St., tel. 442-1369. This Boulder institution, having survived since the '60s, has featured hundreds of big-name acts and can always be relied on for an evening distinctly Boulder, even if it's just a lineup of local college bands. Other clubs and theaters that regularly book live music are **Pennylane,** 18th and Pearl, tel. 443-9516 (also poetry readings, etc.); **Taylor's Bar and Grille,** on the Hill at 1143 13th, tel. 939-8883; the **Boulder Theater,** 2030 14th Street, tel. 444-3600; **Ground Zero,** 1360 College, tel. 444-5333; and **Outback Saloon,** 3141 28th St., tel. 444-0081.

If you have something a little tamer in mind, check out the Mezzanine at the **Hotel Boulderado,** tel. 442-4344, an elegant place to dig some cool jazz—located at 13th and Spruce. **The James Pub and Grille,** tel. 449-1922, 1922 13th St., regularly features live Irish music (to go with the Guinness on draft and the corned beef and cabbage in which they specialize). Tuesday nights, local folk musicians descend on The James, circle up their chairs, and jam—as many as 45 musicians at a time. On the other hand, if you feel like kicking up your heels to some down-home country tunes, saunter on over to **Boulder City Limits,** at 47th and Diagonal, tel. 444-6666.

Another classic Boulder bar is the **West End Tavern,** tel. 444-3535. Now, even if the West End hadn't been named "best neighborhood bar" by both the Boulder *Daily Camera* and the Denver(!) *Post,* this would still be one of the best spots in town to go sip a cold one. On a warm afternoon, it doesn't get much better than sitting up on the roof, with one of Boulder's best views of the Flatirons, and listening to some live music with friends while you work through a Boulder Pale. Located just above the Pearl Street Mall, between 9th and 10th.

For those who like to kill two birds with one stone—eat and be entertained at the same time—there's the **Boulder Dinner Theater,** tel. 449-6000. Summer stock actors, based around the country, perform well-known and lesser-known plays and musicals. Tickets run $22-28.

Other typically Boulder ways to spend the evening include attending the **Shakespeare Festival** (see "Calendar" below), poetry readings, public lectures and workshops, film festivals, and even open-mike nights. Even a simple evening stroll down the Pearl Street Mall guarantees surprises and no small amount of entertainment (see "Shopping" below).

CALENDAR

Boulder's annual events—much like the town itself—are incredibly diverse, from steeply serious to downright silly, and some of them are a little bit of both.

Kinetic Sculpture Challenge

Another only-in-Boulder attraction, this parade and "race" on Boulder Reservoir in early May

THE COLORADO MUSIC FESTIVAL

Every summer for about seven weeks, the Colorado Music Festival fills Chautauqua Auditorium in Boulder with fine music and other artistic projects. Inside this century-old, barnlike structure with bare cement floors, one can hear the rich tones of Mozart, Beethoven, Vivaldi, Mahler, and others. The bare wooden walls inside Chautauqua make for excellent acoustics because, according to conductor Giora Bernstein, the wood is a "live material" and "resonates the sound." As *New York* magazine put it, "Boulder, by any standard, is a fulfilling place, but Giora Bernstein and his brilliantly planned festival make the place extraordinary."

On Thursday and Friday nights, the Colorado Festival Orchestra plays; on Sunday nights the Festival Chamber Orchestra plays. World-renowned guest artists are often featured with both the philharmonic and chamber orchestras. Tuesday nights are for the Celebrity Series, solo and ensemble performances by CFO musicians and guest artists.

The Colorado Music Festival also offers a special humanities project each year: a series of concerts, lectures, and films focussed on a central theme. Projects have included La Belle Epoche—Paris 1885-1914; Stravinsky—The Late Works; WW II through McCarthyism; Music of the Sixties; and Celebration: The Arts of Yamagata, Japan.

The Chautauqua Auditorium sits at the base of a mountain and is elevated just high enough to provide a panoramic view of the town. In front of the hall is a long, lush, sloping lawn, perfect for enjoying the fresh air and sunshine, and maybe even a picnic, before a concert. In addition to the auditorium concerts, the CMF sponsors several free outdoor events, including a Young People's Concert and a Fourth of July Pops Concert.

The CMF is strictly a summer orchestra made up of musicians from all over the world chosen by Bernstein. "This is a very intensive program," says Bernstein. "There's music going on all the time—mornings, afternoons, evenings. It's a pace that would be difficult to keep on a year-round basis. In a concentrated summer, it's very exciting."

Maestro Bernstein's intensity has delivered results. His orchestra has won two awards from the American Society of Composers, Authors, and Publishers, as well as the 1988 Governor's Award for Excellence in the Arts. CFO music has also been featured on National Public Radio and on European radio.

Chautauqua Auditorium is located at Baseline and 9th. For schedule and ticket information, write 1035 Pearl St., Suite 302, Boulder, CO 80302, or phone (303) 449-1397.

—*Thomas Owen Meinen*

combines equal parts competitiveness, engineering savvy, and silliness. A bizarre array of human-powered vehicles tread and float (and often stall and sink) 'cross land and water before thousands of cheering spectators, many of whom have taken advantage of the bountiful food and drink served both at the pre-event parade at the Pearl Street Mall and the race at the lake. For more information, phone (303) 444-5600.

Fourth Of July
From fireworks to Frisbee, Boulder's Fourth-of-July events offer something for every taste and mood. One of the country's largest "Ultimate Frisbee" competitions (a non-contact team sport that combines a bit of basketball, football, and soccer), usually runs three days around the Fourth; phone (303) 443-6343 for more information. Over 50 years old, the annual Independence Day Celebration at Folsom Field features the Boulder Summer Concert Band, a sing-

along, and fireworks. You can also see fireworks over Barker Meadow Reservoir in Nederland. **Note:** Fireworks in the mountains, particularly in the forested areas, are always subject to fire conditions. Recent drought years have seen the cancellations of many Colorado fireworks displays.

Shakespeare Festival
Founded in 1957, Boulder's Shakespeare Festival generally runs from late June through mid-August and tackles the full range of the bard's work—comedy, history, tragedy—with varying degrees of success. 1990's production of *As You Like It* was particularly well received, as was a recent *King Lear* and *Richard III*. Part of what makes this festival so special is the theater itself: the Mary Rippon Outdoor Theater on the University of Colorado campus—surrounded by ivy-covered stone buildings, the amphitheater and stage send even the most

cynical play-goer back to 17th-century Stratford-on-Avon. Tickets to the festival range about $12-25. For information and reservations, phone (303) 492-8181.

Colorado Music Festival

Very highly regarded—both locally and outside the area—Boulder's classical music festival runs for six weeks, from mid-June to early August. Attracting some of the biggest names in the profession—musicians and conductors—the festival typically includes some two dozen concerts, with music by everyone from Bach and Beethoven to Shostakovich and Ravel to Bernstein and Gershwin.

As if the music weren't enough, the concerts are performed in Chautauqua Auditorium, where the shadow-of-the-Flatirons setting, combined with the turn-of-the-century structures, makes for the ideal concert locale.

For information on the Colorado Music Festival, phone (303) 449-1397. See also accompanying special topic.

Gilbert And Sullivan Festival

For music lovers whose tastes run a little less *profundo* than the classical music of the Colorado Music Festival, Boulder also offers Gilbert and Sullivan. Begun in 1980, the fest runs matinees and evening shows through July. For information, phone (303) 492-4205.

Colorado Indian Market

Taking place in early or mid-July each year, the Colorado Indian Market draws artists, dancers, storytellers, and other craftspeople from tribes throughout the United States, as well as South and Central America. Jan Esty, the original organizer of the event, which first came to Boulder in 1982, feels that since there were no borders in the Americas before it was colonized all New World natives should be allowed to participate. The inside scoop: If you're looking for art—from sand paintings to sculpture, from jewelry to basketry—you'll get better deals on the show's last day, usually a Sunday. The selection won't be as good, but artisans, not excited about packing up their work and moving it, will be more inclined to bargain over the prices.

For current information on the Indian Market, phone (303) 447-9967.

SHOPPING

Pearl Street Mall

Boulder's famous Pearl Street Mall is certainly as much an attraction as it is a place to go shopping, for here's where you can see Boulder at its most crazy, colorful, and cosmopolitan, hip, happy, and unhomogenous. Join the parade of street musicians and jugglers, tourists from Tennessee, kids, families, and local students—everyone's having a good time. And if you get tired of strolling, there are several cafés, restaurants, bars, and snack shops—many with sidewalk seating—where you can rest and refuel while the mall continues to buzz about you. Even in the evening after the shops are closed, street activities continue and the strollers keep strolling.

Among the more interesting shops are **Old Tibet** at 948 Pearl, a small import store with authentic clothing, jewelry, and other items from Tibet and Nepal. In the same building, **Narayan's Gateway to Nepal,** tel. (303) 440-0331, specializes in treks and tours to Nepal, Tibet, and India—run by native Nepalese.

State of the Arts is a large import and craft store with everything from Grateful Dead T-shirts to African and South American jewelry and clothing. **El Loro Jewelry and Clog Company** is the closest thing I've seen in a long time to a late '60s "head shop" (a true remembrance of things passed), selling incense, jewelry, T-shirts, and, yes, clogs; my only question is, Where're the black-light posters? Across the street, **Ecology House,** much more than a faddy I-heart-baby-seals limousine liberal store, carries *good* books on survival (personal and environmental), posters, T-shirts, jewelry, bumper stickers, and lots of stuff for kids, with 10% of each sale going to environmental organizations. **Boulder Arts and Crafts Cooperative** is a large shop with jewelry, pottery, woodcarvings, weavings, stained glass, etc., by local artisans. A couple of fun novelty shops are **Golden Oldies,** which carries a fine selection of funky vintage men's and women's clothing, from ties and hats to vests and dresses; and **Into the Wind,** which specializes in, well, wind toys—kites, wind chimes, weather vanes, Frisbees. Be sure to check out **Peppercorn,** too, which

the Boulder courthouse, just off Pearl Street Mall

STEPHEN METZGER

carries a huge array of gourmet kitchenware, as well as zillions of cookbooks and a huge selection of coffee beans. **The Page** has great children's books, carrying everything from Dr. Seuss to international mythology retold for kids.

A block below the mall, still on Pearl St., **Boulder Army Surplus Store** carries a wide array of backpacking and camping supplies, including topo maps, while a block above the mall is one of the state's most interesting bookstores. **Rue Morgue Mystery Bookshop** carries *only* mystery/murder/detective novels (the name is from a story by Edgar Alan Poe, the grandfather of the mystery novel). Not only does the little shop carry books by mainstream authors (Raymond Chandler, Tony Hillerman, Robert Parker, etc.), but it also has hundreds of titles by lesser-known writers as well—both new and used books.

If you're looking for food on the mall, you don't have to look far, but you do have to be able to make decisions—because there's a *lot* from which to choose, from Mexican to Chinese, from pasta to popcorn. There's also a crepe cart, a vegetarian take-out place, and a pizza-by-the-slice shop. The **Trident Cafe,** just west of the mall, is an Old-World-style coffee house, serving espressos and other coffees, as well as pastries. Adjoining the Trident is **Bookseller Used Books** (you can walk between the two without stepping out onto the sidewalk), lending the place a legitimate literary air. **Public restrooms** are located about mid-mall, at the corner of Pearl and 13th.

The Hill

Located at 13th and College just west of the campus, the Hill is a collage of cafés, taverns, boutiques, and record stores. Bordering one of the city's densest concentrations of student housing, The Hill is a way hip hangout: Coeds tressed and dressed in black linger solo over cappuccinos, Camus, and clove cigarettes; Lycra-shorted frat studs pound beers and trade insider information on papers in their fraternity files; transients hit up passers-by for spare change; freshmen, always walking a few steps ahead, give their parents the grand tour; and the music, incense, and even patchouli oil waft from open doorways. A must for anyone visiting Boulder.

Particularly impressive are the book and record stores (three of each within a few hundred yards). Check out **Albums on the Hill,** 1128 13th St., specializing in rare albums; when you see some of the price tags you'll wish you hadn't donated your Herman's Hermits records to your little sister. While you're at it, wander into **Rock and Roll Posters,** 1091 13th St., or **Art to Go,** 1118 13th, for excellent full-sized rock, film, and celebrity posters and prints. For books of all kinds, as well as University of Colorado mementos, be sure to hit the university bookstore at the corner of College and Broadway.

If the youthful nature of The Hill gets to be too much, or your kids were last seen looking at skull-and-crossbone earrings in **All the Rage Audio and Video,** take time out at **Kinsley & Co.,** 1155 13th Street—not only does this shop sell upscale men's and women's clothing, but they also have a fly-fishing department, with Orvis gear and other equipment up-nose from the bait plunker. On the corner of 13th and College, **Espresso Roma** is one of the best places in town to cop a cappuccino and read the morning news, while eavesdropping on what the local students are up to (and were the night before). Around the corner, at 1322 College, **Brillig Works Café and Bakery** also serves cappuccino and other gourmet coffees, as well as dynamite baked goods and vegetarian specials—with background music from the Dead to Miles Davis to Brahms.

Farmers Market

In the summer (through October) on Sat. mornings from 8 a.m.-1 p.m., an average of between 35 and 40 local farmers set up stands in Boulder City Park, at 13th and Canyon, and sell their wares directly to the consuming public. Whether it's apples or apricots, pears or peaches, honey or honeydew, these fruits, vegetables, and other products are fresh and pesticide-free, and this is the place to stock up. (Growers are required to display explanations of their farming methods, and most will gladly discuss their theories with you.)

SERVICES

The **Boulder Police Department** can be reached by calling (303) 441-4444 (911 in emergencies). The offices of the **Boulder County Sheriff** are at 1777 6th St.; phone 441-4444. **Boulder Community Hospital** is located at 1100 Balsam (corner of N. Broadway); phone 440-2037 (emergency care) or 440-2273 (hospital switchboard). The central **post office** is at 1905 15th; phone 938-1100.

Recycling

Drop off aluminum, glass, newspaper, and plastic at the three **King Soopers** (6550 Lookout Rd., 3600 Table Mesa Rd., and 1650 30th St.) and at both **Safeways** (4800 E. Baseline and 2798 Arapahoe). For information, phone **Recycle Boulder** at (303) 441-4234.

INFORMATION

If you drive into Boulder from Denver, you'll notice the Boulder information bus on the hill south of town. A subtle introduction to the distinctness that is Boulder, the old school bus is more reminiscent of the Merry Pranksters than of Colorado's railroad history, which so many of the state's other towns try to capture by locating their information booths in old railroad cars. Stop in for maps, brochures, current papers and newsletters, directions to many of the area's highlights, and listings of events. The central office of the **Boulder Chamber of Commerce** is at 2440 Pearl (corner of Folsom); phone (303) 442-2911.

The Boulder **public library** is located at 1000 Canyon Dr.; phone 441-3111 for hours and information. The historical library is at 1125 Pine; phone 441-3110.

For **road and weather information,** phone 639-1234 (I-25 and east) or 639-1111 (Denver and west). Tune to Boulder's public radio station, KGNU, at 88.5 FM.

Bookstores

With one of the highest per-capita number of bookstores in the west (the phone book lists over 30), Boulder could (and does) entertain bibliophiles for days on end—it would take you that long to make the rounds from Waldenbooks and B. Dalton to shops specializing in rare books or politics. **Stage House Books and Prints** would be an excellent place to start. This two-story shop on Pearl a block above the mall is a used-booklover's dream. Not only will you find every kind of book imaginable, but there are chairs for plunking down and actually *reading,* while books are literally *everywhere*—strewn on the stairs, cluttered on the countertops, lined and piled up on the floor. Stage House has a special section of first editions and signed books.

Almost directly aross the street are the **Rue Morgue Mystery Bookshop** and **The Bookseller** (adjacent to the Trident Café). On the Hill, **Aion Bookshop** has used and out-of-print books on most subjects, with a focus on literature, science, and the humanities. The **Boulder Bookstore,** with stores in both the Pearl Street Mall and the Village Shopping Center, carries a wide range of books, with lots on Colorado and the West. **Left Hand Books and Records,** 1200 Pearl, carries books of political interest, specializing in feminism and other progressive issues.

Naropa Institute

Offering an educational and intellectual environment alternative to traditional universities, Naropa is a fully accredited undergraduate and graduate school inspired by a 5th-12th century Buddhist university in India. Though the general tenor and underlying philosophy of the school reflects its Buddhist model, the courses are non-sectarian and wide ranging, with a general emphasis in arts, humanities, and social sciences. In addition to the classes and seminars available to students, many programs and events—from poetry readings to deep-ecology workshops—are open to the public. Semi-regular faculty members include Gary Snyder and Allen Ginsberg.

For more information, phone (303) 444-0202.

Boulder Graduate School

This is a small nonprofit institution offering a variety of workshops and seminars, most of which are oriented toward holistic living and peaceful coexistence—with lovers, neighbors, the environment, and the Earth. Catalogues are available free in racks around town. For more information, phone (303) 444-1946.

Boulder Peace Institute

Offering a rotating series of lectures, seminars, and concentrated one- and two-week workshops, the Boulder Peace Institute is dedicated to resolving conflict in all aspects of our lives—from personal through global levels. Phone (303) 444-4150 for more information.

Further Reading

Anyone who's poked her head into any one of Boulder's many bookstores can tell you there's a lot written about the town and area. For starters, check out *A Look at Boulder, From Settlement to City,* a thorough and illustrated history by Phyllis Smith (Pruett Publishing Company).

TRANSPORTATION

If you're coming into Boulder via Denver and Stapleton Airport, you can get here quite easily. **Rocky Mountain Super Coach** offers door-to-door service for about $14 each way; phone (303) 499-1951. **Boulder Airporter** offers the same service; phone 321-3222.

Getting around in Boulder is quite easy, what with the excellent public transportation system, the fine network of bike trails, and the straightforward way in which the town's laid out. For starters, remember that the numbered streets run parallel to the mountains—north to south—as do Broadway, which runs along the west end of Boulder between town and the mountains, and Folsom, running pretty much through the center of town. (Highway 36 through town is 28th Street.) The main drags running east to west, crossing the numbered streets, are Baseline, Arapahoe, Canyon, Pearl, and Valmont. Iris Avenue, which runs east from Broadway, becomes the Diagonal Hwy., CO 119, to Niwot.

In addition, **The Ride!,** Denver's bus system, has regular service to Boulder, as well as a depot at 14th and Walnut; phone 299-6000 for route and schedule information.

For 24-hour taxi service, phone **Boulder Yellow Cab** at 442-2277.

WEST OF BOULDER

NEDERLAND

Colorado 119 winds west out of Boulder into Boulder Creek Canyon. Just a few miles out of town, you enter Roosevelt National Forest, and at Nederland, 17 miles out of Boulder, the road tees into CO 72. From there, you can either turn north toward Estes Park and Rocky Mountain National Park or turn south for Central City and Black Hawk.

Nederland (pop. 1,200; elev. 8,236 feet) is a quirky little town in three parts: the funky, one-block old town, with a natural-foods store, gift shop, and a couple of cafés; the restored old town, with restaurants and liquor stores; and a new shopping center with City Market, video store, and Coast to Coast hardware.

Barker Meadow Reservoir is located a stone's throw from town and is a favorite fishing lake (stocked regularly). No camping or boating allowed. Public parking and restrooms are in the center of town at the junction of CO 119 and CO 72. **Chipeta Park** behind City Market has a nice playground and picnic area.

CENTRAL CITY AND BLACK HAWK

Long known as the home of the Central City Opera, which has been attracting well-known performers and discriminating fans since 1932, Central City and Black Hawk have recently undergone a serious makeover that will greatly affect the area's complexion as it enters its third century: Legalized gambling came to the two communities in October of 1991. Though maximum bets are only $5, and gaming is limited to blackjack, poker, and slots, the new diversion has already divided locals and thrown a bizarre variable at real estate. Property values skyrocketed as soon as the measure passed (summer, 1990), casinos were built seemingly overnight (as of April 1993, there were 17 casinos in Central City and 21 in Black Hawk!), and the atmosphere of the area was one of excitement mixed with general chaos.

Whatever the result, gambling is guaranteed to draw even greater numbers of travelers to the region, and the two communities, located in a narrow gulch where traffic was a problem well before legal betting showed up, will be forced to rethink local transportation, as well as housing, and other sundry business concerns.

HISTORY

When gold was first discovered in Gregory Gulch in 1859, word spread quickly to the gold camps of Auraria and Denver City, where disgruntled miners were cursing the "Pikes Peak Hoax." Many of them immediately headed for the hills, and soon the Central City area was teeming with newly hopeful prospectors. Horace Greeley, the New York *Tribune* editor, researching a piece on the West's goldfields, visited the camp and was given a tour by a group of miners. Unbeknownst to Greeley, the men had "salted" a placer mine by shooting gold dust into it with a shotgun. Greeley's subsequent report dramatically increased East Coast interest in the area, and soon even more miners were pouring into the gulch.

Originally, Gregory Gulch was dotted with a number of small camps, including Gregory Point, Mountain City, Black Hawk, and Nevadaville. Soon, though, Central City, named for its location about midway up the gulch, became the hub of the area's action, informally incorporating some of the other camps. Greeley, in addition to writing about the easily extractable gold, described the camps and the miners themselves: "I doubt there is as yet a table or chair in these diggings . . . the entire population sleep in tents or under pine boughs."

Between 1859 and 1867, the gulch produced $9 million in gold, earning it the nickname, "The richest square mile on earth." During this time, engineers were perfecting mining techniques, smelters were built in Central City and Black Hawk, and more and more prospectors were arriving in the gulch hoping to strike it rich. Central City's mid-1860s population was 15,000.

STEPHEN METZGER

downtown Central City

From its very beginnings, Central City had a reputation for being more "cultured" and sophisticated than some of the other mountain mining camps, and its diverse groups of miners—Russians, Welshmen, French, Germans, Italians, blacks, among others—lent the little community a cosmopolitan air. In 1861, the Central City Opera House hosted its first production, *Camille,* and throughout the decade the town was well known for its Vaudeville and minstrel shows.

The railroad came to Black Hawk in 1872 and was extended to Central shortly thereafter, making the community much more accessible. In 1874, a fire swept through Central City, destroying many buildings, including the opera house, although the theater was rebuilt four years later—with four-foot-thick stone walls—and by the late '70s was attracting some of the biggest names in American theater, including Sarah Bernhardt, Lillian Russell, and Edwin Booth.

Like most other Colorado mining towns, Central City and Black Hawk were all but abandoned by the early 20th century once silver was devalued and production in the gold mines had slowed to almost nothing. The opera house was boarded up. Then in 1932, the newly formed Central City Opera Association pulled down the boards, restored the seats and interior, and reopened the opera house. In honor of the old building's history, the first show put on was, again, *Camille.* The Central City Opera remains one of the town's primary draws.

During the 1950s, Central City was known as a wild and woolly anything-goes outpost town, with more than its share of colorful characters. Among those who showed up to raise hell here were Jack Kerouac and gang. In *On the Road,* Kerouac describes his adventures: "It was a wonderful night. Central City is two miles high; at first you get drunk on the altitude, then you get tired, and there's a fever in your soul. We approached the lights around the opera house down the narrow dark street; then we took a sharp right and hit some old saloons with swinging doors. . . . Beyond the back door was a view of the mountainsides in the moonlight. I let out a yahoo. The night was on."

Through the '60s, '70s, and '80s, Central City continued to appeal to tourism. In addition to the opera, boosters bragged about the museums, mine tours, and the century-old buildings. And with its proximity to Denver, Central City attracted large numbers of travelers. In fact, during this time, traffic was often bumper to bumper through town in the summer, and on particularly busy days (weekends), cars were often backed up well below town. The little streets and sidewalks, meanwhile, would swell with tourists; the gift and souvenir shops, T-shirt shops, and restaurants would be jammed with camera-toting visitors.

And now, with legalized gambling and increased tourism, the little towns are changing even more. Precisely how and to what degree remains to be seen.

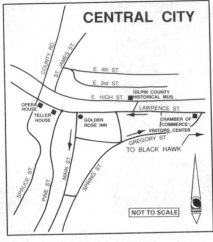

© MOON PUBLICATIONS, INC.

ATTRACTIONS

Gilpin County Historical Museum

Displaying a huge array of authentic items and artifacts from the area's fascinating history, this is one of Central City's less touristy attractions. The museum's rooms represent various eras and themes, including early travel, education, fashion, business, and medicine. In addition, historical photos and miniature reproductions of a Victorian-era mining town combine to give the visitor a very real sense of life in the rough-and-tumble Colorado of the late 19th century.

The museum, located at 228 E. High St. (a half block east of Eureka), is open daily 9 a.m.-5 p.m., Memorial Day through Labor Day, and weekends 9 a.m.-5 p.m. the rest of the year. Admission is $3. For more information, write Box 244, Central City, CO 80427, or phone (303) 582-5283.

Teller House And Opera House Tour

Tours of the Central City Opera House and adjoining Teller House, at one time one of the West's most luxurious hotels, are offered June through August from late morning to early evening. Small fee. In the bar of the Teller House, you'll see the famous **Face on the Barroom Floor,** painted in 1936 by a Denver journalist.

The tours begin at 120 Eureka St. and take about a half-hour. For exact times, phone (303) 582-3200.

ACCOMMODATIONS

Lodging in Central City and Black Hawk includes the **Golden Gate Casino Bed and Breakfast** (five rooms available), tel. (303) 582-1650, where rooms start at about $55; the **Winfield Scott Bed and Breakfast,** tel. 582-3433, doubles starting at about $80 (with a one-bedroom suite available); and the **Carriage House Inn,** tel. 642-3636. The **Gold Dust Lodge,** tel. 582-5415, located two miles off Hwy. 119, has doubles for about $45 (including free shuttle service to casinos).

Camping And RVing

A **KOA** campground is located four miles north of Black Hawk on CO 72; phone (303) 582-9979. There's also camping at **Golden Gate Canyon State Park,** also just north of Black Hawk on CO 72. In addition, the 8,500-acre park offers hiking, horseback riding, and cross-country skiing. For information, phone 592-1502. Also see "Parks and Recreation" under "Boulder" above.

FOOD

The dining scene in Central City and Black Hawk changed considerably when the casinos arrived—essentially, all independent restaurants were offered big bucks to hit the road and make room for the casinos. These days, dining is pretty limited to restaurants in the casinos, many of which offer excellent deals (prime-rib dinner at the Glory Hole for $3.95). A note of caution, though. Most of the deals are offered simply to get you in the door, and few are those who eat and leave without making a few bets on the way in or out; your $3.95 dinner can wind up costing you $15 or $20 before you can say "craps."

ENTERTAINMENT

Part of the entertainment in Central City and Black Hawk of course is simply wandering around the steep streets and into gift shops and saloons—as well as watching all the other folks doing just about the same thing. At the heart of the entertainment scene, though, is the **Central City Opera,** which takes place in the town's 1878 opera house. With produc

face on the barroom floor

BOB RACE

tions ranging from the classical (*The Magic Flute*) to more modern (*The Merry Widow*), the Central City troupe is the oldest summer opera company in the country; since its re-opening in 1932, it's developed a loyal following, from tourists who simply enjoy the novelty to hard-core opera buffs. The season generally runs mid-July through mid-August. For information and reservations, write Central City Opera House Association, 621 7th St., Suite 1601, Denver, CO 80293, or phone (303) 292-6500.

CALENDAR

The highlight of Central City's tourist season is the opera, which runs mid-July to mid-August (see above). In addition, there are a number of other festivals of note, some serious, some silly. The **Jazz Festival** is in mid-August, while early June marks the **Lou Bunch Days** "Bed Races"

(contestants feel like sheet afterwards . . .). For information on annual events in Central City and Black Hawk, contact the Gilpin County Chamber of Commerce.

SERVICES

Phone the **Central City Police** at (303) 582-5411 and the **Gilpin County Sheriff** at 582-5511. The **post office** is located on Gregory just east of Spring Street.

Recycling
The closest recycling centers are in **Nederland**, about 25 miles north on CO 72. The **Boulder County Transfer Station** on County Rd. 128 E, tel. (303) 258-7878, takes aluminum, glass, and newspaper, and the **BF Super Foods**, 60 Lakewood Dr., tel. 258-3105, takes aluminum.

INFORMATION

Be sure to stop in at the offices of the **Gilpin County Chamber of Commerce,** located at the east end of town. For information before your visit, write Box 343, Black Hawk, CO 80422, tel. (303) 582-5077, or phone the **Central City Public Relations Office** at 582-5251. You can also get information about the area by phoning **Central City Public Information** toll-free at (800) 542-2999.

TRANSPORTATION

Central City and Black Hawk are close to the metro Denver area and easily accessible. From Denver, take I-70 or US 6 about 45 miles west and turn north on CO 119 (the turnoff is well marked), and continue for about eight miles. You can also get there from Boulder by going west on CO 119 and continuing south through Nederland, a distance of about 35 miles.

BOOKLIST

HISTORY

Buchholtz, C.W. *Rocky Mountain National Park: A History*. Boulder: Colorado Associated University Press, 1983. Exhaustive story of the park area, from the Native Americans who once called this region of the Rockies home to National Park designation in 1915 and the problems of overcrowding in the 1970s and '80s. A refreshing blend of academic research and pleasantly readable writing—full of details, anecdotes, and colorful characters.

Bueler, William M. *Roof of the Rockies: A History of Colorado Mountaineering*. Evergreen: Cordillera Press, Inc., 1986. Bueler, who had climbed all of Colorado's "14ers" by 1952, divides Colorado climbing into two periods: exploration and modern mountaineering. Very well written and thorough, with maps, charts, and photos.

Burroughs, John Rolfe. *Steamboat in the Rockies*. Fort Collins: The Old Army Press, 1974. The story of Steamboat Springs, from the discovery of the springs in 1839 to the development of the ski resort in the 1970s—as seen through the loving eyes of a 50-year resident of the Steamboat area. Burroughs, who has written extensively on the west—fiction, nonfiction, and poetry—has won several prestigious awards for his writing and draws on both local lore and published reports in the Routt County Sentinel; the result is a pleasant blend of homespun folksiness and footnotey history.

Conlin, Joseph H. *Bacon, Beans, and Galatines*. Reno: University of Nevada Press, 1988. A well-researched and witty account of "chow" on the western frontier.

Dodds, Joane West, photography by Edwin Lloyd Dodds. *Pueblo: A Pictorial History*. Norfolk, VA: Donning Company, 1982. A coffee table-style book on the history of Pueblo, with excellently detailed text accompanying the photos.

Gilliland, Mary Ellen. *Frisco! A Colorful Colorado Community*. Silverthorne: Alpenrose Press, 1984. A history of Frisco and Summit County, with profiles of major players, contributors, and characters.

Henderson, Junious, ed. *Colorado: Short Studies of its Past and Present*. New York: AMS Press, 1969. A series of academic essays on Colorado—from prehistoric peoples through the gold rush to 20th-century education. Particularly interesting, if only because the subject is otherwise so scantily written about, is Irene Pettit McKeehan's "Colorado in Literature." McKeehan's piece is a scholarly examination of the state's well-known as well as lesser-known writers and writings—from Whitman and Parkman to obscure poets whose works have only recently been rediscovered.

Lee, Mabel Barbee, foreward by Lowell Thomas. *Cripple Creek Days*. Lincoln: University of Nebraska Press, 1984. Well-written and personal narrative account of Cripple Creek, from first word of gold to the early 1900s, and the author's return in mid-century (her father had been one of Cripple Creek's original miners).

Lister, Florence, and Robert Lister. *Those Who Came Before*. Tucson: University of Arizona Press, 1983. A fascinating study of the Native Americans who lived in and/or passed through the Southwest, including Arizona, Colorado, New Mexico, and Utah. The Anasazi, Mogollon, and Hohokam cultures are examined in depth, as are the later Pueblo peoples. Beautiful color and black-and-white photos.

Marks, Paula Mitchell. *And Die in the West*. New York: William Morrow and Company, Inc., 1989. An exhaustive socio-historical examination of the famous gunfight at the OK Corral. Though not specifically about Colorado (the shootout took place in Tombstone, Arizona), this book will be of interest to any fan of the American West (besides, Doc Holliday, one of the fight's participants, is buried in Glenwood Springs, Colorado). Combining the scholar's eye for detail and passion for accuracy with a lively writing style, Marks debunks many of the fictionalized accounts of the gunfight, putting it into a larger context and looking at the conflicting loyalties that led to the showdown.

Marshall, Muriel. *Red Hole in Time*. College Station, TX: A and M University Press, 1988. A poetic and heartfelt study of the geology and history of the remote Escalante Canyon, a sharp crease in the Uncompahgre Plateau. Treated as a microcosm of the settling of the west itself, the story of Escalante is rich in its people, landscapes, and folklore.

McTighe, James. *Roadside History of Colorado*. Boulder: Johnson Publishing Company, 1984. Route-by-route (milepost-by-milepost!) look at the state's history.

Riley, Glenda. *Women and Indians on the Frontier, 1825-1915*. Albuquerque: University of New Mexico Press, 1985. In a refreshingly unique look at the settling of the West, Riley argues that women were less likely to prejudge the natives than were men, and that women both greatly contributed to and were significantly liberated by westward expansion.

Rohrbough, Malcolm J. *Aspen: The History of a Silver Mining Town, 1879-1893*. New York: Oxford University Press, 1986. Detailed and scholarly look at the influences of both mining and the railroad, ending with the collapse of the silver market.

Smith, Duane A. *Silver Saga*. Boulder: Pruett Publishing Company, 1974. A close-up, historical examination of the mining town of Caribou, discovered in 1869, with special emphasis on the characters who populated it and the reason "a generation's struggle to plant a lasting settlement failed."

Smith, Duane A. *Rocky Mountain Boom Town: A History of Durango, Colorado*. Boulder: Pruett Publishing Company, 1986. Very thorough and well-written account of Durango's history, with tables, charts, historical photos, etc.

Smith, Phyllis. *A Look at Boulder, From Settlement to City*. Boulder: Pruett Publishing Company, 1981. Meticulously researched and detailed history of Boulder, with excellent historical photos.

Sprague, Marshall. *Money Mountain*. New York: Ballantine Books, 1971. A detailed and highly readable history of Cripple Creek, from the discovery of gold to the early days of reconstruction.

Ubbelohde, Carl, Maxine Benson, and Duane A. Smith. *A Colorado History*. Boulder: Pruett Publishing Company, 1972 (third edition). A nicely readable narrative of the state, from the first cliff dwellers through 20th-century economic challenges. Particularly interesting and well written is the section on frontier Colorado and the Pikes Peak gold rush.

DESCRIPTION AND TRAVEL

Abbey, Edward. *Desert Solitaire: A Season in the Wilderness*. New York: Ballantine Books (through arrangement with McGraw-Hill Book Co.), 1968. Abbey's notes and observations as a May-to-September Park Service ranger, spent in virtual solitude in the Southwest desert (actually Arches National Monument in southeastern Utah). Some of the most poetic, emotional, and inspiring writing to come out of the Southwest.

Casewit, Curtis. *Colorado Off the Beaten Path*. Chester, CT: Globe Pequot Press, 1987. A selective guide to Colorado's less-traveled roads and places. A quirky book with lots of oddball tips and information, it's a good companion to other available guides.

Caughey, Bruce, and Dean Winstanley. *The Colorado Guide*. Golden: Fulcrum Press, 1989. An exceptional general guide to Colorado with an emphasis on recreation. Excellent discussions and descriptions of backcountry hiking trails and tips on out-of-the-way lodges and restaurants.

Chronic, Halka. *Roadside Geology of Colorado.* Missoula, MT: Mountain Press Publishing Company, 1980. Part of the popular series, this is an immensely informative book detailing Colorado's fascinating geology along the state's major and minor roads and highways.

Eberhart, Perry. *Guide to the Colorado Ghost Towns and Mining Camps.* Denver: Sage Books, 1959. Another difficult-to-find but fascinating and useful book, Perry's guide is fraught with maps, historical photos, and descriptions of the old towns, camps, and characters.

Gregory, Lee. *Colorado Scenic Guide, Northern Region.* Boulder: Johnson Books, 1990. Full of facts, maps, and advice for hikers, jeepers, cross-country skiers, and anyone else who wants to explore Colorado's outdoors. Focuses on areas north of Cañon City, particularly on Colorado Springs and Front Range areas.

Gregory, Lee. *Colorado Scenic Guide, Southern Region.* Boulder: Johnson Books, 1990. Same as above, with most sites concentrated south and west of Cañon City, particularly in the Telluride-Creede-Pagosa Springs areas.

Hillestadt, Charles, and Toni Knapp. *Absolutely Every Bed and Breakfast in Colorado.* Colorado Springs: Rockrimmon Press, Inc., 1991. A just-the-facts-ma'am guide to the state's bed and breakfasts, with locations, prices, and amenities—written by the co-owner (Hillestadt) of Denver's Queen Anne Inn.

Houk, Rose. *A Guide to the Rimrock Drive of Colorado National Monument.* Fruita: Colorado National Monument Association, 1987. Photos, history, anecdotes, and suggestions for tours.

Layton, Marie T. *Colorado Bed and Breakfast Guide.* Boulder: Fulcrum Publishing, 1990. Insider's guide to over 50 bed and breakfasts throughout the state. Detailed descriptions of inns, individual rooms, and specific highlights.

Robbins, Michael, photos by Paul Chesley. *High Country Trails Along the Continental Divide.* Washington, D.C.: National Geographic Society, 1981. Excellent photos and exhilarating narrative/descriptive text discussing Continental Divide Trail from New Mexico to Canada—profiles of people, examinations of history, etc.

Smith, Duane A. *Mesa Verde National Park.* Lawrence: University Press of Kansas, 1988. The story of one of Colorado's most visited tourist attractions. Includes descriptions of the life of the Anasazi, who dwelled in the cliffside palaces from about A.D. 1000 to 1300, as well as a look at contemporary park policies and problems.

Work Projects Administration. *The WPA Guide to 1930s Colorado.* Lawrence: University Press of Kansas, 1987 (originally published in 1941 as *Colorado: A Guide to the Highest State*). Reprint from the classic WPA guidebook series, the book is most useful when discussing the state's history (pre-1940). The original now long out of print (sometimes available in bookstores specializing in rare books), this is a wonderful way to get a sense of what Colorado (and traveling) was like between the world wars. Exceptionally thorough discussions of back roads, as well as sites and incidents of relatively minor historical consequence.

RECREATION

Alley, Jean, and Hartley Alley. *Colorado Cycling Guide.* Boulder: Pruett Publishing Company, 1990. A thorough look at back-road and main-route tours in Colorado, including Stapleton Airport to Boulder and various scenic rides in the San Juan Mountains. Photos, maps, degrees of difficulty, brief histories of some towns, and listings of campgrounds, motels, and restaurants.

Boddie, Caryn, and Peter Boddie. *A Hiker's Guide to Colorado.* Billings and Helena, MT: Falcon Press, 1984. Seventy-five hikes with descriptions, maps, and advice.

Borneman, Walter R., and Lyndon J. Lampert. *A Climbing Guide to Colorado's Fourteeners.* Boulder: Pruett Publishing Company, 1988. Peak-by-peak discussions of routes, dangers, what to bring. With maps and photos.

Cahill, Rick. *Colorado Hot Springs Guide.* Boulder: Pruett Publishing Company, 1986. Dozens of springs around the state are covered, with maps, photos, history, and technicalities, such as water flow.

Coello, Dennis. *Bicycle Touring Colorado.* Flagstaff, AZ: Northland Publishing Company, 1989. A look at longer rides around the state, full of suggestions and tips. Lots of first-person anecdotes, lively writing.

de Haan, Vici. *Bike Rides of the Colorado Front Range.* Boulder: Pruett Publishing Company, 1989. Nicely detailed discussions of dozens of rides in and out of the Boulder, Golden, Lyon, and Estes Park areas, with maps, photos, difficulty ratings, etc.

de Haan, Vici. *Hiking Trails of the Boulder Mountain Parks and Plains.* Boulder: Pruett Publishing Company, 1989. Excellent descriptions of scores of hikes in the Boulder area, with photos, maps, difficulty ratings, etc.

Kelly, Tim. *Tim Kelly's Colorado Hunting, Fishing, and Outdoor Guide.* Denver: Don Hart Publishing, 1990. Wonderfully detailed maps, photos, charts, and textual discussions of Colorado's streams, lakes, hiking trails, and backcountry. Full of expert advice.

Lund, Morten, Bob Gillen, and Michael Bartlett, eds. *The Ski Book.* New York: Arbor House, 1982. With a foreword by winter Olympic gold medalist Jean-Claude Killy, this is an anthology of some of the best ski writing of the century. Essays and articles from *Skiing, Ski, Powder,* and *Sports Illustrated,* as well as from many fine books on the subject, with pieces by Percy Bysshe Shelley, Robert Frost, Ernest Hemingway, Gay Talese, Thomas Mann, John Updike, Art Buchwald, and other writers who have written over the years for ski magazines.

Martin, Bob. *Hiking the Highest Passes of Colorado.* Boulder: Pruett Publishing Company, 1988. Based on the premise that hiking Colorado's high passes (the author includes 60) is more rewarding than "bagging peaks," this book offers road directions, hiking routes, advice, and suggests other points of interest en route. Includes maps, charts, and photos.

Mays, Buddy. *Guide to Western Wildlife.* San Francisco: Chronicle Books, 1988. Pocket-sized guide to the huge variety of the West's critters.

Muller, Dave. *Colorado Mountain Hikes For Everyone.* Denver: Quality Press, 1987. A very accessible book with over 100 hikes throughout Colorado, with maps, charts, photos, advice, directions, etc.

Ormes, Robert M. *Guide to the Colorado Mountains.* Colorado Springs: 1986. Amazingly detailed climber's guide, with maps, photos, suggested routes and trails.

Pixler, Paul. *Hiking Trails of Southwestern Colorado.* Boulder: Pruett Publishing Company, 1981. Maps, charts, text descriptions, degrees of difficulty, and time allowances for trails in some of the state's finest and most scenic hiking areas.

Schmidt, Jeremy. *Adventuring in the Rockies: The Sierra Club Travel Guide to the Rocky Mountain Regions of the United States and Canada.* San Francisico: Sierra Club Books, 1986. Guide to hiking, camping, and sightseeing in the Rockies, with an emphasis on low-impact exploration.

Stienstra, Tom. *Rocky Mountain Camping.* San Francisco: Foghorn Press, 1989. Campground-by-campground guide to over 1,200 spots in Colorado, Wyoming, and Montana, with number of sites, fees, other activities in the area, etc., as well as whom to contact.

Stoehr, William L. *Bicycling the Back Country: A Mountain Bike Guide to Colorado.* Boulder: Pruett Publishing Company, 1987. Maps, charts, descriptions of a huge range of rides in just about every imaginable corner of the state. A must for the serious off-road rider.

Wheat, Doug. *The Floater's Guide to Colorado.* Billings and Helena, MT: Falcon Press Publishing Company, 1983. An immeasurably detailed and well-written book exhaustively discussing the state's rivers—fit for kayak, canoe, or raft. Wheat is a biologist and geologist who pioneered many of the rivers covered in the book. The *Denver Post* called it "the American Express card for river running. Don't leave home without it."

POLITICS AND GOVERNMENT

Prucha, Francis Paul. *The Great Father: The United States Government and the American Indian.* Lincoln: University of Nebraska Press, 1984. This huge (1,300 pages) two-volume set is one of the definitive reference works on the delicate and often stormy relationship between Native Americans and those who subdued and govern them.

Wright, James Edward. *The Politics of Populism: Dissent in Colorado.* New Haven: Yale University Press, 1974. Tracing the beginnings of Colorado's progressive politics from the gold rush of the late 1850s through the Populist revolution of the latter part of the century, Wright, a history professor at Dartmouth, argues that the state's mining origins were largely what led to its strident support of unionism and other movements that defined 20th-century labor and politics.

BIOGRAPHY, AUTOBIOGRAPHY, AND MEMOIR

Conner, Daniel Ellis. *A Confederate in the Colorado Gold Fields.* Norman: University of Oklahoma Press, 1970. Reworked by editors Donald J. Berthong and Odessa Davenport from a manuscript written in the late 1860s, this book tells the story of a gold seeker who during the Civil War sympathizes and becomes involved with a group of Colorado Confederates hiding out near Pueblo. Especially interesting are Conner's descriptions

of modes of travel (using a gold pan for a snow sled, for example) and of other Colorado pioneers.

French, Emily, edited by Janet Lecompte. *Emily: The Diary of a Hard-Worked Woman.* Lincoln: University of Nebraska Press, 1987. An extraordinary collection of diary entries by French, a 47-year-old laundress, cleaning woman, and nurse, who wrote daily of her life on the Colorado plains and in Denver from January 1 to December 31, 1890. "I got up so early, thinking of the one that now seems to fill all my cravings for a companion, will he be all to me," she writes on June 17, and on November 8: "Another day, oh when will I have my time all to rest, will it ever come, I try to be kind, it does no good."

Hamil, Harold. *Colorado Without Mountains: A High Plains Memoir.* Kansas City, MO: The Lowell Press, 1976. A story of growing up in the "other" Colorado, the cattle ranches east of the Rockies, at a time when the West had been won and the way it was being run was changing dramatically. The author, a former AP reporter and journalism professor, tells his story in short, chatty chapters—one particularly intriguing as well as disturbing anecdote is about the appearance of the Ku Klux Klan at Hamil's high school graduation in 1924.

Townshend, Robert T. *A Tenderfoot in Colorado.* Norman: University of Oklahoma Press, 1968 (originally published in 1923). "In 1869 I found myself five thousand miles to the westward of Old England, in a car on the newly opened Union Pacific Railroad, with a good hope of being safely landed by it in the part of the Far West known as Wyoming Territory, U.S.A. I was a tenderfoot, though the title was strange to me; but I was out to learn." Thus begins Townshend's first-person account of his exploration of the central Rockies. Though the prose is rather archaic and some of his observations seem racist ("He was an Indian with brains"), the book does exude a certain charm. And if we can assume that Townshend's rendering of Old-West dialogue is accurate, we get a good idea of how folks spoke in them days.

ENVIRONMENT/ECOLOGY

Devall, Bill, and John Sessions. *Deep Ecology: Living as If Nature Mattered.* Salt Lake City: Peregrine Smith Books, 1985. A mind-bogglingly important tome that instructs us in how to live in a world that is falling victim to "progress"—that is, the book asks us literally to reconstruct our thinking about our relationship to Nature and the Earth: "The nature of deep ecology is to keep asking more searching questions about human life, society, and Nature as in the Western philosophical tradition of Socrates. . . . Deep ecology goes beyond the so-called factual level to the level of self and Earth wisdom."

Seed, John, et al. *Thinking Like a Mountain: Toward a Council of All Beings.* Philadelphia and Santa Cruz: New Society Publishers, 1988. An anthology of writings, prose and poetry, most dealing to some degree with the *gaia* concept, of the earth as a spiritual lifeforce. Includes pieces by Robinson Jeffers, Chief Seattle, Gary Snyder, and others.

ETHNIC COLORADO

de Onis, Jose, ed. *The Hispanic Contribution to the State of Colorado.* Boulder: Westview Press, 1976. A collection of essays looking at the many facets that make up Hispanic Colorado, from early Spanish contacts and original Spanish and Mexican land grants to Hispanic folklore and close-up examinations of specific regions—including the San Luis Valley, where the Spanish language is more alive than perhaps anywhere else in the state.

NATIVE AMERICANA

Bruchas, Joseph. *Survival This Way: Interviews With American Indian Poets.* Tucson: University of Arizona Press, 1988. Interviews with Joy Harjo, N. Scott Momaday, Simon Ortíz, and 18 others.

Dodge, Robert K., and Joseph B. McCullough, eds. *Voices from Wah'Kon-Tah.* New York: International Publishers, Inc., 1976. A widely varied collection of Native American poetry, uneven in quality, but always evocative, stirring, and often disturbing. Contributors include such well-known Native American writers as Paula Gunn-Allen, N. Scott Momaday, Simon Ortíz, Marnie Walsh, and James Welch. Excellent introduction by Vine Deloria, Jr.

Eagle/Walking Turtle. *Indian America: A Traveler's Companion.* Santa Fe: John Muir Publications, 1989. A state-by-state guide to many of the country's Native American tribes, reservations, visitor-information centers, art forms, museums, and public festivals. Although there's not a whole lot on Colorado, the book suggests the variety and scope of the hundreds of tribes and their involvements.

Marriot, Alice, and Carol K. Rachlin, eds. *American Indian Mythology.* New York: New American Library, 1968. One of the best available collections of Native American myths, including many from Southwestern tribes. Meet Coyote, Spider Woman, the War Twins, and many others, and watch for the huge difference and fascinating parallels between Native American and Judeo-Christian mythology. Introduction alone is worth the price of admission.

Murphy, James E., and Sharon M. Murphy, eds. *Let My People Know.* Norman: University of Oklahoma Press, 1981. Scholarly study of Native American journalism, from confiscated presses of the mid-19th-century to modern journals and newspapers.

Neihardt, John G. *Black Elk Speaks.* New York: Washington Square Press, 1959. Told to Neihardt by the Sioux warrior and medicine man, the story recounts Black Elk's youth on the plains, his Vision, the coming of the white man, and the battle of Wounded Knee. Though not specifically about Colorado, the book offers a unique insight into Native American life in the late 19th century. A painful yet important book.

Olson, James S., and Raymond Wilson. *Native Americans in the 20th Century.* Chicago: University of Illinois Press, 1984. A somewhat academic but highly readable account of the forces working against the 20th-century Native American. The authors look at past government attempts at "helping" the natives, from Compensation to Termination and Relocation, as well as Native American responses—from passive resistance to militancy. Excellent historical and contemporary photographs.

Witt, Shirley Hill, and Stan Steiner, eds. *The Way, An Anthology of Native American Literature.* New York: Alfred A. Knopf, Inc., 1972. Wonderfully eclectic collection of songs, poetry, oratory, mythology, and contemporary journalism by Native Americans. Includes poetry by Simon Ortíz and N. Scott Momaday, oratory by Tecumsah, and Geronimo's surrender speech to General Cook.

ART AND PHOTOGRAPHY

Dallas, Sandra. *Yesterday's Denver.* Miami: E.A. Seemann Publishing Company, 1974. Collection of historical photographs of Denver, from 1859 through WW II. Excellent shots of pioneers, transportation, and architecture, as well as of visiting celebrities, including Billy Sunday, Dwight Eisenhower, and Gary Cooper.

Muench, David, text by David Sumner. *Colorado.* Portland, OR: Graphic Arts Center Publishing Company, 1978. Most readers are familiar with Muench's work—some of the most glorious nature photography of the century—so suffice it to say this is Muench at his best, working one of the most gorgeous spots on the planet. Accompanying text, as always, is as informative, eloquent, and inspiring as the photos.

Shapiro, Michael Edward, and Peter H. Hassrick (with other contributors). *Frederick Remington: The Masterworks.* New York: Harry N. Abrams Press, Inc. 1988. An impressively large study of both the work and the man who helped define western art and gave

many Americans their only view of late-19th-century cowboys, soldiers, Indians, and mountain men.

LANGUAGE

Cobos, Ruben. *A Dictionary of New Mexican and Southern Colorado Spanish.* Santa Fe: Museum of New Mexico Press, 1983. Like the remote pockets in rural Appalachia where small, linguistically incestuous groups, isolated from outside influences, still speak an English very much like 17th and 18th century "King's English," some areas of the Southwest are so similarly isolated that the people living there speak a Spanish much like that of 16th and 17th century Spaniards. This fascinating dictionary gives the background of the phenomenon and translates Spanish words unlikely to be encountered outside small rural pockets of New Mexico and southern Colorado.

Smith, Cornelius C. *A Southwestern Vocabulary: The Words They Used.* Glendale, CA: Arthur H. Clark Co., 1984. Over 500 words brought to the southwest by its various settlers and passers-through: Spanish, Anglo, Native American, and U.S. military.

FICTION

Abbey, Edward. *The Monkey Wrench Gang.* New York: Avon Books, 1976. The founding father of modern environmentalism tackles the money-hungry bureaucrats wrecking the Southwest's deserts and rivers.

Hillerman, Tony. *Dance Hall of the Dead; Skinwalker; People of Darkness; The Ghostway; Listening Woman; The Fly on the Wall; The Blessing Way; Thief of Time; Talking God, Coyote Waits.* Most available in Avon paperback. Hillerman's murder mysteries, most of which take place on the Navajo reservation in the Four Corners area, are universally acclaimed for their authenticity and brilliant depictions of the Southwest. Readers trying to unravel the crimes along with Detective Jim

Chee and Lieutenant Joe Leaphorn learn intimate and fascinating details about Indian culture.

Michener, James. *Centennial.* New York: Random House, 1974. A typically Michenerian (that is, l-o-n-g) historical novel of the Colorado plains. Follow professor Lewis Vernor to Greeley and the surrounding area as he researches the geology, prehistory, Native American history, and settlement of the region while on assignment for a major magazine. Meet a colorful cast of characters—some real, some invented—as you absorb the story of this fascinating area.

Momaday, N. Scott. *House Made of Dawn.* New York: Perennial Library, 1977. A young Native American attempts to return to the traditions of his pueblo after fighting in WW II. Beautifully written by one of our great American novelists and poets, the story draws on the mythology, vision, and spirit of the Pueblo peoples.

Shuler, Linda Lay. *She Who Remembers.* New York: William Morrow and Company, 1988. (Also available in paperback from New American Library.) Imagine *Clan of the Cave Bear* in a Four Corners setting. A historical bodice-ripper (with a strong heroine who's not above a little loincloth-ripping herself). The story of Kwani and her attraction to the Anasazi stud, Kokopelli. Very well researched, providing good background reading on Mesa Verde and the Anasazi people. Ideal vacation reading.

Silko, Leslie Marmon. *Ceremony.* New York: Viking Press, 1977. Powerful story of the spiritual healing of a Navajo veteran of WW II. Blends Native American mythology and storytelling with conventional fictional devices. A must for anyone interested in southwestern tribes, and especially their literature.

COOKBOOKS

Junior League of Denver. *Creme de Colorado Cookbook.* Three hundred pages of Colorado cooking, from the relatively tame (Creamy Banana Coffee Cake) to wild (Minted Grouse Breasts and Gunnison Trapper Game Pie).

Volunteers of the State Historical Society of Colorado. *Pioneer Potluck: Stories and Recipes of Early Colorado.* Boulder, 1963. Though difficult to find (check libraries and used bookstores), this little loose-bound paperback is a western bouillabaisse of characters, cooks, and recipes of pioneer Colorado. Each contributor is described briefly (oftentimes by a daughter or granddaughter), and then some of his or her specialties are described. Learn how to make pickled peaches, beaver tail, vinegar pie, squatter's soup, posole, Rocky Mountain oysters, and son-of-a-bitch stew ("From a freshly killed beef take the following: liver, heart, brains, sweetbreads, kidneys, and marrow-gut. Wash them carefully, then cut them up into pieces a little bit bigger than the wrapped cubes of sugar you find in a restaurant . . .").

ODDS AND ENDS

Stegner, Wallace. *The American West as Living Space.* Ann Arbor: University of Michigan Press, 1987. Stegner shares his insights and offers intriguing analyses of why folks are drawn to, live in, and love the West.

MAGAZINES

Backpacker. Subtitled "The Magazine of Wilderness Travel," this publication mixes hard-hitting stories on environmental issues with destination pieces spotlighting backcountry areas around the world. The magazine also reviews equipment and runs stories on health and safety in the woods. Excellent photo essays, too. Available at most newsracks. For subscription information, write 33 East Minor Street, Emmaus, PA 18098.

Colorado Woman News. A monthly news magazine focusing on women's issues, with regular departments, feature stories, and a broad editorial slant—ranging from black feminism to health and day care problems to softball coverage. Available in newsstands around the state.

Denver Magazine. Standard metropolitan production, with a variety of well-written and entertaining pieces, from profiles of local artists to looks at successful Denver businesses—also dining guides and suggested trips around Colorado. $2/copy around the state. Subscription information: Box 1673, Inglewood, CO 80150, or phone (303) 322-6400.

Icon. Billing itself the "arts alternative," this little monthly newspaper/magazine is actually being quite modest. With intelligently written art, music, film, and drama reviews, as well as features on the arts in the Denver area, *Icon* is a must for anyone interested at all in any of the various art media. If the reviews and features aren't enough for you, the schedules of events, concerts, gallery openings, and club bookings should convince you. Available free throughout the Denver and Boulder areas. For subscription and other information, write 2548 15th St., Denver, CO 80211, or phone (303) 455-4643.

Powder. A monthly ski magazine for chutes-shredders, powderhounds, and cornice-jumpers (including pinheads and snowboarders). Never taking itself too seriously, *Powder* is an excellent blend of intelligent writing, humor, and just the right amount of smugness. Tons of outrageous photos, lots of expert advice. Published seven times a year. Box 1028, Dana Point, CA 92629; tel. (714) 496-5922.

Rocky Mountain Sports Fitness. Monthly oversized newsprint magazine crammed with information on competitive and noncompetitive sports events of all kinds. Find out where the next 100-mile mountain run is, or when the next five-km walk/jog/wheelchair competition around Lake Dillon is. *Sports Fitness* also profiles local athletes and runs stories on fishing, boardsailing, mountain biking, hiking, kayaking, skiing, triathlons, and just about every other outdoor sport. Distributed free around the mountain area. For information, write 1919 14th St., Boulder, CO 80302, or phone (303) 440-5111.

Ski and *Skiing.* The two biggest and most widely read ski magazines in the country, both are Times Mirror publications and run many of the same types of pieces—from annual equipment reviews and instructional articles to exotic travel (from Heavenly Valley to the Himalayas), as well as profiles and reader surveys. Watch *Ski* and *Skiing* for pieces by the country's best ski writers, including Peter Shelton, Andrew Slough, Lito Tejada-Flores. *Ski* and *Skiing* are available at newsstands, grocery stores, and ski shops around the U.S.

Snow Country. Upscale guide to year-round resort living and vacationing, aimed at the traveler with the bucks to consider investing in properties he finds to his liking. Very well edited and written, and with a sometimes paradoxical social attitude: It's pro-development yet gives its writers free reign to explore environmentally sensitive issues. Also includes profiles of "snow country" celebrities. Published monthly (10 issues); costs $1.95 at newsstands. Executive and editorial offices are at 5520 Park Ave., Trumbull, CT 06611-0395; tel. (203) 373-7000.

Trail And Timberline. Monthly publication of the venerable Colorado Mountain Club featuring stories on all aspects of Colorado mountaineering, plus pieces on hiking and climbing around the world. Regular departments include "Book Reviews" and "Outings," which lists upcoming hikes and other CMC-sponsored events. For information, write the club at 2530 W. Alameda Ave., Denver, CO 80219, or phone (303) 922-8315.

Vail Magazine. Nicely packaged blend of views on Vail real estate, architecture, and history, as well as photo essays, promotional pieces, ads for galleries, and a monthly calendar. $3.25/copy at bookstores and newsracks throughout the state. Subscription information: Box 368, Vail, CO 81658, or phone (303) 476-6600.

NEWSPAPERS

The Aspen Times. Weekly paper focusing on Aspen's development, real estate, politics, and sports, with a big emphasis on skiing (not surprisingly). Ranges in tone from lighthearted and tongue-in-cheek to stern editorializing. Also includes dining and lodging supplements. Published every Thursday and available throughout the Aspen area at 35 cents a copy. For subscriptions, write Box E, Aspen, CO 81612.

Colorado Daily. University of Colorado (Boulder) paper, emphasizing local and campus news but also with short pieces of national and international interest. Good entertainment listings and reviews, also provocative editorial and op-ed pages. "Colorado Daily Trail Guide" column examines riding and hiking trails in the area, and offers advice on what to see and do along the way, as well as what to take along for a safe and enjoyable trip. Available free in newsracks throughout Boulder. Phone (303) 443-6272 for subscription information.

Daily Camera. Boulder's daily, with large national and international news and sports sections, and editorials of local and worldwide interest. Good source for what's happenin' in Boulder. Phone (303) 442-1202, or write Box 591, Boulder, CO 80306.

Denver Post. The best paper in Colorado, in fact one of the best in the west. Progressive editorial slant, in-depth reporting (longer stories than those in the *Rocky Mountain News)*, excellent columnists. Printed on recycled paper. Pick one up daily while you're visiting the state for local, national, and international news.

Gazette Telegraph. Daily newspaper of Colorado Springs and Pikes Peak area. For subscription, phone (719) 632-5511.

The Parent. This small monthly more than makes up for its lack of size with its excellent articles and listings of interest to Colorado parents, as well as those passing through. Regular features focusing on kids and their folks in-

clude the calendar of events, profiles of local teachers and other educators, lists of classes and workshops, as well as a regular Q-and-A column, where readers' questions about their kids are answered. Free throughout the Denver area, though not as easy to find as some publications. For information, write Denver Parent, Inc., 818 E. 19th Ave., Denver, CO 80218, or phone (303) 832-7822.

Rocky Mountain News. Founded on April 23, 1859 by William N. Byers, the *News* is Colorado's oldest paper and with the *Denver Post* one of the two largest. Stories shorter and less developed than the *Post's,* and the editorial slant a bit more conservative.

Summit Daily News. The refreshingly brazen regional paper of Summit County, with a wide range of stories on international and national politics, as well as the standard local fare: sports, dining guides, real estate. Write 120 3rd Ave., Frisco, CO 80443, or phone (303) 668-3998.

Westword. This is Denver's controversial news and arts weekly, irreverently written by committed journalists whose aim is to "comfort the afflicted and afflict the comfortable." Particularly good—and eagerly awaited by the entire city—is the annual "Best of Denver" edition, which comes out in late June. Here you'll find the editors' recommendations—as well as those of their readers—for everything from best neighborhood bar and best Mexican restaurant to "Best Ethnic Selection in a Megamarket," and "Best Massage for Those Who Are Embarrassed About Their Bodies" to "Best Gay Rodeo." *Westword* is also one of the best sources for entertainment in and around the Denver area—from comedy clubs to jazz concerts to gallery openings. For information, phone (303) 296-7744, or write Box 5970, Denver, CO 80217.

INDEX

Page numbers in **boldface** indicate the primary reference. *Italicized* page numbers indicate information in captions, special topics, charts, illustrations, or maps.

ABOUT THE AUTHOR

Stephen Metzger lives in Northern California with his wife Betsy, daughters Hannah and Gina, and golden retriever Murphy. He has written for the San Francisco *Chronicle* and *Examiner,* for several national and international skiing, health and fitness, and in-flight magazines, and is the author of *California Downhill* and *New Mexico Handbook* (Moon Publications). He has also published poetry and short fiction in literary journals and is a member of the English Department at California State University Chico. When not writing, traveling, or teaching, Steve enjoys reading, playing basketball and softball, running, bicycling, brewing beer, and playing music (guitar and banjo).

THE METRIC SYSTEM

1 inch = 2.54 centimeters (cm)
1 foot = .304 meters (m)
1 mile = 1.6093 kilometers (km)
1 km = .6124 miles
1 fathom = 1.8288 m
1 chain = 20.1168 m
1 furlong = 201.168 m
1 acre = .4047 hectares
1 sq km = 100 hectares
1 sq mile = 2.59 square km
1 ounce = 28.35 grams
1 pound = .4536 kilograms
1 short ton = .90718 metric ton
1 short ton = 2000 pounds
1 long ton = 1.016 metric tons
1 long ton = 2240 pounds
1 metric ton = 1000 kilograms
1 quart = .94635 liters
1 US gallon = 3.7854 liters
1 Imperial gallon = 4.5459 liters
1 nautical mile = 1.852 km

To compute centigrade temperatures, subtract 32 from Fahrenheit and divide by 1.8. To go the other way, multiply centigrade by 1.8 and add 32.

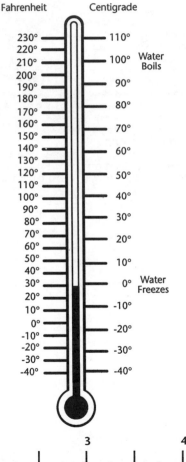

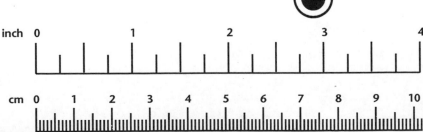

MOON HANDBOOKS—THE IDEAL TRAVELING COMPANIONS

Open a Moon Handbook and you're opening your eyes and heart to the world. Thoughtful, sensitive, and provocative, Moon Handbooks encourage an intimate understanding of a region, from its culture and history to essential practicalities. Fun to read and packed with valuable information on accommodations, dining, recreation, plus indispensable travel tips, detailed maps, charts, illustrations, photos, glossaries, and indexes, Moon Handbooks are ideal traveling companions: informative, entertaining, and highly practical.

To locate the bookstore nearest you that carries Moon Travel Handbooks or to order directly from Moon Publications, call: (800) 345-5473, Monday-Friday, 9 a.m.-5 p.m. PST.

THE PACIFIC/ASIA SERIES

BALI HANDBOOK   by Bill Dalton
Detailed travel information on the most famous island in the world. 428 pages.   **$12.95**

BANGKOK HANDBOOK   by Michael Buckley
Your tour guide through this exotic and dynamic city reveals the affordable and accessible possibilities. Thai phrasebook. 214 pages.   **$10.95**

BLUEPRINT FOR PARADISE: How to Live on a Tropic Island   by Ross Norgrove
This one-of-a-kind guide has everything you need to know about moving to and living comfortably on a tropical island. 212 pages.   **$14.95**

FIJI ISLANDS HANDBOOK   by David Stanley
The first and still the best source of information on travel around this 322-island archipelago. Fijian glossary. 198 pages.   **$11.95**

INDONESIA HANDBOOK   by Bill Dalton
This one-volume encyclopedia explores island by island the many facets of this sprawling, kaleidoscopic island nation. Extensive Indonesian vocabulary. 1,000 pages.   **$19.95**

JAPAN HANDBOOK   by J.D. Bisignani
In this comprehensive new edition, award-winning travel writer J.D. Bisignani offers to inveterate travelers, newcomers, and businesspeople alike a thoroughgoing presentation of Japan's many facets. 950 pages.   **$22.50**

MICRONESIA HANDBOOK: Guide to the Caroline, Gilbert, Mariana, and Marshall Islands
by David Stanley
Micronesia Handbook guides you on a real Pacific adventure all your own. 345 pages.   **$11.95**

NEW ZEALAND HANDBOOK   by Jane King
Introduces you to the people, places, history, and culture of this extraordinary land. 571 pages.
$18.95

OUTBACK AUSTRALIA HANDBOOK   by Marael Johnson
Australia is an endlessly fascinating, vast land, and *Outback Australia Handbook* explores the
cities and towns, sheep stations, and wilderness areas of the Northern Territory, Western
Australia, and South Australia. Full of travel tips and cultural information for adventuring,
relaxing, or just getting away from it all. 355 pages.   **$15.95**

PHILIPPINES HANDBOOK   by Peter Harper and Evelyn Peplow
Crammed with detailed information, *Philippines Handbook* equips the escapist, hedonist, or
business traveler with thorough coverage of the Philippines's colorful history, landscapes, and
culture. 600 pages.   **$17.95**

SOUTHEAST ASIA HANDBOOK   by Carl Parkes
Helps the enlightened traveler discover the real Southeast Asia. 873 pages.   **$16.95**

SOUTH KOREA HANDBOOK   by Robert Nilsen
Whether you're visiting on business or searching for adventure, *South Korea Handbook* is an
invaluable companion. Korean glossary with useful notes on speaking and reading the
language. 548 pages.   **$14.95**

SOUTH PACIFIC HANDBOOK   by David Stanley
The original comprehensive guide to the 16 territories in the South Pacific. 740 pages.   **$19.95**

TAHITI-POLYNESIA HANDBOOK   by David Stanley
All five French-Polynesian archipelagoes are covered in this comprehensive guide by
Oceania's best-known travel writer. 235 pages.   **$11.95**

THAILAND HANDBOOK   by Carl Parkes
Presents the richest source of information on travel in Thailand. 568 pages.   **$16.95**

THE HAWAIIAN SERIES

BIG ISLAND OF HAWAII HANDBOOK   by J.D. Bisignani
An entertaining yet informative text packed with insider tips on accommodations, dining, sports
and outdoor activities, natural attractions, and must-see sights. 347 pages.   **$11.95**

HAWAII HANDBOOK   by J.D. Bisignani
Winner of the 1989 Hawaii Visitors Bureau's Best Guide Award and the Grand Award for
Excellence in Travel Journalism, this guide takes you beyond the glitz and high-priced hype and
leads you to a genuine Hawaiian experience. Covers all 8 Hawaiian Islands. 879 pages.   **$15.95**

KAUAI HANDBOOK   by J.D. Bisignani
Kauai Handbook is the perfect antidote to the workaday world. Hawaiian and pidgin glossaries.
236 pages.   **$9.95**

MAUI HANDBOOK   by J.D. Bisignani
"No fool-'round" advice on accommodations, eateries, and recreation, plus a comprehensive
introduction to island ways, geography, and history. Hawaiian and pidgin glossaries. 350 pages.
$11.95

OAHU HANDBOOK   by J.D. Bisignani
A handy guide to Honolulu, renowned surfing beaches, and Oahu's countless other diversions. Hawaiian and pidgin glossaries. 354 pages.   **$11.95**

THE AMERICAS SERIES

ALASKA-YUKON HANDBOOK   by Deke Castleman and Don Pitcher
Get the inside story, with plenty of well-seasoned advice to help you cover more miles on less money. 384 pages.   **$13.95**

ARIZONA TRAVELER'S HANDBOOK   by Bill Weir
This meticulously researched guide contains everything necessary to make Arizona accessible and enjoyable. 505 pages.   **$14.95**

BAJA HANDBOOK   by Joe Cummings
A comprehensive guide with all the travel information and background on the land, history, and culture of this untamed thousand-mile-long peninsula. 356 pages.   **$13.95**

BELIZE HANDBOOK   by Chicki Mallan
Complete with detailed maps, practical information, and an overview of the area's flamboyant history, culture, and geographical features, *Belize Handbook* is the only comprehensive guide of its kind to this spectacular region. 263 pages.   **$14.95**

BRITISH COLUMBIA HANDBOOK   by Jane King
With an emphasis on outdoor adventures, this guide covers mainland British Columbia, Vancouver Island, the Queen Charlotte Islands, and the Canadian Rockies. 381 pages. **$13.95**

CANCUN HANDBOOK   by Chicki Mallan
Covers the city's luxury scene as well as more modest attractions, plus many side trips to unspoiled beaches and Mayan ruins. Spanish glossary. 257 pages.   **$12.95**

CATALINA ISLAND HANDBOOK: A Guide to California's Channel Islands
by Chicki Mallan
A complete guide to these remarkable islands, from the windy solitude of the Channel Islands National Marine Sanctuary to bustling Avalon. 245 pages.   **$10.95**

COLORADO HANDBOOK   by Stephen Metzger
Essential details to the all-season possibilities in Colorado fill this guide. Practical travel tips combine with recreation—skiing, nightlife, and wilderness exploration—plus entertaining essays. 416 pages.   **$17.95**

COSTA RICA HANDBOOK   by Christopher P. Baker
Experience the many wonders of the natural world as you explore this remarkable land. Spanish-English glossary. 700 pages.   **$17.95**

IDAHO HANDBOOK   by Bill Loftus
A year-round guide to everything in this outdoor wonderland, from whitewater adventures to rural hideaways. 275 pages.   **$12.95**

JAMAICA HANDBOOK by Karl Luntta
From the sun and surf of Montego Bay and Ocho Rios to the cool slopes of the Blue Mountains, author Karl Luntta offers island-seekers a perceptive, personal view of Jamaica. 230 pages. **$14.95**

MONTANA HANDBOOK by W.C. McRae and Judy Jewell
The wild West is yours with this extensive guide to the Treasure State, complete with travel practicalities, history, and lively essays on Montana life. 393 pages. **$13.95**

NEVADA HANDBOOK by Deke Castleman
Nevada Handbook puts the Silver State into perspective and makes it manageable and affordable. 400 pages. **$14.95**

NEW MEXICO HANDBOOK by Stephen Metzger
A close-up and complete look at every aspect of this wondrous state. 375 pages. **$13.95**

NORTHERN CALIFORNIA HANDBOOK by Kim Weir
An outstanding companion for imaginative travel in the territory north of the Tehachapis. 800 pages. **$19.95**

OREGON HANDBOOK by Stuart Warren and Ted Long Ishikawa
Brimming with travel practicalities and insiders' views on Oregon's history, culture, arts, and activities. 461 pages. **$15.95**

PACIFIC MEXICO HANDBOOK by Bruce Whipperman
Explore 2,000 miles of gorgeous beaches, quiet resort towns, and famous archaeological sites along Mexico's Pacific coast. Spanish-English glossary. 428 pages. **$15.95**

TEXAS HANDBOOK by Joe Cummings
Seasoned travel writer Joe Cummings brings an insider's perspective to his home state. 483 pages. **$13.95**

UTAH HANDBOOK by Bill Weir
Weir gives you all the carefully researched facts and background to make your visit a success. 445 pages. **$14.95**

WASHINGTON HANDBOOK by Dianne J. Boulerice Lyons and Archie Satterfield
Covers sights, shopping, services, transportation, and outdoor recreation, with complete listings for restaurants and accommodations. 433 pages. **$13.95**

WYOMING HANDBOOK by Don Pitcher
All you need to know to open the doors to this wide and wild state. 495 pages. **$14.95**

YUCATAN HANDBOOK   by Chicki Mallan
All the information you'll need to guide you into every corner of this exotic land. Mayan and Spanish glossaries. 391 pages.   **$14.95**

THE INTERNATIONAL SERIES

EGYPT HANDBOOK   by Kathy Hansen
An invaluable resource for intelligent travel in Egypt. Arabic glossary. 522 pages.   **$18.95**

MOSCOW-ST. PETERSBURG HANDBOOK   by Masha Nordbye
Provides the visitor with an extensive introduction to the history, culture, and people of these two great cities, as well as practical information on where to stay, eat, and shop. 260 pages. **$13.95**

NEPAL HANDBOOK   by Kerry Moran
Whether you're planning a week in Kathmandu or months out on the trail, *Nepal Handbook* will take you into the heart of this Himalayan jewel. 378 pages.   **$12.95**

NEPALI AAMA   by Broughton Coburn
A delightful photo-journey into the life of a Gurung tribeswoman of Central Nepal. Having lived with Aama (translated, "mother") for two years, first as an outsider and later as an adopted member of the family, Coburn presents an intimate glimpse into a culture alive with humor, folklore, religion, and ancient rituals. 165 pages.   **$13.95**

PAKISTAN HANDBOOK   by Isobel Shaw
For armchair travelers and trekkers alike, the most detailed and authoritative guide to Pakistan ever published. Urdu glossary. 478 pages.   **$15.95**

STAYING HEALTHY IN ASIA, AFRICA, AND LATIN AMERICA
by Dirk G. Schroeder, Sc D, MPH
Don't leave home without it! Besides providing a complete overview of the health problems that exist in these areas, this book will help you determine which immunizations you'll need beforehand, what medications to take with you, and how to recognize and treat infections and diseases. Includes extensively illustrated first-aid information and precautions for heat, cold, and high altitude. 200 pages.   **$10.95**

MOONBELTS

Made of heavy-duty Cordura nylon, the Moonbelt offers maximum protection for your money and important papers. This all-weather pouch slips under your shirt or waistband, rendering it virtually undetectable and inaccessible to pickpockets. One-inch-wide nylon webbing, heavy-duty zipper, one-inch quick-release buckle. Accommodates traveler's checks, passport, cash, photos. Size 5 x 9 inches. Black.   **$8.95**

**New travel handbooks may be available that are not on this list.
To find out more about current or upcoming titles,
call us toll-free at (800) 345-5473.**

IMPORTANT ORDERING INFORMATION

FOR FASTER SERVICE: Call to locate the bookstore nearest you that carries Moon Travel Handbooks or order directly from Moon Publications:

(800) 345-5473 • **Monday-Friday** • **9 a.m.-5 p.m. PST** • **fax (916) 345-6751**

PRICES: All prices are subject to change. We always ship the most current edition. We will let you know if there is a price increase on the book you ordered.

SHIPPING & HANDLING OPTIONS: 1) Domestic UPS or USPS first class (allow 10 working days for delivery): $3.50 for the first item, 50 cents for each additional item.

Exceptions:
- **Moonbelt** shipping is $1.50 for one, 50 cents for each additional belt.
- Add $2.00 for same-day handling.
- UPS 2nd Day Air or Printed Airmail requires a special quote.
- International Surface Bookrate (8-12 weeks delivery):
  $3.00 for the first item, $1.00 for each additional item. Note: Moon Publications cannot guarantee international surface bookrate shipping.

FOREIGN ORDERS: All orders that originate outside the U.S.A. must be paid for with either an International Money Order or a check in U.S. currency drawn on a major U.S. bank based in the U.S.A.

TELEPHONE ORDERS: We accept Visa or MasterCard payments. Minimum order is US$15.00. Call in your order: (800) 345-5473, 9 a.m.-5 p.m. Pacific Standard Time.

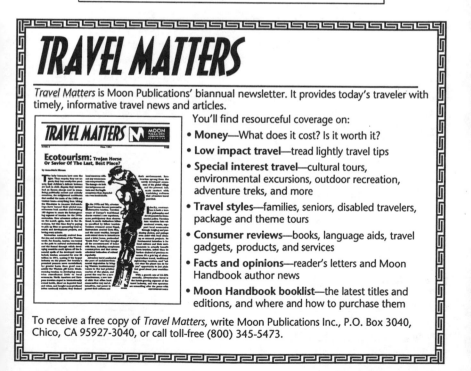

ORDER FORM

Be sure to call (800) 345-5473 for current prices and editions or for the name of the bookstore nearest you that carries Moon Travel Handbooks • 9 a.m.–5 p.m. PST
(See important ordering information on preceding page)

Name: _____ Date: _____

Street: _____

City: _____ Daytime Phone: _____

State or Country: _____ Zip Code: _____

QUANTITY	TITLE	PRICE

Taxable Total_____

Sales Tax (7.25%) for California Residents_____

Shipping & Handling_____

TOTAL_____

Ship: ☐ UPS (no PO Boxes)   ☐ 1st class   ☐ International surface mail

Ship to: ☐ address above   ☐ other _____

_____

Make checks payable to: **MOON PUBLICATIONS, INC**. P.O. Box 3040, Chico, CA 95927-3040 U.S.A. We accept Visa and MasterCard. **To Order:** Call in your Visa or MasterCard number, or send a written order with your Visa or MasterCard number and expiration date clearly written.

Card Number: ☐ **Visa**   ☐ **MasterCard**

☐ ☐ ☐ ☐   ☐ ☐ ☐ ☐   ☐ ☐ ☐ ☐   ☐ ☐ ☐ ☐

Exact Name on Card: _____

expiration date: _____

signature_____